People on People

The Oxford Dictionary of Biographical Quotations

People
on **People**

The Oxford Dictionary of Biographical Quotations

Edited by **Susan Ratcliffe**

OXFORD
UNIVERSITY PRESS

OXFORD
UNIVERSITY PRESS

Great Clarendon Street, Oxford OX2 6DP

Oxford University Press is a department of the University of Oxford.
It furthers the University's objective of excellence in research, scholarship,
and education by publishing worldwide in

Oxford New York

Athens Auckland Bangkok Bogotá Buenos Aires Cape Town
Chennai Dar es Salaam Delhi Florence Hong Kong Istanbul Karachi
Kolkata Kuala Lumpur Madrid Melbourne Mexico City Mumbai Nairobi
Paris São Paulo Shanghai Singapore Taipei Tokyo Toronto Warsaw

with associated companies in Berlin Ibadan

Oxford is a registered trade mark of Oxford University Press
in the UK and in certain other countries

Published in the United States
by Oxford University Press Inc., New York

© Oxford University Press 2001

Database right Oxford University Press (maker)

First published 2001

British Library Cataloguing in Publication Data

Data available

Library of Congress Cataloging in Publication Data

Data available

ISBN 0-19-866261-0

10 9 8 7 6 5 4 3 2 1

Designed by Jane Stevenson
Typeset in Swift and Frutiger
by Interactive Sciences Ltd, Gloucester
Printed in Great Britain
on acid-free paper by
T. J. International Ltd, Padstow, Cornwall

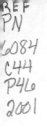
Project Team

Managing Editor	Elizabeth Knowles
Editor	Susan Ratcliffe
Library Research	Ralph Bates Marie G. Diaz
Reading Programme	Jean Harker Verity Mason Richard Ramage Helen Rappaport
Data Capture	Muriel Summersgill
Proof-reading	Kim Allen Fabia Claris Carolyn Garwes

Contents

Foreword   ix

Quotations   1

Index   375

Foreword

'There is only one thing in the world worse than being talked about, and that is not being talked about,' said Oscar Wilde. This collection of quotations brings together what all sorts of people have had to say about each other: whether admiring, disapproving, cruel, or just witty.

Most of the quotations are from people who are just as famous as the people they are talking about. So Albert Einstein describes Marie Curie as 'very intelligent, but as cold as a herring', Danny Blanchflower talks about George Best who has 'ice in his veins, warmth in his heart, and timing and balance in his feet', and Pablo Casals comments on Jacqueline du Pré: 'Oh, I *like* it—she moves *with* the music.' But in real life people do not restrict themselves to their own field: Oscar Wilde talks about Chopin and John Stuart Mill as well as more obvious targets such as Aubrey Beardsley and George Bernard Shaw. John Milton talks about 'the famous Galileo grown old', Martin Luther thinks Copernicus 'will turn the whole art of astronomy inside out', and Bob Dylan 'learned as much from Cézanne as . . . from Woody Guthrie.'

As Francis Ford Coppola says, 'Your work parallels your life, but in the sense of a glass full of water where people look at it and say, "Oh the water's the same shape as the glass!"'. This book concentrates on the lives and personalities, but in many cases the links are such that a comment on the work may also illuminate the person. Pete Townsend says 'It's the most psychedelic experience I ever had, going to see Hendrix play. When he started to play, something changed: colours changed, everything changed', while Henry Moore tells us 'The first hole made through a piece of stone is a revelation'.

It is in general true that what people have to say about others can be very revealing of themselves. Wilhelm II's comment 'The machine is running away with *him* as it ran away with *me*' tells us as much about the Kaiser's perception of his own experience as it does of Hitler. John Gielgud's tactless remark to Elizabeth Taylor 'I don't know what's happened to Richard Burton. I think he married some terrible film star and had to live abroad' is another instance. Yves Saint Laurent's comparison of his own creativity with that of Proust communicates as much about Saint Laurent as about Proust. Indeed, a self-image can often be illuminating, and assessments of people by themselves are frequently included: Sigmund Freud describes himself as 'nothing but a conquistador', while Margaret Thatcher is 'extraordinarily patient, provided I get my own way in the end', and A. E. Housman thinks that his 'photograph is not quite true to my own notion of my gentleness and sweetness of nature, but neither perhaps is my external appearance'.

Straightforward remarks along the lines 'So-and-so is the best artist (or musician, or tennis player)' have been excluded, except where the speaker or context gives the remark more interest. So the self-proclaimed 'greatest' Muhammed Ali's comment on Joe Louis 'I just give lip service to being the greatest. He was the greatest' is included. Likewise, Elizabeth Hurley's apparently banal comment on Anna Kournikova 'She is a very pretty girl' is given point by its relationship to Kournikova's description of Hurley 'She's sooo ugly'.

The people talking and talked about include philosophers, sportsmen, scientists, dancers, musicians, writers, politicians, actors, and those famous simply for being celebrities. Major figures have long entries reflecting the influence they continue to exert, with comments from contemporaries to the present day: from Ben Jonson to Richard Eyre on Shakespeare, from Voltaire to Einstein on Newton, and from Mozart to Ringo Starr on Beethoven. However, the length of entries varies from a single quotation to a whole spectrum of viewpoints, and the number of comments does not always reflect the relative importance of the subject. Some people seem to attract notice much more than others, perhaps because of their personalities or situations. Thus two princesses with marital difficulties have numerous supporters and detractors among their contemporaries. On Caroline of Brunswick, Jane Austen's view 'Poor woman, I shall support her as long as I can, because she *is* a woman and because I hate her husband' is opposed by the the Duke of Wellington, forced to cheer by a mob, 'God save the Queen, and may all your wives be like her!', while two hundred years later Diana, Princess of Wales, is variously described as 'the people's princess' and 'a silly Sloane turned secular saint'.

Most of the quotations can stand alone, but occasionally one quotation is directly linked to another: sometimes a personal response such as Neil Kinnock's reply to Michael Heseltine's description of him as 'Self-appointed king of the gutter of politics', 'If I was in the gutter, which I ain't, he'd still be looking up at me from the sewer'. Elsewhere, it can be a comment on a comment, such as Squire's verse on Einstein 'In continuation of Pope on Newton'. In such cases a cross-reference is supplied.

The people talked about range from the medieval scholar Peter Abelard to the French footballer Zinédine Zidane. Each entry begins with a short description of the subject, followed by the quotations in alphabetical order of author. The names of people mentioned in the biographical descriptions who have their own entries elsewhere in the book appear in bold type. Brief details of the date of the quotation, or a source where appropriate, follow the text. Where required, information on the context of the quotation is also given. Since the emphasis of the book is on people, the reader has not been burdened with extensive bibliographic detail. The author index gives brief biographical details of each author, and provides short context lines and a finding reference for each of their quotations. It is thus possible to find out not only what has been said about someone, but also to see what they have to say about others.

Creating this book would not have been possible without the assistance of many people. Most of all, I should like to thank Elizabeth Knowles, Managing Editor of Oxford Quotations Dictionaries, for her unfailing encouragement, suggestions, and assistance. More than half of the quotations are new, and this is due in no small measure to Jean Harker, Verity Mason, Richard Ramage, and Helen Rappaport, who contributed quotations to the Reading Programme, and to Ralph Bates and Marie Diaz who undertook library research. My thanks are due to them, and also to Alysoun Owen of OUP Reference Department, who played a large part in planning the form and identity of the book, to Muriel Summersgill for data capture, to Emma Lenz for supplementary research, and to Kim Allen, Fabia Claris, and Carolyn Garwes for proofreading the text.

Working on this book has been a pleasure, with continual surprising and interesting insights into people of many different times and places, some familiar and others new, at least to me. I hope the reader will experience the same enjoyment in the discovery of how varied people and their reactions to each other can be.

SUSAN RATCLIFFE

Oxford 2001

A

Peter Abelard 1079–1142

French scholar, theologian, and philosopher, famous for his tragic love affair with his pupil Héloise.

Héloise
c.1098–1164

1 I was more pleased with possessing your heart than with any other happiness . . . the man was the thing I least valued in you.
first letter to Abelard, c.1122

Bella Abzug 1920–98

American politician. She took particular interest in feminist, peace, and welfare issues.

Bella Abzug
1920–98

1 They call me Battling Bella, Mother Courage, and a Jewish mother with more complaints than Portnoy . . . But whatever I am—and this ought to be made very clear at the outset—I am a very serious woman.
Mel Ziegler (ed.) *Bella!* (1972)

Norman Mailer
1923–

2 [Bella Abzug] could boil the fat off a taxicab driver's neck.
attributed

Robert Adam 1728–92

Scottish architect. He was influenced by neoclassical theory and initiated a lighter, more decorative style than the previously fashionable Palladianism.

Horace Walpole
1717–97

1 Adam, our most admired, is all gingerbread, filigraine, and fan painting.
letter, April 1775

Abigail Adams 1744–1818

American wife of **John Adams** and mother of **John Quincy Adams**.

John Adams
1735–1826

1 You bid me burn your letters. But I must forget you first.
letter, April 1776

Ansel Adams 1902–84

American photographer, noted for his black-and-white photographs of American landscapes.

Henri Cartier-Bresson
1908–

2 The world is going to pieces and people like Adams and [Edward] Weston are photographing rocks!
during the Depression of the 1930s
Vicki Goldberg *Margaret Bourke-White* (1986)

Gerry Adams 1948–

Northern Irish politician, leader of Sinn Fein.

Gerry Adams
1948–

3 I don't know who said politics is the art of the possible, but whoever said it was reducing it to mediocrity—politics has to be the art of the *impossible*.
Lynn Barber *Demon Barber* (1998)

David Trimble
1944–

4 A Sinn Fein president in a government of Northern Ireland? That's like Hitler in a synagogue.
discounting the view that Gerry Adams might take a seat on the Ulster Executive
in April 1998

John Adams 1735–1826

American Federalist statesman, President 1797–1801; husband of **Abigail Adams**.

Abigail Adams
1744–1818

5 I cannot say that I think you are very generous to the ladies; for, whilst you are proclaiming peace and good will to men, emancipating all the nations, you insist upon retaining an absolute power over wives.
  letter, May 1776

Thomas Jefferson
1743–1826

6 He is vain, irritable, and a bad calculator of the force and probable effect of the motives which govern men.This is all the ill which can possibly be said of him. He is as disinterested as the Being who made him.
  letter, 1787

Thomas Paine
1737–1809

7 It has been the political career of this man to begin with hypocrisy, proceed with arrogance, and finish with contempt.
  in November 1802

John Quincy Adams 1767–1848

American statesman, President 1825–9; son of **John Adams**. He helped to shape the Monroe doctrine and after leaving office he was prominent in the anti-slavery campaign.

Ralph Waldo Emerson
1803–82

8 When they talk about his old age and venerableness and nearness to the grave he knows better. He is like one of those old cardinals, who as quick as he is chosen Pope, throws away his crutches and his crookedness, and is as straight as a boy. He is an old roué, who cannot live on slops, but must have sulphuric acid in his tea.
  Journals

Joseph Addison 1672–1719

English essayist, poet, dramatist, and Whig politician, co-founder in 1711 of *The Spectator* with **Richard Steele**.

Joseph Addison
1672–1719

1 Thus I live in the world rather as a Spectator of mankind, than as one of the species, by which means I have made myself a speculative statesman, soldier, merchant, and artisan, without ever meddling with any practical part of life.
  in March 1711

Joseph Addison
1672–1719

2 See in what peace a Christian can die.
  dying words

Edward Gibbon
1737–94

3 The style of Mr Addison is adorned by the female graces of elegance and mildness.
  Memoirs of My Life (1796)

Samuel Johnson
1709–84

4 Whoever wishes to attain an English style, familiar but not coarse, and elegant but not ostentatious, must give his days and nights to the volumes of Addison.
  Lives of the English Poets (1779–81)

Alexander Pope
1688–1744

5 Statesman, yet friend to Truth! of soul sincere,
  In action faithful, and in honour clear;
  Who broke no promise, served no private end,
  Who gained no title, and who lost no friend.
  'To Mr Addison' (1720)

Thomas Tickell
1686–1740

6 There taught us how to live; and (oh! too high
  The price for knowledge) taught us how to die.
  'To the Earl of Warwick. On the Death of Mr Addison' (1721)

Virginia Woolf
1882–1941

7 Undoubtedly it is due to Addison that prose is now prosaic—the medium which makes it possible for people of ordinary intelligence to communicate their ideas to the world.
The Common Reader (1925)

Anna Akhmatova 1889–1966

Russian poet. The personal and Christian tone of her poems brought her into official disfavour.

Anna Akhmatova
1889–1966

1 Fate did not leave anything out for me. Everything anyone could possibly experience fell to my lot.
G. A. Adamovich *Vuzdushnye puti* (1967)

Nadezhda Mandelstam
1899–1980

2 She was the stern and overbearing abbess of a convent in which the rules were strict to a fault and all sins had to be atoned for.
Hope Abandoned (1974)

Osip Mandelstam
1891–1938

3 Upon you is the mark of God.
remark, 1910

Andrei Zhdanov
1896–1948

4 The gloomy tones of hopelessness before death, mystic experiences intermingled with eroticism—this is the spiritual world of Akhmatova, a leftover from the old aristocratic culture which has sunk once and for all into the oblivion of 'the good old days of Catherine'. Half nun, half harlot, or rather a harlot-nun whose sin is mixed with prayer.
Roberta Reeder *Anna Akhmatova: Poet and Prophet* (1995)

Prince Albert 1819–61

Consort to **Queen Victoria** and prince of Saxe-Coburg-Gotha. He was involved in planning the Great Exhibition of 1851, and died prematurely from typhoid fever.

Prince Albert
1819–61

1 In my home life I am very happy and contented; but the difficulty of filling my place with proper dignity is that I am only the husband, and not the master in the house.
letter, May 1840

Prince Albert
1819–61

2 Gentlemen—I conceive it to be the duty of every educated person closely to watch and study the time in which he lives, and, as far as in him lies, to add his humble mite of individual exertion to further the accomplishment of what he believes providence to have ordained.
in 1850

Alfred, Lord Tennyson
1809–92

3 Wearing the white flower of a blameless life,
Before a thousand peering littlenesses,
In that fierce light which beats upon a throne,
And blackens every blot.
Idylls of the King (1862 ed.) dedication

Queen Victoria
1819–1901

4 It was with some emotion . . . that I beheld Albert—who is beautiful.
of her first meeting with Prince Albert, c.1838; attributed

Louisa May Alcott 1832–88

American novelist. Best known for the novel *Little Women* and its sequels, she was also a supporter of women's suffrage.

Louisa May Alcott
1832–88

1 Resolved to take Fate by the throat and shake a living out of her.
Ednah D. Cheney *Louisa May Alcott: Her Life, Letters, and Journals* (1889)

Julie Burchill
1960–

2 If Louisa May Alcott had really been sound, she'd have written a trilogy, and called the last one *Divorced Lesbian Sluts*.
in December 1995

Alexander the Great 356–323 BC

King of Macedon 336–323. He conquered Persia, Egypt, Syria, Mesopotamia, Bactria, and the Punjab, but after his death from a fever at Babylon his empire quickly fell apart.

Alexander the Great
356–323 BC

1 Is it not worthy of tears that, when the number of worlds is infinite, we have not yet become lords of a single one?
when asked why he wept on hearing from Anaxarchus that there was an infinite number of worlds
Plutarch *Moralia*

Montaigne
1533–92

2 I can easily imagine Socrates in the place of Alexander; Alexander in that of Socrates, I cannot.
Essais (1580)

Horace Walpole
1717–97

3 Alexander at the head of the world never tasted the true pleasure that boys of his own age have enjoyed at the head of school.
letter, May 1736

Muhammed Ali 1942–

American boxer; born Cassius Clay. He won the world heavyweight title in 1964, 1974, and 1978, becoming the only boxer to be world champion three times.

Muhammad Ali
1942–

1 I'm the greatest.
adopted as his catchphrase from 1962

Muhammad Ali
1942–

2 Float like a butterfly, sting like a bee.
summary of his boxing strategy
G. Sullivan *Cassius Clay Story* (1964); probably originated by Drew 'Bundini' Brown

Henry Cooper
1934–

3 He was quickly dubbed the 'Louisville Lip', as he drummed up business with a tongue that was even faster than his fists.
attributed

Coretta Scott King
1927–

4 He's not only a champion of boxing, he's a champion of justice, peace and human dignity.
in 1967

Christopher Logue
1926–

5 Two blacks on a 15 bus,
Ali for king, their quid pro quo:
'He may be quick—but is he strong?'
'Is Ali strong?—O daddy-O.
When that Muhammad pats your cheek
It breaks your little toe!'
attributed

Norman Mailer
1923–

6 For Ali to compose a few words of real poetry would be equal to an intellectual throwing a good punch.
The Fight (1976)

Woody Allen 1935–

American film director, writer, and actor. He stars in most of his own films, which humorously explore themes of neurosis and sexual inadequacy.

Woody Allen
1935–

1 My one regret in life is that I am not someone else.
Eric Lax *Woody Allen and his Comedy* (1975)

Woody Allen
1935–

2 I don't sit at home drinking liquor with writer's block. I don't have a bad relationship with my sister. I didn't kidnap my kid. I didn't grow up in Coney Island, and my father did not work bumper cars.
denying he resembles his film characters
in December 1999

Helena Bonham Carter
1966–

3 He did not just keep his clothes on under the sheet, but he kept his shoes on too. When I asked him why, he said it was in case there was a fire.
attributed, 1995

Mia Farrow 1945–	4 He had polyester sheets and I wanted to get cotton sheets. He discussed it with his shrink many times before he made the switch. *in February 1997*
Mia Farrow 1945–	5 A lovable *nebbish*, endlessly and hilariously whining and quacking, questioning moral and philosophical issues great and small. He was a guy with his heart and his conscience on his sleeve . . . A guy who is nothing like the real Woody Allen. *of Allen's screen persona* *What Falls Away* (1997)
Meryl Streep 1949–	6 Woody has the potential to be America's Chekhov, but instead he's still caught up in the jet-set crowd type of life, trivializing his talent. *of the film* Manhattan *(1979)* *in March 1980*
Gene Wilder 1933–	7 The way Woody makes a movie, it's as if he was lighting ten thousand safety matches to illuminate a city. Each one of them is a little epiphany. *in October 1978*

Kingsley Amis 1922–95

English novelist and poet, father of **Martin Amis**. He achieved popular success with his first novel *Lucky Jim* (1954), a satire on middle-class aspirations set in a provincial university.

Martin Amis 1949–	1 How he loved that dictionary . . . When it was near by and he was praising it ('This, this is the one'), he would sometimes pat and even stroke the squat black book, as if it were one of his cats. *of the* Concise Oxford Dictionary *in June 2000*
	of appreciations of other writers in Amis's Memoirs*:*
Craig Brown 1957–	2 It is as if Amis is swimming slowly but surely under water, carefully slogging through the praise stroke by stroke, when all of a sudden he feels he can't go any further without rising to the surface and taking a quick slug of the air of misanthropy. *Craig Brown's Greatest Hits* (1993)
Robertson Davies 1913–95	3 Kingsley Amis never writes a novel without bellyaching about something. It's an awful bore. *in April 1995*
Robert Graves 1895–1985	4 That's Kingsley Amis, and there's no known cure. *on spotting him looking disgruntled at a party* *attributed*

Martin Amis 1949–

English novelist, son of **Kingsley Amis**. Chiefly set against a background of contemporary urban life, his works are notable for their black humour and inventive use of language.

Kingsley Amis 1922–95	5 If I was reviewing Martin under a pseudonym, I would say he works too hard and it shows. *in August 1995*
A. S. Byatt 1936–	6 A kind of male turkeycocking which is extremely bad for the industry. *on Martin Amis's demands for a large advance on a new book* *in January 1995*
Craig Raine 1944–	7 The greatest pyrotechnician of his generation . . . he's got serious, he's got ideas. The GUT—Great Universal Themes—are all there now, aren't they. *attributed*

Roald Amundsen 1872–1928

Norwegian explorer. Amundsen was the first to navigate the North-West Passage (1903–6) and in 1911 he became the first to reach the South Pole.

Apsley Cherry-Garrard
1882–1959

1 For a dash to the pole and nothing else, [give me] Amundsen.
F. A. Worsley *Shackleton's Boat Journey* (1999); see **Shackleton** 1

Captain Lawrence Oates
1880–1912

2 I must say that man must have had his head screwed on right.
on Amundsen's reaching the South Pole first
diary, January 1912

Elizabeth Garrett Anderson 1836–1917

English physician. Debarred from medical courses because of her sex, she studied privately, obtaining a licence to practise in 1865. She opened a dispensary for women and children in London, which later became a hospital.

Josephine Butler
1828–1906

1 I gained more from her than from any other doctor, for she not only repeated what all of the others had said, but entered much more into my mental state and way of life than they could do, because I was able to *tell* her so much more than I ever could or would tell to any *man*.
E. Moberly Bell *Josephine Butler* (1962)

Lord John Russell
1792–1878

2 I am much pleased at Miss Garrett's success. She ought to have a vote for Westminster, but not to sit in Parliament. It would make too much confusion.
letter, 1870

Maya Angelou 1928–

American novelist and poet. The first volume of her autobiography, *I Know Why the Caged Bird Sings* recounts her harrowing experiences as a black child in the American South.

Maya Angelou
1928–

1 What I would really like said about me is that I dared to love.
interview, March 1985

Queen Anne 1665–1714

Queen of Great Britain and Ireland 1702–14. She was the daughter of the Catholic **James II**, but herself a Protestant. None of her children survived into adulthood, and the throne passed to the House of Hanover on her death.

John Arbuthnot
1667–1735

1 I believe sleep was never more welcome to a weary traveller than death was to her.
letter, August 1713

Walter Bagehot
1826–77

2 Queen Anne was one of the smallest people ever set in a great place.
The English Constitution (1867)

Winston Churchill
1874–1965

3 She was not very wise, nor clever, but she was very like England.
Marlborough, His Life and Times (1933–8)

Louis XIV
1638–1715

4 It means I'm growing old when ladies declare war on me.
in 1702

Sarah, Duchess of Marlborough
1660–1744

5 Her friendships were flames of extravagant passion, ending in aversion.
Characters of her contemporaries (1838)

Alexander Pope
1688–1744

6 Here thou, great Anna! whom three realms obey,
Dost sometimes counsel take—and sometimes tea.
The Rape of the Lock (1714)

G. M. Trevelyan
1876–1962

7 The friendship of Anne Stuart and Sarah Churchill was rooted in genuine human affection. Anne's mind was as slow as a lowland river. Sarah kept her sharp and witty tongue in constant use.
England Under Queen Anne (1930–4)

Anne of Cleves 1515–57

Fourth wife of **Henry VIII**. Henry was initially deceived by a flattering portrait of Anne by **Holbein**; the marriage was dissolved after only six months.

Henry VIII
1491–1547

8 The King found her so different from her picture . . . that . . . he swore they had brought him a Flanders mare.

Tobias Smollett *A Complete History of England* (3rd ed., 1759)

Anne, Princess Royal 1950–

Daughter of **Elizabeth II**. She is a skilled horsewoman (riding for Great Britain in the 1976 Olympics) and is president of Save the Children Fund.

Anne, Princess Royal
1950–

9 When I appear in public people expect me to neigh, grind my teeth, paw the ground and swish my tail—none of which is easy.

in May 1977

Anne, Princess Royal
1950–

10 I don't work that way . . . The very idea that all children want to be cuddled by a complete stranger, I find completely amazing.

on her work for Save the Children
in January 1998

Prince Philip, Duke of Edinburgh
1921–

11 If the man had succeeded in abducting Anne, she'd have given him the hell of a time while in captivity.

of an attempt to kidnap Princess Anne in 1974
Philip Ziegler *Elizabeth's Britain* (1986)

Michelangelo Antonioni 1912–

Italian film director. His films concentrate upon the study of character and illuminate such themes as suicide and humankind's alienation from the environment.

Orson Welles
1915–85

1 The critics tell me he's a stylist of the cinema. But how can you be a stylist if you don't understand grammar?

Kenneth Tynan *Tynan Right and Left* (1967)

Guillaume Apollinaire 1880–1918

French poet. His poems, which are written without punctuation, are a conscious attempt to be resolutely modern. He coined the term surrealist.

Christopher Logue
1926–

1 Come to the edge.
We might fall.
Come to the edge.
It's too high!
COME TO THE EDGE!.
And they came
and he pushed
and they flew . . .

'Come to the edge' (1969)

Diane Arbus 1923–71

American photographer. She is best known for her disturbing images of people on the streets of US cities.

Diane Arbus
1923–71

1 I do feel I have some slight coma or something about the quality of things. I mean it's very subtle and a little embarrassing to me, but I really believe there are things which nobody would see unless I photographed them.

Cecil Beaton *The Magic Image* (1975)

Jeffrey Archer 1940–

British Conservative politician and best-selling novelist, husband of Mary **Archer**. His political career collapsed after it was revealed that he had attempted to establish a false alibi in his 1987 libel case.

Mary Archer
1944–

1 My husband's talent for inaccurate précis.
attributed

Mary Archer
1944–

2 I am cross with Jeffrey, but I have formed the judgement that he is a decent and generous spirited man over 35 years and that will not change over one weekend.
following the revelation that her husband had planned to establish a false alibi in his 1987 libel case
in November 1999

Nancy Banks-Smith

3 I'm still suffering from the big dénouement in [Jeffrey Archer's book] Not A Penny More when 'the three stood motionless like sheep in the stare of a python.' The whole thing keeps me awake at night. Here are these sheep, gambolling about in the Welsh jungle, when up pops a python. A python, what's more, who thinks he's a cobra.
in March 1990

William Hague
1961–

4 This candidate is a candidate of probity and integrity—I am going to back him to the full.
on Archer's candidacy for the position of Mayor of London
at the Conservative party conference, October 1999

Ian Hislop
1960–

5 He can't write fiction and he can't write non-fiction, so he's invented a bogus category in between.
*on Jeffrey Archer's 'novelography', based on **Rupert Murdoch** and **Robert Maxwell***
in April 1996

Barry Humphries
1934–

6 The prigs who attack Jeffrey Archer should bear in mind that we all, to some extent, reinvent ourselves. Jeffrey has just gone to a bit more trouble.
in December 1999

Mary Archer 1944–

British scientist, wife of Jeffrey **Archer**.

Jeffrey Archer
1940–

7 She has had a remarkable life with me with remarkable privileges.
in December 2000

Mr Justice Caulfield
1914–

8 Remember Mary Archer in the witness box. Your vision of her will probably never disappear. Has she elegance? Has she fragrance? Would she have—without the strain of this trial—a radiance?
summing up of the court case between Jeffrey Archer and the Star, *July 1987*

Archimedes c.287–212 BC

Greek mathematician and inventor, of Syracuse. He is famous for his discovery of Archimedes' principle (supposedly while taking a bath, after which he ran through the streets shouting 'Eureka!').

Dannie Abse
1923–

1 That Greek one then is my hero, who watched the bath water rise above his navel and rushed out naked, 'I found it, I found it' into the street in all his shining, and forgot that others would only stare at his genitals.
Walking under Water (1952)

G. H. Hardy
1877–1947

2 Archimedes will be remembered when Aeschylus is forgotten, because languages die and mathematical ideas do not. 'Immortality' may be a silly word, but probably a mathematician has the best chance of whatever it may mean.
Simon Singh *Fermat's Last Theorem* (1997)

Plutarch
AD c.46–c.120

3 Though he was the author of many curious and excellent discoveries, yet he is said to have desired his friends only to place on his tombstone a cylinder containing a sphere, and to set down the proportion which the containing solid bears to the contained.
Parallel Lives

Ernest Renan
1823–92

4 The most ordinary schoolchild now knows the truths for which Archimedes would have given his life.
Souvenirs d'enfance et de jeunesse (1883)

Hannah Arendt 1906–75

German-born American philosopher and political theorist. She wrote on totalitarianism and on **Eichmann**'s trial.

Hannah Arendt
1906–75

1 Things I have been thinking about in recent years. The whole question of inner life, its turmoil, muliplication, the splitting-into-two (consciousness), the curious fact that I am One only in company.
letter, August 1969

Aristotle 384–322 BC

Greek philosopher and scientist. A pupil of **Plato** and tutor to **Alexander the Great**, he founded a school (the Lyceum) outside Athens. His work was central to Arabic and medieval philosophy.

Dante Alighieri
1265–1321

1 *Il maestro di color che sanno.*
The master of those who know.
Divina Commedia 'Inferno'

Bertrand Russell
1872–1970

2 Aristotle maintained that women have fewer teeth than men; although he was twice married, it never occurred to him to verify this statement by examining his wives' mouths.
The Impact of Science on Society (1952)

Robert South
1634–1716

3 An Aristotle was but the rubbish of an Adam, and Athens but the rudiments of Paradise.
Twelve Sermons . . . (1692)

Giorgio Armani 1935–

Italian fashion designer. He established his own company in 1975 and rapidly became one of Italy's best-known ready-to-wear designers for both men and women.

Gianni Versace
1946–97

1 You dress elegant and sophisticated women, I dress sluts.
attributed by Armani, 2000

Louis Armstrong 1900–71

American jazz musician; known as Satchmo. A major influence on Dixieland jazz, he was a trumpet and cornet player as well as a bandleader and singer.

Kingsley Amis
1922–95

1 Louis shown in vaudeville garb, coloured derby, waistcoat with brass buttons, check pants, Dizzy in beret, suit, hornrims. Louis is America, entertainment; Dizzy is the world, art. K. Abé sees all this, of course.
*of photographs of Louis Armstrong and **Dizzy Gillespie** by K. Abé*
in February 1989

Dizzy Gillespie
1917–93

2 If it hadn't been for him, there wouldn't have been none of us. I want to thank Mr Louis Armstrong for my livelihood.
in 1970

Philip Larkin
1922–85

3 For me the biggest thrill is to imagine what the other players felt like. Did they feel that they were making great jazz with a Genius? I wonder.
letter, June 1941

Matthew Arnold 1822–88

English poet, essayist, and social critic. He criticized the Victorian age in terms of its materialism, philistinism, and complacency.

Elizabeth Barrett Browning
1806–61

1 He is an admirable poet in one sense—an admirable *poetical writer*. But he must break up all his ice of meditation, and consent to feel like a child and attain to seeing like a seer, before we call him a poet in the absolute sense.
letter, February 1854

Henry James
1843–1916

2 I met Matthew Arnold and had a few words with him. He is not as handsome as his photographs—or as his poetry.
letter, March 1873

George Meredith
1828–1909

3 Arnold is a dandy Isaiah, a poet without passion, whose verse, written in a surplice, is for freshmen and for gentle maidens who will be wooed to the arms of these future rectors.
in July 1909

Edith Sitwell
1887–1964

4 Matthew Arnold's chilblained, mittened musings.
Alexander Pope (1930)

Roseanne Arnold 1953–

American actress, noted for her popular television comedy series.

Roseanne Arnold
1953–

5 I used to think I was an interesting person, but I must tell you how sobering a thought it is to realize your life's story fills about thirty-five pages and you have, actually, not much to say.
Roseanne (1990)

Thomas Arnold 1795–1842

English historian and educator. He was Headmaster of Rugby School from 1828, and influential in the development of the public school system.

Thomas Arnold
1795–1842

6 My love for any place, or person, or institution, is exactly the measure of my desire to reform them.
letter, March 1835

Walter Bagehot
1826–77

7 He worked, he pounded, if the phrase may be used, into the boy a belief, or at any rate a floating, confused conception, that there are great subjects, that there are strange problems, that knowledge has an indefinite value, that life is a serious and solemn thing.
'Mr Clough's Poems' (1862)

Sydney Smith
1771–1845

8 Arnold seems to have been a very pious, honest, learned, and original man, without five grains of common sense. He divided mankind into two parts—Dr Arnold, and *other people*: with the former part remained all the sense, philosophy, wisdom, and liberality.
letter, 1844

Arthur Ashe 1943–93

American tennis player. He won the US Open championship in 1968 and Wimbledon in 1975, and was the first black male player to achieve world rankings.

Arthur Ashe
1943–93

1 I learned to play tennis because the tennis courts were the closest athletic facility to my house. But I liked tennis best anyway. I wasn't big enough then for football; I wasn't tall enough for basketball; and soccer wasn't in vogue yet.
in July 1985

Frederick Ashton 1904–88

British ballet dancer, choreographer, and director. As a choreographer he created successful new works as well as popular adaptations of classical ballets.

Cecil Beaton
1904–80

1 He was by nature an Indian—extremely lazy and hated any power, loathed making decisions and only wanted to do—if any work at all— only creative things.
Julie Kavanagh *Secret Muses* (1996)

Roy Strong
1935–

2 Fred really ought to be kept off the stage. For one of the most creative, lazy, and mean-spirited people one has ever met, he thrives on adulation. His curtain-calls are now a complete act in themselves.
diary, October 1979

Isaac Asimov 1920–92

Russian-born American writer and scientist, particularly known for his works of science fiction and books on science for non-scientists.

Martin Amis
1949–

1 I expected cheerful volubility, but Asimov gives off an air of irritated preoccupation, as if silently completing a stint of mental arithmetic.
in 1980

Isaac Asimov
1920–92

2 It has always been my ambition to die in harness with my head face down on a keyboard and my nose caught between two of the keys.
'Farewell—Farewell' (1992)

Herbert Asquith 1852–1928

British Liberal statesman, Prime Minister 1908–16. He had to deal with demands for Irish Home Rule and women's suffrage.

Leo Amery
1873–1955

1 For twenty years he has held a season-ticket on the line of least resistance and has gone wherever the train of events has carried him, lucidly justifying his position at whatever point he has happened to find himself.
in July 1914

Winston Churchill
1874–1965

2 The difference between him and Arthur is that Arthur is wicked and moral, Asquith is good and immoral.
*comparing Asquith with **Arthur Balfour***
E. T. Raymond *Mr Balfour* (1920)

John Maynard Keynes
1883–1946

3 I am not sure that this want of originality was not one of the most necessary of the ingredients to produce the successful combination. His mind was was built for the purpose of dealing with the given facts of the outside world.
of Asquith's intellect
Essays in Biography (1951)

David Lloyd George
1863–1945

4 Asquith worries too much about small points. If you were buying a large mansion he would come to you and say 'Have you thought that there is no room for the cat?'
letter, 1915

Ottoline Morrell
1873–1938

5 I feel that he is always a spectator in life and doesn't really feel the war or anything else very deeply.
Miranda Seymour *Ottoline Morrell* (1992)

Margot Asquith 1864–1945

British political hostess; wife of **Herbert Asquith**.

Harold Laski
1893–1950

6 As scandal is the second breath of life my name is down for an early copy.
on Margot Asquith's forthcoming memoirs
letter, March 1920

Dorothy Parker
1893–1967

7 The affair between Margot Asquith and Margot Asquith will live as one of the prettiest love stories in all literature.

reviewing Margot Asquith's Lay Sermons
in October 1927

Fred Astaire 1899–1987

American dancer, singer, and actor. He is famous for starring in a number of film musicals, including *Top Hat* (1935) and *Shall We Dance?* (1937), in a successful partnership with **Ginger Rogers**.

Anonymous

1 Can't act. Slightly bald. Also dances.

studio official's comment
Bob Thomas *Astaire* (1985)

George Balanchine
1904–83

2 He is the most interesting, the most inventive, the most elegant dancer of our times . . . You see a little bit of Astaire in everybody's dancing—a pause here, a move there. It was all Astaire's originally.

Bob Thomas *Astaire* (1985)

Margot Fonteyn
1919–91

3 There is never a trace of effort, and that is because he had devoted infinite patience to rehearsing and perfecting every detail. His technique is astounding, yet everything is accomplished with the air of someone sauntering through the park on a spring morning.

The Magic of Dance (1979)

Graham Greene
1904–91

4 Mr Astaire is the nearest approach we are ever likely to have to a human Mickey Mouse . . . with his quick physical wit, his incredible agility. He belongs to a fantasy world almost as free as Mickey's from the law of gravity.

in 1936

Lorenz Hart
1895–1943

5 Fred Astaire once worked so hard
He often lost his breath.
And now he taps all the other chaps to death.

'Do It the Hard Way' (1940 song)

Audrey Hepburn
1929–93

6 One look at this most debonair and distinguished of legends, and I could feel myself turn into solid lead while my heart sank into my two left feet. Then suddenly I felt a hand around my waist and with his inimitable grace and lightness, Fred literally swept me off my feet.

recalling rehearsals for Funny Face *(1956), in 1981*

Kenneth Tynan
1927–80

7 Was it unadventurous for Astaire to stick to tap-dancing instead of venturing into ballet? On the contrary, it was brave, and it was what made him (and will keep him forever) a classic.

letter, April 1979

Nancy Astor 1879–1964

American-born British Conservative politician. She became the first woman to sit in the House of Commons when she succeeded her husband as MP for Plymouth in 1919.

Nancy Astor
1879–1964

1 My vigour, vitality, and cheek repel me. I am the kind of woman I would run from.

comment, March 1955

Winston Churchill
1874–1965

2 NANCY ASTOR: If I were your wife I would put poison in your coffee!
CHURCHILL: And if I were your husband I would drink it.

Consuelo Vanderbilt Balsan *Glitter and Gold* (1952)

Clement Attlee 1883–1967

British Labour statesman, Prime Minister 1945–51. His term saw the creation of the modern welfare state and the nationalization of major industries.

Clement Attlee
1883–1967

1 Few thought he was even a starter
There were many who thought themselves smarter
But he ended PM
CH and OM
An earl and a knight of the garter.
letter, April 1956

R. A. Butler
1902–82

2 Little Attlee, who had a habit of biting people in the pants.
on Attlee's governing style
Alistair Horne *Macmillan 1957–1986* (1989)

Winston Churchill
1874–1965

3 A modest man who has a good deal to be modest about.
in June 1954

Winston Churchill
1874–1965

4 A sheep in sheep's clothing.
Lord Home *The Way the Wind Blows* (1976)

Hugh Dalton
1887–1962

5 It is a wretched disheartening result! And a little mouse shall lead them.
on the choice of leader of the Labour Party
diary, November 1935

George VI
1894–1952

6 I gather they call the Prime Minister 'Clem'. 'Clam' would be more appropriate.
after Attlee's audience to kiss hands, in July 1945

Douglas Jay
1907–96

7 He never used one syllable where none would do.
Peter Hennessy *Muddling Through* (1996)

James Margach
d. 1979

8 The little indiarubber man.
The Anatomy of Power (1979)

Harold Nicolson
1886–1968

9 Attlee is a charming and intelligent man, but as a public speaker he is, compared to Winston [Churchill], like a village fiddler after Paganini.
diary, November 1947

George Orwell
1903–50

10 Attlee reminds me of nothing so much as a recently dead fish, before it has had time to stiffen.
diary, May 1942

Margaret Atwood 1939–

Canadian novelist, poet, critic, and short-story writer.

Margaret Atwood
1939–

1 I am like the Jeremy Bentham of the Booker, the taxidermist's special, just there to encourage the others.
in November 2000

Robert Fulford
1932–

2 I'd like to be one of the young journalists who gather . . . for her eightieth-birthday interview. I can't imagine what such people will want to ask her, but I can pretty well describe her answers—they'll be tart, aphoristic, defiant, confident.
Best Seat in the House: Memoirs of a Lucky Man (1988)

W. H. Auden 1907–73

British-born poet, resident in America from 1939. *Look, Stranger!* (1936) and *Spain* (1937, on the Civil War) secured his position as a leading left-wing poet.

Hannah Arendt
1906–75

1 As if life itself had delineated a kind of face-scape to make manifest the 'heart's invisible furies'.
of Auden's famous wrinkles
Richard Davenport-Hines *W. H. Auden* (1995)

W. H. Auden
1907–73

2 My face looks like a wedding-cake left out in the rain.
  Humphrey Carpenter *W. H. Auden* (1981)

W. H. Auden
1907–73

3 Nothing I wrote in the thirties saved one Jew from Auschwitz.
  attributed

Roy Campbell
1901–57

4 The most violent action he ever saw was when he was playing table tennis at Tossa del Mar on behalf of the Spanish Republicans—apart from the violent exercise he got with his knife and fork.
  commenting on Auden's war record
  Nine (1950)

Seamus Heaney
1939–

5 Auden of the last years, when he had begun to resemble in his own person an ample, flopping, ambulatory volume of the *OED* in carpet slippers.
  in June 1987

Randall Jarrell
1914–65

6 One never steps twice into the same Auden.
  The Third Book of Criticism (1969)

Philip Larkin
1922–85

7 Auden killed his own poetry by going to America where, having sacrificed the capacity to make art out of life, he tried to make art out of art instead.
  Required Writing (1983)

George Orwell
1903–50

8 The high-water mark, so to speak, of Socialist literature is W. H. Auden, a sort of gutless Kipling.
  The Road to Wigan Pier (1937)

Stephen Spender
1909–95

9 People sometimes divide others into those you laugh at and those you laugh with. The young Auden was someone you could laugh-at-with.
  W. H. Auden (1973)

Igor Stravinsky
1882–1971

10 He is the dirtiest man I have ever liked.
  Richard Davenport-Hines *W. H. Auden* (1995)

Dylan Thomas
1914–53

11 I sometimes think of his poetry as a great war, admire intensely the mature, religious, and logical fighter, and deprecate the boy bushranger.
  in November 1937

Evelyn Waugh
1903–66

12 It seems one had to know Mr Auden to appreciate him. Nothing in his written work explains the dominating position he held. There was something, apparently, in the tone of his voice reading his and his friends' work which greatly excited his hearers.
  in May 1951

St Augustine of Hippo AD 354–430

Doctor of the Church. After a series of spiritual crises in his early life he was baptized by St Ambrose and became bishop of Hippo in 396. His writings, such as *Confessions* and the *City of God*, dominated subsequent Western theology.

St Augustine of Hippo
AD 354–430

1 Give me chastity and continency—but not yet!
  Confessions (AD 397–8)

Augustus 63 BC–AD 14

The first Roman emperor, also called (until 27 BC) Octavian. He was adopted by the will of his great-uncle **Julius Caesar** and gained supreme power by his defeat of Antony in 31 BC.

Cicero
106–43 BC

1 The young man should be praised, decorated, and got rid of.
  of Octavian, the future Emperor Augustus
  referred to in a letter from Decimus Brutus to Cicero

Aung San Suu Kyi 1945–

Burmese political leader. She was kept under house arrest from 1989 to 1995, and the military government refused to recognize her party's victory in the 1990 elections.

Aung San Suu Kyi
1945–

1 I am not a martyr. I have suffered, but there are many more in my country who have suffered much more than me.
interview, March 1996

Aung San Suu Kyi
1945–

2 There are two main reasons why I do not find my work a burden in spite of the difficulties involved. First, I have dedicated and honourable (and good-humoured) colleagues whom I can trust and respect, and second, I gather strength from each day satisfactorily accounted for, including the brief days of rest which I would like to think are well-earned.
Letters from Burma (1997)

James Mawdsley

3 Not just a treasure to Burma, but a treasure to the world.
in October 2000

Jane Austen 1775–1817

English novelist. Her six major novels are notable for skilful characterization, dry wit, and penetrating social observation.

W. H. Auden
1907–73

1 You could not shock her more than she shocks me;
Beside her Joyce seems innocent as grass,
It makes me most uncomfortable to see
An English spinster of the middle class
Describe the amorous effects of 'brass',
Reveal so frankly and with such sobriety
The economic basis of society.
Letter to Lord Byron (1936)

Jane Austen
1775–1817

2 Let other pens dwell on guilt and misery. I quit such odious subjects as soon as I can.
Mansfield Park (1814)

Jane Austen
1775–1817

3 What should I do with your strong, manly, spirited sketches, full of variety and glow?—How could I possibly join them on to the little bit (two inches wide) of ivory on which I work with so fine a brush, as produces little effect after much labour?
letter, December 1816

Charlotte Brontë
1816–55

4 Miss Austen being, as you say, without 'sentiment', without *poetry*, maybe *is* sensible, real (more *real* than *true*), but she cannot be great.
letter, January 1848

J. M. Coetzee
1940–

5 Jane Austen finds sex as demonic as Sade does. She finds it demonic and therefore locks it out.
Giving Offence (1996)

D. W. Harding
1906–

6 Regulated hatred.
title of an article on the novels of Jane Austen, March 1940

Mary Russell Mitford
1787–1855

7 Till 'Pride and Prejudice' showed what a precious gem was hidden in that unbending case, she was no more regarded in society than a poker or a fire-screen, or any other thin upright piece of wood or iron that fills its corner in peace and quietness. The case is very different now: she is still a poker—but a poker of whom everyone is afraid.
letter, 1815

Sir Walter Scott
1771–1832

8 The Big Bow-Wow strain I can do myself like any now going; but the exquisite touch, which renders ordinary commonplace things and characters interesting, from the truth of the description and the sentiment, is denied to me.
diary, March 1826

Emma Thompson
1959–

9 I hope she knows how big she is in Uruguay.

accepting an Oscar for the screenplay of Sense and Sensibility *(1995 film)*
in Los Angeles, March 1996

Mark Twain
1835–1910

10 When I take up one of Jane Austen's books . . . I feel like a barkeeper entering the kingdom of heaven.

Q. D. Leavis *Fiction and the Reading Public* (1932)

Revd W. Awdry 1911–97

English author. He began to tell his railway stories to his three-year-old son when the boy had measles; they developed into the immensely popular *Thomas the Tank Engine* series.

Revd W. Awdry
1911–97

1 I should like my epitaph to say, 'He helped people see God in the ordinary things of life, and he made children laugh.'

attributed

A. J. Ayer 1910–89

English philosopher. Involved with the Vienna Circle in 1932, he was an important proponent of logical positivism.

A. J. Ayer
1910–89

1 I have made a mess of my personal life, but I have taught my students to find the truth.

Ben Rogers *A. J. Ayer: A Life* (1999)

e. e. cummings
1894–1962

2 You walk on tightropes as if they lay on the ground,
and always, bird eyed, notice more than we notice you notice; and the
observation follows always with the clarity
of a wire slicing cheese.

'AJA'

C. S. Lewis
1898–1963

3 A cross between a rodent and a firefly.

attributed, 1977

J. B. Priestley
1894–1984

4 God can stand being told by Professor Ayer and Marghanita Laski that He doesn't exist.

in July 1965

Bernard Williams
1929–

5 Like a lot of militant atheists, he found the Church of England rather exasperating. He preferred having Jesuits whom he would really argue against.

in 1989

B

Charles Babbage 1791–1871

English mathematician, inventor, and pioneer of machine computing. He designed a mechanical computer with **Ada Lovelace** but was unable to complete it in his lifetime.

Charles Darwin
1809–82

1 Carlyle . . . silenced everyone by haranguing during the whole dinner on the advantages of silence. After dinner, Babbage, in his grimmest manner, thanked Carlyle for his very interesting lecture on silence.

Francis Darwin (ed.) *The Life and Letters of Charles Darwin* (1887)

Joseph Henry
1797–1878

2 All the overflowings of a mind so rich that its very waste became valuable to utilize.

Report of the Smithsonian (1873)

Harriet Martineau
1802–76

3 His patience in explaining his machine in those days was really exemplary . . . A lady, to whom he had sacrificed some very precious time, on the supposition that she understood as much as she assumed to do, finished by saying, 'Now, Mr Babbage, there is only one thing that I want to know. If you put the question in wrong, will the answer come out right?'
Autobiography (1877)

Lauren Bacall 1924–

American actress. She co-starred with her husband, **Humphrey Bogart**, in a number of successful thrillers, including *The Big Sleep* and *Key Largo*.

Lauren Bacall
1924–

1 I think your whole life shows in your face and you should be proud of that.
interview, March 1988

Humphrey Bogart
1899–1957

2 PLEASE FENCE ME IN BABY THE WORLD'S TOO BIG OUT HERE AND I DON'T LIKE IT WITHOUT YOU.
telegram to Lauren Bacall; Lauren Bacall *By Myself* (1978)

Johann Sebastian Bach 1685–1750

German composer. An exceptional and prolific baroque composer, his works included more than 250 sacred cantatas.

Thomas Beecham
1879–1961

1 Too much counterpoint; what is worse, Protestant counterpoint.
attributed

Ludwig van Beethoven
1770–1827

2 The immortal god of harmony.
letter, April 1801

Neville Cardus
1889–1975

3 Unaccompanied Bach is for me one of the severest hardships of the calling of musical critic. It is probably good, even jolly to play, but to have to listen to it is worse than breaking stones.
The Delights of Music (1966)

Catherine Carswell
1879–1946

4 Bach is for me the bread and wine of music.
John Carswell (ed.) *Lying Awake* (1950)

Edward Elgar
1857–1934

5 Bach—who heals and pacifies all men and all things.
letter, July 1902

Roger Fry
1866–1934

6 Bach almost persuades me to be a Christian.
Virginia Woolf *Roger Fry* (1940)

W. S. Gilbert
1836–1911

7 QUESTION: Mr. Sullivan's music . . . reminds me so much of dear Baytch. Do tell me: what is Baytch doing just now? Is he still composing? GILBERT: Just now, as a matter of fact, dear Baytch is by way of decomposing.
Hesketh Pearson *Gilbert and Sullivan* (1947)

Johann Wolfgang von Goethe
1749–1832

8 It is as though eternal harmony were conversing with itself, as it may have happened in God's bosom shortly before he created the world.
on hearing Bach's organ works
Karl and Irene Geiringer *The Bach Family* (1954)

Edna St Vincent Millay
1892–1950

9 I find that I never lose Bach. I don't know why I have always loved him so. Except that he is so pure, so relentless and incorruptible, like a principle of geometry.
letter September 1920

Michael Torke
1961–

10 Why waste money on psychotherapy when you can listen to the B Minor Mass?
in September 1990

Francis Bacon 1561–1626

English statesman and philosopher. He was Lord Chancellor under **James I** before impeachment on charges of corruption. As a scientist he advocated the inductive method.

Francis Bacon
1561–1626

1 I have as vast contemplative ends, as I have moderate civil ends; for I have taken all knowledge to be my province.
letter, 1592

Francis Bacon
1561–1626

2 I do not look *about* me, I look *above* me.
on being advised to look about him on finding himself in disfavour
John Aubrey *Brief Lives*

William Hazlitt
1778–1830

3 His strength was in reflection, not in production: he was the surveyor, not the builder of science.
Lectures chiefly on the dramatic literature of the age of Elizabeth (1820)

Ben Jonson
c.1573–1637

4 The fear of every man that heard him was, lest he should make an end.
Timber, or Discoveries made upon Men and Matter (1641)

Lord Macaulay
1800–59

5 He who first treated legislation as a science was among the last English men who used the rack . . . he who first summoned philosophers to the great work of interpreting nature was among the last Englishmen who sold justice.
in July 1837

Alexander Pope
1688–1744

6 If parts allure thee, think how Bacon shined,
The wisest, brightest, meanest of mankind.
An Essay on Man Epistle 4 (1734)

Lytton Strachey
1880–1932

7 Francis Bacon has been described more than once with the crude vigour of antithesis . . . He was no striped frieze; he was shot silk.
Elizabeth and Essex (1928)

Izaak Walton
1593–1683

8 The great Secretary of Nature and all learning, Sir Francis Bacon.
Life of Herbert (1670 ed.)

Francis Bacon 1909–92

Irish painter. His work chiefly depicts human figures in grotesquely distorted postures, their features blurred or erased, and set in confined interior spaces.

Francis Bacon
1909–92

9 Who can I tear to pieces, if not my friends? . . . If they were not my friends, I could not do such violence to them.
John Russell *Francis Bacon* (1979)

Graham Sutherland
1903–80

10 He seems to have a very special sense of luxury. When you go to him for a meal, it is unlike anyone else's. It is all very casual and vague; there is no timetable; but the food is wonderful.
Cecil Beaton's diary, February 1960

Robert Baden-Powell 1857–1941

English soldier and founder of the Boy Scout movement. He became a national hero after his successful defence of Mafeking (1899–1900) in the Boer War.

Anonymous

1 The wolf that never sleeps.
traditional nickname of Baden-Powell, said to derive from a Matabele name

Robert Baden-Powell
1857–1941

2 The whole secret of my getting on lay with my mother.
Lessons from the Varsity of Life (1933)

John Hargrave
1894–82

3 It was the Boy-Poltergeist in Baden-Powell—that made rapport with the primitive fraternity gang spirit of boyhood.
Tim Jeal *Baden-Powell* (1989)

Douglas Bader 1910–82

British airman. Despite having lost both legs in a flying accident in 1931, he saw action as a fighter pilot during the Battle of Britain (1940–1).

Douglas Bader
1910–82

1 How do I want to be remembered when I die? As a fighter pilot? Look, I want to be remembered so that other people, when they talk about me, smile. That's how I want to be remembered. I don't give a damn about being a fighter pilot. The thing is this: I want to leave warmth behind.
speech, September 1982

Kenneth More
1914–82

2 If I was in a tight corner, I'd rather be in a tight corner with Douglas Bader—legs or no legs—than anyone else alive. He looks after people.
John Frayn Turner *Douglas Bader* (1995)

Joan Baez 1941–

American folk singer. She is best known for her performances at civil rights demonstrations in the early 1960s.

Joan Baez
1941–

1 Screaming at people may not be the most efficient way. I'm going to stay back a little from now on. I'm learning how to listen to people instead of preaching at them so much.
in January 1976

David Bailey 1938–

English photographer. He was a prominent figure of 1960s pop culture.

David Bailey
1938–

1 I never cared for fashion much. Amusing little seams and witty little pleats. It was the girls I liked.
in November 1990

Diana Vreeland
1903–89

2 [He looked] just like a Shetland pony.
attributed, August 1989

Joan Bakewell 1933–

British writer and broadcaster. Her television series included *Late Night Line Up* and *The Heart of the Matter*.

Frank Muir
1920–98

1 The thinking man's crumpet.
attributed

Stanley Baldwin 1867–1947

British Conservative statesman, Prime Minister 1923–4, 1924–9, and 1935–7. He handled the abdication of King **Edward VIII** skilfully, and opposed demands for rearmament.

Lord Beaverbrook
1879–1964

1 His successive attempts to find a policy remind me of the chorus of a third-rate revue. His evasions reappear in different scenes and in new dresses, and every time they dance with renewed and despairing vigour. But it is the same old jig.
in October 1930

Lord Beaverbrook
1879–1964

2 The Flying Scotsman is no less splendid a sight when it travels north to Edinburgh than when it travels south to London. Mr Baldwin denouncing sanctions was as dignified as Mr Baldwin imposing them.
in May 1937

Winston Churchill
1874–1965

3 COMMENT: One never hears of Baldwin nowadays—he might as well be dead.
CHURCHILL: No, not dead. But the candle in that great turnip has gone out.
Harold Nicolson's diary, August 1950

Lord Curzon
1859–1925

4 Not even a public figure. A man of no experience. And of the utmost insignificance.

of Baldwin's appointment as Prime Minister in 1923
Harold Nicolson *Curzon: the Last Phase* (1934)

George Orwell
1903–50

5 One could not even dignify him with the name of stuffed shirt. He was simply a hole in the air.

The Lion and the Unicorn (1941)

F. E. Smith
1872–1930

6 I think Baldwin has gone mad. He simply takes one jump in the dark: looks round; and then takes another.

letter, August 1923

G. M. Trevelyan
1876–1962

7 In a world of voluble hates, he plotted to make men like, or at least tolerate one another.

in *Dictionary of National Biography 1941–50* (1959)

Cristóbal Balenciaga 1895–1972

Spanish couturier. His garments were noted for their simplicity, elegance, and boldness of design. In the 1950s he contributed to the move away from the New Look.

Cecil Beaton
1904–80

1 It is a phenomenon that the son of an ordinary Spanish boatman, a poor boy with no opportunity to glimpse the grand world, should be born with such innate taste.

diary, February 1960

Arthur James Balfour 1848–1930

British Conservative statesman, Prime Minister 1902–5. In 1917, as Foreign Secretary, Balfour issued the declaration in favour of a Jewish national home in Palestine that came to be known as the Balfour Declaration.

Aung San Suu Kyi
1945–

1 I liked what I learned about the 'happy Prime Minister'. I particularly like him for the fact that in spite of the metaphysical dabbling, which troubled some of his political colleagues, he possessed a healthy appreciation for the detective story.

Letters from Burma (1997)

Winston Churchill
1874–1965

2 The difference between him and Arthur is that Arthur is wicked and moral, Asquith is good and immoral.

*comparing **H. H. Asquith** with Balfour*
E. T. Raymond *Mr Balfour* (1920)

Winston Churchill
1874–1965

3 Like a powerful graceful cat walking delicately and unsoiled across a rather muddy street.

*of Balfour's moving from **Asquith**'s Cabinet to that of **Lloyd George***
Great Contemporaries (1937)

David Lloyd George
1863–1945

4 He will be just like the scent on a pocket handkerchief.

on being asked what place Balfour would have in history
Thomas Jones' diary June 1922

Zoë Ball 1970–

British radio and television presenter.

Zoë Ball
1970–

1 People ask me what I do and I say I don't really know. I get paid to be a fool.

in September 2000

Severiano Ballesteros 1957–

Spanish golfer. In 1979 he became the youngest player in the 20th century to win the British Open; the following year he was the youngest-ever winner of the US Masters.

Severiano Ballesteros
1957–

1 I'm not nearly as bingo, bango, bongo in the head as people think.

in 1994

Honoré de Balzac 1799–1850

French novelist. He is chiefly remembered for his series of ninety-one interconnected novels and stories known collectively as *La Comédie humaine*.

Honoré de Balzac
1799–1850
1 If I'm not a genius, I'm done for.
letter, 1819

Honoré de Balzac
1799–1850
2 I am not deep, but I am very wide, and it takes time to walk round me.
letter, 1837

Régis Debray
1940–
3 Balzac observed all the things that Marx did not.
Teachers, Writers, Celebrities (1981)

Gustave Flaubert
1821–80
4 What a man Balzac would have been if he had known how to write!
letter, 1852

James Joyce
1882–1941
5 I am inclined to think that Balzac's reputation rests on a lot of neat generalizations about life.
Frank Budgen *James Joyce and the Making of Ulysses* (1934)

Alphonse de Lamartine
1790–1869
6 He has the face of an element . . . he possessed so much soul that his heavy body seemed not to exist.
Ruth Butler *Rodin: The Shape of Genius* (1993)

Auguste Rodin
1840–1917
7 Hair in disorder, eyes lost in a dream, a genius who, in his little room, is able to reconstruct bit by bit the entire structure of his society and to expose life in all its tumultuousness for his contemporaries and for all generations to come.
in February 1900

Edmund White
1940–
8 Someone once said Balzac's only fault is that he makes all of his characters into geniuses, like himself. What a wonderful fault!
interview, 1988

Émile Zola
1840–1902
9 What a man! . . . He crushes the entire century.
letter, May 1867

Tallulah Bankhead 1903–68

American actress. She became noted for her uninhibited public persona, rich laugh, and harsh drawl.

Tallulah Bankhead
1903–68
1 I'm as pure as the driven slush.
in April 1947

Tallulah Bankhead
1903–68
2 I read Shakespeare and the Bible and I can shoot dice. That's what I call a liberal education.
attributed

John Mason Brown
1900–69
3 Tallulah Bankhead barged down the Nile last night as Cleopatra—and sank.
in November 1937

Mrs Patrick Campbell
1865–1940
4 Tallulah Bankhead is always skating on thin ice. Everyone wants to be there when it breaks.
attributed

Joseph Banks 1743–1820

English botanist. He accompanied Captain **James Cook** on his first voyage to the Pacific, and helped to establish the Royal Botanic Gardens at Kew.

Fanny Burney
1752–1840
1 Sir Joseph was so exceedingly shy that we made no sort of acquaintance at all. If instead of going round the world he had only fallen from the moon, he could not appear less versed in the usual modes of a tea-drinking party. But what, you will say, has a tea-drinking party to do with a botanist, a man of science, a president of the Royal Society?
diary, March 1788

Horace Walpole
1717–97

2 This, however, is better than his going to draw naked savages, and be scalped, with that wild man Banks, who is poaching in every ocean for the fry of little islands that escaped the drag-net of Spain.
   letter, September 1772

Roger Bannister 1929–

British middle-distance runner and neurologist. In May 1954 he became the first man to run a mile in under 4 minutes.

Roger Bannister
1929–

1 I sometimes think that running has given me a glimpse of the greatest freedom a man can ever know, because it results in the simultaneous liberation of both body and mind.
   First Four Minutes (1955)

Samuel Barber 1910–81

American composer. He developed a style based on romanticism allied to classical forms; his music includes operas and orchestral and chamber music.

Samuel Barber
1910–81

1 I have always believed that I need a circumference of silence. As to what happens when I compose, I really haven't the faintest idea.
   David Ewen *American Composers* (1982)

Brigitte Bardot 1934–

French actress. The film *And God Created Woman* (1956) established her reputation as an international sex symbol. She later became an active supporter of animal welfare.

Brigitte Bardot
1934–

1 I really am a cat transformed into a woman.
   Tony Crawley *Bébé: The Films of Brigitte Bardot* (1975)

Brigitte Bardot
1934–

2 I gave my beauty and my youth to men. I am going to give my wisdom and experience to animals.
   attributed, June 1987

Simone de Beauvoir
1908–86

3 Garbo's visage had a kind of emptiness into which anything could be projected—nothing can be read into Bardot's face.
   Brigitte Bardot and the Lolita Syndrome (1959)

Roger Vadim
1927–2000

4 She was a wanton woman who had sacrificed her body to the god of Success, perpetuating the myth of the film world in which depravity pays better than talent.
   Memoirs of the Devil (1975)

Ronnie Barker 1929–

English comic actor. His many television appearances include both situation comedies and shows such as *The Two Ronnies* with Ronnie Corbett.

Peter Hall
1930–

1 He completely inhabited what it was he was being, even if it was a north country charlady.
   Bob McCabe *Ronnie Barker* (1998)

Syd Barrett 1946–

English pop singer, a member of Pink Floyd.

Roger Waters
1944–

1 Syd was a visionary, an extraordinary musician, he started Pink Floyd . . . Syd was the key that unlocked the door to rock 'n' roll for me.
   Julian Palacios *Lost in the Woods: Syd Barrett and the Pink Floyd* (1998)

J. M. Barrie 1860–1937

Scottish dramatist and novelist. Barrie's most famous play is *Peter Pan* (1904), a fantasy for children about a boy who would not grow up.

J. M. Barrie
1860–1937

1 I can't abide children, never could. It was merely pretend on my part to get round their mothers and so spend an idle hour in dalliance. I know a boy of four who, when he wakes up and sees the sun, calls out 'Good morning, God.' His own idea. Horrible.
speech, December 1930

Mrs Patrick Campbell
1865–1940

2 A little child whom the Gods have whispered to.
letter, January 1913

Philip Guedalla
1889–1944

3 The cheerful clatter of Sir James Barrie's cans as he went round with the milk of human kindness.
Supers and Supermen (1920)

George Jean Nathan
1882–1958

4 The triumph of sugar over diabetes.
Robin May *The Wit of the Theatre* (1969)

John Barrymore 1882–1942

American actor. A light comedian as well as a serious actor, his most celebrated role was on stage as Hamlet.

John Barrymore
1882–1942

1 My only regret in the theatre is that I could never sit out front and watch me.
Eddie Cantor *The Way I See It* (1959)

Michael Barrymore 1952–

British entertainer and television game show host.

Bob Monkhouse

2 Are fans likely to confuse the real-life Barrymore with the big-headed, foul-mouthed, envious, ungrateful, petty-minded game show host he portrays so convincingly and effortlessly?
on Barrymore's first straight acting role
in April 2000

Béla Bartók 1881–1945

Hungarian composer. His work owes much to Hungarian folk music and includes six string quartets, three piano concertos, and the *Concerto for Orchestra* (1943).

Zoltán Kodály
1882–1967

1 Bartók's name . . . stands for the principle of and the demand for regeneration stemming from the people, both in art and politics.
in 1956

Yehudi Menuhin
1916–99

2 As he elevated folk music to universal validity, so he gave noble dimensions to human emotion. Strong with the earthy, primeval strength of its origins, his music has also the cultivated strength of a steely, ruthless discipline which refuses all indulgence.
Unfinished Journey (1976)

Colin Wilson
·1931–

3 He not only never wears his heart on his sleeve; he seems to have deposited it in some bank vault.
Brandy of the Damned (1964)

Charles Baudelaire 1821–67

French poet and critic. He is largely known for *Les Fleurs du mal*, a series of poems that explore his isolation and melancholy and the attraction of evil and the macabre.

Arthur Rimbaud
1854–91

1 Baudelaire is the first seer, king of poets, *a true God*.
letter, May 1871

Aubrey Beardsley 1872–98

English artist and illustrator, associated with art nouveau and the Aesthetic movement. He is known for original and controversial illustrations, such as those for **Oscar Wilde**'s *Salome* (1894).

Max Beerbohm
1872–1956

1 Beardsley always seemed to know, by instinctive erudition, all about everything.
in January 1955

Edward Burne-Jones
1833–98

2 I've always wondered what people saw in Beardsley's drawings. Lust does frighten me. I say it looks like such despair—despair of any happiness and search for it in new degradation.
Mary Lago (ed.) *Burne-Jones Talking* (1981)

Roger Fry
1866–1934

3 The Fra Angelico of Satanism.
Stanley Weintraub *Beardsley* (1967)

Oscar Wilde
1854–1900

4 There were great possibilities always in the cavern of his soul, and there is something macabre and tragic in the fact that one who added another terror to life should have died at the age of a flower.
letter, March 1898

Cecil Beaton 1904–80

English photographer famous for his fashion features and portraits of celebrities, particularly the British royal family. He later diversified into costume and set design.

Anonymous

1 BEATON: What on earth can I become?
FRIEND: I shouldn't bother too much. Just become a friend of the Sitwells and see what happens.
at the outset of Beaton's career; Laurence Whistler *The Laughter and the Urn* (1985)

Cecil Beaton
1904–80

2 Cocteau says I am Malice in Wonderland and I have succeeded in spending my life in an unreality made up of fun, so much too much fun and my interests are limited to the joys of certain superficial forms of beauty.
diary, 1935

Truman Capote
1924–84

3 It is not difficult to discern Beaton's influence in the work of others; a harder task is to identify those who have influenced him.
The Best of Beaton (1968) introduction

Noël Coward
1899–1973

4 Though Waterloo was won upon the playing fields of Eton,
The next war will be photographed, and lost, by Cecil Beaton.
'Bright Young People' (1931)

Grace Kelly
1928–82

5 The epitome of Ewardian elegance.
Hugo Vickers *Cecil Beaton* (1993)

Warren Beatty 1937–

American actor, film director, and screenwriter. He gained a reputation as a suave, handsome leading man, and later became involved in film production.

Anonymous

1 If I were to be reincarnated, I'd like it to be as Warren Beatty's fingertips.
widely attributed to **Woody Allen**, but denied by him
John Baxter *Woody Allen* (1998)

Ray Connally

2 Listening to Warren Beatty being interviewed was like waiting for speech to finish being invented.
Shadows on a Wall (1994)

Shirley MacLaine
1934–

3 Can you believe that Warren Beatty is half-Canadian—the top half.
attributed

Lord Beaverbrook 1879–1964

Canadian-born British Conservative politician and owner of the *Daily Express*. He was also Minister of Aircraft Production in **Churchill**'s cabinet (1940).

Beverley Baxter
1891–1964

1 Beaverbrook is so pleased to be in the Government that he is like the town tart who has finally married the Mayor!
Henry ('Chips') Channon's diary June 1940

Rudyard Kipling
1865–1936

2 Power without responsibility: the prerogative of the harlot throughout the ages.
summing up Lord Beaverbrook's political standpoint vis-à-vis *the* Daily Express
quoted by Stanley Baldwin, March 1931

on being told by Lord Beaverbrook's butler that, 'The Lord is out walking':

David Lloyd George
1863–1945

3 Ah, on the water, I presume.
Lord Cudlipp letter September 1993

Malcolm Muggeridge
1903–90

4 Working for [C. P.] Scott [of the *Manchester Guardian*] was like waltzing with some sedate old dowager at a mayoral reception in Manchester; for Beaverbrook, like taking the floor in a night-club in the early hours of the morning, when everyone is more or less drunk.
The Infernal Grove (1975)

Evelyn Waugh
1903–66

5 Of course, I believe in the Devil. How otherwise would I account for the existence of Lord Beaverbrook?
L. Gourlay *The Beaverbrook I Knew* (1984)

H. G. Wells
1866–1946

6 If Max gets to Heaven he won't last long. He will be chucked out for trying to pull off a merger between Heaven and Hell . . . after having secured a controlling interest in key subsidiary companies in both places, of course.
A. J. P. Taylor *Beaverbrook* (1972)

Boris Becker 1967–

German tennis player. In 1985 he became the youngest man and first unseeded player to win the men's singles championship at Wimbledon. He won at Wimbledon again in 1986 and 1989.

Nikki Pilic

1 He is all contradiction. He is *all* contradiction. For me he is like the painter Van Gogh. He's not . . . *usual*.
in 1992

Thomas à Becket c. 1118–70

English prelate and statesman, Archbishop of Canterbury 1162–70. He openly opposed **Henry II**, who uttered words in anger which led four knights to assassinate Becket in his cathedral.

Thomas Carlyle
1795–1881

1 Your Becket was a noisy egoist and hypocrite; getting his brains spilt on the floor of Canterbury cathedral, to secure the main chance,—somewhat uncertain how!
Past and Present (1843)

T. S. Eliot
1888–1965

2 This is the creature that crawled upon the King; swollen with blood and
swollen with pride.
Creeping out of the London dirt,
Crawling up like a louse on your shirt,
The man who cheated, swindled, lied; broke his oath and betrayed his
King.
Murder in the Cathedral (1935)

Henry II
1133–89

3 Will no one rid me of this turbulent priest?
oral tradition, conflating a number of variant forms

Margaret Beckett 1943–

British Labour politician. She was acting leader of the Labour Party after the sudden death of John Smith, and became President of the Board of Trade in the **Blair** government.

Margaret Beckett
1943–

1 Being effective is more important to me than being recognised.
in January 2000

Samuel Beckett 1906–89

Irish dramatist, novelist, and poet. He is best known for his plays, especially *Waiting for Godot* (1952), a seminal work in the Theatre of the Absurd.

Samuel Beckett
1906–89

2 I couldn't have done it otherwise, gone on I mean. I could not have gone on through the awful wretched mess of life without having left a stain upon the silence.
Deirdre Bair *Samuel Beckett* (1978)

Samuel Beckett
1906–89

3 I am what her savage loving has made me.
of his mother
James Knowlson *Damned to Fame* (1996)

Peter Hall
1930–

4 The eyes pale and watering, the appearance sometimes hawk-like, sometimes child-like, but definitely a bird—a bird in his movements, his shyness, and because of occasionally a certain predatory hauteur.
diary, May 1976

David Beckham 1975–

English footballer. He has attracted considerable media attention while playing for Manchester United and England, and for his marriage to Victoria 'Posh Spice' Adams.

Victoria Adams
1974–

1 David and I haven't got that many friends. We could have our wedding in a post box.
in April 1999

George Best
1946–

2 He's been unbelievable considering the amount of publicity he gets . . . He does what he's paid to do better than anyone, and he does it on the pitch so they can all have a go at him.
in January 2001

Kevin Keegan
1951–

3 I want more from David Beckham. I want him to improve on perfection.
in 2000

Thomas Beecham 1879–1961

English conductor and impresario, founder of the London Philharmonic and the Royal Philharmonic. He did much to stimulate interest in new or neglected composers.

John Barbirolli
1899–1970

1 He conducted like a dancing dervish.
Charles Reid *John Barbirolli* (1971)

Thomas Beecham
1879–1961

2 I am not the greatest conductor in this country. On the other hand I'm better than any damned foreigner.
attributed

Robert Boothby
1900–86

3 Beecham was deeply rooted in provincial England. In this respect and in others he resembled Arnold Bennett. One from Lancashire, one from the Potteries. Both enjoyed being thought of as 'cards' which indeed they were.
My Yesterday, Your Tomorrow (1962)

Neville Cardus
1889–1975

4 A complex character—Falstaff, Puck, Malvolio all mixed up, each likely to overwhelm the others. Witty, then waggish, supercilious, then genial, kindly, and sometimes cruel, an artist in affectation, yet somehow always himself. Lancashire in his bones, yet a man of the world.
Sir Thomas Beecham (1961)

Max Beerbohm 1872–1956

English caricaturist, essayist, and critic. A central figure of the Aesthetic Movement, he is remembered chiefly for his novel, *Zuleika Dobson* (1911).

Vita Sackville-West
1892–1962

1 It always makes me cross when Max is called 'The Incomparable Max'. He is not incomparable at all, and in fact compares very poorly with Harold Nicolson, as a stylist, a wit, and an observer of human nature. He is a shallow, affected, self-conscious fribble—so there.
letter to Harold Nicolson, December 1959

George Bernard Shaw
1856–1950

2 The younger generation is knocking at the door, and as I open it there steps spritely in the incomparable Max.
on handing over the theatre review column to Max Beerbohm
in *Saturday Review* May 1898

Lytton Strachey
1880–1932

3 He has the most remarkable and seductive genius—and I should say about the smallest in the world.
letter, December 1917

Evelyn Waugh
1903–66

4 A delicious little old dandy, very quick in mind still.
diary, May 1947

Oscar Wilde
1854–1900

5 Tell me, when you are alone with Max, does he take off his face and reveal his mask?
W. H. Auden *Forewords and Afterwords* (1973)

Ludwig van Beethoven 1770–1827

German composer. Despite increasing deafness Beethoven was responsible for a prodigious output. He is often seen as bridging the classical and romantic movements.

Michael Bakunin
1814–76

1 Everything will pass, and the world will perish but the Ninth Symphony will remain.
Edmund Wilson *To The Finland Station* (1940)

Thomas Beecham
1879–1961

2 Even Beethoven thumped the tub. The Ninth Symphony was composed by a sort of Mr Gladstone of music.
Harold Atkins and Archie Newman *Beecham Stories* (1978)

Ludwig van Beethoven
1770–1827

3 I will seize Fate by the throat; it shall certainly not bend and crush me completely.
letter, 1801

Anthony Burgess
1917–93

4 I should imagine that the tensions and releases of Beethoven have as much to do with visceral problems as with the fight towards the ecstatic vision.
in 1983

E. M. Forster
1879–1970

5 It will be generally admitted that Beethoven's Fifth Symphony is the most sublime noise that has ever penetrated into the ear of man.
Howards End (1910)

Johann Wolfgang von Goethe
1749–1832

6 His talent amazed me; unfortunately he is an utterly untamed personality, not altogether in the wrong in holding the world to be detestable, but who does not make it any the more enjoyable either for himself or others by his attitude.
Marion M. Scott *Beethoven* (1934)

Franz Liszt
1811–86

7 To us musicians the work of Beethoven parallels the pillars of smoke and fire which led the Israelites through the desert.
letter, 1852

Gustav Mahler
1860–1911

8 I have realized today that articulate art is greater than inarticulate nature.
after seeing Niagara Falls and conducting the Pastoral *symphony on the same day*
Alma Mahler *Gustav Mahler: Memories and Letters* (1946)

Yehudi Menuhin
1916–99

9 A colossus beyond the grasp of most mortals, with his totally uncompromising power, his unsensual and uningratiating way with music as with people.
Unfinished Journey (1976)

Wolfgang Amadeus Mozart
1756–91

10 Keep your eyes on him; some day he will give the world something to talk about.
in 1787

Friedrich Nietzsche
1844–1900

11 Beethoven's music is music about music.
Human All-too-Human (1878)

Simon Rattle
1955–

12 If anyone has conducted a Beethoven performance, and then doesn't have to go to an osteopath, then there's something wrong.
in May 1990

Robert Schumann
1810–56

13 Nature would burst should she attempt to produce nothing save Beethovens.
Alan Walker (ed.) *Robert Schumann: the Man and his Music* (1972)

Ringo Starr
1940–

14 'What do you think of Beethoven?'
'I love him, especially his poems.'
at a press conference during the Beatles' first American tour in 1964

John Tavener
1944–

15 Beethoven's music may be the most extraordinary human cry ever uttered, but it isn't sacred art.
Andrew Ford *Composer to Composer* (1993)

Pyotr Ilich Tchaikovsky
1840–93

16 I bow before the greatness of some of his works—but I do not *love* Beethoven. My attitude toward him reminds me of what I experienced in childhood toward the God Jehovah. I had toward Him . . . a feeling of wonder, but at the same time also of fear.
diary, 1886

Arturo Toscanini
1867–1957

17 With one more drop of blood perhaps we can come a little nearer to what Beethoven wanted.
rehearsing the Ninth Symphony
George R. Marek *Toscanini* (1975)

Colin Wilson
1931–

18 He reminds me of a man driving the car with the handbrake on, but stubbornly refusing to stop, even though there is a strong smell of burning rubber.
Brandy of the Damned (1964)

Isabella Mary Beeton 1836–65

English author on cookery, famous for her best-selling *Book of Cookery and Household Management* (1861).

Elizabeth David
1913–92

1 The great points about Isabella Beeton's *Household Management* were the clarity and detail of her general instructions, her brisk comments, her no-nonsense asides. No doubt she was sometimes a governessy young woman. That was just what made her voice the voice of authority. Mrs Beeton commands . . . Her pupils obey.
in October 1960

Brendan Behan 1923–64

Irish dramatist and poet who supported Irish nationalism and was convicted for terrorism.

on being asked 'What was the message of your play' after a performance of The Hostage:

Brendan Behan
1923–64

1 Message? Message? What the hell do you think I am, a bloody postman?
Dominic Behan *My Brother Brendan* (1965)

Aphra Behn 1640–89

English novelist and dramatist, regarded as the first professional woman writer in England.

Anthony Burgess
1917–93

1 She was involved in an insurrection of slaves, thus going one better than Harriet Beecher Stowe, who merely preached abolitionism.
in December 1980

Anne Finch, Lady Winchilsea
1661–1720

2 He lamented for Behn, o'er that place of her birth,
And said amongst femens was not on the earth
Her superior in fancy, in language, or wit,
Yet owned that a little too loosely she writ.
'The Circuit of Apollo'

Bix Beiderbecke 1903–31

American jazz musician and composer. A self-taught cornettist and pianist, he was one of a handful of white musicians who profoundly influenced the development of jazz.

Philip Larkin
1922–85

1 Bix was an incompetent blaster compared to Louis [Armstrong]!
letter, June 1941

Martin Bell 1938–

British journalist and Independent politician. In 1997 he won the Tatton constituency from Neil Hamilton on an anti-sleaze platform.

Martin Bell
1938–

1 If I go back to a war zone somewhere else, the white suit and the green socks will be there because they have worked for me. I don't expect to convince anybody else of this, I'm only to convince me.
Anthony Clare *In the Psychiatrist's Chair III* (1998)

Neil Hamilton
1949–

2 Martin Bell's father founded *The Times* crossword puzzle, but this book proves that poor Martin doesn't have a clue, about politics at least.
in September 2000

Giovanni Bellini c. 1430–1516

Italian painter. His work is dominated by madonnas and other sacred subjects; he also made a significant contribution towards the treatment of figures within a landscape.

Albrecht Dürer
1471–1528

1 Giovanni Bellini has praised me very highly to many noblemen . . .
Everyone tells me how devout a man he is, which makes me like him.
He is very old, and still the best in painting.
letter, 1505

Hilaire Belloc 1870–1953

French-born British writer, historian, and poet remembered chiefly for *Cautionary Tales*. He also collaborated with **G. K. Chesterton** in works critical of modern industrial society and socialism.

Hilaire Belloc
1870–1953

1 When I am dead, I hope it may be said:
'His sins were scarlet, but his books were read.'
'On His Books' (1923)

Hilaire Belloc
1870–1953

2 Gentlemen, I am a Catholic . . . If you reject me on account of my religion, I shall thank God that He has spared me the indignity of being your representative.
speech to voters of South Salford, 1906

G. K. Chesterton
1874–1936

3 In so far as he is a traditionalist, he is an English traditionalist. But when he was specially a revolutionist, he was in the very exact sense a French Revolutionist. And it might be roughly symbolised by saying that he was an English poet but a French soldier.
Autobiography (1936)

George Bernard Shaw
1856–1950

4 Wells and I, contemplating the Chesterbelloc, recognize at once a very amusing pantomime elephant, the front legs being that very exceptional and un-English individual Hilaire Belloc, and the hind legs that extravagant freak of French nature, G. K. Chesterton.
in February 1908

Saul Bellow 1915–

Canadian-born American novelist, of Russian-Jewish descent. His fiction is both ironic and optimistic in its treatment of the human condition.

Saul Bellow
1915–

1 Nobody likes being written about in their lifetime, it's as though the FBI and the CIA were suddenly to splash your files in the paper.
in September 1997

Robert Benchley 1889–1945

American critic and humorist. His humorous sketches include *My Ten Years in a Quandary*.

Robert Benchley
1889–1945

1 It took me fifteen years to discover that I had no talent for writing, but I couldn't give it up because by that time I was too famous.
Nathaniel Benchley *Robert Benchley* (1955)

Tony Benn 1925–

British Labour politician. He was debarred from the House of Commons on succeeding to the title of Viscount Stansgate in 1960. He renounced his title in 1963 and was re-elected.

Tony Benn
1925–

1 Not a reluctant peer but a persistent commoner.
at a press conference, November 1960

Tony Benn
1925–

2 If I rescued a child from drowning, the Press would no doubt headline the story 'Benn grabs child.'
in March 1975

Bernard Levin
1928–

3 Benn flung himself into the Sixties technology with the enthusiasm (not to say language) of a newly enrolled Boy Scout demonstrating knot-tying to his indulgent parents.
The Pendulum Years (1970)

Ken Livingstone
1945–

4 Tony Benn was the moderniser who went on to become a socialist terror in the minds of Middle England.
in July 1999

John Mortimer
1923–

5 Less of a wide-eyed Trot than a very English phenomenon, a descendent of the Roundheads and non-conformists and, despite his doubts about the Almighty, a 19th-century Christian socialist.
in June 1999

Jimmy Reid

6 He has had more conversions on the road to Damascus than a Syrian long distance lorry driver.
in June 1999

Harold Wilson
1916–95

7 He immatures with age.
in 1981

Alan Bennett 1934–

English dramatist and actor. He achieved fame with the revue *Beyond the Fringe* (1960), the satirical comedy *Forty Years On* (1969), and the television monologues *Talking Heads* (1987).

Alan Bennett
1934–

1 Winsome, lose some.
cancelling an interview with the Independent *after the paper described him as winsome*
in March 1995

Alan Bennett
1934–

2 I'm less genial than people think, but I'm too timid to seem nasty.
in October 1995

Alec Guinness
1914–2000

3 He was wearing a sports jacket, blue shirt with a crumply collar and twisted string of a tie . . . I rejoice that he brings Yorkshire and Camden Town with him wherever he goes.

invited to dine at the Berkeley with Bennett
diary, May 1996

Arnold Bennett 1867–1931

English novelist, dramatist, and critic. His fame rests on the novels and stories set in the Potteries ('the Five Towns') of his youth.

Lord Beaverbrook
1879–1964

4 Arnold, you're a hard man.

regarded by Bennett as 'the most tremendous compliment ever paid to him'
J. A. Gere and John Sparrow (eds.) *Geoffrey Madan's Notebooks* (1981)

D. H. Lawrence
1885–1930

5 I'd like to write an essay on Bennett—sort of pig in clover.

letter, March 1928

Ezra Pound
1885–1972

6 Arnold Bennett knew his eggs. Whatever his interest in good writing, he never showed the public anything but AVARICE. Consequently they adored him.

letter, May 1937

Jack Benny 1894–1974

American comedian and actor. Working notably on radio and then television, he was renowned for his timing, delivery, and mordant, self-effacing humour.

Fred Allen
1894–1956

1 I don't want to say Jack Benny is cheap, but he's got short arms and carries his money low in his pockets.

Irving Fein *Jack Benny* (1976)

Jack Benny
1894–1974

2 HOLDUP MAN: Quit stalling—I said your money or your life.
JACK BENNY: I'm thinking it over!

one of Benny's most successful gags

David Thomson
1941–

3 He walked with the slow-motion splendour of the ghost of Rockefeller.

A Biographical Dictionary of Film (1994)

Jeremy Bentham 1748–1832

English philosopher and jurist. The first major proponent of utilitarianism, Bentham was concerned to reform the law to secure 'the greatest happiness of the greatest number'.

Edward Bulwer-Lytton
1803–73

1 He was the very Theseus of legislative reform,—he not only pierced the labyrinth—he destroyed the monster.

England and the English (1833)

Karl Marx
1818–83

2 The arch-philistine Jeremy Bentham was the insipid, pedantic, leather-tongued oracle of the bourgeois intelligence of the nineteenth century.

Das Kapital (1894)

Gore Vidal
1925–

3 Apparently Bentham thought that human beings had but two desires, gain and pleasure, and he accepted those desires as the facts of our condition (he hated St Paul) and tried to make of them a philosophy whose keystone was an eloquent defence of usury. He would have been at home in New York.

Burr (1973)

Alban Berg 1885–1935

Austrian composer. A pupil of **Schoenberg**, he was one of the leading exponents of twelve-note composition.

Alban Berg
1885–1935

1 When I compose I always feel I am like Beethoven; only afterwards do I become aware that at best I am only Bizet.

Theodor Adorno *Alban Berg* (1968)

Ingmar Bergman 1918–

Swedish film and theatre director. He used haunting imagery and symbolism often derived from Jungian dream analysis.

Ingmar Bergman
1918–

1 After years of playing with images of life and death, life has made me shy.

message sent on winning the Palme of Palmes at the Cannes Film Festival, in May 1997

Ingrid Bergman 1915–82

Swedish actress, remembered particularly for her romantic role opposite **Humphrey Bogart** in *Casablanca* (1942).

Ingrid Bergman
1915–82

2 I am a migratory bird. Ever since I was a little girl, I have looked for new things—I have longed for big adventures.

letter, 1949

Ingrid Bergman
1915–82

3 I am rather proud of my wrinkles, after all, and have never tried to hide my age.

interview, 1969

Federico Fellini
1920–93

4 One had the feeling that she was like a fairy godmother who had just come to Rome. One could expect anything from her. She could work miracles for us, like a Walt Disney character.

Donald Spoto *Notorious* (1997)

John Gielgud
1904–2000

5 Dear Ingrid—speaks five languages and can't act in any of them.

Ronald Harwood *The Ages of Gielgud* (1984)

George Berkeley 1685–1753

Irish philosopher and bishop. He argued that material objects exist solely by being perceived.

Lord Byron
1788–1824

1 When Bishop Berkeley said 'there was no matter',
And proved it—'twas no matter what he said.

Don Juan (1819–24)

Samuel Johnson
1709–84

2 I refute it *thus*.

kicking a large stone by way of refuting Berkeley's theory of the non-existence of matter in August 1763

Irving Berlin 1888–1989

Russian-born American songwriter. He had no formal musical training but wrote many famous songs including 'God Bless America' and 'White Christmas'.

*after meeting Irving Berlin and supposing him to be **Isaiah Berlin**:*

Winston Churchill
1874–1965

1 Berlin's just like most bureaucrats. Wonderful on paper but disappointing when you meet them face to face.

Laurence Bergreen *As Thousands Cheer* (1990)

Oscar Hammerstein II
1895–1960

2 Irving just loves hits. He has no sophistication about it—he just loves hits.

Michael Freedland *Irving Berlin* (1974)

Jerome Kern
1885–1945

3 Irving Berlin has no place in American music—he *is* American music.

Michael Freedland *Irving Berlin* (1974)

Sheridan Morley
1941–

4 Berlin was not a thinker: if among his contemporaries, George Gershwin wrote from the heart, and Cole Porter from the head, then Irving wrote from the gut.

in October 1990

Isaiah Berlin 1909–97

Latvian-born British philosopher who concerned himself with the history of ideas.

Maurice Bowra
1898–1971

5 Like Our Lord and Socrates, Berlin talked much but published little.
in 1971

Winston Churchill
1874–1965

*after meeting **Irving Berlin** and supposing him to be Isaiah Berlin:*
6 Berlin's just like most bureaucrats. Wonderful on paper but disappointing when you meet them face to face.
Laurence Bergreen *As Thousands Cheer* (1990)

Bernard Levin
1928–

7 I believe that Sir Isaiah Berlin is the only man in Britain who talks more rapidly than I do, and even that is a close-run thing.
In These Times (1986)

Stephen Spender
1909–95

8 A baby elephant, always the same baby elephant.
on Berlin's ageing
Michael Ignatieff *Isaiah Berlin: A Life* (1998)

Hector Berlioz 1803–69

French composer. He was one of the most original composers of his time and a major exponent of 19th-century programme music.

Hector Berlioz
1803–69

1 My life is to me a deeply interesting romance.
letter, 1833

Claude Debussy
1862–1918

2 A monster. He is not a musician at all. He creates the illusion of music by means borrowed from literature and painting. Besides, there is, as far as I can see, little that is French in him.
Edward Lockspeiser *Debussy* (1963)

Heinrich Heine
1797–1856

3 He is an immense nightingale, a lark as great as an eagle . . . the music causes me to dream of fabulous empires filled with fabulous sins.
J. H. Elliot *Berlioz* (1967)

Clara Schumann
1819–96

4 Cold, unsympathetic and querulous.
J. H. Elliot *Berlioz* (1967)

Jeffrey Bernard 1932–97

English journalist. His column for the *Spectator* reflected his erratic lifestyle.

Jeffrey Bernard
1932–97

1 My misdeeds are accidental happenings and merely the result of having been in the wrong bar or bed at the wrong time, say most days between midday and midnight.
in July 1992

Keith Waterhouse
1929–

2 Jeffery Bernard is unwell.
the habitual explanation for the non-appearance of Bernard's column
title of play (1989)

Sarah Bernhardt 1844–1923

French actress. Regarded as the greatest tragic actress of her day, she was noted for her clear voice, magnetic personality, and great beauty. She continued to act in seated roles after the amputation of a leg in 1915.

Anonymous

1 How different, how very different from the home life of our own dear Queen!
comment overheard at a performance of Cleopatra by Sarah Bernhardt
Irvin S. Cobb *A Laugh a Day* (1924); probably apocryphal

Maurice Baring
1874–1945

2 She took herself as much for granted as being the greatest actress in the world, as Queen Victoria took it for granted that she was Queen of England.
Puppet Show of Memory (1932)

Leonard Bernstein 1918–90

American composer, conductor, and pianist. As a composer he encompassed a wide range of forms and styles in his music.

Oscar Levant
1906–72

1 He uses music as an accompaniment to his conducting.
Memoirs of an Amnesiac (1965)

Yogi Berra 1925–

American baseball player. He was especially famous as a catcher with the New York Yankees, and became known for his pithy sayings.

A. Bartlett Giamatti
1938–89

1 Talking to Yogi Berra about baseball is like talking to Homer about the Gods.
in April 1987

Chuck Berry 1931–

American rock-and-roll singer, guitarist, and songwriter. He was one of the first great rock-and-roll stars with a large teenage following.

Keith Richards
1943–

1 One of the reasons I worked with Chuck Berry was that I felt I owed him so much. When I started I pinched virtually all of his riffs, you know? But I figure I repaid my debt because he was one of the most difficult persons I've ever worked with apart from Mick Jagger.
Mick St Michael *Keith Richards in His Own Words* (1994)

George Best 1946–

Northern Irish footballer. He was named European Footballer of the Year in 1968, but his career foundered in a succession of personal problems.

George Best
1946–

1 People say I wasted my money. I say 90 per cent went on women, fast cars and booze. The rest I wasted.
in December 1990

Danny Blanchflower
1926–93

2 He has ice in his veins, warmth in his heart, and timing and balance in his feet.
David Meek *Anatomy of a Football Star: George Best* (1970)

*Best was often told by **Matt Busby** not to bother to turn up for Busby's team talks to Manchester United:*

Matt Busby
1909–94

3 It wasn't worth his coming. It was a very simple team talk. All I used to say was: 'Whenever possible, give the ball to George.'
Michael Parkinson *Sporting Lives* (1993)

Barry John
1945–

4 I was able to stay in my natural environment and develop there as a respected member of the community. If I had been fifteen years old and pulled off the streets of Belfast onto the pitch at Old Trafford, I feel I'd have ended up as George Best has.
in 1972

Hugh McIlvanney
1933–

5 With feet as sensitive as a pick-pocket's hands, his control of the ball under the most violent pressure was hypnotic.
Nick Coleman and Nick Hornby (eds) *Picador Book of Sports Writing* (1996)

Peter Stringfellow

6 He is famous, he is rich, he is Irish. Not a good combination.
in July 2000

John Betjeman 1906–84

English poet, noted for his self-deprecating, witty, and gently satirical poems, appointed Poet Laureate in 1972. His essays reflect his interest in Victorian and Edwardian architecture.

Cecil Beaton
1904–80

1 John Betjeman, with trousers too short, walking like a toddler on the sands; he only lacked a bucket and spade.
diary, September 1973

Diarmuid Brennan	2 I came to the conclusion that a man who could give such pleasure with his pen couldn't be much of a secret agent. I may well be wrong. *view of the IRA army council's head of civilian intelligence on Betjeman's role as a press attaché in wartime Dublin* report, c.1941; reported April 2000
Lord Chetwode 1869–1950	3 Well, Betjeman, if you're going to be my son-in-law you needn't go on calling me 'Sir'. Call me 'Field Marshal'. attributed
Gavin Ewart 1916–95	4 So the last date slides into the bracket, that will appear in all future anthologies— And in quiet Cornwall and in London's ghastly racket We are now Betjemanless. 'In Memoriam, Sir John Betjeman (1906–84)' (1985)
Philip Larkin 1922–85	5 The quickest way to start a punch-up between two British literary critics is to ask them what they think of the poems of Sir John Betjeman. *Required Writing* (1983)
Candida Lycett Green 1942–	6 His output was utterly staggering considering he was always having lunch and quite a lot to drink. *a daughter's view* in October 1995

Aneurin Bevan 1897–1960

British Labour politician. A brilliant though often abrasive orator, his most notable contribution was the creation of the National Health Service (1948).

Aneurin Bevan 1897–1960	1 Damn it all, you can't have the crown of thorns *and* the thirty pieces of silver. *on his position in the Labour Party, c.1956* Michael Foot *Aneurin Bevan* vol. 2 (1973)
Ernest Bevin 1881–1951	*on the observation that Aneurin Bevan was sometimes his own worst enemy:* 2 Not while I'm alive 'e ain't! Roderick Barclay *Ernest Bevin and Foreign Office* (1975)
R. A. Butler 1902–82	3 Bevan was the greatest parliamentary orator since Charles James Fox. *The Art of the Possible* (1971)
Iain Macleod 1913–70	4 To have a debate on the National Health Service without the right hon. Gentleman would be like putting on Hamlet with no-one in the part of First Gravedigger. House of Commons, March 1952
Harold Macmillan 1894–1986	5 He enjoys prophesying the imminent fall of the capitalist system and is prepared to play a part, any part, in its burial, except that of mute. Michael Foot *Aneurin Bevan* (1962)

Ernest Bevin 1881–1951

British Labour statesman and trade unionist. He was one of the founders of the Transport and General Workers' Union and a leading organizer of the General Strike (1926).

Clement Attlee 1883–1967	1 It's a good maxim that if you have a good dog you don't bark yourself. I had a very good dog in Mr Ernest Bevin. attributed, 1960
Michael Foot 1913–	2 A speech from Ernest Bevin on a major occasion had all the horrific fascination of a public execution. If the mind was left immune, eyes and ears and emotions were riveted. *Aneurin Bevan* vol. 1 (1962)

Dickie Bird 1933–

English cricketer, notable for his career as a Test umpire.

Dickie Bird
1933–

1 I worry about everything. I even worry about the odd time I'm not worried. I think something must be wrong. I'm one of nature's witterers.

in April 1993

Michael Parkinson
1935–

2 Give Dickie a light meter, low cloud and a light drizzle, and no one, not even the Greeks, could concoct more drama and tragedy from the occasion.

in June 1995

Lord Birkenhead see F. E. Smith

John Birt 1944–

British broadcasting executive. His period as Director-General of the BBC was marked by many controversial organizational changes.

Michael Grade
1943–

1 I always felt that his mindset was fixed when he played with his Meccano set in the nursery.

It Seemed Like a Good Idea at the Time (1999)

Harrison Birtwistle 1934–

English composer and clarinettist. His early work was influenced by **Stravinsky**; later compositions are more experimental.

Harrison Birtwistle
1934–

1 You can't stop. Composing's not voluntary, you know. There's no choice, you're not free. You're landed with an idea and you have responsibility to that idea.

in April 1996

Tony Blair
1953–

2 What you do is more important than what I do.

Deborah Bull *Dancing Away* (1998)

Otto von Bismarck 1815–98

German statesman, known as the Iron Chancellor. He was the driving force behind the unification of Germany.

Otto von Bismarck
1815–98

1 I do not regard the procuring of peace as a matter in which we should play the role of arbiter between different opinions . . . more that of an honest broker who really wants to press the business forward.

speech, February 1878

A. J. P. Taylor
1906–90

2 Bismarck was a political genius of the highest rank, but he lacked one essential quality of the constructive statesman: he had no faith in the future.

in *Encyclopedia Britannica* (1954)

John Tenniel
1820–1914

3 Dropping the pilot.

on Bismarck's departure from office
cartoon caption, March 1890

Conrad Black 1944–

Canadian media entrepreneur. He owns newspapers in Australia, Britain, Canada, and the US.

Robert Fulford
1932–

1 His personality had a staged, directed feel to it. It was also oddly familiar. Where had I seen it before, a large, handsome man with a supercilious and condescending manner and a baroque vocabulary? Of course: Orson Welles in *Citizen Kane*. I was talking to Citizen Black.

Best Seat in the House: Memoirs of a Lucky Man (1988)

Margaret Thatcher
1925–

2 I like Conrad Black because he is the only person I have ever met who makes me feel positively 'wet'.

attributed, 1987

Black Prince 1330–76

Eldest son of Edward III and noted warrior, whose name apparently derives from the black armour he wore when fighting. He predeceased his father.

Edward III
1312–77

1 Also say to them, that they suffre hym this day to wynne his spurres, for if god be pleased, I woll this journey be his, and the honoure therof.

commonly quoted 'Let the boy win his spurs'
at Crécy, 1346

Elizabeth Blackwell 1821–1910

Anglo-American physician. She was the first woman to qualify as a doctor of medicine.

Elizabeth Blackwell
1821–1910

1 I must have something to engross my thoughts, some object in life which will fill this vacuum, and prevent this sad wearing away of the heart.

Pioneer Work in Opening the Medical profession to Women (1895)

Tony Blair 1953–

British Labour statesman, Prime Minister since 1997. His landslide victory in the election of 1997 gave his party its biggest-ever majority.

Tony Blair
1953–

1 I am from the Disraeli school of Prime Ministers in their relations with the Monarch.

in November 1997

Bill Clinton
1946–

2 Either he is a great athlete or I have a career as a golf instructor ahead of me.

after taking Blair through his first round of golf
in May 1998

Frank Field
1942–

3 It will give the public a rest as much it will reward his family.

on whether Blair should take paternity leave
in May 2000

Edward Heath
1916–

4 INTERVIEWER: What adjectives would you use to describe Tony Blair?
HEATH: Popular, effective, shallow.

in November 1998

Peter Mandelson
1953–

5 Few politicians are good at taking the high ground and throwing themselves off it. Tony does it, and takes great care to bring everyone else behind him. He manages the process of risk-taking with great application to detail.

in February 1996

Michael Portillo
1953–

6 It is not that the Prime Minister believes in nothing, it is that he believes in everything.

in October 1998

Margaret Thatcher
1925–

7 I'm worried about that young man, he's getting awfully bossy.

in February 1999

William Blake 1757–1827

English artist and poet. Blake's poems mark the beginning of romanticism and a rejection of the Age of Enlightenment. His watercolours and engravings, like his writings, were only fully appreciated after his death.

William Rose Benét
1886–1950

1 Blake saw a treefull of angels at Peckham Rye,
And his hands could lay hold on the tiger's terrible heart.
Blake knew how deep is Hell, and Heaven how high,
And could build the universe from one tiny part.

'Mad Blake' (1918)

William Blake
1757–1827

2 What it will be questioned when the sun rises do you not see a round disc of fire somewhat like a guinea O no no I see an innumerable company of the heavenly host crying Holy, Holy, Holy is the Lord God Almighty.

A Vision of the Last Judgement (1810)

William Blake
1757–1827

3 Imagination is my world; this world of dross is beneath my notice.

'Painting and the Fine Arts' in *Encyclopaedia Britannica* (7th ed., 1830)

T. S. Eliot
1888–1965

4 He approached everything with a mind unclouded by current opinions. There was nothing of the superior person about him. This makes him terrifying.

The Sacred Wood (1920)

Northrop Frye
1912–91

5 Read Blake or go to hell: That's my message to the modern world.

attributed, 1991

William Wordsworth
1770–1850

6 There is no doubt that this poor man was mad, but there is something in the madness of this man which interests me more than the sanity of Lord Byron and Walter Scott.

Henry Crabb Robinson *Reminiscences*

W. B. Yeats
1865–1939

7 Or that William Blake
Who beat upon the wall
Till truth obeyed his call.

'An Acre of Grass' (c.1938)

Colin Blakemore 1944–

British physiologist, specializing in neuroscience.

Colin Blakemore
1944–

1 If you've a chance as a scientist to make a small contribution to the catalogue of what it is that we know about the world, for me that's immensely satisfying and quite enough.

Anthony Clare *In the Psychiatrist's Chair II* (1995)

Danny Blanchflower 1926–93

Northern Irish footballer. He was British Footballer of the Year 1960–1, and later became a journalist and television commentator.

Stanley Matthews
1915–2000

1 Danny projected his mind where other players projected their bodies; played the game as constructively and intelligently as he thought and talked about it.

The Way It Was (2000)

Karen Blixen 1885–1962

Danish novelist and short-story writer. She is best known for *Seven Gothic Tales* and her autobiography *Out of Africa*, which she wrote after living in Kenya from 1914 to 1931.

Cecil Beaton
1904–80

1 This woman who knows the whole of *King Lear* by heart carries the wisdom of the world in her eyes.

diary, August 1962

Edmund Blunden 1896–1974

English poet and critic. His poetry reveals his love of the English countryside, while his prose work *Undertones of War* (1928) deals with his experiences in the First World War.

Edmund Blunden
1896–1974

1 When I was young I hoped that one day I should be able to go into a post office to buy a stamp without feeling nervous and shy: now I realize that I never shall.

Rupert Hart-Davis, letter, August 1956

Anthony Blunt 1907–83

British art historian, Foreign Office official, and Soviet spy. He was stripped of his knighthood in 1979.

Roy Strong
1935–

1 No one of significance has raised a finger of support for him, although the Establishment, if it had seen any glimmer of repentance, would, as usual, have tried to lift him back.
diary, November 1979

Humphrey Bogart 1899–1957

American actor. He appeared in many gangster roles, and his best-known films include *Casablanca* and *The Big Sleep* (in which he played opposite his wife **Lauren Bacall**).

James Agate
1877–1947

1 He has charm and he doesn't waste energy pretending to act. He has a sinister-rueful countenance which acts for him. He has an exciting personality and lets it do the work.
attributed

Lauren Bacall
1924–

2 He never tried to impress anyone. I've never known anyone who was so completely his own man. He could not be led in any direction unless it was the direction he chose to go.
Earl Wilson *The Show Business Nobody Knows* (1971)

Raymond Chandler
1888–1959

3 Bogart is so much better than any other tough-guy actor. As we say here, Bogart can be tough without a gun. Also he has a sense of humour that contains that grating undertone of contempt.
Dorothy Gardiner and Katherine S. Walker *Raymond Chandler Speaking* (1962)

Katharine Hepburn
1909–

4 His yes meant yes, his no meant no . . . there was no bunkum about Bogart.
Joe Hyams *Bogie* (1966)

Kenneth Tynan
1927–80

5 He looked like a walking ad for that essential Hemingway prop, the built-in shit detector.
in June 1966

Peter Ustinov
1921–

6 It was useless for an actor to act his heart out in a close-up if Humphrey Bogart was smoking a cigarette in the background.
attributed, 1970

Raoul Walsh
1887–1980

7 You can't kill Jimmy Stewart, Gary Cooper or Gregory Peck in a picture. But you can kill off Bogart. The audience doesn't resent it.
Kenneth Tynan *Tynan Right and Left* (1967)

Niels Bohr 1885–1962

Danish physicist. Bohr's theory of the structure of the atom incorporated quantum theory for the first time. He helped to develop the atom bomb in Britain and then in the US.

Albert Einstein
1879–1955

1 Not often in my life has a human being caused me such joy by his mere presence as you have done.
letter to Bohr, May 1920

Albert Einstein
1879–1955

2 He utters his opinions like one who perpetually gropes and never like one who believes to possess the definitive truth.
letter, March 1954

Dwight D. Eisenhower
1890–1969

3 A great man whose mind has explored the mysteries of the inner structure of atoms, and whose spirit has reached into the very heart of man.
in October 1957

Werner Heisenberg
1901–76

4 Primarily a philosopher, not a physicist.
Abraham Pais *A Tale of Two Continents* (1997)

Abraham Pais
1918–

5 To the end, he was one of the most open-minded physicists I have known, forever eager to learn of new developments from younger people and remaining faithful to his own admonition always to be prepared for a surprise.
A Tale of Two Continents (1997)

Marc Bolan 1947–77

British pop singer, member of the rock band T. Rex.

David Bowie
1947–

1 I never had any competition, except Marc Bolan back in England . . . I fought like a *madman* to beat him. Knowing theoretically there was no race. But wanting passionately to do it.
in June 1976

Elton John
1947–

2 On first meeting Marc, I was astounded by the amount of energy he radiated. He lived in a wonderful fantasy world which he never let go of.
in *Marc Bolan* (Virgin Modern Icons, 1997)

Anne Boleyn 1507–36

English wife of **Henry VIII**, mother of **Elizabeth I**. Henry divorced Catherine of Aragon in order to marry Anne, but she was later executed.

Anne Boleyn
1507–36

1 You have chosen me, from a low estate, to be your queen and your companion, far beyond my desert or desire. If then, you find me worthy of such honour, good your Grace, let not any light fancy, or bad counsel of mine enemies, withdraw your princely favour from me.
letter to Henry VIII, 1536

Andrew Bonar Law 1858–1923

Canadian-born British Conservative statesman, Prime Minister 1922–3. He retired as leader of the Conservative Party in 1921, but returned in 1922 to become Prime Minister for six months.

Herbert Henry Asquith
1852–1928

1 It is fitting that we should have buried the Unknown Prime Minister by the side of the Unknown Soldier.
Robert Blake *The Unknown Prime Minister* (1955)

Andrew Bonar Law
1858–1923

2 If I am a great man, then all great men are frauds.
Lord Beaverbrook *Politicians and the War* (1932)

David Lloyd George
1863–1945

3 Bonar would never make up his mind on anything. Once a question had been decided, Bonar would stick to it and fight for it to a finish, but he would never help in the taking of a decision.
A. J. Sylvester *Life with Lloyd George* (1975)

Bono 1960–

Irish rock star, a member of the band U2.

Bono
1960–

1 I've no regrets other than a really awful haircut in the mid-Eighties—a haircut that launched a thousand third division soccer players.
in February 1997

Daniel Boone c. 1734–1820

American pioneer. Boone made trips west from Pennsylvania into the unexplored area of Kentucky, organizing settlements and successfully defending them against hostile American Indians.

Stephen Vincent Benét
1898–1943

1 When Daniel Boone goes by, at night,
The phantom deer arise
And all lost, wild America
Is burning in their eyes.
'Daniel Boone'

Lord Byron
1788–1824

2 Tis true he shrank from men even of his nation,
When they built up unto his darling trees,—
He moved some hundred miles off, for a station
Where there were fewer houses and more ease.
Don Juan (1819–24)

William Booth 1829–1912

English religious leader, founder and first general of the Salvation Army. A Methodist revivalist preacher, in 1865 he established a mission in the East End of London which later became the Salvation Army.

Vachel Lindsay
1879–1931

1 Booth died blind and still by faith he trod,
Eyes still dazzled by the ways of God.
'General William Booth Enters into Heaven' (1913)

Betty Boothroyd 1929–

British Labour politician, the first woman Speaker of the House of Commons, 1992–2000.

Betty Boothroyd
1929–

1 My desire to get here was like miners' coal dust, it was under my fingers and I couldn't scrub it out.
of Parliament
Glenys Kinnock and Fiona Millar (eds.) *By Faith and Daring* (1993)

Teresa Gorman
1931–

2 I get sick of hearing how Betty Boothroyd, the Speaker, was a Tiller Girl. I trained in tap, ballet and jazz and I could high-kick her out of the House.
in June 1999

Charles Kennedy
1959–

3 I address you as Madam Speaker, you call me love.
in July 2000

Björn Borg 1956–

Swedish tennis player. He won five consecutive men's singles titles at Wimbledon (1976–80), beating the record of three consecutive wins held by Fred Perry.

Allan Border
1955–

1 I liked the contrast between his confidence on court and his shyness off it . . . Quiet, but ruthless.
in May 1993

Clive James
1939–

2 Like a Volvo, Borg is rugged, has good after-sales service, and is very dull.
in June 1980

Ilie Nastase
1946–

3 They should send Borg away to another planet. We play tennis. He plays something else.
attributed

Jorge Luis Borges 1899–1986

Argentinian poet, short-story writer, and essayist. The volume of short stories *A Universal History of Infamy* (1935, revised 1954) is regarded as a founding work of magic realism.

Jorge Luis Borges
1899–1986

1 Although at my age almost everyone I know is dead, I prefer to live my life looking forward. The past is a subject for poems, for elegies, but I try not to think about the past. I would rather spend my time thinking of the future, although quite possibly I have little future left.
in 1984

Leonor Acevedo Borges
1876–1975

2 I don't know why you waste your time with Anglo-Saxon, instead of studying something useful like Latin or Greek!
to her son, c.1964

Cesare Borgia 1476–1507

Italian statesman, cardinal, and general. The illegitimate son of Cardinal Rodrigo Borgia (later Pope Alexander VI) and brother of Lucrezia Borgia, he was captain general of the papal army from 1499.

Cesare Borgia
1476–1507

1 *Aut Caesar, aut nihil.*
Caesar or nothing.
motto inscribed on his sword

Max Born 1882–1970

German theoretical physicist, a founder of quantum mechanics. He also wrote on the philosophy of physics and the social responsibility of scientists.

Max Born
1882–1970

1 I am now convinced that theoretical physics is actual philosophy.
Jacob Bronowski *The Ascent of Man* (1973)

Jacob Bronowski
1908–74

2 Born had a remarkable personal, Socratic gift. He drew young men to him, he got the best out of them, and the ideas that he and they exchanged and challenged also produced his best work.
The Ascent of Man (1973)

Hieronymus Bosch c. 1450–1516

Dutch painter. Bosch's highly detailed works are typically crowded with half-human, half-animal creatures and grotesque demons in settings symbolic of sin and folly.

Carl Gustav Jung
1875–1961

1 This master of the monstrous . . . the discoverer of the Unconscious.
Alistair Smith *Early Netherlandish and German Paintings* (1985)

James Boswell 1740–95

Scottish author and biographer. *The Life of Samuel Johnson* (1791) gives a vivid and intimate portrait of **Johnson** and an invaluable panorama of the age and its personalities.

Stanley Baxter
1926–

1 To be so randy . . . and so literate.
in December 1995

Samuel Johnson
1709–84

2 Were you to die, it would be a limb lopped off.
attributed

Lord Macaulay
1800–59

3 Homer is not more decidedly the first of heroic poets, Shakespeare is not more decidedly the first of dramatists, Demosthenes is not more decidedly the first of orators, than Boswell is the first of biographers.
Essays Contributed to the Edinburgh Review (1843)

Sir Walter Scott
1771–1832

4 He was always labouring at notoriety, and, having failed in attracting it in his own person, he hooked his little bark to them whom he thought most likely to leave harbour, and so shone with reflected light, like the rat that eat the malt that lay in the house that Jack built.
letter, January 1829

Horace Walpole
1717–97

5 It is the story of a mountebank and his zany.
of Boswell's Tour of the Hebrides
letter, October 1785

Ian Botham 1955–

English all-round cricketer. In 1978 he became the first player to score 100 runs and take eight wickets in a single test match.

Ian Botham
1955–

1 It seems everything I do people are going out of their way to knock down.
in March 1986

Mike Brearley
1942–

2 He is the greatest match-winner the game has ever known.
in 1985

Harold Larwood
1904–95

3 This fellow is the most over-rated player I have ever seen. He looks too heavy, and the way he's been bowling out here, he wouldn't burst a paper bag.
  attributed

Viv Richards
1952–

4 People used to say he was my white brother. West Indians believed he should have been born in the Caribbean but, equally, Australians thought he would have made a good Aussie.
  Sir Vivian: The Definitive Autobiography (2000, with Bob Harris)

Fred Trueman
1931–

5 He couldn't bowl a hoop downhill.
  in 1985

Sandro Botticelli 1445–1510

Italian painter. He worked in Renaissance Florence under the patronage of the Medicis and is best known for his mythological works such as *Primavera* (c.1478) and *The Birth of Venus* (c.1480).

Kenneth Clark
1903–83

1 Botticelli's Venus is not at all the amorous strumpet of paganism, but, pale and withdrawn, dissolves into his image of the Virgin Mary.
  Civilization (1969)

Peter Ustinov
1921–

2 If Botticelli were alive today he'd be working for *Vogue*.
  in October 1962

Horatio Bottomley 1860–1933

British journalist and financier. He made a large fortune but was eventually found guilty of fraud and disgraced.

Horatio Bottomley
1860–1933

1 What poor education I have received has been gained in the University of Life.
  speech at the Oxford Union, December 1920

Horatio Bottomley
1860–1933

reply to a prison visitor who asked if he were sewing:
2 No, reaping.
  S. T. Felstead *Horatio Bottomley* (1936)

Pierre Boulez 1925–

French composer and conductor. His works explore and develop serialism and aleatory music, making use of both traditional and electronic instruments.

John Cage
1912–92

1 Pierre has the mind of an expert. With that kind of mind you can only deal with the past. You can't be an expert in the unknown.
  Joan Peyser *Boulez* (1976)

Adrian Boult 1889–1983

English conductor. Noted especially for his championship of English composers, he was music director of the BBC and principal conductor of the London Philharmonic Orchestra.

Thomas Beecham
1879–1961

1 He came to see me this morning—positively reeking of Horlicks.
  Ned Sherrin *Cutting Edge* (1984)

Margaret Bourke-White 1906–71

American photojournalist. During the Second World War she was the first female photographer to be attached to the US armed forces, accompanying the Allied forces when they entered the concentration camps.

Margaret Bourke-White
1906–71

1 Nothing attracts me like a closed door. I cannot let my camera rest until I have pried it open.
  Portrait of Myself (1964)

David Bowie 1947–

English rock singer, songwriter, and actor. He is known for his theatrical performances and unconventional stage personae. He also acted in a number of films, especially in the 1980s.

David Bowie
1947–

1 I play my part right the way down the line. That's what 'Bowie' is supposed to be all about.
interview, 1973

Caroline Coon
1945–

2 David Bowie is the one person the growing wave of third-generation rock fans seem to identify with. Although a musical stylist rather than an innovator, he's captured their imagination with a film and stage persona creating him as a mutant alien from another planet.
in August 1976

Bryan Ferry
1945–

3 There doesn't ever seem to be any self-doubt with Bowie and this is to be commended. He seems to be very good at getting the best out of himself. I'm always riddled with doubts and self-criticism.
David Buckley *Strange Fascination: David Bowie* (1999)

John Peel
1939–

4 I liked the idea of him reinventing himself because it was at a time when audiences wanted a kind of predictability, perhaps even more so than now. The one distinguishing feature about early-70s progressive rock was that it didn't progress. Before Bowie came along, people didn't want too much change.
David Buckley *Strange Fascination: David Bowie* (1999)

Nicolas Roeg
1928–

5 What I found so difficult was that he was so hard to reach—not emotionally, just on a purely physical level. There are barriers, a filter system around every star, of course, but they seemed particularly strong around Bowie.
in May 1993

Maurice Bowra 1898–1971

British scholar. As Warden of Wadham College, he became a noted personality in the Oxford of his day.

Maurice Bowra
1898–1971

1 I'm a man more dined against than dining.
John Betjeman *Summoned by Bells* (1960)

Edith Sitwell
1887–1964

2 He is an exceedingly energetic man—like a short express train, complete with steam.
letter, April 1948

John Sparrow
1906–92

3 Without you, Heaven would be too dull to bear,
And Hell would not be Hell if you are there.
epitaph for Bowra, in May 1975

Geoffrey Boycott 1940–

English cricketer. He was an opening batsman for England, captain of Yorkshire 1971–5, and scored more than 150 centuries.

Geoffrey Boycott
1940–

1 People shrink away from frankness. I am not diplomatic because I think that diplomacy sometimes means avoiding the truth.
in January 1995

David Gower
1957–

2 Geoff Boycott is enough of an enigma to puzzle the sphinx.
attributed

Fred Trueman
1931–

3 He is a real tiger who hates bowlers as much as I hate batsman.
attributed

Boy George 1961–

English pop singer and songwriter. He became popular in the early 1980s as a 'new romantic', and was noted for cross-dressing and his fun image.

Boy George
1961–

1 My parents were convinced that I would one day become Mr Average, but almost 30 years on I am still an A1 freak.
in March 1999

Jimmy Boyle 1944–

Scottish murderer. He took part in a rehabilitation programme and subsequently took up sculpture, published his prison diaries, and since his release has worked with young offenders.

Jimmy Boyle
1944–

1 You who sit out there, what the fuck do you know? How can I expect you to understand what it means to be in the control of people who look on me as an animal? I want to destroy your system. I want to live.
The Pain of Confinement (1984)

Robert Boyle 1627–91

Irish-born scientist. Boyle put forward a view of matter based on particles which was a precursor of the modern theory of chemical elements.

Anonymous

2 The son of the Earl of Cork and the father of modern chemistry.
quoting 'a late distinguished professor', in *British Quarterly Review* 1849

John Aubrey
1626–97

3 He is charitable to ingenious men that are in want, and foreign chemists have had large proof of his bounty, for he will not spare for cost to get any rare secret.
Brief Lives

Samuel Pepys
1633–1703

4 I took boat at the Old Swan, and there up the river all alone as high as Putney almost, and then back again, all the way reading, and finishing Mr Boyle's book of Colours, which is so chymical, that I can understand but little of it, but understand enough to see that he is a most excellent man.
diary, June 1667

Bessie Braddock 1899–1970

British trade unionist and Labour politician. She was a strong supporter of her native Liverpool, and of welfare services for working people.

Winston Churchill
1874–1965

1 BESSIE BRADDOCK: Winston, you're drunk.
CHURCHILL: Bessie, you're ugly. But tomorrow I shall be sober.
J. L. Lane (ed.) *Sayings of Churchill* (1992)

Sylvia Pankhurst
1882–1960

2 The finest fighting platform speaker in the country.
attributed

Don Bradman 1908–2001

Australian cricketer. Bradman's test match batting average of 99.94 is well above that of any other cricketer of any era.

Anonymous

1 Give us this day our daily Bradman
For ours is the harbour, the bridge and the Bradman for ever and ever.
Australian parody of the Lord's Prayer, 1930s

Neville Cardus
1889–1975

2 Bradman was the summing up of the Efficient Age which succeeded the Golden Age. Here was brilliance safe and sure, streamlined and without impulse. Victor Trumper was the flying bird; Bradman the aeroplane.
Autobiography (1947)

G. H. Hardy 1877–1947	3 Bradman is a whole class above every batsman who has ever lived: if Archimedes, Newton and Gauss remain in the Hobbs class, I have to admit the possibility of a class above them, which I find difficult to imagine. They had better be moved from now on into the Bradman class. postcard to C. P. Snow, c.1938

Jack Hobbs
1882–1963

4 He got too many runs. The pot calling the kettle black? No, I was human; he got hundreds every time he went in . . . He was mechanical; he was the greatest run-getting machine of all time.
in 1952

Philip Larkin
1922–85

5 Don Bradman was enclosed in a legend that grew bigger daily, like a gigantic indestructible crystal.
attributed

R. C. Robertson-Glasgow
1901–65

6 In the whole game, he was the greatest capitalist of skill. Poetry and murder lived in him together. He would slice the bowling to ribbons, then dance without pity on the corpse.
46 Not Out (1945)

R. S. Whitington
1912–

7 But Bradman the man was not so easy to idolize as Bradman the batsman. He decided . . . to remain encased in a shell that any oyster would have envied.
Cricket Caravan (1950)

Johannes Brahms 1833–97

German composer and pianist. Firmly opposed to the 'New German' school of **Liszt** and the young **Wagner**, he eschewed programme music and opera and concentrated on traditional forms.

Edward Elgar
1857–1934

1 The classical composer *par excellence* of the present day; one who, free from any provincialism of expression or national dialect (the charming characteristic of lesser men: Gade, Dvorak, Grieg) writes for the whole world and for all time—a giant, lofty and unapproachable—Johannes Brahms.
letter, December 1886

Gustav Mahler
1860–1911

2 I have gone all through Brahms pretty well by now. All I can say of him is that he's a puny little dwarf with a rather narrow chest. Good Lord, if a breath from the lungs of Richard Wagner whistled about his ears he would scarcely be able to keep his feet.
letter, c.1903

Yehudi Menuhin
1916–99

3 Take Brahms: the product of the misty landscapes of north Germany, his works are full of groping, dreaminess and introspection. Mist gives a sense of infinity; it may be only two feet deep but equally it may cover the world, there is no knowing.
Unfinished Journey (1976)

Robert Schumann
1810–56

4 I believe Johannes to be the true Apostle, who will also write Revelations.
attributed

George Bernard Shaw
1856–1950

5 Brahms is just like Tennyson, an extraordinary musician, with the brains of a third rate village policeman.
letter, April 1893

Pyotr Ilich Tchaikovsky
1840–93

6 I have played over the music of that scoundrel Brahms. What a giftless bastard!
diary, October 1886

Marlon Brando 1924–

American actor. An exponent of method acting, his career included many memorable roles in films such as *On the Waterfront* and *The Godfather*.

Humphrey Bogart
1899–1957

1 I came out here with one suit and everybody said I looked like a bum. Twenty years later Marlon Brando came out with only a sweatshirt and the town drooled over him. That shows how much Hollywood has progressed.
attributed

Marlon Brando
1924–

2 Movies, to me, are a way of making a living. Any satisfaction one gets beyond that is gratis.
R. Schickel *Brando* (1994)

Francis Ford Coppola
1939–

3 Before we started, I thought of him as this strange, moody Titan. But he turned out to be very simple, very direct.
R. Schickel *Brando* (1994)

John Gielgud
1904–2000

4 He's a funny, intense, egocentric boy . . . He's very nervous and mutters his lines and rehearses by himself all day long . . . I think his sincerity may bring him to an interesting performance.
letter, 1955

Elia Kazan
1909–

5 He is exactly the thing I like in actors. There's a hell of a lot of turmoil there. There's ambivalence there. He's uncertain of himself and he's passionate, both at the same time.
R. Schickel *Brando* (1994)

Tennessee Williams
1911–83

6 Ride out boy and send it solid. From the greasy Polack you will someday arrive at the gloomy Dane.
telegram sent on the opening night of *A Streetcar Named Desire*, 1947

Richard Branson 1950–

English businessman. He made his name with the company Virgin Records, which he set up in 1969. He later influenced the opening up of air routes with Virgin Atlantic Airways, established in 1984.

John Edmonds
1944–

1 You need more than a beard, an open-necked shirt and a failed diploma in ballooning to make the trains run on time.
in September 1998

Brassaï 1899–1984

Hungarian-born French painter and photographer. His photographs of the night-life of Paris in the 1930s caused a sensation.

Henry Miller
1891–1980

1 The eye of Paris.
in November 1937

Wernher von Braun 1912–77

German-born American rocket engineer. Braun led development on the V-2 rockets used by Germany in the Second World War. After the war he moved to the US, where he pioneered the work which resulted in the US space programme.

Wernher von Braun
1912–77

1 No—I never knew what was happening in the concentration camps. But I suspected it, and in my position I could have found out. I didn't, and I despise myself for it.
Arthur C. Clarke *Astounding Days* (1989)

Tom Lehrer
1928–

2 'Once the rockets are up, who cares where they come down? That's not my department,' says Wernher von Braun.
'Wernher von Braun'

Bertolt Brecht 1898–1956

German dramatist, producer, and poet. Collaborating with Kurt Weill, he combined music and drama, for example in *The Threepenny Opera*. Later he experimented with ideas of a Marxist 'epic theatre'.

Peter Hall
1930–

1 I don't regard Brecht as a man of iron-grey purpose and intellect, I think he is a theatrical whore of the first quality.
attributed, 1962

Richard Briers 1934–

British actor. He is particularly well-known for his parts in television series such as *The Good Life*.

Richard Briers
1934–

1 I told the producer: 'I'm very old. I'm a living legend. I must not be pushed around or bullied. No horses or fast cars. I'll be quite amusing sitting in a library.'
refusing to do stunt work
in January 2001

W. A. Darlington
1890–1979

2 Richard Briers played Hamlet like a demented typewriter.
review of a RADA production
Diana Rigg *No Turn Unstoned* (1982)

Benjamin Britten 1913–78

English composer, pianist, and conductor. He founded the Aldeburgh festival with **Peter Pears** in 1948, and in 1976 became the first composer to be made a life peer.

W. H. Auden
1907–73

1 What immediately struck me, about Britten the composer, was his extraordinary musical sensitivity in relation to the English language.
in July 1935

Benjamin Britten
1913–78

2 I do not easily think in words, because words are not my medium.
speech, Hull, 1962

Peter Hall
1930–

3 There is something thoughtful about him, like a precise headmaster who is going to stand no nonsense.
diary, August 1972

Yehudi Menuhin
1916–99

4 If wind and water could write music, it would sound like Ben's.
Christopher Headington *Britten* (1981)

Colin Wilson
1931–

5 There is no reason . . . why innocence should not be a valid theme for music; but to dwell on it for thirty years argues a certain arrested development.
Brandy of the Damned (1964)

Anne Brontë 1820–49

English novelist. She grew up in the Yorkshire village of Haworth with her sisters Charlotte and Emily, and is best known for her novels *Agnes Grey* and *The Tenant of Wildfell Hall*.

George Moore
1852–1933

1 A sort of literary Cinderella.
Conversations in Ebury Street (1924)

Mrs Humphrey Ward
1851–1920

2 The books and poems that she wrote serve as a matter of comparison by which to test the greatness of her two sisters. She is the measure of their genius—like them, but not with them.
preface to the Haworth edition of the Brontë's works (1924)

Charlotte Brontë 1816–55

English novelist. She led a lonely childhood with her sisters in the remote village of Haworth, and achieved fame with her romantic tour-de-force *Jane Eyre* (1847).

Charlotte Brontë
1816–55

3 I shall soon be 30—and I have done nothing yet . . . I feel as if we were all buried here.
    letter, March 1845

Patrick Brontë
1777–1861

4 Charlotte has been writing a book, and it is much better than likely.
    to his younger daughters, on first reading Jane Eyre
    Elizabeth Gaskell *The Life of Charlotte Brontë* (1857)

G. K. Chesterton
1874–1936

5 She showed that abysses may exist inside a governess and eternities inside a manufacturer.
    Twelve Types (1902)

Elizabeth Gaskell
1810–65

6 Her hands are like birds' claws, and she is so shortsighted that she cannot see your face unless you are close to her. She is said to be frightfully shy, and almost cries at the thought of going amongst strangers.
    in 1850

William Makepeace Thackeray
1811–63

7 Rather than have fame, rather than any other earthly good or mayhap heavenly she wants some Tomkins or another to love her and to be in love with. But you see she is a little bit of a creature without a penny worth of good looks, thirty years old I should think, buried in the country, and eating up her own heart there, and no Tomkins will come.
    letter, March 1853

Virginia Woolf
1882–1941

8 She does not attempt to solve the problems of human life; she is even unaware that such problems exist; all her force, and it is the more tremendous for being constricted, goes into the assertion 'I love, I hate, I suffer'.
    The Common Reader (1925)

Emily Brontë 1818–48

English novelist and poet. She died of tuberculosis after the publication (but before the success) of her masterpiece *Wuthering Heights* (1847).

Matthew Arnold
1822–88

9   She—
    (How shall I sing her?)—whose soul
    Knew no fellow for might,
    Passion, vehemence, grief,
    Daring, since Byron died.
    'Haworth Churchyard' (1855)

Charlotte Brontë
1816–55

10 Indeed, I have never seen her parallel in anything, stronger than a man, simpler than a child, her nature stood alone.
    preface to Emily Brontë *Wuthering Heights* (1850 ed.)

Peter Brook 1925–

English theatre director. As co-director of the Royal Shakespeare Company he earned critical acclaim with *King Lear* (1963) and *A Midsummer Night's Dream* (1970).

Kenneth Tynan
1927–80

1 Brook is not the extrovert, Orson Welles, *monstre sacré* kind of boy-genius: non-conformity does not tempt him, he was never a crusader, and he looks about as neurotic as a chipmunk.
    in April 1954

Rupert Brooke 1887–1915

English poet. He is most famous for his wartime poetry *1914 and Other Poems* (1915). He died while on naval service in the Mediterranean.

Frances Cornford
1886–1960

1 A young Apollo, golden-haired,
Stands dreaming on the verge of strife,
Magnificently unprepared
For the long littleness of life.
'Youth' (1910)

Henry James
1843–1916

2 Of course, of course.
on hearing that Rupert Brooke had died on a Greek island
C. Hassall *Rupert Brooke* (1964)

D. H. Lawrence
1885–1930

3 I first heard of him as a Greek god under a Japanese sunshade, reading poetry in his pyjamas, at Grantchester,—at Grantchester upon the lawns where the river goes. Bright Phoebus smote him down. It is all in the saga.
letter, April 1915

F. R. Leavis
1895–1978

4 He energized the Garden-Suburb ethos with a certain original talent and the vigour of a prolonged adolescence . . . rather like Keats's vulgarity with a Public School accent.
New Bearings in English Poetry (1932)

Charles Hamilton Sorley
1895–1915

5 *The Morning Post*, which has always hitherto disapproved of him, is now loud in his praises because he has conformed to their stupid axiom of literary criticism that the only stuff of poetry is violent physical experience, by dying on active service.
having seen the notice of Brooke's death in The Morning Post
letter, April 1915

Lytton Strachey
1880–1932

6 It was impossible not to like him, impossible not to hope that he might like one again; and now . . . The meaninglessness of fate is intolerable; it's all muddle and futility.
letter, April 1915

Trevor Brooking 1948–

English footballer and broadcaster. He played for West Ham United and England.

Brian Clough
1935–

1 Trevor Brooking floats like a butterfly, and stings like one too.
in 1981

Mel Brooks 1926–

American film director and comic actor. His film debut *The Producers* (1968) was followed by the spoof western *Blazing Saddles* (1974).

Woody Allen
1935–

1 I hear the people on his movies love the experience so much that they wish it could go on forever. On my movies, they're *thrilled* when it's over.
Kenneth Tynan *Show People* (1980)

Mel Brooks
1926–

2 I went into show business to make a noise, to *pronounce myself*. I want to go on making the loudest noise to the most people.
in October 1978

Terry Wogan
1938–

3 Perhaps the only American I have ever met who understood irony, he was sarcastic, iconoclastic, anarchic and anything else that ends in -ic, with the possible exception of chic.
Is It Me? (2000)

Christy Brown 1932–81

Irish writer and painter, who worked with his left foot.

Christy Brown
1932–81

1 Painting became everything to me . . . Through it I made articulate all that I saw and felt, all that went on inside the mind that was housed within my useless body like a prisoner in a cell.
My Left Foot (1954)

Gordon Brown 1951–

Scottish Labour politician. As Chancellor of the Exchequer he has been noted for his cautious financial policies.

Anonymous

2 Prudence is the other woman in Gordon's life.
an unidentified aide, in March 1998

Anonymous

3 The chancellor is an anorak. He has the social skills of a whelk.
an unidentified Treasury official, in January 1999

John Redwood
1951–

4 Gordon Brown is a bit like someone who takes great pride in how clean they leave the washing up, hoping we won't notice that they break and throw away all the really dirty plates and cups.
in May 2000

James Brown 1928–

American soul and funk singer and songwriter. He became known as 'Soul Brother Number One' in the 1960s, playing a leading role in the development of funk.

Michael Jackson
1958–

5 I never dared speak to him, but I consider James Brown my greatest teacher. I was too young to think about it as a kid, I just felt it, like an animal senses things.
Gerri Hirshey *Nowhere to Run: the Story of Soul Music* (1985)

Bill Wyman
1936–

6 He does the most incredible dancing, like Mick, only about twenty times faster . . . You could put Jerry Lee Lewis, Little Richard, Chuck Berry, and Bo Diddley on one side of the stage, and James Brown on the other, and you wouldn't even notice the others were there!
Peter Guralnick *Sweet Soul Music* (1986)

John Brown 1800–59

American abolitionist. He was executed after raiding a government arsenal at Harpers Ferry in Virginia, intending to arm black slaves and start a revolt.

Anonymous

7 John Brown's body lies a mould'ring in the grave,
His soul is marching on.
song (1861)

Frederick Douglass
c.1818–95

8 Like Samson, he has laid his hands upon the pillars of this great national temple of cruelty and blood, and when he falls, that temple will speedily crumble to its final doom, burying its denizens in its ruins.
in November 1859

Ralph Waldo Emerson
1803–82

9 That new saint, than whom nothing purer or more brave was ever led by love of men into conflict and death . . . will make the gallows glorious like the cross.
in December 1859

Herman Melville
1819–91

10 But the streaming beard is shown
(Weird John Brown),
The meteor of the war.
'The Portent' (1859)

Thomas Browne 1605–82

English author and physician. He achieved prominence with *Religio Medici* (1642), a collection of imaginative and erudite opinions on a vast number of subjects connected with religion.

William Hazlitt
1778–1830

1 Sir Thomas Browne seemed to be of opinion that the only business of life was to think, and that the proper object of speculation was, by darkening knowledge, to breed more speculation, and 'find no end in wandering mazes lost'.
'Character of Sir T. Brown as a Writer' (1820)

Charles Lamb
1775–1834

2 Who would not be curious to see the lineaments of a man who, having himself been twice married, wished that mankind were propagated like trees!
quoted by William Hazlitt, January 1826

Virginia Woolf
1882–1941

3 His immense egotism has paved the way for all psychological novelists, autobiographers, confession-mongers, and dealers in the curious shades of our private life. He it was who first turned from the contacts of man with man, to their lonely life within.
The Common Reader (1925)

Elizabeth Barrett Browning 1806–61

English poet. She established her reputation with *Poems* (1844). In 1846 she eloped to Italy with **Robert Browning**.

Elizabeth Barrett
Browning
1806–61

1 Beseech for me the indulgence of your father and mother, and ask your sister to love me. I feel so as if I had slipped down over the wall into somebody's garden.
letter to Robert Browning, shortly after their marriage, September 1846

Robert Browning
1812–89

2 The simple truth is that she was the poet, and I the clever person by comparison.
letter, August 1871

Edward Fitzgerald
1809–83

3 Mrs Browning's death is rather a relief to me, I must say: no more Aurora Leighs, thank God! A woman of real genius, I know; but what is the upshot of it all? She and her sex had better mind the kitchen and their children; and perhaps the poor: except in such things as little novels, they only devote themselves to what men do much better, leaving that which men do worse or not at all.
letter, July 1861; see **Fitzgerald** 1

Virginia Woolf
1882–1941

4 Fate has not been kind to Mrs Browning as a writer. Nobody reads her, nobody discusses her, nobody troubles to put her in her place.
The Common Reader: second series (1932)

Robert Browning 1812–89

English poet. In 1842 he established his name with *Dramatic Lyrics*, containing 'The Pied Piper of Hamelin' and 'My Last Duchess'. In 1846 he eloped with **Elizabeth Barrett**.

W. H. Auden
1907–73

5 Robert Browning
Immediately stopped frowning
And started to blush
When fawned on by Flush.
Academic Graffiti (1971)

Elizabeth Barrett
Browning
1806–61

6 Or from Browning some 'Pomegranate', which, if cut deep down the
middle,
Shows a heart within blood-tinctured, of a veined humanity.
'Lady Geraldine's Courtship' (1844)

Robert Browning 1812–89	7 When it was written, God and Robert Browning knew what it meant; now only God knows. *on* Sordello attributed
Henry James 1843–1916	8 A great gossip and a very 'sympathetic' easy creature. letter, January 1877
Ezra Pound 1885–1972	9 Hang it all, Robert Browning, There can be but the one 'Sordello'. *Draft of XXX Cantos* (1930)
Alfred, Lord Tennyson 1809–92	10 He has plenty of music in him, but he cannot get it out. Hallam Tennyson *Alfred Lord Tennyson* (1897)
Robert Yelverton Tyrrell 1844–1914	11 The original Greek is of great use in elucidating Browning's translation of the *Agamemnon*. habitual remark to students; Ulick O'Connor *Oliver St John Gogarty* (1964)
Oscar Wilde 1854–1900	12 Meredith's a prose Browning, and so is Browning. *Intentions* (1891)

Lenny Bruce 1925–66

American comedian. He gained notoriety for flouting the bounds of respectability with his humour, and was imprisoned for obscenity in 1961. He died following an accidental drugs overdose.

Lenny Bruce 1925–66	1 People should be taught what is, not what should be. All my humour is based on destruction and despair. If the whole world were tranquil, without disease and violence, I'd be standing in the breadline. *The Essential Lenny Bruce* (1967)
Kenneth Tynan 1927–80	2 The cynicism is just a façade. Bruce has the heart of an unfrocked evangelist. *How to Talk Dirty and Influence People* (1965)

Anton Bruckner 1824–96

Austrian composer and organist. He wrote ten symphonies, four masses, and a *Te Deum*. He was often persuaded by well-meaning friends to alter his scores.

Hugo Wolf 1860–1903	1 One single cymbal clash by Bruckner is worth all the four symphonies of Brahms with the serenades thrown in. Derek Watson *Bruckner* (1975)

Pieter Bruegel c. 1525–69

Flemish artist. He produced landscapes, religious allegories, and satires of peasant life. Both his sons also worked as painters.

W. H. Auden 1907–73	1 About suffering they were never wrong, The Old Masters . . . In Bruegel's *Icarus*, for instance, how everything turns away Quite leisurely from the disaster. 'Musée des Beaux Arts' (1940)
Charles Baudelaire 1821–67	2 The devilish pandemonium of Bruegel, that can only be interpreted as a kind of special satanic grace. 'Quelques caricaturistes étrangers' (1857)
William Carlos Williams 1883–1963	3 Bruegel saw it all and with his grim humour faithfully recorded it. *Pictures from Brueghel* (1962) 'Children's Games'

Isambard Kingdom Brunel 1806–59

English engineer. The chief engineer of the Great Western Railway, his achievements include designing the Clifton suspension bridge and the first transatlantic steamship, the *Great Western*.

Isambard Kingdom Brunel
1806–59

1 Shall I make a good husband?—Am doubtful—my ambition, or whatever it may be called (it is not the mere wish to be rich) is rather extensive.
diary, 1827

Daniel Gooch
1816–89

2 The greatest of England's engineers . . . the man with the greatest originality of thought and power of execution, bold in his plans but right. The commercial world thought him extravagant; but although he was so, great things are not done by those who sit down and count the cost of every thought and act.
diary, 1859

Frank Bruno 1961–

English boxer. In 1995 he became the WBC world heavyweight champion; by this time he was a popular media personality in Britain.

Frank Bruno
1961–

1 My aim is to become another Diego Maradona—the man with the golden fist.
in 1986

Mike Tyson
1966–

2 Listen, if I chopped off one of my arms, he still couldn't beat me.
in October 1988

Bill Bryson 1951–

American travel writer, author of *Notes From a Small Island* and *A Walk in the Woods*.

Bill Bryson
1951–

1 I do not see myself as a travel writer. To me a travel writer is someone who goes off and faces some really extreme danger . . . I enjoy making jokes.
interview, July 2000

Deborah Bull 1963–

English ballet dancer. She is a Principal Dancer with the Royal Ballet.

Deborah Bull
1963–

1 I'm a Salieri not a Mozart, a Damon Hill not a Michael Schumacher. I wouldn't flounce away from the track muttering about the engine letting me down. Like Damon in his unreliable Arrows car, I'd stay and help the mechanics push it clear.
diary, May 1997

Ninette de Valois
1898–

2 Oh yes. Lovely dancer. Dreadful name.
Deborah Bull *Dancing Away* (1998)

John Bunyan 1628–88

English writer. A Nonconformist, he was imprisoned twice for unlicensed preaching, during which time he began his major work *The Pilgrim's Progress* (1678–84).

Christopher Hill
1912–

1 Just as Oliver Cromwell aimed to bring about the kingdom of God on earth and founded the British Empire, so Bunyan wanted the millennium and got the novel.
A Turbulent, Seditious, and Factious People: John Bunyan and his Church, 1628-1688 (1988)

Rudyard Kipling
1865–1936

2 A tinker out of Bedford,
A vagrant oft in quod,
A private under Fairfax,
A minister of God.
'The Holy War' (1917)

W. B. Yeats
1865–1939

3 Why do you call Bunyan a mystic? It is not possible to make a definition of mysticism to include him.
letter, June 1918

Richard Burbage c.1567–1619

English actor. He was the creator of most of **Shakespeare**'s great tragic roles, and was also associated with the building of the Globe Theatre.

Thomas Middleton
c.1580–1627

1 Astronomers and star-gazers this year,
Write but of four eclipses—five appear;
Death interposing Burbage, and their staying,
Hath made a visible eclipse of playing.
'On the death of that great master in his art . . . R. Burbage'

Julie Burchill 1960–

English journalist and writer.

Lynn Barber
1944–

1 She is a difficult so-and-so, what might be called a proper little madam were she not such an improper and enormous madam.
Demon Barber (1998)

Julie Burchill
1960–

2 I always cry when I talk about my parents. I must say I cry quite easily—psychopaths do.
Lynn Barber *Demon Barber* (1998)

Eric Burdon 1941–

British pop singer, a member of The Animals.

George Melly
1926–

1 Yet it was possible to produce hit records and remain 'in', socially at any rate. Eric Burdon of the Animals did it because he seemed so desperate, so sincere, so drunk, so willing to shoot his mouth off, so excessive. In the pop world of the middle 60s nothing succeeded like excess.
Revolt into Style (1970)

Anthony Burgess 1917–93

English novelist and critic. One of his best-known novels is *A Clockwork Orange* (1962), a disturbing, futuristic vision of juvenile delinquency, violence, and high technology.

Anthony Burgess
1917–93

1 The ideal reader of my novels is a lapsed Catholic and a failed musician, short-sighted, colour-blind, auditorily biased, who has read the books that I have read. He should also be about my age.
George Plimpton (ed.) *Writers at Work* 4th Series (1977)

Edmund Burke 1729–97

British man of letters and Whig politician. Burke wrote particularly on the issues of political emancipation and moderation.

Charles James Fox
1749–1806

1 Burke was a most impractical person, a most unmanageable colleague—he would never support any measure, however convinced he might be in his heart of its utility, if it has first been proposed by another.
Samuel Rogers *Table Talk* (1856)

Edward Gibbon
1737–94

2 I admire his eloquence, I approve his politics, I adore his chivalry, and I can even forgive his superstition.

letter, February 1791

Oliver Goldsmith
1728–74

3 Too nice for a statesman, too proud for a wit.

Retaliation (1774)

Warren Hastings
1732–1818

4 Oft have I wondered that on Irish ground
No poisonous reptiles ever yet were found;
Revealed the secret strands of nature's work,
She saved her venom to create a Burke.

A. Mervyn Davies *Warren Hastings* (1935)

William Hazlitt
1778–1830

5 From the first time I cast my eyes on anything of Burke's . . . I said to myself, 'This is true eloquence: this is a man pouring out his mind on paper.' All other styles seemed to me pedantic and impertinent . . . I conceived too that he might be wrong in his main argument, and yet deliver fifty truths in arriving at a false conclusion.

'On Reading Old Books' (1826)

Samuel Johnson
1709–84

6 If a man were to go by chance at the same time with Burke under a shed, to shun a shower, he would say—'this is an extraordinary man.'

comment, May 1784

Thomas Paine
1737–1809

7 As he rose like a rocket, he fell like the stick.

on Burke's losing the debate on the French Revolution to **Charles James Fox***, in the House of Commons*
Letter to the Addressers on the late Proclamation (1792)

Thomas Paine
1737–1809

8 [He] is not affected by the reality of distress touching his heart, but by the showy resemblance of it striking his imagination. He pities the plumage, but forgets the dying bird.

on Burke's Reflections on the Revolution in France
The Rights of Man (1791)

Richard Brinsley Sheridan
1751–1816

9 When posterity read the speeches of Burke, they will hardly be able to believe that, during his lifetime, he was not considered as a first-rate speaker, not even as a second-rate one.

Samuel Rogers *Table Talk* (1856)

Edward Burne-Jones 1833–98

English painter and designer. His work, which included tapestry and stained-glass window designs, reflected his interest in medieval and literary themes and is typical of the later Pre-Raphaelite style.

Edward Burne-Jones
1833–98

1 I mean by a picture a beautiful romantic dream of something that never was, never will be—in a light better than any light that ever shone—in a land no one can define or remember, only desire—and the forms divinely beautiful.

in *Eminently Victorian* (1974)

Henry James
1843–1916

2 In the palace of art there are many chambers, and that of which Mr Burne-Jones holds the key is a wondrous museum. His imagination, his fertility of invention, his exquisiteness of work, his remarkable gifts as a colorist . . . all these things constitute a brilliant distinction.

in 1877

Dante Gabriel Rossetti
1828–82

3 One of the nicest young fellows in Dreamland.

on meeting Burne-Jones, in 1855

Ellen Terry
1847–1928

4 I generally go and see Burne-Jones when there's a fog. He looks so angelic, painting away there by candlelight.

letter, October 1896

Fanny Burney 1752–1840

English novelist. Her first novels, *Evelina* (1778) and *Cecilia* (1782), brought her fame and the patronage of **Dr Johnson**. She served Queen Charlotte at court from 1786.

Samuel Johnson
1709–84

1 Miss Burney is a real wonder. What she is, she is intuitively. Dr Burney told me she had the fewest advantages of any of his daughters, from some peculiar circumstances. And such has been her timidity, that he himself had not any suspicion of her powers.
in June 1779

Lord Macaulay
1800–59

2 All those whom we have been accustomed to revere as intellectual patriarchs seemed children when compared to her; for Burke sat up all night to read her writings, and Johnson had pronounced her superior to Fielding.
in January 1843

Sir Walter Scott
1771–1832

3 An elderly lady with no remains of personal beauty but a gentle manner and a pleasing expression of countenance.
diary, November 1826

Robert Burns 1759–96

Scottish poet, best known for poems such as 'The Jolly Beggars' (1786) and 'Tam o' Shanter' (1791), and for old Scottish songs which he collected, including 'Auld Lang Syne'.

Robert Burns
1759–96

1 The Poetic Genius of my Country found me as the prophetic bard Elijah did Elisha—at the plough; and threw her inspiring mantle over me.
Poems 1787 (2nd ed.); dedication

Robert Burns
1759–96

2 Some rhyme a neebor's name to lash;
Some rhyme (vain thought!) for needfu' cash;
Some rhyme to court the countra clash,
An' raise a din;
For me, an aim I never fash;
I rhyme for fun.
'To J. S[mith]' (1786)

Lord Byron
1788–1824

3 What an antithetical mind!—tenderness, roughness—delicacy, coarseness—sentiment, sensuality—soaring and grovelling, dirt and deity—all mixed up in that one compound of inspired clay!
diary, December 1813

Thomas Carlyle
1795–1881

4 A Burns is infinitely better educated than a Byron.
Notebooks November 1831

Catherine Carswell
1879–1946

5 Any notion of Robert as a dreamy-eyed young man weaving rhymes while loitering behind the plough, is as prettified as his portraits. An unwelcome energy informed his speech and his movements. Into his Freemasonry, his friendships and loves, he poured the full violence of living.
The Life of Robert Burns (1930)

Ralph Waldo Emerson
1803–82

6 The Confession of Augsburg, the Declaration of Independence, the French Rights of Man, and the 'Marseillaise', are not more weighty documents in the history of freedom than the songs of Burns.
speech, January 1859

William Hazlitt
1778–1830

7 Someone said, that if you had shaken hands with him, his hand would have burnt yours.
Lectures on the English Poets (1818)

Hugh MacDiarmid
1892–1978

8 Mair nonsense has been uttered in his name
Than in ony's barrin' liberty and Christ.
A Drunk Man Looks at the Thistle (1926)

Sir Walter Scott
1771–1832

9 I would have taken the poet, had I not known what he was, for a very sagacious country farmer of the old Scotch school.
J. G. Lockhart *Life of Robert Burns* (1828)

Richard Burton 1821–90

English explorer, anthropologist, and translator. He and John Hanning Speke were the first Europeans to see Lake Tanganyika (1858). He translated the *Arabian Nights* and the *Kama Sutra*.

Richard Burton
1821–90

1 I struggled for forty-seven years, I distinguished myself in every way I possibly could. I never had a compliment nor a 'Thank you', nor a single farthing. I translated a doubtful book in my old age, and I immediately made sixteen thousand guineas.
Arthur Symons *Dramatis Personae* (1923)

Alan Moorehead
1910–83

2 An orchestra without a conductor.
preface to Richard Burton *The Lake Regions of Central Africa* (1961 ed.)

Ouida
1839–1908

3 He was a man who looked like Othello and lived like the Three Mousquetaires blended in one.
in June 1906

Henry Morton Stanley
1841–1904

4 His face struck me for its keen, audacious look. He spoke well and avoided jarring my nerves. If he were not so wicked—I have a strong feeling that I should like him.
diary, September 1872

Richard Burton 1925–84

Welsh actor. He played a number of Shakespearean roles on stage before becoming well known in films. He often co-starred with **Elizabeth Taylor** (to whom he was twice married).

Richard Burton
1925–84

5 You may be as vicious about me as you please. You will only do me justice.
interview, April 1963

Alistair Cooke
1908–

6 It manages to reveal what two years' abandonment to the fleshpots has made us forget: his unsleeping intelligence so exquisitely articulated in his hands and eyes, his marvellous low-key cunning, his capacity, which out-Oliviers Olivier, for the wildest Oedipus agonies.
of Burton as Hamlet
in March 1964

John Gielgud
1904–2000

7 I don't know what's happened to Richard Burton. I think he married some terrible film star and had to live abroad.
remark to Elizabeth Taylor; attributed

Emlyn Williams
1905–87

8 He's miscast and she's Miss Taylor.
on the Burton-Taylor Private Lives *in 1964*
James Harding *Emlyn Williams* (1987)

Matt Busby 1909–94

Scottish-born footballer and football manager. As manager of Manchester United 1945–69 he reconstructed the team after an air crash at Munich airport in 1958 and won the European Cup in 1968.

Hugh McIlvanney
1933–

1 No man in my experience ever exemplified better the ability to treat you as an equal while leaving you with the sure knowledge that you were less than he was.
in January 1994

Harold Wilson
1916–95

2 Matt Busby is a symbol of everything that is best in our great national game.
attributed

Barbara Bush 1925–

American First Lady, wife of President **George Bush**.

asked why she thought she was a popular First Lady:

Barbara Bush
1925–

1 It was because I threatened no one. I was old, white-headed and large.
   in December 1994

George Bush 1924–

American Republican statesman, President 1989–93.

Barbara Bush
1925–

2 Remember, they only name things after you when you're dead or really old.
   at the naming ceremony for the George Bush Centre for Intelligence
   in April 1999

George Bush
1924–

3 Oh, the vision thing.
   responding to the suggestion that he turn his attention from short-term campaign objectives and look to the longer term
   in January 1987

George Bush
1924–

4 What's wrong with being a boring kind of guy?
   campaigning for the Republican nomination, in April 1988

Barbara Ehrenreich
1941–

5 Consider the Vice-president, George Bush, a man so bedevilled by bladder problems that he managed, for the last eight years, to be in the men's room whenever an important illegal decision was made.
   'The Unbearable Being of Whiteness' (1988)

Clive James
1939–

6 Every sentence he manages to utter scatters its component parts like pond water from a verb chasing its own tail.
   The Dreaming Swimmer (1992)

Richard Milhous Nixon
1913–94

7 Bush will be like Ford. As soon as he leaves town, he'll no longer matter. I've been gone 20 years, but I still matter.
   in December 1992

Ann Richards
1933–

8 Poor George, he can't help it—he was born with a silver foot in his mouth.
   keynote speech at the Democratic convention, 1988

George W. Bush 1946–

American Republican statesman, President from 2001; son of **George Bush**. His victory over **Al Gore** was subject to considerable legal debate.

George W. Bush
1946–

9 I do not reinvent myself at every turn. I am not running in borrowed clothes.
   speech accepting the Republican nomination, August 2000

on the prospect of an empty house after their twin daughters had left for college:

Laura Bush
1946–

10 Everyone deals with it in different ways. But I told George I thought running for president was a little extreme.
   speech, August 2000

Molly Ivins
1944–
and **Lou Dubose**

11 If you think his daddy had trouble with 'the vision thing', wait till you meet this one.
   Shrub (2000)

Darcey Bussell 1969–

British ballet dancer. She is a Principal Ballerina with the Royal Ballet.

Anonymous

1 LITTLE GIRL: Mommy, why is Darcee Boucelle such a good dancer?
   MOTHER: It's because she's pretty on the inside and she's doubly pretty on the outside.
   Deborah Bull *Dancing Away* (1998)

R. A. Butler 1902–82

British Conservative politician. He introduced the Education Act of 1944, and narrowly lost the leadership of his party to **Alec Douglas-Home** in 1963.

R. A. Butler
1902–82

1 I think a Prime Minister has to be a butcher and know the joints. That is perhaps where I have not been quite competent, in knowing all the ways that you can cut up a carcass.
in June 1966

Harold Macmillan
1894–1986

2 He would have been marvellous in medieval politics, creeping about the Vatican; a tremendous intriguer, he always had some marvellous plan . . . and he loved the press.
Alistair Horne *Macmillan* (1988)

Lord Byron 1788–1824

English poet. Though criticized on moral grounds, Byron's poetry exerted considerable influence on the romantic movement, particularly on the Continent, and introduced the concept of the Byronic hero.

Matthew Arnold
1822–88

1 What helps it now, that Byron bore,
With haughty scorn which mocked the smart,
Through Europe to the Aetolian shore
The pageant of his bleeding heart?
That thousands counted every groan,
And Europe made his woe her own?
'Stanzas from the Grande Chartreuse' (1855)

Max Beerbohm
1872–1956

2 Byron!—he would be all forgotten today if he had lived to be a florid old gentleman with iron-grey whiskers, writing very long, very able letters to *The Times* about the Repeal of the Corn Laws.
Zuleika Dobson (1911)

Henry Brougham
1778–1868

3 He is at best, he says, but an intruder into the groves of Parnassus; he never lived in a garret, like thorough-bred poets; and 'though he once roved a careless mountaineer in the Highlands of Scotland', he has not of late enjoyed this advantage.
in January 1808

Lord Byron
1788–1824

4 Oh, talk not to me of a name great in story;
The days of our youth are the days of our glory;
And the myrtle and ivy of sweet two-and-twenty
Are worth all your laurels, though ever so plenty.
'Stanzas Written on the Road between Florence and Pisa, November 1821'

Lord Byron
1788–1824

5 I awoke one morning and found myself famous.
on the instantaneous success of Childe Harold
Thomas Moore *Letters and Journals of Lord Byron* (1830)

Jane Welsh Carlyle
1801–66

6 If they had said that the sun or the moon had gone out of the heavens, it could not have struck me with the idea of a more awful and dreary blank in creation than the words: 'Byron is dead!'
letter, May 1824

Claire Clairmont
1798–1879

7 I shall ever remember the gentleness of your manners and the wild originality of your countenance.
letter to Lord Byron, April 1816

John Constable
1776–1837

8 The world is rid of Lord Byron, but the deadly slime of his touch still remains.
letter, May 1824

Johann Wolfgang von
Goethe
1749–1832

9 It still saddens me that Lord Byron, who showed such impatience with the fickle public, wasn't aware of how well the Germans can understand him and how highly they esteem him. With us the moral and political tittle-tattle of the day falls away, leaving the man and the talent standing alone in all their brilliance.
letter, March 1831

Johann Wolfgang von
Goethe
1749–1832

10 Lord Byron is great only as a poet; as soon as he reflects, he is a child.
Johann Peter Eckermann *Conversations with Goethe* (1836–48)

John Keats
1795–1821

11 You speak of Lord Byron and me—there is this great difference between us. He describes what he sees—I describe what I imagine. Mine is the hardest task.
letter, September 1819

Lady Caroline Lamb
1785–1828

12 Mad, bad, and dangerous to know.
of Byron, after their first meeting at a ball
diary, March 1812

Lord Macaulay
1800–59

13 I never heard a single expression of fondness for him fall from the lips of any of those who knew him well.
letter, June 1831

Lord Macaulay
1800–59

14 From the poetry of Lord Byron they drew a system of ethics, compounded of misanthropy and voluptuousness, a system in which the two great commandments were, to hate your neighbour, and to love your neighbour's wife.
Essays Contributed to the Edinburgh Review (1843)

Enoch Powell
1912–98

15 Always looking at himself in mirrors to make sure he was sufficiently outrageous.
in May 1988

Mary Shelley
1797–1851

16 Our Lord Byron—the fascinating—faulty—childish—philosophical being—daring the world—docile to a private circle—impetuous and indolent—gloomy and yet more gay than any other.
letter, January 1830

Percy Bysshe Shelley
1792–1822

17 I have not the smallest influence over Lord Byron, in this particular, and if I had, I certainly should employ it to eradicate from his great mind the delusions of Christianity, which, in spite of his reason, seem perpetually to recur.
letter, April 1822

Julius Caesar 100–44 BC

Roman general and statesman. He conquered Gaul and invaded Britain, and after a civil war he became dictator of Rome. He was assassinated.

Julius Caesar
100–44 BC

1 Caesar had rather be first in a village than second at Rome.
Francis Bacon *The Advancement of Learning*; based on Plutarch

Thomas Campbell
1777–1844

2 What millions died—that Caesar might be great!
Pleasures of Hope (1799)

Curio

3 Every woman's man and every man's woman.
Suetonius *Lives of the Caesars*

George Bernard Shaw
1856–1950

4 A man of great common sense and good taste, meaning thereby a man without originality or moral courage.
Notes to Caesar and Cleopatra (1901)

John Cage 1912–92

American composer, pianist, and writer. He was notable for his experimental approach, which included the use of randomness and periods of silence.

Pierre Boulez
1925–

1 He was refreshing but not very bright. His freshness came from an absence of knowledge.

Joan Peyser *Boulez: Composer, Conductor, Enigma* (1976)

asked about the noise of New York:

John Cage
1912–92

2 Many people have not learned to enjoy it as harmony. I'm surprised at that. They find it nerve-racking. And I have never found a sound to be nerve-racking; not even a burglar alarm.

Andrew Ford *Composer to Composer* (1993)

Arnold Schoenberg
1874–1951

3 He is not a composer, but an inventor—of genius.

Peter Yates *Twentieth Century Music* (1968)

Nicolas Cage 1964–

American actor. His films include *Leaving Las Vegas*.

Jim Carrey
1962–

4 Nic is representative of the Picasso school of acting. He doesn't mind putting the two eyes on one side of the face.

Douglas Thompson *Uncaged: the Biography of Nicolas Cage* (1997)

David Lynch
1946–

5 You give him an idea and he grabs onto it like crazy. He's like a wild dog on a leash.

Douglas Thompson *Uncaged: the Biography of Nicolas Cage* (1997)

James Cagney 1899–1986

American actor. He is chiefly remembered for playing gangster roles in films, but he was also a skilled dancer and comedian.

Alistair Cooke
1908–

1 That jaunty, bouncing, forever cocky little figure, successfully pretending through so many rowdy films to be a scamp but rarely managing to conceal the candid, decent Everyman underneath.

Fun and Games with Alistair Cooke (1994)

Kenneth Tynan
1927–80

2 Cagney, even with sub-machine gun hot in hand and corpses piling at his ankles, can still persuade many people that it was not his fault.

in May 1951

Michael Caine 1933–

English film actor. He achieved fame in laconic, anti-heroic roles, and later appeared in a wide variety of films.

Michael Caine
1933–

1 My career must be slipping. This is the first time I've been available to pick up an award.

at the Golden Globe awards, January 1999

Michael Caine
1933–

2 Just because I have made a point of never losing my accent it doesn't mean I am an eel-and-pie yob.

in April 2000

James Callaghan 1912–

British Labour statesman, Prime Minister 1976–9. He became Prime Minister as the leader of a minority government, but was defeated in the election following the 'winter of discontent'.

Tony Benn
1925–

1 Jim was an old trade unionist who believed that you ought to discuss. The IMF meetings were riveting. He set me up to talk first so that he could knock me down and say there was no alternative.

talk, January 1999

| James Callaghan 1912– | 2 | When I am shaving in the morning I say to myself that if I were a young man I would emigrate. By the time I am sitting down to breakfast I ask myself, 'where would I go?'
Barbara Castle's diary, November 1974 |

| Roy Jenkins 1920– | 3 | There is nobody in politics I can remember and no case I can think of in history where a man combined such a powerful political personality with so little intelligence.
Richard Crossman's diary, September 1969 |

| Harold Wilson 1916–95 | 4 | He's inordinately ambitious and inordinately weak. So weak that as Chancellor of the Exchequer he used to weep on my shoulder and then go away and intrigue against me.
Richard Crossman's diary, September 1968 |

Maria Callas 1923–77

American-born operatic soprano, of Greek parentage. She was a coloratura soprano whose bel canto style of singing was especially suited to early Italian opera.

| Maria Callas 1923–77 | 1 | First I lost weight, then I lost my voice, and now I've lost Onassis.
Barbara McDowell and Hana Umlauf *Woman's Almanac* (1977) |

| Marguerite Duras 1914– | 2 | Behind the dazzling fires of footlights no one is so beautiful as this ugly woman.
attributed |

Julia Margaret Cameron 1815–79

English photographer, credited with being the first to use soft-focus techniques. Her work often reflects the influence of contemporary painting.

| Julia Margaret Cameron 1815–79 | 1 | I longed to arrest all beauty that came before me, and at length the longing has been satisfied.
Annals of My Glass House (1874) |

| Victor Hugo 1802–85 | 2 | No one has ever captured the rays of the sun as you have. I throw myself at your feet.
Sylvia Wolf *Julia Margaret Cameron's Women* (1999) |

| Emily Tennyson 1813–96 | 3 | Mrs Cameron is making endless Madonnas and May Queens and Foolish Virgins and Wise Virgins and I know not what besides. It really is wonderful how she puts her spirit into people.
Sylvia Wolf *Julia Margaret Cameron's Women* (1999) |

Naomi Campbell 1970–

British fashion model.

| Naomi Campbell 1970– | 1 | I make my boyfriends famous.
attributed |

Mrs Patrick Campbell 1865–1940

English actress. Renowned for her wit and beauty, she played many major roles on the London stage, but later declined in popularity.

| James Agate 1877–1947 | 2 | This was an actress who, for twenty years, had the world at her feet. She kicked it away, and the ball rolled out of her reach.
diary, April 1940 |

| Mrs Patrick Campbell 1865–1940 | 3 | I'm out of a job. London wants flappers, and I can't flap.
on herself, in 1927 |

| George Bernard Shaw 1856–1950 | 4 | It is greatly to Mrs Patrick Campbell's credit that, bad as the play was, her acting was worse.
review of Sardou's *Fedora*, June 1895 |

| Alexander Woollcott 1887–1943 | 5 | She was like a sinking ship firing on the rescuers.
While Rome Burns (1944) |

Henry Campbell-Bannerman 1836–1908

British Liberal statesman, Prime Minister 1905–8.

Nicolas Bentley
1907–78

1 He is remembered chiefly as the man about whom all is forgotten.
An Edwardian Album (1974)

R. B. Cunninghame Graham
1852–1936

2 He has all the qualifications for a great Liberal Prime Minister. He wears spats and he has a beautiful set of false teeth.
James Bridie *One Way of Living* (1930)

Albert Camus 1913–60

French novelist, dramatist, and essayist. He achieved fame with his first novel, *The Outsider* (1942); it conveys his conception of the absurdity of human existence.

Albert Camus
1913–60

1 What I know most surely about morality and the duty of man I owe to sport.
often quoted as ' . . . I owe to football'
Herbert R. Lottman *Albert Camus* (1979)

George Canning 1770–1827

British Tory statesman, Prime Minister 1827. As Foreign Secretary he presided over a reversal of Britain's hitherto conservative foreign policy.

Lord Byron
1788–1824

1 Even thy genius, Canning, may permit,
Who, bred a statesman, still was born a wit.
'The Age of Bronze' (1823)

George IV
1762–1830

2 Very well, gentlemen, since you are determined to have him, take him in God's name, but remember I tell you he will throw you all overboard.
in September 1822

William Hazlitt
1778–1830

3 Mr Canning has the luckless ambition to play off the tricks of a political rope-dancer, and he chooses to do it on the nerves of humanity!
The Spirit of the Age (1824)

Eric Cantona 1966–

French footballer. A gifted but volatile forward, he was suspended for eight months by the FA in 1995 for a flying kick against a spectator who had insulted him.

Eric Cantona
1966–

1 We are not on Earth to be imposed upon, or to accept things that bug us and make us unhappy. I, for one, don't have the strength to say yes all the time.
in January 2000

Truman Capote 1924–84

American writer. His works range from the light-hearted *Breakfast at Tiffany's* to *In Cold Blood*, a meticulous re-creation of a brutal multiple murder.

Dominick Dunne
1925–

1 What happened to Truman Capote was that he got inside the establishment and tried to stay. It's just a place to visit.
interview, October 2000

of Truman Capote's death:

Gore Vidal
1925–

2 Good career move.
attributed

Pierre Cardin 1922–

French couturier, the first designer in the field of haute couture to show a collection of clothes for men as well as women.

Pierre Cardin
1922–

1 I always told myself that if ever I made my fortune, I would never try to impress people better off than myself: they would simply find me ridiculous. And if I was to show off in front of those poorer, it would be humiliating for them.
Nicholas Coleridge *The Fashion Conspiracy* (1988)

George Carey 1935–

English Anglican churchman, Archbishop of Canterbury since 1991. He comes from a broadly evangelical background.

George Carey
1935–

1 People have described me as a 'management bishop' but I say to my critics, 'Jesus was a management expert too.'
in March 1991

Thomas Carlyle 1795–1881

Scottish historian and political philosopher, author of *History of the French Revolution* (1837). Many of his works advocate a benevolent autocracy.

Matthew Arnold
1822–88

1 I never much liked Carlyle. He seemed to me to be 'carrying coals to Newcastle', as our proverb says; preaching earnestness to a nation which had plenty of it by nature, but was less abundantly supplied with several other useful things.
letter, March 1881

Samuel Butler
1835–1902

2 It was very good of God to let Carlyle and Mrs Carlyle marry one another and so make only two people miserable instead of four.
letter, November 1884

Julia Margaret Cameron
1815–79

3 When I have had such men before my camera my whole soul has endeavoured to do its duty towards them in recording faithfully the greatness of the inner as well as the features of the outer man . . . The photograph thus taken has been almost the embodiment of a prayer.
on photographing Carlyle
Sylvia Wolf *Julia Margaret Cameron's Women* (1999)

John Carey
1934–

4 Carlyle was so poisonous it's a wonder his mind didn't infect his bloodstream.
in 1983

Jane Welsh Carlyle
1801–66

5 I am not at all the sort of person you and I took me for.
letter to Thomas Carlyle, May 1822

Charles Darwin
1809–82

6 He has been all-powerful in impressing some grand moral truths on the minds of men. On the other hand, his views about slavery were revolting. In his eyes might was right. His mind seemed to me a very narrow one; even if all branches of science, which he despised, are excluded.
Francis Darwin (ed.) *The Life and Letters of Charles Darwin* (1887)

Friedrich Nietzsche
1844–1900

7 Thomas Carlyle, that arrogant old muddle-head and grumbler, spent his long life trying to romanticize the common sense of his Englishmen—but in vain!
Human, All-too-Human vol. 2 (1878)

Alfred, Lord Tennyson
1809–92

8 Carlyle is a poet to whom nature has denied the faculty of verse.
letter, c.1870

Mark Twain 1835–1910	9	At bottom he was probably fond of them [Americans], but he was always able to conceal it. *in December 1899*
Walt Whitman 1819–92	10	Rugged, mountainous, volcanic, he was himself more a French revolution than any of his volumes. *Specimen Days February 1881*

Andrew Carnegie 1835–1919

Scottish-born American industrialist and philanthropist. He built up a fortune in the steel industry, then retired from business and devoted his wealth to charitable purposes.

Andrew Carnegie 1835–1919	1	I was brought up among Chartists and Republicans. . . . My childhood's desire was to get to be a man and kill a king. *J. F. Wall Andrew Carnegie (1970)*
Billy Connolly 1942–	2	Still, they [the Americans] got Andrew Carnegie about whom it was said that he gave money away as silently as a waiter falling down a flight of stairs with a tray of glasses. *Gullible's Travel (1982)*
Albert Einstein 1879–1955	3	I am absolutely convinced that no wealth in the world can help humanity forward, even in the hands of the most devoted worker in this cause . . . Can anyone imagine Moses, Jesus, or Gandhi with the moneybags of Carnegie? *Mein Weltbild (1934)*

Caroline of Ansbach 1683–1737

Queen of George II, over whom she had considerable influence.

Lady Mary Wortley Montagu 1689–1762	1	Superior to her waiting nymphs, As lobster to attendant shrimps. *of Queen Caroline when dressed in pink* 'Epistle to Lord Hervey on the King's Birthday'

Caroline of Brunswick 1768–1821

Wife of **George IV**. The marriage was a failure, and the king attempted unsuccessfully to divorce her.

Anonymous	2	Most Gracious Queen, we thee implore To go away and sin no more, But if that effort be too great, To go away at any rate. *letter from Francis Burton to Lord Colchester, November 1820*
Jane Austen 1775–1817	3	I suppose all the world is sitting in judgement upon the Princess of Wales's letter. Poor woman, I shall support her as long as I can, because she *is* a woman and because I hate her husband. *letter, February 1813*
Max Beerbohm 1872–1956	4	Fate wrote her a most tremendous tragedy, and she played it in tights. *The Yellow Book (1894)*
Princess Charlotte 1796–1817	5	My mother was bad, but she would not have become as bad as she was if my father had not been infinitely worse. *Ernst Stockmar Memoirs of Baron Stockmar (1873)*
George IV 1762–1830	6	Harris, I am not well; pray get me a glass of brandy. *on first seeing his future wife* *Earl of Malmesbury's diary, April 1795*

when forced by a mob to cheer Caroline of Brunswick:

Duke of Wellington
1769–1852

7 God Save the Queen, and may all your wives be like her!

Elizabeth Longford *Wellington: Pillar of State* (1972); also attributed to Lord Anglesey and others

Dora Carrington 1893–1932

English painter. She became involved with the Bloomsbury Group, in particular **Lytton Strachey**. When he died in 1932 she committed suicide.

Gerald Brenan
1894–1987

1 I was as proud of my affair with her as I was of having been in the line at Passchendaele. The tears I shed for her were, I thought, my true medals.

Jane Hill *The Art of Dora Carrington* (1994)

Dora Carrington
1893–1932

2 I often hope I shall die at forty, I could not bear the ignominy of becoming a stout boring elderly lady with a hobby of sketching in watercolours.

letter, 1932

Lewis Carroll 1832–98

English writer. He was a mathematics lecturer at Oxford University and wrote the children's classics *Alice's Adventures in Wonderland* (1865) and *Through the Looking Glass* (1871).

Ellen Terry
1847–1928

1 He was as fond of me as he could be of anyone over the age of ten.

Derek Hudson *Lewis Carroll* (1954)

Henri Cartier-Bresson 1908–

French photographer and film director. Intent on capturing the 'decisive moment' of a scene or event, he recorded the lives of ordinary people without artificial composition.

Cecil Beaton
1904–80

1 His cherubic, almost simpleton, appearance is most disconcerting—for it gives no indication of the far from simple character of this somewhat twisted artist of the secret, prying lens.

diary, October 1944

Barbara Cartland 1901–2000

English writer. A prolific author, she specialized in light romantic fiction.

Barbara Cartland
1901–2000

1 I was shown round Tutankhamun's tomb in the 1920s. I saw all this wonderful pink on the walls and the artefacts. I was so impressed that I vowed to wear it for the rest of my life.

in March 1998

Alan Clark
1928–

2 A magnificent sight presents itself: Barbara Cartland wearing an electric pink chiffon dress, with false eyelashes, as thick as those caterpillars that give you a rash if you handle them, was draped on the central staircase with her dress arranged like a caricature of the celebrated Cecil Beaton photograph of the Countess of Jersey.

diary May 1984

Pablo Casals 1876–1973

Spanish cellist, conductor, and composer. He went into voluntary exile during the Franco regime.

Jacqueline du Pré
1945–87

1 It gave me pleasure to talk with him about the music and to play for him, but I didn't find him daunting. He was surrounded by all these old ladies who just wanted to lie at his feet. He listened but he was dogmatic. He wanted everything to be played his way.

Carol Easton *Jacqueline du Pré* (1989)

Mary Cassatt 1844–1926

American painter. Cassatt worked mostly in Paris and was persuaded by **Degas** to exhibit with the Impressionists. Her paintings display a close interest in everyday subject matter.

Edgar Degas
1834–1917

1 I will not admit that a woman can draw so well.
Ellen Wilson *American Painter in Paris* (1971)

Barbara Castle 1910–

British Labour politician. As Minister for Transport she introduced the breathalyser test and the 70 mph speed limit. She campaigns in support of pension reform.

Anonymous

1 If she wrote a note for the milkman she would bring socialism into it.
attributed

Gordon Brown
1951–

2 She is my mentor and my tormentor.
attributed

Barbara Castle
1910–

3 I will fight for what I believe in until I drop dead. And that's what keeps you alive.
in January 1998

Lord Castlereagh 1769–1822

British Tory statesman. He became Foreign Secretary in 1812 and represented Britain at the Congress of Vienna (1814–15); he committed suicide apparently as a result of pressure of work.

Lord Byron
1788–1824

1 The intellectual eunuch Castlereagh.
Don Juan (1819–24)

Lord Byron
1788–1824

2 So he has cut his throat at last!—He! Who?
The man who cut his country's long ago.
'Epigram on Lord Castlereagh'

Percy Bysshe Shelley
1792–1822

3 I met Murder on the way—
He had a mask like Castlereagh.
'The Mask of Anarchy' (1819)

Fidel Castro 1927–

Cuban statesman, Prime Minister 1959–76 and President since 1976. He set up a communist regime which survived the abortive Bay of Pigs invasion, the Cuban Missile Crisis, and the collapse of the Soviet bloc.

Richard Milhous Nixon
1913–94

1 Castro couldn't even go to the bathroom unless the Soviet Union put the nickel in the toilet.
interview, September 1980

Catherine the Great 1729–96

Empress of Russia. She became empress in her own right after her husband was deposed and assassinated.

Catherine the Great
1729–96

1 I shall be an autocrat: that's my trade. And the good Lord will forgive me: that's his.
attributed

Denis Diderot
1713–84

2 The soul of Brutus and the charms of Cleopatra.
Henri Troyat *Catherine the Great* (1978)

Elizabeth Montagu
1720–1800

3 This Empress is a monster with talents.
letter, June 1765

Cato the Younger 95–46 BC

Roman politician. He was an opponent of the dictatorial ambitions of **Julius Caesar**.

Cicero
106–43 BC

1 He delivers his opinions as though he were living in Plato's Republic rather than among the dregs of Romulus.
Ad Atticum

Margaret Cavendish, Duchess of Newcastle c.1624–74

English woman of letters. *Poems and Fancies* (1653) was followed by many other works on a wide range of themes.

Margaret Cavendish
c.1624–74

1 Greek, Latin poets, I could never read,
Nor their historians, but our English Speed;
I could not steal their wit, nor plots out take;
All my plays' plots, my own poor brain did make.
Plays (1662) 'To the Readers'

Charles Lamb
1775–1834

2 A dear favourite of mine, of the last century but one—the thrice noble, chaste, and virtuous,—but again somewhat fantastical, and original-brained, generous Margaret Newcastle.
Essays of Elia (1823)

Samuel Pepys
1633–1703

3 The whole story of this lady is a romance, and all she doth is romantic. Her footmen in velvet coats, and herself in an antique dress as they say, and was the other day at her own play, *The Humorous lovers*; the most ridiculous thing that ever was wrote, but yet she and her Lord mightily pleased with it.
diary, April 1667

Robert Cecil c.1563–1612

English statesman. Secretary of State for **Elizabeth I**, he helped to smooth the succession of **James I**, and continued to hold office under him.

Anonymous

1 Here lieth Robin Crookback, unjustly reckoned
A Richard the Third, he was Judas the Second.
contemporary verse on Robert Cecil's death; P. M. Handover *The Second Cecil* (1959)

Francis Bacon
1561–1626

2 He was no fit counsellor to make affairs better, yet he was fit to stop them from getting worse.
David Cecil *The Cecils of Hatfield House* (1973)

William Cecil
1520–98

3 I advise thee not to affect, or neglect, popularity too much. Seek not to be Essex; shun to be Raleigh.
advice to his son, given in the 1570s

William Cecil 1520–98

English statesman. He was **Elizabeth I**'s most trusted councillor and minister and the driving force behind many of her government's policies.

Elizabeth I
1533–1603

4 This judgement I have of you that you will not be corrupted by any manner of gift and that you will be faithful to the state; and that without respect of my private will you will give me that counsel which you think best.
in 1558

Elizabeth I
1533–1603

5 My lord, we make use of you, not for your bad legs, but for your good head.
referring to Cecil's gout
F. Chamberlin *Sayings of Queen Elizabeth* (1923)

Ben Jonson
c.1573–1637

6 The only faithful watchman for the realm,
That in all tempests never quit the helm,
But stood unshaken in his deeds and name,
And laboured in the work; not with the fame.
'Epigram on William Lord Burghley'

Paul Celan 1920–70

Romanian-born poet, who wrote in German. His poem 'Death Fugue' reflects his experiences in a Nazi labour camp.

Paul Celan
1920–70

1 There's nothing in the world for which a poet will give up writing, not even when he is a Jew and the language of his poems is German.
letter, August 1948

Benvenuto Cellini 1500–71

Italian goldsmith and sculptor. His work is characterized by its elaborate virtuosity.

Michelangelo
1475–1564

1 For years I have known you to be the greatest goldsmith ever heard of; and from this time I shall look on you as a sculptor of like merit.
letter to Cellini, c. 1554

Cervantes 1547–1616

Spanish novelist and dramatist. His most famous work is *Don Quixote* (1605–15), a satire on chivalric romances that greatly influenced the development of the novel.

Lord Byron
1788–1824

1 Cervantes smiled Spain's chivalry away.
Don Juan (1819–24)

Paul Cézanne 1839–1906

French painter. He is closely identified with post-Impressionism. His later work is dominated by the increasing use of simplified geometrical forms; this was an important influence on the development of cubism.

Mary Cassatt
1844–1926

1 Cézanne is one of the most liberal artists I have ever seen. He prefaces every remark with *Pour moi* it is so and so, but he grants that everyone may be as honest and as true to nature from their convictions; he doesn't believe that everyone should see alike.
letter, 1894

Paul Cézanne
1839–1906

2 I believe I become more lucid before nature. Unfortunately, with me, the realization of my sensations is always very painful. I can't attain the intensity which is developed in my senses; I don't get that magnificent richness of colouring which animates nature . . . Look at that cloud—I would like to be able to paint that. Now Monet, he could do it. He has the muscles.
Herbert Read *The Meaning of Art* (3rd ed., 1951)

Bob Dylan
1941–

3 In writing songs I've learned as much from Cézanne as I have from Woody Guthrie.
Clinton Heylin *Dylan: Behind the Shades* (1991)

Émile Zola
1840–1902

4 To convince Cézanne of anything is like teaching the towers of Notre Dame to dance.
Lawrence Gowing 'The Great Transformation'

Marc Chagall 1887–1985

Russian-born French painter and graphic artist. His work was characterized by the use of rich emotive colour and dream imagery, and had a significant influence on surrealism.

Marc Chagall
1887–1985

1 I don't know if colour chose me or I chose colour, but since childhood I've been married to colour in its pure state.
R. McMullen and I. Bidermass *The World of Marc Chagall* (1968)

Neville Chamberlain 1869–1940

British Conservative statesman, Prime Minister 1937–40. He pursued a policy of appeasement with Germany, but was forced to abandon this policy in 1939.

Aneurin Bevan
1897–1960

1 Listening to a speech by Chamberlain is like paying a visit to Woolworth's: everything in its place and nothing above sixpence.
Michael Foot *Aneurin Bevan* vol. 1 (1962)

Winston Churchill
1874–1965

2 In the depths of that dusty soul is nothing but abject surrender.
Leon Harris *The Fine Art of Political Wit* (1965)

David Lloyd George
1863–1945

3 Neville has a retail mind in a wholesale business.
in 1935

David Lloyd George
1863–1945

4 He might make an adequate Lord Mayor of Birmingham in a lean year.
Leon Harris *The Fine Art of Political Wit* (1965)

David Lloyd George
1863–1945

5 [He] saw foreign policy through the wrong end of a municipal drainpipe.
Leon Harris *The Fine Art of Political Wit* (1965); also attributed to Churchill

Harold Nicolson
1886–1968

6 Chamberlain (who has the mind and manner of a clothes-brush) aims only at assuring temporary peace at the price of ultimate defeat.
diary, June 1938

George Orwell
1903–50

7 He was merely a stupid old man doing his best according to his very dim lights.
Collected Essays, Journalism and Letters (1968)

Raymond Chandler 1888–1959

American novelist. He is remembered as the creator of the private detective Philip Marlowe and as one of the exponents of the tough, realistic style of hard-boiled detective fiction.

Raymond Chandler
1888–1959

1 If my books had been any worse, I should not have been invited to Hollywood, and if they had been any better, I should not have come.
letter, December 1945

Raymond Chandler
1888–1959

2 Having just read the admirable profile of Hemingway in the *New Yorker* I realize that I am much too clean to be a genius, much too sober to be a champ, and far, far too clumsy with a shotgun to live the good life.
Philip Durham *Down These Mean Streets a Man Must Go* (1963)

Subrahmanyan Chandrasekhar 1910–95

Indian-born American astronomer. He worked on stellar evolution.

Subrahmanyan Chandrasekhar
1910–95

1 I had no mentor. And nobody 'influenced' me. I wrote my thesis on my own. I have always been alone. This is not criticism. It is the character of my work.
Kameshwar C. Wali *S. Chandrasekhar: The Man Behind the Legend* (1997)

Coco Chanel 1883–1971

French couturière. Her simple but sophisticated garments were a radical departure from the stiff corseted styles of the early twentieth century.

Cecil Beaton
1904–80

1 She was a female Brummell. Just as the Beau got rid of frills and furbelows overnight, so too Chanel demonstrated that nothing was more chic than fine linen, navy-blue serge, and lots of soap.
diary, 1971

Coco Chanel
1883–1971

2 God knows I wanted love. But the moment I had to choose between the man I loved and my dresses, I chose the dresses.
Marcel Haedrich *Coco Chanel* (1987)

Karl Lagerfeld
1939–

3 Chanel never liked knees.
in July 1990

Charlie Chaplin 1889–1977

English film actor and director. He directed and starred in many short silent comedies, mostly playing a bowler-hatted tramp, a character which was his trademark for more than twenty-five years.

Charlie Chaplin
1889–1977

1 I remain one thing and one thing only, and this is a clown. It places me on a much higher plane than any politician.
My Autobiography (1964)

W. C. Fields
1880–1946

2 He's the best ballet dancer that ever lived, and if I get a good chance I'll kill him with my bare hands.
Kenneth Tynan *Profiles* (1989)

Sam Goldwyn
1882–1974

3 Chaplin is no business man. All he knows is that he can't take less.
My Autobiography (1964)

W. Somerset Maugham
1874–1965

4 He does not give you the impression of a happy man. I have a notion that he suffers from a nostalgia of the slums. The celebrity he enjoys, his wealth, imprison him in a way of life in which he finds only constraint. I think he looks back to the freedom of his struggling youth.
in 1922

Ottoline Morrell
1873–1938

5 I found in Charlie Chaplin something of the same intense poignancy as there was in Nijinsky.
Robert Gathorne-Hardy (ed.) *Ottoline* (1963)

Will Rogers
1879–1935

6 The Zulus know Chaplin better than Arkansas knows Garbo.
in August 1939

Mae West
1892–1980

7 Chaplin was a really great artist who also created his own character.
Charlotte Chandler *The Ultimate Seduction* (1984)

Charlemagne 742–814

King of the Franks 768–814 and Holy Roman emperor 800–14. His court became the cultural centre of the Carolingian Renaissance.

Alcuin
c.735–804

1 Happy is the people for whom divine mercy has provided so good and wise a ruler.
letter to Charlemagne, 801

Einhard
c.770–840

2 He was large and strong and of lofty stature, though not disproportionately tall; the upper part of his head was round, his eyes very large and animated, nose a little long, hair fair, and face laughing and merry. Thus his appearance was always stately and dignified, whether he was standing or sitting; although his neck was somewhat short, and his belly rather prominent; but the symmetry of the rest of his body concealed these defects.
The Life of Charlemagne (ed. S. Painter, 1960)

Charles I 1600–49

King of England, Scotland, and Ireland 1625–49. His reign was dominated by the deepening religious and constitutional crisis that resulted in the English Civil War. He was tried by a special court and beheaded.

Charles I
1600–49

1 If I would have given way to an arbitrary way, for to have all laws changed according to the power of the sword, I needed not to have come here; and therefore I tell you (and I pray God it be not laid to your charge) that I am the martyr of the people.
speech on the scaffold, January 1649

Earl of Clarendon
1609–74

2 He was always an immoderate lover of the Scottish nation, having not only been born there but educated by that people and besieged by them always, having few English about him till he was King.
History of the Great Rebellion (1703)

Earl of Clarendon
1609–74

3 He was very fearless in his person, but not enterprising, and had an excellent understanding, but was not confident enough of it; which made him often times change his opinion for a worse, and follow the advice of a man that did not judge so well as himself.
History of the Great Rebellion (1703)

Oliver Cromwell
1599–1658

4 Cruel necessity.
on the execution of Charles I
Joseph Spence *Anecdotes* (1820)

William Laud
1573–1645

5 A mild and gracious prince who knew not how to be, or how to be made, great.
P. Heylin *Cyprianus Angelicus* (1688)

Andrew Marvell
1621–78

6 *He* nothing common did or mean
Upon that memorable scene:
But with his keener eye
The axe's edge did try.
on the execution of Charles I
'An Horatian Ode upon Cromwell's Return from Ireland' (written 1650)

Charles II 1630–85

King of England, Scotland, and Ireland 1660–85. He displayed considerable adroitness in handling the difficult constitutional situation, but continuing religious and political strife dogged his reign.

Gilbert Burnet
1643–1715

7 A secularist, he shook off Presbyterianism as a viper, utilised Episcopacy as the readiest political tool, and finally put on Popery as a comfortable shroud to die in.
History of My Own Time (1724)

Charles II
1630–85

8 This is very true: for my words are my own, and my actions are my ministers'.
reply to Lord Rochester's epitaph on him
Thomas Hearne: *Remarks and Collections* (1885–1921); see 11 below

Daniel Defoe
1660–1731

9 His lazy, long, lascivious reign.
The True-Born Englishman (1701)

Lord Rochester
1647–80

10 A merry monarch, scandalous and poor.
'A Satire on King Charles II' (1697)

Lord Rochester
1647–80

11 Here lies a great and mighty king
Whose promise none relies on;
He never said a foolish thing,
Nor ever did a wise one.
an alternative first line reads: 'Here lies our sovereign lord the King'
'The King's Epitaph'

Charles XII 1682–1718

King of Sweden 1697–1718. Initially successful in the Great Northern War against Denmark, Poland-Saxony, and Russia, his later invasion of Russia ended in the destruction of his army.

Samuel Johnson
1709–84

12 A frame of adamant, a soul of fire,
No dangers fright him, and no labours tire.
The Vanity of Human Wishes (1749)

Voltaire
1694–1778

13 The only person in history who was free from all human weakness.
Life of Charles XII (1731)

Charles, Prince of Wales 1948–

Heir apparent to **Elizabeth II**. His interests include architecture, the environment, and education. He married Lady **Diana** Spencer in 1981; the couple had two children, and were divorced in 1996.

Margaret Atwood 14 If he weren't the prince or the duke or whatever he is, he would be
1939–   considered a valuable eccentric person going against the grain and speaking out. A sort of Bertrand Russell or Albert Schweitzer of the food chain.
in September 2000

Noël Coward 15 I told the Queen how moved I had been by Prince Charles's Investiture
1899–1973   [as Prince of Wales], and she gaily shattered my sentimental illusions by saying that they were both struggling not to giggle because at the dress rehearsal the crown was too big and extinguished him like a candle-snuffer!
diary, July 1969

Ray Charles 1930–

American pianist and singer. Totally blind from the age of 6, he drew on blues, jazz, and country music for his inspiration.

Ray Charles 16 My people made me what I am, because you have to become big in your
1930–   own community first, but as far as leaving that black audience exclusively, I never even thought twice about it.
Peter Guralnick *Sweet Soul Music* (1986)

Leonard Cohen 17 Ray Charles is the greatest. I think in terms of just the sheer perfection
1934–   of his style, I don't think there's anybody that touches him.
Jim Devlin *Leonard Cohen in His Own Words* (1998)

Bobby Charlton 1935–

English footballer. An outstanding Manchester United striker, he scored a record forty-nine goals for England and was a member of the side that won the World Cup in 1966.

Bobby Charlton 1 Some folks tell me that we professional players are soccer slaves. Well,
1935–   if this is slavery, give me a life sentence.
in 1960

Jimmy Greaves 2 Bobby Charlton almost rivals Churchill as the best known Briton of all
1940–   the 20th century. Britain never had a greater sporting ambassador.
attributed

Thomas Chatterton 1752–70

English poet, chiefly remembered for his fabricated poems professing to be those of a 15th-century monk. He committed suicide at the age of 17.

John Keats 1 Oh Chatterton! how very sad thy fate!
1795–1821   Dear child of sorrow! Son of misery!
How soon the film of death obscured that eye,
Whence genius wildly flashed.
'To Chatterton' (written 1815)

Horace Walpole 2 He was an instance that a complete genius and a complete rogue can be
1717–97   formed before a man is of age.
letter, July 1778

William Wordsworth 3 I thought of Chatterton, the marvellous boy,
1770–1850   The sleepless soul that perished in its pride.
'Resolution and Independence' (1807)

Geoffrey Chaucer c.1343–1400

English poet. His most famous work, the *Canterbury Tales* (c.1387–1400), is a cycle of linked tales told by a group of pilgrims.

William Caxton
c.1421–91

1 The worshipful father and first founder and embellisher of ornate eloquence in our English, I mean Master Geoffrey Chaucer.
in c.1478

John Dryden
1631–1700

2 'Tis sufficient to say, according to the proverb, that here is God's plenty.
of Chaucer
Fables Ancient and Modern (1700)

John Dryden
1631–1700

3 [Chaucer] is a perpetual fountain of good sense.
Fables Ancient and Modern (1700)

James Joyce
1882–1941

4 Of all English writers Chaucer is the clearest. He is as precise and slick as a Frenchman.
Frank Budgen *James Joyce and the Making of Ulysses* (1934)

John Lydgate
c.1370–c.1451

5 Sithe off oure language he was the lodesterre.
The Fall of Princes (1431–8)

Edmund Spenser
c.1552–99

6 Dan Chaucer, well of English undefiled.
The Faerie Queen (1596)

Virginia Woolf
1882–1941

7 He was a staunch churchman, but he laughed at priests. He was an able public servant and courtier, but his views on sexual morality were extremely lax. He sympathized with poverty, but did nothing to improve the lot of the poor . . . And yet, as we read him, we are absorbing morality at every pore.
The Common Reader (1925)

Anton Chekhov 1860–1904

Russian dramatist and short-story writer. His work portrays upper-class life in pre-revolutionary Russia with a blend of naturalism and symbolism and almost imperceptible shifts from comedy to tragedy.

John Carey
1934–

1 Chekhov must have been the sanest person in 19th-century Europe. He was sanity raised to the power of genius.
in 1987

Anton Chekhov
1860–1904

2 Medicine is my lawful wife and literature is my mistress. When I get tired of one I spend the night with the other.
letter, September 1888

V. S. Pritchett
1900–97

3 Chekhov had the art of showing us art as inverted poetry.
Chekhov: A Spirit Set Free (1988)

Leo Tolstoy
1828–1910

4 You know I can't stand Shakespeare's plays, but yours are even worse.
remark to Chekhov, after seeing Uncle Vanya
P. P. Gnedich *Kniga Zhizni Vospominaniya* (1929)

Cher 1946–

American pop singer and actress. She began her career as a singer but went on to win awards as a film actress.

Cher
1946–

1 I'm the female equivalent of a counterfeit $20 bill. Half of what you see is a pretty good reproduction, the rest is a fraud.
Doug McClelland *Star Speak: Hollywood on Everything* (1987)

Lord Cherwell 1886–1957

German-born British physicist, who was Churchill's scientific and aeronautical adviser during the war.

Lord Cherwell
1886–1957

1 I think it more important to know about the properties of chlorine than about the improprieties of Clodius; or about the behaviour of crystals than about the misbehaviour of Christina. Surely it is more important to know what a calorie is than what Caligula did; and anyhow what catalysts do is certainly more useful and less objectionable than what Catiline did.
in 1954

Lord Chesterfield 1694–1773

English writer and politician. His *Letters to his Son* became famous as a guide to manners and behaviour.

Samuel Johnson
1709–84

1 This man I thought had been a Lord among wits; but, I find, he is only a wit among Lords.
remark, 1754

Samuel Johnson
1709–84

2 They teach the morals of a whore, and the manners of a dancing master.
of Chesterfield's Letters
remark, 1754

Voltaire
1694–1778

3 The only Englishman who ever argued for the art of pleasing as the first duty of life.
letter, August 1774

Horace Walpole
1717–97

4 His speeches were fine, but as much laboured as his extempore sayings.
in 1751

G. K. Chesterton 1874–1936

English essayist, novelist, and critic. His novels include *The Napoleon of Notting Hill* and a series of stories featuring Father Brown, a priest with a talent for detection.

Hilaire Belloc
1870–1953

1 Remote and ineffectual Don
That dared attack my Chesterton.
'Lines to a Don' (1910)

John Carey
1934–

2 Chesterton had a body like a slag heap, but a mind like the dawn sky. He saw the world new, as if he'd just landed from another planet.
in 1978

G. K. Chesterton
1874–1936

3 My real judgement of my own work is that I have spoilt a number of jolly good ideas in my time.
Autobiography (1936)

E. V. Lucas
1868–1938

4 Poor G.K.C., his day is past—
Now God will know the truth at last.
mock epitaph; Dudley Barker G. K. Chesterton (1973)

H. L. Mencken
1880–1956

5 A reader who really follows him starts out in the Nineteenth Century and lands in the Thirteenth.
Minority Report (1956)

Ezra Pound
1885–1972

6 Chesterton is like a vile scum on a pond ... all his slop—it is really modern Catholicism to a great extent, the *never* taking a hedge straight, the mumbo-jumbo of superstition dodging behind clumsy fun and paradox ... I believe he creates a milieu in which art is impossible.
letter, August 1917

George Bernard Shaw 1856–1950	7 Wells and I, contemplating the Chesterbelloc, recognize at once a very amusing pantomime elephant, the front legs being that very exceptional and un-English individual Hilaire Belloc, and the hind legs that extravagant freak of French nature, G. K. Chesterton. in February 1908
George Bernard Shaw 1856–1950	8 Chesterton's resolute conviviality is about as genial as an *auto da fé* of teetotallers. *Pen Portraits and Reviews* (1932)
Humbert Wolfe 1886–1940	9 Here lies Mr Chesterton, who to heaven might have gone, but didn't, when he heard the news that the place was run by Jews. 'G. K. Chesterton' (1925)

Maurice Chevalier 1888–1972

French singer and actor. He gained an international reputation in the Paris music-halls of the 1920s, and went on to star in successful Hollywood musicals.

	asked what he felt about the advancing years on his seventy-second birthday:
Maurice Chevalier 1888–1972	1 Considering the alternative, it's not too bad at all. Michael Freedland *Maurice Chevalier* (1981)
Jeannette MacDonald 1903–65	2 The fastest derrière-pincher in the West. Edward Baron Turk *Hollywood Diva* (1998)
David Thomson 1941–	3 A sort of male duenna with a leer face-lifted into a smile. *A Biographical Dictionary of Film* (1994)

Francis Chichester 1901–72

English yachtsman. In his yacht *Gipsy Moth IV* he was the first person to sail alone round the world with only one stop (1966–7).

Alistair Cooke 1908–	1 A very rum sort of hero, Popeye in the flesh. 'Chichester: The Master Mariner' (1967)

Melanie Chisholm 1974–

English pop singer; a member of the Spice Girls, known as 'Mel C.' and 'Sporty Spice'.

Melanie Chisholm 1974–	1 You know, I would like to like reading. I've been trying to get myself to read for such a long time. I've got piles of books that I wanna read, but I just get distracted. in March 2000

Frédéric Chopin 1810–49

Polish-born French composer and pianist. Writing almost exclusively for the piano, he composed numerous mazurkas and polonaises inspired by Polish folk music, as well as nocturnes, preludes, and two piano concertos.

Frédéric Chopin 1810–49	1 I'm a revolutionary, money means nothing to me. Arthur Hedley *Chopin* (1947)
Eugène Delacroix 1798–1863	2 He is the truest artist I have ever met. Arthur Hedley *Chopin* (1947)
Robert Schumann 1810–56	3 Hats off, gentlemen—a genius! 'An Opus 2' (1831)
Oscar Wilde 1854–1900	4 After playing Chopin, I feel as if I had been weeping over sins that I had never committed, and mourning over tragedies that were not my own. *The Critic as Artist* (1891)

Agatha Christie 1890–1976

English writer of detective fiction. Her novels are characterized by brisk, humorous dialogue and ingenious plots; many of them feature the Belgian Hercule Poirot or the resourceful Miss Marple.

Agatha Christie
1890–1976

1 I'm a sausage machine, a perfect sausage machine.
G. C. Ramsey *Agatha Christie* (1972)

Julian Symons
1912–94

2 She shows us the ace of spades face up. Then she turns it over, but we still know where it is, so how has it been transformed into the five of diamonds?
Bloody Murder (1972)

Jennie Churchill 1854–1921

American-born society hostess, wife of Lord **Randolph Churchill** and mother of Sir **Winston Churchill**.

Jennie Churchill
1854–1921

1 I shall never get used to not being the most beautiful woman in the room. It was an intoxication to sweep in and know that every man had turned his head. It kept me in form.
in 1914

Randolph Churchill 1849–94

British Conservative politician, the father of Sir **Winston Churchill**. He supported a group known as the 'Fourth Party'.

Lord Randolph Churchill
1849–94

2 I never could make out what those damned dots [decimal points] meant.
W. S. Churchill *Lord Randolph Churchill* (1906)

W. E. Gladstone
1809–98

3 There never was a Churchill from John of Marlborough down that had either morals or principles.
in conversation in 1882

Cuthbert Morley Headlam
1876–1964

4 Someone said of Randolph Churchill that he was the kind of man who would like to be the bride at a wedding, and the corpse at the funeral.
diary July 1927

Lord Rosebery
1847–1929

5 There was no retirement, no concealment. He died by inches in public, sole mourner at his own protracted funeral.
attributed

Randolph Churchill 1911–68

British journalist, the son of Sir **Winston Churchill**.

Evelyn Waugh
1903–66

6 A typical triumph of modern science to find the only part of Randolph that was not malignant and remove it.
on hearing that Randolph Churchill's lung, when removed, proved non-malignant
in March 1964

Winston Churchill 1874–1965

British Conservative statesman, Prime Minister 1940–5, 1951–5. A consistent opponent of appeasement between the wars, he led Britain throughout the Second World War.

Anonymous

7 Winston is back.
on Churchill's reappointment as First Sea Lord
Board of Admiralty signal to the Fleet, September 1939

Herbert Henry Asquith
1852–1928

8 He is a Chimborazo or Everest among the sandhills of the Baldwin Cabinet.
Roy Jenkins *Asquith* (1964)

Clement Attlee
1883–1967
9 The voice we heard was that of Mr Churchill but the mind was that of Lord Beaverbrook.
speech on radio, June 1945

Clement Attlee
1883–1967
10 A monologue is not a decision.
to Churchill, who had complained that a matter had been raised several times in Cabinet
Francis Williams *A Prime Minister Remembers* (1961)

Arthur James Balfour
1848–1930
11 I thought he was a young man of promise, but it appears he is a young man of promises.
Winston Churchill *My Early Life* (1930)

Max Beerbohm
1872–1956
12 The youthful Churchill had dry hair like a waxwork, no wrinkles, and the pallor of one who has lived in the limelight.
Cecil Beaton's diary, September 1953

Aneurin Bevan
1897–1960
13 He does not talk the language of the 20th century but that of the 18th. He is still fighting Blenheim all over again. His only answer to a difficult situation is send a gun-boat.
speech, October 1951

Aneurin Bevan
1897–1960
14 He is a man suffering from petrified adolescence.
Vincent Brome *Aneurin Bevan* (1953)

Aneurin Bevan
1897–1960
15 He never spares himself in conversation. He gives himself so generously that hardly anybody else is permitted to give anything in his presence.
attributed, April 1954

R. A. Butler
1902–82
16 The greatest adventurer of modern political history.
John Colville's diary, May 1940

Jennie Churchill
1854–1921
17 You seem to have no real purpose in life and won't realize at the age of twenty-two that for a man life means work, and hard work if you mean to succeed.
letter, February 1897

Winston Churchill
1874–1965
18 Anyone can rat, but it takes a certain amount of ingenuity to re-rat.
on rejoining the Conservatives twenty years after leaving them for the Liberals, c.1924
Kay Halle *Irrepressible Churchill* (1966)

Winston Churchill
1874–1965
19 NANCY ASTOR: If I were your wife I would put poison in your coffee!
CHURCHILL: And if I were your husband I would drink it.
Consuelo Vanderbilt Balsan *Glitter and Gold* (1952)

Winston Churchill
1874–1965
20 It was the nation and the race dwelling all round the globe that had the lion's heart. I had the luck to be called upon to give the roar.
speech, November 1954

Winston Churchill
1874–1965
21 We are all worms. But I do believe that I am a glow-worm.
Violet Bonham-Carter *Winston Churchill as I Knew Him* (1965)

Stafford Cripps
1889–1952
22 CHURCHILL: I am the humble servant of the Lord Jesus Christ and of the House of Commons.
CRIPPS: I hope you treat Jesus better than you treat the H of C.
diary, April 1950

Cuthbert Morley Headlam
1876–1964
23 He is a terrible burden for any Govt. to carry—someone said of Randolph Churchill that he was the kind of man who would like to be the bride at a wedding, and the corpse at the funeral—the same applies to his more brilliant son.
diary July 1927

Eric Hobsbawm
1917–
24 This great romantic, whose political judgement had been almost consistently wrong on every matter since 1914.
Age of Extremes (1994)

Harold Laski 25 He searched always to end a sentence with a climax. He looked for
1893–1950 antithesis like a monkey looking for fleas.
letter, May 1927

David Lloyd George 26 Winston would go up to his Creator and say that he would very much
1863–1945 like to meet His Son, of Whom he had heard a great deal and, if
possible, would like to call on the Holy Ghost. Winston *loves* meeting
people.
A. J. Sylvester's diary January 1937

David Lloyd George 27 He would make a drum out of the skin of his mother in order to sound
1863–1945 his own praises.
Peter Rowland *Lloyd George* (1975)

Lady Lytton 28 The first time you meet Winston you see all his faults and the rest of
1874–1971 your life you spend in discovering his virtues.
letter, December 1905

John Masefield 29 This Man, in darkness saw; in doubtings led;
1878–1967 In danger, did; in uttermost despair,
Shone, with a Hope that made the midnight fair.
The world he saved calls blessing on his head.
'On the Birthday of a Great Man' (1954)

Ed Murrow 30 He mobilized the English language and sent it into battle to steady his
1908–65 fellow countrymen and hearten those Europeans upon whom the long
dark night of tyranny had descended.
broadcast, 30 November 1954

Lord Reith 31 He is the greatest menace we have ever had—country and Empire
1889–1971 sacrificed to his megalomania, to his monstrous obstinacy and wrong-
headedness.
diary, October 1942

Franklin D. Roosevelt 32 It is fun to be in the same decade with you.
1882–1945 *acknowledging congratulations on his 60th birthday*
cabled reply to Winston Churchill, January 1942

Beatrice Webb 33 Restless, almost intolerably so, without capacity for sustained and
1858–1943 unexcited labour, egotistical, bumptious, shallow-minded and
reactionary, but with a certain personal magnetism, great pluck and
some originality, not of intellect but of character.
in 1903

Cicero 106–43 BC

Roman statesman, orator, and writer. As an orator and writer Cicero established a model
for Latin prose. A supporter of Pompey against **Julius Caesar**, in the *Philippics* he attacked
Mark Antony, who had him put to death.

Catullus 1 Catullus gives you warmest thanks,
c.84–c.54 BC And he the worst of poets ranks;
As much the worst of bards confessed,
As you of advocates the best.
letter of thanks to Cicero
Carmina no. 49 (translated by Sir William Marris)

Cicero 2 O happy Rome, born when I was consul!
106–43 BC Juvenal *Satires*

Plutarch 3 The man who is thought to have been the first to see beneath the
AD c.46–c.120 surface of Caesar's public policy and to fear it, as one might fear the
smiling surface of the sea.
Parallel Lives

Eric Clapton 1945–

English blues and rock guitarist, singer, and composer. His group Cream (1966–8) was influential in the development of rock music.

Ginger Baker
1939–

1 The majority of the world is convinced that Cream was Eric Clapton's band and he enjoys it. Cream was *my* band. I formed it. I did most of the hard work. And I got the least out of it . . . I hate that stuff Clapton does now.
in February 1990

Eric Clapton
1945–

2 I felt through most of my youth that my back was against the wall and that the only way to survive was with dignity, pride and courage. I heard that in certain forms of music and I heard it most of all in the blues, because it was always an individual. It was one man and his guitar versus the world.
Christopher Sandford *Clapton: Edge of Darkness* (1994)

Tom McGuinness
1941–

3 The idea that he was a purist is nonsense. Eric loved the blues, but he wasn't above other types of music . . . It was the image of the blues that attracted him . . . He really *did* think that it was him against the world. On the other hand, he could play the guitar.
Christopher Sandford *Clapton: Edge of Darkness* (1994)

John Mayall
1933–

4 There was always a chameleon thing with Eric, a sense of impermanence. When he joined the band we were very, *very* close on a social level. A year later he walked out.
Christopher Sandford *Clapton: Edge of Darkness* (1994)

Alan Clark 1928–99

British Conservative politician. He was noted for his independence and colourful lifestyle.

Lynn Barber
1944–

1 It is as if, as a teenager, he adopted some gruesome old buffer's view of what being 'a man of the world' entailed and has persisted in it ever since. He is like a little boy trying to pass for a grown-up but eternally getting it wrong.
Demon Barber (1998)

Alastair Campbell
1957–

2 Labour spin doctors aren't supposed to like Tory MPs. But Alan Clark was an exceptional man.
in September 1999

Alan Clark
1928–99

3 If you have bright plumage, people will take pot shots at you.
in June 1994

Matthew Parris
1949–

4 Why waste it on some vanilla-flavoured pixie. Bring on the fruitcakes, we want a fruitcake for an unlosable seat. They enliven the Commons.
the day before the Kensington and Chelsea association chose Alan Clark as their parliamentary candidate, January 1997

Arthur C. Clarke 1917–

English writer of science fiction. He co-wrote (with Stanley Kubrick) the screenplay for the film *2001: A Space Odyssey* (1968).

Kingsley Amis
1922–95

1 His writing is sharp, lucid and logical, embodying imagination in the true sense of the word: common sense with wings.
in August 1973

Anonymous

2 Our next speaker is the only person I know who can be unambiguously introduced by a four-digit number—2001.
at Massachusetts Institute of Technology, March 1976

Arthur C. Clarke
1917–

3 He never grew up, but he never stopped growing.
suggested epitaph for himself
Neil McAleer *Odyssey: the Authorized Biography of Arthur C. Clarke* (1992)

Stanley Kubrick
1928–99

J. B. Priestley
1894–1984

4 Arthur is not an anecdotable character.
  Neil McAleer *Odyssey: the Authorized Biography of Arthur C. Clarke* (1992)

5 I think Mr Clarke is the happiest writer I have ever met.
  Neil McAleer *Odyssey: the Authorized Biography of Arthur C. Clarke* (1992)

Julian Clary 1959–

British comedian and entertainer.

Julian Clary
1959–

1 My mother wanted me to be a nice boy. I didn't let her down. I don't smoke, drink or mess around with women.
  comment on himself, March 1996

Claude 1600–82

French painter. By 1630 he had achieved great fame in Italy as a landscape painter. His mature works concentrate on the poetic power of light and atmosphere.

John Constable
1776–1837

1 In Claude's landscape all is lovely—all amiable—all is amenity and repose;—the calm sunshine of the heart.
  lecture, June 1836

William Hazlitt
1778–1830

2 Claude's landscapes, perfect as they are, want gusto . . . He saw the atmosphere, but he did not feel it.
  'On Gusto' (1817)

John Cleese 1939–

English comic actor and writer, famous for *Monty Python's Flying Circus* and the situation comedy *Fawlty Towers*.

David Thomson
1941–

1 There is nothing funnier than a huge man trying to inspire order in the world.
  A Biographical Dictionary of Film (1994)

Georges Clemenceau 1841–1929

French statesman, Prime Minister 1906–9 and 1917–20. At the Versailles peace talks he pushed hard for a punitive settlement with Germany.

Georges Clemenceau
1841–1929

1 I have no political system, and I have abandoned all political principles. I am a man dealing with events as they come in the light of my experience.
  Winston Churchill *Great Contemporaries* (1937)

John Maynard Keynes
1883–1946

2 He felt about France what Pericles felt of Athens—unique value in her, nothing else mattering; but his theory of politics was Bismarck's. He had one illusion—France; and one disillusion—mankind, including Frenchmen, and his colleagues not least.
  The Economic Consequences of the Peace (1919)

David Lloyd George
1863–1945

3 M. Clemenceau . . . is one of the greatest living orators, but he knows that the finest eloquence is that which gets things done and the worst is that which delays them.
  speech at Paris Peace Conference, January 1919

Cleopatra 69–30 BC

Queen of Egypt 47–30. After a brief liaison with **Julius Caesar** she formed a political and romantic alliance with Mark Antony. She and Antony were defeated by Rome at the battle of Actium.

Leigh Hunt
1784–1859

1 The laughing queen that caught the world's great hands.
  'The Nile' (1818)

Blaise Pascal
1623–62

2 Had Cleopatra's nose been shorter, the whole face of the world would have changed.
  Pensées (1670)

William Shakespeare
1564–1616

3 Age cannot wither her, nor custom stale
Her infinite variety.
Antony and Cleopatra (1606–7)

Bill Clinton 1946–

American Democratic statesman, President 1993–2001. He was impeached in 1998 on charges of perjury and obstruction of justice, but was acquitted.

Pat Buchanan
1938–

1 Everyone has a skeleton in their closet. The difference between Bill Clinton and myself is that he has a walk-in closet.
in November 1999

Bill Clinton
1946–

2 I experimented with marijuana a time or two. And I didn't like it, and I didn't inhale.
in March 1992

Bill Clinton
1946–

3 The comeback kid!
description of himself after coming second in the New Hampshire primary in the 1992 presidential election (since 1952, no presidential candidate had won the election without first winning in New Hampshire)

Hillary Rodham Clinton
1947–

4 I am not standing by my man, like Tammy Wynette. I am sitting here because I love him, I respect him, and I honour what he's been through and what we've been through together.
television interview, January 1992

Hillary Rodham Clinton
1947–

5 A hard dog to keep on the porch.
in August 1999

Jay Leno
1950–

6 This Ken Starr report is now posted on the Internet. I'll bet Clinton's glad he put a computer in every classroom now.
in September 1998

Peter Mandelson
1953–

7 I think he is a one-off. He is a cross between a thoroughly charming, charismatic human being and a political computer.
in December 2000

Sinéad O'Connor
1966–

8 Does impeachment mean they are going to turn him into a peach? If so, can I eat him?
in February 1999

Harold Pinter
1930–

9 Milosevic is undoubtedly ruthless and savage. So is Clinton.
in April 1999

Barbra Streisand
1942–

10 We elected a President, not a Pope.
to journalists at the White House, February 1998

Hillary Rodham Clinton 1947–

American lawyer and Democratic politician. Her support proved invaluable to her husband **Bill Clinton**, both in campaigning for the Presidency and in various scandals.

Bill Clinton
1946–

11 Presidents have feelings too.
after William Safire had called Hillary Clinton 'a congenital liar'
in January 1996

Hillary Rodham Clinton
1947–

12 I could have stayed home and baked cookies and had teas. But what I decided was to fulfil my profession, which I entered before my husband was in public life.
comment on questions raised by rival Democratic contender Edmund G. Brown Jr., in March 1992

Camille Paglia
1947–

13 A raisin-eyed, carrot-nosed, twig-armed straw-stuffed mannequin trundled in on a go-cart by the mentally bereft powerbrokers of the state Democratic Party.
in February 2000

Lord Clive 1725–74

British general and colonial administrator. In 1757 he recaptured Calcutta, following the Black Hole incident. He was implicated in the East India company's corruption scandals and committed suicide.

Edmund Clerihew Bentley
1875–1956

1 What I like about Clive
Is that he is no longer alive.
There is a great deal to be said
For being dead.
'Clive' (1905)

Lord Clive
1725–74

2 By God, Mr Chairman, at this moment I stand astonished at my own moderation!
reply during Parliamentary cross-examination, 1773

Lord Clive
1725–74

3 I feel that I am reserved for some end or other.
when his pistol twice failed to fire, while attempting to take his own life
G. R. Gleig *The Life of Robert, First Lord Clive* (1848)

Brian Clough 1935–

English football player and manager. He managed Derby County and Nottingham Forest.

Malcolm Allison

1 He is a kind of Rolls Royce Communist.
in 1973

Brian Clough
1935–

2 If I'm ever feeling a bit uppity, whenever I get on my high horse, I go and take another look at my dear Mam's mangle that has pride of place in the dining-room.
Clough: The Autobiography (1994)

Archie Gemmill
1947–

3 A player can never feel too sure of himself with Clough. That's his secret.
Peter Taylor *With Clough* (1980)

Martin Clunes 1962–

English actor. His television work includes the comedy series *Men Behaving Badly*.

Martin Clunes
1962–

1 I wish I had led as wild a life as some people have made out.
interview, May 2000

William Cobbett 1762–1835

English writer and political reformer. He started his political life as a Tory, but later became a radical.

Thomas Carlyle
1795–1881

1 The pattern John Bull of his century, strong as the rhinoceros, and with singular humanities and genialities shining through his thick skin.
'Sir Walter Scott' (1838)

G. K. Chesterton
1874–1936

2 There was something cool about Cobbett, for all his fire; and that was his educational instinct, his love of alphabetical and objective teaching. He was a furious debater; but he was a mild and patient schoolmaster. His dogmatism left off where most dogmatism begins. He would always bully an equal; but he would never have bullied a pupil.
William Cobbett (1925)

William Cobbett
1762–1835

3 From a very early age, I had imbibed the opinion, that it was every man's duty to do all that lay in his power to leave his country as good as he had found it.
in December 1832

William Hazlitt
1778–1830

4 He is a kind of fourth estate in the politics of the country.
The Spirit of the Age (1825)

Richard Cobden 1804–65

English political reformer, one of the leading spokesmen of the free-trade movement in Britain. With John Bright, he led the Anti-Corn Law League in its successful campaign for the repeal of the Corn Laws.

Thomas Carlyle 1 Cobden is an inspired bagman, who believes in a calico millennium.
1795–1881   T. W. Reid *Life, Letters and Friendships of Richard Monckton* (1890)

Jean Cocteau 1889–1963

French dramatist, novelist, and film director. His plays are noted for their striking blend of poetry, irony, and fantasy.

Cecil Beaton 1 As with most artists, the eyes communicate their owner's deepest
1904–80   secrets. As silent as Jean's mouth is talkative, the dilated pupils of his
bulging fishy eyes, anguished and tortured, aghast and helpless, seem
to be looking into another existence.
diary, spring 1936

Sebastian Coe 1956–

British middle-distance runner and Conservative politician, an Olympic gold medal winner in the 1,500 metres in 1980 and 1984.

Sebastian Coe 1 For me championships are what athletics has always been about.
1956–   in January 1990

Steve Ovett 2 The public has always known that I was never the beast that I was
1955–   painted and Seb was never the saint some people made him out to be.
attributed

Leonard Cohen 1934–

Canadian singer and writer.

Leonard Cohen 1 Sometimes my voice can make *me* cry.
1934–   in November 1988

Leonard Cohen 2 I don't consider myself a pessimist. I think of a pessimist as someone
1934–   who is waiting for it to rain. And I feel soaked to the skin.
in May 1993

Elton John 3 He's kinda got a non-voice but it's like one of those great voices, like a
1947–   Dylan or a Lou Reed.
Jim Devlin *Leonard Cohen in His Own Words* (1998)

Samuel Taylor Coleridge 1772–1834

English poet, critic, and philosopher. His *Lyrical Ballads* (1798), written with **William Wordsworth**, marked the start of English romanticism.

Lord Byron 1 And Coleridge, too, has lately taken wing,
1788–1824   But, like a hawk encumbered with his hood,
Explaining metaphysics to the nation—
I wish he would explain his explanation.
Don Juan (1819–24)

Lord Byron 2 Let simple Wordsworth chime his childish verse,
1788–1824   And brother Coleridge lull the babe at nurse.
English Bards and Scotch Reviewers (1809)

Thomas Carlyle 3 He has no resolution, he shrinks from pain or labour in any of its
1795–1881   shapes. His very attitude bespeaks this: he never straightens his knee
joints, he stoops with his fat ill-shapen shoulders, and in walking he
does not tread but shovel and slide.
letter, June 1824

Thomas Carlyle
1795–1881

4 How great a possibility; how small a realized result.
  letter, August 1834

Samuel Taylor Coleridge
1772–1834

5 O, lift one thought in prayer for S. T. C.;
  That he who many a year with toil of breath
  Found death in life, may here find life in death.
  'Epitaph for Himself' (1834)

E. M. Forster
1879–1970

6 If life is a lesson, he never learnt it.
  attributed

William Hazlitt
1778–1830

7 He talked on for ever; and you wished him to talk on for ever.
  Lectures on the English Poets (1818)

William Hazlitt
1778–1830

8 The owner of a mind which keeps open house, and entertains all comers.
  Spirit of the Age (1825)

Leigh Hunt
1784–1859

9 His forehead was prodigious—a great piece of placid marble; and his fine eyes, in which all the activity of his mind seemed to concentrate, moved under it with a sprightly ease, as if it was pastime to them to carry all that thought.
  Autobiography (1850)

John Keats
1795–1821

10 Coleridge, for instance, would let go by a fine isolated verisimilitude caught from the penetralium of mystery, from being incapable of remaining content with half knowledge.
  letter, December 1817

Charles Lamb
1775–1834

11 Cultivate simplicity, Coleridge.
  letter, November 1796

Charles Lamb
1775–1834

12 An Archangel a little damaged.
  letter, April 1816

Percy Bysshe Shelley
1792–1822

13 A cloud-encircled meteor of the air,
  A hooded eagle among blinking owls.
  'Letter to Maria Gisborne' (1820)

Colette 1873–1954

French novelist. Colette made her name as a serious writer with her novels *Chéri* and *La Fin de Chéri*, telling of a passionate relationship between a young man and an older woman.

Brigid Brophy
1929–95

1 Colette wrote of vegetables as if they were love objects and of sex as if it were an especially delightful department of gardening.
  Anne Stibbs (ed.) *Like a Fish Needs a Bicycle* (1992)

Violet Trefusis
1894–1972

2 She was essentially domesticated, *une femme d'intérieur*, who loved receiving in her own home. To use a word that must astonish those who do not know Colette, she was 'cosy' . . . her kitchen was more familiar to her than her drawing-room. She adored comfort and disdained luxury.
  Don't Look Round (1952)

Joan Collins 1933–

English actress, a sex symbol in films such as *Our Girl Friday* (1953) and known more recently for the television series *Dynasty* (1981–9).

Joan Collins
1933–

1 I've never yet met a man who could look after me. I don't need a husband. What I need is a wife.
  in December 1987

Alex Comfort 1920–2000

British physician and writer. His work focused particularly on the problems of ageing, though he was best-known to the public for his book *The Joy of Sex*.

Nicholas Comfort 1 I always felt his brain might blow up. He used to think so hard that it hurt.
a son's view
in April 2000

Denis Compton 1918–97

English cricketer. He played for Middlesex and England, and also played football for Arsenal and England.

John Arlott
1914–91
1 Recorded centuries leave no trace,
On memories of that timeless grace.
attributed

Len Hutton
1916–90
2 There was no way I could compete with him in the popularity stakes, and the debonair way he played his cricket attracted both the powers-that-be and the public.
Gerald Howat *Len Hutton* (1988)

Michael Parkinson
1935–
3 He did not simply play at Lord's, he possessed it. When he walked out to the middle he was not a cricketer coming out to bat on his home turf, he was an impresario performing a one-man show in an auditorium he owned.
in September 1994

Ivy Compton-Burnett 1884–1969

English novelist. Her novels typically portray life at the turn of the 19th century and are characterized by ironic wit and an emphasis on dialogue.

Ivy Compton-Burnett
1884–1969
1 There's not much to say. I haven't been at all deedy.
on being asked about herself
in August 1969

Anthony Powell
1905–2000
2 She saw life in the relentless terms of a Greek tragedy, its cruelties, ironies—above all its passions—played out against a background of triviality and ennui.
in September 1969

William Congreve 1670–1729

English dramatist. A close associate of **Swift**, **Pope**, and **Steele**, he wrote plays which epitomize the wit and satire of Restoration comedy.

William Congreve
1670–1729
1 For my part I keep the Commandments, I love my neighbour as my self, and to avoid coveting my neighbour's wife I desire to be coveted by her; which you know is quite another thing.
letter, September 1700

Kenneth Tynan
1927–80
2 William Congreve is the only sophisticated playwright England has produced; and like Shaw, Sheridan and Wilde, his nearest rivals, he was brought up in Ireland.
Curtains (1961)

Voltaire
1694–1778
3 The language is everywhere that of men of honour, but their actions are those of knaves; a proof that he was perfectly well acquainted with human nature, and frequented what we call polite company.
Lettres Philosophiques (1733)

Gerry Conlon 1954–

First member of the Guildford Four to be released from prison.

Gerry Conlon
1954–

1 The life sentence goes on. It's like a runaway train that you can't just get off.

of life after his conviction was quashed by the Court of Appeal
in September 1997

Sean Connery 1930–

Scottish film actor best known for his portrayal of James Bond.

Sean Connery
1930–

1 The problem within interviews of this sort is to get across the fact, without breaking your arse, that one is not Bond, that one was functioning reasonably well before Bond, and that one is going to function reasonably well after Bond.

interview, November 1965

Sean Connery
1930–

2 I suppose more than anything else I'd like to be an old man with a good face, like Hitchcock or Picasso. They know life is not a popularity contest.

Eddie Dick (ed.) *From Limelight to Satellite* (1990)

John Huston
1906–87

3 As long as actors are going into politics, I wish, for Christ's sake, that Sean Connery would become king of Scotland.

Eddie Dick (ed.) *From Limelight to Satellite* (1990)

Steven Spielberg
1947–

4 Sean Connery is not like anybody else; he's an original.

Robert Sellers *The Films of Sean Connery* (1990)

Terence Young
1915–94

5 All his success hasn't changed Sean one iota, subtly or unsubtly, period.

Andrew Yule *Sean Connery* (1992)

Cyril Connolly 1903–74

English writer and journalist. His works include one novel, *The Rock Pool* (1936), and collections of essays, aphorisms, and reflections.

Cyril Connolly
1903–74

1 I have always disliked myself at any given moment. The sum total of such moments is my life.

in March 1954

E. M. Forster
1879–1970

2 He gave pleasure a bad name.

Noel Annan *Our Age* (1990)

Kenneth Tynan
1927–80

3 Cyril Connolly is either a bon viveur with a passion for literature, or a *littérateur* with a passion for high living.

in March 1954

Virginia Woolf
1882–1941

4 Apes are considerably preferable to Cyril.

attributed

Jimmy Connors 1952–

American tennis player. He won Wimbledon in 1974 and 1982, and the US Open championship five times.

Martin Amis
1949–

1 Jimmy was such an out-and-out 'personality' that he managed to get into a legal dispute with the president of his own fan club.

in September 1994

Jimmy Connors
1952–

2 I like my image. It's me. I'm a louse, but if you're going to be a louse, I say be a good one. I play to win and I play to entertain.

Rich Koster *The Tennis Bubble* (1976)

Jimmy Connors
1952–

3 Nobody reminds me of me, I'm an original.

in 1989

Rod Laver 1938–	4 The guy seems to make himself more unpopular every time he plays. Rich Koster *The Tennis Bubble* (1976)
Roger Taylor	5 Look at Jimmy Connors. No one walked away from a match he was in because no matter what the score, he was never beaten until the last gasp. in April 1995

Joseph Conrad 1857–1924

Polish-born British novelist. His long career at sea (1874–94) inspired many of his most famous works. Much of his work, including his story *Heart of Darkness*, explores the darkness within human nature.

Joseph Conrad 1857–1924	1 A Polish nobleman, cased in British tar! letter, May 1890
Ford Madox Ford 1873–1939	2 Conrad spent a day finding the *mot juste*; then killed it. Robert Lowell *Notebook 1967–68* (1969)
E. M. Forster 1879–1970	3 The secret casket of his genius contains a vapour rather than a jewel. *reviewing Conrad's* Notes on Life and Letters *(1921)* Cedric Watts *Joseph Conrad* (1994)
D. H. Lawrence 1885–1930	4 Why this giving in before you start, that pervades all Conrad and such folks—the Writers among the Ruins. I can't forgive Conrad for being so sad and giving in. letter, October 1912
Thomas Mann 1875–1955	5 Joseph Conrad's *Heart of Darkness* prophetically inaugurated the twentieth century. attributed
George Moore 1852–1933	6 What is Conrad but the wreck of Stevenson floating about on the slip-slop of Henry James? letter from G. W. Lyttelton, March 1956
Bertrand Russell 1872–1970	7 He thought of civilized and morally tolerable human life as a dangerous walk on a thin crust of barely cooled lava which at any moment might break and let the unwary sink into fiery depths. Norman Sherry *Conrad and his World* (1972)
Jeanette Winterson 1959–	8 The Salieri of letters. *Art Objects* (1995)

John Constable 1776–1837

English painter. Among his best-known works are early paintings inspired by the landscape of his native Suffolk. Later he became fascinated by the painting of changing weather patterns.

William Blake 1757–1827	1 Why, this is not drawing, but *inspiration*. C. R. Leslie *Memoirs of the Life of John Constable* (1843)
John Constable 1776–1837	2 The sound of water escaping from mill-dams, etc., willows, old rotten planks, slimy posts, and brickwork . . . those scenes made me a painter and I am grateful. letter, October 1821
Henry Fuseli 1741–1825	3 I like de landscapes of Constable; he is always picturesque, of a fine colour, and de lights always in de right places; but he makes me call for my greatcoat and umbrella. C. R. Leslie *Memoirs of the Life of John Constable* (1843)
John Ruskin 1819–1900	4 Unteachableness seems to have been a main feature of his character, and there is a corresponding want of veneration in the way he approaches nature herself. *Modern Painters* (1843–60)

on a Constable painting of the Thames:

Sylvia Townsend Warner
1893–1978

5 It is as though Constable had taken a long steady appraising stare at Canaletto and then charged straight through him.
  letter, February 1969

James Cook 1728–79

English explorer. On his first expedition to the Pacific (1768–71), he charted the coasts of New Zealand and New Guinea as well as exploring the east coast of Australia and claiming it for Britain.

James Boswell
1740–95

1 A plain, sensible man with an uncommon attention to veracity.
  Alan Moorehead *The Fatal Impact* (1966)

William Plomer
1903–73

2 The story of his life does not lend itself to exploitation by cheap biographers. He was not a 'great lover', he was a great worker; there was nothing scandalous or equivocal or cheaply sensational in his career; and nobody ever made fewer mistakes.
  Bonamy Dobrée *From Anne to Victoria* (1937)

Peter Cook 1937–95

English satirist and actor. He came to notice in *Beyond the Fringe* and later collaborated with **Dudley Moore** in *Not Only . . . But Also.*

Alan Bennett
1934–

3 He proved that a life of self-indulgence, if led with a whole heart, may also bring a certain wisdom.
  in 1995

Jeffrey Bernard
1932–97

4 It is as though God is stooping down to pick the wings off his butterflies.
  of the deaths of Cook and **John Osborne**
  in 1995

Peter Cook
1937–95

5 Life is a matter of passing the time enjoyably. There may be other things in life, but I've been too busy passing my time enjoyably to think very deeply about them.
  in January 1994

Robin Cook 1946–

British Labour politician, Foreign Secretary from 1997.

Margaret Cook

6 If anyone sends me a card with a robin on it I'll never speak to them again. It is strange that such an aggressive creature has come to symbolise the season of goodwill.
  after her husband left her, in January 1998

Frederick Forsyth
1938–

7 If a man cannot keep a measly affair secret, what is he doing in charge of the Intelligence Service?
  on the break-up of Cook's marriage
  in January 1998

Alistair Cooke 1908–

British-born American journalist and broadcaster. He has commented on American affairs for the BBC since 1938.

Michael Parkinson
1935–

1 One of the few men in the entire world acquainted with the work of both Isaiah and Irving Berlin and able to write about the two of them with the same enthusiasm.
  Alistair Cooke *Fun and Games* (1994) foreword

Kenneth Tynan
1927–80

2 Cooke is one of the great reporters. Nobody can reproduce events, giving the feel as well as the facts, the pith as well as the husk, with greater clarity or gentler wit.
  Persona Grata (1953)

Calvin Coolidge 1872–1933

American Republican statesman, President 1923–9. He was seen as an embodiment of thrift and honesty in a decade when corruption in public life was common.

Anonymous 1 Though I yield to no one in my admiration for Mr Coolidge, I do wish he did not look as if he had been weaned on a pickle.
Alice Roosevelt Longworth *Crowded Hours* (1933)

Calvin Coolidge 2 Perhaps one of the most important accomplishments of my
1872–1933 administration has been minding my own business.
in March 1929

Walter Lippmann 3 Mr Coolidge's genius for inactivity is developed to a very high point. It
1889–1974 is far from being an indolent activity. It is a grim, determined, alert inactivity which keeps Mr Coolidge occupied constantly. Nobody has ever worked harder at inactivity, with such force of character, with such unremitting attention to detail, with such conscientious devotion to the task.
Men of Destiny (1927)

H. L. Mencken 4 He slept more than any other President, whether by day or by night.
1880–1956 Nero fiddled, but Coolidge only snored.
in April 1933

Dorothy Parker 5 How do they know?
1893–1967 *on being told that Calvin Coolidge had died*
Malcolm Cowley *Writers at Work* 1st Series (1958)

Alice Cooper 1948–

American rock singer, lead singer of the band of the same name, noted for his sensational and theatrical style.

Ian Kilminster 1 I still can't believe Alice Cooper plays golf!
1945– interview, July 2000

Gary Cooper 1901–61

American actor. His laconic, understated performance in such westerns as *The Virginian* and *High Noon* established his reputation in tough cowboy films.

John Barrymore 2 That fellow is the world's greatest actor. He can do with no effort what
1882–1942 the rest of us spent years trying to learn; to be perfectly natural.
Jane Mercer *Great Lovers of the Movies* (1975)

Frank Capra 3 Every line in his face spelled honesty. So innate was his integrity he
1897–1991 could be cast in phoney parts, but never look phoney himself.
The Name Above the Title (1971)

Alistair Cooke 4 To the moviegoer, Cooper was the matinee idol toughened and tanned,
1908– into something at once glamorous and primitive. He was notoriously known as the actor who couldn't act.
'The Legend of Gary Cooper' (1961)

Henry Cooper 1934–

English boxer, the only man to win a Lonsdale belt outright three times. He beat **Muhammad Ali** in 1963, but lost to him in 1966 in his only world title fight.

Muhammad Ali 5 Cooper hit me so hard, he didn't only shake me, he shook my relations
1942– in Africa!
Howard L. Bingham *Muhammad Ali: a Thirty-Year Journey* (1993)

Nicolaus Copernicus 1473–1543

Polish astronomer. He proposed a model of the solar system in which the planets orbited in perfect circles around the sun.

Martin Luther
1483–1546

1 The fool will turn the whole art of astronomy inside out! But, as the Holy Scripture reports, Joshua ordered the sun to stand still and not the earth.

in June 1539

Francis Ford Coppola 1939–

American film director, writer, and producer. His reputation rests chiefly on *The Godfather* (1972) and its two sequels, which chart the fortunes of a New York Mafia family over several generations.

Francis Ford Coppola
1939–

1 I probably have genius, but no talent.

in March 1982

Francis Ford Coppola
1939–

2 Your work parallels your life, but in the sense of a glass full of water where people look at it and say, 'Oh, the water's the same shape as the glass!'

interview, October 1988

George Lucas
1944–

3 All directors have egos and are insecure. But of all the people I know, Francis has the biggest ego and the biggest insecurities.

Garry Jenkins *Harrison Ford: Imperfect Hero* (1997)

Pierre Corneille 1606–84

French dramatist, generally regarded as the founder of classical French tragedy.

Victor Hugo
1802–85

1 To my mind, the style of Racine has aged much more than the style of Corneille. Corneille is wrinkled, Racine has withered. Corneille remains magnificent, venerable, and powerful. Corneille has aged like an old man, Racine like an old woman.

Tas de pierres (1942)

Samuel Johnson
1709–84

2 Corneille is to Shakespeare . . . as a clipped hedge is to a forest.

Hester Lynch Piozzi *Anecdotes of . . . Johnson* (1786)

Correggio c. 1489–1534

Italian painter. The soft, sensual style of his devotional and mythological paintings influenced the rococo of the 18th century. He is best known for his frescoes in Parma cathedral.

Correggio
c.1489–1534

1 I, too, am a painter!

on seeing Raphael's St Cecilia *at Bologna, c.1525*
L. Pungileoni *Memorie Istoriche de . . . Correggio* (1817)

David Coulthard 1971–

Scottish motor-racing driver, now resident in Monte Carlo.

Prince Rainier
1923–

1 Pay your parking tickets, Mr Coulthard.

presenting the trophy for the Monaco Grand Prix
in June 2000

Gustave Courbet 1819–77

French painter. A leader of the 19th-century realist school of painting, he favoured an unidealized choice of subject matter.

Gustave Courbet
1819–77

1 I hope always to earn my living by my art without having ever deviated by even a hair's breadth from my principles, without having lied to my conscience for a single moment, without painting even as much as can be covered by a hand only to please anyone or to sell more easily.

letter, 1854

Noël Coward 1899–1973

English dramatist, actor, and composer. He is remembered for witty, satirical plays, such as *Hay Fever* (1925) and *Private Lives* (1930), as well as revues and musicals featuring songs such as 'Mad Dogs and Englishmen'.

Cecil Beaton
1904–80

1 He has become a fat old turtle with slits for eyes—no upper teeth—the lower lip bulging outwards—hunched—bent—the lot. How sad. He was once the very spirit of youth.
diary, October 1968

Noël Coward
1899–1973

2 The only thing that really saddens me over my demise is that I shall not be here to read the nonsense that will be written about me . . . There will be lists of apocryphal jokes I never made and gleeful misquotations of words I never said. *What* a pity I shan't be here to enjoy them!
diary, March 1955

Ernest Hemingway
1899–1961

3 I can't bear another minute of Noël's inane chatter. Who's interested in a bunch of old English actresses he's picked up from the gutter? Not me. If he wags that silly finger once more I may hit him.
Alec Guinness *Blessings in Disguise* (1985)

Anita Loos
1893–1981

4 So bloated with conceit.
G. Carey *Anita Loos* (1988)

Kenneth Tynan
1927–80

5 Taut, facially, as an appalled monolith; gracious, socially, as a royal bastard; tart, vocally, as a hollowed lemon.
in 1952

Kenneth Tynan
1927–80

6 Forty years ago he was Slightly in *Peter Pan*, and you might say that he has been wholly in *Peter Pan* ever since.
Curtains (1961)

Thomas Cranmer 1489–1556

English Protestant cleric. Appointed Archbishop of Canterbury after helping to negotiate **Henry VIII**'s divorce from Catherine of Aragon, he was responsible for the compilation of the Book of Common Prayer.

Charles, Prince of Wales
1948–

1 The genius of Cranmer's Prayer Book—in my humble opinion—lies in the conveyance of that sense of the sacred through the power and majesty of the language.
speech, April 1997

Thomas Cranmer
1489–1556

2 This was the hand that wrote it [his recantation], therefore it shall suffer first punishment.
at the stake for heresy, Oxford, March 1556

Henry VIII
1491–1547

3 That man hath the sow by the right ear.
of Cranmer's suggestions on the royal divorce
in June 1529

Joan Crawford 1908–77

American actress. Her film career lasted for over forty years, during which she played the female lead, and later appeared in mature roles, such as *Whatever Happened to Baby Jane?*

Christina Crawford
1939–

1 Everything was new and modern and plastic. Even the flowers and plants were plastic. Mother preferred them because they could be kept sparkling clean, and were regularly washed in soapy water.
Mommie Dearest (1979)

Joan Crawford
1908–77

2 I'd play Wally Beery's grandmother if it's a good part!
Fred Guiles *Joan Crawford: The Last Word* (1995)

George Cukor
1899–1983

3 The camera saw, I suspect, a side of her that no flesh-and-blood lover ever saw.
attributed

Anita Loos
1893–1981

4 Nothing she did was without calculation.
G. Carey *Anita Loos* (1988)

Francis Crick 1916–

English biophysicist. Together with **James D. Watson** he proposed the double helix structure of the DNA molecule.

Francis Crick
1916–

1 See my hand? Five fingers? If you think I have the faintest clue why I have five and only five fingers you are badly mistaken.
on being congratulated on his work on DNA
Abraham Pais *A Tale of Two Continents* (1997)

James D. Watson
1928–

2 I have never seen Francis Crick in a modest mood. Perhaps in other company he is that way, but I have never had reason so to judge him.
The Double Helix (1968)

Oliver Cromwell 1599–1658

English general and statesman, Lord Protector of the Commonwealth 1653–8. Cromwell was the leader of the victorious Parliamentary forces in the English Civil War.

Earl of Clarendon

1 He will be looked upon by posterity as a brave bad man.
The History of the Rebellion (1703)

Oliver Cromwell
1599–1658

2 Remark all these roughnesses, pimples, warts, and everything as you see me; otherwise I will never pay a farthing for it.
to Lely, commonly quoted as 'warts and all'
Horace Walpole *Anecdotes of Painting in England* vol. 3 (1763)

John Dryden
1631–1700

3 For he was great, ere fortune made him so.
on the death of Cromwell
Heroic Stanzas (1659)

George Fox
1624–91

4 O Oliver, hadst thou been faithful and thundered down the deceit . . . the King of France should have bowed his neck under thee, the Pope should have withered as in winter, the Turk in all his fatness should have smoked.
in c.1657; William Braithwaite *The Beginnings of Quakerism* (1970)

Christopher Hill
1912–

5 Oliver Cromwell aimed to bring about the kingdom of God on earth and founded the British Empire.
A Turbulent, Seditious, and Factious People: John Bunyan and his Church, 1628-1688 (1988)

John Milton
1608–74

6 Cromwell, our chief of men.
'To the Lord General Cromwell' (written 1652)

Samuel Pepys
1633–1703

7 At dinner we talked much of Cromwell, all saying he was a brave fellow and did owe his crown he got to himself, as much as any man that ever got one.
diary, February 1667

Alexander Pope
1688–1744

8 See Cromwell, damned to everlasting fame!
An Essay on Man Epistle 4 (1734)

William Waller
1598–1668

9 Whilst he was cautious of his own words, (not putting forth too many, lest they should betray his thoughts) he made others talk until he had, as it were, sifted them, and known their most intimate designs.
Christopher Hill *God's Englishman* (1970)

Bing Crosby 1903–77

American singer and actor, whose songs include 'White Christmas'. He starred in the *Road* films (1940–62) with **Bob Hope** and Dorothy Lamour.

Bing Crosby
1903–77

1 He was an average guy who could carry a tune.
suggestion for his own epitaph; attributed

Bob Hope
1903–

2 Once Bing hit success, he placed himself in a little Cellophane bag and he zipped it up and he just will not allow anyone to get inside that bag. He doesn't want to be told that he's good.

Charles Thompson *Bing* (1976)

Richard Crossman 1907–74

British Labour politician. His diaries, which were published after his death, give a detailed picture of the working of government.

Tina Brown
1953–

1 [Richard Crossman] has the jovial garrulity and air of witty indiscretion that shows he intends to give nothing away.

Loose Talk (1979)

Winston Churchill
1874–1965

2 The Hon. Member is never lucky in the coincidence of his facts with the truth.

in July 1954

Hugh Dalton
1887–1962

3 He is loyal to his own career but only incidentally to anything or anyone else.

diary, September 1941

Marie Curie 1867–1934

Polish-born French physicist. Working with her husband **Pierre Curie**, she discovered the elements polonium and radium. She died of leukaemia.

Marie Curie
1867–1934

1 In science, we must be interested in things, not in persons.

in c.1904; Eve Curie *Madame Curie* (1937)

Albert Einstein
1879–1955

2 Madame Curie is very intelligent but as cold as a herring, meaning that she is lacking in all feelings of joy and sorrow. Almost the only way in which she expresses her feelings is to rail at things she doesn't like.

letter, August 1913

Albert Einstein
1879–1955

3 Full of goodness and obstinacy at the same time, and it is for that that I like you, and I am happy that I have been able, during the peaceful days we spent together, to glimpse the depth of your mind where everything gets figured out in private.

in December 1923

Albert Einstein
1879–1955

4 Marie Curie is, of all celebrated beings, the only one whom fame has not corrupted.

Eve Curie *Madame Curie* (1938)

Maurice Rostand

5 No, you have never led an army,
No voices whispered stern commands.
But your sincere consuming ardour
Far outshines the burning brands.

'Ode to Marie Curie' (1921)

Pierre Curie 1859–1906

French physicist, pioneer of radioactivity. Working with his wife **Marie Curie**, he discovered the elements polonium and radium. He died in a street accident.

Marie Curie
1867–1934

6 I endure life, but I believe that never again will I be able to enjoy it . . . Because I don't have a gay or serene soul by nature and I leaned on the sweet serenity of Pierre . . . and the source is gone.

diary, June 1906

Emile Gautier

7 No one in truth, could have been more distracted, more detached from material life, than this great bearded boy, who looked more like an old student, a bohemian sculptor or a nihilist than a professor and member of the Institute. He was always 'out of it' . . . chasing after some transcendent problem.

in May 1906

Paul Langevin
1872–1946

8 An elegance of mind which produced in him the habit of believing nothing, of doing nothing, of saying nothing, of accepting nothing in his thought or in his actions which was not perfectly clear and which he did not entirely understand.
in June 1906

Lord Curzon 1859–1925

British statesman. He was Viceroy of India 1898–1905.

Anonymous

1 My name is George Nathaniel Curzon,
I am a most superior person.
My face is pink, my hair is sleek,
I dine at Blenheim once a week.
The Masque of Balliol (c.1870)

Lord Beaverbrook
1879–1964

2 Often undecided whether to desert a sinking ship for one that might not float, he would make up his mind to sit on the wharf for a day.
Men and Power (1956)

Lord Beaverbrook
1879–1964

3 For all the rest of his life Curzon was influenced by his sudden journey to heaven at the age of thirty-nine, and then by his return seven years later to earth, for the remainder of his mortal existence.
of Curzon as Viceroy
Men and Power (1956)

of the career of Lord Curzon:

Winston Churchill
1874–1965

4 The morning had been golden; the noontide was bronze; and the evening lead. But all were solid, and each was polished till it shone after its fashion.
Great Contemporaries (1937)

Jawaharlal Nehru
1889–1964

5 After every other Viceroy has been forgotten, Curzon will be remembered because he restored all that was beautiful in India.
Kenneth Rose Superior Person (1969)

George Custer 1839–76

American cavalry general. He served with distinction in the American Civil War but led his men to their deaths in a clash (popularly known as Custer's Last Stand) with the Sioux at Little Bighorn in Montana.

Crazy Horse
c.1842–1877

1 They say we massacred him, but he would have massacred us had we not defended ourselves and fought to the death.
E. A. Brininstool Crazy Horse (1949)

Sitting Bull
c.1831–90

2 Where the last stand was made, the Long Hair stood like a sheaf of corn with all the ears fallen around him.
in 1877

D

Dalai Lama 1935–

Spiritual head of Tibetan Buddhism and formerly the ruler of Tibet. He escaped to exile in India in 1959 following the invasion by the Chinese.

Rupert Murdoch
1931–

1 I have heard cynics who say he's a very political old monk shuffling around in Gucci shoes.
interview, September 1999

Salvador Dali 1904–89

Spanish painter. A surrealist, he portrayed dream images with almost photographic realism against backgrounds of arid Catalan landscapes.

Salvador Dali
1904–89

1 At the age of six I wanted to be a cook. At seven I wanted to be Napoleon. And my ambition has been growing steadily ever since.
The Secret Life of Salvador Dali (1948)

Salvador Dali
1904–89

2 Picasso is Spanish, I am too. Picasso is a genius. I am too. Picasso will be seventy-two and I about forty-eight. Picasso is known in every country of the world; so am I. Picasso is a Communist; I am not.
lecture in Madrid, October 1951

Timothy Leary
1920–96

3 Dali is the only painter of LSD without LSD.
Salvador Dali *Dali by Dali* (1970)

George Orwell
1903–50

4 He is as antisocial as a flea. Clearly, such people are undesirable, and a society in which they can flourish has something wrong with it.
'Benefit of Clergy: Some Notes on Salvador Dali' (1944)

George Orwell
1903–50

5 If it were possible for a book to give a physical stink off its pages, this one would.
on Dali's memoirs
'Benefit of Clergy: Some Notes on Salvador Dali' (1944)

John Dalton 1766–1844

English chemist, father of modern atomic theory. He argued that elements are composed of atoms and produced the first table of comparative atomic weights.

Humphrey Davy
1778–1829

1 His voice was harsh and brawling, his gait stiff and awkward; his style of writing and conversation dry and almost crabbed. In person he was tall, bony, and slender. He never could learn to swim: on investigating this circumstance he found that his specific gravity as a mass was greater than that of water.
W. C. Henry *Memoirs of the Life and Scientific Researches of John Dalton* (1854)

J. J. Thomson
1856–1940

2 He was not a fluent speaker, and when, as President, he had to make a few remarks when the reader of a paper stopped, he is reported to have sometimes contented himself by saying, 'This paper will no doubt be found interesting by those who take an interest in it'.
Recollections and Reflections (1936)

Dante Alighieri 1265–1321

Italian poet. His epic poem *The Divine Comedy* described his spiritual journey through Hell, Purgatory, and Paradise.

William Blake
1757–1827

1 It appears to me that men are hired to run down men of genius under the mask of translators, but Dante gives too much of Caesar: he is not a republican.
Annotations to Boyd's Dante (written c.1800)

Robert Browning
1812–89

2 Dante, who loved well because he hated,
Hated wickedness that hinders loving.
'One Word More' (1855)

Geoffrey Chaucer
c.1343–1400

3 Redeth the grete poete of Ytaille
That highte Dant, for he kan al devyse
Fro point to point; nat o word wol he faille.
The Canterbury Tales

T. S. Eliot
1888–1965

4 There is no poet in any tongue—not even Latin or Greek—who stands so firmly as a model for all poets.
Dante (1929)

William Hazlitt
1778–1830

5 He stood bewildered, not appalled, on that dark shore which separates the ancient and the modern world . . . He is power, passion, self-will personified.
Lectures on the English Poets (1818)

Dorothy L. Sayers
1893–1957

6 He was a very great comic writer—which was quite the last thing one would ever have inferred from the things people say in their books.
Further Papers on Dante (1957)

Percy Bysshe Shelley
1792–1822

7 His very words are instinct with spirit; each is as a spark, a burning atom of inextinguishable thought; and many yet lie covered in the ashes of their birth and pregnant with a lightning which has yet found no conductor.
A Defence of Poetry (written 1821)

Georges Jacques Danton 1759–94

French revolutionary. A noted orator, he was initially an ally of **Robespierre** but later revolted against the severity of the Revolutionary Tribunal and was executed.

Georges Jacques Danton
1759–94

1 Thou wilt show my head to the people: it is worth showing.
to his executioner, April 1794

Charles Darwin 1809–82

English natural historian and geologist. The material which Darwin collected as naturalist on HMS *Beagle* became the basis for his ideas on natural selection, expressed in his works *On the Origin of Species* and *The Descent of Man*.

Charles Darwin
1809–82

1 Everything about which I thought or read was made to bear directly on what I had seen or was likely to see; and this habit of mind was continued during the five years of the voyage. I feel sure that it was this training which has enabled me to do whatever I have done in science.
of the voyage of the Beagle
Francis Darwin (ed.) *The Life and Letters of Charles Darwin* (1887)

Charles Darwin
1809–82

2 If I had to live my life again, I would have made a rule to read some poetry and listen to some music at least once every week; for perhaps the parts of my brain now atrophied would thus have been kept active through use. The loss of these tastes is a loss of happiness, and may possibly be injurious to the intellect, and more probably to the moral character, by enfeebling the emotional part of our nature.
Francis Darwin (ed.) *The Life and Letters of Charles Darwin* (1887)

Francis Darwin
1848–1925

3 It is a proof of the terms on which we were, and also of how much he was valued as a play-fellow, that one of his sons when about four years old tried to bribe him with sixpence to come and play in working hours.
quoting one of his sisters; 'Reminiscences of My Father's Everyday Life' (1887)

Stephen Jay Gould
1941–

4 He spent about eight or ten years working on barnacles in between 1838, when he developed the theory of natural selection, and 1859 when he published it. I think it was largely displacement activity.
Lewis Wolpert and Alison Richards *A Passion for Science* (1988)

John Stuart Mill
1806–73

5 Though he cannot be said to have proved the truth of his doctrine, he does seem to have proved that it *may* be true, which I take to be as great a triumph as knowledge and ingenuity could possibly achieve on such a question.
letter, April 1860

Bertrand Russell
1872–1970

6 What Galileo and Newton were to the seventeenth century, Darwin was to the nineteenth.
History of Western Philosophy (1945)

Robert Louis Stevenson
1850–94

7 I never know whether to be more surprised at Darwin himself for making so much of Natural Selection, or at his opponents for making so little of it.

'Selections from his note-book' (1923)

Elizabeth David 1913–92

British cookery writer. She played a leading role in introducing Mediterranean cuisine to Britain in the 1950s and 1960s.

Auberon Waugh
1939–2001

1 If I had to choose one woman this century who had brought about the greatest improvement in English life, my vote would go to Elizabeth David.

attributed

Ray Davies 1944–

English pop singer and songwriter, of The Kinks.

Ned Sherrin
1931–

1 Almost all popular singers and songwriters have been influenced by America, and many of them sing in an American fashion. Ray shone out as someone who was not doing that and was in a way celebrating the Englishness, which in the first place had an appeal and a reality for the people in his native country. But it's so vivid that it's been able to leap across the Atlantic.

Neville Marten and Jeffrey Hudson *The Kinks: Well-Respected Men* (1996)

Robertson Davies 1913–95

Canadian novelist.

Robertson Davies
1913–95

2 It's an excellent life of somebody else. But I've really lived inside myself, and she can't get in there.

on a biography of himself
interview, April 1995

John Kenneth Galbraith
1908–

3 Davies I discovered when it was still possible to drop his name and have presumptively informed friends say, 'Who is that?'

Andrea D. Williams (ed.) *A View from the Stands of People, Politics, Military Power and the Arts* (1986)

Norman Mailer
1923–

4 I met him in New York, and I couldn't believe that anybody that pompous could be that good a writer.

in September 1987

Bette Davis 1908–89

American actress. She established her Hollywood career playing a number of strong, independent female characters, while her flair for suggesting the macabre and menacing emerged in later films.

Christina Crawford
1939–

1 Bette Davis was the consummate match for my mother's storehouse of tricks. She was a shrewd professional and every bit as indomitable as her co-star. Years later, mother would only have to hear her name mentioned to start a tirade.

*view of **Joan Crawford**'s daughter*
Mommie Dearest (1979)

Bette Davis
1908–89

2 'Playing our parts.' Yes, we all have to do that and from childhood on, I have found that my own character has been much harder to play worthily and far harder at times to comprehend than any of the roles I have portrayed.

in July 1956

Sam Goldwyn
1882–1974

3 Who wasted my time with *that* one?

on Bette Davis' first screen test, in 1929

Graham Greene
1904–91

4 That precise nervy voice, the pale ashblonde hair, the popping neurotic eyes, a kind of corrupt and phosphorescent prettiness.
  quoted by Kenneth Tynan, letter, November 1972

John Huston
1906–87

5 There is something elemental about Bette—a demon within her which threatens to break out and eat everybody, beginning with their ears.
  An Open Book (1980)

Colin Davis 1927–

British conductor.

Colin Davis
1927–

6 When I was nine I remember one of my most secret vices was to wait till everybody had gone out and listen to the last scene of Siegfried again. I was so worried about this I didn't want anyone to know.
  Anthony Clare *In the Psychiatrist's Chair III* (1998)

Jefferson Davis 1808–89

American statesman, President of the Confederate States 1861–5.

William Yancey
1814–63

7 The man and the hour have met.
  of Davis as President-elect of the Confederacy
  in 1861

Miles Davis 1926–91

American jazz trumpeter, composer, and bandleader. In the 1950s he played in a new style which became known as 'cool' jazz. In the 1960s he pioneered the fusion of jazz and rock.

Kenneth Tynan
1927–80

8 Then Miles alone leaning back with his trumpet aimed at the footlights, composing bleak, illuminating footnotes to what the ensemble had stated, each note hanging in the air like ripe fruit.
  in February 1963

Sammy Davis Jnr. 1925–90

American entertainer. A friend of **Frank Sinatra**, he was a member of the Hollywood 'Rat Pack'.

Sammy Davis Jnr.
1925–90

on golf:
9 QUESTION: What is your handicap?
  DAVIS: I'm a coloured, one-eyed Jew—do I need anything else?
  Yes I Can (1965)

Sammy Davis Jnr.
1925–90

10 Being a star has made it possible for me to get insulted in places where the average Negro could never *hope* to go and get insulted.
  Yes I Can (1965)

Humphrey Davy 1778–1829

English chemist. He discovered nitrous oxide (laughing gas) and the elements sodium, potassium, magnesium, calcium, strontium, and barium. In 1815 he invented the miner's safety lamp.

Anonymous

1 Sir H. Davy's greatest discovery was Michael Faraday.
  Paul Harvey *Oxford Companion to English Literature* (1932)

Edmund Clerihew Bentley
1875–1956

2 Sir Humphrey Davy
  Abominated gravy.
  He lived in the odium
  Of having discovered Sodium.
  'Sir Humphrey Davy' (1905)

Richard Dawkins 1941–

English biologist. Dawkins's book *The Selfish Gene* (1976) did much to popularize the theory of sociobiology.

John Carey
1934–

1 The way Dawkins writes about science is not just a brain-tonic. It is more like an extended stay on a brain health-farm . . . You come out feeling lean, tuned and enormously more intelligent.
attributed

Doris Day 1924–

American actress and singer. She became a film star in the 1950s with roles in light-hearted musicals, comedies, and romances.

Groucho Marx
1895–1977

1 I've been around so long, I knew Doris Day before she was a virgin.
Max Wilk *The Wit and Wisdom of Hollywood* (1972)

Robin Day 1923–2000

British journalist and broadcaster. He introduced a more probing style of political interview.

Robin Day
1923–2000

2 I was never a journalist. I was always an institution.
attributed

Frankie Howerd
1922–92

3 Such cruel glasses.
in *That Was The Week That Was* (BBC TV series, from 1963)

John Humphrys
1943–

4 He was the father of the modern political interview. If you don't like Paxman and me, then you've got Robin Day to blame for it . . . Robin broke the taboo that you only asked the questions politicians wanted asked.
in August 2000

Moshe Dayan 1915–81

Israeli statesman and general. As Minister of Defence he oversaw Israel's victory in the Six Day War and as Foreign Minister he played a prominent role in negotiations towards the Camp David agreements of 1979.

Moshe Dayan
1915–81

1 War is the most exciting and dramatic thing in life. In fighting to the death you feel terribly relaxed when you manage to come through.
in February 1972

Chaim Herzog
1918–97

2 Matters of routine, discipline, training, housekeeping and general administration bored him.
The War of Atonement (1975)

James Dean 1931–55

American actor. Although he starred in only three films before dying in a car accident, he became a cult figure closely identified with the title role of *Rebel Without a Cause*.

Alec Guinness
1914–2000

1 It is now ten o'clock, Friday the 23rd of September. If you get in that car you will be found dead in it by this time next week.
to James Dean, whose fatal crash took place a week later
Blessings in Disguise (1985)

Elia Kazan
1909–

2 You can't not like a guy with that much pain in him.
Jeff Young (ed.) *Kazan on Kazan* (1999)

Simone de Beauvoir 1908–86

French existentialist philosopher, novelist, and feminist. Her best-known work is *The Second Sex* (1949), a central book of the 'second wave' of feminism.

Stevie Smith
1902–71

1 Miss de Beauvoir has written an enormous book about women and it is soon clear that she does not like being a woman.
reviewing *The Second Sex* in the 1950s

Louis de Bernières 1954–

British novelist and short-story writer.

Louis de Bernières
1954–

1 The trouble with fulfilling your ambitions is you think you will be transformed into some sort of archangel and you're not. You still have to wash your socks.

in February 1999

Claude Debussy 1862–1918

French composer and critic. Debussy carried the ideas of Impressionist art and symbolist poetry into music.

Claude Debussy
1862–1918

1 The colour of my soul is iron-grey and sad bats wheel about the steeple of my dreams.

letter, 1894

Nikolai Rimsky-
Korsakov
1844–1908

2 Better not listen to it; you risk getting used to it, and then you would end by liking it.

of Debussy's music
Igor Stravinsky *Chronicle of my Life* (1936)

Edgar Degas 1834–1917

French painter and sculptor. An Impressionist painter, Degas is best known for his paintings of ballet dancers.

Edgar Degas
1834–1917

1 Everybody has talent at twenty-five. The difficult thing is to have it at fifty.

R. H. Ives Gammell *The Shop-Talk of Edgar Degas* (1961)

Paul Gauguin
1848–1903

2 You know how greatly I respect the work of Degas, yet I feel occasionally that he lacks something which carries him beyond himself—a heart which beats.

letter, 1889

Charles de Gaulle 1890–1970

French general and statesman, President 1959–69. A wartime leader of the Free French movement, he is remembered for his assertive foreign policy.

Winston Churchill
1874–1965

1 What can you do with a man who looks like a female llama surprised when bathing?

comment, 1944

Winston Churchill
1874–1965

2 The hardest cross I have to bear is the Cross of Lorraine.

Harold Wilson *A Prime Minister on Prime Ministers* (1977)

Charles de Gaulle
1890–1970

3 Since they whose duty it was to wield the sword of France have let it fall shattered to the ground, I have taken up the broken blade.

speech, July 1940

Charles de Gaulle
1890–1970

4 I always thought I was Jeanne d'Arc and Bonaparte. How little one knows oneself.

*on being compared to **Robespierre***
in June 1958

Henry Kissinger
1923–

5 One had the sense that if he moved to a window the centre of gravity might shift and the whole room might tilt everyone into the garden.

The White House Years (1979)

Sylvia Townsend
Warner
1893–1978

6 General de Gaulle is again pictured in our newspapers, looking as usual like an embattled codfish. I wish he could be filleted and put quietly away in a refrigerator.

letter, September 1948

Eugène Delacroix 1798–1863

French painter, the chief painter of the French romantic school. He is known for his use of vivid colour, free drawing, and exotic, violent, or macabre subject matter.

Charles Baudelaire 1 Delacroix, lake of blood haunted by bad angels.
1821–67   'Les Phares' (1857)

Charles Baudelaire 2 A curious mixture of scepticism, politeness, dandyism, ardour,
1821–67   cunning, despotism, and finally a certain species of kindness or
moderated tenderness which always accompanies genius.
Herbert Read *The Meaning of Art* (3rd ed., 1951)

Charles Baudelaire 3 The truth is that in the last years of his life, all that might be called
1821–67   pleasure had disappeared from his life, a single, avid, exacting, terrible
passion having taken its place—work—which was no longer merely a
passion, but would have been better described as a fury.
Herbert Read *The Meaning of Art* (3rd ed., 1951)

Jean Ingres 4 They have let the wolf into the sheepfold!
1780–1867   *on Delacroix being elected to the Academy*
P. Amaury-Duval *L'atelier d'Ingres* (1878)

Walter de la Mare 1873–1956

English poet. Essentially a lyric poet, he is known particularly for his verse for children.

Siegfried Sassoon 1 I have never been in his company without a sense of heightened and
1886–1967   deepened perception. After talking to him, one goes away seeing the
world, for a while, with rechristened eyes.
Siegfried's Journey (1945)

Frederick Delius 1862–1934

English composer, of German and Scandinavian descent. He is best known for pastoral works such as *Brigg Fair*, but he also wrote songs, concertos, and choral and theatre music.

Frederick Delius 1 I have seen the best of the earth and done everything that is worth
1862–1934   doing.
Eric Fenby *Delius as I knew him* (1936)

Colin Wilson 2 In Delius the apples of decadence have turned slightly more rotten.
1931–   *Brandy of the Damned* (1964)

Cecil B. de Mille 1881–1959

American film producer and director, famous for his spectacular epics, including *The Ten Commandments* and *Samson and Delilah*.

Anonymous 1 Cecil B. de Mille
Rather against his will,
Was persuaded to leave Moses
Out of 'The Wars of the Roses'.
J. W. Carter (ed.) *Clerihews* (1938); attributed to Nicolas Bentley

George Cukor 2 Preposterous, illiterate, ludicrous, *but*—what a master storyteller!
1899–1983   Kenneth Tynan *Tynan Right and Left* (1967)

Agnes de Mille 3 His success was a world success, and he enjoyed every minute of it, and
1908–   it lasted. He kept sex, sadism, patriotism, real estate, religion and
public relations dancing in mid-air like jugglers' balls for fifty years.
Speak to Me, Dance with Me (1973)

Billy Graham 4 Another early film which made an impact on me was Cecil B. DeMille's
1918–   *King of Kings*. This probably taught me more about the life of Christ than
did a great deal of the Sunday school training I had as a boy.
in April 1963

Gloria Swanson
1899–1983

5 Working for Mr De Mille was like playing house in the world's most expensive department store.
Swanson on Swanson (1980)

King Vidor
1895–1982

6 When I saw one of his pictures, I wanted to quit the business.
Kevin Brownlow *The Parade's Gone By* (1968)

Jack Dempsey 1895–1983

American boxer. He was world heavyweight champion 1919–26. His defence of the title in 1921 was the first fight at which a million dollars was taken at the gate.

Jack Dempsey
1895–1983

1 Tall men come down to my height when I hit 'em in the body.
attributed

Judi Dench 1934–

English classical actress, who has also appeared in numerous West End, film, and television productions.

Judi Dench
1934–

1 I feel for eight minutes on screen, I should only get a little bit of him.
accepting an Oscar for her role as Queen Elizabeth in Shakespeare in Love
at the Academy Awards, Los Angeles, March 1999

Catherine Deneuve 1943–

French actress. She is best known for her roles in such films as *Repulsion* (1965) and *Belle de jour* (1967).

Catherine Deneuve
1943–

1 Why would I talk about the men in my life? For me, life is not about men.
on writing her autobiography
in April 1997

Thomas De Quincey 1785–1859

English essayist and critic. He achieved fame with his *Confessions of an English Opium Eater*, a study of his addiction to opium and its psychological effects.

D. H. Lawrence
1885–1930

1 He is a *very* nice man—I can go on reading and reading him. I laughed over *Goethe* yesterday. I like him, De Quincey, because he also dislikes such people as Plato and Goethe, whom I dislike.
letter, 1919

Dorothy Wordsworth
1771–1855

2 He is a remarkable and very interesting young man; very diminutive in person, which, to strangers, makes him appear insignificant; and so modest, and so very shy that even now I wonder how he ever had the courage to address himself to my brother by letter.
letter, December 1807

Edward Stanley, 14th Earl of Derby 1799–1869

British Conservative statesman, Prime Minister 1852, 1858–9, and 1866–8. He led the protectionists in the House of Lords and as Prime Minister he carried the second Reform Act (1867) through Parliament.

Edward Bulwer-Lytton
1803–73

1 Here Stanley meets,—how Stanley scorns, the glance!
The brilliant chief, irregularly great,
Frank, haughty, rash,—the Rupert of Debate!
The New Timon (1846)

Benjamin Disraeli
1804–81

2 The noble Lord is the Prince Rupert of Parliamentary discussion.
speech, April 1844

Lord Derby 1865–1948

British Conservative politician.

Earl Haig
1861–1928

3 A very weak-minded fellow I am afraid, and, like the feather pillow, bears the marks of the last person who has sat on him!

letter, January 1918

René Descartes 1596–1650

French philosopher, mathematician, and man of science. He concluded that everything was open to doubt except his own conscious experience.

Alain
1868–1951

1 Descartes' mistake is of higher quality than the truth of a pedant.

Propos d'un Normand

John Aubrey
1626–97

2 He was too wise a man to encumber himself with a wife; but as he was a man, he had the desires and appetites of a man; he therefore kept a good conditioned handsome woman that he liked, and by whom he had some children (I think two or three). 'Tis a pity, but coming from the brain of such a father, they should be well cultivated.

Brief Lives

Thomas Hobbes
1588–1679

3 Mr Hobbes was wont to say that had Descartes kept himself wholly to geometry, that he had been the best geometer in the world. He did very much admire him, but said that he could not pardon him for writing in the defence of transubstantiation which he knew to be absolutely against his judgement.

John Aubrey *Brief Lives*

Jean de la Fontaine
1621–95

4 Descartes, this mortal who has been made a god among the pagans, and who holds the place between man and spirit.

Fables

Blaise Pascal
1623–62

5 I cannot forgive Descartes: in all his philosophy he would very much have liked to be able to do without God, but he could not resist making him give a flick to set the world in motion; after that, God had nothing more to do with it.

Pensées (1670)

Gilbert Ryle
1900–76

6 The dogma of the Ghost in the Machine.

on the mental-conduct concepts of Descartes
The Concept of Mind (1949)

Madame de Staël 1766–1817

French novelist and critic. A precursor of the French romantics, she wrote two semi-autobiographical novels, and her critical work introduced late 18th-century German writers and thinkers to France.

Lord Byron
1788–1824

1 She thinks like a man, but alas! she feels like a woman.

J. Christopher Herold *Mistress to an Age* (1959)

Eamon de Valera 1882–1975

American-born Irish statesman, Taoiseach 1937–48, 1951–4, and 1957–9 and President of the Republic of Ireland 1959–73. He was the founder of the Fianna Fáil Party.

Michael Collins
1890–1922

1 How could one argue with a man who was always drawing lines and circles to explain his position?

attributed

Eamon de Valera
1882–1975

2 Whenever I wanted to know what the Irish people wanted, I had only to examine my own heart and it told me straight off what the Irish people wanted.

in Dáil Éireann, January 1922

**Oliver St John
Gogarty**
1878–1957

3 We rose to bring about Eutopia,
But all we got was Dev's myopia.
Ulick O'Connor *Oliver St John Gogarty* (1964)

David Lloyd George
1863–1945

4 Negotiating with de Valera . . . is like trying to pick up mercury with a fork.
to which de Valera replied, 'Why doesn't he use a spoon?'
M. J. MacManus *Eamon de Valera* (1944)

Ninette de Valois 1898–2001

Irish choreographer, ballet dancer, and teacher. A former soloist with Diaghilev's Ballets Russes, she formed the Royal Ballet and the Sadler's Wells ballet school.

Frederick Ashton
1904–88

1 I feel rather like James the First succeeding Queen Elizabeth.
on becoming director of the Royal Ballet in 1963

Sergei Diaghilev
1872–1929

2 Half tart, half royal family of France.
on Ninette de Valois' choice of name
John Drummond *Speaking of Diaghilev* (1997)

Lincoln Kirstein
1907–96

3 Ninette is a combination of Montgomery of Alamein and Mrs Bowdler.
Julie Kavanagh *Secret Muses* (1996)

Sergei Diaghilev 1872–1929

Russian ballet impresario. In 1909 he formed the Ballets Russes, with **Nijinsky**, and later Massine, as his star performer.

Cecil Beaton
1904–80

1 Very grandiose. Very *grand seigneur*. Immaculate. He moved slowly. He had to turn his whole head round, his whole body round, if he wanted to look over his shoulder.
John Drummond *Speaking of Diaghilev* (1997)

Osbert Lancaster
1908–80

2 He was as ruthless as any American impresario, or any of the big tycoons of the theatre, but at the same time he had enormous taste.
John Drummond *Speaking of Diaghilev* (1997)

Marie Rambert
1888–1982

3 But here came in the greatness of Diaghilev. He knew when he loved those young people, say Nijinsky or Massine or Lifar, he made them into gods. They couldn't sustain it after his death.
John Drummond *Speaking of Diaghilev* (1997)

Diana, Princess of Wales 1961–97

former wife of **Prince Charles**. Married in 1981 and divorced in 1996, she became a popular figure through her charity work and glamorous media appearances, and her death gave rise to intense national mourning.

Tony Blair
1953–

1 She was the People's Princess, and that is how she will stay . . . in our hearts and in our memories forever.
on hearing of the death of Diana, Princess of Wales, August 1997

Julie Burchill
1960–

2 Now, at last, this sad, glittering century has an image worthy of it: a wandering, wondering girl, a silly Sloane turned secular saint, coming home in her coffin to RAF Northolt like the good soldier she was.
in September 1997

**Diana, Princess of
Wales**
1961–97

3 I'd like to be a queen in people's hearts but I don't see myself being Queen of this country.
television interview, November 1995

Maureen Dowd
1952–

4 The Princess of Wales was the queen of surfaces, ruling over a kingdom where fame was the highest value and glamour the most cherished attribute.
in September 1997

Elton John	5	Goodbye England's rose;
1947–		May you ever grow in our hearts.
and **Bernie Taupin**		'Candle in the Wind' (song, revised version, 1997)
1950–		

Elton John	6	And it seems to me you lived your life
1947–		Like a candle in the wind:
and **Bernie Taupin**		Never fading with the sunset
1950–		When the rain set in.
		'Candle in the Wind' (song, revised version, 1997); see **Monroe** 9

Andrew Motion	7	Beside the river, swerving under ground.
1952–		your future tracked you, snapping at your heels:
		Diana, breathless, hunted by your own quick hounds.
		'Mythology' (1997)

Lord Spencer	8	She needed no royal title to continue to generate her particular brand
1964–		of magic.
		funeral tribute, September 1997

Lord Spencer	9	A girl given the name of the ancient goddess of hunting was, in the
1964–		end, the most hunted person of the modern age.
		funeral tribute, September 1997

Charles Dickens 1812–70

English novelist. His novels are notable for their satirical humour and treatment of contemporary social problems, including the plight of the urban poor and the corruption and inefficiency of the legal system.

Kingsley Amis	1	My own experience in reading Dickens . . . is to be bounced between
1922–95		violent admiration and violent distaste almost every couple of
		paragraphs, and this is too uncomfortable a condition to be much
		alleviated by an inward recital of one's duty not to be fastidious, to gulp
		the stuff down in gobbets like a man.
		What Became of Jane Austen? (1970)

Walter Bagehot	2	He describes London like a special correspondent for posterity.
1826–77		in October 1858

Alan Bennett	3	We were put to Dickens as children but it never quite took. That
1934–		unremitting humanity soon had me cheesed off.
		The Old Country (1978)

Henry James	4	The greatest of superficial novelists . . . It were, in our opinion, an
1843–1916		offence against humanity to place Mr Dickens among the greatest
		novelists.
		'Our Mutual Friend' (1865)

Milan Kundera	5	Heartlessness masked by a style overflowing with feeling.
1929–		*of Dickens's novels*
		Testaments Betrayed (1995)

George Orwell	6	A man who is always fighting against something, but who fights in the
1903–50		open and is not frightened . . . a man who is *generously angry*.
		Collected Essays, Journalism and Letters (1968)

Dorothy Parker	7	Who call him spurious and shoddy
1893–1967		Shall do it o'er my lifeless body.
		I heartily invite such birds
		To come outside and say those words!
		'Sunset Gun'

Sydney Smith	8	The soul of Hogarth has migrated into the body of Dickens.
1771–1845		letter, 1837

Queen Victoria	9	He had a large loving mind and the strongest sympathy with the poorer
1819–1901		classes. He felt sure a better feeling, and much greater union of classes,
		would take place in time. And I pray earnestly it may.
		diary, June 1870

Emily Dickinson 1830–86

American poet. From the age of 24 she led the life of a recluse. Only seven of her poems were published in her lifetime.

Hart Crane
1899–1932

1 You who desired so much—in vain to ask—
Yet fed your hunger like an endless task,
Dared dignify the labor, bless the quest—
Achieved that stillness ultimately best,
Being, of all, least sought for: Emily, hear!
'To Emily Dickinson' (1927)

Emily Dickinson
1830–86

2 They shut me up in prose—
As when a little girl
They put me in the closet—
Because they liked me 'still'.
'They shut me up in prose' (c. 1862)

Amy Lowell
1874–1925

3 Sappho would speak, I think, quite openly,
And Mrs Browning guard a careful silence,
But Emily would set doors ajar and slam them
And love you for your speed of observation.
'The Sisters' (1925)

Adrienne Rich
1923–

4 and in your halfcracked way you chose
silence for entertainment,
chose to have it out at last
on your own premises.
attributed

John G. Diefenbaker 1895–1979

Canadian Progressive Conservative statesman, Prime Minister 1957–63.

Joe Clark
1939–

1 In a very real sense, his life was Canada. Over eight decades, he spanned our history, from the ox cart on the prairies to the satellite in space. He shaped much of that history—all of it shaped him.
in August 1979

John G. Diefenbaker
1895–1979

2 While there's snow on the roof, it doesn't mean the fire has gone out in the furnace.
approaching his 80th birthday, in September 1975

Marlene Dietrich 1901–92

German-born American actress and singer. She became famous for her part as Lola in *The Blue Angel* (1930). From the 1950s she was also successful as an international cabaret star.

Alistair Cooke
1908–

1 A beauty so overwhelming that it allows her own character never to come into play and therefore never to be called into question . . . it is because the Dietrich character has no home, no passport, no humdrum loyalties, that the memory can hold her only in permanent soft-focus.
Sheridan Morley *Marlene Dietrich* (1978)

Noël Coward
1899–1973

2 Though we all might enjoy
Seeing Helen of Troy
As a gay cabaret entertainer,
I doubt that she could
Be one quarter as good
As our legendary, lovely Marlene.
in 1954

Marlene Dietrich
1901–92

3 If it's true that my legs are my fortune, why should I show them to you for nothing?
to a photographer, c. 1950; L. Frewin *Blond Venus* (1955)

Ernest Hemingway
1899–1961

4 That Kraut is the best that ever came into the ring.
Sheridan Morley *Marlene Dietrich* (1978)

Kenneth Tynan
1927–80

5 She has sex, but no particular gender. Her masculinity appeals to women, and her sexuality to men.
Curtains (1961)

Josef von Sternberg
1894–1969

6 I then put her into the crucible of my conception, blended her image to correspond with mine, and, pouring lights on her until the alchemy was complete, proceeded with a screen test.
Sheridan Morley *Marlene Dietrich* (1976)

Joe DiMaggio 1914–99

American baseball player. Star of the New York Yankees team 1936–51, he was briefly married to **Marilyn Monroe** in 1954.

Yogi Berra
1925–

1 I don't know if it's good for baseball but it sure beats the hell out of rooming with Phil Rizzuto!
*on the announcement of the marriage of Joe DiMaggio and **Marilyn Monroe***
attributed

Diogenes c.400–c.325 BC

Greek philosopher. The most famous of the Cynics, he lived ascetically in Athens (according to legend, in a tub).

Alexander the Great
356–323 BC

1 If I were not Alexander, I would be Diogenes.
Plutarch *Parallel Lives*

Diogenes
c.400–c.325 BC

Alexander the Great asked him if he lacked anything:
2 Yes, that I do: that you stand out of my sun a little.
Plutarch *Parallel Lives*

Christian Dior 1905–57

French couturier. He introduced the New Look in 1947.

Cecil Beaton
1904–80

1 In appearance Dior is like a bland country curate made out of pink marzipan.
The Glass of Fashion (1954)

Coco Chanel
1883–1971

2 Clothes by a man who doesn't know women, never had one, and dreams of being one!
of Dior's New Look
attributed

Walt Disney 1901–66

American animator and film producer. He made his name with the creation of cartoon characters such as Mickey Mouse, Donald Duck, Goofy, and Pluto.

Walt Disney
1901–66

1 Fancy being remembered around the world for the invention of a mouse!
*during his last illness; Leonard Mosley *Disney's World* (1985)

Henry Miller
1891–1980

2 He's the master of the nightmare. He's the Gustave Doré of the world of Henry Ford and Co., Inc.
The Air-Conditioned Nightmare (1945)

Benjamin Disraeli 1804–81

British Tory statesman, Prime Minister 1868 and 1874–80; later Lord Beaconsfield. He introduced the second Reform Act, ensured that Britain bought a controlling interest in the Suez Canal, and made **Queen Victoria** Empress of India.

Otto von Bismarck
1815–98

1 The old Jew! That is the man.
of Disraeli at the Congress of Berlin, 1878; attributed

Thomas Carlyle
1795–1881

2 A superlative Hebrew conjuror.
Shooting Niagara: and After? (1867)

Benjamin Disraeli 1804–81	3 I have climbed to the top of the greasy pole. on becoming Prime Minister; W. Monypenny and G. Buckle *Life of Benjamin Disraeli* vol. 4 (1916)

to Queen Victoria after the publication of Leaves from the Journal of our Life in the Highlands*:*

Benjamin Disraeli 1804–81	4 We authors, Ma'am. in 1868
Mary Anne Disraeli d. 1872	5 I wish you could only see Dizzy in his bath, then you would know what a white skin is. *of her husband* attributed; William Gregory *An Autobiography* (1894)
Michael Foot 1913–	6 Disraeli was my favourite Tory. He was an adventurer pure and simple, or impure and complex. I'm glad to say Gladstone got the better of him. in March 1975
W. E. Gladstone 1809–98	7 A man who is *never beaten*. Every reverse, every defeat is to him only an admonition to wait and catch his opportunity of retrieving his position. letter, August 1877
Harold Macmillan 1894–1986	8 The English, they don't like clever people. The whole Tory Party spent 1868–74 trying to get rid of Dizzy. in August 1975
Lord Salisbury 1830–1903	9 Too clever by half. *of Disraeli's amendment on Disestablishment* speech, March 1868
Lord Salisbury 1830–1903	10 What with deafness, ignorance of French, and Bismarck's extraordinary mode of speech, Beaconsfield has the dimmest idea of what is going on—understands everything crossways—and imagines a perpetual conspiracy. letter from the Congress of Berlin, June 1878

Frank Dobson 1940–

British Labour politician. He resigned from the government to run for Mayor of London, but was defeated by **Ken Livingstone**.

Frank Dobson 1940–	1 I trudge the streets rather than trade the soundbite. I . . . would not know a focus group if I met one. I am unspun. in February 2000
Ann Widdecombe 1947–	2 How dare he tell me what to do when he has a circumference to rival the Equator. *on the Health Minister's advice that a healthy diet should include more bran and fibre* in July 1998

John Donne 1572–1631

English poet and preacher. A metaphysical poet, he wrote love poems and religious poems, and was one of the most celebrated preachers of his age.

Thomas Carew c.1595–1640	1 Here lies a king, that ruled as he thought fit The universal monarchy of wit. 'An Elegy upon the Death of Dr John Donne' (1640)
Samuel Taylor Coleridge 1772–1834	2 With Donne, whose muse on dromedary trots, Wreathe iron pokers into true-love knots. 'On Donne's Poetry' (1818)
John Donne 1572–1631	3 John Donne, Anne Donne, Un-done. *in a letter to his wife, on being dismissed from the service of his father-in-law, Sir George More* Izaak Walton *The Life of Dr Donne* (1640)
James I 1566–1625	4 Dr Donne's verses are like the peace of God; they pass all understanding. remark recorded by Archdeacon Plume (1630–1704)

Ben Jonson
c.1573–1637

5 Donne, for not keeping of accent, deserved hanging.

in *Conversations with William Drummond of Hawthornden* (written 1619)

Alexander Pope
1688–1744

6 Donne had no imagination, but as much wit, I think, as any writer can possibly have.

Joseph Spence *Anecdotes* (ed. J. Osborn, 1966)

R. S. Thomas
1913–2000

7 Donne's thin, cerebral laughter.

Laboratories of the Spirit (1975)

Izaak Walton
1593–1683

8 But God, who is able to prevail, wrestled with him, as the Angel did with Jacob, and marked him; marked him for his own.

Life of Donne (1670 ed.)

Fedor Dostoevsky 1821–81

Russian novelist. Dostoevsky's novels reveal his psychological insight, savage humour, and concern with the religious, political, and moral problems posed by human suffering.

Joseph Conrad
1857–1924

1 The grimacing, haunted creature . . . fierce mouthings from prehistoric ages.

Cedric Watts *Joseph Conrad: Writers and their Work* (1994)

Anna Dostoevsky
1846–1918

2 It seems to me that he has never loved, that he has only imagined that he has loved, that there has been no real love on his part. I even think that he is incapable of love; he is too much occupied with other thoughts and ideas to become strongly attached to anyone earthly.

a wife's view
in 1887

W. Somerset Maugham
1874–1965

3 The humour of Dostoevsky is the humour of a bar-loafer who ties a kettle to a dog's tail.

A Writer's Notebook (1949) written in 1917

W. Somerset Maugham
1874–1965

4 He has the look of a man who has been in hell and seen there, not a hopeless suffering, but meanness and frippery.

A Writer's Notebook (1949) written in 1917

Frederick Douglass c.1818–95

American civil rights campaigner. Born a slave, after escaping he lectured on slavery and set up an abolitionist journal, the *North Star*.

Susan B. Anthony
1820–1906

1 Frederick Douglass used to tell me that when he was a Maryland slave, and a good Methodist, he would go into the farthest corner of the tobacco fields and pray to God to bring him liberty; but God never answered his prayers until he prayed with his heels.

R. C. Dorr *Susan B. Anthony* (1928)

Frederick Douglass
c.1818–95

2 You have seen how a man was made a slave; you shall see how a slave was made a man.

Narrative of the Life of Frederick Douglass (1845)

Booker T. Washington
1856–1915

3 The life of Frederick Douglass is the history of American slavery epitomized in a single human experience. He saw it all, lived it all, and overcame it all.

Frederick Douglass (1907)

Arthur Conan Doyle 1859–1930

Scottish novelist and short-story writer, chiefly remembered for his creation of the private detective Sherlock Holmes.

Joseph Bell
1837–1911

1 Why bother yourself about the cataract of drivel for which Conan Doyle is responsible? I am sure he never imagined that such a heap of rubbish would fall on my devoted head in consequence of his stories.

Bell was the inspiration for Sherlock Holmes
Joseph Bell: an Appreciation by an Old Friend (1913)

P. G. Wodehouse
1881–1975

2 Don't you find as you age in the wood, as we are both doing, that the tragedy of life is that your early heroes lose their glamour? . . . Now, with Doyle I don't have this feeling. I still revere his work as much as ever. I used to think it swell, and I still think it swell.
Performing Flea (1953)

Francis Drake c.1540–96

English sailor and explorer. He was the first Englishman to circumnavigate the globe (1577–80), in his ship the *Golden Hind*. He helped defeat the Spanish Armada.

Anonymous

1 The Sun himself cannot forget
His fellow traveller.
Wit's Recreations (1640)

Henry Newbolt
1862–1938

2 Drake he's in his hammock an' a thousand mile away
(Capten, art tha sleepin' there below?)
Slung atween the round shot in Nombre Dios Bay
An' dreamin' arl the time o' Plymouth Hoe.
'Drake's Drum' (1897)

John Dryden 1631–1700

English poet, critic, and dramatist of the Augustan Age. He popularized the heroic couplet as a verse form, and his prose writing style is often considered the model for modern English literature.

W. H. Auden
1907–73

1 There *Dryden* sits with modest smile,
The master of the middle style.
New Year Letter (1941)

Samuel Taylor Coleridge
1772–1834

2 Dryden's genius was of that sort which catches fire by its own motion: his chariot-wheels got hot by driving fast.
Table Talk (1836)

Thomas Gray
1716–71

3 Remember Dryden, and be blind to all his faults.
letter, October 1765

Gerard Manley Hopkins
1844–89

4 He is the most masculine of our poets; his style and rhythms lay the strongest stress of all our literature on the naked thew and sinew of the English language.
letter, November 1887

Samuel Johnson
1709–84

5 The father of English criticism.
Lives of the English Poets (1779–81)

Lord Macaulay
1800–59

6 His mind was of a slovenly character,—fond of splendour, but indifferent to neatness. Hence most of his writings exhibit the sluttish magnificence of a Russian noble, all vermin diamonds, dirty linen and inestimable sables.
in January 1828

Alexander Pope
1688–1744

7 Ev'n copious Dryden, wanted, or forgot,
The last and greatest art, the art to blot.
Imitations of Horace (1737)

Marcel Duchamp 1887–1968

French-born American artist. A leading figure of the Dada movement and originator of conceptual art, he invented 'ready-mades', mass-produced articles selected at random and displayed as works of art.

Guillaume Apollinaire
1880–1918

1 Perhaps it will be the task of an artist as detached from aesthetic preoccupations and as intent on the energetic as Marcel Duchamp to reconcile art and the people.
Les Peintres cubistes (1913)

Robert Dudley c.1532–88

English nobleman. After the mysterious death of his wife Amy Robsart in 1560 it was rumoured that he would marry **Elizabeth I**.

Ben Jonson
c.1573–1637

1 Here lies a valiant warrior
Who never drew a sword;
Here lies a noble courtier
Who never kept his word.
attributed

Isadora Duncan 1878–1927

American dancer and teacher. She was a pioneer of modern dance, famous for her 'free' barefoot dancing.

Frederick Ashton
1904–88

1 She was really a kind of intellectual strip teaser, taking off gauze veils one by one and draping them over the piano.
Peter Hall's diary, December 1975

Isadora Duncan
1878–1927

2 The only dance masters I could have were Jean-Jacques Rousseau, Walt Whitman and Nietzsche.
My Life (1927)

Ken Russell
1927–

3 Isadora seemed to embody the best and worst of an artist. She had genuine talent, some mystical insight, but she was a bit bogus as well. She had that touch of vulgarity which I think art and people connected with it could well profit by.
John Baxter An Appalling Talent (1973)

George Bernard Shaw
1856–1950

4 A woman whose face looked as if it had been made of sugar and someone had licked it.
Hesketh Pearson Bernard Shaw (1961)

Edith Wharton
1862–1937

5 I beheld the dance I had always dreamed of, a flowing of movement into movement, an endless interweaving of motion and music, satisfying every sense as a flower does, or a phrase of Mozart's.
attributed

Jacqueline du Pré 1945–87

English cellist. She made her solo debut at the age of 16. Her performing career was halted in 1972 by multiple sclerosis.

John Barbirolli
1899–1970

1 Jackie is sometimes accused of excessive emotions . . . but I love it. When you are young, you should have an excess of everything. If you haven't got an excess when you are young, what are you going to pare off as the years go by?
Carol Easton Jacqueline du Pré (1989)

Pablo Casals
1876–1973

2 QUESTION: Doesn't she *move* an awful lot?
CASALS: Oh, I *like* it—she moves *with* the music!
Carol Easton Jacqueline du Pré (1989)

Jacqueline du Pré
1945–87

3 It gave me everything I needed and wanted. Playing was the cream. When I played, it never bothered me what happened. But I realized later that it didn't necessarily equip one to deal with one's fellow humans.
Carol Easton Jacqueline du Pré (1989)

Zubin Mehta
1936–

4 Women usually have a small tone—they are all Mozart specialists. This girl plays like five men.
Carol Easton Jacqueline du Pré (1989)

Yehudi Menuhin
1916–99

5 Those very qualities: strength and joy, passion and directness that were her musical voice are palpably her true character.
William Wordsworth (ed.) Jacqueline du Pré: Impressions (1983)

Paul Tortelier
1914–90

6 With her short blond hair and clear blue eyes, she was a Wagner heroine. She was Siegfried. When we played together, she knew what I would do before I did it.
in 1962

Albrecht Dürer 1471–1528

German engraver and painter. He was the leading German artist of the Renaissance, important for his technically advanced woodcuts and copper engravings and also noted for his watercolours and drawings.

Albrecht Dürer
1471–1528

1 I have many friends among the Italians who warn me not to eat and drink with their painters. Many of them are my enemies; they copy my works in the churches and wherever they can find them; and then they decry my work and say it was not in the manner of the classics and therefore it was no good.
letter, 1505

William Hogarth
1697–1764

2 Albert Dürer, who drew mathematically, never deviated into grace.
The Analysis of Beauty (1753)

John Keats
1795–1821

3 Living in such warlike times [he] perhaps was forced to paint in his gauntlets.
letter, 1819

Henry Wadsworth Longfellow
1807–82

4 *Emigravit* is the inscription on the tombstone where he lies;
Dead he is not, but departed,—for the artist never dies.
'Nuremberg' (1844)

Gerald Durrell 1925–95

English zoologist and writer, brother of **Lawrence Durrell**. He founded the Jersey Wildlife Preservation Trust.

Lawrence Durrell
1912–90

1 Don't you think the little devil writes well? His style's like fresh, crisp lettuce.
attributed

Lawrence Durrell 1912–90

English novelist, poet, and travel writer, brother of **Gerald Durrell**. He spent much of his life abroad, and wrote prolifically in an ornate, poetic style.

Gerald Durrell
1925–95

2 Larrie writes for posterity. I write for money.
attributed

Bob Dylan 1941–

American singer and songwriter. The leader of an urban folk-music revival in the 1960s, he became known for political and protest songs such as 'The Times They Are A-Changin'' (1964).

Joan Baez
1941–

1 Bob walks into a room and every eye in the place is on him. There are eyes on Bob even when he is hiding. All that has probably not been easy for him.
in January 1976

Bob Dylan
1941–

2 I think that's just another word for a washed-up has-been.
on being described as an 'icon'
in January 1998

Marianne Faithfull
1946–

3 Dylan was so cryptic that everything seemed to take on at least one other meaning. When he asked for something with which to stir his coffee people did a fast double take. Did he mean spoon?
Faithfull (1995, with David Dalton)

Allen Ginsberg
1926–97

4 Dylan has sold out to God. That is to say, his command was to spread his beauty as wide as possible. It was an artistic challenge to see if great art can be done on a jukebox. And he proved that it can.
  Alice Echols *Scars of Sweet Paradise* (2000)

Woody Guthrie
1912–67

5 That boy's got a voice. Maybe he won't make it with his writing, but he can sing it. He can really sing it.
  Joe Klein *Woody Guthrie: a life* (1980)

Tom Jones
1940–

6 I don't like Bob Dylan. I don't like his attitude and his records. All he stands for is a bad influence. Being cheeky with the press was bad. He says he's not a singer—so why does he sing? . . . I don't *hate* listening to his records, but I can't stand it when people say he's a genius.
  in 1966

Ewan MacColl
1915–89

7 Dylan is to me the perfect symbol of the anti-artist in our society. He is against everything—the last resort of someone who doesn't really want to change the world . . . Dylan's songs accept the world as it is.
  interview, September 1965

Bruce Springsteen
1949–

8 Bob freed your mind the way Elvis freed your body. He showed us that just because music was innately physical did not mean that it was anti-intellectual. He had the vision and the talent to make a pop record that contained the whole world.
  speech, January 1988

Esther Dyson 1951–

American businesswoman. She is influential in the information technology industry.

Esther Dyson
1951–

1 I think of who I am as what I've done.
  in January 1999

E

Arthur Eddington 1882–1944

English astronomer, founder of astrophysics. He established the fundamental principles of stellar structure, and wrote one of the finest presentations of **Einstein**'s theory of relativity.

Erwin Schrödinger
1887–1961

1 Like a Shakespearean fool, his laughing manner often encloses a deep truth in a bad joke.
  in 1929

Anthony Eden 1897–1977

British Conservative statesman, Prime Minister 1955–7. His premiership was dominated by the Suez crisis of 1956; widespread opposition to Britain's role in this led to his resignation.

R. A. Butler
1902–82

1 REPORTER: Mr Butler, would you say that this is the best Prime Minister we have?
  R. A. BUTLER: Yes.
  interview at London Airport, January 1956

R. A. Butler
1902–82

2 That's the trouble with Anthony—half mad baronet, half beautiful woman.
  attributed

Noël Coward
1899–1973

3 Poor Anthony has resigned, given up, and is on his way to New Zealand, a tragic figure who had been cast in a star part well above his capabilities.
  diary January 1957

Beatrice Eden
d. 1957

4 [Adlai] Stevenson is just like Anthony Eden. Both are excellent Number Two men.

Fleur Cowles *She Made Friends and Kept Them* (1996)

Malcolm Muggeridge
1903–90

5 He was not only a bore; he bored for England.

Tread Softly (1966)

Reginald Paget
1908–90

6 There is no disguise or camouflage about the Prime Minister. He is the original banana man, yellow outside and a softer yellow inside.

speech, September 1956

Maria Edgeworth 1767–1849

English-born Irish novelist. Her novel *Castle Rackrent* was the first true historical novel in English.

Lord Byron
1788–1824

1 She was a nice little unassuming 'Jeanie Deans-looking body' as we Scotch say—and, if not handsome, certainly not ill-looking. Her conversation was as quiet as herself. One would never have guessed she could write *her name*.

in January 1821

Sir Walter Scott
1771–1832

2 I have not the pen of our friend Maria Edgeworth, who writes all the while she laughs, talks, eats, and drinks—and I believe, though I do not pretend to be so far in the secret, all the time she sleeps too. She has good luck in having a pen which walks at once so unweariedly and so well.

letter, 1825

Edward VII 1841–1910

King from 1901. He was kept away from the conduct of affairs during the long reign of **Queen Victoria**. On coming to the throne, his popularity helped revitalize the monarchy.

Prince Albert
1819–61

1 He is lively, quick and sharp when his mind is set on anything, which is seldom . . . But usually his intellect is of no more use than a pistol packed at the bottom of a trunk if one were attacked in the robber-infested Apennines.

letter, December 1858

Anonymous

2 We shall not pretend that there is nothing in his long career which those who respect and admire him would wish otherwise.

on Edward VII's accession to the throne

in *The Times* January 1901, leading article

Lord Fisher
1841–1920

3 He wasn't clever, but he always did the right thing, which is better than brains.

letter, May 1910

Queen Victoria
1819–1901

4 Poor Bertie—his is not a nature made to bear sorrow, or a life without amusement and excitement—he gets bitter and irritable.

letter, June 1892

Beatrice Webb
1858–1943

5 There is something comic in the great British nation with its infinite variety of talents, having this undistinguished and limited-minded German bourgeois to be its social sovereign.

diary, February 1897

Edward VIII 1894–1972

King in 1936 but not crowned. Edward abdicated eleven months after coming to the throne in order to marry the American divorcee Mrs **Wallis Simpson**, and was created Duke of Windsor.

Stanley Baldwin
1867–1947

6 From the very first he insisted that he would marry her. He had *no* spiritual conflict *at all*. There was no battle in his will . . . There was simply no moral struggle. It appalled me.

Frances Donaldson *Edward VIII* (1974)

Lord Beaverbrook
1879–1964

7 Our cock won't fight.

to **Winston Churchill**, during the abdication crisis of 1936

Edward VIII
1894–1972

8 At long last I am able to say a few words of my own . . . you must believe me when I tell you that I have found it impossible to carry the heavy burden of responsibility and to discharge my duties as King as I would wish to do without the help and support of the woman I love.

radio broadcast following his abdication, December 1936

George V
1865–1936

9 After I am dead, the boy will ruin himself in twelve months.

Keith Middlemas and John Barnes *Baldwin* (1969)

Keir Hardie
1856–1915

10 From his childhood onward this boy will be surrounded by sycophants and flatterers by the score—[*Cries of* 'Oh, oh!']—and will be taught to believe himself as of a superior creation. [*Cries of* 'Oh, oh!'] A line will be drawn between him and the people whom he is to be called upon some day to reign over. In due course, following the precedent which has already been set, he will be sent on a tour round the world, and probably rumours of a morganatic alliance will follow—[*Loud cries of* 'Oh, oh!' *and* 'Order!']—and the end of it all will be that the country will be called upon to pay the bill. [*Cries of* Divide!]

speech in the House of Commons, June 1894

Lord Kitchener
1850–1916

11 I don't mind your being killed, but I object to your being taken prisoner.

to the Prince of Wales during the First World War
quoted by Viscount Esher, December 1914

Queen Mary
1867–1953

12 I do not think you have ever realised the shock, which the attitude you took up caused your family and the whole nation. It seemed inconceivable to those who had made such sacrifices during the war that you, as their King, refused a lesser sacrifice.

letter to the Duke of Windsor, July 1938

Graham Payn

13 To be honest, the Duke of Windsor was an extremely dull man. Noël [Coward] said he even danced a boring Charleston, which is no mean feat.

in November 1999

Duchess of Windsor
1896–1986

14 He was born to be a salesman. He would be an admirable representative of Rolls Royce. But an ex-King cannot start selling motor-cars.

Harold Nicolson's diary, May 1947

Duchess of Windsor
1896–1986

15 He was my entire life. I can't begin to think what I am going to do without him, he gave up so much for me, and now he has gone. I always hoped I would die before him.

looking at her husband's coffin, in June 1972

Ilya Ehrenburg 1891–1967

Russian novelist and journalist. He became famous during the Second World War for his anti-German propaganda in *Pravda* and *Red Star*. His novels include *The Thaw* (1954), a work criticizing Stalinism.

Nadezhda Mandelstam
1899–1980

1 He was as helpless as everybody else, but at least he tried to do something for others.

Hope Abandoned (1974)

Adolf Eichmann 1906–62

German Nazi administrator who was responsible for administering the concentration camps. In 1960 he was traced by Israeli agents and executed after trial in Israel.

Hannah Arendt
1906–75

1 It was as though in those last minutes he was summing up the lessons that this long course in human wickedness had taught us—the lesson of the fearsome, word-and-thought-defying *banality of evil*.

Eichmann in Jerusalem (1963)

Albert Einstein 1879–1955

German-born American theoretical physicist. Although his special and general theories of relativity, which revolutionized physics, led indirectly to the atom bomb, he remained a committed pacifist.

Anonymous

1 I don't like the family Stein!
There is Gert, there is Ep, there is Ein.
Gert's writings are punk,
Ep's statues are junk,
Nor can anyone understand Ein.
rhyme current in the US in the 1920s

Roland Barthes
1915–80

2 Through the mythology of Einstein, the world blissfully regained the image of knowledge reduced to a formula.
Mythologies (1957)

Jacob Bronowski
1908–74

3 Einstein was a man who could ask immensely simple questions. And what his life showed, and his work, is that when the answers are simple too, then you hear God thinking.
The Ascent of Man (1973)

Albert Einstein
1879–1955

4 If my theory of relativity is proven correct, Germany will claim me as a German and France will declare that I am a citizen of the world. Should my theory prove untrue, France will say that I am a German and Germany will declare that I am a Jew.
address at the Sorbonne, Paris, possibly early December 1929

Albert Einstein
1879–1955

5 If I would be a young man again and had to decide how to make my living, I would not try to become a scientist or scholar or teacher. I would rather choose to be a plumber or a peddler in the hope to find that modest degree of independence still available under present circumstances.
in November 1954

Albert Einstein
1879–1955

6 One must divide one's time between politics and equations. But our equations are much more important to me.
C. P. Snow 'Einstein'

Paul Langevin
1872–1946

7 It is as important an event as would be the transfer of the Vatican from Rome to the New World. The pope of physics has moved and the United States will now become the centre of the natural sciences.
on Einstein's move to America
Abraham Pais *A Tale of Two Continents* (1997)

Lise Meitner
1878–1968

8 For all my great admiration and affection for Einstein during the Berlin years I often stumbled inwardly over his absolute lack of personal relationships . . . Only later did I understand that this separation from individuals was necessary for his love and responsibility toward humanity.
letter, February 1955

Robert Oppenheimer
1904–67

9 He was almost wholly without sophistication and wholly without worldliness . . . There was always with him a wonderful purity at once childlike and profoundly stubborn.
in March 1966

Pablo Picasso
1881–1973

10 Every positive value has its price in negative terms . . . The genius of Einstein leads to Hiroshima.
F. Gilot and C. Lake *Life With Picasso* (1964)

Bertrand Russell
1872–1970

11 He removed the mystery from gravitation, which everybody since Newton had accepted with a reluctant feeling that it was unintelligible.
G. J. Whitrow *Einstein: The Man and His Achievement* (1967)

Erwin Schrödinger
1887–1961

12 When kings build, the hod-carriers have something to do.
letter to Einstein, 1925–6

Albert Schweitzer 13 Even though without writing each other, we are in mental
1875–1965 communication for we respond to our dreadful times in the same way
and tremble together for the future of mankind . . . I like it that we
have the same given name.
letter, February 1955

George Bernard Shaw 14 Ptolemy made a universe, which lasted 1400 years. Newton, also, made
1856–1950 a universe, which lasted 300 years. Einstein has made a universe, and I
can't tell you how long that will last.
David Cassidy *Einstein and Our World* (1995)

J. C. Squire 15 It did not last: the Devil howling 'Ho!
1884–1958 Let Einstein be!' restored the status quo.
'In continuation of Pope on Newton' (1926); see **Newton** 9

H. G. Wells 16 Einstein must have been like a gentle bright kitten trying to make
1866–1946 friends with a child's balloon, very large and unaccountably
unpuncturable.
of *Einstein's meeting with* **J. B. S. Haldane**
Experiment in Autobiography (1934)

Dwight D. Eisenhower 1890–1969

American general and Republican statesman, President 1953–61. In the Second World
War he was Supreme Commander of allied forces in western Europe 1943–5.

Dean Acheson 1 I doubt very much if a man whose main literary interests were in works
1893–1971 by Mr Zane Grey, admirable as they may be, is particularly equipped to
be the chief executive of this country, particularly where Indian Affairs
are concerned.
attributed

Anonymous 2 I like Ike.
US button badge first used in 1947 when Eisenhower was seen as a potential presidential
nominee; coined by Henry D. Spalding (d. 1990)

Alistair Cooke 3 The best thing about Eisenhower's Presidency was his Jeffersonian
1908– conviction that there should be as little government and as much golf
as possible.
in 1973

Barry Goldwater 4 A dime store New Dealer.
1909–98 Alistair Cooke *Memories of the Great and the Good* (1999)

Janis Joplin 5 Fourteen heart attacks and he had to die in my week. In MY week.
1943–70 *when ex-President Eisenhower's death prevented her photograph appearing on the cover of*
Newsweek
in April 1969

Douglas MacArthur 6 He'll make a fine president. He was the best clerk who ever served
1880–1964 under me.
attributed, 1952

Adlai Stevenson 7 If I talk over people's heads, Ike must talk under their feet.
1900–65 during the Presidential campaign of 1952; Bill Adler *The Stevenson Wit* (1966)

Adlai Stevenson 8 The General has dedicated himself so many times he must feel like the
1900–65 cornerstone of a public building.
Leon Harris *The Fine Art of Political Wit* (1964)

the White House in the time of President Eisenhower:
Emlyn Williams 9 The Tomb of the Well-Known Soldier.
1905–87 James Harding *Emlyn Williams* (1987)

Alfred Eisenstaedt 1898–1995

German-born American photographer, best known for his work with *Life* magazine.

Alfred Eisenstaedt 1 Although I am 92, my brain is 30 years old.
1898–1995 to a reporter in 1991

Alfred Eisenstaedt
1898–1995

2 It's more important to click with people than to click the shutter.
attributed

Edward Elgar 1857–1934

British composer. He is known particularly for the *Enigma Variations*, the oratorio *The Dream of Gerontius*, and for patriotic pieces such as the five *Pomp and Circumstance* marches.

Thomas Beecham
1879–1961

1 The musical equivalent of the Towers of St Pancras Station.
of Elgar's 1st Symphony
Neville Cardus *Sir Thomas Beecham* (1961)

Edward Elgar
1857–1934

2 I have worked hard for forty years and at last, Providence denies me a decent hearing of my work: so I submit—I always said God was against art and I still believe it.
letter, October 1900

Edward Elgar
1857–1934

3 I am very busy with a symphony—twenty years ago I should have thoughtlessly said 'my' symphony: but I have lived long enough to know nothing is mine—certainly not the sounds one is permitted to weave together.
letter, July 1908

Hubert Parry
1848–1918

4 The English public is curious. It can only recognise one composer at a time. Once it was Sullivan. Now it is Elgar.
Michael Kennedy *Portrait of Elgar* (1968)

George Bernard Shaw
1856–1950

5 Edward Elgar, the figurehead of music in England, is a composer whose rank it is neither prudent nor indeed possible to determine. Either it is one so high that only time and posterity can confer it, or else he is one of the Seven Humbugs of Christendom.
Music and Letters (1920)

El Greco 1541–1614

Cretan-born Spanish painter. El Greco's portraits and religious works are characterized by distorted perspective, elongated figures, and strident use of colour.

Stevie Smith
1902–71

1 Just see how Theotocopoulos
Throws on his canvas
Colours of hell.
'Spanish School' (1937)

George Eliot 1819–80

English novelist; pseudonym of Mary Ann Evans. Famed for her intellect, scholarly style, and moral sensibility, she is regarded as one of the great English novelists.

Thomas Carlyle
1795–1881

1 I found out in the first two pages that it was a woman's writing—she supposed that in making a door, you last of all put in the *panels*!
Gordon S. Haight *George Eliot* (1968)

J. W. Cross
1840–1924

2 She told me that, in all she considered her best writing there was a 'not herself' which took possession of her, and that she felt her own personality to be merely the instrument through which the spirit as it were was acting.
Life of George Eliot (1884)

George Eliot
1819–80

3 Few women, I fear, have had such reason as I have to think the long sad years of youth were worth living for the sake of middle age.
letter, 1857

Elizabeth Gaskell
1810–65

4 I *have* tried to be moral, and dislike her and dislike her books—but it won't do. There is not a wrong word, or a wrong thought in them, I do believe,—and though I should have been more 'comfortable' for some indefinable reason, if a *man* had written them instead of a *woman*, yet I think the author must be a noble creature; and I shut my eyes to the awkward blot in her life.
letter, 1856

Henry James
1843–1916

5 She is magnificently ugly—deliciously hideous . . . Now in this vast ugliness resides a most powerful beauty which, in a very few minutes, steals forth and charms the mind, so that you end as I ended, in falling in love with her.
letter, May 1869

Mrs Lynn Lynton
1822–98

6 She was a made woman . . . made by self-manipulation, as one makes a statue or a vase. I have never known anyone who seemed to me so purely artificial as George Eliot.
My Literary Life (1899)

George Meredith
1828–1909

7 George Eliot had the heart of Sappho; but the face, with the long proboscis, the protruding teeth of the Apocalyptic horse, betrayed animality.
in July 1909

Mrs Margaret Oliphant
1828–97

8 How I have been handicapped in life! Should I have done better if I had been kept, like her, in a mental greenhouse and taken care of?
Autobiography and Letters of Mrs Margaret Oliphant (1899)

V. S. Pritchett
1900–97

9 Hers is a mind that has grown by making judgements, as Mr Gladstone's head was said to have grown by making speeches.
attributed

Edith Sitwell
1887–1964

10 In later years the great novelist who was known as George Eliot had, in spite of her ugliness, a monolithic, mysterious, primeval grandeur of countenance, like that of an Easter Island statue, washed by oceans of light.
English Eccentrics (1958)

Anthony Trollope
1815–82

11 She was one whose private life should be left in privacy, as may be said of all who have achieved fame by literary merits.
letter, January 1881

T. S. Eliot 1888–1965

American-born British poet, critic, and dramatist. He was established as the voice of a disillusioned generation by *The Waste Land* (1922). *Four Quartets* (1943) revealed his increasing involvement with Christianity.

Anonymous

12 Many of my colleagues . . . think a banker has no business whatever to be a poet. They don't think the two things can combine. But I believe that anything a man does, whatever his *hobby* may be, it's all the better if he is really keen on it and does well. I think it helps him with his work . . . I don't see why—in time, of course, in time—he mightn't even become a Branch Manager.
view of a senior official of Lloyds Bank where Eliot was employed
in conversation c.1920

Anthony Burgess
1917–93

13 With Eliot, the past was not a dull and venerable ancestor but a living force which modified the present and was in turn modified by it. Time was not an army of unalterable law; time was a kind of ectoplasm.
Urgent Copy (1968)

John Carey
1934–

14 Even the greatest poets need something to cling to. Keats had Beauty; Milton had God. T. S. Eliot's standby was Worry.
in September 1988

T. S. Eliot
1888–1965

15 How unpleasant to meet Mr Eliot!
With his features of clerical cut,
And his brow so grim
And his mouth so prim
And his conversation, so nicely
Restricted to What Precisely
And If and Perhaps and But.
'Five-Finger Exercises' (1936)

T. S. Eliot
1888–1965

16 To me . . . [*The Waste Land*] was only the relief of a personal and wholly insignificant grouse against life; it is just a piece of rhythmical grumbling.
The Waste Land (ed. Valerie Eliot, 1971) epigraph

Queen Elizabeth, the Queen Mother
1900–

17 Then we had this rather lugubrious man in a suit, and he read a poem . . . I think it was called The Desert. And first the girls got the giggles and then I did and then even the King.
describing T. S. Eliot reading from The Waste Land *an evening at Windsor during the war*

F. R. Leavis
1895–1978

18 Self-contempt, well-grounded.
on the foundation of T. S. Eliot's work
attributed

Harold Nicolson
1886–1968

19 He is without pose and full of poise. He makes one feel that all cleverness is an excuse for thinking hard.
in March 1932

George Orwell
1903–50

20 Eliot has remained aloof, but if forced at the pistol's point to choose between Fascism and some more democratic form of Socialism, would probably choose Fascism.
Inside the Whale (1940)

Edmund Wilson
1895–1972

21 'Mr Eliot' was a fictional character and Tom himself helped to create him. Among the roles the poet deftly played were The Anglican Clergyman, The Formidable Professor, Dr Johnson and the Genteel Bostonian.
attributed

Elizabeth I 1533–1603

Queen from 1558. Her reign, which was dominated by the threat of a Catholic restoration and by war with Spain, saw a flowering of national culture. Although frequently courted, she never married.

The Bible (Authorized Version)
1611

1 Upon the setting of that bright Occidental Star, Queen Elizabeth of most happy memory.
The Epistle Dedicatory

William Cecil
1520–98

2 I pray you diligently and effectually let her majesty understand, how her singular kindness doth overcome my power to acquit it; who, though she will not be a mother, yet she sheweth herself, by feeding me with her own princely hand, as a careful nurse.
letter, July 1598

Elizabeth I
1533–1603

3 I am your anointed Queen. I will never be by violence constrained to do anything. I thank God that I am endued with such qualities that if I were turned out of the Realm in my petticoat, I were able to live in any place in Christome.
speech to Members of Parliament, November 1566

Elizabeth I
1533–1603

4 I know I have the body of a weak and feeble woman, but I have the heart and stomach of a king, and of a king of England too; and think foul scorn that Parma or Spain, or any prince of Europe, should dare to invade the borders of my realm.
speech to the troops at Tilbury on the approach of the Armada, 1588

Elizabeth I 1533–1603	5 Though God hath raised me high, yet this I count the glory of my crown: that I have reigned with your loves. The Golden Speech, 1601
Christopher Hatton 1540–91	6 The queen did fish for men's souls, and had so sweet a bait that no one could escape her network. Eric St John Brooks *Sir Christopher Hatton* (1946)
Walter Raleigh c.1552–1618	7 A lady whom Time had surprised. at his trial, November 1603
William Shakespeare 1564–1616	8 This royal infant,—heaven still move about her!— Though in her cradle, yet now promises Upon this land a thousand blessings, Which time shall bring to ripeness. *Henry VIII* (1613, with John Fletcher)

Elizabeth II 1926–

Queen of the United Kingdom since 1952. She has always shown a strong personal commitment to the Commonwealth, and is one of the most travelled 20th-century monarchs.

Hardy Amies 1909–	9 She is only 5ft 4in, and to make someone that height look regal is difficult. Fortunately she holds herself very well. interview, February 1997
R. A. Butler 1902–82	10 She seemed fascinated by Parliament—who was rising, who falling. Like all clever women she was very interested in personalities and, apart from the national interest, she enjoyed evaluating to what degree the Government had suffered a setback or had scored points in political terms. Robert Lacey *Majesty* (1983)
James Callaghan 1912–	11 But each [Prime Minister] thinks he is treated in a much more friendly way than the one before! Though I'm sure that's not true. The Queen is more even-handed. What one gets is friendliness but not friendship. Elizabeth Longford *Elizabeth R* (1983)
Elizabeth II 1926–	12 I declare before you all that my whole life, whether it be long or short, shall be devoted to your service and the service of our great Imperial family to which we all belong. broadcast speech, as Princess Elizabeth, to the Commonwealth from Cape Town, April 1947
Queen Elizabeth, the Queen Mother 1900–	13 Yes, she has youth on her side, and an extraordinary calmness and serenity which will come in very useful in the years ahead. Cecil Beaton's diary, 1952
John Paul Getty 1892–1976	14 Ah'm sorry your Queen has to pay taxes. She's not a wealthy woman. attributed
John Grigg 1924–	15 The personality conveyed by the utterances which are put into her mouth is that of a priggish schoolgirl, captain of the hockey team, a prefect, and a recent candidate for confirmation. It is not thus that she will be able to come into her own as an independent and distinctive character. in August 1958
Laurie Lee 1914–97	16 She has sometimes a look of pain on her face and yet she always carries on with the job. I think people have responded to that. in 1977
Harold Macmillan 1894–1986	17 She took her Commonwealth responsibilities very seriously and rightly so, for the responsibilities of the UK monarchy had so shrunk that if you left it at that you might as well have a film star. in November 1961

Ian Paisley 18 She has become a parrot.
1926– *on the perceived readiness of the Queen to repeat the views of her Prime Minister*
in May 1998

Michael Parkinson 19 She's head of a dysfunctional family—if she lived on a council estate in
1935– Sheffield, she'd probably be in council care.
in January 1999

Prince Philip, Duke of 20 Tolerance is the one essential ingredient . . . You can take it from me
Edinburgh that the Queen has the quality of tolerance in abundance.
1921– *his recipe for a successful marriage*
in November 1997

Patrick White 21 Poor girl, she might loosen up if one took her in hand, but as it is she
1912–90 struck me as being quite without charm, except of a perfectly
stereotyped English county kind, and hard as nails under the Little-
Thing-in-Blue appearance.
letter, March 1963

Elizabeth, the Queen Mother 1900–

Wife of George VI. She married **George VI** in 1923, when he was Duke of York; they had
two daughters, **Elizabeth II** and **Princess Margaret**.

Cecil Beaton 22 If the Queen Mother were anyone other than she is (ridiculous
1904–80 supposition) would one come so readily under her spell?
diary 1952

Lord Charteris 23 She is a bit of an ostrich, she has learned to protect herself. What she
1913– doesn't want to see, she doesn't look at.
in January 1995

*Nicolson had failed to recognize immediately that the 'dear little woman in black' to whom he
was talking was the Duchess of York:*
Harold Nicolson 24 I steered my conversation onwards in the same course as before but
1886–1968 with different sails: the dear old jib of comradeship was lowered and
very slowly the spinnaker of 'Yes Ma'am' was hoisted in its place.
diary, February 1936

Will Self 25 The *éminence cerise*, the bolster behind the throne.
1961– in August 1999

Duke Ellington 1899–1974

American jazz pianist, composer, and bandleader. Coming to fame in the early 1930s,
Ellington was one of the first popular musicians to write extended pieces.

Percy Grainger 1 The three greatest composers who ever lived are Bach, Delius, and
1882–1961 Duke Ellington. Unfortunately Bach is dead, Delius is very ill but we are
happy to have with us today The Duke.
John Bird *Percy Grainger* (1999)

Ben Elton 1959–

British writer and performer. Originally a stand-up comedian, he has co-written many
successful television comedy shows as well as stage plays and novels.

Ben Elton 1 I always say that the bottom of a stand-up comedian ages at three times
1959– the speed of his body. I mean I'm only 29 but my bottom remembers
the Second World War.
in May 1989

Ralph Waldo Emerson 1803–82

American philosopher and poet. He evolved the concept of Transcendentalism, a philosophy based on a belief that divinity pervades the whole of nature and humankind.

Thomas Carlyle
1795–1881

1 What I loved in the man was his health, his unity with himself; all people and all things seemed to find their quite peaceable adjustment with him, not a proud domineering one, as after a doubtful *contest*, but a spontaneous-looking peaceable, even humble one.
letter, September 1833

Arthur Hugh Clough
1819–61

2 What shall we do without you? Think where we are. Carlyle has led us all out into the desert, and he has left us there.
parting words to Emerson, July 1848

William James
1842–1910

3 Rarely has a man so accurately known the limits of his genius or so unfailingly kept within them.
address, 1903

Herman Melville
1819–91

4 Yet I think Emerson is more than a brilliant fellow. Be his stuff begged, borrowed, or stolen, or of his own domestic manufacture he is an uncommon man. Swear he is a humbug—then he is no common humbug.
letter, March 1849

Friedrich Nietzsche
1844–1900

5 Such a man as instinctively feeds on pure ambrosia and leaves alone the indigestible in things.
Twilight of the Idols (1889)

**Algernon Charles
Swinburne**
1837–1909

6 I called him a wrinkled and toothless baboon, who, first hoisted in notoriety on the shoulders of Carlyle, now spits and splutters on a filthier platform of his own finding and fouling.
account of a letter, sent to Emerson, which did not receive a reply
in conversation with Edmund Gosse; Evan Charteris *Life and Letters of Sir Edmund Gosse* (1931)

Tracey Emin 1963–

English artist. She was nominated for the Turner prize for 'My Bed' in 1999.

Tracey Emin
1963–

1 I'm not an outsider at all. I'm on every bloody A-list there is in the art world.
in July 2000

Brian Sewell

2 I don't know what art is, but I do know what it isn't. And it isn't someone . . . embroidering the name of everyone they have slept with on the inside of a tent.
in April 1999

Brian Epstein 1934–67

English manager of the Beatles.

Andrew Loog Oldham
1944–

1 When you sat down with Brian, you knew you were dealing with a man who had a vision for the Beatles and nobody was going to get in the way of that vision. He was convinced that eventually everybody was going to agree with him. That gave him the power to make people listen.
Stoned (2000)

Jacob Epstein 1880–1959

American-born British sculptor. A founder member of the vorticist group, many of his works aroused violent criticism for their use of distortion and alleged obscenity.

Anonymous 2 A form of statuary which no careful father would wish his daughter, or no discerning young man his fiancée, to see.
on Epstein's sculptures for the former BMA building in the Strand, London
in *Evening Standard* June 1908

Anonymous 3 I don't like the family Stein!
There is Gert, there is Ep, there is Ein.
Gert's writings are punk,
Ep's statues are junk,
Nor can anyone understand Ein.
rhyme current in the US in the 1920s

Jacob Epstein
1880–1959
4 Why don't they stick to murder and leave art to us?
on hearing that his statue of Lazarus in New College chapel, Oxford, kept **Khrushchev** *awake at night*
attributed

Ezra Pound
1885–1972
5 Epstein is a great sculptor. I wish he would wash, but I believe Michelangelo *never* did, so I suppose it is part of the tradition.
Charles Norman *The Case of Ezra Pound* (1948)

Max Ernst 1891–1976

German artist. He was a leader of the Dada movement and developed the techniques of collage, photomontage, and frottage. He is probably best known for his surrealist paintings.

habitual reply as a child to the question 'What do you like doing most of all?':
Max Ernst
1891–1976
1 Looking.
Hans Richter *Dada: art and anti-art* (1965)

Earl of Essex 1566–1601

English soldier and courtier. Although a favourite of **Elizabeth I**, he was eventually executed for treason.

Francis Bacon
1561–1626
1 I love few persons better than yourself . . . I was ever sorry that your Lordship should fly with waxen wings, doubting Icarus's fortune.
letter, July 1600

Elizabeth I
1533–1603
2 God may pardon you, but I never can.
to the dying Countess of Nottingham, for her part in the death of Essex
in February 1603; almost certainly apocryphal

Euclid c.300 BC

Greek mathematician. He taught at Alexandria, and his great work *Elements of Geometry* was the standard work until other kinds of geometry were discovered in the 19th century.

Edna St Vincent
Millay
1892–1950
1 Euclid alone
Has looked on Beauty bare.
The Harp-Weaver and Other Poems (1923)

Linda Evangelista 1965–

Canadian supermodel.

Linda Evangelista
1965–
1 I don't get out of bed for less than $10,000 a day
attributed

Chris Evans 1966–

British disc jockey and broadcaster. He has presented breakfast shows on both radio and television.

Spike Milligan
1918–

1 He's all small talk. The smartest thing I've ever heard him say is, 'Good morning'.

in July 1999

Edith Evans 1888–1976

English actress. She appeared in a wide range of roles but is particularly remembered as Lady Bracknell in **Oscar Wilde**'s *The Importance of Being Earnest*.

Noël Coward
1899–1973

2 She took her curtain calls as though she had just been un-nailed from the cross.

diary, October 1964

John Gielgud
1904–2000

3 Edith has a weird, earthly sense of stagecraft; she's got a *badger's* way of sniffing out things, of isolating what's best and most actable in a part.

in July 1952

John Gielgud
1904–2000

4 Edith Evans was savage as Lady Bracknell. You see, she came from a family of servants whom the Lady Bracknells of this world rang for to put a lump of coal on the fire. Her performance was pure revenge.

John Mortimer *In Character* (1984)

Kenneth Tynan
1927–80

5 Her voice has been said to caress, to ripple and to cascade; it has been likened to silk, satin and even bombazine; it has been compared to a river in flood and the sea in a Cornish cove, not to mention lark-song and the music of the nightingale.

in January 1956

Chris Evert 1954–

American tennis player. She won both the US and French Open championships six times and three Wimbledon titles (1974; 1976; 1981).

Chris Evert
1954–

1 You get labelled. people tell me every day how great I am, and they don't know me. I'm no angel. I'm a control freak—on and off the court.

attributed

Ted Tinling

2 Chrissie is the Sugar Plum Fairy of the lot.

attributed

F

Douglas Fairbanks 1883–1939

American actor. He co-founded United Artists in 1919 and became famous for his swashbuckling film roles. He was married to **Mary Pickford** 1919–36.

Douglas Fairbanks Jr
1909–

1 He was by nature very athletic, and enjoyed doing stunts just for the fun of it, off stage. If he saw a gate, rather than go through the gate he'd hop over it. If he saw a desk, he'd rather vault over the desk than walk round it.

John Baxter *Stunt* (1973)

D. W. Griffith
1875–1948

2 Send him to Sennett. He belongs with the slapstick cops.

remark, c.1915

Mary Pickford
1893–1979

3 Douglas has always faced a situation the only way he knew how, by running away from it.

Sunshine and Shadow (1955)

Marianne Faithfull 1946–

English pop singer. She was popular in the 1960s, when her relationship with **Mick Jagger** attracted considerable attention.

Andrew Loog Oldham
1944–

1 The moment I caught sight of Marianne I recognised my next adventure, a true star. In another century you'd have set sail for her; in 1964 you'd record her.
Stoned (2000)

Nick Faldo 1957–

English golfer. He won the British Open championship in 1987 and 1990 and the US Masters Tournament in 1989, 1990, and 1996.

Nick Faldo
1957–

1 Then they accuse me of being 'Mechanical Man'. This really gets my goat. Makes me sound like a battery toy. What my game is about is control.
in May 1993

Greg Norman
1955–

2 Nick played great and I played poor. There were no two ways about it.
on losing the Masters tournament, in April 1996

Michael Faraday 1791–1867

English physicist and chemist. One of the greatest experimentalists, Faraday was largely self-educated. His most important work was in electromagnetism.

Anonymous

1 Sir H. Davy's greatest discovery was Michael Faraday.
Paul Harvey *Oxford Companion to English Literature* (1932)

Albert Einstein
1879–1955

2 This man loved mysterious Nature as a lover loves his distant beloved.
letter, December 1952

Michael Faraday
1791–1867

3 Tyndall, I must remain plain Michael Faraday to the last; and let me now tell you, that if I accepted the honour which the Royal Society desires to confer upon me, I would not answer for the integrity of my intellect for a single year.
on being offered the Presidency of the Royal Society
J. Tyndall *Faraday as a Discoverer* (1868)

Aldous Huxley
1894–1963

4 Even if I could be Shakespeare, I think I should still choose to be Faraday.
in 1925, attributed

T. H. Huxley
1825–95

5 The prince of scientific expositors, Faraday, was once asked, 'How much may a popular lecturer suppose his audience knows?' He replied emphatically, 'Nothing.'
L. Huxley *Life and Letters of Thomas Henry Huxley* (1900)

James Clerk Maxwell
1831–79

6 Faraday, on the other hand, shews up his unsuccessful as well as his successful experiments, and his crude ideas as well as his developed ones, and the reader, however inferior to him in inductive power, feels sympathy even more than admiration, and is tempted to believe that, if he had the opportunity, he too would be a discoverer.
A Treatise on Electricity and Magnetism (1873)

Mia Farrow 1945–

American actress, wife of **Frank Sinatra** and **Woody Allen**.

Mia Farrow
1945–

1 I want a big career, a big man, and a big life. You have to think big. That's the only way to get it.
Kitty Kelley *His Way* (1986)

William Faulkner 1897–1962

American novelist. His works deal with the history and legends of the American South and have a strong sense of a society in decline.

Clifton Fadiman
1904–

1 Even those who call Mr Faulkner our greatest literary sadist do not fully appreciate him, for it is not merely his characters who have to run the gauntlet but also his readers.
in April 1934

William Faulkner
1897–1962

2 He made the books and he died.
his own 'sum and history of my life'
letter, February 1949

Ernest Hemingway
1899–1961

3 Poor Faulkner. Does he really think big emotions come from big words?
A. E. Hotchner *Papa Hemingway* (1966)

Gabriel Fauré 1845–1924

French composer and organist. His best-known work is the *Requiem* for solo voices, choir, and orchestra.

Gabriel Fauré
1845–1924

1 I have been reserved all my life . . . and have only been able to let myself go in certain situations.
letter, 1921

Marcel Proust
1871–1922

2 I not only admire, adore and venerate your music, I have been and still am in love with it.
letter, 1897

Mohamed Al Fayed 1933–

Egyptian businessman. A longstanding feud with Tiny Rowland followed his takeover of Harrods department store. He has failed in his attempts to gain British citizenship.

Mohamed Al Fayed
1933–

1 I am happy with my Egyptian passport. When you were wearing the animal skin and fighting with sticks, we were building the pyramids.
in July 1999

Tiny Rowland
1917–98

2 A hero from zero.
title of book, 1988

Enrico Fermi 1901–54

Italian-born American atomic physicist, who directed the first controlled nuclear chain reaction in 1942 and joined the Manhattan Project to work on the atom bomb.

Luis Walter Alvarez
1911–88

1 There is no democracy in physics. We can't say that some second-rate guy has as much right to opinion as Fermi.
D. S. Greenberg *The Politics of Pure Science* (1969)

Kathleen Ferrier 1912–53

English contralto. She is particularly famous for her performance in 1947 of Mahler's song cycle *Das Lied von der Erde*.

Judy Holliday
1922–65

1 There was a young lady called Ferrier,
Whose voice is just like her exterrier,
She sings so delicious
That all I do wish is
That no one will ever bury her.
in 1950

Tennessee Williams
1911–83

2 But what can I write about that heavenly voice? One feels so inadequate in front of such a voice.
in 1978

Richard Feynman 1918–88

American theoretical physicist, noted for his work on quantum electrodynamics.

Freeman Dyson
1923–

1 He was somebody with this completely clear-headed view of things. That was what impressed me most strongly—that he was a sort of *Bhagavad-Gita* ideal of somebody who was engaged in action, but at the same time totally detached.
    Christopher Sykes (ed.) *No Ordinary Genius* (1994)

Richard Feynman
1918–88

2 What I cannot create, I do not understand. Know how to solve every problem that has been solved.
    written on his blackboard at Caltech, as he left it for the last time in January 1988

Marvin Minsky
1927–

3 The important thing is not to persist; I think the reason most people fail is that they are too determined to make something work only because they are attached to it. Talking to Feynman, whatever came up he would say, 'Well, here's another way to look at it.' The least stuck person I have ever known.
    Christopher Sykes (ed.) *No Ordinary Genius* (1994)

Henry Fielding 1707–54

English novelist. His plays provoked the introduction of censorship in theatres in 1737. He then turned to writing picaresque novels, and was also responsible for the formation of the Bow Street Runners.

George Borrow
1803–81

1 The most singular genius which their island ever produced, whose works it has long been the fashion to abuse in public and to read in secret.
    The Bible in Spain (1843)

Charlotte Brontë
1816–55

2 [Thackeray] resembles Fielding as an eagle does a vulture: Fielding could stoop on carrion, but Thackeray never does.
    Jane Eyre (2nd ed., 1848) preface

**Samuel Taylor
Coleridge**
1772–1834

3 How charming, how wholesome, Fielding always is! To take him up after Richardson is like emerging from a sick room heated by stoves into an open lawn, on a breezy day in May.
    Table Talk (1836)

Samuel Richardson
1689–1761

4 His spurious brat, Tom Jones.
    letter, February 1752

W. C. Fields 1880–1946

American comedian. Having made his name as a comedy juggler he became a vaudeville star. His films established him as an internationally famous comic.

Louise Brooks
1906–85

1 He was an isolated person. As a young man he stretched out his hand to Beauty and Love and they thrust it away. Gradually he reduced reality to exclude all but his work, filling the gaps with alcohol whose dim eyes transformed the world into a distant view of harmless shadows.
    Kenneth Tynan *Show People* (1980)

W. C. Fields
1880–1946

2 Here lies W. C. Fields. I would rather be living in Philadelphia.
    suggested epitaph for himself, in June 1925

Leo Rosten
1908–97

3 Any man who hates dogs and babies can't be all bad.
    of W. C. Fields, and often attributed to him
    speech, February 1939

Kenneth Tynan
1927–80

4 His nose, resembling a doughnut pickled in vinegar or an eroded squash ball, was unique; so, too, was his voice. He both looked and sounded like a cement-mixer.
    in February 1951

Ralph Fiennes 1962–

British actor. His films include *Schindler's List*, *The English Patient*, and *The End of the Affair*.

Camille Paglia
1947–

1 Rumours of Ralph Fiennes's acting ability are wildly exaggerated. He is as asexual as an adenoid.
  in August 1998

Bobby Fischer 1943–

American chess player. He defeated Boris Spassky in 1972 to take the world championship, which he held until 1975.

Bobby Fischer
1943–

1 There was something that didn't turn me on about games like Chinese Chequers. I like to watch my opponent's egos crumble.
  attributed

Mary Kenny

2 Bobby Fischer is a chess phenomenon, it is true, but is also a social illiterate, a political simpleton, a cultural ignoramus, and an emotional baby.
  attributed

Edward Fitzgerald 1809–83

English scholar and poet. He is remembered for his free poetic translation of *The Rubáiyát of Omar Khayyám* (1859).

Robert Browning
1812–89

1 Ay, dead! and were yourself alive, good Fitz,
How to return your thanks would pass my wits.
Kicking you seems the common lot of curs—
While more appropriate greeting lends you grace:
Surely to spit there glorifies your face—
Spitting from lips once sanctified by Hers.
  in July 1889; see **Browning** 3

F. Scott Fitzgerald 1896–1940

American novelist. His novels, in particular *The Great Gatsby* (1925), provide a vivid portrait of the US during the jazz era of the 1920s.

F. Scott Fitzgerald
1896–1940

2 I am not a great man, but sometimes I think the impersonal and objective quality of my talent and the sacrifices of it, in pieces, to preserve its essential value has some sort of epic grandeur.
  letter, 1940

Zelda Fitzgerald
1900–47

3 Don't you think I was made for you? I feel like you had me ordered—and I was delivered to you—to be worn—I want you to wear me, like a watch-charm or a button hole bouquet—to the world.
  letter to F. Scott Fitzgerald, 1919

Ernest Hemingway
1899–1961

4 Scott took LITERATURE so solemnly. He never understood that it was just writing as well as you can and finishing what you start.
  letter, May 1950

Jay McInerney
1955–

5 I think he was more interested in capturing time and freezing it. I think very early on he decided that he'd been to a dance and danced with a girl, and even if he couldn't remember which dance or which girl, that it represented some glorious high point of his life, and everything he did was an attempt to recapture that moment.
  in June 1996

Penelope Fitzgerald 1916–2000

English novelist and biographer.

Penelope Fitzgerald
1916–2000

6 I'm a sort of back-of-the-envelopes writer, and then I lose the envelopes.
  interview, December 1991

Gustave Flaubert 1821–80

French novelist and short-story writer. He achieved fame with his first published novel, *Madame Bovary* (1857), for which he was tried for immorality (and acquitted).

John Carey
1934–

1 Flaubert was a perpetual adolescent. His distinction lay in never outgrowing the hatred and contempt that the normal teenager feels when confronted with adult human beings.
  in April 1989

Gustave Flaubert
1821–80

2 My deplorable mania for analysis exhausts me. I doubt everything, even my doubt.
  letter, August 1846

Henry James
1843–1916

3 It was in his nature to be more conscious of one broken spring in the couch of fate, more wounded by a pin-prick, more worried by an assonance, than he could ever be warmed or pacified from within.
  'Gustave Flaubert' (1893)

Mary McCarthy
1912–89

4 An interviewer asked me what book I thought best represented the modern American woman. All I could think of to answer was *Madame Bovary*.
  On the Contrary (1961)

Dorothy Parker
1893–1967

5 And there was that sucker Flaubert rolling around on his floor for three days looking for the right word.
  Malcolm Cowley (ed.) *Writers at Work* (1958) 1st Series

Alexander Fleming 1881–1955

Scottish bacteriologist. In 1928, Fleming discovered the effect of penicillin on bacteria. Twelve years later **Howard Florey** and Ernst Chain established its therapeutic use as an antibiotic.

Gwyn Macfarlane
1907–87

1 Fleming was like a man who stumbles on a nugget of gold, shows it to a few friends, and then goes off to look for something else. Florey was like a man who goes back to the same spot and creates a gold mine.
  Howard Florey (1979)

Ian Fleming 1908–64

English novelist. He is known for his spy novels whose hero is the secret agent James Bond.

Kingsley Amis
1922–95

2 Fleming technologized the fairy-tale for us, making marvellous things seem familiar, and familiar things marvellous.
  What Became of Jane Austen (1970)

Rosamond Lehmann
1901–90

3 The trouble with Ian is that he gets off with women because he can't get on with them.
  John Pearson *The Life of Ian Fleming* (1966)

Howard Florey 1898–1968

Australian pathologist. With Ernst Chain he isolated and purified penicillin, developed techniques for its large-scale production, and performed the first clinical trials.

Howard Florey
1898–1968

1 If you do the experiment you may not be certain to get an answer, but if you don't do it you can be certain not to get one.
  Gwyn Macfarlane *Howard Florey* (1979)

Gwyn Macfarlane
1907–87

2 Fleming was like a man who stumbles on a nugget of gold, shows it to a few friends, and then goes off to look for something else. Florey was like a man who goes back to the same spot and creates a gold mine.
  Howard Florey (1979)

Errol Flynn 1909–59

Australian-born American actor. His usual role was the swashbuckling hero of romantic film costume dramas.

Bette Davis
1908–89

1 [He] was certainly one of the great male beauties of his time, but a terrible actor—not because he didn't have the basic talent, but because he was lazy, self-indulgent, refused to take his work seriously, and tended to throw away his lines and scenes.
James Spada *More Than a Woman* (1993)

Errol Flynn
1909–59

2 My problem lies in reconciling my gross habits with my net income.
Jane Mercer *Great Lovers of the Movies* (1975)

David Niven
1910–83

3 You always knew precisely where you stood with him because he *always* let you down.
Bring on the Empty Horses (1975)

Jack Warner
1892–1978

4 He had a mediocre talent, but to all the Walter Mittys of the world he was all the heroes in one magnificent, sexy, animal package.
My Hundred Years in Hollywood (1965)

Jane Fonda 1937–

American actress. In the 1980s she became known for her fitness routine, *Jane Fonda's Workout*.

Jane Fonda
1937–

1 I will go to my grave regretting the photograph of me on an anti-aircraft gun, which looks like I was trying to shoot at American planes. It galvanized hostility.
of her visit to Hanoi during the Vietnam War
in June 2000

Margot Fonteyn 1919–91

English ballet dancer. In 1962 she began a celebrated partnership with **Rudolf Nureyev**. In 1979 she was named *prima ballerina assoluta*.

Cecil Beaton
1904–80

1 The ugly little frog that she is becomes a beauty through the quality of her spirit.
diary, 1963

Richard Buckle
1916–

2 She has perfected the art of answering questions at length and saying absolutely nothing. She would never, even under torture, admit that pink was her favourite colour for fear of offending orange and mauve.
in March 1969

Margot Fonteyn
1919–91

3 I explained it when I danced it.
on being asked to explain one of her performances
Alastair Macaulay *Margot Fonteyn* (1998)

Gerald Ford 1909–

American Republican statesman, President 1974–7. He became President on the resignation of **Richard Nixon** in the wake of the Watergate affair.

Bella Abzug
1920–98

1 Richard Nixon impeached himself. He gave us Gerald Ford as his revenge.
in *Rolling Stone*; Linda Botts *Loose Talk* (1980)

Gerald Ford
1909–

2 I am a Ford, not a Lincoln.
on taking the vice-presidential oath, December 1973

Lyndon Baines Johnson
1908–73

3 So dumb he can't fart and chew gum at the same time.
Richard Reeves *A Ford, not a Lincoln* (1975)

Lyndon Baines Johnson
1908–73

4 He played too much football without a helmet.
Denys Cook *Presidents of the USA* (1981)

Harrison Ford 1942–

American actor. He became internationally famous with his leading roles in the film *Star Wars* and as Indiana Jones.

Harrison Ford
1942–

5 [I'm] nothing more than a worker in a service occupation . . . It's like being a waiter or a gas-station attendant, but I'm waiting on six million people a week if I'm lucky.
Garry Jenkins *Harrison Ford: Imperfect Hero* (1997)

Henry Ford 1863–1947

American motor manufacturer. A pioneer of large-scale mass production, he founded the Ford Motor Company, which in 1909 produced his famous Model T.

Thomas Alva Edison
1847–1931

6 Ford is a 'natural businessman' just as he is a 'natural mechanic', and he is the rarest of all types, in that he is a combination of the two.
J. K. Galbraith *The Liberal Hour* (1960)

Flann O'Brien
1911–66

7 Could Henry Ford produce the Book of Kells? Certainly not. He would quarrel initially with the advisability of such a project and then prove it was impossible.
Myles Away from Dublin (1990)

John Ford 1895–1973

American film director. He is chiefly known for his westerns of which many, including *Stagecoach* and *She Wore a Yellow Ribbon*, starred **John Wayne**.

Frank Capra
1897–1991

8 John Ford is the Compleat Director . . . the dean of directors,— undoubtedly the greatest and most versatile in films. A megaphone has been to John Ford what the chisel was to Michelangelo: his life, his passion, his cross.
The Name Above the Title (1971)

John Ford
1895–1973

9 My name's John Ford. I am a director of Westerns.
introducing himself at a meeting of the Screen Directors' Guild
Geoffrey Nowell-Smith *The Oxford History of World Cinema* (1996)

Edward G. Robinson
1893–1972

10 Whatever John Ford wants, John Ford gets.
All My Yesterdays (1974)

Orson Welles
1915–85

11 I like the old masters, by which I mean John Ford, John Ford . . . and John Ford.
Walter Wagner *You Must Remember This* (1975)

George Foreman 1948–

American boxer. He won the world heavyweight title in 1973–4, regaining it in 1994–5 to become the oldest world heavyweight champion.

George Foreman
1948–

1 Why am I coming back? I'll make a long story short. I can spell it. M-o-n-e-y.
resuming his career at 39; attributed

E. M. Forster 1879–1970

English novelist and literary critic. His novels include *A Room with a View* (1908) and *A Passage to India* (1924).

E. M. Forster
1879–1970

1 If I had to choose between betraying my country and betraying my friend, I hope I should have the guts to betray my country.
Two Cheers for Democracy (1951)

John Maynard Keynes
1883–1946

2 The elusive colt of a dark horse.
Michael Holroyd *Lytton Strachey* (1994 rev. ed.)

T. E. Lawrence 3 Forster's world seemed a comedy, neatly layered and staged in a garden
1888–1935 whose trim privet hedges were delicate with gossamer conventions.
About its lawns he rolled thunderstorms in teacups, most lightly,
beautifully.
in August 1927

Katherine Mansfield 4 E. M. Forster never gets any further than warming the teapot. He's a
1888–1923 rare fine hand at that. Feel this teapot. Is it not beautifully warm? Yes,
but there ain't going to be no tea.
diary, May 1917

Gore Vidal 5 He was always in court, seated on the high bench, passing judgements,
1925– a black cloth on his head.
Palimpsest (1995)

Rebecca West 6 I don't belong to a world where E. M. Forster, a self-indulgent old liberal
1892–1983 with hardly a brain in his head, could be taken as a national symbol of
moral power.
letter, December 1973

Charles James Fox 1749–1806

British Whig statesman. At the age of 19 he entered Parliament advocating American
independence, and later welcomed the French Revolution. He remained in opposition from
1783 to 1806.

Georgiana, Duchess 1 He seems to have the particular talent of knowing more about what he
of Devonshire is saying and with less pains than anybody else—his conversation is
1757–1806 like a brilliant player of billiards, the strokes follow one another, piff,
paff.
E. Lascelles *Charles James Fox* (1936)

George III 2 That young man has so thoroughly cast off every principle of common
1738–1820 honour and honesty, that he must become as contemptible as he is
odious.
letter, February 1774

Edward Gibbon 3 Let him do what he will I must love the dog.
1737–94 letter, January 1793

on hearing a report that his son Charles James Fox was to be married:
Lord Holland 4 He will be obliged to go to bed at least one night of his life.
1705–74 Christopher Hobhouse *Fox* (1934)

Samuel Johnson 5 Fox divided the kingdom with Caesar; so that it was a doubt whether
1709–84 the nation should be ruled by the sceptre of George III or the tongue of
Fox.
on the Parliamentary defeat of Charles James Fox, and the subsequent dissolution
in 1784

Charles Shaw-Lefevre, 6 What is that fat gentleman in such a passion about?
Lord Eversley *as a child, on hearing Charles James Fox speak in Parliament*
1794–1888 G. W. E. Russell *Collections and Recollections* (1898)

Aretha Franklin 1942–

American soul and gospel singer. Her best-known songs include 'I Say a Little Prayer'
(1967).

Ray Charles 1 Well, far as I'm concerned, she's the right one, baby. I'm not much for
1930– hanging out, but I *will* go see Aretha. She's my one and only sister.
Jerry Wexler *Rhythm and Blues: a life in American music* (1993)

Rev. C. L. Franklin 2 If you want to know the truth, Aretha has never left the church. If you have the ability to feel, and you have the ability to hear, you know that Aretha is still a gospel singer.
Peter Guralnick *Sweet Soul Music* (1986)

Keith Richards 3 The amazing thing about Aretha is there is this voice, which is almost
1943– like a national monument in America, and when she sings, she's chain-smoking . . . Maybe I should smoke more!
Mick St Michael *Keith Richards in His Own Words* (1994)

Benjamin Franklin 1706–90

American statesman, inventor, and scientist. A wealthy printer and publisher, his main scientific achievements were in the field of electricity.

Thomas Jefferson 4 COMTE DE VERGENNES: You replace Mr Franklin.
1743–1826 JEFFERSON: I succeed him; no one could replace him.
attributed, on becoming envoy to France, 1784

John Keats 5 A philosophical Quaker full of mean and thrifty maxims.
1795–1821 letter, October 1818

D. H. Lawrence 6 Printer, philosopher, scientist, author and patriot, impeccable husband
1885–1930 and citizen, why isn't he an archetype? Pioneers, Oh Pioneers! Benjamin was one of the greatest pioneers of the United States. Yet we just can't do with him. What's wrong with him then? Or what's wrong with us?
Studies in Classic American Literature (1923)

Comte de Mirabeau 7 Antiquity would have raised altars to this mighty genius, who, to the
1749–91 advantage of mankind, compassing in his mind the heavens and the earth, was able to restrain alike thunderbolts and tyrants.
address to the French National Assembly upon the death of Franklin

Robert Louis 8 Prudence is a wooden Juggernaut, before whom Benjamin Franklin
Stevenson walks with the portly air of a high priest.
1850–94 *Virginibus Puerisque* (1881)

A. R. J. Turgot 9 He snatched the lightning shaft from heaven, and the sceptre from
1727–81 tyrants.
inscription for a bust of Benjamin Franklin

Franz Josef 1830–1916

Emperor of Austria from 1848 and king of Hungary from 1867. The assassination in Sarajevo of his heir apparent, Archduke Franz Ferdinand, precipitated the First World War.

Franz Josef 1 Nothing has been spared me in this world.
1830–1916 *on hearing of the assassination of the Empress Elizabeth* in September 1898

Joe Frazier 1944–

American boxer. He first won the world title in 1968, lost it to **George Foreman** in 1973, and subsequently lost to **Muhammad Ali** twice before retiring in 1976.

Muhammad Ali 1 Frazier is so ugly that he should donate his face to the US Bureau of
1942– Wild Life.
in 1972

Muhammad Ali 2 It's gonna be a thrilla, a chilla, and a killa,
1942– When I get the gorilla in Manila.
in 1975

Frederick, Prince of Wales 1707–1751

British prince. The son of George II and **Caroline of Ansbach**, he died before his father.

Anonymous 1 Here lies Fred,
Who was alive and is dead:
Had it been his father,
I had much rather;
Had it been his brother,
Still better than another.
Horace Walpole *Memoirs of George II* (1847)

Caroline of Ansbach 2 My dear firstborn is the greatest ass, and the greatest liar, and the
1683–1737 greatest *canaille*, and the greatest beast in the whole world, and I
heartily wish he was out of it.
in *Dictionary of National Biography* (1917–)

Frederick the Great 1712–86

King of Prussia from 1740. His campaigns in the War of the Austrian Succession (1740–8)
and the Seven Years War (1756–63) considerably strengthened Prussia.

Frederick the Great 3 My people and I have come to an agreement which satisfies us both.
1712–86 They are to say what they please, and I am to do what I please.
his interpretation of benevolent despotism
attributed

Lord Macaulay 4 In order that he might rob a neighbour whom he had promised to
1800–59 defend, black men fought on the coast of Coromandel, and red men
scalped each other by the Great Lakes of North America.
Biographical Essays (1857)

Lucian Freud 1922–

German-born British painter. His subjects, typically portraits and nudes, are painted in a
powerful naturalistic style based on firm draughtsmanship and often using striking angles.

Francis Bacon 1 That's what so awful about having to sit to Lucian. He makes you sit by
1909–92 the hour without moving an eyelash, and I find sitting very unnerving,
exhausting work.
Cecil Beaton's diary, 1960

Sigmund Freud 1856–1939

Austrian neurologist and psychotherapist. He was the first to emphasize the significance of
unconscious processes in normal and neurotic behaviour, and was the founder of
psychoanalysis.

W. H. Auden 2 To us he is no more a person
1907–73 now but a whole climate of opinion.
'In Memory of Sigmund Freud' (1940)

Alan Bullock 3 No single man, probably, has exercised a greater influence on the ideas,
1914– literature and art of the twentieth century than Freud.
'The Double Image' (1991)

Salvador Dali 4 Without hesitation, I place Freud among the heroes. He dispossessed
1904–89 the Jewish people of the greatest and most influential of all heroes—
Moses.
diary, May 1957

Ken Dodd 5 Freud's theory was that when a joke opens a window and all those bats
1931– and bogeymen fly out, you get a marvellous feeling of relief and
elation. The trouble with Freud is that he never had to play the old
Glasgow Empire on a Saturday night after Rangers and Celtic had both
lost.
quoted in many, usually much contracted, forms since the mid-1960s

Albert Einstein
1879–1955

6 The old one . . . had a sharp vision; no illusions lulled him to sleep except for an often exaggerated faith in his own ideas.
letter, July 1949

Sigmund Freud
1856–1939

7 I am actually not at all a man of science, not an observer, not a thinker. I am by temperament nothing but a conquistador—an adventurer, if you want it translated—with all the curiosity, daring, and tenacity characteristic of a man of this sort.
letter, February 1900

John Irving
1942–

8 Sigmund Freud was a novelist with a scientific background. He just didn't know he was a novelist. All those damn psychiatrists after him, they didn't know he was a novelist either.
George Plimpton (ed.) *Writers at Work* (8th Series, 1988)

R. D. Laing
1927–89

9 Freud was a hero. He descended to the 'Underworld' and met there stark terrors. He carried with him his theory as a Medusa's head which turned these terrors to stone.
The Divided Self (1959)

Vladimir Nabokov
1899–1977

10 Let me say at once that I reject completely the vulgar, shabby, fundamentally medieval world of Freud, with its crankish quest for sexual symbols (something like searching for Baconian acrostics in Shakespeare's works) and its bitter little embryos spying, from their natural nooks, upon the love life of their parents.
Speak, Memory (1951)

Elisabeth Frink 1930–93

English sculptor and graphic artist. She made her name with angular bronzes, often of birds.

Laurie Lee
1914–97

1 A hoarder of myths, a familiar of spirits, a courage-giver, a buckler-on of swords. Her iconography is brutal, uncompromising, virile and sharp as knives.
in 1958

Laurie Lee
1914–97

2 Possessed of an archaic beauty and gold-bronze finish as though she herself were self-created, or was some oracular Delphic presence.
in 1958

David Frost 1939–

English broadcaster and writer. After presenting *That Was The Week That Was*, he went on to present many other television programmes, and was a founder of TV-AM.

Carina Frost
1952–

when asked if her future husband were religious:
1 Yes, he thinks he's God Almighty.
in July 1985

David Frost
1939–

2 John Smith said to me, 'You have a way of asking beguiling questions with potentially lethal consequences.' I would be content to have that on my tombstone.
interview, November 2000

Kitty Muggeridge
1903–94

3 David Frost has risen without trace.
said c.1965 to Malcolm Muggeridge

Robert Frost 1874–1963

American poet, noted for his ironic tone and simple language.

Alistair Cooke
1908–

4 To the great mass of Americans, I suppose, he was simply a noble old man, said to be a great poet, who had come to be a colourful human adjunct to the refurbishing of the White House.
Memories of the Great and the Good (1999)

Roger Fry 1866–1934

English art critic. A supporter of the post-Impressionists, he favoured a very formal theory of aesthetics.

Jeanette Winterson
1959–

1 [Roger Fry] gave us the term 'Post-Impressionist', without realising that the late twentieth century would soon be entirely fenced in with posts.
Art Objects (1995)

Stephen Fry 1957–

English comedian, actor, and writer. His temporary disappearance in 1995 caused a sensation.

Stephen Fry
1957–

2 My known peculiarities and preferences make me a member of what one might call the Millicent Tendency, not just a Champagne Socialist, but a Pink Champagne Socialist to boot.
in November 1996

Stephen Fry
1957–

3 It is quite difficult to feel that I am placed somewhere between Alan Bennett and the Queen Mother, a sort of public kitten.
in November 1999

Northrop Frye 1912–91

Canadian literary critic. His work explores the use of myth and symbolism.

Robertson Davies
1913–95

1 Only Ulysses can bend the bow of Ulysses.
when asked who would 'replace' Northrop Frye
in January 1991

Louis Dudek
1918–

2 Oh, Frye has all the answers, he just doesn't seem to have any questions.
John Metcalf (ed.) *The Bumper Book* (1986)

Northrop Frye
1912–91

3 Read Blake or go to hell: That's my message to the modern world.
attributed, 1991

Marshall McLuhan
1911–80

4 Norrie is not struggling for his place in the sun. He is the sun.
attributed, 1989

R. Buckminster Fuller 1895–1983

American designer and architect. He is best known for his invention of the geodesic dome and for his ideals of using the world's resources with maximum purpose and least waste.

Arthur C. Clarke
1917–

1 Bucky may be our first engineering saint.
J. Baldwin *BuckyWorks* (1996)

R. Buckminster Fuller
1895–1983

2 I'd like to introduce myself as the world's most successful failure.
J. Baldwin *BuckyWorks* (1996)

G

Clark Gable 1901–60

American actor. He became famous for his numerous roles in Hollywood films of the 1930s, such as *Gone with the Wind*.

Gable asked Faulkner whom he considered the best living writers:

William Faulkner
1897–1962

1 FAULKNER: Ernest Hemingway . . . and William Faulkner.
GABLE: Do you write, Mr Faulkner?
FAULKNER: Yes, Mr Gable; what do you do?
Bruce F. Kawin *Faulkner and Film* (1977)

Howard Hughes Jr.
1905–76

2 That man's ears make him look like a taxi-cab with both doors open.
Charles Higham and Joel Greenberg *Celluloid Muse* (1969)

David O. Selznick
1902–65

3 Gable has enemies all right—but they all like him.
David Niven *Bring On the Empty Horses* (1975)

Spencer Tracy
1900–67

4 Gable was a star, all right, and he put it on the line that he was not an actor . . . but he made an impression with what he *did*.
Larry Swindell *Spencer Tracy* (1969)

Thomas Gainsborough 1727–88

English painter. Although he was famous for his society portraits, landscape was his preferred subject.

Thomas Gainsborough
1727–88

1 I am sick of portraits and wish very much to take my viol-da-gamba and walk off to some sweet village where I can paint landskips and enjoy the fag-end of life in quietness and ease. But these fine ladies and their tea-drinkings, dancings, husband-huntings etc. etc. etc. will fob me out of the last ten years.
letter, c.1770

William Hazlitt
1778–1830

2 His subjects are softened and sentimentalised too much, it is not simple unaffected nature that we see, but nature sitting for her picture.
in July 1814

Horace Walpole
1717–97

3 Pieces of land and sea so natural that one steps back for fear of being splashed.
of two landscapes by Gainsborough, exhibited in 1781
in *Dictionary of National Biography* (1917–)

Hugh Gaitskell 1906–63

British Labour statesman. He opposed the government over the Suez crisis and resisted calls within his own party for unilateral disarmament.

Aneurin Bevan
1897–1960

1 The right kind of leader for the Labour Party . . . a desiccated calculating machine.
*generally taken as referring to Gaitskell, although **Bevan** specifically denied it in an interview with **Robin Day** in April 1959*
Michael Foot *Aneurin Bevan* vol. 2 (1973)

Richard Crossman
1907–74

2 While there is death there is hope.
on the death of Gaitskell
Tam Dalyell *Dick Crossman* (1989)

Hugh Gaitskell
1906–63

3 There are some of us . . . who will fight and fight and fight again to save the Party we love.
speech at Labour Party Conference, October 1960

Roy Jenkins
1920–

4 Morally, he was in the bravest of all categories: he flinched, but he always went on.
W. T. Rodgers (ed.) *Hugh Gaitskell 1906–63* (1964)

Galileo Galilei 1564–1642

Italian astronomer and physicist. His acceptance of the Copernican system was rejected by the Catholic Church, and under threat of torture from the Inquisition he recanted his heretical views.

Albert Einstein
1879–1955

1 Alas, you find [vanity] in so many scientists. It has always hurt me that Galileo did not acknowledge the work of Kepler.
in April 1955

Albert Einstein
1879–1955

2 Pure logical thinking cannot yield us any knowledge of the empirical world; all knowledge of reality starts from experience and ends in it . . . Because Galileo saw this, and particularly because he drummed it into the scientific world, he is the father of modern physics—indeed, of modern science altogether.
    Ray Spangenburg and Diane K. Moser *The History of Science from the Ancient Greeks to the Scientific Revolution* (1993)

Galileo Galilei
1564–1642

3 Alas . . . Galileo, your devoted friend and servant, has been for a month totally and incurably blind; so that this heaven, this earth, this universe, which by my remarkable observations and clear demonstrations I have enlarged a hundred, nay, a thousand fold beyond the limits universally accepted by the learned men of all previous ages, are now shrivelled up for me into such a narrow compass as is filled by my own bodily sensations.
    in c.1637

Stephen Jay Gould
1941–

4 A man does not attain the status of Galileo merely because he is persecuted; he must also be right.
    Ever since Darwin (1977)

John Milton
1608–74

5 There [in Italy] it was that I found and visited the famous Galileo grown old, a prisoner to the Inquisition, for thinking in astronomy otherwise than the Franciscan and Dominican licenser thought.
    Areopagita (1644)

Liam Gallagher 1972–

English pop singer, a member of Oasis.

Cilla Black
1943–

1 There's not many men my own age I'd even look at. I know Liam Gallagher is free now, but I'm afraid he's not my type, chuck.
    in September 2000

Noel Gallagher
1967–

2 If I wasn't related to Liam I would have sacked him four years ago.
    in July 2000

Noel Gallagher 1967–

English pop singer, a member of Oasis.

Noel Gallagher
1967–

3 We are lads. We have burgled houses and nicked car stereos, and we like girls and swear and go to the football and take the piss.
    interview, March 1996

Noel Gallagher
1967–

4 I would hope we mean more to people than putting money in a church basket and saying ten Hail Marys on a Sunday. Has God played Knebworth recently?
    on the drawing power of Oasis
    in July 1997

Thomas Gallagher

5 I feel like the roots of a great bunch of flowers. The grower gets all the praise, the flowers get the adoration, while the roots that started it all must remain under the ground unnoticed.
    view of the father of Noel and Liam
    in August 1997

Indira Gandhi 1917–84

Indian stateswoman, Prime Minister 1966–77 and 1980–4. The daughter of **Jawaharlal Nehru**, she was assassinated by her own Sikh bodyguards.

Indira Gandhi
1917–84

1 Even if I died in the service of the nation, I would be proud of it. Every drop of my blood, I am sure, will contribute to the growth of this nation and make it strong and dynamic.
    speech, Delhi, October 1984

Mahatma Gandhi 1869–1948

Indian nationalist and spiritual leader. He opposed British rule in India, pursuing a policy of non-violent civil disobedience, but was assassinated following partition.

Tony Benn
1925–

2 What I do remember, something that you would remember, this great man, sitting on the floor, devoted his whole attention to this little boy of six and my older brother. Now not many adults do that, they pat you on the head and talk to your dad.

on meeting Gandhi as a child; Anthony Clare *In the Psychiatrist's Chair III* (1998)

Winston Churchill
1874–1965

3 It is . . . alarming and also nauseating to see Mr Gandhi, a seditious Middle Temple lawyer, now posing as a fakir of a type well-known in the East, striding half-naked up the steps of the Viceregal Palace, while he is still organizing and conducting a defiant campaign of civil disobedience, to parley on equal terms with the representative of the King Emperor.

speech, February 1931

Stafford Cripps
1889–1952

4 I know of no other man in our time, or indeed in recent history, who so convincingly demonstrated the power of the spirit over material things.

speech, October 1948

Albert Einstein
1879–1955

5 I believe that Gandhi held the most enlightened views of all the political men in our time. We should strive to do things in his spirit; not to use violence in fighting for our cause and to refrain from taking part in anything we believe is evil.

in June 1950

Mahatma Gandhi
1869–1948

6 Non-violence is the first article of my faith. It is also the last article of my creed.

speech, March 1922, on a charge of sedition

Mary McCarthy
1912–89

7 The horror of Gandhi's murder lies not in the political motives behind it or in its consequences for Indian policy or for the future of non-violence; the horror lies simply in the fact that any man could look into the face of this extraordinary person and deliberately pull a trigger.

On the Contrary (1961)

Sarojini Naidu
1879–1949

8 If only Bapu knew the cost of setting him up in poverty!

A. Campbell-Johnson *Mission with Mountbatten* (1951)

Jawaharlal Nehru
1889–1964

9 The light has gone out of our lives and there is darkness everywhere.

following Gandhi's assassination
broadcast, January 1948

George Orwell
1903–50

10 Regarded simply as a politician, and compared with other leading political figures of our times, how clean a smell he has managed to leave behind!

Collected Essays, Journalism and Letters

Greta Garbo 1905–90

Swedish-born American actress. She gained instant recognition for her compelling screen presence and enigmatic beauty. In 1941 she retired and lived as a recluse for the rest of her life.

Tallulah Bankhead
1903–68

1 Her mystery was as thick as a London fog.

attributed

Cecil Beaton
1904–80

2 The same wild untamed quality of genius—of not fitting. But Greta is subtle and sensitive and has a sense of humanity even if she is utterly self centred.

in 1963; Diane Solway *Nureyev: His Life* (1998)

Alistair Cooke
1908–

3 In the first five minutes of the film [*Anna Karenina*], when the smoke artfully provided by the train clears away and reveals the Garbo's face, you might just as well pick up your hat and go home if you too can't guess the end.
   Garbo and the Night Watchmen (1937)

Simone de Beauvoir
1908–86

4 Garbo's visage had a kind of emptiness into which anything could be projected—nothing can be read into Bardot's face.
   Brigitte Bardot and the Lolita Syndrome (1959)

Greta Garbo
1905–90

5 I want to be alone.
   Grand Hotel (1932 film), the phrase already being associated with Garbo

Greta Garbo
1905–90

6 Life has been difficult for me. You must realize I am a sad person: I am a misfit in life.
   Cecil Beaton's diary, 1947

Greta Garbo
1905–90

7 NIVEN: Why *did* you give up the movies?
   GARBO: I had made enough faces.
   David Niven *Bring on the Empty Horses* (1975)

Lillian Gish
1896–1993

8 Garbo's temperament reflected the rain and the gloom of the long, dark Swedish winters.
   The Movies, Mr Griffith and Me (1969)

Graham Greene
1904–91

9 A great actress? Oh, undoubtedly, one wearily assents, but what dull pompous films they make for her, hardly movies at all so retarded are they by her haggard equine renunciations, the slow consummation of her noble adulteries.
   Halliwells Filmgoer's Companion (1997 ed.)

Christopher Isherwood
1904–86

10 She wanted to be told the secret of eternal youth, the meaning of life—but quickly, in one lesson, before her butterfly attention wandered away again.
   meeting the Indian spiritual leader Krishnamurti
   diary, November 1939

Clare Booth Luce
1903–87

11 A deer in the body of a woman, living resentfully in the Hollywood zoo.
   attributed

Groucho Marx
1895–1977

12 *approaching an unwelcoming Greta Garbo and peering up under the brim of her floppy hat:*
Pardon me, Ma'am . . . I thought you were a guy I knew in Pittsburgh.
   David Niven *Bring on the Empty Horses* (1975)

Kenneth Tynan
1927–80

13 What, when drunk, one sees in other women, one sees in Garbo sober.
   Curtains (1961)

Mae West
1892–1980

14 She didn't let other people make her live her life the way they wanted her to live it. She had style; she was her own person.
   Charlotte Chandler *The Ultimate Seduction* (1984)

James Abram Garfield 1831–81

American Republican statesman, President March–September 1881. He was assassinated within months of becoming President.

James Abram Garfield
1831–81

1 Assassination can no more be guarded against than death by lightning; and it is best not to worry about either.
   John M. Taylor *Garfield of Ohio: The Available Man* (1970)

Ulysses S. Grant
1822–85

2 Garfield has shown that he is not possessed of the backbone of an angle-worm.
   John M. Taylor *Garfield of Ohio: The Available Man* (1970)

William Roscoe Thayer
1859–1923

3 From log-cabin to White House.
   title of biography (1910) of Garfield

Judy Garland 1922–69

American singer and actress. Her most famous early film role was in *The Wizard of Oz*. She apparently died of a drug overdose after suffering many personal problems.

Ray Bolger
1904–87

1 Judy Garland never found that land, never really heard that lullaby, never saw a rainbow that wasn't manufactured in a studio. Judy's world was the wicked Witch's world. Bubble, bubble, toil and trouble. Oh yes, she had her triumphs. But, while she triumphed on the stage, the pot was boiling for Judy. She never had a chance.
view of the Scarecrow
Anne Edwards *Judy Garland* (1976)

Judy Garland
1922–69

2 If I'm such a legend, then why am I so lonely? If I'm a legend, then why do I sit at home for hours staring at the damned phone?
John Gruen *Close-Up* (1968)

Vincente Minnelli
1910–84

3 If she could never belong to one man, Judy would always belong to the people. She might exasperate them or try their patience, but she would remain a national addiction.
I Remember It Well (1974)

Kenneth Tynan
1927–80

4 She incarnates a dream. She embodies the persistence of youth so completely that we forbid her to develop, and permit her no maturity. Even in middle age, she must continue to sing about adolescence and all the pain and nostalgia that go with it.
in May 1959

David Garrick 1717–79

English actor and dramatist. He was equally successful in tragic and comic roles, and later became the manager of the Drury Lane Theatre.

Samuel Foote
1720–77

1 God's revenge against vanity.
to David Garrick, who had asked him what he thought of a heavy shower of rain falling on the day of the Shakespeare Jubilee, organized by and chiefly starring Garrick himself
W. Cooke *Memoirs of Samuel Foote* (1805)

on attempting to paint two actors, David Garrick and Samuel Foote:

Thomas Gainsborough
1727–88

2 Rot them for a couple of rogues, they have everybody's faces but their own.
Allan Cunningham *The Lives of the Most Eminent Painters, Sculptors and Architects* (1829)

Oliver Goldsmith
1728–74

3 Our Garrick's a salad; for in him we see
Oil, vinegar, sugar, and saltness agree.
Retaliation (1774)

Oliver Goldsmith
1728–74

4 On the stage he was natural, simple, affecting;
'Twas only that when he was off he was acting.
Retaliation (1774)

Samuel Johnson
1709–84

5 I am disappointed by that stroke of death, which has eclipsed the gaiety of nations and impoverished the public stock of harmless pleasure.
on the death of Garrick
Lives of the English Poets (1779–81)

Paul Gascoigne 1967–

English footballer; known as Gazza. A gifted though controversial attacking midfielder, he played for clubs including Tottenham Hotspur, Lazio, and Glasgow Rangers.

George Best
1946–

1 He is accused of being arrogant, unable to cope with the press, and a boozer. Sounds like he's got a chance to me.
attributed

Germaine Greer
1939–

2 In his lumpy long shorts and up-and-down socks he seemed more like a boy than a man, the Just William of the side.
in June 1996

Mr Justice Harman
1930–

3 Isn't there an operetta called *La Gazza Ladra*?
in October 1990

Alf Ramsey
1920–

4 Gifted? Yes. But it takes more than that and a silly grin to make your mark in international football.
attributed

Terry Venables
1943–

5 The boy's a very sensitive boy.
in June 1990

Elizabeth Gaskell 1810–65

English novelist. An active humanitarian from a Unitarian background, she is famous for novels such as *Cranford* and *North and South* which display her interest in social concerns.

Charlotte Brontë
1816–55

1 Mrs Gaskell herself is a woman of whose conversation and company I should not tire. She seems to me kind, clever, animated, and unaffected.
letter, July 1851

Jane Welsh Carlyle
1801–66

2 A natural unassuming woman whom they have been doing their best to spoil by making a lioness of her.
letter, May 1849

Arthur Hugh Clough
1819–61

3 She is neither young (past 30) nor beautiful; very retiring, but quite capable of talking when she likes—a good deal of the clergyman's wife about her.
letter, February 1849

Bill Gates 1955–

American computer entrepreneur. He co-founded the computer software company Microsoft and became the youngest multi-billionaire in American history.

Randall E. Stross

1 American anti-intellectualism will never again be the same because of Bill Gates. Gates embodies what was supposed to be impossible—the practical intellectual.
The Microsoft Way (1996)

Paul Gauguin 1848–1903

French painter. From 1891 on he lived mainly in Tahiti, painting in a post-Impressionist style that was influenced by primitive art.

Paul Gauguin
1848–1903

1 Art for Art's sake. Why not?
Art for Life's sake. Why not?
Art for Pleasure's sake. Why not?
What does it matter, as long as it is Art?
Gauguin's formula for his work
Herbert Read *The Meaning of Art* (3rd ed., 1951)

John Gay 1685–1732

English poet and dramatist. He is chiefly known for *The Beggar's Opera* (1728), a low-life ballad opera combining burlesque and political satire.

John Gay
1685–1732

1 Life is a jest; and all things show it.
I thought so once; but now I know it.
'My Own Epitaph' (1720)

Alexander Pope
1688–1744

2 Of manners gentle, of affections mild;
In wit, a man; simplicity, a child;
With native humour temp'ring virtuous rage,
Formed to delight at once and lash the age.
'Epitaph: On Mr Gay in Westminster Abbey' (1733)

Martha Gellhorn 1908–98

American journalist.

Martha Gellhorn
1908–98

1 I believed that all one did about a war was go to it, as a gesture of solidarity, and get killed, or survive if lucky until the war was over . . . I had no idea you could be what I became, an unscathed tourist of wars.
The Face of War (1959)

Genghis Khan 1162–1227

Founder of the Mongol empire. He took the name Genghis Khan ('ruler of all') in 1206 after uniting the nomadic Mongol tribes, and by the time of his death his empire extended from China to the Black Sea.

Genghis Khan
1162–1227

1 Happiness lies in conquering one's enemies, in driving them in front of oneself, in taking their property, in savouring their despair, in outraging their wives and daughters.
Witold Rodzinski *The Walled Kingdom: A History of China* (1979)

Artemisia Gentileschi 1593–1652/3

Italian painter.

Artemisia Gentileschi
1593–1652/3

1 I have the greatest sympathy for your lordship, because the name of a woman makes one doubtful until one has seen the work.
letter to her patron, January 1649

George I 1660–1727

King from 1714. He succeeded to the British throne as a result of the Act of Settlement (1701). Unpopular in England as a foreigner who never learned English, he left administration to his ministers.

George I
1660–1727

1 I hate all Boets and Bainters.
John Campbell *Lives of the Chief Justices* (1849)

Samuel Johnson
1709–84

2 George the First knew nothing, and desired to know nothing; did nothing, and desired to do nothing; and the only good thing that is told of him is, that he wished to restore the crown to its hereditary successor.
comment, April 1775

George III 1738–1820

King from 1760. He exercised considerable political influence, but it declined from 1788 after bouts of mental illness, as a result of which his son, later **George IV**, was made regent in 1811.

Walter Bagehot
1826–77

3 Throughout the greater part of his life George III was a kind of 'consecrated obstruction'.
The English Constitution (1867)

Edmund Clerihew
Bentley
1875–1956

4 George the Third
Ought never to have occurred.
One can only wonder
At so grotesque a blunder.
'George the Third' (1929)

Lord Byron
1788–1824

5 And when the gorgeous coffin was laid low,
It seemed the mockery of hell to fold
The rottenness of eighty years in gold.
on the burial of George III
The Vision of Judgement (1822)

George III
1738–1820

6 Born and educated in this country, I glory in the name of Briton.
speech to House of Lords, November 1760

Samuel Johnson
1709–84

7 Sir, they may talk of the King as they will; but he is the finest gentleman I have ever seen.

in 1767

Percy Bysshe Shelley
1792–1822

8 An old, mad, blind, despised, and dying king.

'Sonnet: England in 1819' (written 1819)

Horace Walpole
1717–97

9 He lost his dominions in America, his authority over Ireland, and all influence in Europe, by aiming at despotism in England; and exposed himself to more mortifications and humiliations than can happen to a quiet Doge of Venice.

Memoirs of the Reign of King George III (1845)

George IV 1762–1830

King from 1820. Known as a patron of the arts and *bon viveur*, he gained a bad reputation which was further damaged by his attempt to divorce his estranged wife **Caroline of Brunswick** just after coming to the throne.

Anonymous

10 The first gentleman in Europe.

nickname given to George IV; applied satirically by Cruikshank in a caricature (1820)

Beau Brummell
1778–1840

11 Who's your fat friend?

referring to the Prince of Wales, later George IV
Capt. Jesse *Life of George Brummell* (1844)

Caroline of Brunswick
1768–1821

12 My God! is the Prince always like that? I find him very fat and not at all as handsome as his portrait.

Earl of Malmesbury's diary, April 1795

Leigh Hunt
1784–1859

13 This Adonis in loveliness was a corpulent man of fifty.

in March 1812

Charles Lamb
1775–1834

14 Not a fatter fish than he
Flounders round the polar sea.
See his blubber—at his gills
What a world of drink he swills . . .
By his bulk and by his size
By his oily qualities
This (or else my eyesight fails)
This should be the Prince of Wales.

anonymously written in 1812

Sir Walter Scott
1771–1832

15 [George IV] converses himself with so much ease and elegance that you lose thoughts of the prince in admiring the well-bred and accomplished gentleman. He is in many respects the model of a British monarch.

diary, October 1826

George V 1865–1936

King from 1910. He won respect for his punctilious attitude towards royal duties and responsibilities, and exercised restrained but important influence over British politics.

Margot Asquith
1864–1945

16 How dull the royal family is, only interested in buttons and things.

Sarah Bradford *Elizabeth* (1996)

John Betjeman
1906–84

17 Spirits of well-shot woodcock, partridge, snipe
Flutter and bear him up the Norfolk sky.

'Death of King George V' (1937)

Lord Dawson of Penn
1864–1945

18 The King's life is moving peacefully towards its close.

bulletin, drafted on a menu card at Buckingham Palace on the eve of the king's death, January 1936

Edward VIII
1894–1972

19 He disapproved of Soviet Russia, painted fingernails, women who smoked in public, cocktails, frivolous hats, American jazz and the growing habit of going away for weekends.

A King's Story (1951)

*on **H. G. Wells**'s comment on 'an alien and uninspiring court':*

George V 20 I may be uninspiring, but I'll be damned if I'm an alien!
1865–1936 Sarah Bradford *George VI* (1989); attributed

George V 21 My father was frightened of his mother; I was frightened of my father,
1865–1936 and I am damned well going to see to it that my children are frightened
of me.
attributed in Randolph S. Churchill *Lord Derby* (1959), but said by Kenneth Rose in *George V* (1983) to be almost certainly apocryphal

George V 22 I am not a clever man, but if I had not picked up something from all
1865–1936 the brains I've met, I would be an idiot.
Robert Rhodes James *Victor Cazalet* (1976)

Owen Morshead 23 The House of Hanover, like ducks, produce bad parents—they trample
1893–1977 on their young.
letter from Harold Nicolson to Vita Sackville-West, January 1949

Harold Nicolson 24 For seventeen years he did nothing at all but kill animals and stick in
1886–1968 stamps.
diary, August 1949

George VI 1894–1952

King from 1936–52. Despite a retiring disposition he became a popular monarch, gaining respect for the staunch example he and his family set during the London Blitz.

Edward VIII 25 He has one matchless blessing, enjoyed by so many of you and not
1894–1972 bestowed on me—a happy home with his wife and children.
speech, December 1936

George V 26 I pray to God that my eldest son will never marry and have children,
1865–1936 and that nothing will come between Bertie and Lilibet and the throne.
Sarah Bradford *George VI* (1989)

George V 27 Bertie has more guts than the rest of them put together.
1865–1936 Sarah Bradford *Elizabeth* (1996)

Richard Gere 1949–

American actor, who appeared in films such as *American Gigolo* and *Pretty Woman*.

David Thomson 1 There are times when Richard Gere has the warm effect of a wind
1941– tunnel at dawn, waiting for work, all sheen, inner curve, and posed
emptiness.
A Biographical Dictionary of Film (1994)

Geronimo c. 1829–1909

Apache chief. He led his people in resistance to white encroachment on tribal reservations in Arizona, waging war in a series of raids before surrendering in 1886.

Geronimo 1 Once I moved about like the wind. Now I surrender to you and that is
c. 1829–1909 all.
surrendering to General Crook, March 1886

George Gershwin 1898–1937

American composer and pianist, of Russian-Jewish descent. He composed many successful songs and musicals, the orchestral work *Rhapsody in Blue*, and the opera *Porgy and Bess*.

George Gershwin 1 RUMOURS ABOUT HIGHBROW MUSIC RIDICULOUS STOP AM OUT TO WRITE HITS.
1898–1937 telegram to his Hollywood agent, 1930s

Ira Gershwin 2 I now belong, I see, to the rank of Brothers of the Great.
1896–1983 *thanking a friend for clippings about his brother George's success*
Philip Furia *Ira Gershwin* (1966)

Oscar Hammerstein II 1895–1960	3 He was a lucky young man Lucky to be so in love with the world Lucky because the world was so in love with him. Merle Armitage (ed.) *George Gershwin* (1938)
Oscar Levant 1906–72	4 Tell me, George, if you had to do it all over would you fall in love with yourself again. David Ewen *The Story of George Gershwin* (1943)
Arnold Schoenberg 1874–1951	5 Many musicians do not consider George Gershwin a serious composer. But they should understand that, serious or not, he is a composer—that is, a man who lives in music and expresses everything, serious or not, sound or superficial, by means of music, because it is his native language. Robert Kimball and Alfred Simon *The Gershwins* (1973)

J. Paul Getty 1892–1976

American industrialist. He made a large fortune in the oil industry and was also a noted art collector. He founded the J. Paul Getty Museum in Los Angeles.

Bernard Levin 1928–	1 Paul Getty ... had always been vastly, immeasurably wealthy, and yet went about looking like a man who cannot quite remember whether he remembered to turn the gas off before leaving home. *The Pendulum Years* (1970)
Roy Thomson 1894–1976	2 He's richer than me, but then again he's six months older. *on Getty, when both were in their eighties* Diane Francis *Controlling Interest: Who Owns Canada?* (1986)

Edward Gibbon 1737–94

English historian. He is best known for his multi-volume work *The History of the Decline and Fall of the Roman Empire*, which aroused controversy for its critical account of the spread of Christianity.

James Boswell 1740–95	1 I think it is right that as fast as infidel wasps or venomous insects, whether creeping or flying, are hatched, they should be crushed. letter, April 1776
James Boswell 1740–95	2 He is an ugly, affected, disgusting fellow, and poisons our literary club to me. letter, May 1779
Lord Byron 1788–1824	3 Sapping a solemn creed with solemn sneer. *Childe Harold's Pilgrimage* (1812–18)
George Colman, the Younger 1762–1836	4 Johnson's style was grand and Gibbon's elegant; the stateliness of the former was sometimes pedantic, and the polish of the latter was occasionally finical. Johnson marched to kettle-drums and trumpets; Gibbon moved to flute and hautboys: Johnson hewed passages through the Alps, while Gibbon levelled walks through parks and gardens. *Random Records* (1830)
Edward Gibbon 1737–94	5 To the University of Oxford I acknowledge no obligation; and she will as cheerfully renounce me for a son, as I am willing to disclaim her for a mother. I spent fourteen months at Magdalen College: they proved the fourteen months the most idle and unprofitable of my whole life. *Memoirs of My Life* (1796)
Edward Gibbon 1737–94	6 The captain of the Hampshire grenadiers ... has not been useless to the historian of the Roman empire. *of his own army service* *Memoirs of My Life* (1796)
William Henry, Duke of Gloucester 1743–1805	7 Another damned, thick, square book! Always scribble, scribble, scribble! Eh! Mr Gibbon? Henry Best *Personal and Literary Memorials* (1829); D. M. Low *Edward Gibbon* (1937) notes alternative attributions to the Duke of Cumberland and King George III

when his apparently flattering reference to Gibbon as the 'luminous' author of The Decline and Fall *was queried:*

Richard Brinsley Sheridan
1751–1816

8 Luminous! oh, I meant—voluminous.
during the trial of Warren Hastings in 1785

John Gielgud 1904–2000

English actor and director. A notable Shakespearean actor, particularly remembered for his interpretation of the role of Hamlet.

Peter Brook
1925–

1 He is like an aircraft circling before it can land . . . He will change and change indefinitely, in search of rightness.
on Gielgud as a director
in May 2000

Alec Guinness
1914–2000

2 A silver trumpet muffled in silk.
describing Gielgud's voice
attributed

Peter Hall
1930–

3 John Gielgud to me was mercury—quicksilver in his wit, always ahead of the audience, always reassessing his performance.
in May 2000

Ralph Richardson
1902–83

4 I was always rather amazed at him—a kind of brilliant butterfly, while I was a gloomy sort of boy.
on first meeting Gielgud in 1929; Clive Francis *Sir John* (1994)

Lee Strasberg
1901–82

5 When Gielgud speaks the verse I can hear Shakespeare thinking.
attributed

Kenneth Tynan
1927–80

6 The finest actor on earth from the neck up.
in 1959

Emlyn Williams
1905–87

7 All nose and passion and dragging calves and unbridled oboe of a voice—no peering at the back of the furniture for this beginner.
in c.1924, attributed

W. S. Gilbert 1836–1911

English dramatist. He is best known as a librettist who collaborated on light operas with the composer Sir **Arthur Sullivan**.

Anthony Hope
1863–1933

1 His foe was folly and his weapon wit.
inscription on W. S. Gilbert's memorial on the Victoria Embankment, London, 1915

Arthur Sullivan
1842–1900

2 You say that in serious opera, you must more or less sacrifice yourself. I say that this is just what I have been doing in all our joint pieces.
letter, March 1889

Eric Gill 1882–1940

English sculptor, engraver, and typographer. His best-known sculptures are the relief carvings *Stations of the Cross* at Westminster Cathedral and the *Prospero and Ariel* on Broadcasting House in London.

Kingsley Amis
1922–95

1 In the words of that old idiot and very bad artist Eric Gill, 'The artist is not a special kind of man; every man is a special kind of artist.' That's only possible if making mud pies counts as art.
in October 1979

Alec Guinness
1914–2000

2 Gill was revealed in a biography a few years ago as having abused practically his whole family. Too bad and too sad, if so; but his work still shines out as a magnificent expression of the human spirit and man's skill with his hands.
diary, April 1998

Dizzy Gillespie 1917–93

American jazz trumpet player and bandleader. He was a virtuoso trumpet player and a leading exponent of the bebop style.

Kingsley Amis
1922–95

1 Louis shown in vaudeville garb, coloured derby, waistcoat with brass buttons, check pants, Dizzy in beret, suit, hornrims. Louis is America, entertainment; Dizzy is the world, art. K. Abé sees all this, of course.

*of photographs of **Louis Armstrong** and Dizzy Gillespie by K. Abé*
in February 1989

Philip Larkin
1922–85

2 I didn't relish his addiction to things Latin-American and I found his sense of humour rudimentary.

Required Writing (1983)

Allen Ginsberg 1926–97

American poet. A leading poet of the beat generation, he was later influential in the hippy movement of the 1960s.

Allen Ginsberg
1926–97

1 Oh that's easy. Beat writer, Blake scholar, Buddhist harmonium-player, Jewish punk rocker, once dangerous subversive. Or maybe just poet.

defining himself, in 1997

Giotto c. 1267–1337

Italian painter. He rejected the flat, formulaic, and static images of Italo-Byzantine art in favour of a more naturalistic style showing human expression.

Boccaccio
1313–75

1 Mortal sight was often puzzled, face to face with his creations, and took the painted thing for the actual object.

of the painting of Giotto
Decameron (1348–58)

Dante Alighieri
1265–1321

2 In painting Cimabue was thought to hold the field; now Giotto has the palm, so that he has obscured the other's fame.

Divina Commedia

Lillian Gish 1896–1993

American actress. She and her sister Dorothy (1898–1968) appeared in a number of **D. W. Griffith**'s films, including *Hearts of the World* (1918) and *Orphans of the Storm* (1922).

Simon Callow
1949–

1 The spirit of absolution and healing . . . with a kind of secular sanctity that cannot be forged.

of Lillian Gish in The Night of the Hunter *(1955)*
Geoffrey Nowell-Smith *The Oxford History of World Cinema* (1996)

Mrs Patrick Campbell
1865–1940

2 Lillian Gish may be a charming person, but she is not Ophelia. She comes on stage as if she'd been sent for to sew rings on the new curtains.

Cecil Beaton's diary, 1938

Lillian Gish
1896–1993

3 When Dorothy arrives the party begins. When I arrive it usually ends.

contrasting herself with her sister
Geoffrey Nowell-Smith *The Oxford History of World Cinema* (1996)

D. W. Griffith
1875–1948

4 She is the best actress I know. She has the most brain.

Geoffrey Nowell-Smith *The Oxford History of World Cinema* (1996)

W. E. Gladstone 1809–98

British Liberal statesman, Prime Minister 1868–74, 1880–5, 1886, and 1892–4. His ministries saw the introduction of elementary education and the third Reform Act, and his campaign in favour of Home Rule for Ireland.

Anonymous

1 He talked shop like a tenth muse.

on Gladstone's Budget speeches
G. W. E. Russell *Collections and Recollections* (1898)

Walter Bagehot
1826–77

2 He believes, with all his heart and soul and strength, that there *is* such a thing as truth; he has the soul of a martyr with the intellect of an advocate.
Biographical Studies (1881)

E. F. Benson
1867–1940

3 Always there was this huge concentration of force; purpose at white heat roared like a furnace in every action of his life. When once he had convinced himself on any subject it ceased to be his opinion and became a cosmic truth which it was the duty of every right-minded person to uphold.
As We Were (1930)

Thomas Carlyle
1795–1881

4 An almost spectral kind of phantasm of a man—nothing in him but forms and ceremonies and outside wrappings.
letter, March 1873

Lord Randolph Churchill
1849–94

5 The forest laments in order that Mr Gladstone may perspire.
on Gladstone's hobby of felling trees
speech, January 1884

Lord Randolph Churchill
1849–94

6 An old man in a hurry.
address, June 1886

Winston Churchill
1874–1965

7 Mr Gladstone read Homer for fun, which I thought served him right.
My Early Life (1930)

Benjamin Disraeli
1804–81

8 Mr Gladstone not only appeared but rushed into the debate . . . the new members trembled and fluttered like small birds when a hawk is in the air.
of Gladstone in the House of Commons
letter, March 1875

Benjamin Disraeli
1804–81

9 A sophistical rhetorician, inebriated with the exuberance of his own verbosity.
in July 1878

Benjamin Disraeli
1804–81

10 If Gladstone fell into the Thames, that would be misfortune; and if anybody pulled him out, that, I suppose, would be a calamity.
Leon Harris *The Fine Art of Political Wit* (1965)

Catherine Gladstone
1812–1900

to her husband:
11 Oh, William dear, if you weren't such a great man you would be a terrible bore.
Roy Jenkins *Gladstone* (1995)

T. H. Huxley
1825–95

12 Why, put him in the middle of a moor, with nothing in the world but his shirt, and you could not prevent him being anything he liked.
Roy Jenkins *Gladstone* (1995)

Henry Labouchere
1831–1912

13 He [Labouchere] did not object to the old man always having a card up his sleeve, but he did object to his insinuating that the Almighty had placed it there.
on Gladstone's 'frequent appeals to a higher power'
Earl Curzon *Modern Parliamentary Eloquence* (1913)

W. C. Sellar
1898–1951
and **R. J. Yeatman**
1898–1968

14 Gladstone . . . spent his declining years trying to guess the answer to the Irish Question; unfortunately whenever he was getting warm, the Irish secretly changed the Question.
1066 and All That (1930)

Queen Victoria
1819–1901

15 The danger to the country, to Europe, to her vast Empire, which is involved in having all these great interests entrusted to the shaking hand of an old, wild, and incomprehensible man of 82, is very great!
on Gladstone's last appointment as Prime Minister
letter, August 1892

Queen Victoria
1819–1901

16 He speaks to Me as if I was a public meeting.
G. W. E. Russell *Collections and Recollections* (1898)

Garnet Wolseley 17 God must be very angry with England when he sends back Mr
1833–1913 Gladstone to us as first minister.
> letter, 1886

Evelyn Glennie 1965–

Scottish percussion player. She is an outstanding percussion player who has won many awards. She lost her hearing as a teenager.

Evelyn Glennie 1 The loneliest period for a musician is immediately after a concert.
1965– interview, November 2000

Johann Wolfgang von Goethe 1749–1832

German poet, dramatist, and scholar. Involved at first with the *Sturm und Drang* movement, Goethe changed to a more measured and classical style.

Albert Einstein 1 I feel in him a certain condescending attitude toward the reader, a
1879–1955 certain lack of humble devotion which, especially in great men, has such a comforting effect.
> letter, April 1932

Johann Wolfgang von 2 I do not know myself, and God forbid that I should.
Goethe remark, April 1829
1749–1832

Sir Walter Scott 3 Goethe is different and a wonderful fellow, the Ariosto at once, and
1771–1832 almost the Voltaire of Germany.
> *Anne of Geierstein* (1829)

Charles Hamilton 4 If Goethe really died saying 'more light', it was very silly of him: what
Sorley he wanted was more warmth.
1895–1915 letter, July 1914

Oliver Goldsmith 1728–74

Irish novelist, poet, essayist, and dramatist. He settled in London, where he practised as a physician before beginning his literary career.

David Garrick 1 Here lies Nolly Goldsmith, for shortness called Noll,
1717–79 Who wrote like an angel, but talked like poor Poll.
> 'Impromptu Epitaph' (written 1773–4)

Samuel Johnson 2 To Oliver Goldsmith, A Poet, Naturalist, and Historian, who left scarcely
1709–84 any style of writing untouched, and touched none that he did not adorn.
> epitaph, 1776

Samuel Johnson 3 No man was more foolish when he had not a pen in his hand, or more
1709–84 wise when he had.
> comment, 1780

Sam Goldwyn 1882–1974

Polish-born American film producer. With **Louis B. Mayer**, he founded the film company Metro-Goldwyn-Mayer (MGM) in 1924.

Learned Hand 1 A self-made man may prefer a self-made name.
1872–1961 *on Samuel Goldfish's changing his name to Samuel Goldwyn*
Bosley Crowther *Lion's Share* (1957)

Ben Hecht 2 [Goldwyn] filled the room with wonderful panic and beat at your mind
1894–1964 like a man in front of a slot machine, shaking it for a jackpot.
A. Scott Berg *Goldwyn* (1989)

George Bernard Shaw 3 The trouble, Mr Goldwyn, is that you are only interested in art and I am
1856–1950 only interested in money.
> *telegraphed version of the outcome of a conversation between **Shaw** and Sam Goldwyn*
Alva Johnson *The Great Goldwyn* (1937)

Maud Gonne 1867–1953

Irish nationalist and actress. She was a founder of Sinn Fein. The poet **Yeats** fell in love with her, and she inspired many of his poems.

Maud Gonne
1867–1953

1 Our children were your poems of which I was the Father sowing the unrest and storm which made them possible and you the mother who brought them forth in suffering and in the highest beauty and our children had wings.

letter to W. B. Yeats, September 1911

W. B. Yeats
1865–1939

2 How many loved your movements of glad grace,
And loved your beauty with love false or true;
But one man loved the pilgrim soul in you,
And loved the sorrows of your changing face.

'When You are Old' (1893)

Mikhail Sergeevich Gorbachev 1931–

Soviet statesman, General Secretary of the Communist Party 1985–91 and President 1988–91. His foreign policy brought about an end to the cold war, while at home he introduced major reforms known as glasnost and perestroika.

Sean Connery
1930–

1 I can't answer for women, but I find him very attractive as a man's man. He has an extraordinary combination of intelligence, baldness and serenity. Almost Buddha-like.

in May 1999

Michael Foot
1913–

2 In my estimation, he did more than any other single individual engaged in the ugly trade of world politics to make possible a peaceful ending of our war-ridden century . . . whatever else he was or was not, he was the most passionate nuclear disarmer who ever appeared on the planet.

Dr Strangelove, I Presume (1999)

Andrei Gromyko
1909–89

3 Comrades, this man has a nice smile, but he's got iron teeth.

speech, March 1985

Richard Milhous Nixon
1913–94

4 Gorbachev is Wall Street and Yeltsin is Main Street; Gorbachev is Georgetown drawing rooms and Yeltsin is Newark factory gate.

in April 1991

Margaret Thatcher
1925–

5 We can do business together.

in December 1984

Mikhail Zhvanetsky
1934–

6 We enjoyed . . . his slyness. He mastered the art of walking backward into the future. He would say 'After me'. And some people went ahead, and some went behind, and he would go backward.

in September 1994

Charles George Gordon 1833–85

British general and colonial administrator. He made his name by crushing the Taiping Rebellion in China. In 1884 he fought Mahdist forces in Sudan but was trapped at Khartoum and killed.

Evelyn Baring
1841–1917

1 A man who habitually consults the Prophet Isaiah when he is in a difficulty is not apt to obey the orders of any one.

letter, 1884

Lord Kitchener
1850–1916

2 Never was a garrison so nearly rescued, never was a commander so sincerely lamented.

report, 1885

Al Gore 1948–

American Democratic politician, vice-president of **Bill Clinton**. In 2000 he narrowly lost the Presidential contest to **George W. Bush**.

Fergal Keane
1961–

1 The skeletons in his closet are calcium deficient.

in November 2000

Ralph Nader
1934–

2 Only Al Gore can beat Al Gore. And he's been doing a pretty good job of that.

responding to claims that his candidacy could split the liberal vote and cost Gore the election
in November 2000

explaining why he would support Ralph Nader for the presidency in preference to his own cousin
Al Gore:

Gore Vidal
1925–

3 In the long run Gore is thicker than Nader.

in August 2000

Stephen Jay Gould 1941–

American palaeontologist. A noted popularizer of science, he has proposed the concept of punctuated equilibrium, and written on the social context of scientific theory.

Stephen Jay Gould
1941–

1 One thing I'm good at is lateral and tangential thinking. I can see connections among things. That's why the essays I write work. I can see connections that most people think are odd, or peculiar, but are apposite once they're pointed out. And so my work has been integrative, that's what I'm best at doing. I do figure out Dorothy Sayers' mysteries because Peter Wimsey is constructed as that kind of thinker.

Lewis Wolpert and Alison Richards A Passion for Science (1988)

John Maynard Smith
1920–

2 The evolutionary biologists with whom I have discussed his work tend to see him as a man whose ideas are so confused as to be hardly worth bothering with, but as one who should not be publicly criticized because he is at least on our side against the creationists. All of this would not matter, were it not that he is giving non-biologists a largely false picture of the state of evolutionary theory.

in November 1995

David Gower 1957–

English cricketer. A consistent rather than heavy scorer, he captained England in the mid 1980s.

Frances Edmonds

1 Difficult to be more laid back without being actually comatose.

in 1985

David Gower
1957–

2 'For fun, style and excellence.' If I had the choice of words to be chiselled on my tombstone . . . it would be those.

Gower: The Autobiography (1992)

Len Hutton
1916–90

3 David Gower makes batting look as easy as drinking tea.

attributed

Michael Parkinson
1935–

4 Cricket is littered with gibbering wrecks of people who have tried to fathom what goes on in Gower's head.

in July 1993

Goya 1746–1828

Spanish painter and etcher. He is famous for his works treating the French occupation of Spain, including *The Shootings of May 3rd 1808* and *The Disasters of War*, depicting the cruelty and horror of war.

Charles Baudelaire
1821–67

1 Goya, nightmare full of unknown things.

'Les Phares' (1857)

Charles Baudelaire
1821–67

2 He is a sad, sceptical Cervantes-turned-Voltairean. The light of Velasquez and the colour of Greco died with him.
Jean Chabrun *Goya* (1965)

Goya
1746–1828

3 I had three masters: Nature, Velasquez and Rembrandt.
Jean Chabrun *Goya* (1965)

Seamus Heaney
1939–

4 He painted with his fists and elbows, flourished
The stained cape of his heart as history charged.
'Summer 1969' (1975)

W. G. Grace 1848–1915

English cricketer. In a first-class career that lasted until 1908, he made 126 centuries, scored 54,896 runs, and took 2,864 wickets.

Anonymous

1 They have paid to see Dr Grace bat, not to see you bowl.
said to the bowler when the umpire had called 'not out' after W. G. Grace was unexpectedly bowled first ball
Harry Furniss *A Century of Grace* (1985); perhaps apocryphal

Edmund Clerihew Bentley
1875–1956

2 Dr W. G. Grace
Had hair all over his face.
Lord! How all the people cheered,
When a ball got lost in his beard.
'Dr W. G. Grace'

C. P. Snow
1905–80

3 Grace was the star cricketer and one of the greatest of all Victorian heroes. He played as an amateur, and amateurs were not supposed to be paid. That did not prevent Grace making large sums of money out of the game. He was a cheat, on and off the cricket field.
introduction to Arthur Conan Doyle *The Case-book of Sherlock Holmes* (1974 ed.)

Lew Grade 1906–

British television producer and executive, born in Russia. A pioneer of British commercial television, he served as president of ATV (Associated Television) from 1977 to 1982.

Lew Grade
1906–

1 All my shows are great. Some of them are bad. But they are all great.
in September 1975

Harry Secombe
1921–

2 These days a star is anyone who can hold a microphone. A superstar is someone who has shaken hands with Lew Grade, and a super-super-star is one who has refused to shake hands with Lew Grade.
in 1972

Steffi Graf 1969–

German tennis player. She was ranked top women's player at the age of 16 and won her seventh Wimbledon singles title in 1996.

Martin Amis
1949–

1 Steffi Graf is something unbelievable on the tennis court, a miracle of speed, balance and intense athleticism. She looks like a skater but she moves like a puck.
Visiting Mrs Nabokov and Other Excursions (1993)

Martha Graham 1893–1991

American dancer, teacher, and choreographer. She evolved a new dance language using more flexible movements intended to express psychological complexities and emotional power.

Woody Allen
1935–

1 Graham is the other side of the comic prism, of the comic perspective. [She] is overpowering. The movements are so primordial that they're terrifying and irresistible.
in November 1975

Percy Grainger 1882–1961

Australian-born American composer and pianist. From 1901 he lived in London, where he collected, edited, and arranged English folk songs, writing works such as *Country Gardens* (1919).

Percy Grainger
1882–1961

1 The Country Garden in the English sense is not a flower garden. It is a small vegetable garden. So you can think of turnips if you like as I play it.
radio broadcast, January 1937

Percy Grainger
1882–1961

2 Anyway I thought it was better to kill him and get the song that let him live and not get the song.
on collecting a song from an elderly man too sick to sing
John Amis *A Miscellany* (1985)

Edvard Grieg
1843–1907

3 I like your fresh healthy outlook on Art, I like your unspoiled nature which not even 'High Life' has been able to corrupt, and then I like your deep feeling for folk-song and all the possibilities it carries within itself.
letter, June 1906

Hugh Grant 1960–

British actor. His films include *Four Weddings and a Funeral* and *Notting Hill*.

Elizabeth Hurley
1965–

1 Hugh has been my north, my south, my east, and my west for so long that I can't really imagine life with anyone else yet.
in 2000

Ulysses S. Grant 1822–85

American general and President 1869–77. As supreme commander of the Unionist armies, he defeated the Confederate army in 1865 with a policy of attrition.

Ulysses S. Grant
1822–85

2 A verb is anything that signifies to be; to do; to suffer. I signify all three.
Horace Green *General Grant's Last Stand* (1936)

Abraham Lincoln
1809–65

3 I can't spare this man; he fights.
J. F. C. Fuller *The Generalship of Ulysses S. Grant* (1929)

William Tecumsah Sherman
1820–91

4 [Grant] stood by me when I was crazy, and I stood by him when he was drunk; and now we stand by each other always.
of his relationship with his fellow Union commander
in 1864; Geoffrey C. Ward *The Civil War* (1991)

Robert Graves 1895–1985

English poet, novelist, and critic, known for his individualistic later work and keen interest in classics and mythology.

John Carey
1934–

1 Robert Graves was unique. He followed no fads and set no fashions. He had a mind like an alchemist's laboratory: everything that got into it came out new, weird and gleaming.
in December 1985

Alastair Reid
1926–

2 He was fond of declaring that 'he bred show dogs in order to be able to afford a cat', the dogs being prose, the cat poetry.
Whereabouts (1987)

Thomas Gray 1716–71

English poet, best known for *'Elegy Written in a Country Church-Yard'* (1751).

Thomas Gray
1716–71

1 Too poor for a bribe, and too proud to importune,
He had not the method of making a fortune.
'Sketch of his own Character' (written 1761)

Samuel Johnson
1709–84

2 He was dull in a new way, and that made many people think him *great*.
comment, March 1775

James Wolfe
1727–59

3 The General . . . repeated nearly the whole of Gray's Elegy . . . adding, as he concluded, that he would prefer being the author of that poem to the glory of beating the French to-morrow.
J. Playfair *Biographical Account of J. Robinson* (1815)

Jimmy Greaves 1940–

English footballer. He played as a striker for Chelsea, AC Milan, Tottenham Hotspur, and West Ham United and won 57 international caps. After his retirement he became a television football commentator.

Jimmy Greaves
1940–

1 My name is Jimmy Greaves. I am a professional footballer. And I am an alcoholic.
This One's On Me (1979)

Peter Greenaway 1942–

English film director. His contrived and controversial works explore sex, human mutability, and gamesmanship.

David Thomson
1941–

1 When Greenaway's camera makes its rapid, sidelong tracking movements from space to space it resembles a rat in the skirting boards, thrilled by human squalor.
on Greenaway's camera style
A Biographical Dictionary of Film (1994)

Graham Greene 1904–91

English novelist. The moral paradoxes he saw in his Roman Catholic faith underlie much of his work. Well-known works which explore religious themes include *Brighton Rock* and *The Power and the Glory*.

Muriel Spark
1918–

1 It was typical of Graham that with the monthly cheques he often sent a few bottles of red wine to 'take the edge off cold charity'.
of the financial help he gave her as a struggling writer
Alec Guinness *My Name Escapes Me* (1996)

Kenneth Tynan
1927–80

2 His talk is not so much kindly as commiserating, and his demeanour is that of a scholar at a jam session, rather than a saint in the market place.
in February 1953

Evelyn Waugh
1903–66

3 I wouldn't give up writing about God at this stage, if I was you. It would be like P. G. Wodehouse dropping Jeeves half way through the Wooster series.
Christopher Sykes *Evelyn Waugh* (1975)

Germaine Greer 1939–

Australian feminist and writer. She first achieved recognition with her influential book *The Female Eunuch* (1970).

Germaine Greer
1939–

1 Why couldn't I have a mother who was motherly instead of a frustrated pin-up?
Daddy, We Hardly Knew You (1989)

Germaine Greer
1939–

2 I haven't lost my sense of humour or my tolerance of dreadful behaviour.
on being held captive in her home by an obsessive student
in April 2000

Christina Hardyment

3 Greer is a Snow Queen, her vision forever marred by some internal splinter of glass that makes the world seem implacably hostile.
Alistair Horne (ed.) *Telling Lives: From W. B. Yeats to Bruce Chatwin* (2000)

Lady Jane Grey 1537–54

Queen of England 1553. The dying Edward VI named his cousin Jane as his successor. She was deposed after nine days and later executed.

Lady Jane Grey
1537–54

1 One of the greatest benefits that God ever gave me is that he sent me so sharp and severe parents and so gentle a schoolmaster.
Roger Ascham *The Schoolmaster* (1570)

Edvard Grieg 1843–1907

Norwegian composer, conductor, and violinist. He took much of his inspiration from Norwegian folk music. He wrote the incidental music to **Ibsen**'s play *Peer Gynt*.

Claude Debussy
1862–1918

1 One has in one's mouth the bizarre and charming taste of a pink sweet stuffed with snow.
of Grieg's music
Gil Blas (1903)

Edvard Grieg
1843–1907

2 I am sure my music has a taste of codfish in it.
speech, 1903

Franz Liszt
1811–86

3 Persevere; I tell you, you have the gifts, and—do not let them intimidate you!
attributed

George Bernard Shaw
1856–1950

4 Grieg's Peer Gynt music . . . consists of two or three catchpenny phrases served up with plenty of orchestral sugar.
in 1892

D. W. Griffith 1875–1948

American film director. A pioneer in film, he is responsible for introducing many cinematic techniques, including flashback and fade-out.

Cecil B. de Mille
1881–1959

1 Above all, he taught us how to photograph thought, not only by bringing the camera close to a player's eyes, but by such devices, novel and daring in their time, as focusing it on a pair of hands clasped in anguish or on some symbolic object that mirrored what was in the player's mind.
The Autobiography of Cecil B. DeMille (1959)

Lillian Gish
1896–1993

2 With him, we never felt that we were working for a salary. He inspired in us his belief that we were involved in a medium that was powerful enough to influence the whole world.
The Movies, Mr Griffith and Me (1969)

Hedda Hopper
1885–1966

3 His footprints were never asked for, yet no one ever filled his shoes.
From Under My Hat (1952)

Woodrow Wilson
1856–1924

4 It is like writing history with lightning.
on seeing Griffith's film The Birth of a Nation
in February 1915

Alec Guinness 1914–2000

English actor. His stage career ranged from **Shakespeare** to contemporary drama. He gave memorable performances in the films *Kind Hearts and Coronets*, *Bridge on the River Kwai*, and *Star Wars*.

Martin Bell
1938–

1 I knew when Sir Alec Guinness endorsed my campaign that the force was with us.
on winning the Tatton constituency, in May 1997

John Gielgud
1904–2000

2 Alec, dear, I just can't think why you want to play the big parts. Why don't you stick to the little people you do so well?
attributed

Alec Guinness
1914–2000

3 Essentially I'm a small-part actor who's been lucky enough to play leading roles for most of his life.
attributed

John Le Carré
1931–

4 His genuis was to propose the character, but not to shove it in your face. He almost let George Smiley lie on the printed page, and left most of him to the viewer's imagination.
in August 2000

Ronald Neame
1911–

5 He was like a chameleon—he became the character he was playing.
in August 2000

Laurence Olivier
1907–89

6 Marvellous, old cock! I never realized Malvolio could be played as a bore.
Alec Guinness *My Name Escapes Me* (1996)

Kenneth Tynan
1927–80

7 The people Guinness plays best are all ice-berg characters, nine-tenths concealed, whose fascination lies not in how they look but in how their minds work.
Alec Guinness (1961)

Woody Guthrie 1912–67

American folk singer and songwriter. His radical politics and the rural hardships of the Depression inspired many of his songs.

Woody Guthrie
1912–67

1 Left wing, chicken wing, it's all the same to me.
Joe Klein *Woody Guthrie: a life* (1980)

Woody Guthrie
1912–67

2 I ain't a communist necessarily, but I been in the red all my life.
Joe Klein *Woody Guthrie: a life* (1980)

Burl Ives
1909–95

3 He had a chip on his shoulder. His mind worked so fast that you couldn't keep up with him, and sometimes I just felt like decking him, but Woody was so small and delicate that it just didn't seem fair.
Joe Klein *Woody Guthrie: a life* (1980)

John Steinbeck
1902–68

4 Harsh voiced and nasal, his guitar hanging like a tire iron on a rusty rim, there is nothing sweet about Woody, and there is nothing sweet about the songs he sings. But there is something more important for those who will listen. There is the will of the people to endure and fight against oppression. I think we call this the American spirit.
introduction to Alan Lomax, Pete Seeger and Woody Guthrie *Hard-hitting Songs for Hard Hit People* (1962)

Nell Gwyn 1650–87

English actress. Originally an orange seller, she became famous as a comedienne at the Theatre Royal, Drury Lane, London. She was a mistress of **Charles II**.

Charles II
1630–85

1 Let not poor Nelly starve.
last words; Bishop Gilbert Burnet *History of My Own Time* (1724)

Nell Gwyn
1650–87

2 Pray, good people, be civil. I am the Protestant whore.
at Oxford, during the Popish Terror, 1681

Samuel Pepys
1633–1703

3 Pretty witty Nell.
diary, April 1665

H

Gene Hackman 1931–

American actor. He is a noted character actor.

Gene Hackman   1 I want to keep myself as common as I can, so that I can be uncommon
1931–   in my work.
interview, July 2000

William Hague 1961–

British Conservative politician, leader of the Conservative party from 1997.

Tony Banks   1 To make matters worse they have elected a foetus as party leader. I bet
1943–   a lot of them wish they had not voted against abortion now.
remark, October 1997

Tony Blair   2 Mr Hague may be good at telling jokes, but every time you come to a
1953–   critical question of judgement like this he gets it wrong.
*on Hague's endorsement of **Jeffrey Archer** as mayoral candidate for London*
in November 1999

Neil Kinnock   3 I have a lot of sympathy with him. I too was once a young, bald Leader
1942–   of the Opposition.
in October 1999

Norman Tebbit   4 As he gets more interesting, people forget that he's bald, he's got an
1931–   unusual voice and he's small.
in June 2000

Earl Haig 1861–1928

British Field Marshal. During the First World War he served as Commander-in-Chief of British forces in France, maintaining a strategy of attrition.

Lord Beaverbrook   1 With the publication of his Private Papers in 1952, he committed
1879–1964   suicide 25 years after his death.
Men and Power (1956)

Alan Bennett   2 People always complain about muck-raking biographers saying 'Leave
1934–   us our heroes.' 'Leave us our villains' is just as important.
of an attempt to rehabilitate Haig
diary, February 1996

David Lloyd George   3 [Haig is] brilliant—to the top of his boots.
1863–1945   attributed

J. B. S. Haldane 1892–1964

Scottish mathematical biologist. As well as contributing to the development of population genetics, Haldane became well known as a popularizer of science and as an outspoken Marxist.

J. B. S. Haldane   1 My final word, before I'm done,
1892–1964   Is 'Cancer can be rather fun'.
Thanks to the nurses and Nye Bevan
The NHS is quite like heaven
Provided one confronts the tumour
With a sufficient sense of humour.
'Cancer's a Funny Thing' (1968)

Peter Medawar   2 J. B. S. Haldane, in some ways the cleverest and in others the silliest
1915–87   man I have ever known.
Memoirs of a Thinking Radish (1986)

Peter Medawar
1915–87

3 His liking and admiration for the working classes was purely notional and his colleagues soon formed the opinion that he couldn't bear the sight of them; it was the laugh of the Department when electricians whose duty it was to rewire his office demanded danger money for working in it.
Memoirs of a Thinking Radish (1986)

John Maynard Smith
1920–

4 He really was very, very clever indeed. So he made you feel stupid. He also made you feel very small and he had a very short temper, and it was rather like sitting on a landmine which was liable to blow up at any minute.
Lewis Wolpert and Alison Richards *A Passion for Science* (1988)

H. G. Wells
1866–1946

5 Einstein must have been like a gentle bright kitten trying to make friends with a child's balloon, very large and unaccountably unpuncturable.
*of **Einstein**'s meeting with Haldane*
Experiment in Autobiography (1934)

Jerry Hall 1956–

American model and actress, former wife of **Mick Jagger**.

Jerry Hall
1956–

1 My mother said it was simple to keep a man, you must be a maid in the living room, a cook in the kitchen and a whore in the bedroom. I said I'd hire the other two and take care of the bedroom bit.
in October 1985

Geri Halliwell 1972–

English pop singer. Formerly a member of the Spice Girls, known as 'Ginger Spice', she left to take up a solo career.

Geri Halliwell
1972–

1 Maybe I'm not going to be Meryl Streep, but I think I can do something honest and that the audience will leave the cinema feeling filled up.
on being an actress
in May 2000

Lady Emma Hamilton c.1765–1815

English beauty and mistress of **Lord Nelson**. She had a daughter by Nelson in 1801 and lived with him after her husband's death in 1803.

Horatio, Lord Nelson
1758–1805

1 I leave Emma Lady Hamilton, therefore, a legacy to my king and country, that they will give her an ample provision to maintain her rank in life.
will, October 1805

John Hampden 1594–1643

English politician. He opposed the policies of **Charles I** and died in a skirmish in the early stages of the Civil War.

Earl of Clarendon
1609–74

1 Without question, when he first drew the sword, he threw away the scabbard.
The History of the Rebellion (1703)

Earl of Clarendon
1609–74

2 He had a head to contrive, a tongue to persuade, and a hand to execute any mischief.
The History of the Rebellion (1703)

Lord Macaulay
1800–59

3 He knew that the essence of war is violence, and that moderation in war is imbecility.
Essays Contributed to the Edinburgh Review (1843)

Tony Hancock 1924–68

English comedian. He made his name in 1954 with the radio series *Hancock's Half Hour*, later adapted to television (1956–61). He committed suicide in 1968.

Warren Mitchell
1926–

1 Comedy comes from conflict, from hatred. Hancock hated Sid James for not recognising him as a star. In fact Hancock hated the world.
  in January 1991

George Frederick Handel 1685–1759

German-born composer and organist, resident in England from 1712. A prolific composer, he is chiefly remembered for his choral works, especially the oratorio *Messiah*.

Ludwig van
Beethoven
1770–1827

1 He was the greatest composer that ever lived. I would uncover my head, and kneel before his tomb.
  Percy M. Young *Handel* (1947)

John Byrom
1692–1763

2 Some say, that Signor Bononcini,
  Compared to Handel's a mere ninny;
  Others aver, that to him Handel
  Is scarcely fit to hold a candle.
  Strange! that such high dispute should be
  'Twixt Tweedledum and Tweedledee.
  'On the Feuds between Handel and Bononcini' (1727)

Isaac Newton
1642–1727

3 I found . . . nothing worthy to remark but the elasticity of his fingers.
  hearing Handel play
  John Hawkins *Life of Samuel Johnson* (1787)

Hannibal 247–182 BC

Carthaginian general. In the second Punic War he attacked Italy via the Alps, repeatedly defeating the Romans, but failed to take Rome itself.

Juvenal
AD c.60–c.130

1 Off you go, madman, and hurry across the horrible Alps, duly to delight schoolboys and become a subject for practising speech-making.
  Satires

Harald Hardrada 1015–1066

King of Norway from 1045. Invading England, he was defeated and killed by **Harold II** at Stamford Bridge in September 1066.

Harold II
c.1019–66

1 He will give him seven feet of English ground, or as much more as he may be taller than other men.
  King Harald's Saga (c.1260)

Keir Hardie 1856–1915

Scottish Labour politician. A miner before becoming an MP in 1892, he became the first leader of both the Independent Labour Party (1893) and the Labour Party (1906).

Keir Hardie
1856–1915

1 I am of that unfortunate class who never knew what it was to be a child in spirit. Even the memories of boyhood and young manhood are gloomy.
  Kenneth O. Morgan *Keir Hardie* (1967)

Beatrice Webb
1858–1943

2 [He] deliberately chooses this policy as the only one he can boss. His only chance of leadership lies in the creation of an organization 'agin the government'; he knows little and cares less for any constructive thought or action.
  Kitty Muggeridge and Ruth Adam *Beatrice Webb* (1967)

G. H. Hardy 1877–1947

English mathematician. A pure mathematician, he worked on analytic number theory with John Littlewood.

Graham Greene
1904–91

1 When *A Mathematician's Apology* was first published, Graham Greene in a review wrote that along with Henry James's notebooks, this was the best account of what it was like to be a *creative artist*.
C. P. Snow *Variety of Men* (1967)

G. H. Hardy
1877–1947

2 [Hardy] said, with his usual clarity, that if the word meant anything he was not a genius at all. At his best, he said, he was for a short time the fifth best pure mathematician in the world.
C. P. Snow *Variety of Men* (1967)

C. P. Snow
1905–80

3 His mind . . . was brilliant and concentrated: so much so that by his side anyone else's seemed a little muddy, a little pedestrian and confused.
Variety of Men (1967)

Thomas Hardy 1840–1928

English novelist and poet. Much of his work deals with the struggle against the indifferent force that inflicts the sufferings and ironies of life.

W. H. Auden
1907–73

4 Thomas Hardy
Was never Tardy
When summoned to fulfil
The Immanent Will.
Academic Graffiti (1971)

J. M. Barrie
1860–1937

5 Hardy could scarcely look out of the window at twilight without seeing something hitherto hidden from mortal eye.
in November 1928

G. K. Chesterton
1874–1936

6 Hardy went down to botanize in the swamp, while Meredith climbed towards the sun. Meredith became, at his best, a sort of daintily dressed Walt Whitman: Hardy became a sort of village atheist brooding and blaspheming over the village idiot.
Victorian Age in Literature (1912)

Thomas Hardy
1840–1928

7 If this sort of thing continues no more novel-writing for me. A man must be a fool to deliberately stand up and be shot at.
of a hostile review of Tess of the D'Urbervilles, *1891*
Florence Hardy *The Early Life of Thomas Hardy* (1928)

D. H. Lawrence
1885–1930

8 What a commonplace genius he has, or a genius for the commonplace, I don't know which. He doesn't rank so terribly high, really. But better than Bernard Shaw, even then.
letter, July 1928

Jean Harlow 1911–37

American film actress. **Howard Hughes**'s *Hell's Angels* (1930) launched her career, her platinum blonde hair and sex appeal bringing immediate success.

Margot Asquith
1864–1945

1 The *t* is silent, as in *Harlow*.
to Jean Harlow, who had been mispronouncing 'Margot'
T. S. Matthews *Great Tom* (1973)

George Cukor
1899–1983

2 Jean Harlow was very soft about her toughness.
Gavin Lambert *On Cukor* (1973)

Graham Greene
1904–91

3 There is no sign that her acting would ever have progressed beyond the scope of the restless shoulders and the protruberant breasts; her technique was the gangster's technique; she toted a breast like a man totes a gun.
in August 1937

Harold II c. 1019–66

King 1066. He resisted the Norse king **Harald Hardrada** at Stamford Bridge, but was killed and his army defeated by **William I** at the Battle of Hastings.

Orderic Vitalis 1 This Englishman was very tall and handsome, remarkable for his
1075–c.1142   physical strength, his courage and eloquence, his ready jests and acts of
    valour. But what were all these gifts to him without honour, which is
    the root of all good?
    Ecclesiastical History

George Harrison 1943–

English rock and pop guitarist, the lead guitarist of the Beatles. His fascination with India was reflected in the solo career that he pursued after the group's break-up in 1970.

Brian Epstein 1 He is a good listener and shows a genuine interest in the outside world.
1934–67   He wants to know and I find this an enchanting trait in a young man
    who is so successful and so rich that if he never learned anything new
    he would not suffer any loss.
    A Cellarful of Noise (1964)

John Lennon 2 I wouldn't have minded being George, the invisible man, and learning
1940–80   what he learned. Maybe it was hard for him sometimes, because Paul
    and I are such egomaniacs, but that's the game.
    in 1970

Rex Harrison 1908–90

English actor. His most famous role was as Professor Higgins in the stage and film musical *My Fair Lady*. Other films include *Blithe Spirit* and *Dr Dolittle*.

Noël Coward 3 If you weren't the finest light-comedy actor in the world next to me,
1899–1973   you'd be good for only one thing—selling cars in Great Portland Street.
    in c.1964

William Harvey 1578–1657

English physician, discoverer of the circulation of the blood.

John Aubrey 1 I have heard him say, that after his book of the *Circulation of the Blood*
1626–97   came out, that he fell mightily in his practice, and that it was believed
    by the vulgar that he was crack-brained; and all the physicians were
    against his opinion, and envied him.
    Brief Lives

Thomas Hobbes 2 He is the only man, perhaps, that ever lived to see his own doctrine
1588–1679   established in his life time.
    John Aubrey *Brief Lives*

Warren Hastings 1732–1818

British colonial administrator and India's first Governor General. He was later impeached for corruption but acquitted after a seven-year trial.

Lord Macaulay 1 The Chief Justice was rich, quiet, and infamous.
1800–59   *Essays Contributed to the Edinburgh Review* (1843)

Charles Haughey 1925–

Irish statesman, Taoiseach 1979–81, 1982, 1987–92.

Conor Cruise O'Brien 1 If I saw Mr Haughey buried at midnight at a crossroads, with a stake
1917–   driven through his heart—politically speaking—I should continue to
    wear a clove of garlic round my neck, just in case.
    in October 1982

Václav Havel 1936–

Czech dramatist and statesman. His plays were critical of totalitarianism and he was twice imprisoned as a dissident. He was elected president of Czechoslovakia in 1989.

Václav Havel
1936–

1 That special time caught me up in its wild vortex and—in the absence of leisure to reflect on the matter—compelled me to do what had to be done.
> on his election to the Presidency
> Summer Meditations (1992)

Franz Joseph Haydn 1732–1809

Austrian composer. A major exponent of the classical style, he taught both **Mozart** and **Beethoven**. His output was prolific, and he played a significant role in the development of the symphony.

Franz Joseph Haydn
1732–1809

1 But all the world understands my language.
> on being advised by **Mozart**, in 1790, not to visit England because he knew too little of the world and too few languages
> Rosemary Hughes Haydn (1950)

Friedrich Nietzsche
1844–1900

2 So far as genius can exist in a man who is merely virtuous, Haydn had it. He went as far as the limits that morality sets to intellect.
> The Will to Power (1888)

William Hazlitt 1778–1830

English essayist and critic. His diverse essays, collected in Table Talk (1821), were marked by a clarity and conviction which brought new vigour to English prose writing.

Samuel Taylor Coleridge
1772–1834

1 Beneath this stone does William Hazlitt lie,
Thankless of all that God or man could give.
He lived like one who never thought to die,
He died like one who dared not hope to live.
> 'Epitaph on a Bad Man'

Robert Louis Stevenson
1850–94

2 Though we are mighty fine fellows nowadays, we cannot write like Hazlitt.
> Virginibus Puerisque (1881)

William Wordsworth
1770–1850

3 He is not a proper person to be admitted into respectable society, being the most perverse and malevolent creature that ill luck has ever thrown in my way.
> letter, 1817

Seamus Heaney 1939–

Irish poet. He was born in Northern Ireland, and his early poetry reflects the rural life of his youth. In 1972 he took Irish citizenship and his poetry began to deal with wider social and cultural themes.

Gavin Ewart
1916–95

1 He's very popular among his mates.
I think I'm Auden. He thinks he's Yeats.
> 'Seamus Heaney' (1986)

Seamus Heaney
1939–

2 Don't be surprised
If I demur, for, be advised
My passport's green.
No glass of ours was ever raised
To toast The Queen.
> rebuking the editors of The Penguin Book of Contemporary British Poetry for including him among its authors
> Open Letter (1983)

Clive James
1939–

3 He looks such a woolly cuddle and sounds smoother than a pint of Guinness going down a dry throat.
> in February 1981

A. N. Wilson
1950–

4 It has to be said that if Heaney belonged to an unfashionable race—
were he a Welshman for instance—his poetry—perfectly pleasant, mild
stuff—would have been lucky to make it into the parish magazine.
in January 1997

William Randolph Hearst 1863–1951

American newspaper publisher and tycoon. His introduction of features such as large
headlines and sensational crime reporting revolutionized American journalism. He was the
model for the film *Citizen Kane*.

William Randolph Hearst
1863–1951

1 You furnish the pictures and I'll furnish the war.
*message to the artist Frederic Remington in Havana, Cuba, during the Spanish-American War
of 1898*
attributed

Edward Heath 1916–

British Conservative statesman, Prime Minister 1970–4. He negotiated Britain's entry into
the European Economic Community and faced problems caused by inflation and
widespread strikes.

Anonymous

1 Beneath that extraordinary exterior there is a little pink, quivering Ted
trying to get out.
comment of a former Cabinet colleague, in 1993; Peter Hennessy The Prime Minister: the
Office and its Holders since 1945 *(2000)*

Tony Benn
1925–

2 Ted Heath is to the left of new Labour. I told him this and he said, 'I do
wish you wouldn't say that, it annoys my colleagues.'
interview, August 2000

Edward Heath
1916–

3 Music means everything to me when I'm alone. And it's the best way of
getting that bloody man Wilson out of my hair.
James Margach The Abuse of Power *(1978)*

Douglas Hurd
1930–

4 He's an educator, Ted. If he hadn't been a politician I think he would
have been a don or a schoolmaster. He believes that people are entitled
to the truth.
interview, September 1996

Roy Jenkins
1920–

5 A great lighthouse which stands there, flashing out beams of light,
indifferent to the waves which beat against him.
in September 1990

James Margach
d. 1979

6 Power, which has the ability to mellow some of those who achieve it . . .
in Heath's case changed his personality overnight. When Prime
Minister he became authoritarian and intolerant.
The Abuse of Power *(1978)*

Yehudi Menuhin
1916–99

7 With all the respect I have for Edward Heath's integrity and
intelligence, I feel he is most fulfilled and relaxed among musicians.
Unfinished Journey *(1976)*

Margaret Thatcher
1925–

8 I'll always be fond of dear Ted, but there's no sympathy in politics.
attributed, 1975

Harold Wilson
1916–95

9 We must kick Ted in the groin. We must be rough with him.
Richard Crossman's diary, October 1969

Werner Heisenberg 1901–76

German mathematical physicist and philosopher. He developed a system of quantum
mechanics based on matrix algebra in which he stated his famous uncertainty principle.

Albert Einstein
1879–1955

1 Marvellous, what ideas the young people have these days. But I don't
believe a word of it.
of the uncertainty principle
in 1927

Joseph Heller 1923–99

American novelist. His experiences in the US air force during the Second World War inspired his best-known novel *Catch-22* (1961), an absurdist black comedy satirizing war.

Lynn Barber
1944–

1 He is one of those loud-laughing, wisecracking, back-slapping, supposedly 'jovial' characters who always, in my experience, have a heart the size of a pea.
Demon Barber (1998)

Joseph Heller
1923–99

2 When I read something saying I've not done anything as good as *Catch-22* I'm tempted to reply, 'Who has?'
in June 1993

Joseph Heller
1923–99

3 Comedy doesn't make me laugh. Tragedy does!
Lynn Barber *Demon Barber* (1998)

Lillian Hellman 1905–84

American dramatist. She was blacklisted as an alleged communist in the early 1950s.

Lillian Hellman
1905–84

1 I cannot and will not cut my conscience to fit this year's fashions.
letter, May 1952

Mary McCarthy
1912–89

2 Every word she writes is a lie, including 'and' and 'the'.
in February 1980

Robert Helpmann 1909–86

Australian ballet dancer, choreographer, director, and actor. In 1935 he began a long partnership with **Margot Fonteyn**. He was noted for his dramatic ability.

Kenneth Tynan
1927–80

1 Dancing is poetry with arms and legs, and Helpmann is dancing incarnate.
letter, December 1944

Felicia Hemans 1793–1835

English poet. She wrote many books of verse, including the poem 'Casabianca' ('The boy stood on the burning deck . . . ').

Sir Walter Scott
1771–1832

1 Too many flowers . . . too little fruit.
describing the work of Felicia Hemans
letter, July 1823

Ernest Hemingway 1899–1961

American novelist, short-story writer, and journalist. His early work reflects the disillusionment of the post-war 'lost generation', while later his theme is the strength and dignity of the human spirit.

Raymond Chandler
1888–1959

1 Having just read the admirable profile of Hemingway in the *New Yorker* I realize that I am much too clean to be a genius, much too sober to be a champ, and far, far too clumsy with a shotgun to live the good life.
Philip Durham *Down These Mean Streets a Man Must Go* (1963)

Cyril Connolly
1903–74

2 He is the bully on the Left Bank, always ready to twist the milksop's arm.
in May 1964

Marlene Dietrich
1901–92

3 He is gentle, as all real men are gentle; without tenderness, a man is uninteresting.
A. E. Hotchner *Papa Hemingway* (1966 ed.)

F. Scott Fitzgerald
1896–1940

4 Ernest's quality of a stick hardened in the fire.
letter, September 1930

Zelda Fitzgerald
1900–47

5 [*The Sun Also Rises* is about] bullfighting, bullslinging, and bull—.
Marion Meade *What Fresh Hell Is This?* (1988)

Ernest Hemingway
1899–1961

6 I started out very quiet and I beat Mr Turgenev. Then I trained hard and I beat Mr de Maupassant. I've fought two draws with Mr Stendhal, and I think I had an edge in the last one. But nobody's going to get me in any ring with Mr Tolstoy unless I'm crazy or I keep getting better.
in May 1950

Dorothy Parker
1893–1967

7 He has a capacity for enjoyment so vast that he gives away great chunks to those about him, and never even misses them . . . He can take you to a bicycle race and make it raise your hair.
in November 1929

Gertrude Stein
1874–1946

8 Anyone who marries three girls from St Louis hasn't learned much.
J. R. Mellow *Charmed Circle: Gertrude Stein and Company* (1974)

Gore Vidal
1925–

9 What other culture could have produced someone like Hemingway and *not* seen the joke?
Pink Triangle and Yellow Star (1982)

Jimi Hendrix 1942–70

American rock guitarist and singer, remembered for the flamboyance and originality of his improvisations.

Eric Clapton
1945–

1 His courage came from a fantastic conviction that everything he did was correct.
Myles Palmer (ed.) *Small Talk, Big Quotes* (1993)

Germaine Greer
1939–

2 We have lost the best rock guitarist we ever had because we did not know how to keep him.
in October 1970

Jimi Hendrix
1942–70

3 QUESTION: Do you play the guitar with your teeth?
HENDRIX: No, with my ears.
in February 1968

Jimi Hendrix
1942–70

4 I've just got to get out. Maybe to Venus or somewhere. Some place *you* won't be able to find me.
Tony Palmer *All You Need Is Love* (1976)

Ian Kilminster
1945–

5 He was the perfect gentleman. Like me. I always open doors for women. It's just good manners. With Jimi, when a woman came into the room, he'd stand up as if he'd been goosed. And this even though he was a snake for women.
interview, July 2000

Patti Smith
1946–

6 Anyway, nobody—man, woman, or horse—has topped what Jimi Hendrix has done. His gender is totally beside the point; the real question is, what planet did he come from?
in December 1975

Pete Townshend
1945–

7 It's the most psychedelic experience I ever had, going to see Hendrix play. When he started to play, something changed: colours changed, everything changed.
Charles Shaar Murray *Crosstown Traffic: Jimi Hendrix and Post-war Pop* (1989)

Henry II 1133–89

King from 1154. The first Plantagenet king, he restored order after the reigns of Stephen and Matilda. Opposition to his policies on reducing the power of the Church was led by **Thomas à Becket**.

St Bernard of Clairvaux
1090–1153

1 From the Devil he came and to the Devil he shall return.
attributed

Walter Map
c.1140–c.1209

2 He passed nights without sleep and was untiring in his activities. Whenever in his dreams passion mocked him with vain shapes, he used to curse his body, because neither toil nor fasting was able to break or weaken it. I, however, ascribe his activities not to his incontinence but to his fear of becoming too fat.
De Nugis Curialum

Henry V 1387–1422

King from 1413. He renewed the Hundred Years War soon after coming to the throne and defeated the French at Agincourt in 1415.

Michael Drayton
1563–1631

3 O when shall English men
With such acts fill a pen?
Or England breed again
Such a King Harry?
'The Ballad of Agincourt' (1606)

William Shakespeare
1564–1616

4 Cry 'God for Harry! England and Saint George!
Henry V (1599)

Henry VII 1457–1509

King from 1485. He inherited the Lancastrian claim to the throne through his mother. He defeated **Richard III** at Bosworth Field and eventually established an unchallenged Tudor dynasty.

Francis Bacon
1561–1626

5 He was a prince, sad, serious, and full of thoughts, and secret observations, and full of notes and memorials in his own hand, especially touching persons. As, who to employ, whom to reward, whom to inquire of, whom to beware of.
History of the Reign of King Henry VII (1622)

Henry VIII 1491–1547

King from 1547. Henry had six wives; he executed two and divorced two. His first divorce, from Catherine of Aragon, led to England's break with the Roman Catholic Church.

Jane Austen
1775–1817

6 Nothing can be said in his vindication, but that his abolishing Religious Houses and leaving them to the ruinous depredations of time has been of infinite use to the landscape of England in general.
The History of England (written 1791)

Erasmus
c.1469–1536

7 In the midst stood Prince Henry, who showed already something of royalty in his demeanour, in which there was a certain dignity combined with a singular courtesy.
meeting Henry aged 8 in 1499

Thomas More
1478–1535

8 Son Roper, I may tell thee I have no cause to be proud thereof, for if my head could wish him a castle in France it should not fail to go.
after the King had entertained him at Chelsea
William Roper *Life of Sir Thomas More*

Walter Raleigh
c.1552–1618

9 If all the pictures and patterns of a merciless prince were lost in the world, they might all be painted to the life, out of the story of this king.
The History of the World (1614)

Thomas Wolsey
c.1475–1530

10 He is a prince of royal courage and hath a princely heart; and rather than he will miss or want part of his appetite, he will hazard the loss of one-half of his kingdom.
comment, November 1530

Audrey Hepburn 1929–93

British actress, born in Belgium. After pursuing a career as a stage and film actress in England, she moved to Hollywood, where she starred in such films as *My Fair Lady* (1964).

Cecil Beaton
1904–80

1 A new type of beauty: huge mouth, flat Mongolian features, heavily painted eyes, a coconut coiffure, long nails without varnish, a wonderfully lithe figure, a long neck, but perhaps too scraggy.
diary, July 1953

Peter Ustinov
1921–

2 Statistics tell us that Audrey died young. What no statistics can show is that Audrey would have died young at any age.
Quotable Ustinov (1995)

Katharine Hepburn 1909–

American actress. Making her screen debut in 1932, she starred in a wide range of films, often opposite **Spencer Tracy**.

Cecil Beaton
1904–80

3 She has a face that belongs to the sea and the wind, with large rocking horse nostrils and teeth that you know just bite an apple every day.
in March 1954

John Ford
1895–1973

4 A split personality, half pagan, half puritan.
remark, c.1932

Katharine Hepburn
1909–

5 I have lived my life as a man.
looking back over her career
James Spada *More Than a Woman* (1993)

Dorothy Parker
1893–1967

6 She ran the whole gamut of the emotions from A to B.
comment at a Broadway premiere, 1933; attributed

Ginger Rogers
1911–95

7 She is snippy, you know, which is too bad. She was never on my side.
interview, December 1991

Kenneth Tynan
1927–80

8 Her vitality is deafening. If anything, she has a Huckleberry Finn complex, a sheer love of truancy, which never fails to worry those whose view of life is impaired by the grindstones in front of their noses.
in June 1952

Barbara Hepworth 1903–75

English sculptor. A pioneer of abstraction in British sculpture, she worked in wood, stone, and bronze and is noted for her simple monumental works in landscape and architectural settings.

Barbara Hepworth
1903–75

1 My left hand is my thinking hand. The right is only a motor hand.
A Pictorial Autobiography (1970)

George Herbert 1593–1633

English metaphysical poet. His poems are pervaded by simple piety and reflect his spiritual conflicts.

Seamus Heaney
1939–

1 For three centuries and more, George Herbert exemplified the body heat of a healthy Anglican life.
The Redress of Poetry (1995)

Izaak Walton
1593–1683

2 Thus he lived, and thus died like a saint, unspotted of the world, full of alms-deeds, full of humility, and all the examples of a virtuous life.
Life of George Herbert (1670)

Robert Herrick 1591–1674

English poet. He is best known for his collection *Hesperides* (1648), containing both secular and religious poems.

Elizabeth Barrett Browning
1806–61

1 The Ariel of poets, sucking 'Where the bee sucks' from the rose-heart of nature, and reproducing the fragrance idealized.
The Greek Christian Poets and the English Poets (1842)

Roy Fuller
1912–91

2 How enviable Herrick's
Fourteen hundred lyrics!
Though, as the Scot complained when they dealt him all
The trumps, a lot of them were small.
'Quatrains of an Elderly Man: Poetry and Whist'

Robert Southey
1774–1843

3 Of all our poets this man appears to have had the coarsest mind. Without being intentionally obscene, he is thoroughly filthy, and has not the slightest sense of decency.
Commonplace Book (1849–51)

Sylvia Townsend Warner
1893–1978

4 I think the most indigestible poets are the purely lyrical, poetical ones. Very few people can swallow Herrick. He is so small they bolt him in pellets.
diary, August 1929

Caroline Herschel 1750–1848

German-born astronomer. She became an assistant to her brother **William Herschel**, and made many discoveries of her own.

Fanny Burney
1752–1840

1 The comet was very small, and had nothing grand or striking in its appearance; but it is the first lady's comet, and I was very desirous to see it.
diary, 1786

Caroline Herschel
1750–1848

2 You see, sir, I do own myself to be vain, because I would not wish to be singular; and was there ever a woman without vanity? or a man either? only with this difference that among gentlemen the commodity is generally styled ambition.
in September 1798

John Herschel 1792–1871

English astronomer and physicist, son of **William Herschel**. He extended the sky survey to the southern hemisphere, carried out pioneering work in photography.

John Herschel
1792–1871

3 *Light* was my first love!
Sylvia Wolf *Julia Margaret Cameron's Women* (1999)

William Herschel 1738–1822

German-born British astronomer. His cataloguing of the skies resulted in the discovery of the planet Uranus. He was the first to appreciate the great remoteness of stars.

Fanny Burney
1752–1840

4 The King has not a happier subject than this man, who owes wholly to His Majesty that he is not wretched: for such was his eagerness to quit all other pursuits to follow astronomy solely, that he was in danger of ruin, when his talents, and great and uncommon genius, attracted the King's patronage.
diary, 1786

Horace Walpole
1717–97

5 Oh, I must stop: I shall turn my own brain, which, while it is launching into an ocean of universes, is still admiring pismire Herschel. That he should have a *wise* look does not surprise me—he may be stupified by his own discoveries.
letter, September 1787

Lord Hervey 1696–1743

English politician and writer. He was satirized by **Alexander Pope** with increasing bitterness.

Lord Hervey
1696–1743

1 I am fit for nothing but to carry candles and set chairs all my life.
letter to Robert Walpole, 1737

Alexander Pope
1688–1744

2 A cherub's face, a reptile all the rest.
'An Epistle to Dr Arbuthnot' (1735)

Michael Heseltine 1933–

British Conservative politician. He was thought to be instrumental in the defeat of **Margaret Thatcher** in 1990, but failed to succeed her.

Gordon Brown
1951–

1 The tiger, once the king of the jungle, now just the fireside rug, decorative and ostentatious certainly, but there essentially to be walked all over.
in July 1992

Julian Critchley
1930–2000

2 He could not see a parapet without ducking beneath it.
Heseltine (1987)

Michael Jopling
1930–

3 The trouble with Michael is that he had to buy all his furniture.
Alan Clark's diary, June 1987

Neil Kinnock
1942–

4 If I was in the gutter, which I ain't, he'd still be looking up at me from the sewer.
Robert Harris *The Making of Neil Kinnock* (1984); see **Kinnock 1**

Norman Tebbit
1931–

5 I have always called him a one-ball juggler, and a good politician really has to be a multi-ball juggler, and to be Prime Minister you have to be a six, eight, or ten-ball juggler, and Michael's not that.
in September 2000

Rudolf Hess 1894–1987

German Nazi politician. In 1941 he secretly parachuted into Scotland to negotiate peace with Britain. At the Nuremberg war trials he was sentenced to life imprisonment in Berlin, where he died.

Winston Churchill
1874–1965

1 He is the maggot in the Nazi apple.
Guy Eden *Portrait of Churchill* (1945)

John Hewson 1946–

Australian Liberal politician. Before entering politics he was an economist.

Paul Keating
1944–

1 This little flower, this delicate little beauty, this cream puff, is supposed to be beyond personal criticism . . . He is simply a shiver looking for a spine to run up.
attributed

Alex 'Hurricane' Higgins 1949–

Northern Irish snooker player, World Champion in 1972 and 1982.

Steve Davis
1957–

1 A lot of people are using two-piece cues nowadays. Alex Higgins hasn't got one, because they don't come with instructions.
attributed

Clive James
1939–

2 He smokes the way he plays—as if there was not only no tomorrow, but hardly anything left of today. With adrenalin instead of blood, and dynamite instead of adrenalin, he sprints around the table, mowing down the referee.
in May 1980

Jimmy Hill

English footballer and football commentator.

Tommy Docherty
1928–

1 Jimmy Hill is to football what King Herod was to babysitting.
interview, June 1992

Nicholas Hilliard 1547–1619

English miniaturist.

John Donne
1572–1631

1   A hand or eye
By Hilliard drawn is worth an history
By a worse painter made.
'The Storm'

Paul Hindemith 1895–1963

German composer. A leading figure in the neoclassical trend which began in the 1920s, he believed that music should have a social purpose.

Joseph Goebbels
1897–1945

1 Purely German his blood may be, but this only provides drastic confirmation of how deeply the Jewish intellectual infection has eaten into the body of our own people.
speech, 1934

Paul Hindemith
1895–1963

2 I am gradually beginning to feel like a cornerstone on which every passerby can pass the water of his artistic opinion.
letter, 1946

Damien Hirst 1965–

English artist. His more controversial works have included the use of dead animals.

Damien Hirst
1965–

1 It's amazing what you can do with an E in A-level art, twisted imagination and a chainsaw.
after winning the 1995 Turner Prize
in December 1995

Alfred Hitchcock 1899–1980

English film director. He moved to Hollywood in 1939. Among his later works, notable for their suspense and their technical ingenuity, are the thrillers *Strangers on a Train*, *Psycho*, and *The Birds*.

Tippi Hedren
1935–

1 [Alfred Hitchcock] thought of himself as looking like Cary Grant. That's tough, to think of yourself one way and look another.
interview in California, 1982

Alfred Hitchcock
1899–1980

2 If I made Cinderella, the audience would immediately be looking for a body in the coach.
in June 1956

François Truffaut
1932–84

3 Hitchcock filmed scenes of murder as if they were love scenes, and love scenes as if they were murder.
Donald Spoto *The Art of Alfred Hitchcock* (1992)

Adolf Hitler 1889–1945

Austrian-born Nazi leader. He became Chancellor of Germany in 1933. His expansionist foreign policy precipitated the Second World War, while his fanatical anti-Semitism led to the Holocaust.

Vernon Bartlett
1894–1983

1 I, and many others who had interviews with him, were at first impressed by his sincerity, and later realized that he was sincere only in his belief that he was destined to rule the world.
I Know What I Liked (1974)

Frank Buchman
1878–1961

2 I thank heaven for a man like Adolf Hitler, who built a front line of defence against the anti-Christ of Communism.

in August 1936

Albert Camus
1913–60

3 It is true that this man was nothing but an elemental force in motion, directed and made more effective by extreme cunning and by a relentless tactical clairvoyance . . . Hitler was history in its purest form.

The Rebel (1951)

Winston Churchill
1874–1965

4 A monster of wickedness, insatiable in his lust for blood and plunder . . . this bloodthirsty guttersnipe.

radio broadcast, June 1941

Albert Einstein
1879–1955

5 A man with limited intellectual abilities and unfit for any useful work, bursting with envy and bitterness against all whom circumstance and nature had favoured over him.

unpublished manuscript, 1935

Joseph Goebbels
1897–1945

6 This man's got everything to be king. The born popular leader! The coming dictator.

diary, November 1925

Paul von Hindenburg
1847–1934

7 That man for a Chancellor? I'll make him a postmaster and he can lick the stamps with my head on them.

to Meissner, August 1932

Adolf Hitler
1889–1945

8 I go the way that Providence dictates with the assurance of a sleepwalker.

speech in Munich, March 1936

William Morris Hughes
1862–1952

9 If you paved the way from here to Broken Hill with Bibles, and if that man Hitler swore an oath on every one of them, I wouldn't believe a goddam bloody word he said.

John Thompson On Lips of Living Men (1962)

Lord Jakobovits
1921–

10 Silence, indifference and inaction were Hitler's principal allies.

in December 1989

Diana Mosley
1910–

11 Hitler was extremely clever, incredibly frank, and wonderful, charming. We were very great friends.

in November 2000

A. J. Muste
1885–1967

12 If I can't love Hitler, I can't love at all.

at a Quaker meeting, 1940

George Orwell
1903–50

13 I have reflected that I would certainly kill him if I could get within reach of him, but that I could feel no personal animosity. The fact is that there is something deeply appealing about him.

Collected Essays, Journalism and Letters (1968)

Ezra Pound
1885–1972

14 Adolf Hitler was a Jeanne d'Arc, a saint. He was a martyr. Like many martyrs, he held extreme views.

interview, May 1945

John Simon
1873–1954

15 If Joan of Arc had been born in Austria and worn a moustache, she might have conveyed much the same impression.

on meeting Hitler for the first time
letter March 1935

A. J. P. Taylor
1906–90

16 A racing tipster who only reached Hitler's level of accuracy would not do well for his clients.

The Origins of the Second World War (1961)

Leon Trotsky
1879–1940

17 Anyone who expects to meet a lunatic brandishing a hatchet and instead finds a man hiding a revolver in his trouser pocket is bound to feel relieved. But that doesn't prevent a revolver from being more dangerous than a hatchet.

in 1933

Wilhelm II
1859–1941

18 The machine is running away with *him* as it ran away with *me*.

remark, August 1939

Thomas Hobbes 1588–1679

English philosopher. Hobbes was a materialist, claiming that there was no more to the mind than the physical motions discovered by science.

John Aubrey
1626–97

1 His extraordinary timorousness Mr Hobbes doth very ingeniosely confess and attributes it to the influence of his mother's dread of the Spanish invasion in 88, she being then with child of him.
   Brief Lives

John Aubrey
1626–97

2 The wits at court were wont to bait him, but he feared none of them, and would make his part good. The king called him *the bear*; 'here comes the bear to be baited.'
   Brief Lives

William Hazlitt
1778–1830

3 His strong mind and body appear to have resisted all impressions but those which were derived from the downright blows of matter: all his ideas seemed to lie like substances in his brain: what was not a solid, tangible, distinct, palpable object was to him nothing.
   lecture, 1813

Harold Laski
1893–1950

4 I read Hobbes again with a hopelesss sense of despairing infirmity. The others in English theory I would have a shot at equalling, but that old rascal leaves me with a sense of how high above all others he is.
   letter, January 1919

Jonathan Swift
1667–1745

5 Hobbes clearly proves, that every creature
   Lives in a state of war by nature.
   'On Poetry' (1733)

Jack Hobbs 1882–1963

English cricketer. During his career (1905–1934) he scored 61,237 runs and 197 centuries, and made 61 test appearances for England.

John Arlott
1914–91

1 Others scored faster; hit the ball harder; more obviously murdered bowling. No one else, though, ever batted with more consummate skill than his, which was based essentially on an infallible sympathy with the bowled ball.
   Jack Hobbs: Profile of 'The Master' (1982)

David Hockney 1937–

English painter and draughtsman. He is best known for his association with pop art and for his Californian work of the mid 1960s, which depicts flat, almost shadowless architecture, lawns, and swimming pools.

Cecil Beaton
1904–80

1 He is never blasé; never takes anything for granted. Life is a delightful wonderland for him; much of the time he is wreathed in smiles.
   diary, 1969

John Gielgud
1904–2000

2 David Hockney did a drawing of me when I was 70 and I thought that if I really looked like that, I must kill myself tomorrow.
   attributed

David Hockney
1937–

3 I've got Bradford; they'll never take that away from me.
   on his roots
   Lynn Barber *Demon Barber* (1998)

Glenn Hoddle 1957–

English football player and manager. A former international, Hoddle's career as manager of England ended after he made remarks about the disabled.

Danny Blanchflower
1926–93

1 Hoddle a luxury? It's the bad players who are a luxury.
   in 1981

David Blunkett
1947–

2 If Hoddle is right, I must have been a failed football coach in a previous incarnation.
following Hoddle's remarks on disability
in January 1999

Dorothy Hodgkin 1910–94

British chemist. She applied the X-ray diffraction technique to complex organic compounds and determined the structures of penicillin, vitamin B_{12}, and insulin.

Dorothy Hodgkin
1910–94

1 I'm really an experimentalist. I used to say, I think with my hands. I just like manipulation. I began to like it as a child and it's continued to be a pleasure.
Lewis Wolpert and Alison Richards *A Passion for Science* (1988)

William Hogarth 1697–1764

English painter and engraver. Notable works include his series of engravings on 'modern moral subjects', such as *A Rake's Progress*, which satirized the vices of both high and low life in 18th-century England.

David Garrick
1717–79

1 Farewell, great painter of mankind!
Who reached the noblest point of art,
Whose pictured morals charm the mind
And through the eye correct the heart.
monument in Chiswick churchyard (1772)

Charles Lamb
1775–1834

2 Other pictures we look at—his prints we read.
Essays and Sketches 'On the Genius and Character of Hogarth' (1811)

James Hogg 1770–1835

Scottish poet. A shepherd in the Ettrick Forest whose poetic talent was discovered by **Sir Walter Scott**.

Lord Byron
1788–1824

1 The said Hogg is a strange being, but of great, though uncouth, powers. I think very highly of him, as a poet; but he, and half of these Scotch and Lake troubadours, are spoilt by living in little circles and petty societies.
letter, August 1814

Sir Walter Scott
1771–1832

2 The poor fellow has just talent enough to spoil him for his own trade without having enough to support him by literature.
letter, August 1810

Sir Walter Scott
1771–1832

3 The honest grunter.
diary, December 1825

Hans Holbein 1497–1543

German painter and engraver. He became a well-known court portraitist in England and was commissioned by **Henry VIII** to supply portraits of the king's prospective brides.

Nicholas Hilliard
1547–1619

1 The most excellent painter and limner . . . the greatest master truly in both those arts after the life that ever was.
Derek Wilson *Hans Holbein: Portrait of an Unknown Man* (1996)

Michael Holding 1954–

West Indian cricketer, a fast bowler.

Dickie Bird
1933–

1 You can hear most bowlers pounding up, grunting and snorting. But often I'd stand there when Michael was bowling my end and wonder where he had got to. And then he'd flow past me like a ghost.
Michael Parkinson *Sporting Profiles* (1995)

Billie Holiday 1915–59

American jazz singer. She began her recording career with Benny Goodman's band in 1933, going on to perform with many small jazz groups.

Miles Davis
1926–91

1 She doesn't need any horns. She sounds like one anyway.
   Nat Hentoff *Jazz Is* (1978)

Billie Holiday
1915–59

2 The stuff they wrote about me in Europe made me feel alive. Over here some damn body is always trying to embalm me. I'm always making a comeback, but nobody ever tells me where I've been.
   Lady Sings the Blues (1956, with William Duffy)

Billie Holiday
1915–59

3 You can be up to your boobies in white satin, with gardenias in your hair and no sugar cane for miles, but you can still be working on a plantation.
   Lady Sings the Blues (1956, with William Duffy)

Buddy Holly 1936–59

American rock-and-roll singer, guitarist, and songwriter. He recorded such hits as 'That'll be the Day' with his band, The Crickets, before going solo in 1958. He was killed in an aircraft crash.

Don McLean
1945–

1 Something touched me deep inside
   The day the music died.
   on the death of Buddy Holly
   'American Pie' (1972 song)

Alec Douglas-Home, Lord Home 1903–95

British Conservative statesman, Prime Minister 1963–4. He relinquished his hereditary peerage to become Prime Minister.

Cyril Connolly
1903–74

1 In the eighteenth century he would have become Prime Minister before he was thirty; as it was he appeared honourably ineligible for the struggle of life.
   Enemies of Promise (1938)

Peter Hennessy
1947–

2 He was like the very last of the steam locomotives which were on their twilight journeys at exactly this time. Perhaps he was a kind of human Coronation Scot. Or more likely, given his country pursuits, he was 'Mallard', pulling one last express from King's Cross to Edinburgh and sounding its distinctive whistle in a plaintive farewell as it crossed the Royal Border Bridge above the River Tweed at Berwick.
   The Prime Minister: the Office and its Holders since 1945 (2000)

**Alec Douglas-Home,
Lord Home**
1903–95

3 When I have to read economic documents I have to have a box of matches and start moving them into position to simplify and illustrate the points to myself.
   in September 1962

Hugh MacDiarmid
1892–1978

4 If you ask: Do I have a personal antipathy to Sir Alec Home, I say yes I have. This campaign is a personal issue. After all, I have a personality, and Home doesn't.
   opposing Home as a Communist candidate, in October 1964

Harold Macmillan
1894–1986

5 A wonderful little man—iron painted to look like wood.
   John Gunther *Procession* (1965)

Lord Peyton
1919–

6 The great thing about Alec Home is that he was not media driven. He would have had some difficulty in spelling the word 'image'.
   in conversation, 1997

Homer 8th century BC

Greek epic poet. He is traditionally held to be the author of the *Iliad* and the *Odyssey*, though modern scholarship has revealed the place of the Homeric poems in a pre-literate oral tradition.

Anonymous
1 Seven wealthy towns contend for HOMER dead
Through which the living HOMER begged his bread.
Aesop at Tunbridge (1698)

Dante Alighieri
1265–1321
2 Homer, the sovereign poet.
Divina Commedia

Thomas Heywood
c.1574–1641
3 Seven cities warred for Homer, being dead,
Who, living, had no roof to shroud his head.
'The Hierarchy of the Blessed Angels' (1635)

Horace
65–8 BC
4 I'm aggrieved when sometimes even excellent Homer nods.
Ars Poetica

Rudyard Kipling
1865–1936
5 When 'Omer smote 'is bloomin' lyre,
He'd 'eard men sing by land an' sea;
An' what he thought 'e might require,
'E went an' took—the same as me!
'When 'Omer smote 'is bloomin' lyre' (1896)

Robert Hooke 1635–1703

English scientist. He formulated the law of elasticity and introduced the term *cell* to biology. He also invented or improved many scientific instruments and mechanical devices.

John Aubrey
1626–97
1 Now when I have said his inventive faculty is so great, you cannot imagine his memory to be excellent, for they are like two buckets, as one goes up, the other goes down. He is certainly the greatest mechanic this day in the world.
Brief Lives

Samuel Pepys
1633–1703
2 Mr Hooke, who is the most, and promises the least, of any man in the world that ever I saw.
diary, February 1664

J. Edgar Hoover 1895–1972

American lawyer and director of the FBI 1924–72. He reorganized the FBI into a scientific law-enforcement agency, but was criticized for the organization's role during the McCarthy era.

Lyndon Baines Johnson
1908–73
1 Better to have him inside the tent pissing out, than outside pissing in.
David Halberstam *The Best and the Brightest* (1972)

Bob Hope 1903–

British-born American comedian. He often adopted the character of a cowardly incompetent, cheerfully failing to become a romantic hero, as in the *Road* films (1940–62) in which he starred with **Bing Crosby** and Dorothy Lamour.

Woody Allen
1935–
1 A woman's man, a coward's coward and always brilliant.
in 1978

Bob Hope
1903–
2 Well, I'm still here.
after erroneous reports of his death, marked by tributes paid to him in Congress in June 1998

Anthony Hopkins 1937–

Welsh actor. He won an Oscar for his performance in *The Silence of the Lambs* (1991).

Lynn Barber
1944–

1 His favourite novel is *The Great Gatsby* and one can see why—like Jay Gatsby, he is someone who has concocted the externals of a life, but not the inner workings. He has succeeded in everything he set out to do, except somehow being himself.
Demon Barber (1998)

Gerard Manley Hopkins 1844–89

English poet. Becoming a Jesuit in 1868, he wrote little poetry until 1876, when a shipwreck inspired him to write 'The Wreck of the Deutschland', making use of his 'sprung rhythm' technique.

Gerard Manley
Hopkins
1844–89

2 I am surprised you should say fancy and aesthetic tastes have led me to my present state of mind; these would be better satisfied in the Church of England, for bad taste is always meeting one in the accessories of Catholicism.
on his adoption of the Catholic faith
letter to his father, October 1866

Gerard Manley
Hopkins
1844–89

3 The fine pleasure is not to do a thing but to feel that you could . . . If I could but get on, if I could but produce a work I should not mind its being buried, silenced, and going no further; but it kills me to be time's eunuch and never to beget.
letter, September 1885

Philip Larkin
1922–85

4 'The Wreck of the Deutschland' would have been markedly inferior if Hopkins had been a survivor from the passenger list.
attributed

Horace 65–8 BC

Roman poet of the Augustan period. A notable satirist and literary critic, he is best known for his *Odes*, much imitated by later ages. His other works include *Satires* and *Ars Poetica*.

W. H. Auden
1907–73

1 As I get older, and the times get gloomier and more difficult, it is to poets like Horace and Pope that I find myself more and more turning for the kind of refreshment I require.
in February 1969

Horace
65–8 BC

2 And if you include me among the lyric poets, I'll hold my head so high it'll strike the stars.
Odes

Rudyard Kipling
1865–1936

3 C—taught me to loathe Horace for two years; to forget him for twenty, and then to love him for the rest of my days and through many sleepless nights.
of his school classics master
Something of Myself (1937)

Petronius
d. AD 65

4 Horace's careful felicity.
Satyricon

A. E. Housman 1859–1936

English poet and classical scholar. He is now chiefly remembered for the poems collected in *A Shropshire Lad* (1896), a series of nostalgic verses largely based on ballad forms.

W. H. Auden
1907–73

1 To my generation, no other English poet seemed so perfectly to express the sensibility of a male adolescent.
Humphrey Carpenter *W. H. Auden* (1981)

John Carey
1934–

2 Housman was a kind of human cactus. Hard and prickly outside, and mushy in the middle, he flowered briefly and surprisingly about twice a year. The poems he produced on these rare occasions are among the most beautiful and miserable in the language.
in 1979

A. E. Housman
1859–1936

3 Cambridge has seen many strange sights. It has seen Wordsworth drunk and Porson sober. It is now destined to see a better scholar than Wordsworth and a better poet than Porson betwixt and between.
speech at University College, London, March 1911

A. E. Housman
1859–1936

4 The photograph is not quite true to my own notion of my gentleness and sweetness of nature, but neither perhaps is my external appearance.
letter, June 1922

A. E. Housman
1859–1936

5 Experience has taught me, when I am shaving of a morning, to keep watch over my thoughts, because, if a line of poetry strays into my memory, my skin bristles so that the razor ceases to act.
lecture, May 1933

Hugh Kingsmill
1889–1949

6 What still alive at twenty-two,
A clean upstanding chap like you?
Sure, if your throat 'tis hard to slit,
Slit your girl's, and swing for it.
'Two Poems, after A. E. Housman' (1933)

Philip Larkin
1922–85

7 Housman is the poet of unhappiness; no one else has reiterated his single message so plangently.
in 1979

George Orwell
1903–50

8 Housman was Masefield with a dash of Theocritus.
Inside the Whale (1940)

Ezra Pound
1885–1972

9 O woe, woe,
People are born and die,
We also shall be dead pretty soon
Therefore let us act as if we were dead already.
Mr Housman's Message (1911)

Tom Stoppard
1937–

10 Life's a curse, love's a blight, God's a blaggard, cherry blossom is quite nice.
summarizing Housman
The Invention of Love (1997)

Michael Howard 1941–

British Conservative politician. As Home Secretary 1993–7 he pursued controversial policies on prisons.

Ann Widdecombe
1947–

1 He has something of the night in him.
of Michael Howard as a contender for the Conservative leadership
in May 1997

Geoffrey Howe 1926–

British Conservative politician. His resignation speech was seen as a crucial factor in the downfall of **Margaret Thatcher**.

Denis Healey
1917–

1 Like being savaged by a dead sheep.
on being criticized by Geoffrey Howe in the House of Commons
in June 1978

Fred Hoyle 1915–

English astrophysicist and writer, one of the proponents of the steady state theory of cosmology. His later work has included the controversial suggestion that life on the earth has an extraterrestrial origin.

Fred Hoyle
1915–

1 When I was young, the old regarded me as an outrageous young fellow, and now that I'm old the young regard me as an outrageous old fellow.
   in March 1995

Howard Hughes 1905–76

American industrialist, film producer, and aviator. For the last twenty-five years of his life he lived as a recluse.

Joan Didion
1934–

1 In a nation which increasingly appears to prize social virtues, Howard Hughes remains not merely antisocial but grandly, brilliantly, surpassingly antisocial. He is the last private man, the dream we no longer admit.
   Slouching Towards Bethlehem (1968)

Ted Hughes 1930–98

English poet. His vision of the natural world as a place of violence, terror, and beauty pervades his work. He was married to **Sylvia Plath**.

David Holloway
1924–

2 As our leading nature poet, he might find some sort of inspiration from the wild life of Balmoral.
   on the appointment of Hughes as Poet Laureate, in 1984

Ted Hughes
1930–98

3 I was a post-war, utility son-in-law!
   Not quite the Frog-Prince. Maybe the Swineherd.
   Birthday Letters (1998) 'A Pink Wool Knitted Dress'

Philip Larkin
1922–85

4 We had the old crow over at Hull recently, looking like a Christmas present from Easter Island.
   letter, 1975

Laurie Lee
1914–97

5 I was an expert on badgers when he was still mewling and puking in a buzzard's nest.
   in 1960

Sylvia Plath
1932–63

6 We will publish a bookshelf of books between us before we perish! And a batch of brilliant healthy children!
   diary, 1957

Victor Hugo 1802–85

French poet, novelist, and dramatist. A leading figure of French romanticism, he brought a new freedom to French poetry. His political and social concern is shown in his novels.

Jean Cocteau
1889–1963

1 Victor Hugo was a madman who thought he was Victor Hugo.
   Opium (1930)

André Gide
1869–1951

2 Hugo—alas!
   when asked who was the greatest 19th-century poet
   Claude Martin *La Maturité d'André Gide* (1977)

Basil Hume 1923–99

English cardinal. Abbot of Ampleforth until he became Archbishop of Westminster in 1976, he pursued a course which balanced liberal and conservative wings of the Catholic church.

Basil Hume
1923–99

1 Deep down, we remain human, very human and have all the desires to love and be loved by one person . . . Every time I did a marriage, every time I see people married, I say: 'That could have been me.'
   attributed; in 1992

David Hume 1711–76

Scottish philosopher, economist, and historian. He rejected the possibility of certainty in knowledge and claimed that all the data of reason stem from experience.

David Hume
1711–76

2 I do not believe there is one Englishman in fifty, who, if he heard that I had broke my neck tonight, would not be rejoiced with it. Some hate me because I am not a Tory, some because I am not a Whig, some because I am not a Christian, and all because I am a Scotsman.

J. Y. T. Greig (ed.) *Letters of David Hume* (1932)

Adam Smith
1723–90

3 Upon the whole, I have always considered him, both in his lifetime and since his death, as approaching as nearly to the idea of a perfectly wise and virtuous man, as perhaps the nature of human frailty will permit.

letter, November 1776

John Humphrys 1943–

British broadcaster, a presenter of the *Today* programme on BBC Radio 4.

John Humphrys
1943–

1 I've got the perfect face for radio.

interview, October 2000

Leigh Hunt 1784–1859

English poet and essayist. He travelled with **Shelley** and **Byron**, and was imprisoned for his comments on **George IV**.

Lord Byron
1788–1824

1 I cannot describe to you the despairing sensation of trying to do something for a man who seems incapable or unwilling to do any thing further for himself,—at least, to the purpose. It is like pulling a man out of a river who directly throws himself in again.

letter, April 1823

Percy Bysshe Shelley
1792–1822

2 You will see Hunt—one of those happy souls
Which are the salt of the earth, and without whom
This world would smell like what it is—a tomb.

'Letter to Maria Gisborne' (1820)

Virginia Woolf
1882–1941

3 A light man, I daresay, but civilized.

diary, August 1921

William Holman Hunt 1827–1910

English painter, one of the founders of the Pre-Raphaelite Brotherhood. He painted biblical scenes with extensive use of symbolism.

Beatrix Potter
1866–1943

4 Whatever one may think of his work, one must respect the man, amongst the crowds of painters who dish off vulgar pictures to sell—Mr Millais might well remark, here is poor Hunt been seven years at his picture, and I shall finish mine in seven weeks.

diary, March 1885

Elizabeth Hurley 1965–

British model and actress.

Edwina Currie
1946–

1 What has she ever done apart from abolish cellulite? Does that deserve admiration?

in September 2000

Anna Kournikova
1981–

2 She's sooo ugly!

in 2000; see **Kournikova** 1

Geoff Hurst 1941–

English footballer, the only player ever to score three goals in a World Cup final, in 1966.

Jimmy Greaves
1940–

1 Geoff Hurst had a hammer in his left boot and good left feet are like bricks of gold.
attributed

John Huston 1906–87

American-born film director. He made his debut as a film director in 1941 with *The Maltese Falcon*, and also directed *The African Queen* and *Prizzi's Honor*.

Michael Caine
1933–

1 John had one theme, and it was attaining the impossible dream.
Lawrence Grobel *The Hustons* (1990)

Katharine Hepburn
1909–

2 That fool John. Funny as a baby's open grave.
after filming *The African Queen*; Lawrence Grobel *The Hustons* (1990)

Edna O'Brien
1932–

3 He was really a cowboy who wished he was an intellectual.
in 1982

Len Hutton 1916–90

English cricketer. He played for Yorkshire and for England, scoring a record 364 in the 1938 test against Australia and became the first professional captain of the England team.

Edmund Blunden
1896–1974

1 His body and his bat were as truly one as love itself.
Gerald Howat *Len Hutton* (1988)

Harold Pinter
1930–

2 His bat was part of his nervous system.
'Hutton and the Past' (1978)

Aldous Huxley 1894–1963

English novelist and essayist. His best-known novel is *Brave New World* (1932). In 1937 he moved to California and pursued his interests in Eastern mysticism and parapsychology, experimenting with psychedelic drugs.

Elizabeth Bowen
1899–1973

1 He is at once the truly clever person and the stupid person's idea of the clever person; he is expected to be relentless, to administer intellectual shocks.
in December 1936

**Henry ('Chips')
Channon**
1897–1958

2 I met Aldous Huxley slinking out of a bank, as if he was afraid to be seen emerging from a capitalist institution, from where he had doubtless withdrawn large sums.
diary, December 1935

G. K. Chesterton
1874–1936

3 People will call Mr Aldous Huxley a pessimist; in the sense of one who makes the worst of it. To me he is that far more gloomy character; the man who makes the best of it.
The Common Man (1950)

**Christopher
Isherwood**
1904–86

4 Stupidity afflicts him like a nasty smell—and how eagerly he sucks at the dry teats of books!
diary, January 1940

Anita Loos
1893–1981

5 The trouble with Aldous is he's a genius who just once in a while isn't very smart.
G. Carey *Anita Loos* (1988)

Bertrand Russell
1872–1970

6 You could always tell by his conversation which volume of the *Encyclopedia Britannica* he'd been reading. One day it would be Alps, Andes and Apennines, and the next it would be the Himalayas and the Hippocratic Oath.
letter, July 1965

T. H. Huxley 1825–95

English biologist. A surgeon and leading supporter of Darwinism, he coined the word *agnostic* to describe his own beliefs.

Charles Darwin
1809–82

7 My good and admirable agent for the promulgation of damnable heresies.

Adrian Desmond *Huxley: The Devil's Disciple* (1994)

T. H. Huxley
1825–95

8 Morals and religion are one wild whirl to me—of them the less said the better. In the region of the intellect alone can I find free and innocent play for such faculties as I possess.

J. MacGillivray *Narrative of the Voyage of H. M. S. Rattlesnake* (1852)

T. H. Huxley
1825–95

9 I am too much of a sceptic to deny the possibility of anything.

letter, March 1886

Henry James
1843–1916

10 Huxley is a very genial, comfortable being—yet with none of the noise and windy geniality of some folks here.

letter, March 1877

Herbert Spencer
1820–1903

11 I have sometimes described him as one who is continually taking two irons out of the fire and putting three in; and necessarily, along with the external congestion entailed, there is apt to come internal congestion.

Autobiography (1904)

Samuel Wilberforce
1805–73

12 Was it through his grandfather or his grandmother that he claimed his descent from a monkey?

addressed to Huxley in a debate on **Darwin**'s theory of evolution, June 1860

Henrik Ibsen 1828–1906

Norwegian dramatist. He is credited with being the first major dramatist to write tragedy about ordinary people in prose.

Gustav Mahler
1860–1911

1 Shakespeare is the positive, the productive; Ibsen merely analysis, negation, barrenness.

letter, June 1904

Sean O'Casey
1880–1964

2 Ibsen can sit serenely in his Doll's House, while Strindberg is battling with his heaven and his hell.

letter, August 1927

C. P. Snow
1905–80

3 The only writer of world class who seems to have had an understanding of the industrial revolution was Ibsen in his old age: and there wasn't much that old man didn't understand.

The Two Cultures and the Scientific Revolution (1959)

Ice-T 1958–

American rap musician.

Ice-T
1958–

1 When they call you articulate, that's another way of saying 'He talks good for a black guy'.

interview, in 1995

Richard Ingrams 1937–

English journalist. He was a co-founder and editor of the satirical magazine *Private Eye*.

Richard Ingrams
1937–

1 My motto is publish and be sued.
   comment, May 1977

Richard Ingrams
1937–

2 I don't trust photographers. I'm now a relaxed, contented 60-year-old, but look at my pictures and you see a crazy, bug-eyed serial killer.
   in August 1997

Henry Irving 1838–1905

English actor-manager. He managed the Lyceum Theatre from 1878 to 1902, during which period he entered into a celebrated acting partnership with **Ellen Terry**.

Peter Hall
1930–

1 Like many of us, he worked furiously in the theatre because he wished to avoid life.
   diary, August 1978

Henry James
1843–1916

2 The actor, of course, at moments presents to the eye a remarkably sinister figure. He strikes us, however, as superficial—a terrible fault for an archfiend.
   of Irving as Mephistopheles in **Goethe**'s *Faust*
   The Scenic Art (1948)

George Bernard Shaw
1856–1950

on returning his ticket for Irving's funeral:
3 Literature, alas, has no place in his death as it had no place in his life. Irving would turn in his coffin if I came, just as Shakespeare will turn in his coffin when Irving comes.
   letter, November 1905

Ellen Terry
1847–1928

4 His *self* was to him on a first night what the shell is to a lobster on dry land.
   The Story of My Life (1907)

Isabella of France 1292–1358

Wife of Edward II of England. She invaded England in 1326 with her lover Roger de Mortimer, murdering Edward and replacing him with her son, Edward III.

Thomas Gray
1716–71

1 She-wolf of France, with unrelenting fangs,
   That tear'st the bowels of thy mangled mate.
   The Bard (1757)

Christopher Isherwood 1904–86

British-born American novelist. His 1930s novels *Mr Norris Changes Trains* and *Goodbye to Berlin* (filmed as *Cabaret*, 1972) vividly portray Germany on the eve of **Hitler**'s rise to power.

Christopher
Isherwood
1904–86

1 I am a camera with its shutter open, quite passive, recording, not thinking.
   Goodbye to Berlin (1939)

Charles Ives 1874–1954

American composer, noted for his use of polyrhythms, polytonality, quarter-tones, and aleatoric techniques.

Arnold Schoenberg
1874–1951

1 He has solved the problem how to preserve one's self and to learn. He responds to negligence by contempt. He is not forced to accept praise or blame.
   H. and S. Cowell *Charles Ives and his Music* (1955)

Igor Stravinsky
1882–1971

2 This fascinating composer . . . was exploring the 1960s during the heyday of Strauss and Debussy.
   Dialogues and a Diary (1963)

J

Andrew Jackson 1767–1845

American general and Democratic statesman, President 1829–37; known as Old Hickory. He defeated a British army at New Orleans in 1815 and invaded Florida, then held by the Spanish, in 1818.

Henry Clay
1777–1852

1 [Andrew Jackson] is ignorant, passionate, hypocritical, corrupt, and easily swayed by the basest men who surround him.
letter, August 1833

Glenda Jackson 1936–

English actress and politician. After a successful film career she became a Labour MP in 1992.

Roy Hodges

2 If she'd gone into politics she'd be prime minister; if she'd gone into crime she'd be Jack the Ripper.
a husband's view
David Nathan *Glenda Jackson* (1984)

Glenda Jackson
1936–

3 When I heard the BBC was putting on a retrospective season of my films I thought, 'Oh my God, I must have died.'
David Nathan *Glenda Jackson* (1984)

Glenda Jackson
1936–

4 If I am one of Blair's babes, well I've been called a damn sight worse.
in August 1999

Trevor Nunn
1940–

5 She has a capacity for work that's phenomenal. There's immense power of concentration, a great deal of attack, thrust, determination. She searches hard. It's quite ruthless.
David Nathan *Glenda Jackson* (1984)

Janet Suzman
1939–

6 Some actors go towards the parts and transform themselves into them, becoming the characters they play. Glenda draws the role towards her and it becomes her with her silhouette, her persona. But it is the character all the same.
David Nathan *Glenda Jackson* (1984)

Michael Jackson 1958–

American singer and songwriter. Having started singing with his four brothers, as the Jackson Five, he became the most commercially successful American star of the 1980s.

Julie Burchill
1960–

7 Michael Jackson is harmless enough—that's why he's so popular—but he is not a big talent, let alone a big brain, and his attempts to recreate the perfect Disneyland childhood sometimes seem in danger of driving him mad.
Damaged Gods: Cults and Heroes Reappraised (1986)

Madonna
1958–

8 As a teenager I was a Michael Jackson wannabe. I thought to myself 'I can do everything he can do only I'm a girl'.
Mick St Michael *Madonna in Her Own Words* (1990)

Diana Ross
1944–

9 There was always an identification between Michael and me. He kind of idolized me, and he wanted to sing like me.
Gerri Hirshey *Nowhere to Run: the Story of Soul Music* (1985)

Thomas Jonathan Jackson 1824–63

American Confederate general; known as Stonewall Jackson. During the American Civil War he became the deputy of **Robert E. Lee**.

Barnard Elliott Bee
1823–61

10 There is Jackson with his Virginians, standing like a stone wall. Let us determine to die here, and we will conquer.
at the battle of Bull Run, July 1861

Ulysses S. Grant
1822–85

11 He was a gallant soldier, and a Christian gentleman.
in 1864

Robert E. Lee
1807–70

12 You are better off than I am, for while you have lost your *left*, I have lost my *right* arm.
note to Jackson when he was wounded, May 1863

Mick Jagger 1943–

English rock singer and songwriter. He formed the Rolling Stones c. 1962 with guitarist **Keith Richards**, a childhood friend.

Cecil Beaton
1904–80

1 The mouth is almost too large; he is beautiful and ugly, feminine and masculine: a rare phenomenon.
diary, March 1967

Marianne Faithfull
1946–

2 Mick's genius was in his lyrics, but his great talent has always been artifice, inflation and swagger and gradually he developed his by now well-known pneumatic personality, a flexible and cartoon-like envelope that eventually became his all-purpose self.
Faithfull (1995, with David Dalton)

Paul McCartney
1942–

3 Mick could never get totally involved with anybody or anything. He would just flit about. I don't think he was ever hooked on anything. I'm sure he's tried everything, taken what he wants and left the rest alone.
Marianne Faithfull with David Dalton *Faithfull* (1995)

George Melly
1926–

4 There is a great deal of hate in the Stones' best records. Jagger was pop's Byronic hero, its Rimbaud, its Maldoror.
Revolt into Style (1970)

George Melly
1926–

5 Surely nothing could be that funny.
on being told by Mick Jagger that his wrinkles were laughter lines
in 1994

William Rees-Mogg
1928–

6 Who breaks a butterfly on a wheel?
defending Mick Jagger after his arrest for cannabis possession
leader in *The Times* June 1967, quoting **Alexander Pope**

Muddy Waters
1915–83

7 He took my music. But he gave me my name.
Tony Palmer *All You Need Is Love* (1976)

James I 1566–1625

King of Scotland (as James VI) from 1567, and of England and Ireland from 1603; son of **Mary Queen of Scots**.

Henri IV
1553–1610

1 The wisest fool in Christendom.
attributed both to Henri IV and Sully

James I
1566–1625

2 Were I not a king, I would be a University man. And if it were so that I must be a prisoner, if I might have my wish, I would have no other prison than this library, and be chained together with these good authors.
referring to the Bodleian Library, Oxford; attributed

James II 1633–1701

King from 1685–8. Unpopular for his Catholicism, he was deposed in favour of his Protestant daughter **Mary II** and her husband **William of Orange**. He died in exile in France.

Charles II
1630–85

3 Nobody will kill me to make James king.
when urged not to expose himself to the risk of assassination by strolling in St James's Park in c.1673, perhaps apocryphal

Duchess of Orleans
1652–1722

4 Our dear King James is good and honest, but the most incompetent man I have ever seen in my life. A child of seven years would not make such silly mistakes as he does.
letter June 1692

Henry James 1843–1916

American-born British novelist and critic. His early novels, notably *The Portrait of a Lady*, deal with the relationship between European civilization and American life, while his later works depict English life.

Mrs Henry Adams
1843–85

5 He chaws more than he bites off.
letter, December 1881

Ivy Compton-Burnett
1884–1969

6 A curious talent. One has to respect him. But how one would like to give him a push.
Hilary Spurling *Secrets of a Woman's Heart: the Later Life of Ivy Compton-Burnett* (1984)

Joseph Conrad
1857–1924

7 He is never in deep gloom or in violent sunshine. But he feels deeply and vividly every delicate shade. We cannot ask for more.
letter, February 1899

T. S. Eliot
1888–1965

8 He had a mind so fine no idea could violate it.
in January 1918

Philip Guedalla
1889–1944

9 The work of Henry James has always seemed divisible by a simple dynastic arrangement into three reigns: James I, James II, and the Old Pretender.
Supers and Supermen (1920)

Henry James
1843–1916

10 I should so much have loved to be popular!
Alfred Sutro *Celebrities and Simple Souls* (1933)

W. Somerset Maugham
1874–1965

11 Poor Henry, he's spending eternity wandering round and round a stately park and the fence is just too high for him to peep over and they're having tea just too far away for him to hear what the countess is saying.
Cakes and Ale (1930)

W. Somerset Maugham
1874–1965

12 He did not live, he observed life from a window, and too often was inclined to content himself with no more than what his friends told him they saw when *they* looked out of a window.
in 1937

George Moore
1852–1933

13 The interviewer in us would like to ask Henry James why he never married; but it would be in vain to ask, so much does he write like a man to whom all action is repugnant. He confesses himself on every page, as we all do. On every page James is a prude.
Confessions of a Young Man (1888)

H. G. Wells
1866–1946

14 It is leviathan retrieving pebbles. It is a magnificent but painful hippopotamus resolved at any cost, even at the cost of its dignity, upon picking up a pea which has got into a corner of its den.
Boon (1915)

Edith Wharton
1862–1937

15 We who knew him well know how great he would have been if he had never written a line.
letter, March 1916

Oscar Wilde 16 Mr Henry James writes fiction as if it were a painful duty.
1854–1900 *Intentions* (1891)

P. D. James 1920–

English writer of detective fiction. She is noted for her novels featuring the poet-detective Adam Dalgleish.

P. D. James 17 I had an interest in death from an early age. It fascinated me. When I
1920– heard 'Humpty Dumpty sat on a wall,' I thought, 'Did he fall or was he pushed?'
in 1995

Thomas Jefferson 1743–1826

American Democratic Republican statesman, President 1801–9. He played a key role in the American leadership during the War of Independence and was the principal drafter of the Declaration of Independence (1776).

John Adams 1 You and I ought not to die before we have explained ourselves to each
1735–1826 other.
letter to Thomas Jefferson, July 1813

John F. Kennedy 2 Probably the greatest concentration of talent and genius in this house
1917–63 except for perhaps those times when Thomas Jefferson ate alone.
of a dinner for Nobel prizewinners at the White House
in April 1962

Gertrude Jekyll 1843–1932

English horticulturalist and garden designer. She designed over 300 gardens for buildings designed by **Edwin Lutyens**, promoting colour design in garden planning and 'wild' gardens.

Christopher Hussey 1 Perhaps the greatest *artist* in horticulture and garden-planting that
1899–1970 England has produced—whose influence on garden design has been as widespread as Capability Brown's in the eighteenth century.
The Life of Sir Edwin Lutyens (1953)

Gertrude Jekyll 2 I have been more or less a gardener all my life.
1843–1932 *Children and Gardens* (1908)

Edwin Lutyens 3 [The] best friend a man could ever have found.
1869–1944 Sally Festing *Gertrude Jekyll* (1991)

Russell Page 4 A dumpy figure in a heavy gardener's apron, her vitality shining from a
1906–85 face half concealed by two pairs of spectacles and a battered and yellowed straw hat.
The Education of a Gardener (1962)

Logan Pearsall Smith 5 Miss Jekyll was as ready as ever for a scrap . . . it was impossible, or
1865–1946 almost impossible, when she held a view strongly, to make her give way an inch.
Reperusals and Recollections (1936)

John Rushworth Jellicoe 1859–1935

British admiral, commander of the Grand Fleet at the Battle of Jutland, 1916.

Winston Churchill 1 Jellicoe was the only man on either side who could lose the war in an
1874–1965 afternoon.
The World Crisis (1927)

St Joan of Arc c.1412–31

French national heroine. She led the French armies in the Hundred Years War. Captured by the Burgundians, she was handed over to the English and burnt at the stake.

Christine de Pisan
c.1364–c.1430

1 She seemeth fed by that same armour's touch,
Nurtured on iron.
'O Thou! ordained Maid of very God!' (1429)

Victor Hugo
1802–85

2 The French soul is stronger than the French mind, and Voltaire shatters against Joan of Arc.
Tas de pierres (1942)

King John 1165–1216

King of England 1199–1216; known as John Lackland. He lost most of his French possessions to Philip II of France. In 1209 he was excommunicated, and in 1215 he was forced to sign Magna Carta by his barons.

A. A. Milne
1882–1956

1 King John was not a good man—
He had his little ways.
And sometimes no one spoke to him
For days and days and days.
'King John's Christmas' (1927)

Pope John XXIII 1881–1963

Italian pope. He favoured modernizing the Catholic church and encouraged moves towards ecumenism, convening the second Vatican Council.

Pope John XXIII
1881–1963

2 Anybody can be pope; the proof of this is that I have become one.
Henri Fesquet *Wit and Wisdom of Good Pope John* (1964)

Augustus John 1878–1961

Welsh painter, brother of **Gwen John**. He was noted for his portraits, particularly of prominent writers.

**Oliver St John
Gogarty**
1878–1957

3 You who revel in the quick
And are Beauty's Bolshevik;
For you know how to undress
And expose her loveliness.
'To Augustus John'

Augustus John
1878–1961

4 If it's beauty, it's love in my case.
Michael Holroyd *Augustus John* (1996)

Augustus John
1878–1961

5 In case it is one of mine.
patting children in Chelsea on the head as he passed by
Michael Holroyd *Augustus John* (1975)

W. B. Yeats
1865–1939

6 The most innocent, wicked man I have ever met.
letter, October 1907

Elton John 1947–

English pop and rock singer, pianist, and songwriter. His tribute to **Diana, Princess of Wales**, 'Candle in the Wind', became the highest-selling single in history.

Michael Jackson
1958–

7 I had to set my hair on fire to make news. You only had to get married.
wedding telegram, February 1984

Elton John
1947–

8 A review in the *Financial Times* said I was an extremely funky pub pianist. That was a good summing-up of what I am.
in September 1997

Elton John
1947–

9 When I write a song it's like a child to me.
in November 2000

Gwen John 1876–1939

Welsh painter. The sister of **Augustus John**, she settled in France and worked as **Rodin**'s model, becoming his mistress.

Augustus John
1878–1961
10 Fifty years hence I shall be remembered only as the brother of Gwen John.
in 1946

Pope John Paul II 1920–

Polish cleric, pope since 1978. The first non-Italian pope since 1522, he has travelled abroad extensively during his papacy and has upheld the Church's traditional position on many issues.

Mikhail Sergeevich Gorbachev
1931–
1 All that has happened in East Europe over these last few years would not have been possible without the presence of this Pope.
in 1992

Margaret Hebblethwaite
1951–
2 John Paul reminds me of that foot in the Monty Python series that squelches anything in sight. No one can criticise and so you get a conspiracy of silence, a silence that breeds widespread hypocrisy and promotes court flatterers.
attributed, 1995

Muriel Spark
1918–
3 I wouldn't take the Pope too seriously. He's a Pole first, a pope second, and maybe a Christian third.
in May 1989

Amy Johnson 1903–41

English aviator. In 1930 she became the first woman to fly solo to Australia. She later set records with her solo flights to Tokyo (1931) and to Cape Town (1932).

Amy Johnson
1903–41
1 Had I been a man I might have explored the Poles, or climbed Mount Everest, but as it was, my spirit found outlet in the air.
Margot Asquith (ed.) *Myself When Young* (1938)

Earvin Johnson 1959–

American basketball player; known as Magic Johnson. He played for the Los Angeles Lakers from 1979 to 1991. After being diagnosed HIV-positive he won an Olympic gold medal in 1992 and then returned to the Lakers.

Earvin Johnson
1959–
2 Magic is who I am on the basketball court. Earvin is who I am.
My Life (1992, with William Novak)

Rony Seikaly
3 The NBA players are smart enough to know you get the [Aids] virus from unprotected sex, and we're not going to have unprotected sex on the basketball court.
on the return of Johnson in February 1996

Lyndon Baines Johnson 1908–73

American Democratic statesman, President 1963–9. He continued the programme of reforming initiated by **John F. Kennedy**, but the increasing involvement of the US in the Vietnam War undermined his popularity.

Anonymous
4 Hey, hey, LBJ, how many kids did you kill today?
anti-Vietnam marching slogan, 1960s

Lyndon Baines Johnson
1908–73
5 I am a free man, an American, a United States Senator, and a Democrat, in that order.
in 1958

Peter Ustinov
1921–
6 I once wrote a short story which wasn't published because of the accusation of hitting President Johnson below the belt. It's hardly my fault if LBJ wears his belt like a crown.
Quotable Ustinov (1995)

Theodore H. White
1915–86

7 Johnson's instinct for power is as primordial as a salmon's going upstream to spawn.

The Making of the President (1964)

Samuel Johnson 1709–84

English lexicographer, writer, critic, and conversationalist. A leading figure in the literary London of his day, he is noted particularly for his *Dictionary of the English Language* (1755).

James Boswell
1740–95

8 When I put down Mr Johnson's sayings, I do not keep strictly to chronology. I am glad to collect the gold dust, as I get by degrees as much as will be an ingot.

diary, April 1775

Fanny Burney
1752–1840

9 The freedom with which Dr Johnson condemns whatever he disapproves is astonishing.

in August 1778

Thomas Carlyle
1795–1881

10 Figure him there, with his scrofulous diseases, with his great greedy heart, and unspeakable chaos of thoughts; stalking mournful as a stranger in this earth; eagerly devouring what spiritual thing he could come at: school-languages and other merely grammatical stuff, if there were nothing better! The largest soul that was in all England.

On Heroes and Hero-Worship (1841)

George Colman, the Younger
1762–1836

11 Johnson's style was grand and Gibbon's elegant; the stateliness of the former was sometimes pedantic, and the polish of the latter was occasionally finical. Johnson marched to kettle-drums and trumpets; Gibbon moved to flute and hautboys: Johnson hewed passages through the Alps, while Gibbon levelled walks through parks and gardens.

Random Records (1830)

William Cowper
1731–1800

12 Oh! I could thresh his old jacket till I made his pension jingle in his pockets.

on Johnson's inadequate treatment of Paradise Lost

letter, October 1779

Oliver Goldsmith
1728–74

13 There is no arguing with Johnson; for when his pistol misses fire, he knocks you down with the butt end of it.

comment, October 1769

Nathaniel Hawthorne
1804–64

14 Dr Johnson's morality was as English an article as a beefsteak.

Our Old Home (1863)

Samuel Johnson
1709–84

15 The black dog I hope always to resist, and in time to drive, though I am deprived of almost all those that used to help me . . . When I rise my breakfast is solitary, the black dog waits to share it, from breakfast to dinner he continues barking, except that Dr Brocklesby for a little keeps him at a distance.

on his attacks of melancholia

letter, June 1783

Mary Knowles
1733–1807

16 He gets at the substance of a book directly; he tears out the heart of it.

in April 1778

Lord Macaulay
1800–59

17 The gigantic body, the huge massy face, seamed with the scars of disease, the brown coat, the black worsted stockings, the grey wig with the scorched foretop, the dirty hands, the nails bitten and pared to the quick.

Essays Contributed to the Edinburgh Review (1843)

Samuel Parr
1747–1825

18 Ay, now that the old lion is dead, every ass thinks he may kick at him.

in December 1784

Lord Pembroke
1734–94

19 Dr Johnson's sayings would not appear so extraordinary, were it not for his bow-wow way.

in March 1775

George Bernard Shaw
1856–1950

20 I have not wasted my life trifling with literary fools in taverns as Johnson did when he should have been shaking England with the thunder of his spirit.
preface to *Misalliance* (1914)

Tobias Smollett
1721–71

21 That great Cham of literature, Samuel Johnson.
letter, March 1759

Horace Walpole
1717–97

22 It is the story of a mountebank and his zany.
of **Boswell**'s Tour of the Hebrides
letter, October 1785

Al Jolson 1886–1950

Russian-born American singer, film actor, and comedian. He appeared in the first full-length talking film, *The Jazz Singer* (1927).

George Burns
1896–1996

1 It was easy enough to make Jolson happy at home. You just had to cheer him for breakfast, applaud wildly for lunch, and give him a standing ovation for dinner.
Michael Freedland *Al Jolson* (1972)

Eddie Cantor
1892–1964

2 There was something electric about him that sent a thrill up your spine. He sang and talked; but he was more than just a singer or an actor—he was an *experience*.
Take My Life (1957)

Al Jolson
1886–1950

3 You think that's noise—you ain't heard nuttin' yet!
first said in a café, competing with the din from a neighbouring building site
in 1906; subsequently an aside in *The Jazz Singer*

Brian Jones 1942–69

British rock musician, a member of the Rolling Stones. He had severe drug problems and was found drowned in his swimming pool.

Marianne Faithfull
1946–

1 For Brian, relations with other people always took place in the extreme. The only kind of affection or friendship he could tolerate was unconditional love. From men, women, girlfriends, chauffeurs, waiters. Even with that, he could only just about cope with life. Anything less he found a bit tricky.
Faithfull (1995, with David Dalton)

Lou Reed
1944–

2 After the Beatles came the Stones and of the Stones one could never have ignored Brian Jones with his puffed-up Pisces, all-knowing, suffering fish eyes, his incredible clothes, those magnificent scarves, Brian always ahead of style, perfect Brian.
Clinton Heylin (ed.) *The Penguin Book of Rock and Roll Writing* (1992)

Grace Jones 1952–

Jamaican-born rock star.

Grace Jones
1952–

3 These are my favourite, favourite thing. If I'm depressed, if I'm feeling ill, if I'm feeling whatever, once I get my oysters, my toes start to twinkle.
interview, September 2000

Inigo Jones 1573–1652

English architect and stage designer. He introduced the Palladian style to England, and also pioneered the use of the proscenium arch and movable stage scenery.

George Chapman
c.1559–1634

4 Our only learned architect.
'The Divine Poem of Musaeus' (1616) dedication

Ben Jonson
c.1573–1637

5 Dominus do-all.
attributed

Anthony Van Dyck 1599–1641	6 Not to be equalled by whatsoever great masters in his time for boldness, softness, sweetness, and sureness of touch. John Webb *A Vindication of Stone-Heng Restored* (1665)

Tom Jones 1940–

Welsh pop singer. In 1963 he met the songwriter Gordon Mills, who promoted his powerful voice and masculine image.

Tom Jones 1940–	7 People never talked about my music. They just counted how many knickers were on the stage. in June 2000
George Melly 1926–	8 Tom Jones though was respected as a kind of latter-day Elvis and he later preserved that respect by coming on like a vulgar caricature of a show-biz success. What's more he appealed not so much to the teeny-boppers as to young housewives, a more loyal, less fickle class and sufficiently far removed from the pop world as to cause it little embarrassment. *Revolt into Style* (1970)
Scott Walker 1944–	9 Every time I hear Tom Jones I want to jump out of a window . . . I hear Tom Jones destroying a song, and yet he and I are always being compared as singers. Mike Watkinson and Pete Anderson *Scott Walker: A Deep Shade of Blue* (1994)

Vinnie Jones 1965–

Welsh footballer. He played for Wimbledon and Wales, and subsequently took up an acting career.

Vinnie Jones 1965–	10 I was born in the real world, not with a silver spoon in my mouth. If you plant a rose in the best soil it'll grow whatever you do. It's a lot harder growing in concrete, understand what I'm saying? interview, July 2000

Ben Jonson c. 1573–1637

English dramatist and poet. With his play *Every Man in his Humour* he established his 'comedy of humours', whereby each character is dominated by a particular obsession. He became the first Poet Laureate in the modern sense.

Anonymous	1 O rare Ben Jonson. inscription on the tomb of Jonson in Westminster Abbey
Nevill Coghill 1899–1980	2 The comedies of Ben Jonson are clearly no laughing matter if we compare them with Shakespeare. *Collected Papers of Nevill Coghill* (1988)
William Collins 1721–59	3 Too nicely Jonson knew the critic's part, Nature in him was almost lost in Art. 'Verses addressed to Sir Thomas Hanmer' (1743)
Michael Drayton 1563–1631	4 Next these, learn'd Jonson, in this list I bring, Who had drunk deep of the Pierian spring. 'To Henry Reynolds, of Poets and Poesy' (1627)
John Dryden 1631–1700	5 He invades authors like a monarch; and what would be theft in other poets, is only victory in him. *An Essay of Dramatic Poesy* (1668)
Craig Raine 1944–	6 Pioneer of the bizarre, racy, and often grotesque urban poetry of modern life. *Haydn and the Valve Trumpet* (1990)
Alfred, Lord Tennyson 1809–92	7 I can't read Ben Jonson, especially his comedies. To me he appears to move in a wide sea of glue. Hallam Tennyson *Alfred Lord Tennyson* (1897)

Janis Joplin 1943–70

American singer. She died from a heroin overdose just before her most successful album, *Pearl*, and her number-one single 'Me and Bobby McGee' were released.

Leonard Cohen
1934–

1 She was that good that you feel the body of work she left behind is just too brief. There are certain kinds of artist that blaze in a very bright light for a very brief time, the Rimbauds, the Shelleys, Tim Buckley, people like that. And Janis was one of them.
in 1976

Jerry Garcia
1942–95

2 It was the best possible time for her death. If you know any people who passed that point into decline . . . really getting messed up, old, senile, done in. But going up, it's like a skyrocket, and Janis was a skyrocket chick.
David Dalton *Janis: Janis Joplin* (1972)

Janis Joplin
1943–70

3 I just made love to 25,000 people, and I'm goin' home alone.
after a concert at Harvard Stadium
in August 1970

Michael Jordan 1963–

American basketball player, known as an exceptional all-rounder and nicknamed 'Air Jordan'.

Mike Tyson
1966–

1 Anyone who can fly deserves respect.
Bill Hughes and Patrick King (eds) *Come Out Writing* (1991)

Josephine 1763–1814

Empress of France 1804–9. She married **Napoleon** in 1796. Their marriage proved childless and she was divorced by Napoleon in 1809.

Napoleon I
1769–1821

1 I still love you, but in politics there is no heart, only head.
on their divorce
C. Barnett *Bonaparte* (1978)

Benjamin Jowett 1817–93

English classicist. He was Master of Balliol College, Oxford, and noted for his translations from Greek.

H. C. Beeching
1859–1919

1 First come I; my name is Jowett.
There's no knowledge but I know it.
I am Master of this college:
What I don't know isn't knowledge.
The Masque of Balliol (c.1870)

James Joyce 1882–1941

Irish writer. His novel *Ulysses* revolutionized the structure of the modern novel and developed the stream-of-consciousness technique. *Finnegans Wake* pushed linguistic experimentation to the extreme.

Samuel Beckett
1906–89

1 His writing is not about something. It is the thing itself.
Our Exagmination Round His Factification for Incamination of Work in Progress (1929)

E. M. Forster
1879–1970

2 A dogged attempt to cover the universe with mud, an inverted Victorianism, an attempt to make crossness and dirt succeed where sweetness and light failed.
of Joyce's Ulysses
Aspects of the Novel (1927)

Alec Guinness
1914–2000

3 A pornographer worthy of the name; a true artist from his head to his crotch.
A Positively Final Appearance (1999)

James Joyce
1882–1941

4 When a young man came up to him in Zurich and said, 'May I kiss the hand that wrote *Ulysses*?' Joyce replied, somewhat like King Lear, 'No, it did lots of other things too.'
Richard Ellmann *James Joyce* (1959)

D. H. Lawrence
1885–1930

5 My God, what a clumsy *olla putrida* James Joyce is! Nothing but old fags and cabbage-stumps of quotations from the Bible and the rest, stewed in the juice of deliberate, journalistic dirty-mindedness.
letter, August 1928

Harold Nicolson
1886–1968

6 [James Joyce] has the most lovely voice I know—liquid and soft with undercurrents of gurgle.
letter, February 1934

Sean O'Casey
1880–1964

7 Joyce for all his devotion to his art, terrible in its austerity, was a lad born with a song on one side of him, a dance on the other—two gay guardian angels every human ought to have.
Sunset and Evening Star (1954)

George Orwell
1903–50

8 Joyce is a poet and also an elephantine pedant.
Inside the Whale and Other Essays (1940)

George Bernard Shaw
1856–1950

9 I could not write the words Mr Joyce uses: my prudish hands would refuse to form the letters.
Table Talk of G. B. S. (1925)

Virginia Woolf
1882–1941

10 The scratching of pimples on the body of the bootboy at Claridges.
of Joyce's Ulysses
letter, April 1922

W. B. Yeats
1865–1939

11 A cruel playful mind like a great soft tiger cat—I hear, as I read, the report of the rebel sergeant in '98: 'O he was a fine fellow, a fine fellow. It was a pleasure to shoot him.'
letter, March 1922

K

Franz Kafka 1883–1924

Czech novelist, who wrote in German. His work is characterized by its portrayal of an enigmatic and nightmarish reality where the individual is perceived as lonely, perplexed, and threatened.

D. J. Enright
1920–

1 Kafka was a tough, neurasthenic unetiolated visionary who lived from the inside out, spinning his writing out of his guts.
in August 1984

Herbert von Karajan 1908–89

Austrian conductor, chiefly remembered as the principal conductor of the Berlin Philharmonic Orchestra (1955–89).

Thomas Beecham
1879–1961

1 A kind of musical Malcolm Sargent.
Harold Atkins and Archie Newman *Beecham Stories* (1978)

Anatoli Karpov 1951–

Russian chess player. He was world champion from 1975 until defeated by Gary Kasparov in 1985.

Viktor Korchnoi
1931–

1 Karpov beat me unfairly. It was the struggle of the state against the individual.
in 1979

Angelica Kaufman 1740–1807

Swiss painter. In London from 1766, she became well known for her neoclassical and allegorical paintings. She was a founder member of the Royal Academy of Arts (1768).

Johann Wolfgang von Goethe
1749–1832

1 For a woman, she has extraordinary talent. One must look for what she does, not what she fails to do.
Italian Journey (1816–7)

Edmund Kean 1787–1833

English actor, renowned for his interpretations of Shakespearean tragic roles, notably those of Macbeth and Iago.

Samuel Taylor Coleridge
1772–1834

1 To see him act, is like reading Shakespeare by flashes of lightning.
in April 1823

William Hazlitt
1778–1830

2 There is in Mr Kean, an infinite variety of talent, with a certain monotony of genius.
in December 1815

Paul Keating 1944–

Australian Labor statesman, Prime Minister 1991–96. His term of office was notable for a vociferous republican campaign.

Conrad Black
1944–

1 The king of all larrikins, a coarse autodidact with a wicked wit and a tongue that could clip a hedge, he was decisive, cunning, extremely knowledgeable and an unforgettable raconteur. Even now, after all he put us to, I find it a little hard not to like him.
in December 1996

John Hewson
1946–

2 I decided the worst thing you can call Paul Keating, quite frankly, is Paul Keating.
Michael Gordon *A Question of Leadership* (1993)

Paul Keating
1944–

3 I'm a bastard. But I'm a bastard who gets the mail through. And they appreciate that.
in 1994, to a senior colleague

John Keats 1795–1821

English poet. Particularly noted for his contemplation of beauty, he wrote all of his most famous poems, including 'La Belle Dame sans Merci', 'Ode to a Nightingale', and 'Ode on a Grecian Urn', in 1818.

Elizabeth Bishop
1911–79

1 Except for his unpleasant emphasis on the *palate*, he strikes me as almost everything a poet should have been in his day.
letter, March 1959

Lord Byron
1788–1824

2 Such writing is a sort of mental masturbation—he is always f—gg—g his *imagination*.—I don't mean that he is indecent but viciously soliciting his own ideas into a state which is neither poetry nor any thing else but a Bedlam vision produced by raw pork and opium.
letter, November 1820

Lord Byron
1788–1824

3 'Tis strange the mind, that very fiery particle,
Should let itself be snuffed out by an article.
on Keats 'who was killed off by one critique'
Don Juan (1819–24)

Thomas Carlyle
1795–1881

4 Keats is a miserable creature, hungering after sweets which he can't get; going about saying, 'I am so hungry; I should so like something pleasant!'
Wemyss Reid *Life of Richard Monckton Milnes* (1891)

F. Scott Fitzgerald 1896–1940	5 For awhile after you quit Keats all other poetry seems to be only whistling or humming. letter, August 1940
Robert Graves 1895–1985	6 He reversed the traditional metaphor by making Poetry, as a dominant female, pursue the shrinking, womanish poet with masculine lustfulness. attributed
John Keats 1795–1821	7 I do think better of womankind than to suppose they care whether Mister John Keats five feet high likes them or not. letter, July 1818
John Keats 1795–1821	8 'If I should die,' said I to myself, 'I have left no immortal work behind me—nothing to make my friends proud of my memory—but I have loved the principle of beauty in all things, and if I had had time I would have made myself remembered.' letter, 1820
John Keats 1795–1821	9 Here lies one whose name was writ in water. epitaph for himself; Richard Monckton Milnes *Life, Letters and Literary Remains of John Keats* (1848)
John Gibson Lockhart 1794–1854	10 It is a better and a wiser thing to be a starved apothecary than a starved poet; so back to the shop Mr John, back to 'plasters, pills, and ointment boxes.' *reviewing Keats's* Endymion in August 1818
Percy Bysshe Shelley 1792–1822	11 I weep for Adonais—he is dead! O, weep for Adonais! though our tears Thaw not the frost which binds so dear a head! *Adonais* (1821)
W. B. Yeats 1865–1939	12 I see a schoolboy when I think of him With face and nose pressed to a sweet-shop window. 'Ego Dominus Tuus' (1917)

John Keble 1792–1866

English churchman. His sermon on national apostasy (1833) is generally held to mark the beginning of the Oxford Movement, which he founded with **John Henry Newman** and Edward Pusey.

John Keble 1792–1866	1 If the Church of England were to fail, it would be found in my parish. D. Newsome *The Parting of Friends* (1966)

Kevin Keegan 1951–

English footballer and manager. He played as an attacker for clubs including Liverpool and Hamburg, and played for England 1972–82. He managed Newcastle United and England.

Lawrie McMenemy	1 Kevin Keegan is so famous that when we were in the Casbah even the blind men were calling out his name. in 1983

Helen Keller 1880–1968

American writer and social reformer. Blind and deaf from the age of 19 months, she learned how to read, type, and speak with the help of a tutor.

Helen Keller 1880–1968	1 The mystery of language was revealed to me. I knew then that 'w-a-t-e-r' meant the wonderful cool something that was flowing over my hand. That living word awakened my soul, gave it light, joy, set it free! *The Story of My Life* (1902)

Gene Kelly 1912–96

American dancer and choreographer. He performed in and choreographed many film musicals, including *An American in Paris* and *Singin' in the Rain*.

Anonymous 1 A woman might give her heart and soul to Fred Astaire but she saves her body for Gene Kelly.

comment of a young film student at UCLA; Sheridan Morley and Ruth Leon *Gene Kelly: A Celebration* (1996)

Bob Hope 2 Every time Gene Kelly starts dancing, Fred Astaire starts counting his
1903– money.
attributed

Gene Kelly 3 If Fred Astaire is the Cary Grant of dance, I'm the Marlon Brando.
1912–96 attributed

John Updike 4 We still think of Gene Kelly as a guy in loafers and a tight T-shirt, tap-
1932– dancing up a storm all by his lonesome.
in August 1994

Grace Kelly 1928–82

American film actress. She starred in *High Noon* and also made three Hitchcock films, before retiring from films in 1956 on her marriage to Prince Rainier III of Monaco.

Cary Grant 5 Grace acted the way Johnny Weissmuller swam or Fred Astaire danced.
1904–86 She made it look so easy. Some people said that Grace was just being herself. Well, that's the toughest thing to do if you're an actor.
Robert Lacey *Grace* (1994)

Pete Martin 6 Writing about her is like trying to wrap up 115 pounds of smoke.
1901– attributed

Barry Norman 7 She had a quality that is much more important in the cinema than
1933– acting ability. She was, and remains, totally memorable.
in October 1998

James Stewart 8 If you ever played a love scene with her, you'd know she's not cold.
1908–97 Robert Lacey *Grace* (1994)

Lord Kelvin 1824–1907

British physicist and natural philosopher. He is best known for introducing the absolute scale of temperature.

J. J. Thomson 1 His mind was extraordinarily fertile in ideas . . . Even in a lecture, if a
1856–1940 new idea occurred to him, he would start off on a new tack. This made him very discursive and often very lengthy . . . He has been known to have lectured for the hour before reaching the subject of his lecture.
Recollections and Reflections (1936)

John Philip Kemble 1757–1823

English actor-manager, brother of **Sarah Siddons**. Noted for his performances in Shakespearean tragedy, he was manager of Drury Lane and Covent Garden theatres.

William Hazlitt 1 He is the very still life and statuary of the stage; a perfect figure of a
1778–1830 man; a petrification of sentiment, that heaves no sigh and sheds no tear; an icicle upon the bust of tragedy.
in May 1816

Edward 'Teddy' Kennedy 1932–

American Democratic politician. His political career has been overshadowed by his
involvement in a car accident at Chappaquiddick Island (1969), in which his assistant Mary
Jo Kopechne drowned.

Rose Kennedy   1 Now Teddy must run.
1890–1995
to her daughter, on hearing of the assassination of **Robert Kennedy**
attributed, perhaps apocryphal

when asked if she were happy that Edward Kennedy had withdrawn from the Presidential race:

Rose Kennedy   2 If my sons are born to be murdered, they might as well be President
1890–1995   first.
Fleur Cowles *She Made Friends and Kept Them* (1996)

John F. Kennedy 1917–63

American Democratic statesman, President 1961–3. A popular advocate of civil rights, he
was assassinated in Dallas, Texas.

Violet Bonham-Carter   3 My impression was of a man well over life-size with power in reserve—
1887–1969   who carried the world on his shoulders with buoyancy and gaiety and
without a trace of self-importance or swollen head.
diary, May 1963

Fidel Castro   4 Kennedy was an intelligent bandit, while Johnson is a mediocre bandit.
1927–   in 1966

Frederick Forsyth   5 Everyone seems to remember with great clarity what they were doing
1938–   on November 22nd, 1963, at the precise moment they heard President
Kennedy was dead.
The Odessa File (1972)

Eric Hobsbawm   6 The most overrated US president of the century.
1917–   *Age of Extremes* (1994)

Bob Hope   7 I must say the Senator's victory in Wisconsin was a triumph for
1903–   democracy. It proves that a millionaire has just as good a chance as
anybody else.
in 1960; William Robert Faith *Bob Hope* (1983)

Lyndon Baines   8 He never said a word of importance in the Senate and he never did a
Johnson   thing. But somehow he managed to create the image of himself as a
1908–73   shining intellectual, a youthful leader who would change the face of
the country.
Robert Dallek *Flawed Giant* (1998)

Lyndon Baines   9 The enviably attractive nephew who sings an Irish ballad for the
Johnson   company then winsomely disappears before the table-clearing and dish-
1908–73   washing begin.
Matthew Parris *Scorn* (1994)

John F. Kennedy   10 It was involuntary. They sank my boat.
1917–63   *on being asked how he became a war hero*
Arthur M. Schlesinger Jr. *A Thousand Days* (1965)

Joseph P. Kennedy   11 We're going to sell Jack like soapflakes.
1888–1969   *when his son John made his bid for the Presidency*
John H. Davis *The Kennedy Clan* (1984)

Harold Macmillan   12 A sort of Duke of Wellington of America.
1894–1986   Nigel Fisher *Harold Macmillan* (1982)

Jacqueline Kennedy   13 The lines he loved to hear were: 'Don't let it be forgot, that once there
Onassis   was a spot, for one brief shining moment that was known as Camelot.'
1929–94   . . . There'll be great Presidents again . . . but there'll never be another
Camelot again.
quoting Alan Jay Lerner, in December 1963

P. J. O'Rourke
1947–

14 We have no one to blame for the Kennedys but ourselves. We took the Kennedys to heart of our own accord. And it is my opinion that we did it not because we respected them or thought what they proposed was good, but because they were pretty.
Give War a Chance (1992)

Adlai Stevenson
1900–65

15 Do you remember that in classical times when Cicero had finished speaking, the people said, 'How well he spoke', but when Demosthenes had finished speaking, they said, 'Let us march.'
introducing Kennedy in 1960; Bert Cochran *Adlai Stevenson* (1969)

Nigel Kennedy 1956–

English violinist. His punk image contrasted with his early successful classical career.

Nigel Kennedy
1956–

16 I suppose I've devoted myself unconditionally to the violin and the music . . . I know the violin is going to be there so any relationship which has finished, I've still got the music. A lot of my emotional needs are met by the violin.
Anthony Clare *In the Psychiatrist's Chair III* (1998)

Yehudi Menuhin
1916–99

17 Classical music has suffered at the hands of the dogmatic and the mechanical; young musicians need to be able to rediscover spontaneous expressiveness and poetry. Nigel Kennedy became a sensation because the world of classical music had not before experienced a musician of that type.
Unfinished Journey (1976)

Robert Kennedy 1925–68

American Democratic politician. He closely assisted his brother **John F. Kennedy** in domestic policy. He was assassinated during his campaign for the presidential nomination.

Alice Roosevelt Longworth
1884–1980

18 I see Jack in older years as the nice rosy-faced old Irishman with the clay pipe in his mouth, a rather nice broth of a boy. Not Bobby. Bobby could have been a revolutionary priest.
Jean Stein *American Journey: The Times of Robert Kennedy* (1970)

Gore Vidal
1925–

19 His obvious characteristics are energy, vindictiveness, and simple mindedness about human motives which may yet bring him down. To Bobby the world is black or white. Them and Us. He has none of his brother's human ease or charity.
in March 1963

Rose Kennedy 1890–1995

American wife of Joseph P. Kennedy, mother of the American politicians **John**, **Robert**, and **Edward Kennedy**.

Rose Kennedy
1890–1995

20 I would much rather be known as the mother of a great son than the author of a great book or the painter of a great masterpiece.
attributed

Johannes Kepler 1571–1630

German astronomer. His analysis of Tycho Brahe's planetary observations led him to discover the three laws governing orbital motion.

Albert Einstein
1879–1955

1 Kepler was one of the few who are simply incapable of doing anything but stand up openly for their convictions in every field . . . [His] lifework was possible only once he succeeded in freeing himself to a great extent from the intellectual traditions into which he was born.
introduction to Carola Baumgardt *Johannes Kepler: life and letters* (1952)

Galileo Galilei
1564–1642

2 I should indeed dare to bring forward my speculations, if there were many like you; but since there are not, I shrink from a subject of this description.
letter to Kepler, 1597

Alice Keppel 1868–1947

English society hostess, mistress of **Edward VII**.

James Lees-Milne
1908–97

1 Old Mrs Keppel has died. It was curious to see that little, bent old woman scuttling about the Ritz this year, with the white face of a grey mare, and to know that she was King Edward VII's magnificent, upstanding, beautiful, powerful mistress.
diary, September 1947

Jerome Kern 1885–1945

American composer. A major influence in the development of the musical, he wrote several musical comedies, including *Showboat* (1927).

Jerome Kern
1885–1945

1 HAMMERSTEIN: Here is a story laid in China about an Italian told by an Irishman. What kind of music are you going to write?
KERN: It'll be good Jewish music.
discussing with Oscar Hammerstein II a musical to be based on Donn Byrne's novel Messer Marco Polo
Gerald Bordman *Jerome Kern* (1980)

John Maynard Keynes 1883–1946

English economist. An adviser to the Treasury during both world wars, he laid the foundations of modern macroeconomics. His theories influenced **Roosevelt**'s decision to introduce the American New Deal.

John Maynard Keynes
1883–1946

1 I evidently knew more about economics than my examiners.
explaining why he performed badly in the Civil Service examinations
Roy Harrod *Life of John Maynard Keynes* (1951)

Ottoline Morrell
1873–1938

2 A detached, meditating and yet half-caressing interest in those he is speaking to, head on one side, a kindly tolerant smile and very charming eyes wandering, searching and speculating, then probably a frank, intimate and perhaps laughing home-thrust, which may or may not illuminate one's own self-knowledge.
Robert Gathorne-Hardy (ed.) *Ottoline at Garsington* (1974)

Bertrand Russell
1872–1970

3 Keynes's intellect was the sharpest and clearest that I have ever known. When I argued with him, I felt that I took my life in my hands, and I seldom emerged without feeling something of a fool. I was sometimes inclined to feel that so much cleverness must be incompatible with depth, but I do not think this feeling was justified.
Autobiography (1968)

Robert Skidelsky
1939–

4 It is hard to think of any economist who has achieved so much practical good.
John Maynard Keynes vol. 1 (1983)

Nikita Khrushchev 1894–1971

Soviet statesman, Premier 1958–64. He was First Secretary of the Communist Party of the USSR after the death of **Stalin**, whom he denounced in 1956. He came close to war with the US over the Cuban Missile Crisis in 1962.

Jacob Epstein
1880–1959

1 Why don't they stick to murder and leave art to us?
on hearing that his statue of Lazarus in New College chapel, Oxford, kept Khrushchev awake at night
attributed

Lyndon Baines Johnson
1908–73

2 Mr Khrushchev holds out an olive branch and at the same time tries to hit us over the head with it.
in 1960

Nikita Khrushchev
1894–1971

3 When I was forty—your age—I was a clerk in an office, and I've grown to be head of my nation, which shows what wonderful opportunities there are in the Soviet Union.

to **John F. Kennedy**; Cecil Beaton's diary, June 1961

when Khrushchev began banging his shoe on the desk during a speech to the United Nations:

Harold Macmillan
1894–1986

4 Perhaps we could have a translation, I could not quite follow.

in September 1960

Ian Kilminster 1945–

English pop singer, known as 'Lemmy'. In 1975 he formed the punk band Motorhead, noted for the loudness of its music.

Ian Kilminster
1945–

1 If we moved in next to you, your lawn would die.

interview, July 2000

Lord Kilmuir 1900–67

British Conservative politician and lawyer, born David Maxwell Fyfe. He was a prosecutor at the Nuremburg trials.

Anonymous

1 The nearest thing to death in life
Is David Patrick Maxwell Fyfe,
Though underneath that gloomy shell
He does himself extremely well.

said to have been current on the Northern circuit in the late 1930s

Billie Jean King 1943–

American tennis player. She won a record twenty Wimbledon titles, including six singles titles, ten doubles titles, and four mixed doubles titles.

Chris Evert
1954–

1 Billie Jean has to work three times as hard as the rest of us to stay even. When I get out of bed stiff, the morning after a long, tough match, I can't imagine what it must be like for her.

attributed

Billie Jean King
1943–

2 Ask Nureyev to stop dancing, ask Sinatra to stop singing, then you can ask me to stop playing.

in 1982

Martin Luther King 1929–68

American Baptist minister and civil rights leader. He opposed discrimination against blacks by organizing non-violent resistance and peaceful mass demonstrations and was a notable orator. He was assassinated in Memphis.

James Baldwin
1924–87

3 The secret lies, I think, in his intimate knowledge of the people he is addressing be they black or white, and in the forthrightness with which he speaks of those things which hurt and baffle them . . . He allows them their self-respect—indeed, he insists on it.

in February 1961

Nikki Giovanni
1943–

4 His headstone said
FREE AT LAST, FREE AT LAST
But death is a slave's freedom.

'The Funeral of Martin Luther King, Jr' (1970)

Don King
1931–

5 Martin Luther King took us to the mountain top: I want to take us to the bank. I'm not fighting the Civil War, I'm fighting the poverty war.

attributed

Martin Luther King
1929–68

6 I want to be the white man's brother, not his brother-in-law.

in September 1962

Martin Luther King
1929–68

7 I just want to do God's will. And he's allowed me to go up to the mountain. And I've looked over, and I've seen the promised land . . . So I'm happy tonight. I'm not worried about anything. I'm not fearing any man.
   speech in Memphis, April 1968, on the day before his assassination

Yevgeny Yevtushenko
1933–

8 He was a Negro, but with
   a soul as pure as the white snow.
   He was killed by whites
   with black souls.
   When I received this news
   that same bullet entered me.
   That bullet killed him,
   but by that bullet I was reborn,
   and I was reborn a Negro.
   William Robert Miller *Martin Luther King, Jr* (1968)

Neil Kinnock 1942–

British Labour politician. He was leader of the Labour Party 1983–92, opposing the governments of **Margaret Thatcher** and **John Major**.

Michael Heseltine
1933–

1 Self-appointed king of the gutter of politics.
   Robert Harris *The Making of Neil Kinnock* (1984); see **Heseltine** 4

Neil Kinnock
1942–

2 Why am I the first Kinnock in a thousand generations to be able to get to a university?
   later plagiarized by the American politician Joe Biden
   speech in party political broadcast, May 1987

Neil Kinnock
1942–

3 When I go home nowadays, I get the sort of kindliness normally reserved for dead people.
   in March 1996

Margaret Thatcher
1925–

4 Of course you hate choice: you are a socialist—a crypto-Communist.
   in October 1990

Rudyard Kipling 1865–1936

British novelist, short-story writer, and poet. Born in India, he is known for his poems, such as 'If' and 'Gunga Din' and his children's tales, notably *The Jungle Book* and the *Just So Stories*.

W. H. Auden
1907–73

1 His virtuosity with language is not unlike that of one of his drill sergeants with an awkward squad . . . The vulgarest words learn to wash behind their ears and to execute complicated movements at the word of command, but they can hardly be said to learn to think for themselves.
   in October 1943

Rudyard Kipling
1865–1936

2 My Daemon was with me in the *Jungle Books*, *Kim*, and both Puck books, and good care I took to walk delicately lest he should withdraw. I know that he did not, because when these books were finished they said so themselves with, almost, the water-hammer click of a tap turned off.
   Something of Myself (1937)

T. E. Lawrence
1888–1935

3 [He is] a very wonderful fellow and a very mean fellow.
   letter, September 1929

C. S. Lewis
1898–1963

4 Kipling is intensely loved and hated. Hardly any reader likes him a little.
   in 1950

Harold Nicolson
1886–1968

5 Rudyard Kipling's eyebrows are very odd indeed! They curl up black and furious like the moustache of a Neapolitan tenor.
   diary, January 1930

George Orwell
1903–50

6 I worshipped Kipling at thirteen, loathed him at seventeen, enjoyed him at twenty, despised him at twenty-five, and now again rather admire him. The one thing that was never possible, if one had read him at all, was to forget him.

in January 1936

Ezra Pound
1885–1972

7 Rudyard the dud yard,
Rudyard the false measure,
Told 'em that glory
Ain't always a pleasure,
But said it wuz glorious nevertheless
To lick the boots of the bloke
That makes the worst mess.

'Poems of Alfred Venison: Alf's Fourth Bit' (1949)

Dylan Thomas
1914–53

8 Mr Kipling . . . stands for everything in this cankered world which I would wish were otherwise.

letter, 1933

Mark Twain
1835–1910

9 He is a most remarkable man—and I am the other one. Between us we cover all knowledge; he knows all that can be known and I know the rest.

Autobiography (1924)

Hugh Walpole
1884–1941

10 'Carrie,' he says, turning to Mrs K., and at once you see that she is the only real person here to him—so she takes him, wraps him up in her bosom and conveys him back to their uncomfortable hard-chaired home. He is quite content.

on meeting Kipling at a house-party
Charles Carrington *Rudyard Kipling* (ed. 3, 1978)

Oscar Wilde
1854–1900

11 From the point of view of literature Mr Kipling is a genius who drops his aspirates. From the point of view of life, he is a reporter who knows vulgarity better than anyone has ever known it.

Intentions (1891)

P. G. Wodehouse
1881–1975

12 It's odd, this hostility to Kipling. How the intelligentsia do seem to loathe the poor blighter, and how we of the *canaille* revel in his stuff.

Performing Flea (1953)

Henry Kissinger 1923–

German-born American statesman and diplomat. In 1973 he helped negotiate the withdrawal of US troops from South Vietnam, for which he shared the Nobel Peace Prize. He later restored US diplomatic relations with Egypt.

Tommy Docherty
1928–

1 There's a hell of a lot of politics in football. I don't think Henry Kissinger would have lasted forty-eight hours at Old Trafford.

attributed

Joseph Heller
1923–99

2 Kissinger brought peace to Vietnam the same way Napoleon brought peace to Europe: by losing.

Good as Gold (1979)

Henry Kissinger
1923–

3 I am being frank about myself in this book. I tell of my first mistake on page 850.

of his autobiography Years of Upheaval
in January 1983

Lord Kitchener 1850–1916

British soldier and statesman. He served against the Mahdist forces at Omdurman and in the Boer War. At the outbreak of the First World War he became Secretary of State for War, and his image appeared on recruiting posters.

Margot Asquith
1864–1945

1 Kitchener is a great poster.

More Memories (1933)

David Lloyd George
1863–1945

2 One of those revolving lighthouses which radiate momentary gleams of light far out into the surrounding gloom, and then suddenly relapse into complete darkness. There were no intermediate stages.
of Kitchener as War Minister
attributed

Paul Klee 1879–1940

Swiss painter. His work is characterized by his sense of colour and moves freely between abstraction and figuration.

Paul Klee
1879–1940

1 Colour has taken hold of me; no longer do I have to chase after it. I know that it has hold of me for ever. That is the significance of this blessed moment.
on a visit to Tunis in 1914; Herbert Read A Concise History of Modern Painting *(1968)*

Calvin Klein 1942–

American fashion designer, known for his understated fashions for both men and women.

Anonymous

1 Nothing comes between me and my Calvin's.
advertisement, 1978

Marci Klein

2 My only complaint about having a father in fashion is that every time I'm about to go to bed with a guy I have to look at my dad's name all over his underwear.
in October 1994

Otto Klemperer 1885–1973

German-born American conductor and composer. While a conductor in Berlin, he was noted as a champion of new work.

Lotte Lehmann
1888–1976

1 Klemperer sat at the piano like an evil spirit, thumping on it with long hands like tigers' claws, dragging my terrified voice into the fiery vortex of his fanatical will.
Wings of Song (1938)

John Knox c. 1505–72

Scottish Protestant reformer. Knox led opposition to the Catholic **Mary, Queen of Scots** from 1561.

Matthew Arnold
1822–88

1 One is tempted almost to say that there was more of Jesus in St Theresa's little finger than in John Knox's whole body.
Literature and Dogma (1873)

Thomas Carlyle
1795–1881

2 They go far wrong who think that Knox was a gloomy, spasmodic, shrieking fanatic. Not at all; he is one of the solidest of men. Practical, cautious-hopeful, patient; a most shrewd, observing, quietly discerning man.
On Heroes, Hero-Worship, and the Heroic (1841)

James Douglas, Earl of Morton
c. 1516–81

3 Here lies he who neither feared nor flattered any flesh.
said as Knox was buried, November 1572

Dorothy Parker
1893–1967

4 Whose love is given over-well
Shall look on Helen's face in hell
Whilst they whose love is thin and wise
Shall see John Knox in Paradise.
'Partial Comfort' (1937)

Robert Louis Stevenson
1850–94

5 He had a grim reliance in himself, or rather, in his mission; if he were not sure he was a great man, he was at least sure that he was one set apart to do great things.
Familiar Studies of Men and Books (1882)

Käthe Kollwitz 1867–1945

German sculptor and graphic artist.

Käthe Kollwitz
1867–1945

1 I have never done any work cold . . . I have always worked with my blood, so to speak.

letter, April 1917

Alexander Korda 1893–1956

Hungarian-born British film producer and director. Notable productions include *The Private Life of Henry VIII*, *Things to Come*, and *The Third Man*.

Cecil Beaton
1904–80

1 I was surprised that anyone with a moving-picture background could be so well-read and generally intelligent.

diary, 1946

Ralph Richardson
1902–83

2 Alexander Korda was continually making people do things against their will but seldom against their interest.

in 1956

Anna Kournikova 1981–

Russian tennis player.

Elizabeth Hurley
1965–

1 I think she looked smashing. She is a very pretty girl.

in 2000; see **Hurley** 2

Anna Kournikova
1981–

2 The world believes all blondes are stupid and brunettes are smarter. Well, I disagree.

in June 2000

Hans Krebs 1900–81

German-born British biochemist. He discovered the cycle of reactions now known as the Krebs cycle.

Hans Krebs
1900–81

1 Only by trying lots of things, has one a chance of hitting the right one sometimes.

Frederick Holmes *Hans Krebs* (1993)

Nadezhda Krupskaya 1869–1939

Russian revolutionary. As wife of **Lenin**, she supported him, and took a particular interest in education.

Frau Kammerer

1 Frau Lenin would have made a good Hausfrau, but she always had her mind on other work.

a landlady's view
in c.1917; Edmund Wilson *To the Finland Station* (1940)

Joseph Stalin
1879–1953

2 She may use the same lavatory as Lenin, but that doesn't mean she knows anything about Leninism.

remark to Molotov, Party Congress, 1925

Karl Lagerfeld 1939–

German fashion designer.

Karl Lagerfeld
1939–

1 We're not curing cancer. We're not putting people into space. It's only clothes. Let's not take ourselves too seriously.

Nicholas Coleridge *The Fashion Conspiracy* (1988)

Charles Lamb 1775–1834

English essayist and critic. Together with his sister Mary he wrote *Tales from Shakespeare* (1807). He is also noted for his *Essays of Elia* (1823).

Samuel Taylor Coleridge 1772–1834

1 　　　A charm
For thee, my gentle-hearted Charles, to whom
No sound is dissonant which tells of life.
'This Lime-Tree Bower my Prison' (1800)

William Hazlitt 1778–1830

2 His sayings are generally like women's letters; all the pith is in the postscript.
Conversations of James Northcote (1826–7)

Charles Lamb 1775–1834

3 I have something more to do than feel.
on the death of his mother, killed by his sister Mary
letter to Coleridge, September 1796

k. d. lang 1962–

Canadian country and pop singer.

Roy Acuff 1903–92

1 You look like a boy, dress like a girl, and sing like a bird.
in June 1990

k. d. lang 1962–

2 I wanted to develop the idea of torch *and* twang, that's what's inside me and it pretty much sums up the kind of music that interests me.
in October 1989

Lillie Langtry 1853–1929

British actress, known as the Jersey Lily. She became the mistress of the Prince of Wales, later **Edward VII**.

James Agate 1877–1947

1 In her early days she had that beatific expression characteristic of Victorian prettiness—like a sheep painted by Raphael.
diary, April 1940

Philip Larkin 1922–1985

English poet. His poetry is characterized by an air of melancholy and bitterness, and by stoic wit.

Kingsley Amis 1922–95

1 There isn't anybody whose way of talking will interest me and make me laugh as much as yours does . . . There is nobaddy esle but you who contributes as much as I contribute to the total of interest, and who HATES the thigns I HATE as much as I HATE them.
letter to Larkin, September 1946

Alan Bennett 1934–

2 Made a habit of being 60; he made a profession of it. Like Lady Dumbleton, he has been 60 for the last 25 years.
Writing Home (1995)

John Carey 1934–

3 His attitude to most accredited sources of pleasure would make Scrooge seem unduly frolicsome.
in 1983

Clive James 1939–

4 Larkin was so English that he didn't even care much about Britain, and he rarely mentioned it.
The Dreaming Swimmer (1992)

Philip Larkin 1922–85

5 Deprivation is for me what daffodils were for Wordsworth.
Required Writing (1983)

Philip Larkin 1922–85

6 Happiness writes white.
attributed

Harold Larwood 1904–95

English cricketer. In the 1932–3 MCC tour of Australia he bowled fast short-pitched 'bodyline' deliveries, and was involved in controversy when several batsmen were badly injured.

Jack Fingleton
1908–81

1 One could tell his art by his run to the wicket. It was a poem of athletic grace, as each muscle gave over to the other with perfect balance and the utmost power.
Michael Parkinson *Sporting Profiles* (1995)

Niki Lauda 1949–

Austrian motor-racing driver. World champion in 1975, he suffered severe injuries in the 1976 German Grand Prix, but won two more championships (1977 and 1984).

Niki Lauda
1949–

1 The rat was always my role model in the animal kingdom, with its high intelligence and instinct for survival.
attributed, 2000

Harry Lauder 1870–1950

Scottish music-hall comedian. He became highly popular singing songs such as 'I Love a Lassie' and 'Roamin' in the Gloamin' ', and entertained troops at home and abroad in both world wars.

Hugh MacDiarmid
1892–1978

1 The problems o' the Scottish soul
Are nocht to Harry Lauder . . .
To Circumjack Cencrastus, or the Curly Snake (1930)

Charles Laughton 1899–1962

British-born American actor. He is remembered for character roles such as Henry VIII; he also played Quasimodo in *The Hunchback of Notre Dame*.

Kenneth Tynan
1927–80

1 [Charles Laughton] walks top-heavily, like a salmon standing on its tail.
Profiles (ed. Kathleen Tynan, 1989)

Peter Ustinov
1921–

2 He was always hovering around waiting to be offended. We'd see him floating in his own pool and it was just the reverse of an iceberg— ninety per cent of him was visible.
Quotable Ustinov (1995)

Ralph Lauren 1939–

American fashion designer. He is famous for styles such as the 'prairie look' and 'frontier fashions'.

Ralph Lauren
1939–

1 I always wanted to make movies, but I'm just doing them in a different way, creating the dreams, the dream lifestyle. My life helps me with my job, and my job helps me with my life.
interview, May 1997

Antoine Lavoisier 1743–94

French scientist. He caused a revolution in chemistry by his description of combustion. He was guillotined in the French Revolution.

Joseph Louis
Lagrange
1736–1813

1 Only a moment to cut off that head, and a hundred years may not give us another like it.
on the execution of Lavoisier
D. McKie *Antoine Lavoisier* (1962)

Denis Law 1940–

Scottish footballer. Most of his career was spent in England, particularly with Manchester United.

Denis Law
1940–

1 I've always been two different people on the park and off it. It's like looking at a stranger and I can hardly bear to watch.
Grant Jarvie and Graham Walker (eds) *Scottish Sport in the Making of a Nation* (1994)

D. H. Lawrence 1885–1930

English novelist, poet, and essayist. His work is characterized by its condemnation of industrial society and by its frank exploration of sexual relationships.

Kingsley Amis
1922–95

1 One of the great denouncers, the great missionaries the English send to themselves to tell them that they are crass, gross, lost, dead, mad and addicted to unnatural vice.
What Became of Jane Austen? (1970)

John Carey
1934–

2 Lawrence's passion for travel was only equalled by his dislike of the places he arrived at. He would have been a tour operator's nightmare.
in 1987

Catherine Carswell
1879–1946

3 Lawrence was as little morose as any open clematis flower, as little tortured or sinister or hysterical as a humming-bird.
in March 1930

John Galsworthy
1867–1933

4 Interesting, but a type I could not get on with. Obsessed with self. Dead eyes and a red beard, long narrow pale face. A strange bird.
diary November 1917

Robert Graves
1895–1985

5 He was a bum poet, of course, being a bum person.
letter, December 1935

Aldous Huxley
1894–1963

6 Isn't it remarkable how everyone who knew Lawrence has felt compelled to write about him? Why, he's had more books written about him than any writer since Byron!
George Plimpton (ed.) *Writers at Work* (2nd series, 1963)

D. H. Lawrence
1885–1930

7 I like to write when I feel spiteful; it's like having a good sneeze.
letter, November 1913

Frieda Lawrence
1879–1956

8 He loved me absolutely, that's why he hates me absolutely.
letter, c.1914

W. Charles Pilley

9 I do not claim to be a literary critic, but I know dirt when I smell it and here it is in heaps—festering putrid heaps which smell to high heaven.
review of Women in Love
in September 1921

John Robinson
1919–83

10 I think Lawrence tried to portray this [sex] relation as in a real sense an act of holy communion. For him flesh was sacramental of the spirit.
as defence witness in the case against Penguin Books for publishing Lady Chatterley's Lover
in October 1960

Bertrand Russell
1872–1970

11 Gradually I discovered that he had no wish to make the world better but only to indulge in eloquent soliloquy about how bad it was.
Noel Annan *Our Age* (1990)

Virginia Woolf
1882–1941

12 He's like an express train running through a tunnel—one shriek, sparks, smoke and gone.
letter, June 1935

Ruth Lawrence 1971–

English mathematician. A child prodigy who went to the University of Oxford at 12, she is now a university lecturer.

Ruth Lawrence
1971–

13 I now have a completely different view of life. Having a baby cannot possibly be compared to academic results. It is miraculous, it is not like passing an O-level.
in June 2000

T. E. Lawrence 1888–1935

British soldier and writer. From 1916 onwards he helped to organize the Arab revolt against the Turks in the Middle East. In 1922, seeking anonymity, he enlisted in the RAF under an assumed name.

Lord Berners
1883–1950

14 He's always backing into the limelight.
oral tradition

Noël Coward
1899–1973

15 Dear 338171 (May I call you 338?).
letter to T. E. Lawrence, August 1930

Robert Graves
1895–1985

16 He made so many mysteries; told one person one set of facts, another, another. If most compared notes most would be known, but not all.
letter, 1931

W. Somerset Maugham
1874–1965

17 Nothing ever made me more doubtful of T. E. Lawrence's genuineness than that he so heartily trusted two persons whom I knew to be bogus.
A Writer's Notebook (1949)

Edward Lear 1812–88

English humorist and illustrator. He wrote *A Book of Nonsense* (1845) and *Laughable Lyrics* (1877). He also published illustrations of birds and of his travels around the Mediterranean.

W. H. Auden
1907–73

1 Children swarmed to him like settlers. He became a land.
'Edward Lear' (1939)

Edward Lear
1812–88

2 'How pleasant to know Mr Lear!'
Who has written such volumes of stuff!
Some think him ill-tempered and queer,
But a few think him pleasant enough.
Nonsense Songs (1871) preface

Timothy Leary 1920–96

American psychologist. After experimenting with consciousness-altering drugs including LSD, he was dismissed from his teaching post at Harvard University in 1963 and became a figurehead for the hippy drug culture.

Anonymous

1 Timothy has passed . . .
message on Leary's Internet home page, announcing his death, May 1996

F. R. Leavis 1895–1978

English literary critic. Founder and editor of the quarterly *Scrutiny* (1932–53), he emphasized the value of critical study of English literature to preserving cultural continuity.

Noel Annan
1916–

1 He cultivated to perfection the sneer which he used like an oyster-knife, inserting it into the shell of his victim, exposing him with a quick turn of the wrist, and finally flipping him over and inviting his audience to discard him as tainted and inedible.
Our Age (1990)

F. R. Leavis
1895–1978

2 A Roundhead? I'd have been Cromwell.
replying to a student who had asked him whether he would have been a Roundhead in the Civil War
attributed

Edith Sitwell
1887–1964

3 It is sad to see Milton's great lines bobbing up and down in the sandy desert of Dr Leavis's mind with the grace of a fleet of weary camels.
Aspects of Modern Poetry (1934)

Le Corbusier 1887–1965

French architect and town planner, born in Switzerland. A pioneer of the international style, he developed theories on functionalism and the use of new materials and industrial techniques.

Salvador Dali
1904–89

1 Le Corbusier was a pitiable creature working in reinforced concrete. Mankind will soon be landing on the moon, and just imagine: that buffoon claimed we'd be taking along sacks of reinforced concrete. His heaviness and the heaviness of the concrete deserve one another.
Alain Bosquet *Conversations with Dali* (1969)

Le Corbusier
1887–1965

2 One concern has been uppermost in my mind: to make the family sacred, to make a temple of the family home. Once I had thought of this everything changed. A cubic centimetre of housing was worth its weight in gold, so much happiness did it represent.
Mise au point (1965)

Laurie Lee 1914–97

English writer. He is best known for his autobiographical novel *Cider With Rosie*.

Cyril Connolly
1903–74

1 One is a Van Gogh, the other a Samuel Palmer, a maker of ravishing verbal woodcuts.
comparing **Dylan Thomas** and *Laurie Lee*
in May 1955

Clare Francis
1946–

2 Totally un-English in the sense that not only did he love conversation and people, but he liked women and set up an immediate easy intimacy which is very, very rare. He made you feel like a co-conspirator.
Valerie Grove *Laurie Lee: The Well-loved Stranger* (1999)

Laurie Lee
1914–97

3 I am a person of concealment. No one has ever managed to get through.
attributed, 1997

Rosamond Lehmann
1901–90

4 I think you are, without perhaps deliberately meaning to be, rather a dangerous person for women! You seem to expand with such warmth and freedom towards them, it goes to their heads . . . Then suddenly they discover they've come to a walled enclosure with a sign: Keep Off. Keep Out. No Visitors. No Inquiries. No One At Home.
letter, c.1945

Robert E. Lee 1807–70

American general. He was the commander of the Confederate army of Northern Virginia for most of the American Civil War. His invasion of the North was repulsed at the Battle of Gettysburg (1863).

Stephen Vincent Benét
1898–1943

5 And kept his heart a secret to the end
From all the picklocks of biographers.
John Brown's Body (1928)

Thomas Jackson
1824–63

6 Lee is the only man I know whom I would follow blindfold.
letter, May 1862

Robert E. Lee
1807–70

7 I should be trading on the blood of my men.
refusing an offer to write his memoirs
attributed, perhaps apocryphal

Gottfried Wilhelm Leibniz 1646–1716

German rationalist philosopher, mathematician, and logician. He believed that the world is fundamentally harmonious and good. He also devised a method of calculus independently of **Newton**.

Montesquieu
1689–1755

1 It is rare to find learned men who are clean, do not stink, and have a sense of humour.
Lettres Persanes (1721)

Vivien Leigh 1913–67

British actress, born in India. She won Oscars for her performances in *Gone with the Wind* (1939) and *A Streetcar Named Desire* (1951). She was married to **Laurence Olivier** from 1940 to 1961.

Elia Kazan
1909–

1 She had a small talent, but the greatest determination to excel of any actress I've known. She'd have crawled over broken glass if she thought it would help her performance.
R. Schickel *Brando* (1994)

Laurie Lee
1914–97

2 Cheap, pretty face she has, with the spiky selfish personality of a vixen behind it.
diary, February 1944

Kenneth Tynan
1927–80

3 As Lavinia, Vivien Leigh receives the news that she is about to be ravished on her husband's corpse with little more than the mild annoyance of one who would have preferred Dunlopillo.
review of *Titus Andronicus*, 1955

Vladimir Ilich Lenin 1870–1924

Russian revolutionary, Premier of the Soviet Union 1918–24. In 1917 he established Bolshevik control after the overthrow of the tsar. With **Trotsky** he defeated counter-revolutionary forces.

Winston Churchill
1874–1965

1 The Germans turned upon Russia the most grisly of all weapons. They transported Lenin in a sealed truck, like a plague bacillus, from Switzerland into Russia.
The World Crisis (1929)

Arthur Ransome
1884–1967

2 I think . . . he is the first great leader who discounts the value of his own personality. He is quite without personal ambition.
Six Weeks in Russia in 1919 (1919)

Arthur M. Schlesinger Jr.
1917–

3 Suppose . . . that Lenin had died of typhus in Siberia in 1895 and Hitler had been killed on the western front in 1916. What would the twentieth century have looked like now?
The Cycles of American History (1986)

Leon Trotsky
1879–1940

4 The execution of the Tsar's family was needed not only to frighten, horrify and dishearten the enemy, but also to shake up our own ranks, to show them that there was no turning back, that ahead lay either complete victory or complete ruin. *This* Lenin sensed very well.
Diary in Exile (1963)

John Lennon 1940–80

English pop and rock singer, guitarist, and songwriter. A founder member of the Beatles, he wrote most of their songs in collaboration with **Paul McCartney**. He was assassinated outside his home in New York.

Donovan
1946–

1 John certainly had a wicked tongue all right, but he was honest to a fault. Therefore, many people often considered him to be very hard and forward. Actually, that's how he protected his sensitivities, by saying exactly what he felt.
Geoffrey Giuliano *The Beatles: a Celebration: 30th Anniversary Edition* (1992)

Philip Larkin 2 When you get to the top, there is nowhere to go but down, but the
1922–85 Beatles could not get down. There they remain, unreachable, frozen,
fabulous.
in October 1983

John Lennon 3 I'm not gonna change the way I look or the way I feel to conform to
1940–80 anything. I've always been a freak. So I've been a freak all my life and I
have to live with that, you know. I'm one of those people.
interview, September 1980

Sean Taro Ono 4 The most important thing in my father's life? World peace. Me and my
Lennon brother. My mom.
1975– Andrew Solt and Sam Egan *Imagine: John Lennon* (1988)

Paul McCartney 5 He could be a manoeuvring swine, which no one ever realized.
1942– Hunter Davies *The Beatles* (1985)

Yoko Ono 6 Maybe we were naïve, but still we were very honest about everything
1933– we did.
interview, December 1980

Paul Simon 7 I don't know what his motivations are. Many things he's done, I think,
1942– have been pointless. Some have been in bad taste. Others have been
courageous. I think he's generally a well-intentioned guy. I don't know,
it's not my style.
in July 1972

Frank Sinatra 8 Lennon was a most talented man and above all, a gentle soul.
1915–98 Geoffrey Giuliano *The Beatles: a Celebration: 30th Anniversary Edition* (1992)

Joanna Trollope 9 As far as I am concerned, Yoko was welcome to him. He had the sex
1943– appeal of old socks. A dank and dreary man, and physically
unappealing. I don't know what everyone else saw in him.
in December 1995

Karl Wallinger 10 At the end of the Asterix comics they always tie the bard up and hang
1957– him upside down from a tree while all the warriors—all the serious
people—have a slap-up meal . . . Lennon's thing with the American
government was very like that. They just wanted to hang him upside
down from a tree while they got on with things. 'You're just a musician,
we're the blokes who go around killing people.'
interview, August 2000

Sugar Ray Leonard 1956–

American boxer. He became undisputed world welterweight champion in 1981.

Sugar Ray Leonard 1 We're all endowed with God-given talents. Mine happens to be hitting
1956– people in the head.
Thomas Hauser *The Black Lights* (1986)

Ferdi Pacheco 2 Sugar Ray Leonard has a cash register for a brain and a bank vault for a
heart.
in 1989

Leonardo da Vinci 1452–1519

Italian painter, scientist, and engineer. His paintings include *The Last Supper*, and the *Mona
Lisa*. His interests ranged from anatomy and biology to mechanics and hydraulics.

Kenneth Clark 1 He was the most relentlessly curious man in history. Everything he saw
1903–83 made him ask how and why. Why does one find sea-shells in the
mountains? How do they build locks in Flanders? How does a bird fly?
What accounts for cracks in walls? What is the origin of winds and
clouds? Find out; write it down; if you can see it, draw it.
Civilization (1969)

Leonardo da Vinci 1452–1519	2 While I thought I was learning how to live, I have been learning how to die. *Notebooks*
Auguste Renoir 1841–1919	3 He bores me. He ought to have stuck to his flying machines. attributed
Giorgio Vasari 1511–74	4 He might have been a scientist if he had not been so versatile. *Lives of the Artists* (1568)

Graeme Le Saux 1968–

English football player. He has played for Chelsea and England.

Graeme Le Saux 1968–	1 Throughout my career I've been described as 'cerebral'. But I had to look up that word in a dictionary. in March 1999
Piers Morgan 1965–	2 Nobody cares if Le Saux is gay or not. It is the fact that he openly admits to reading *The Guardian* that makes him the most reviled man in football. in March 1999

Monica Lewinsky 1973–

American political trainee. Her relationship with **Bill Clinton** led to his impeachment.

Christine Keeler 1942–	1 Being in the public eye, as Monica Lewinsky will be for the rest of her life, is like being the lady with the moustache at the circus. You're a curiosity—and you will never stop being one. in March 1999
Monica Lewinsky 1973–	2 I have become an accidental celebrity. And, truly, it wasn't hard to do. in November 2000
Philip Roth 1933–	3 This isn't Deep Throat. This is Big Mouth. *The Human Stain* (2000)

Carl Lewis 1961–

American athlete. He won Olympic gold medals in 1984, 1988, 1992, and 1996 (his ninth) for sprinting and the long jump.

Carl Lewis 1961–	1 Men—athletes especially—have to be like King Kong. When we lose, we can't cry and we can't pout. in July 1984

C. S. Lewis 1898–1963

British novelist, religious writer, and literary scholar, born in Northern Ireland. He created the imaginary land of Narnia for a series of children's books.

J. R. R. Tolkien 1892–1973	2 You must always look for the *Ulsterior motive*. A. N. Wilson *Life of C. S. Lewis* (1986)
Kenneth Tynan 1927–80	3 As a man, he combines the manner of Friar Tuck with the mind of St Augustine. *Persona Grata* (1953)

Lennox Lewis 1965–

English boxer, world heavyweight champion.

Lennox Lewis 1965–	4 I'm proud to call myself a mother's boy. Who gives you more in life than your mother? in November 2000

Wyndham Lewis 1882–1957

British novelist, critic, and painter, born in Canada. He was a leader of the vorticist movement, and with **Ezra Pound** edited the magazine *Blast* (1914–15).

T. S. Eliot
1888–1965

5 A man of undoubted genius, but genius for what precisely it would be remarkably difficult to say.

Paul O'Keefe *Some Sort of Genius* (2000)

Ernest Hemingway
1899–1961

6 I do not think I have ever seen a nastier-looking man. Under the black hat, when I had first seen them, the eyes were those of an unsuccessful rapist.

A Moveable Feast (1964)

Wyndham Lewis
1882–1957

7 I have been called a Rogue Elephant, a Cannibal Shark, and a Crocodile. I am none the worse. I remain a caged, and rather sardonic, Lion in a particularly contemptible and ill-run Zoo.

Blasting and Bombardiering (1937)

Edith Sitwell
1887–1964

8 Mr Lewis's pictures appeared, as a very great painter said to me, to have been painted by a mailed fist in a cotton glove.

Taken Care Of (1965)

Liberace 1919–87

American pianist and entertainer. He was known for his romantic arrangements of popular piano classics and for his flamboyant costumes.

William Neil Connor
1909–67

1 Without doubt, he is the biggest sentimental vomit of all time. Slobbering over his mother, winking at his brother, and counting the cash at every second, this superb piece of calculating candy-floss has an answer for every situation.

Liberace successfully sued Connor for libel
in the *Daily Mirror*, 1956

Clive James
1939–

2 It was like being forcibly fed with warm peppermint creams.

of Liberace's performance
in February 1980

Liberace
1919–87

3 When the reviews are bad I tell my staff that they can join me as I cry all the way to the bank.

Autobiography (1973)

Roy Lichtenstein 1923–97

American painter and sculptor. A leading exponent of pop art, he became known for paintings inspired by comic strips.

Roy Lichtenstein
1923–97

1 I want my work to look programmed or impersonal but I don't believe I'm being impersonal while I do it.

interview, c.1964

Eric Liddell 1902–45

Scottish athlete and missionary, born in China. In the 1924 Olympic Games he won the 400 metres in a world record time. His exploits were celebrated in the film *Chariots of Fire*.

Eric Liddell
1902–45

1 The secret of my success over the 400 metres is that I run the first 200 metres as hard as I can. Then, for the second 200 metres, with God's help, I run faster.

D. P. Thomas *Eric H. Liddell: Athlete and Missionary* (1971)

Abraham Lincoln 1809–65

American Republican statesman, President 1861–5. His election on an anti-slavery platform helped precipitate the American Civil War; he was assassinated shortly after the war ended.

Anonymous 1 The silly, flat, dishwatery utterances of the man who has to be pointed out to intelligent observers as the President of the United States.
review of Lincoln's Gettysburg Address, in November 1863

Stephen Vincent 2 Lincoln, six feet one in his stocking feet,
Benét The lank man, knotty and tough as a hickory rail,
1898–1943 Whose hands were always too big for white-kid gloves,
Whose wit was a coonskin sack of dry, tall tales,
Whose weathered face was homely as a ploughed field.
John Brown's Body (1928)

Elizabeth Gaskell 3 My heart burnt within me with indignation and grief; we could think
1810–65 of nothing else . . . All night long we had only snatches of sleep, waking up perpetually to the sense of a great shock and grief. Every one is feeling the same. I never knew so universal a feeling.
of Lincoln's assassination
letter, April 1865

Millard Lampell 4 A lonesome train on a lonesome track,
1919–97 Seven coaches painted black . . .
A slow train, a quiet train,
Carrying Lincoln home again.
'The Lonesome Train' (1943)

Abraham Lincoln 5 I claim not to have controlled events, but confess plainly that events
1809–65 have controlled me.
letter, April 1864

Vachel Lindsay 6 The prairie-lawyer, master of us all.
1879–1931 'Abraham Lincoln Walks at Midnight' (1914)

Carl Sandburg 7 When Abraham Lincoln was shovelled into the tombs,
1878–1967 he forgot the copperheads and the assassin . . .
in the dust, in the cool tombs.
'Cool Tombs' (1918)

Edwin Mcmasters 8 Now he belongs to the ages.
Stanton *following Lincoln's assassination*
1814–69 remark, April 1865

Walt Whitman 9 This dust was once the man,
1819–92 Gentle, plain, just and resolute, under whose cautious hand,
Against the foulest crime in history known in any land or age,
Was saved the Union of these States.
'This dust was once the man' (1881)

Charles Lindbergh 1902–74

American aviator. In 1927 he made the first solo transatlantic flight. He moved to Europe with his wife to escape the publicity surrounding the kidnap and murder of his two-year-old son in 1932.

Neil Armstrong 1 Slim [Lindbergh] flew through miserable weather and stretched science
1930– and the art of navigation to find Le Bourget. We could see our destination throughout our entire voyage.
in May 1997

Anne Morrow 2 I envy C. his terrific drive . . . which he applies without discrimination
Lindbergh to crossing the Atlantic, writing a book . . . or finding out the price of
1906– butter!
diary, 1953

Charles Lindbergh 1902–74	3 Science, freedom, beauty, adventure; what more could you ask of life? *The Spirit of St Louis* (1953)
Charles Scribner 1921–95	4 He was the most fussy of authors, living or dead. He would measure the difference between a semicolon and a colon to make sure each was what it ought to be. To him, every detail in the book has as much significance as if it were a moving part in his airplane. *In the Company of Writers* (1990)

Gary Lineker 1960–

English footballer. A striker, Lineker scored forty-eight goals for England, one short of **Bobby Charlton**'s record.

Hunter Davies 1936–	1 Gary, one of nature's Boy Scouts. in May 1992
Vinnie Jones 1965–	2 He's not the sort of bloke I'd have a pint with. A top-class footballer, but how can someone play so many games and never be booked? Did he play for himself or the team? interview, July 2000
Arthur Smith and **Chris England**	3 [Gary Lineker is] the Queen Mother of football. *An Evening with Gary Lineker* (1990)

Sonny Liston 1932–70

American boxer. He started boxing while serving a prison sentence for robbery. In 1962 he became world heavyweight champion but in 1964 lost his title to **Muhammad Ali**.

Muhammad Ali 1942–	1 Here I predict Sonny Liston's dismemberment, I'll hit him so hard, he'll forget where October-November went. in 1964

Franz Liszt 1811–86

Hungarian composer and pianist. He was a key figure in the romantic movement; many of his piano compositions combine lyricism with great technical complexity.

Frédéric Chopin 1810–49	1 When I think of Liszt as a creative artist, he appears before my eyes rouged, on stilts, and blowing into Jericho trumpets *fortissimo* and *pianissimo*. Walter Beckett *Liszt* (1963)

Ken Livingstone 1945–

British Labour politician. He was a controversial leader of the Greater London Council in the 1980s, and in 2000 became the first Mayor of London, as an independent.

Jeffrey Archer 1940–	1 If the Archangel Gabriel had stood with the name of Winston Churchill, Ken would still have won. of the election of the Mayor of London, in May 2000
Frank Dobson 1940–	2 The ego has landed. of Livingstone's candidacy for Mayor of London, in March 2000
William Hague 1961–	3 Why does he [Tony Blair] not split the job of mayor of London? The former health secretary [Frank Dobson] can run as his 'day mayor' and Ken Livingstone can run as his 'night mayor'. speech, November 1999
Arthur Scargill 1938–	4 I wouldn't vote for Ken Livingstone if he were running for mayor of Toytown. in May 2000

Marie Lloyd 1870–1922

English music-hall entertainer. She achieved fame for her risqué songs and extravagant costumes and took her act to the US, South Africa, and Australia.

Marie Lloyd
1870–1922

1 Every performance of Marie Lloyd is a performance by command of the British Public.
Tony Palmer *All You Need Is Love* (1976)

David Lloyd George 1863–1945

British Liberal statesman, Prime Minister 1916–22. As Chancellor of the Exchequer, he introduced old-age pensions and national insurance. His coalition government was threatened by economic problems and trouble in Ireland.

Margot Asquith
1864–1945

1 He can't see a belt without hitting below it.
quoted by Lady Violet Bonham Carter in June 1953

Stanley Baldwin
1867–1947

2 He spent his whole life in plastering together the true and the false and therefrom manufacturing the plausible.
attributed

Lord Beaverbrook
1879–1964

3 He did not seem to care which way he travelled providing he was in the driver's seat.
The Decline and Fall of Lloyd George (1963)

Arnold Bennett
1867–1931

4 Seventy minutes had passed before Mr Lloyd George arrived at his proper theme. He spoke for a hundred and seventeen minutes, in which period he was detected only once in the use of an argument.
Things that have Interested Me (1921)

Winston Churchill
1874–1965

5 The Happy Warrior of Squandermania.
in April 1929

Winston Churchill
1874–1965

6 When the English history of the first quarter of the twentieth century is written, it will be seen that the greater part of our fortunes in peace and in war were shaped by this one man.
in October 1951

Georges Clemenceau
1841–1929

7 What do you expect when I'm between two men of whom one [Lloyd George] thinks he is Napoleon and the other [Woodrow Wilson] thinks he is Jesus Christ?
on being asked why he always gave in to Lloyd George at the Paris Peace Conference, 1918
letter from Harold Nicolson to his wife, May 1919

John Grigg
1924–

8 Lloyd George would have a better rating in British mythology if he had shared the fate of Abraham Lincoln.
attributed, 1963

John Maynard Keynes
1883–1946

9 This extraordinary figure of our time, this syren, this goat-footed bard, this half-human visitor to our age from the hag-ridden magic and enchanted woods of Celtic antiquity.
Essays in Biography (1933)

A. J. P. Taylor
1906–90

10 He aroused every feeling except trust.
English History 1914–1945 (1965)

Andrew Lloyd Webber 1948–

English composer. His many successful musicals include *Jesus Christ Superstar*, *Cats*, and *The Phantom of the Opera*.

Malcolm Williamson
1931–

1 Lloyd Webber's music is everywhere, but then so is Aids.
in January 1992

John Locke 1632–1704

English philosopher, a founder of empiricism and political liberalism. He argued that the authority of rulers has a human origin and is limited, and that all knowledge is derived from sense-experience.

Thomas De Quincey
1785–1859

1 Against Locke's philosophy I think it an unanswerable objection that, although he carried his throat about with him in this world for seventy-two years, no man ever condescended to cut it.

'Murder Considered as one of the Fine Arts' (1827)

Bertrand Russell
1872–1970

2 Locke is the most fortunate of all philosophers. He completed his work in theoretical philosophy just at the moment when the government of his country fell into the hands of men who shared his political opinions. Both in practice and in theory, the views which he advocated were held, for many years to come, by the most vigorous and influential politicians and philosophers.

History of Western Philosophy (1945)

Henry Wadsworth Longfellow 1807–82

American poet. He is known for 'The Wreck of the Hesperus' and 'The Village Blacksmith' (both 1841) and *The Song of Hiawatha* (1855).

John Betjeman
1906–84

1 The New World meets the Old World and the sentiments expressed
Are melodiously mingled in my warm New England breast.

'Longfellow's Visit to Venice' (1958)

Lord Longford 1905–

British Labour politician and philanthropist. He has campaigned for prison reform and for the release of Myra Hindley.

Brian Masters
1939–

1 My only criticism of Frank Longford . . . is that he has a tendency to forgive other people for things that they didn't do to him.

Anthony Clare *In the Psychiatrist's Chair III* (1998)

Hendrik Antoon Lorentz 1853–1928

Dutch theoretical physicist. He worked on the forces affecting electrons and realized that electrons and cathode rays were the same thing.

Albert Einstein
1879–1955

1 Lorentz is a marvel of intelligence and exquisite tact. A living work of art!

letter, November 1911

Louis XIV 1638–1715

King of France from 1643. Known as the Sun King, his reign represented the high point of the Bourbon dynasty and of French power in Europe.

Louis XIV
1638–1715

1 *L'État c'est moi.*
I am the State.

before the Parlement de Paris, April 1655; probably apocryphal

on Louis's deathbed remark to her: 'We shall meet again soon':

Francoise de Maintenon
1635–1719

2 Behold the fine appointment he makes with me! That man never did love anyone but himself.

remark, September 1715

Louis XVI 1754–93

King of France 1774–92. His minor concessions and reforms in the face of the emerging French Revolution proved disastrous, and he was executed.

L'Abbé Edgeworth de Firmont
1745–1807

3 Son of Saint Louis, ascend to heaven.

to Louis as he mounted the steps of the guillotine
attributed

Joe Louis 1914–81

American boxer; known as the Brown Bomber. He was heavyweight champion of the world 1937–49, defending his title twenty-five times during that period.

Muhammad Ali
1942–

4 Joe Louis was my inspiration. I idolize him. I just give lip service to being the greatest. He was the greatest.
in 1981

James Braddock
1905–74

5 Like someone jammed an electric bulb in your face and busted it.
on being hit by Joe Louis
George Plimpton *Shadow Box* (1977)

Ernest Hemingway
1899–1961

6 The most beautiful fighting machine I have ever seen.
attributed

Ada Lovelace 1815–52

English mathematician. The daughter of **Lord Byron**, she became assistant to **Charles Babbage** and worked with him on his mechanical computer.

Ada Lovelace
1815–52

1 Far be it from *me* to disclaim the influence of *ambition* and *fame*. No living soul ever was more imbued with it than myself.
letter, August 1843

James Lovelock 1919–

English scientist. He is best known for the Gaia hypothesis, that the planet is like a vast self-regulating organism, first presented by him in 1972.

James Lovelock
1919–

1 It is comforting to think that I am a part of her [Gaia], and that my destiny is to merge with the chemistry of our living planet.
in September 2000

Amy Lowell 1874–1925

American poet. A leading imagist poet, she is known for her polyphonic prose and sensuous imagery.

D. H. Lawrence
1885–1930

1 How much nicer, finer, bigger you are intrinsically, than your poetry is.
letter, November 1914

Ezra Pound
1885–1972

2 When I get through with that girl she'll think she was born in free verse.
Horace Gregory *Amy Lowell* (1958)

James Russell Lowell 1819–91

American poet and critic. His works include the satirical *Biglow Papers*.

Walt Whitman
1819–92

3 Lowell was not a grower—he was a builder. He *built* poems: he didn't put in the seed, and water the seed, and send down his sun—letting the rest take care of itself: he measured his poems—kept them within the formula.
Edgar Lee Masters *Whitman* (1937)

Oscar Wilde
1854–1900

4 A poet, a statesman, and an American all in one! A sort of three-headed Cerberus of Civilization, who barks when he is baited, and is often mistaken for a lion, at a distance.
letter, February 1881

L. S. Lowry 1887–1976

English painter. He painted small matchstick figures set against the iron and brick expanse of urban and industrial landscapes, settings provided by his life in Salford, near Manchester.

Michael Coleman
and **Brian Burke**

1 He painted matchstalk men and matchstalk cats and dogs.
'Matchstalk Men and Matchstalk Cats and Dogs' (1977 song)

L. S. Lowry
1887–1976

2 I'm a simple man, and I use simple materials.
   Mervyn Levy *Paintings of L. S. Lowry* (1975)

George Lucas 1944–

American film director, producer, and screenwriter. He wrote and directed *Star Wars* and its sequels.

Harrison Ford
1942–

1 You can type this shit, George, but you sure can't say it.
   of the script of Star Wars
   Garry Jenkins *Harrison Ford: Imperfect Hero* (1997)

Alec Guinness
1914–2000

2 What I didn't tell him was that I just couldn't go on speaking those bloody awful, banal lines. I'd had enough of the mumbo-jumbo.
   of his desire to kill off his Star Wars *character Obi-Wan Kenobi*
   attributed, September 1998

Lucretius c.94–55 BC

Roman poet and philosopher. His poem *On the Nature of Things* is an exposition of the atomist physics of Epicurus, based on a materialistic view of the universe.

Virgil
70–19 BC

1 Lucky is he who has been able to understand the causes of things.
   Georgics

Ludwig II 1845–86

King of Bavaria from 1864. He became a recluse and built a series of elaborate castles. He was declared insane and deposed in 1886.

Ludwig II
1845–86

1 If I didn't have my hair curled every day I couldn't enjoy my food.
   Wilfrid Blunt *The Dream King* (1970)

Joanna Lumley 1946–

British actress. She is best-known for her role as Patsy in the television series *Absolutely Fabulous*.

Joanna Lumley
1946–

1 My painted smile is always genuine but sometimes I think it gives off no warmth.
   in August 2000

Martin Luther 1483–1546

German Protestant theologian. He preached the doctrine of justification by faith rather than by works and attacked the sale of indulgences and papal authority. In 1521 he was excommunicated at the Diet of Worms.

Charles V
1500–58

1 A single friar who goes counter to all Christianity for a thousand years must be wrong.
   in April 1521

Martin Luther
1483–1546

2 Here stand I. I can do no other. God help me. Amen.
   speech at the Diet of Worms, April 1521; attributed

Robert Montgomery
1807–55

3 The solitary monk who shook the world.
   Luther: a Poem (1842)

Edwin Lutyens 1869–1944

English architect. He established his reputation designing country houses, but is particularly known for his plans for New Delhi, and for the Cenotaph in London.

Nikolaus Pevsner
1902–

1 Sir Edwin Lutyens was without any doubt the greatest folly builder England has ever seen.
   in April 1954

Vita Sackville-West
1892–1962

2 That most delightful, good-natured, irresponsible, imaginative jester of genius.
   Pepita (1937)

David Lynch 1946–

American film director. His films include *Eraserhead*, *Blue Velvet*, and *The Elephant Man*.

Nicolas Cage
1964–

1 He's constantly sculpting and fishing. A scene can turn into a comedy or into a heavy horror in a fraction of a second. He's very much a sculptor, a spontaneous sculptor.
Douglas Thompson *Uncaged* (1997)

Isabella Rossellini
1952–

2 When David speaks, he sounds like he just got off the Greyhound bus from Iowa. But underneath that Jimmy Stewart look you find a darker side.
Douglas Thompson *Uncaged* (1997)

M

Bernadette Devlin McAliskey 1947–

Irish nationalist. In 1969 she became the youngest MP since **Pitt** the Younger, standing for the Independent Unity party.

Ian Paisley
1926–

1 International Socialist Playgirl of the Year.
in c.1969, G. W. Target *Bernadette* (1975)

Douglas MacArthur 1880–1964

American general. He was Commander of US (later Allied) forces in the SW Pacific during the Second World War. He was relieved of his command of UN forces in Korea in 1951.

Douglas MacArthur
1880–1964

1 I still remember the refrain of one of the most popular barracks ballads of that day, which proclaimed most proudly that old soldiers never die; they just fade away. I now close my military career and just fade away.
speech, April 1951

Harry S. Truman
1884–1972

2 I didn't fire him because he was a dumb son of a bitch, although he was, but that's not against the law for generals. If it was, half to three-quarters of them would be in jail.
Merle Miller *Plain Speaking* (1974)

Lord Macaulay 1800–59

English historian, essayist, and philanthropist. Notable works include *The Lays of Ancient Rome* and *History of England*.

Matthew Arnold
1822–88

1 The great apostle of the Philistines, Lord Macaulay.
Essays in Criticism First Series (1865)

Thomas Carlyle
1795–1881

2 Macaulay is well for a while, but one wouldn't *live* under Niagara.
R. M. Milnes *Notebook* (1838)

Lord Macaulay
1800–59

3 Thank you, madam, the agony is abated.
aged four, having had hot coffee spilt over his legs
G. O. Trevelyan *Life and Letters of Lord Macaulay* (1876)

Lord Melbourne
1779–1848

4 I wish I was as cocksure of anything as Tom Macaulay is of everything.
Lord Cowper's preface to *Lord Melbourne's Papers* (1889)

Florence Nightingale
1820–1910

5 His conversation was a procession of one.
Cecil Woodham Smith *Florence Nightingale* (1950)

John Ruskin
1819–1900

6 A sentence of Macaulay's . . . may have no more sense in it than a blot pinched between doubled paper.
Praeterita (1887)

Sydney Smith
1771–1845

7 He has occasional flashes of silence, that make his conversation perfectly delightful.
Lady Holland *Memoir* (1855)

Joseph McCarthy 1908–57

American Republican politician. Between 1950 and 1954 he was the instigator of widespread investigations into alleged communist infiltration in US public life.

Alice Roosevelt Longworth
1884–1980

1 The truckman, the trashman and the policeman on the block may call me Alice but you may not.
Michael Teague *Mrs. L* (1981)

Joseph McCarthy
1908–57

2 McCarthyism is Americanism with its sleeves rolled.
speech, 1952

Ed Murrow
1908–65

3 No one can terrorize a whole nation, unless we are all his accomplices.
broadcast, March 1954

Paul McCartney 1942–

English pop and rock singer and songwriter. A founder member of the Beatles, he wrote most of their songs in collaboration with **John Lennon**. After the group broke up in 1970 he formed the band Wings.

Mick Jagger
1943–

1 I went to one of those 'smashing happenings' at the London Roundhouse. I thought everyone would be freaking out and wearing weird clothes but they were all wandering around in dirty macs—it was the most boring thing I've ever seen. Paul McCartney thought everyone would be wearing weird clothes and he went as an Arab, which must have been very lonely for him, because when I went there wasn't another Arab in sight.
David Dalton *The Rolling Stones* (1981)

Philip Larkin
1922–85

2 When you get to the top, there is nowhere to go but down, but the Beatles could not get down. There they remain, unreachable, frozen, fabulous.
in October 1983

Paul McCartney
1942–

3 Ballads and babies. That's what happened to me.
on reaching the age of fifty, in June 1992

Ringo Starr
1940–

4 Paul is the greatest bass player in the world. But he is also very determined; he goes on and on to see if he can get his own way. While that may be a virtue it did mean that musical disagreements inevitably arose from time to time.
Geoffrey Giuliano *Two of Us* (1999)

Liz McColgan 1964–

Scottish athlete. She won the 10,000 metres gold medal at the 1986 Commonwealth Games, and the silver medal at the Seoul Olympics 1988.

Liz McColgan
1964–

1 If you want it you've got to go for it, so I just kept saying to myself 'work, work, work'. I proved I wanted it more than anybody else.
on winning the 10,000 metres at the World Championship, about a year after giving birth in Tokyo, 1991

Don McCullin 1935–

British photojournalist, noted for his coverage of wars and revolutions.

Don McCullin
1935–

1 The photographer must be a humble and patient creature, ready to move forward or disappear into thin air. If I am alone and witness to happiness or shame, or even death, and no one is near, I may have had choices, one to be the photographer, the other the man; but what I try to be is human.
Cecil Beaton *The Magic Image* (1975)

Hugh MacDiarmid 1892–1978

Scottish poet and nationalist. The language of his poems drew on the language of various regions of Scotland and historical periods. He was a founder member of the National Party of Scotland.

John Bellany
1942–

1 He wasn't a one-to-one man in the pub, like Sydney Goodsir Smith. He might let you tug the hem of his garment once in a while, but that was all. He was an élitist; a platform man.
John McEwen *John Bellany* (1994)

Norman MacCaig
1910–96

2 He would walk into my mind as if it were a town and he a torchlight procession of one, lighting up the streets of my mind and some of the nasty little things that were burrowing into the corners.
in September 1978

Hugh MacDiarmid
1892–1978

3 My function in Scotland during the past twenty to thirty years has been that of the catfish that vitalises the other torpid denizens of the aquarium.
Lucky Poet (1943)

Irvine Welsh
1957–

4 A symbol of all that's perfectly hideous about Scotland.
in January 1996

Jeanette MacDonald 1903–65

American actress and singer, noted for her roles in musical films, particularly with Nelson Eddy.

Dirk Bogarde
1921–

1 Remember a lady called Jeanette MacDonald? She sang, rather badly, with tears in her eyes all through the thirties.
letter, January 1970

Maurice Chevalier
1888–1972

2 Her red-haired beauty, her figure, her unusually rare acting ability for a singer, and on top of all that, a crystal voice, fresh as spring water . . . with that nightingale talent tossed into the bargain, she became what she became: unbeatable.
Ma route et mes chansons (1947)

Noël Coward
1899–1973

3 Like watching an affair between a mad rocking-horse and a rawhide suitcase.
of Jeanette MacDonald and Nelson Eddy in the film of his *Bitter Sweet*
diary, July 1946

Cecil B. de Mille
1881–1959

4 Jeannette comes from Philadelphia, but her voice has nothing in common with the Liberty Bell. She can hold a high C for fifty-five seconds without cracking!
in 1937

Nelson Eddy
1901–67

5 Unbelievable personal strength [like] a silver spoon cutting into frozen custard.
in June 1940

Clark Gable
1901–60

6 Hell, when she starts to sing nobody gets a chance. I'm not going to be a stooge for her while she sings in a big beautiful close-up and the camera shoots the back of my neck.
Edward Baron Turk *Hollywood Diva* (1998)

Hoppy Hopkins 7 The iron butterfly.

    c.1935; Edward Baron Turk *Hollywood Diva* (1998)

Ramsay MacDonald 1866–1937

British Labour statesman, Prime Minister 1924, 1929–31, and 1931–5. He served as Britain's first Labour Prime Minister.

Winston Churchill 8 I remember, when I was a child, being taken to the celebrated
1874–1965 Barnum's circus, which contained an exhibition of freaks and monstrosities, but the exhibit on the programme which I most desired to see was the one described as 'The Boneless Wonder'. My parents judged that that spectacle would be too revolting and demoralizing for my youthful eyes, and I have waited 50 years to see the boneless wonder sitting on the Treasury Bench.

    speech, January 1931

George V 9 You have kept up the dignity of the office without using it to give you
1865–1936 dignity.

    to MacDonald as outgoing Prime Minister
    Ramsay MacDonald's diary, June 1934

Lord Horder 10 I have come to the conclusion that the reason why I have found
1871–1955 nothing is because there is nothing there.

    a doctor's view
    Neville Chamberlain's diary, July 1935

David Lloyd George 11 Sufficient conscience to bother him, but not sufficient to keep him
1863–1945 straight.

    A. J. Sylvester *Life with Lloyd George* (1975)

James Maxton 12 Sit down, man. You're a bloody tragedy.
1885–1946

    to Ramsay MacDonald, who was making his last speech to the House of Commons
    in 1935

Harold Nicolson 13 I am haunted by mental decay such as I saw creeping over Ramsay
1886–1968 MacDonald. A gradual dimming of the lights.

    diary, April 1947

Leon Trotsky 14 There is something of the flunkey running all through him.
1879–1940

    in April 1935

Trevor McDonald 1939–

West-Indian born broadcaster. He became the main presenter of *News at Ten* in 1992.

Trevor McDonald 1 I am a West Indian peasant who has drifted into this business and who
1939– has survived. If I knew the secret, I would bottle it and sell it.

    in April 1996

John McEnroe 1959–

American tennis player. A temperamental player, he dominated the game in the early 1980s.

Arthur Ashe 1 This guy is a stiletto. He has great balance and he just slices people up.
1943–93 He's got a ton of shots. It's slice here, nick there, cut over there. Pretty soon you've got blood all over you, even though the wounds aren't deep. Soon after that you've bled to death.

    attributed

Clive James 2 McEnroe . . . did his complete Krakatoa number.
1939–

    of McEnroe disputing a line call at Wimbledon
    in July 1981

John McEnroe 3 One of me is worth forty thousand of you.
1959–

    to the crowd at the Queen's Club tournament, in June 1984

John McEnroe
1959–

4 People pay to watch me and if they want to boo me, that's fine. I'd rather get some attention than no attention. If it's bad, that's life.
attributed

Roger McGough 1937–

English poet. He became well-known in the 1960s as one of the 'Liverpool Poets'.

Roger McGough
1937–

1 I feel like a poet when I'm writing a poem. Otherwise I feel that I'm on the outside of things.
interview, May 1996

Roger McGuinn 1942–

American pop singer, a member of The Byrds.

John Cale
1942–

1 Roger McGuinn was always at an incredible level. If I had to admit that something called folk-rock existed . . . then the Byrds were it.
Clinton Heylin *From the Velvets to the Voidoids* (1993)

Ernst Mach 1838–1916

Austrian physicist and philosopher of science. He did important work on aerodynamics, while his writings inspired the logical positivist philosophers of the 1920s and influenced major scientists.

Albert Einstein
1879–1955

1 Mach was as good a scholar of mechanics as he was a deplorable philosopher.
in 1922

Niccolò Machiavelli 1469–1527

Italian statesman and political philosopher. His best-known work is *The Prince* (1532), which advises rulers that the acquisition and effective use of power may necessitate unethical methods.

Francis Bacon
1561–1626

1 We are much beholden to Machiavel and others, that write what men do, and not what they ought to do.
The Advancement of Learning (1605)

Victor Hugo
1802–85

2 Machiavelli is not an evil genius, nor a cowardly and miserable writer, he is nothing but the fact. And he is not merely the Italian fact, he is the European fact, the fact of the sixteenth century. He seems hideous, and is so, in presence of the moral idea of the nineteenth.
Les Misérables

Lord Macaulay
1800–59

3 Out of his surname they have coined an epithet for a knave, and out of his Christian name a synonym for the Devil.
Essays Contributed to the Edinburgh Review (1843)

William McKinley 1843–1901

American Republican statesman, President 1897–1901. He was assassinated by an anarchist.

Theodore Roosevelt
1858–1919

1 McKinley has no more backbone than a chocolate éclair!
H. T. Peck *Twenty Years of the Republic* (1906)

Charles Rennie Mackintosh 1868–1928

Scottish architect, designer, and painter. A leading exponent of art nouveau, he pioneered the new concept of functionalism in architecture and interior design.

James Guthrie
1859–1930

1 But hang it, Newbery, this man ought to be an artist!
on being told that a winning watercolour was by Mackintosh, an architectural student
in 1891

Shirley MacLaine 1934–

American actress. She has appeared in many successful films and written several volumes of autobiography.

Alfred Hitchcock
1899–1980

1 My dear, you have the guts of a bank robber.
on seeing Shirley MacLaine's screen test
attributed, c.1954

Shirley MacLaine
1934–

2 There is something in me even now that would push a peanut all the way down a street just to see if I could do it.
Douglas Thompson *Uncaged: the Biography of Nicolas Cage* (1997)

Malcolm McLaren 1946–

English manager of the Sex Pistols and pop singer. The boutique he opened with **Vivienne Westwood** in 1971 was influential in the development of punk fashion.

Malcolm McLaren
1946–

1 Be childish
Be irresponsible
Be disrespectful
Be everything
This society hates.
in 1969

Vivienne Westwood
1941–

2 I was a coin and he showed me the other side.
Jane Mulvagh *Vivienne Westwood: An Unfashionable Life* (1998)

Iain Macleod 1913–70

British Conservative politician. He was a gifted speaker but died only a month after becoming Chancellor of the Exchequer.

R. A. Butler
1902–82

1 I cannot help feeling that a man who always held all the bridge scores in his head, who seemed to know all the numbers, and played *vingt et un* so successfully would have been useful.
on Macleod's likely success as Chancellor
The Art of Memory (1982)

Michael Foot
1913–

2 A perspiration of firm confidence exudes from every political pore.
in October 1962

Lord Salisbury
1893–1972

3 Too clever by half.
of Macleod as Colonial Secretary 'in his relationship to the white communities of Africa'
speech, March 1961; see also **Disraeli** 9

Marshall McLuhan 1911–80

Canadian writer and thinker. He became famous in the 1960s for his phrase 'the medium is the message'.

Kenneth Boulding
1910–

1 McLuhan hits a very large nail not quite on the head.
attributed, 1990

Marshall McLuhan
1911–80

2 I am an intellectual thug who has been slowly accumulating a private arsenal with every intention of using it. In a mindless age every insight takes on the character of a lethal weapon.
letter, June 1951

Marshall McLuhan
1911–80

3 As you know, my detractors work night and day to advance my reputation. It is impossible to buy so invaluable a service!
letter, April 1970

Jonathan Miller
1934–

4 McLuhan is doing for visual space what Freud did for sex.
in February 1965

Harold Macmillan 1894–1986

British Conservative statesman, Prime Minister 1957–63. His term of office saw the signing of the Test-Ban Treaty with the US and the USSR. He advocated the granting of independence to British colonies.

Clement Attlee
1883–1967

1 By far the most radical man I've known in politics wasn't on the labour side at all—Harold Macmillan. If it hadn't been for the war he'd have joined the Labour Party. If that had happened Macmillan would have been Labour Prime Minister, and not me.
James Margach *The Abuse of Power* (1981)

Aneurin Bevan
1897–1960

2 The Prime Minister has an absolute genius for putting flamboyant labels on empty luggage.
speech, November 1959

Cuthbert Morley Headlam
1876–1964

3 He is very clever and takes infinite pains to make himself well informed—but somehow I doubt whether he will ever make much political progress. He bores people too quickly and has little or no sense of humour. However, it is never safe to prophesy about anyone's political prospects and Harold may yet come out on top.
diary, January 1932

Bernard Levin
1928–

4 The Stag at Bay with the mentality of a fox at large.
The Pendulum Years (1970)

Harold Macmillan
1894–1986

5 I was always a shit. Maurice wouldn't be one so that's why he didn't get on in politics like me.
referring to his son; Woodrow Wyatt's diary, January 1987

Malcolm Muggeridge
1903–90

6 H. M. always struck me as a parody of a Conservative politician in a novel by Trollope.
The Infernal Grove (1973)

Jeremy Thorpe
1929–

7 Greater love hath no man than this, that he lay down his friends for his life.
on Macmillan sacking seven of his Cabinet in July 1962
D. E. Butler and Anthony King *The General Election of 1964* (1965)

Peter Ustinov
1921–

8 Talk as though you have a cathedral in your mouth.
on imitating Macmillan
attributed

Peter Ustinov
1921–

9 I remember once watching Harold Macmillan on the box. He kept looking at the camera as though it were a cobra. He was appealing to the nation for calm and his face was frozen with terror.
Quotable Ustinov (1995)

George Walden
1939–

10 [It] was like watching a play by Harley Granville-Barker: you expected it to be passé Edwardian stuff and were agreeably surprised to get so much sense and entertainment from such a dated decor.
Lucky George: Memoirs of an Anti-Politician (1999)

Robert McNamara 1916–

American Democratic politician. As Secretary of Defense under **Kennedy** he supported American involvement in Vietnam.

Robert McNamara
1916–

1 I don't object to it's being called 'McNamara's War' . . . It is a very important war and I am pleased to be identified with it and do whatever I can to win it.
in April 1964

Robert McNamara
1916–

2 We . . . acted according to what we thought were the principles and traditions of this nation. We were wrong. We were terribly wrong.
*of the conduct of the Vietnam War by the **Kennedy** and **Johnson** administrations*
in April 1995

Madonna 1958–

American pop singer and actress. Albums such as *Like a Virgin* (1984) and her image as a sex symbol brought her international stardom in the mid 1980s.

Boy George
1961–

1 She's a gay man trapped in a woman's body.
Take It Like a Man (1995)

Mick Jagger
1943–

2 In a very sophisticated way her music and image characterises that essential dumbness that appeals to just about everybody.
Mick St Michael *Madonna in Her Own Words* (1990)

Madonna
1958–

3 Many people see Eva Perón as either a saint or the incarnation of Satan. That means I can definitely identify with her.
on playing the starring role in the film Evita
in February 1996

Charles Shaar Murray

4 So, finally, is Madonna a negative role model for teenagers? Of course not. She preaches safe sex and hard work: what could be more responsible than that?
in July 1990

Camille Paglia
1947–

5 Madonna is the future of feminism.
in 1990

Gustav Mahler 1860–1911

Austrian composer, conductor, and pianist. Forming a link between romanticism and the experimentalism of **Schoenberg**, his works include nine complete symphonies.

Gustav Mahler
1860–1911

1 What we leave behind us is only the husk, the shell. The *Meistersinger*, The Ninth, *Faust*—all them are only the discarded husk! no more, properly speaking, than our bodies are! I don't of course mean that artistic creation is superfluous. It is a necessity of man for growth and *joy*, which again is a question of health and creative energy.—But what actual need is there of notes?
letter, June 1909

Gustav Mahler
1860–1911

2 My life has all been paper! My life has all been paper!
said during his final illness; Alma Mahler *Gustav Mahler: Memories and Letters* (1946)

John Tavener
1944–

3 Mahler . . . can thump you in the stomach at one moment, then make you feel a kind of joy the next. But his is a neurotic joy—I don't think Mahler ever had a spiritual experience in his life.
interview, September 2000

Moses Maimonides 1135–1204

Jewish philosopher and Rabbinic scholar, born in Spain. His *Guide for the Perplexed* (1190) attempts to reconcile Talmudic scripture with the philosophy of **Aristotle**.

Anonymous

1 From Moses to Moses there was none like unto Moses.
later inscription on the tomb of Moses Maimonides

John Major 1943–

British Conservative statesman, Prime Minister 1990–7. His premiership saw the negotiations leading to the signing of the Maastricht Treaty, but he faced serious divisions within his party over Europe.

Anonymous

1 A decent, honourable man who was screwed up, frankly, by not being up to the job.
an unidentified Cabinet colleague; Peter Hennessy *The Prime Minister* (2000)

Lord Cranborne
1946–

2 There was this odd mixture of misery and the limpet—the miserable limpet if you like—which was a great inhibition to his premiership.
in October 1999

Nicholas Fairbairn
1933–95

3 I don't think he's up to the task. He is vin ordinaire and he should be château-bottled.
in April 1994

Chris Patten
1944–

4 As tough as old boots. The strength of his character is . . . more remarkable given how easily hurt he can be and how socially vulnerable he is.
in October 1999

Gillian Shephard
1940–

5 John Major's self-control in cabinet was rigid. The most angry thing he would ever do was to throw down his pencil.
in November 1999

Margaret Thatcher
1925–

6 I shan't be pulling the levers there but I shall be a very good back-seat driver.
on the appointment of John Major as Prime Minister
in November 1990

William Waldegrave
1946–

7 The problem was that when people began to be disloyal later on, they were not very frightened of him.
of John Major's Cabinet
in October 1999

Malcolm X 1925–65

American political activist. He joined the Nation of Islam in 1946 and became a vigorous campaigner for black rights, initially advocating the use of violence. In 1964 he converted to orthodox Islam.

Gwendolyn Brooks
1917–

1 He opened us—
who was a key,

who was a man.
'Malcolm X' (1968)

Eldridge Cleaver
1935–98

2 Black history began with Malcolm X.
Peter Goldman *The Death and Life of Malcolm X* (1973)

Dick Gregory
1932–

3 He spoke like a poor man and walked like a king.
Peter Goldman *The Death and Life of Malcolm X* (1973)

George Leigh Mallory 1886–1924

English mountaineer. He died in an attempt to climb Mount Everest.

George Leigh Mallory
1886–1924

1 Because it's there.
on being asked why he wanted to climb Everest
in March 1923

Lytton Strachey
1880–1932

2 And a face—oh incredible—the mystery of Botticelli, the refinement and delicacy of a Chinese print, the youth and piquancy of an unimaginable English boy.
letter, May 1909

Thomas Malthus 1766–1834

English economist and clergyman. He argued that without the practice of 'moral restraint' the population tends to increase at a greater rate than its means of subsistence.

Sydney Smith
1771–1845

1 Malthus is a real moral philosopher, and I would almost consent to speak as inarticulately, if I could think and act as wisely.
letter, July 1821

Nelson Mandela 1918–

South African statesman, President 1994–9. He was sentenced to life imprisonment in 1964 as an activist for the African National Congress (ANC). Released in 1990, he engaged in talks on majority rule.

Nelson Mandela
1918–

1 I have dedicated my life to this struggle of the African people. I have fought against white domination, and I have fought against black domination. I have cherished the ideal of a democratic and free society in which all persons live together in harmony with equal opportunities. It is an ideal which I hope to live for, and to achieve. But my lord, if needs be, it is an ideal for which I am prepared to die.
   speech at his trial, April 1964

Nelson Mandela
1918–

2 One of the things I learnt when I was negotiating was that until I changed myself I could not change others.
   in April 2000

Peter Mandelson 1953–

British Labour politician. Generally considered an architect of Labour's 1997 election victory, he resigned from the Cabinet in December 1998, returned in late 1999, and resigned again early in 2001.

William Hague
1961–

1 If Roland Rat were appointed to Northern Ireland, I would tell people to work with him. But I would still point out that he is a rat.
   on Peter Mandelson's appointment as Northern Ireland Secretary
   in October 1999

Simon Hoggart
1946–

2 Peter Mandelson is someone who can skulk in broad daylight.
   in July 1998

Ken Livingstone
1945–

3 Bringing Peter Mandelson back to run our campaigns would be like putting a vampire in charge of a blood bank.
   in December 1999

Matthew Parris
1949–

4 My name is Mandy: Peter B.,
   I'm back in charge—don't mess with me.
   My cheeks are drawn, my face is bony,
   The line I take comes straight from Tony.
   in October 1999

Édouard Manet 1832–83

French painter. He adopted a realist approach which greatly influenced the Impressionists, using pure colour to give a direct unsentimental effect.

Édouard Manet
1832–83

1 One doesn't just paint a landscape or a marine or figure study but the impressions of a moment in time.
   Margaret Shennan *Berthe Morisot: the First Lady of Impressionism* (1996)

Katherine Mansfield 1888–1973

New Zealand short-story writer. Her stories range from extended impressionistic evocations of family life to short sketches.

Bertrand Russell
1872–1970

1 Her talk was marvellous, much better than her writing, especially when she was telling of things she was going to write, but when she spoke about people she was envious, dark, and full of alarming penetration in discovering what they least wished known.
   Autobiography (1968)

Virginia Woolf
1882–1941

2 Her mind is a very thin soil, laid an inch or two upon very barren rock.
   diary, August 1918

Mao Zedong 1893–1976

Chinese statesman, chairman of the Communist Party 1949–76. He introduced measures such as the Hundred Flowers, the Great Leap Forward, and the Cultural Revolution.

Bernard Levin
1928–
1 Whom the mad would destroy, they first make gods.
in 1967

Lord Montgomery
1887–1976
2 Mao has a very fine strong face. He's the sort of man I'd go in the jungle with.
in 1961

Palden Gyatso
3 Mao's name was written all over my suffering and all over the deaths of thousands of prisoners. Mao's name linked us all.
Fire Under the Snow (1997)

Diego Maradona 1960–

Argentinian footballer. He captained the Argentina team that won the World Cup in 1986, arousing controversy when his apparent handball scored a goal in the quarter-final match against England.

Diego Maradona
1960–
1 The goal was scored a little bit by the hand of God, another bit by head of Maradona.
in June 1986

Alf Ramsey
1920–
2 Pele had nearly everything. Maradona *has* everything. He works harder, does more, and is more skilful. Trouble is that he'll be remembered for another reason. He bends the rules to suit himself.
in 1986

Bobby Robson
1933–
3 Maradona can win a game on his own in five minutes.
in June 1986

Marcel Marceau 1923–

French mime artist. He is known for appearing as the white-faced Bip, a character he developed from the French Pierrot character.

Marcel Marceau
1923–
1 I have spent more than half a lifetime trying to express the tragic moment.
in August 1988

Rocky Marciano 1923–69

American boxer. He became world heavyweight champion in 1952 and successfully defended his title six times until he retired, undefeated, in 1956.

Sonny Liston
1932–70
1 This man was one of the greatest champions ever. He refused to accept defeat. And nobody beat him.
in 1969

Joe Louis
1914–81
2 I knew how to beat Rocky. Just jab, jab, jab and cross a right. Rocky was insulted if you missed him.
in May 1979

Rocky Marciano
1923–69
3 If a champion spends his money foolishly, they ridicule him for that, and if he doesn't spend it, they call him cheap. Well, I'd rather have them criticize me for not spending it and wind up keeping my money.
Everett M. Skehan *Rocky Marciano* (1983)

Princess Margaret 1930–

British princess, only sister of **Elizabeth II**. In 1960 she married Antony Armstrong-Jones, who was later created Earl of Snowdon; the marriage was dissolved in 1978.

Princess Margaret
1930–
1 My children are not royal, they just happen to have the Queen as their aunt.
Elizabeth Longford (ed.) *The Oxford Book of Royal Anecdotes* (1989)

Jocelyn Stevens
1932–

2 I have always regarded her as a bird in a gilded cage. She would have loved to break free but was never able to.
Sarah Bradford *Elizabeth* (1996)

Marie-Antoinette 1755–93

French queen, wife of **Louis XVI**. Her extravagant lifestyle led to widespread unpopularity and, like her husband, she was executed during the French Revolution.

Edmund Burke
1729–97

1 I thought ten thousand swords must have leapt from their scabbards to avenge even a look that threatened her with insult.
Reflections on the Revolution in France (1790)

Constance Markievicz 1868–1927

Irish nationalist. She was actively involved in the Easter Rising and sentenced to death, but subsequently reprieved.

Mary Colum
1880?–1957

1 She was like an extinct volcano, her former violent self reduced to something burnt out.
of Constance Markievicz in old age
Life and the Dream (1947)

Elizabeth Coxhead
1909–

2 Hers is not the image of Irish womanhood we want to present to the outside world. The crude, charmless, virago-picture almost imposes itself—and then one meets one of her comrades in arms . . . and it is like coming out of a dark tunnel into the strong, sweet air of her own west coast.
The Daughters of Erin (1979)

Eamon de Valera
1882–1975

3 Whoever misunderstood Madame, the poor did not.
Diana Norman *Terrible Beauty* (1987)

Sean O'Casey
1880–1964

4 One thing she had in abundance—physical courage: with that she was clothed as with a garment.
Drums Under the Window (1945)

Duke of Marlborough 1650–1722

British general. He was commander of British and Dutch troops in the War of the Spanish Succession and won a series of victories (notably at Blenheim in 1704) over the French armies of **Louis XIV**.

Lord Byron
1788–1824

1 The glory and the nothing of a name.
'Churchill's Grave' (1816)

W. E. Gladstone
1809–98

2 There never was a Churchill from John of Marlborough down that had either morals or principles.
in conversation in 1882

John, Duke of Marlborough
1650–1722

3 That was once a man.
contemplating his portrait in old age
Winston Churchill *Marlborough: his life and times* vol. 4 (1938)

Sarah, Duchess of Marlborough
1660–1744

4 The Duke returned from the wars today and did pleasure me in his top-boots.
oral tradition, attributed in various forms

Sarah, Duchess of Marlborough
1660–1744

5 If I were young and handsome as I was, instead of old and faded as I am, and you could lay the empire of the world at my feet, you should never share the heart and hand that once belonged to John, Duke of Marlborough.
refusing an offer of marriage from the Duke of Somerset
W. S. Churchill *Marlborough: His Life and Times* (1938)

Robert Southey
1774–1843

6 'And everybody praised the Duke,
Who this great fight did win.'
'But what good came of it at last?'
Quoth little Peterkin.
'Why that I cannot tell,' said he,
'But 'twas a famous victory.'
'The Battle of Blenheim' (1800)

Garnet Wolseley
1833–1913

7 It was Marlborough who first taught us to be proud of our standing
army as a national institution, and the spirit of confidence which
pervaded Wellington's army in the Peninsula, and to a still more
remarkable degree shows itself now in Queen Victoria's army, may be
said to have been born at Blenheim, baptized at Ramillies, and
confirmed at Oudenarde.
Life of Marlborough (1894)

Christopher Marlowe 1564–93

English dramatist and poet. As a dramatist he brought a new strength and vitality to blank
verse; his work influenced **Shakespeare**'s early historical plays.

Michael Drayton
1563–1631

1 For that fine madness still he did retain
Which rightly should possess a poet's brain.
'To Henry Reynolds, of Poets and Poesy' (1627)

William Hazlitt
1778–1830

2 There is a lust of power in his writings, a hunger and thirst after
unrighteousness, a glow of the imagination unhallowed by any thing
except its own energies. His thoughts burn within him like a furnace
with flickering flames; or throwing out black smoke and mists, that
hide the dawn of genius, or like a poisonous mineral, corrode the heart.
Lectures chiefly on the dramatic literature of the age of Elizabeth (1820)

Seamus Heaney
1939–

3 A kind of cross between Oscar Wilde and Jack the Ripper.
The Redress of Poetry (1995)

Henry Irving
1838–1905

4 It was Marlowe who first wedded the harmonies of the great organ of
blank verse which peals through the centuries in the music of
Shakespeare.
speech, 1891

Ben Jonson
c.1573–1637

5 Marlowe's mighty line.
'To the Memory of . . . Shakespeare' (1623)

George Bernard Shaw
1856–1950

6 The infernal tradition that Marlowe was a great dramatic poet instead
of a xvi century Henley throws all the blame for his wretched half-
achievement on the actor. Marlowe had words and a turn for their
music, but nothing to say—a barren amateur with a great air.
letter, September 1903

Chico Marx 1891–1961

American comedian. The films which he made with his brothers are characterized by their
anarchic humour.

Chico Marx
1891–1961

1 I wasn't kissing her, I was just whispering in her mouth.
on being discovered by his wife with a chorus girl
Groucho Marx and Richard J. Anobile *Marx Brothers Scrapbook* (1973)

Groucho Marx
1895–1977

2 There were three things that Chico was always on—a phone, a horse or
a broad.
Ned Sherrin *Cutting Edge* (1984)

Groucho Marx 1895–1977

American comedian. The films which he made with his brothers are characterized by their anarchic humour.

Groucho Marx
1895–1977

3 Here lies Groucho Marx—and lies and lies and lies. P.S. He never kissed an ugly girl.
his own suggestion for his epitaph
B. Norman *The Movie Greats* (1981)

Groucho Marx
1895–1977

4 PLEASE ACCEPT MY RESIGNATION. I DON'T WANT TO BELONG TO ANY CLUB THAT WILL ACCEPT ME AS A MEMBER.
Groucho and Me (1959)

Mae West
1892–1980

5 I respected Groucho and the Marx brothers because they were funny, but what I admired most was that they created their own characters.
Charlotte Chandler *The Ultimate Seduction* (1984)

Karl Marx 1818–83

German political philosopher and economist, resident in England from 1849. With Friedrich Engels, he wrote the *Communist Manifesto* (1848), and he later enlarged on it in *Das Kapital*.

Tony Benn
1925–

6 It is as wholly wrong to blame Marx for what was done in his name, as it is to blame Jesus for what was done in his.
Alan Freeman *The Benn Heresy* (1982)

Fidel Castro
1927–

7 I believe that Karl Marx could have subscribed to the Sermon on the Mount.
Frei Betto *Fidel and Religion* (1987)

J. K. Galbraith
1908–

8 Much of the world's work is done by men who do not feel quite well. Marx is a case in point.
The Age of Uncertainty (1977)

Karl Marx
1818–83

9 All I know is that I am not a Marxist.
attributed in a letter from Friedrich Engels, August 1890

J. A. Schumpeter
1883–1950

10 The cold metal of economic theory is in Marx's pages immersed in such a wealth of steaming phrases as to acquire a temperature not naturally its own.
Capitalism, Socialism and Democracy (1942)

George Bernard Shaw
1856–1950

11 Das Kapital . . . is the book of a man who took no part in normal German or English society, and wrote of Capitalists and Workmen like a Class War Correspondent and not like a fellow creature.
'What I owe to German Culture' (1911)

Queen Mary 1867–1953

Wife of **George V** and mother of **Edward VIII** and **George VI**.

**Henry ('Chips')
Channon**
1897–1958

1 We saw Queen Mary looking like the Jungfrau, white and sparkling in the sun.
diary, June 1937

Edward VIII
1894–1972

2 From her invincible virtue and correctness she looked out as from a fortress upon the rest of humanity with all of its tremulous uncertainties and distractions.
A King's Story (1951)

Edward VIII
1894–1972

3 The bulletins from Marlborough House proclaim the old lady's condition to be slightly improved. Ice in the place of blood in the veins must be a fine preservative.
letter, 1953

George V
1865–1936

4 Put that paragraph at the very end. I cannot bring myself to speak of the Queen when I think of all I owe her.
preparing a reference to Queen Mary in a Silver Jubilee speech; in 1935

Mary, Queen of Scots 1542–87

Queen from 1542. Deposed by her Protestant lords, she fled to England in 1567. She became the focus of several Catholic plots against **Elizabeth I** and was eventually beheaded.

J. M. Barrie
1860–1937

5 If I ever really love it will be like Mary Queen of Scots, who said of her Bothwell that she could follow him round the world in her nightie.
What Every Woman Knows (1918)

Elizabeth I
1533–1603

6 The daughter of debate, that eke discord doth sow.
George Puttenham (ed.) *The Art of English Poesie* (1589)

Patrick, Lord Gray
d. 1612

7 A dead woman bites not.
pressing for the execution of Mary Queen of Scots in 1587; oral tradition

James V
1512–42

8 It came with a lass, and it will pass with a lass.
of the crown of Scotland, on learning of Mary's birth
in December 1542

John Knox
c.1505–72

9 Greater abomination was never in the nature of any woman than is in her, whereof we have but seen only the buds.
History of the Reformation of Religion within the realm of Scotland (1587)

Mary I 1516–58

Queen from 1553. She was known as 'Bloody Mary' from her persecution of Protestants. Calais, England's last possession in France, was lost in her reign.

Mary I
1516–58

10 When I am dead and opened, you shall find 'Calais' lying in my heart.
Holinshed's Chronicles vol. 4 (1808)

W. C. Sellar
1898–1951
and **R. J. Yeatman**
1898–1968

11 The cruel Queen died and a post-mortem examination revealed the word 'CALLOUS' engraved on her heart.
1066 and All That (1930)

Mary II 1662–94

Queen from 1689. Having been invited to replace her Catholic father **James II** on the throne after his deposition, she insisted that her husband, **William III**, be crowned along with her.

John Evelyn
1620–1706

12 She came into Whitehall laughing and jolly, as to a wedding, so as to seem quite transported.
diary, February 1689

John Masefield 1878–1967

English poet and novelist. His fascination with the sea is reflected in his first published and best-known book of poetry: *Salt-Water Ballads*.

Max Beerbohm
1872–1956

1 A swear-word in a rustic slum
A simple swear-word is to some,
To Masefield something more.
Fifty Caricatures (1912)

Robert Bridges
1844–1930

2 Masefield's sonnet? Ah yes, very nice. Pure Shakespeare. Masefield's *Reynard the Fox*? Very nice too. Pure Chaucer. Masefield's *Everlasting Mercy*? Hm. Yes. Pure Masefield.
Beverley Nichols *Twenty-Five* (1926)

D. H. Lawrence
1885–1930

3 He's a horrible sentimentalist—the cheap Byron of his day.
letter, March 1913

Henri Matisse 1869–1954

French painter and sculptor. His use of non-naturalistic colour led him to be regarded as a leader of the fauvists.

John Berger
1926–

1 It is comparatively easy to achieve a certain unity in a picture by allowing one colour to dominate, or by muting all the colours. Matisse did neither. He clashed his colours together like cymbals and the effect was like a lullaby.
Toward Reality (1962)

Stanley Matthews 1915–2000

English footballer. A winger famous for his dribbling skill, he played for Stoke City, Blackpool, and England and remained a professional player until he was 50.

Danny Blanchflower
1926–93

1 You usually knew how he would beat you. You could not do anything about it though.
David Meek *Anatomy of a Football Star: George Best* (1970)

Arthur Hopcraft
1932–

2 He was the opposite of glamorous: a non-drinker, a non-smoker, careful with his money, brought up among thrift and the everlooming threat of dole and debt. . . . He came from that England which had no reason to know that the Twenties were Naughty and the Thirties had style.
The Football Man (1968)

Pelé
1940–

3 The man who taught us how football should be played.
Stanley Matthews *The Way It Was* (2000)

W. Somerset Maugham 1874–1965

British novelist, short-story writer, and dramatist, born in France. His life and wide travels often provide the background to his writing.

Noël Coward
1899–1973

1 Maugham hated people more easily than he loved them; I love people more easily than I hate them.
in 1966

Malcolm Muggeridge
1903–90

2 It is this preoccupation with physical appetite, which he doesn't feel, that makes Maugham's work so intensely vulgar—rather like Balzac's to the rich, or Evelyn Waugh's to the highly born, or like Graham Greene's to the good.
Noel Annan *Our Age* (1990)

James Clerk Maxwell 1831–79

Scottish physicist. He extended the ideas of **Faraday** and **Kelvin** in his equations of electromagnetism and succeeded in unifying electricity and magnetism.

James Jeans
1877–1946

1 No matter how clearly he saw physical concepts in his mind's eye, he never made the mistake of identifying them with ultimate physical reality. He saw too deeply into things ever to imagine that what he saw was the ultimate stratum of all—final and absolute truth.
J. J. Thomson (ed.) *James Clerk Maxwell: A Commemoration Volume* (1931)

Robert Maxwell 1923–91

Czech-born British publisher and media entrepreneur. He died in obscure circumstances while yachting off Tenerife; it subsequently emerged that he had misappropriated company pension funds.

question in a Christmas quiz:

Stephen Fry
1957–

2 Imagine you are the defence counsel for the late Robert Maxwell. Try and persuade a jury that your client is not megalomaniacally insane.
Paperweight (1992)

Robert Maxwell
1923–91

3 I have played football since I was a toddler. Left wing, as you would expect. I was very fast.
attributed

Desmond Morris
1928–

4 Maxwell has the posture and manners of the dominant male.
in 1983

Louis B. Mayer 1885–1957

Russian-born American film executive. In 1924 he formed Metro-Goldwyn-Mayer (MGM) with **Samuel Goldwyn**; he headed the company until 1951.

Marion Davies
1897–1961

1 Mr Wells, don't you think Louis B. Mayer ought to take a trip to Russia and stop communism?
to H. G. Wells; G. Carey *Anita Loos* (1988)

Jules Mazarin 1602–61

Italian-born French statesman. Sent to Paris as the Italian papal legate, he became a naturalized Frenchman, and was made a cardinal in 1641 and then chief minister of France (1642).

Cardinal de Retz
1613–79

1 One of the greatest failings of Cardinal Mazarin is that he has never been able to believe that someone would speak to him with good intentions.
Mémoires (1715)

Peter Medawar 1915–87

English immunologist. He studied the biology of tissue transplantation, and showed that the rejection of grafts was the result of an immune mechanism.

Peter Medawar
1915–87

1 No working scientist ever thinks of himself as old, and so long as health, the rules of retirement, and fortune allow him to continue with research, he enjoys the young scientist's privilege of feeling himself born anew every morning.
Advice to a Young Scientist (1979)

Herman Melville 1819–91

American novelist and short-story writer. His experiences on a whaling ship formed the basis of several novels, notably *Moby Dick* (1851).

D. H. Lawrence
1885–1930

1 Melville has the strange, uncanny magic of sea-creatures, and some of their repulsiveness. He isn't quite a land animal. There is something slithery about him. Something always half-seas-over.
Studies in Classic American Literature (1924)

David Lodge
1935–

2 Herman Melville who split the atom of the traditional novel in the effort to make whaling a universal metaphor.
Changing Places (1975)

Felix Mendelssohn 1809–47

German composer and pianist. His romantic music is elegant, light, and melodically inventive. Other works include *Fingal's Cave* and *Elijah*.

Hector Berlioz
1803–69

1 There is one god—Bach—and Mendelssohn is his prophet.
J. H. Elliot *Berlioz* (1967)

Richard Wagner
1813–83

2 Mendelssohn has demonstrated that the Jew may be highly talented, greatly cultured, and be possessed of the finest sense of honour, but that these qualities do not enable him ever to imbue us with that deep and heart-piercing effect which we demand of art.
in 1850

Yehudi Menuhin 1916–99

American-born British violinist. His career began as a child prodigy, and he was a noted performer of both classical and contemporary music.

Béla Bartók
1881–1945

1 I did not think music could be played like that until long after the composer was dead.

on hearing Menuhin play **Bartók**'s First Sonata for Piano and Violin
in November, 1943

Nigel Kennedy
1956–

2 He never portrayed anger in his playing.
Anthony Clare In the Psychiatrist's Chair III (1998)

Diana Menuhin

3 All the time Y sat on Cloud Nine, the Bodhisattva destined to carry messages between heaven and earth.
Fiddler's Moll (1984)

Yehudi Menuhin
1916–99

4 My life has been spent in creating Utopias.
Unfinished Journey (1976)

George Steiner
1926–

5 To find genius and happiness united is nearly a scandal. Ordinarily those to whom the gods give their largesse are envied, even hated by their peers and contemporaries. Yehudi Menuhin is probably the most widely loved personality in the history of the performing arts.
'Not a Preface but a word of thanks' in Menuhin Unfinished Journey (1976)

Robert Gordon Menzies 1894–1978

Australian Liberal statesman, Prime Minister 1939–41 and 1949–66; Australia's longest-serving Prime Minister.

**William Morris
Hughes**
1862–1952

1 He couldn't lead a flock of homing pigeons.
Howard Beale This Inch of Time . . . (1977)

Eddy Merckx 1945–

Belgian racing cyclist. During his professional career he won the Tour de France five times (1969–72 and 1974).

asked for the best rider of all:

Marcel Bidot

1 Merckx. You have only to look at the list of his victories. He knew how to lift his backside out of the saddle, not like some champions who are very conscious of their media image but not very daring.
Graeme Fife Tour de France (1999)

Madame Eddy Merckx

2 The trouble with Eddy is that he's been vaccinated with a bicycle spoke. A week away from the bike and nothing works.
Graeme Fife Tour de France (1999)

George Meredith 1828–1909

English novelist and poet. He is noted for his control of narrative, sharp psychological characterization, and intricate style.

G. K. Chesterton
1874–1936

1 Meredith became, at his best, a sort of daintily dressed Walt Whitman.
Victorian Age in Literature (1912)

Oscar Wilde
1854–1900

2 Meredith! Who can define him? His style is chaos illuminated by flashes of lightning.
Intentions (1891)

Michelangelo 1475–1564

Italian sculptor, painter, architect, and poet. A leading figure of the High Renaissance, Michelangelo decorated the ceiling of the Sistine Chapel in Rome.

Eugène Delacroix
1798–1863

1 God! What a man! What beauty!
diary, 1824

El Greco
1541–1614

2 He was a good man, but did not know how to paint.
Francisco Pacheco *The Art of Painting: Its Antiquity and Greatness* (1649)

Michelangelo
1475–1564

3 I have only too much of a wife in this art of mine, who has always kept me in tribulation, and my children shall be the works I leave, which, even if they are naught, will live for a while.
in answer to a friend's comment that he had not married and had children
Giorgio Vasari *Lives of the Artists* (1568)

Joshua Reynolds
1723–92

4 I should desire that the last words which I should pronounce in this Academy, and from this place, might be the name of—Michael Angelo.
in December 1790

Auguste Rodin
1840–1917

5 All his statues are so constrained by agony that they seem to wish to break themselves. They all seem ready to succumb to the pressure of despair that fills them.
On Art and Artists (1911)

Mark Twain
1835–1910

6 Lump the whole thing! say that the Creator made Italy from designs by Michael Angelo!
The Innocents Abroad (1869)

W. B. Yeats
1865–1939

7 Michael Angelo left a proof
On the Sistine Chapel roof,
Where but half-awakened Adam
Can disturb globe-trotting Madam.
'Under Ben Bulben' (1939)

Ludwig Mies van der Rohe 1886–1969

German-born architect and designer. He designed the Seagram Building in New York, and was noted for his tubular steel furniture. He is widely associated with the saying 'Less is more'.

Ludwig Mies van der Rohe
1886–1969

1 I see no reason to invent a new architecture every Monday morning. I don't want to be interesting—I want to be good.
attributed

Robert Venturi
1925–

2 Less is a bore.
Complexity and Contradiction in Architecture (1966)

John Stuart Mill 1806–73

English philosopher and economist. Mill is best known for his political and moral works, especially *On Liberty*, and *Utilitarianism*. He criticized the contemporary treatment of women.

Edmund Clerihew Bentley
1875–1956

1 John Stuart Mill,
By a mighty effort of will,
Overcame his natural *bonhomie*
And wrote 'Principles of Political Economy'.
'John Stuart Mill' (1905)

Thomas Carlyle
1795–1881

2 He is still too fond of demonstrating everything. If John Mill were to get up to heaven, he would hardly be content till he had made out how it all was. For my part, I don't much trouble myself about the machinery of the place; whether there is an operative of angels, or an industrial class, I'm willing to leave all that.
Caroline Fox *Memories of Old Friends* (1882)

Oscar Wilde
1854–1900

3 As for Mill as a thinker—a man who knew nothing of Plato and Darwin gives me very little. His reputation is curious to me. I gain nothing, I have gained nothing from him—an arid, dry man with moods of sentiment.
letter, 1889

John Everett Millais 1829–96

English painter. A founder member of the Pre-Raphaelite Brotherhood, he went on to produce lavishly painted portraits and landscapes.

Henry James
1843–1916

1 This strangely unequal painter—a painter whose imperfectly great powers always suggest to me the legend of the spiteful fairy at the christening feast. The name of Mr Millais's spiteful fairy is vulgarity.
in May 1878

John Everett Millais
1829–96

2 Because in my early days I saw a good deal of Rossetti . . . they assume that my Pre-Raphaelite impulses in pursuit of light and truth were due to him. All nonsense! My pictures would have been exactly the same if I had never seen or heard of Rossetti.
Helen Rossetti Angeli *Dante Gabriel Rossetti: His Friends and Enemies* (1949)

John Ruskin
1819–1900

3 I am not sure whether he may not be destined to surpass all that has yet been done in figure-painting, as Turner did all past landscape.
Academy Notes (1856)

Walter Sickert
1860–1942

4 When Millais said 'Art', he meant British Art. And when he said 'British Art', he meant the painting of John Everett Millais.
in June 1929

Arthur Miller 1915–

American dramatist. He wrote *Death of a Salesman* and *The Crucible*, which used the Salem witch trials of 1692 as an allegory for McCarthyism.

Anonymous

1 Egghead weds hourglass.
on the marriage of Arthur Miller and **Marilyn Monroe**
headline in *Variety* 1956; attributed

Anonymous

2 For Miller, an ivory tower is an uninhabitable slum.
Kenneth Tynan *Profiles* (1989)

Kenneth Tynan
1927–80

3 He is a tall, ascetic folk-hero who might have stepped out of one of John Ford's better films: Lincoln, one might say, in horn-rims, making dry jokes in gnarled, relaxed language.
in October 1956

Henry Miller 1891–1980

American novelist. His 1930s autobiographical novels *Tropic of Cancer* and *Tropic of Capricorn* were banned in the US until the 1960s due to their frank depiction of sex and use of obscenities.

Gerald Brenan
1894–1987

4 Miller is not really a writer but a non-stop talker to whom someone has given a typewriter.
Thoughts in a Dry Season (1978)

Henry Miller
1891–1980

5 It is true I swim in a perpetual sea of sex but the actual excursions are fairly limited.
letter, Febuary 1932

Anaïs Nin
1903–77

6 The very touch of the letter was as if you had taken me all into your arms.
letter to Henry Miller, August 1932

Jonathan Miller 1934–

English writer and director. He qualified as a doctor, has directed many plays and operas, and presented various television series.

Peter Hall
1930–

7 He is the only director I know who always likes his own work.
diary, April 1973

Jonathan Miller
1934–

8 I'm usually called a jack of all trades by people who are scarcely jacks of one.
in 1988

Spike Milligan 1918–

British comedian and writer, born in India. He came to prominence in the cult radio programme *The Goon Show* (1951–9).

Dick Lester
1932–

1 He has a thin skin surrealism which is very rare.
Norma Farnes (ed.) *The Goons: The Story* (1997)

Jonathan Miller
1934–

2 His work had the same importance as Alice in Wonderland and the Pickwick Papers.
Norma Farnes (ed.) *The Goons: The Story* (1997)

Peter Sellers
1925–80

3 [I was] just a vase of flowers, and Milligan arranged me.
Norma Farnes (ed.) *The Goons: The Story* (1997)

A. A. Milne 1882–1956

English writer of stories and poems for children. He created the character Winnie the Pooh for his son Christopher Robin.

Christopher Milne
1920–96

1 My father, who had derived such happiness from his childhood, found in me the companion with whom he could return there . . . When I was three he was three. When I was six he was six. . . . He needed me to escape from being fifty.
The Enchanted Places (1974)

Christopher Milne 1920–96

English bookseller, son of **A. A. Milne**. He was closely identified in the public mind with the character Christopher Robin in his father's books.

A. A. Milne
1882–1956

2 I feel that the legal Christopher Robin has already had more publicity than I want for him. Moreover, since he is growing up, he will soon feel that he has had more publicity than he wants for himself.
By Way of Introduction (1929)

Slobodan Milosevic 1941–

Serbian statesman. His strongly pro-Serbian policies led to bitter warfare and 'ethnic cleansing' in Bosnia and Kosovo.

Bill Clinton
1946–

1 Balkan graveyards are full of the broken promises of Slobodan Milosevic.
statement, October 1998

Harold Pinter
1930–

2 Milosevic is undoubtedly ruthless and savage. So is Clinton.
in April 1999

John Milton 1608–74

English poet. His three major works, the epic poems *Paradise Lost* and *Paradise Regained*, and the verse drama *Samson Agonistes*, were completed after he had gone blind.

John Aubrey
1626–97

1 His harmonical and ingenious soul did lodge in a beautiful and well proportioned body. He was a spare man.
Brief Lives

John Aubrey
1626–97

2 Oval face. His eye a dark grey. He had auburn hair. His complexion exceeding fair—he was so fair that they called him *the lady of* Christ's College.
Brief Lives

William Blake
1757–1827

3 The reason Milton wrote in fetters when he wrote of Angels and God, and at liberty when of Devils and Hell, is because he was a true Poet, and of the Devil's party without knowing it.
The Marriage of Heaven and Hell (1790–3)

Lord Byron
1788–1824

4 Milton's the prince of poets—so we say;
A little heavy, but no less divine.
Don Juan (1819–24)

Thomas Carlyle
1795–1881

5 The words of Milton are true in all things, and were never truer than in this: 'He who would write heroic poems must make his whole life a heroic poem.'
Critical and Miscellaneous Essays (1838)

Charles Darwin
1809–82

6 Formerly Milton's *Paradise Lost* had been my chief favourite, and in my excursions during the voyage of the *Beagle*, when I could take only a single volume, I always chose Milton.
Francis Darwin (ed.) *The Life and Letters of Charles Darwin* (1887)

William Empson
1906–84

7 I should say that Milton's experience of propaganda is what makes his later poetry so very dramatic; that is, though he is a furious partisan, he can always imagine with all its force exactly what the reply of the opponent would be.
Milton's God (1961)

Thomas Gray
1716–71

8 The living throne, the sapphire-blaze,
Where angels tremble, while they gaze,
He saw; but blasted with excess of light,
Closed his eyes in endless night.
The Progress of Poesy (1757)

A. E. Housman
1859–1936

9 And malt does more than Milton can
To justify God's ways to man.
A Shropshire Lad (1896)

Samuel Johnson
1709–84

10 An acrimonious and surly republican.
Lives of the English Poets (1779–81)

Samuel Johnson
1709–84

11 Milton, Madam, was a genius that could cut a Colossus from a rock; but could not carve heads upon cherry-stones.
to Hannah More, who had expressed a wonder that the poet who had written Paradise Lost should write such poor sonnets
comment, June 1784

Andrew Marvell
1621–78

12 Where couldst thou words of such a compass find?
Whence furnish such a vast expense of mind?
Just Heav'n thee, like Tiresias, to requite,
Rewards with prophecy thy loss of sight.
'On Mr Milton's Paradise Lost' (1681)

John Milton
1608–74

13 When I consider how my light is spent,
E're half my days, in this dark world and wide,
And that one talent which is death to hide
Lodged with me useless.
'When I consider how my light is spent' (1673)

Alfred, Lord Tennyson
1809–92

14 O mighty-mouthed inventor of harmonies,
O skilled to sing of time or eternity,
God-gifted organ-voice of England,
Milton, a name to resound for ages.
'Milton: Alcaics' (1863)

Virginia Woolf
1882–1941

15 He was the first of the masculinists. He deals in horror and immensity and squalor and sublimity but never in the passions of the human heart. Has any great poem ever let in so little light upon one's own joys and sorrows? I get no help in judging life; I scarcely feel that Milton lived or knew men and women.
diary, 1918

William Wordsworth
1770–1850

16 Milton! thou shouldst be living at this hour:
England hath need of thee: she is a fen
Of stagnant waters: altar, sword, and pen,
Fireside, the heroic wealth of hall and bower,
Have forfeited their ancient English dower

Of inward happiness.
'Milton! thou shouldst be living at this hour' (1807)

Kylie Minogue 1968–

Australian pop singer and actress. She appeared in the television soap opera *Neighbours* and later developed a career as a pop singer.

Tony Parsons 1 She can loll about in a leather fig-leaf and sing about pumping it up all
1953– night long—but Kylie is half a pint of semi-skimmed milk and she
always will be.
Dispatches from the Front Line of Popular Culture (1994)

Joni Mitchell 1943–

Canadian singer and songwriter. Starting to record in 1968, she moved from folk to a fusion of folk, jazz, and rock.

Leonard Cohen 1 Joni Mitchell, she's probably the Beethoven of pop music.
1934– in 1988

David Crosby 2 Take it from guys who know. Joni Mitchell is about as modest as
1941– Mussolini.
Myles Palmer (ed.) *Small Talk, Big Quotes* (1993)

François Mitterrand 1916–96

French statesman, President 1981–95. As President he initially moved to raise basic wages, increase social benefits, nationalize key industries, and decentralize government, but later reversed some of these policies.

George Walden 1 A man whose ultimate priorities in life are books, trees and women
1939– cannot be all bad.
Lucky George: Memoirs of an Anti-Politician (1999)

Amedeo Modigliani 1884–1920

Italian painter and sculptor, resident in France from 1906. His portraits and nudes are noted for their elongated forms, linear qualities, and earthy colours.

Jean Cocteau 1 Modigliani's portraits, even his self-portraits, are not the reflection of
1889–1963 his external observation, but of his internal vision, of a vision as
gracious, noble, acute, and deadly as the fabulous horn of the unicorn.
Jacques Lipchitz *Amedeo Modigliani* (1967)

Max Jacob 2 Everything in [Modigliani] tended towards purity in art. His
1876–1944 insupportable pride, his black ingratitude, his haughtiness did not
exclude familiarity. Yet all that was nothing but a need for crystalline
purity, a trueness to himself in life as in art. He was cutting, but as
fragile as glass; also as inhuman as glass, so to say.
Charles Douglas *Artist Quarter* (1941)

Amedeo Modigliani 3 I do at least three pictures a day in my head. What's the use of spoiling
1884–1920 canvas when nobody will buy?
Pierre Sichel *Modigliani* (1967)

Molière 1622–73

French dramatist. He wrote more than twenty comic plays about contemporary France.

Victor Hugo 1 Voltaire speaks to a party, Molière speaks to society, Shakespeare
1802–85 speaks to mankind.
Littérature et philosophie mêlées (1834)

Vyacheslav Molotov 1890–1986

Soviet statesman. He negotiated the non-aggression pact with Nazi Germany (1939) and after 1945 represented the Soviet Union at meetings of the United Nations.

Winston Churchill
1874–1965

1 I have never seen a human being who more perfectly represented the modern conception of a robot.
The Second World War vol. 1 (1948)

Harold Macmillan
1894–1986

2 A very pale pasty face . . . large forehead . . . closely cut grey hair . . . respectable black suit . . . a head gardener in his Sunday clothes.
Tides of Fortune, 1945–55 (1969)

Walter Mondale 1928–

American Democratic politician and Vice-President.

Ronald Reagan
1911–

1 I am not going to make age an issue in this campaign. I am not going to exploit for political purposes my opponent's youth and inexperience.
in October 1984

Claude Monet 1840–1926

French painter. A founder member of the Impressionists, he was particularly fascinated with the play of light on objects at different times of day and under different weather conditions.

Paul Cézanne
1839–1906

1 Monet is only an eye, but what an eye!
attributed

Claude Monet
1840–1926

2 I paint as a bird sings.
Gustave Geffroy *Claude Monet, sa vie, son temps, son oeuvre* (1922)

George Moore
1852–1933

3 Monet began by imitating Manet, and Manet ended by imitating Monet.
Vale (1914)

Marilyn Monroe 1926–62

American actress; born Norma Jean Mortenson. She emerged as the definitive Hollywood sex symbol. She is thought to have died of an overdose of sleeping-pills.

Anonymous

1 Egghead weds hourglass.
*on the marriage of **Arthur Miller** and Marilyn Monroe*
headline in *Variety* 1956; attributed

Yogi Berra
1925–

2 I don't know if it's good for baseball but it sure beats the hell out of rooming with Phil Rizzuto!
*on the announcement of the marriage of **Joe DiMaggio** and Marilyn Monroe*
attributed

Julie Burchill
1960–

3 In life she was a man's woman because a lot of men wanted her; now she is a man's woman because a lot of men want to be her.
Girls on Film (1986)

George Cukor
1899–1983

4 Her face *moves*—it catches the light—it's genuinely photogenic. And she *thinks boldly*. She thinks as a dog thinks. *Au fond*, her mind is wonderfully unclouded.
Kenneth Tynan *Tynan Right and Left* (1967)

Tony Curtis
1925–

5 It's like kissing Hitler.
when asked what it was like to kiss Marilyn Monroe
A. Hunter *Tony Curtis* (1985)

Harry Golden

6 Marilyn has married a Protestant, a Catholic and a Jew, in that order, and divorced all of them, impartially, with the proper amount of tears. That's what I call brotherhood.
nominating Marilyn Monroe for his Interfaith Brotherhood Week Award; in March 1961

Elizabeth Hurley
1965–

7 If I were as fat as Marilyn Monroe I'd kill myself.
in January 2000

Clive James
1939–

8 She was good at playing abstract confusion in the same way that a midget is good at being short.
Visions Before Midnight (1977)

Elton John
1947–
and Bernie Taupin
1950–

9 Goodbye Norma Jean . . .
It seems to me you lived your life
Like a candle in the wind.
Never knowing who to cling to
When the rain set in.
'Candle in the Wind' (song, 1973)

Norman Mailer
1923–

10 So we think of Marilyn who was every man's love affair with America, Marilyn Monroe who was blonde and beautiful and had a sweet little rinky-dink of a voice and all the cleanliness of all the clean American backyards.
Marilyn (1973)

Arthur Miller
1915–

11 All my energy and attention were devoted to trying to help her solve her problems. Unfortunately I didn't have much success.
in August 1992

Marilyn Monroe
1926–62

12 I always feel I work for those people who work hard, who go to the box office and put down their money and want to be entertained. I always feel I do it for them. I don't care so much about what the director thinks.
interview, October 1960

Edith Sitwell
1887–1964

13 In repose her face was at moments strangely, prophetically, tragic, like the face of a beautiful ghost—a little Spring-ghost, an innocent fertility-daemon, the vegetation spirit that was Ophelia.
Taken Care Of (1966)

Gloria Steinem
1934–

14 I remember her on the screen, huge as a colossus doll, mincing and whispering and simply hoping her way into total vulnerability.
in August 1972

Billy Wilder
1906–

15 Ah, Marilyn, Hollywood's Joan of Arc, our Ultimate Sacrificial Lamb. Well, let me tell you, she was mean, terribly mean. The meanest woman I have ever known in this town . . . I have never met anyone as utterly mean as Marilyn Monroe. Nor as utterly fabulous on the screen, and that includes Garbo.
interview, 1968

Montesquieu 1689–1755

French political philosopher. His reputation rests chiefly on *L'Esprit des lois* (1748), a comparative study of political systems.

Catherine the Great
1729–96

1 I am but a crow strutting about in peacock feathers. If I were Pope I would certainly canonise Montesquieu, and that without listening to a devil's advocate.
in 1767

Lord Montgomery 1887–1976

British Field Marshal. His victory at El Alamein in 1942 proved the first significant Allied success in the Second World War, and he later commanded the Allied ground forces in the invasion of Normandy.

Winston Churchill
1874–1965

1 In defeat unbeatable: in victory unbearable.
Edward Marsh *Ambrosia and Small Beer* (1964)

Dwight D. Eisenhower
1890–1969

2 He's just a little man, and he's just as little inside as he is outside.
Nigel Hamilton *Monty* (1986)

Alec Guinness 1914–2000	3 A vain actor playing to the gallery, brilliant, of course, but somehow offputting. diary, May 1996
Max Hastings 1945–	4 For all Montgomery's caution in battle, the passion for 'tidiness' that more than once denied him all-embracing victories, this essentially cold, insensitive man was devoted to winning. *Overlord* (1984)
Nancy Mitford 1904–73	5 All my books [are] by his bed and when he gets to a daring passage he washes it down with Deuteronomy! letter, October 1953
Lord Montgomery 1887–1976	6 I've got to go to meet God—and explain all those men I killed at Alamein. in 1976; Nigel Hamilton *Monty* (1986)

Bobby Moore 1941–93

English footballer. A defender who spent most of his career with West Ham United, he captained the English team that won the World Cup in 1966.

Michael Parkinson 1935–	1 His detachment from the hurly-burly was disdainful. He always looked like a king among commoners. Then, when there came a champion worthy of his attention, like Pele, we saw proof, if ever it be needed, that he was one of the greatest footballers of all time. in March 1993

Dudley Moore 1935–

English actor, comedian, and musician. He appeared with **Peter Cook** in the television shows *Beyond the Fringe* and *Not Only . . . But Also*.

Peter Cook
1937–95
	2 I'm glad it hasn't changed him. He's still selfish, vain, greedy. In other words a fully-rounded human being.
	    of Moore's success in the US
	    attributed

Henry Moore 1898–1986

English sculptor and draughtsman. His work is characterized by semi-abstract reclining forms, large upright figures, and family groups, intended to be viewed in the open air.

Geoffrey Grigson 1905–85	3 His stony reclining landscape women need to be nearer women, very often, or else further from them; more natural or else more abstract. *Henry Moore* (1944)
Henry Moore 1898–1986	4 The first hole made through a piece of stone is a revelation. in August 1937
John Prescott 1938–	5 He didn't like heads, did he? opening a Moore exhibition in Beijing, October 2000

Marianne Moore 1887–1972

American poet. Her tone is sophisticated and conversational, and her observations detailed and precise.

Elizabeth Bishop 1911–79	6 If she speaks of a chair you can practically sit on it. notebook, *c.*1934/5
Marianne Moore 1887–1972	7 READER: Miss Moore, your poetry is very difficult to read. MARIANNE MOORE: It is very difficult to write. George Plimpton (ed.) *The Writer's Chapbook* (1989)

Roger Moore 1928–

English actor, best known for his film roles as James Bond.

Roger Moore
1928–

8 Left eyebrow raised, right eyebrow raised.
summary of his acting range
David Brown *Star Billing* (1985)

Suzanne Moore

British journalist.

Germaine Greer
1939–

9 So much lipstick must rot the brain.
in May 1995

Margaret Moran 1955–

British Labour politician, MP for Luton South since 1997.

Margaret Moran
1955–

1 I am not a Blair Babe. I am a Blair Witch.
in September 2000

Hannah More 1745–1833

English writer. A member of the Blue Stocking Circle, she is best known for her religious tracts and her interest in education.

Horace Walpole
1717–97

1 Much as I love your writings, I respect yet more your heart and your goodness. You are so good, that I believe you would go to heaven, even though there were no Sunday, and only six *working* days in the week.
letter, 1788

Thomas More 1478–1535

English scholar and statesman. His *Utopia* established him as a leading humanist of the Renaissance. He was imprisoned after opposing **Henry VIII**'s marriage to **Anne Boleyn**, and beheaded.

Jacob Bronowski
1908–74

2 What did Sir Thomas More die of? He died because his king thought of him as a wielder of power. And what More wanted to be, what Erasmus wanted to be, what every strong intellect wants to be, is a guardian of integrity.
The Ascent of Man (1973)

Charles V
1500–58

3 My Lord Ambassador, we understand that the king your master hath put his faithful servant and grave wise councillor, Sir Thomas More, to death. This will we say, that if we had been master of such a servant of whose doings we ourselves have had these many years no small experience, we would rather have lost the best city of our dominions than have lost such a worthy councillor.
in July 1535

Erasmus
c.1469–1536

4 *Omnium horarum hominem.*
A man of all hours.
In Praise of Folly (1509)

Erasmus
c.1469–1536

5 He has the quickest sense of the ridiculous of any man I ever met.
letter, July 1519

Thomas More
1478–1535

6 If the parties will at my hands call for justice, then, all were it my father stood on the one side, and the Devil on the other, his cause being good, the Devil should have right.
William Roper *Life of Sir Thomas More* (1626)

Robert Whittington

7 As time requireth, a man of marvellous mirth and pastimes, and sometime of as sad gravity, as who say: a man for all seasons.
Vulgaria (1521)

Eric Morecambe 1926–84

English comedian. In 1941 he formed a double act with comedian Ernie Wise that led to the enduringly popular TV series *The Morecambe and Wise Show* (1961–76).

Eric Morecambe
1926–84

1 In old-fashioned double acts the straight man would do something right and the comic would get it wrong. With us, Ernie would probably get it wrong as well.
in September 1973

Kenneth Tynan
1927–80

2 Ernie today is the comic *who is not funny*. And Eric—the dominating character who patronises the comic—is the straight man *who is funny*.
in September 1973

Berthe Morisot 1841–95

French painter, the first woman to join the Impressionists. Her works typically depicted women and children.

Édouard Manet
1832–83

1 The Mademoiselles Morisot are charming. What a pity they're not men. All the same, they could serve the cause of painting, in their capacity as women, by each marrying an academician and bringing trouble to those old fogeys in the enemy camp. Or perhaps that's asking too much self-sacrifice!
letter, August 1868

George Moore
1852–1933

2 Her pictures are the only pictures painted by a woman that could not be destroyed without leaving a blank, a hiatus in the history of art.
Modern Painting (1910)

Berthe Morisot
1841–95

3 I have had no expectations, and the desire for posthumous glory seems to me an inordinate aspiration. My ambition is limited to trying to record something fleeting, anything, the least of things. Yet even this ambition is excessive.
Margaret Shennan *Berthe Morisot: the First Lady of Impressionism* (1996)

Auguste Renoir
1841–1919

4 What an anomaly to see the appearance in our age of realism of a painter so impregnated with the grace and finesse of the eighteenth century: in a word, the last elegant and 'feminine' artist that we have had since Fragonard.
Ambroise Vollard *En écoutant Cézanne, Degas, Renoir* (1938)

Jane Morris c. 1840–1914

Wife of **William Morris**.

Henry James
1843–1916

1 It's hard to say whether she's a grand synthesis of all Pre-Raphaelite pictures ever made—or they a 'keen analysis' of her—whether she's an original or a copy. In either case, she is a wonder.
Letters (1920)

William Morris
1834–96

2 I cannot paint you but I love you.
written on his canvas while she sat for him
Timothy Hilton *The Pre-Raphaelites* (1970); possibly apocryphal

George Bernard Shaw
1856–1950

3 The most silent woman I have ever met.
Christopher Wood *The Pre-Raphaelites* (1981)

William Morris 1834–96

English designer, craftsman, poet, and writer. A leading figure in the Arts and Crafts Movement, in 1861 he established Morris & Company to produce hand-crafted goods for the home.

Max Beerbohm
1872–1956

4 Of course he was a wonderful all-round man, but the act of walking round him has always tired me.
letter, c. 1953

William Morris
1834–96

5 I spend my life ministering to the swinish luxury of the rich.
remark, c.1877

John Ruskin
1819–1900

6 I can't understand how a man who, on the whole, enjoys dinner—and breakfast—and supper—to that extent of fat—can write such lovely poems about Misery.
letter, January 1870

W. B. Yeats
1865–1939

7 The dream-world of Morris was as much the antithesis of daily life as with other men of genius, but he was never conscious of the antithesis and so knew nothing of intellectual suffering.
Autobiographies (1926)

Jim Morrison 1943–71

American rock singer. Morrison was the flamboyant lead singer of the Doors, a group formed in 1965.

John Cale
1942–

1 Jim Morrison was like a spoilt, clean-scrubbed schoolboy in his first day on drink.
Richard Witts *Nico: the Lives and Lies of an Icon* (1993)

Ray Manzarek
1935–

2 Jim was definitely seeking the palace of wisdom through the road of excess. And he was enjoying every intoxicated moment.
Light my Fire: my life with the Doors (1998)

Jim Morrison
1943–71

3 I'm interested in anything about revolt, disorder, chaos, especially activity that appears to have no meaning. It seems to me to be the road toward freedom.
in January 1968

Nico
1938–1988

4 You could say that Jim took drugs because he wanted visions for his poetry. It is like people in the office who drink coffee to help them work. It is really the same.
Richard Witts *Nico: the Lives and Lies of an Icon* (1993)

Van Morrison 1945–

Northern Irish singer, instrumentalist, and songwriter. He has developed a distinctive personal style from a background of blues, soul, folk music, and rock.

Lester Bangs
1948–82

5 Van Morrison is interested, *obsessed* with how much musical or verbal information he can compress into a small space, and, almost conversely, how far he can spread one note, word, sound, or picture.
in 1979

Ray Manzarek
1935–

6 Van Morrison was—and is—the best of the white blues men. No-one has that soul, that torment, that anguish.
Light my Fire: my life with the Doors (1998)

Van Morrison
1945–

7 From the journalistic point of view what I do is rock music, but what I actually perform and do on albums has nothing to do with rock. It's not played like rock music. It's a combination of gospel, blues, folk.
interview, February 1983

Jelly Roll Morton 1885–1941

American jazz pianist, composer, and bandleader. He was one of the principal links between ragtime and New Orleans jazz.

Alistair Cooke
1908–

1 He was a gangling, wide-mouthed, flat-faced man with big wrists. He was playing a sour piano in a really smelly café . . . It was like meeting the President in a shoe-shine parlour.
in 1952

Grandma Moses 1860–1961

American painter. Anna Mary Moses took up painting as a hobby in 1927, producing more than a thousand paintings in naive style, mostly of American rural life.

Anonymous 1 She had become by her hundredth year one of those old people who, as old buildings civilize a city or spindly church spires bind up a landscape, make the world seem safer. Shaw and Brancusi were examples; Churchill and Schweitzer still are. They pay the world the great compliment of being reluctant to leave it, and their reluctance becomes a benediction.

in *New Yorker* December 1961

Grandma Moses 2 I look back on my life like a good day's work, it was done and I am
1860–1961 satisfied with it. I was happy and contented, I knew nothing better and made the best out of what life offered. And life is what we make it, always has been, always will be.

My Life's History (1951)

Lord Mountbatten 1900–79

British admiral and administrator. He was supreme Allied commander in SE Asia (1943–5) and the last viceroy and first Governor General of India. He was killed by an IRA bomb while on his yacht.

Charles, Prince of 1 You really are becoming exactly like Queen Victoria in her old age and
Wales nobody will know what to do when you aren't there to help and advise.
1948– in August 1970

Winston Churchill 2 What could you hope to achieve except to be sunk in a bigger and more
1874–1965 expensive ship this time?
overriding Mountbatten's protests at being appointed to a desk job
in November 1941

Nigel Hamilton 3 A master of intrigue, jealousy and ineptitude. Like a spoilt child he
1944– toyed with men's lives with an indifference to casualties that can only be explained by his insatiable, even psychopathic, ambition.
Montgomery (1981)

Leonard Mosley 4 A man of charm, charm, charm and luck, luck, luck.
1913– *The Last Days of the British Raj* (1962)

Lord Mountbatten 5 I can't think of a more wonderful thanksgiving for the life I have had
1900–79 than that everyone should be jolly at my funeral.
Richard Hough *Mountbatten* (1980)

Viscount Slim 6 Youthful, buoyant, picturesque, with a reputation for gallantry known
1891–1970 everywhere, he talked to the British soldier with irresistible frankness and charm.
Defeat into Victory (1956)

Robert Whinney 7 As a captain in command he was consistently unfortunate, with one glorious defeat after another.
Andrew Roberts *Eminent Churchillians* (1994)

Philip Ziegler 8 Remember. In Spite of Everything, He Was A Great Man.
1929– *notice kept on his desk while working on his biography of Mountbatten*
Andrew Roberts *Eminent Churchillians* (1994)

Marjorie ('Mo') Mowlam 1949–

British Labour politician. As Secretary of State for Northern Ireland she oversaw the early stages of the peace process. She continued working while recovering from a brain tumour.

Lynn Barber 1 She stands too close when talking to you and uses your Christian name
1944– excessively.
in February 1998

Alan Clark
1928–99

2 If I can comport myself with the dignity and competence of Ms Mo Mowlam, I shall be very satisfied.
while recovering from surgery for a brain tumour
in June 1999

Lynda Lee-Potter

3 An only slightly effeminate Geordie trucker.
in April 1997

Mo Mowlam
1949–

4 Ian Paisley said he pitied my husband having to put up with 'the sinner', which is what he often called me.
in April 2000

Wolfgang Amadeus Mozart 1756–91

Austrian composer. A child prodigy and a prolific composer, he came to epitomize classical music in its purity of form and melody.

Maurice Baring
1874–1945

1 In Mozart and Salieri we see the contrast between the genius which does what it must and the talent which does what it can.
Outline of Russian Literature (1914)

Karl Barth
1886–1968

2 It may be that when the angels go about their task of praising God, they play only Bach. I am sure, however, that when they are together *en famille*, they play Mozart.
Wolfgang Amadeus Mozart (1956)

Thomas Beecham
1879–1961

3 If I were a dictator I should make it compulsory for every member of the population between the ages of four and eighty to listen to Mozart for at least a quarter of an hour daily for the coming five years.
Harold Atkins and Archie Newman *Beecham Stories* (1978)

Catherine Carswell
1879–1946

4 Bach is for me the bread and wine of music. But Mozart takes me to the Milky Way and brings me into the Pleiades and Orion's Belt.
John Carswell (ed.) *Lying Awake* (1950)

Colin Davis
1927–

5 If you listen to the greatest composer who has ever lived, which is Mozart, you are confronted with a vision of order which I think is not comparable to anything else we know. You are also confronted with a vision of the Garden of Eden.
Anthony Clare *In the Psychiatrist's Chair III* (1998)

Antonín Dvořák
1841–1904

6 Mozart is sunshine.
Otakar Sourek (ed.) *Antonín Dvořák: Letters and Reminiscences* (1954)

Franz Joseph Haydn
1732–1809

7 I tell you, calling God to witness and speaking as a man of honour, that your son is the greatest composer I know, either personally or by repute!
Leopold Mozart, letter, February 1785

Joseph II
1741–90

8 Too beautiful for our ears, and much too many notes, dear Mozart.
of The Abduction from the Seraglio *(1782)*
attributed; Franz Xaver Niemetschek *Life of Mozart* (1798)

Sören Kierkegaard
1813–55

9 I am in love with Mozart like a young girl. Immortal Mozart! I owe you everything . . . I have you to thank that I did not die without having loved.
Either/Or (1843)

Tom Lehrer
1928–

10 It is sobering to consider that when Mozart was my age he had already been dead for a year.
Nat Shapiro (ed.) *Encyclopedia of Quotations about Music* (1978)

Yehudi Menuhin
1916–99

11 Nowhere in the overpopulated urban centres of the modern world can we find the degree of courtesy, chivalry, ritual convention and the ability to convey serious and tragic thoughts in as civilized and respectful a manner as is to be found in Mozart's works.
Unfinished Journey (1976)

Wolfgang Amadeus
Mozart
1756–91

12 Give me the best clavier in Europe with an audience who understand nothing, desire to understand nothing and do not feel with me in what I play, and I would have no joy in it!
letter, May 1778

Wolfgang Amadeus
Mozart
1756–91

13 But why my productions take from my hand that particular form and style that makes them *Mozartish*, and different from the works of other composers, is probably owing to the same cause which renders my nose so large or so aquiline, or, in short, makes it Mozart's, and different from those of other people.
letter, Edward Holmes *The Life of Mozart* (1845)

Camille Paglia
1947–

14 There is no female Mozart because there is no female Jack the Ripper.
in April 1991

Artur Schnabel
1882–1951

15 Children are given Mozart because of the small *quantity* of the notes; grown-ups avoid Mozart because of the great *quality* of the notes.
My Life and Music (1961)

Artur Schnabel
1882–1951

16 Too easy for children, and too difficult for artists.
of Mozart's sonatas; attributed

Franz Schubert
1797–1828

17 O Mozart, immortal Mozart, how many, how infinitely many inspiring suggestions of a finer, better life have you left in our souls!
diary, 1816

Malcolm Muggeridge 1903–90

British journalist and broadcaster. Originally a radical, in later years he became a prominent opponent of the permissive society.

Clive James
1939–

1 Muggeridge is hard to admire, but he somehow ends up cherishable, like an old boiler that doesn't heat the water, but wins your heart by the way it goes boink-boink in the night.
in March 1981

Malcolm Muggeridge
1903–90

2 On television I feel like a man playing a piano in a brothel; every now and again he solaces himself by playing 'Abide with Me' in the hope of edifying both the clients and the inmates.
television interview, September 1972

George Orwell
1903–50

3 He is looking only on the black side, but it is doubtful whether there is any bright side to look on.
Collected Essays, Journalism and Letters (1968)

Anthony Powell
1905–2000

4 The three persons making up the Muggeridgian Trinity each pulling violently in a different direction from the other . . . He who was not with the Third Muggeridge was against him, including First and Second Muggeridge.
The Strangers All Are Gone (1982)

Kenneth Tynan
1927–80

5 Muggeridge, a garden gnome expelled from Eden, has come to rest as a gargoyle brooding over a derelict cathedral.
Matthew Parris *Scorn: with added vitriol* (1995)

Katharine Whitehorn
1928–

6 He thinks he was knocked off his horse by God, like St Paul on the road to Damascus. His critics think he simply fell off from old age.
in May 1979

Brian Mulroney 1939–

Canadian Progressive Conservative statesman, Prime Minister 1984–93. He won a landslide victory in 1984, but stood down after the Canadian recession caused his popularity to slump in the opinion polls.

Jean Chrétien
1934–

1 We have a prime minister today who's acting as a head waiter. 'What do you guys in the provinces want? I'll give it to you.' Mulroney likes to be loved. In politics you should try to be respected.
in 1989

Sheila Copps 2 His whole life has been built on subservience to American corporations. He's a company boy from a company town. But in this case, the town is Canada and the boy is the prime minister.
Nobody's Baby: A Survival Guide to Politics (1986)

Claire Hoy 3 Watching Mulroney, one got the feeling, as always, that beneath the plastic exterior of the studied politician there was an impenetrable layer of more plastic.
Friends in High Places: Politics and Patronage in the Mulroney Government (1987)

Edvard Munch 1863–1944

Norwegian painter and engraver. He infused his subjects with an intense emotionalism, exploring the use of vivid colour and linear distortion to express feelings about life and death.

August Strindberg 1 Someone has said that music must accompany Munch's pictures if they
1849–1912 are to be well and truly explained. That may be so, but while we are waiting for the composer, I will sing the praises of some of his pictures which are reminiscent of Swedenborg's visions.
in 1895

Iris Murdoch 1919–99

British novelist and philosopher, born in Ireland. Many of her novels explore complex sexual relationships and spiritual life.

John Bayley 1 She is not sailing into the dark: the voyage is over, and under the dark
1925– escort of Alzheimer's she has arrived somewhere. So have I.
her husband's view; *Iris* (1998)

Rachel Billington 2 She is like a character out of Hieronymus Bosch—the very nicest
1942– character.
in April 1983

George Lyttelton 3 I liked the tousled, heel-less, ladder-stockinged little lady—crackling
1883–1962 with intelligence but nothing at all of a prig.
letter, June 1959

Iris Murdoch 4 My problem is not being great. I'm in the second league, not among the
1919–99 gods like Jane Austen and Henry James and Tolstoy.
attributed

Iris Murdoch 5 I'm just wandering, I think of things and then they go away for ever.
1919–99 *on her inability to write; the following February it was announced that she was suffering from Alzheimer's disease*
remark, September 1996

Rupert Murdoch 1931–

Australian-born American publisher and media entrepreneur. He owns major newspapers in Australia, Britain, and the US, together with film and television companies.

Clive James 6 Like a Goth swaggering around Rome wearing an onyx toilet seat for a
1939– collar, he exudes self-confidence.
in October 1989

Mike Royko 7 No self-respecting fish would be wrapped in a Murdoch newspaper.
1932– *before resigning from the Chicago Sun-Times when the paper was sold to Murdoch*
comment, 1984

Ted Turner 8 Rupert's idea of a better world is a world that's better for Rupert.
1938– in November 1997

James Murray 1837–1915

Scottish lexicographer. He was first Editor of the *Oxford English Dictionary*, but did not live to see the work completed.

James Murray
1837–1915

1 I feel that in many respects I and my assistants are simply pioneers, pushing our way experimentally through an untrodden forest, where no white man's axe has been before us.
'Report on the Philological Society's Dictionary' (1884)

Benito Mussolini 1883–1945

Italian Fascist statesman; known as *Il Duce*. He entered the Second World War on Germany's side in 1940. Forced to resign after the Allied invasion of Sicily, he was captured and executed by Italian communist partisans.

Winston Churchill
1874–1965

1 This whipped jackal is frisking by the side of the German tiger.
speech, 1941

Winston Churchill
1874–1965

2 Italy's pinchbeck Caesar.
speech, June 1943

Benito Mussolini
1883–1945

3 The Germans should allow themselves to be guided by me if they wish to avoid unpardonable blunders. In politics it is undeniable that I am more intelligent than Hitler.
in 1934

J. B. Priestley
1894–1984

4 The man's a fraud, a mountebank, a megaphone. He doesn't amount to anything more than a black-shirted bullfrog croaking away in the mud.
interview, September 1934

Alexei Sayle
1952–

5 The theory is that if you're fat, wear silly trousers and you've got a big red nose, you're gonna be funny. Well, it didn't f—in' work for Mussolini, did it?
in October 1988

A. J. P. Taylor
1906–90

6 Mussolini was a great showman whose technique improved as the real situation deteriorated.
in February 1982

N

Vladimir Nabokov 1899–1977

Russian-born American novelist and poet. He is best known for *Lolita* (1958), his novel about a middle-aged man's obsession with a twelve-year-old girl.

Vladimir Nabokov
1899–1977

1 I think like a genius, I write like a distinguished author, and I speak like a child.
Strong Opinions (1973)

Fridtjof Nansen 1861–1930

Norwegian Arctic explorer. In 1888 he led the first expedition to cross the Greenland ice fields, and five years later he sailed from Siberia for the North Pole, which he failed to reach.

Fridtjof Nansen
1861–1930

1 [Faust] never reached a place where he wanted to 'remain'. I cannot even glimpse anywhere worth the attempt.
diary, 1909

Napoleon I 1769–1821

Emperor of France 1804–14 and 1815. After overthrowing the Directory, he became the supreme ruler of France and established an empire stretching from Spain to Poland. He was defeated at Waterloo and exiled.

Tsar Alexander I
1777–1825

1 All this devilish political business is going from bad to worse and that infernal creature who is the curse of all the human race becomes every day more and more abominable.
letter, January 1812

Ludwig van Beethoven
1770–1827

2 He is an ordinary human being after all! Now he will trample underfoot the Rights of Man, being a slave to his own ambition; now he will put himself above everyone else and become a tyrant.
on Napoleon becoming Emperor, in 1804

Jean Baptiste Bernadotte
1763–1844

3 Napoleon has not been conquered by men. He was greater than any of us. God punished him because he relied solely on his own intelligence until that incredible instrument was so strained that it broke.
speech on hearing of the death of Napoleon, 1821

Léon Bloy
1846–1917

4 Napoleon is so great that it could be said that the empire of the world was for him no more than second-best.
Le Pélerin de l'absolu

Lord Byron
1788–1824

5 The arbiter of others' fate
A suppliant for his own!
'Ode to Napoleon Bonaparte' (1814)

Thomas Campbell
1777–1844

6 Gentlemen, you must not mistake me. I admit that the French Emperor is a tyrant. I admit he is a monster. I admit that he is the sworn foe of our nation, and, if you will, of the whole human race. But, gentlemen, we must be just to our great enemy. We must not forget that he once shot a bookseller.
proposing a toast at a literary dinner during the Napoleonic Wars
G. O. Trevelyan *The Life of Lord Macaulay* (1876)

Josephine
1763–1814

7 How many times did I not wish to write to you! But I felt the reason of your silence, and I feared to be importunate by a letter. Yours has been a balm for me.
letter, April 1810

Napoleon I
1769–1821

8 I am the successor, not of Louis XVI, but of Charlemagne.
comment on his coronation as Emperor, December 1804

Napoleon I
1769–1821

9 France has more need of me than I have need of France.
speech, December 1813

Friedrich Nietzsche
1844–1900

10 Napoleon—that synthesis of monster and the Superman.
A Genealogy of Morals (1887)

Sir Walter Scott
1771–1832

11 [Napoleon] might have been a great man and was only a great soldier—he might have been the benefactor of the human race and he was the cause of more blood being spilled than had flowed for a hundred years before.
letter, April 1824

Charles-Maurice de Talleyrand
1754–1838

12 It is not an event, it is an item of news.
remark on hearing of the death of Napoleon, 1821

Duke of Wellington
1769–1852

13 I used to say of him that his presence on the field made the difference of forty thousand men.
in conversation, November 1831

Ogden Nash 1902–71

American poet. His sophisticated light verse comprises puns, epigrams, and other verbal eccentricities.

Phyllis McGinley
1905–78

1 Hurray, Mr Nash, for your writings laughable!
We liked you surly, we love you affable,
And think your poems designed for the nursery
Almost the best in your bulging versery.
  in October 1936

Martina Navratilova 1956–

Czech-born American tennis player. Her major successes include nine Wimbledon singles titles, two world championships, and eight successive grand slam doubles titles.

Martina Navratilova
1956–

1 I came to live in a country I love; some people label me a defector. I have loved men and women in my life; I've been labelled 'the bisexual defector' in print. Want to know another secret? I'm even ambidextrous. I don't like labels. Just call me Martina.
  Martina Navratilova—Being Myself (1985)

Liam Neeson 1952–

Northern Irish actor. He has appeared in films such as *Schindler's List* and *Rob Roy*.

John Lahr
1941–

1 Not since Brando tossed meat up to Stella in *A Streetcar Named Desire* has flesh made such a spectacular entrance.
  in 1990

Jawaharlal Nehru 1889–1964

Indian statesman. An early associate of **Mahatma Gandhi**, Nehru was imprisoned nine times by the British for his nationalist campaigns, but went on to become the first Prime Minister of independent India.

Jawaharlal Nehru
1889–1964

1 I shall be the last Englishman to rule in India.
  J. K. Galbraith *A Life in Our Times* (1981)

Sadashiv Kanoji Patil

2 The Prime Minister is like the great banyan tree. Thousands shelter beneath it, but nothing grows.
  when asked in an interview who would be Nehru's successor
  J. K. Galbraith *A Life in Our Times* (1981)

A. S. Neill 1883–1973

Scottish teacher and educationist. He founded the progressive school Summerhill, which has attracted both admiration and hostility for its anti-authoritarian ethos.

A. S. Neill
1883–1973

1 When I lost my leather tawse for ever I lost my fear of my pupils and they lost their fear of me.
  Jonathan Croall *Neill of Summerhill: the Permanent Rebel* (1983)

Horatio, Lord Nelson 1758–1805

British admiral. Nelson became a national hero as a result of his victories at sea in the Napoleonic Wars, especially the Battle of Trafalgar, in which he was mortally wounded.

Anonymous

1 Our dear Admiral Nelson is killed! . . . all the men in our ship who have seen him are such soft toads, they have done nothing but blast their eyes, and cry, ever since he was killed. God bless you! chaps that fought like the devil sit down and cry like a wench.
  view of Sam, a member of the crew of the Royal Sovereign
  letter, October 1805

Horatio, Lord Nelson
1758–1805

2 I have only one eye,—I have a right to be blind sometimes . . . I really do not see the signal!
  at the battle of Copenhagen, 1801

Horatio, Lord Nelson
1758–1805

3 When I came to explain to them the *'Nelson touch'*, it was like an electric shock. Some shed tears, all approved—'It was new—it was singular—it was simple!'
letter to Lady Hamilton, October 1805

Samuel Rogers
1763–1855

4 Lord Nelson was a remarkably kind-hearted man. I have seen him spinning a teetotum with his *one* hand a whole evening, for the amusement of some children.
Table Talk (1856)

Robert Southey
1774–1843

5 Men started at the intelligence, and turned pale, as if they had heard of the loss of a dear friend.
on the death of Nelson
The Life of Nelson (1813)

John von Neumann 1903–57

Hungarian-born American mathematician and computer scientist. He pioneered game theory and the design and operation of electronic computers.

Anonymous

1 It was said that the Pentagon considered him as important as a whole army division.
Abraham Pais A Tale of Two Continents *(1997)*

Barnett Newman 1905–70

American painter. A seminal figure in colour-field painting, he juxtaposed large blocks of uniform colour with narrow marginal strips of contrasting colours.

David Hockney
1937–

1 Once Newman came to one of the first shows I had in New York, and he said to me, You know, I used to paint like this myself. And I said to him, Do you mean I'm going to finish up painting blue stripes? and he laughed. He was a sweet man.
David Hockney (1976)

John Henry Newman 1801–90

English prelate and theologian. A founder of the Oxford Movement, in 1845 he turned to Roman Catholicism, becoming a cardinal in 1879.

Cardinal Manning
1808–92

2 Poor Newman! He was a great hater!
Lytton Strachey Eminent Victorians *(1918)*

John Henry Newman
1801–90

3 From the age of fifteen, dogma has been the fundamental principle of my religion: I know no other religion; I cannot enter into the idea of any other sort of religion; religion, as a mere sentiment, is to me a dream and a mockery.
Apologia pro Vita Sua (1864)

Lytton Strachey
1880–1932

4 When Newman was a child he 'wished that he could believe the Arabian Nights were true'. When he came to be a man, his wish seems to have been granted.
Eminent Victorians (1918)

Isaac Newton 1642–1727

English mathematician and physicist. He gave a mathematical description of the laws of mechanics and gravitation, and worked on the composition of light and the differential calculus.

W. H. Auden
1907–73

1 And make us as Newton was, who in his garden watching
The apple falling towards England, became aware
Between himself and her of an eternal tie.
'O Love, the interest itself' (1936)

Samuel Taylor Coleridge
1772–1834

2 Newton *was* a great man, but you must excuse me if I think that it would take many Newtons to make one Milton.
Table Talk (1835)

William Cowper
1731–1800

3   Newton, childlike sage!
Sagacious reader of the works of God.
The Task (1785)

Albert Einstein
1879–1955

4 In one person he combined the experimenter, the theorist, the mechanic, and, not least, the artist in exposition.
introduction to Newton's *Opticks* (1932 ed.)

John Maynard Keynes
1883–1946

5 Newton was not the first of the age of reason. He was the last of the magicians, the last of the Babylonians and Sumerians, the last great mind which looked out on the visible and intellectual world with the same eyes as those who began to build our intellectual inheritance rather less than 10,000 years ago.
in 1942

Dmitri Mendeleev
1834–1907

6 We could live at the present time without a Plato, but a double number of Newtons is required to discover the secrets of nature, and to bring life into harmony with its laws.
Bernard Jaffe *Crucibles: The Story of Chemistry from Ancient Alchemy to Nuclear Fission* (1976)

Isaac Newton
1642–1727

7 If I have seen further it is by standing on the shoulders of giants.
letter to Robert Hooke, February 1676

Isaac Newton
1642–1727

8 I don't know what I may seem to the world, but as to myself, I seem to have been only like a boy playing on the sea-shore and diverting myself in now and then finding a smoother pebble or a prettier shell than ordinary, whilst the great ocean of truth lay all undiscovered before me.
Joseph Spence *Anecdotes* (ed. J. Osborn, 1966)

Alexander Pope
1688–1744

9 Nature, and Nature's laws lay hid in night.
God said, *Let Newton be!* and all was light.
'Epitaph: Intended for Sir Isaac Newton' (1730)

Alexander Pope
1688–1744

10 Sir Isaac Newton, though so deep in algebra and fluxions, could not readily make up a common account: and, when he was Master of the Mint, used to get somebody to make up his accounts for him.
Joseph Spence *Anecdotes* (ed. J. Osborn, 1966)

James Thomson
1700–48

11 Even Light itself, which every thing displays,
Shone undiscovered, till his brighter mind
Untwisted all the shining robe of day.
on Newton's Opticks
'To the Memory of Sir Isaac Newton' (1727)

Voltaire
1694–1778

12 A man such as Newton, the like of whom is scarcely to be found in ten centuries, is the truly great man, and the politicians and conquerors, in which no period has been lacking, are usually nothing more than illustrious criminals. It is to the man that rules over minds by the power of truth, not to those who enslave men by violence, it is to the man who understands the universe and not to those who disfigure it, that we owe our respect.
Letters concerning the English Nation (1733)

William Wordsworth
1770–1850

13   The statue stood
Of Newton, with his prism, and silent face:
The marble index of a mind for ever
Voyaging through strange seas of Thought, alone.
The Prelude (1850)

Nicholas II 1868–1918

Tsar of Russia. Forced to abdicate after the Russian Revolution in 1917, he was shot along with his family a year later.

Tsarina Alexandra
1872–1918

1 Be the Emperor, be Peter the Great, John the Terrible, the Emperor Paul—crush them all under you—Now don't you laugh, naughty one,— but I long to see you so with those men who try to govern *you* and it must be the contrary.
letter to Tsar Nicholas II, December 1916

Violet Trefusis
1894–1972

2 In their tiny island of detached domesticity, the Imperial family led an exemplary, if narrow life. A complacency worthy of the three little pigs defying the Big Bad Wolf, possessed them. They were not interested in Russia. The letters they exchanged might have been posted in Kensington and delivered in Hampstead.
Don't Look Round (1952)

Wilhelm II
1859–1941

3 The Tsar is not treacherous but he is weak. Weakness is not treachery, but it fulfils all its functions.
comment, March 1907

Jack Nicklaus 1940–

American golfer. He has won more than eighty tournaments during his professional career.

Alistair Cooke
1908–

1 He was not always 'The Golden Bear' to the crowds. In the days of Palmer's supremacy, he padded along behind Arnie and his howling 'army' stolid and unloved.
in July 1972

Florence Nightingale 1820–1910

English nurse and medical reformer. During the Crimean War she improved sanitation and medical procedures at the army hospital at Scutari, achieving a dramatic reduction in the mortality rate.

Anonymous

1 What a comfort it was to see her pass. She would speak to one, and nod and smile to as many more; but she could not do it to all you know. We lay there by the hundreds; but we could kiss her shadow as it fell and lay our heads on the pillow again content.
a soldier of the Crimean War; Cecil Woodham Smith *Florence Nightingale* (1950)

Henry Wadsworth
Longfellow
1807–82

2 A Lady with a Lamp shall stand
In the great history of the land,
A noble type of good,
Heroic womanhood.
'Santa Filomena' (1857)

Marshall McLuhan
1911–80

3 She began to think, as well as to live, her time, and she discovered the new formula for the electronic age: Medicare.
Understanding Media (1964)

Lytton Strachey
1880–1932

4 Her conception of God was certainly not orthodox. She felt towards Him as she might have felt towards a glorified sanitary engineer; and in some of her speculations she seems hardly to distinguish between the Deity and the Drains.
Eminent Victorians (1918)

Queen Victoria
1819–1901

5 Such a *head*! I wish we had her at the War Office.
on first meeting Florence Nightingale after the Crimean War
Lytton Strachey *Eminent Victorians* (1918)

Vaslav Nijinsky 1890–1950

Russian ballet dancer and choreographer. The leading dancer with **Diaghilev**'s Ballets Russes from 1909, he later choreographed music by **Debussy** and **Stravinsky**.

Ottoline Morrell
1873–1938

1 He always seemed lost in the world outside, and as if he looked on as a visitor from another world, although his powers of observation were intensely rapid.
Robert Gathorne-Hardy (ed.) *Ottoline* (1963)

Marie Rambert
1888–1982

2 Often people say, did he really jump so high? And I always say I don't know how far it was from the ground, but I know it was near the stars.
John Drummond *Speaking of Diaghilev* (1997)

Auguste Rodin
1840–1917

3 [His] beauty is that of antique frescoes and sculpture: he is the ideal model, whom one longs to draw and sculpt.
in 1912

Dennis Nilsen 1945–

British mass-murderer.

Dennis Nilsen
1945–

1 You're writing about the victims of my crimes in a way that is so objective, you're reducing them to objects in a way that I reduced them by killing them.
to Brian Masters, author of Killing for Company
Anthony Clare *In the Psychiatrist's Chair III* (1998)

Richard Milhous Nixon 1913–94

American Republican statesman, President 1969–74. In his period of office the Vietnam War ended and relations with China were restored, but he resigned owing to his involvement in the Watergate scandal.

Anonymous

1 Would you buy a used car from this man?
campaign slogan directed against Nixon, 1968

William S. Burroughs
1914–97

2 I think Richard Nixon will go down in history as a true folk hero, who struck a vital blow to the whole diseased concept of the revered image and gave the American virtue of irreverence and scepticism back to the people.
The Adding Machine (1985)

Barry Goldwater
1909–98

3 [He] lied to the Congress, lied to the people, lied to his own men. He was the most dishonest individual I ever met in my life.
Alistair Cooke 'Goldwater: Jefferson in the Desert' (1998)

Joseph Heller
1923–99

4 If Richard Nixon was second-rate, what in the world *is* third-rate?
Good as Gold (1979)

John F. Kennedy
1917–63

5 Do you realize the responsibility I carry? I'm the only person between Nixon and the White House.
remark, 1960 presidential election campaign

Richard Milhous Nixon
1913–94

6 I welcome this kind of examination because people have got to know whether or not their President is a crook. Well, I'm not a crook.
speech at press conference, November 1973

Richard Milhous Nixon
1913–94

7 I brought myself down. I gave them a sword. And they stuck it in.
television interview, May 1977

Eleanor Roosevelt
1884–1962

8 I cannot, of course, ever feel safe . . . because with Mr Nixon I always have the feeling that he will pull some trick at the last minute.
letter to John F. Kennedy, August 1960

Adlai Stevenson
1900–65

9 The Republican party did not have to . . . encourage the excesses of its Vice-Presidential nominee—the young man who asks you to set him one heart-beat from the Presidency of the United States.
speech, October 1952

Adlai Stevenson
1900–65

10 The kind of politician who would cut down a redwood tree, and then mount the stump and make a speech on conservation.
Fawn M. Brodie *Richard Nixon* (1983)

Gore Vidal
1925–

11 He turned being a Big Loser into a perfect triumph by managing to lose the presidency in a way bigger and more original than anyone else had ever lost it before.
in December 1983

Alfred Nobel 1833–96

Swedish chemist and engineer. He invented dynamite, gelignite, and other high explosives, making a large fortune which enabled him to endow the prizes that bear his name.

Pierre Curie
1859–1906

1 The example of the discoveries of Nobel is a case in point: powerful explosives have allowed men to do admirable work. They are also a terrible means of destruction in the hands of great criminals who lead people into war. I am among those who think with Nobel that humanity will derive more good than bad from new discoveries.
lecture to the Swedish Academy, 1905

Emmy Noether 1882–1935

German mathematician. Despite prejudices against women mathematicians she exercised an enormous influence, and inaugurated the modern period in algebraic geometry and abstract algebra.

Albert Einstein
1879–1955

1 It would not have done the Old Guard at Göttingen any harm, had they picked up a thing or two from her. She certainly knows what she is doing.
letter, June 1919

Sidney Nolan 1917–93

Australian painter, known for his paintings of famous characters and events from Australian history.

Sidney Nolan
1917–93

1 I wanted to know the true nature of the 'otherness' I had been born into. It was not a European thing. I wanted to paint the great purity and implacability of the landscape. I wanted a visual form of the 'otherness' of the thing not seen.
in 1971

Patrick White
1912–90

2 For that matter I have never thought of Sid as an intellectual, though he is inclined to throw off those desperate semi-coded messages, or run up a flag with 'Kierkegaard' on it during the soup.
Flaws in the Glass (1981)

Lord Northcliffe 1865–1922

British newspaper proprietor. He built up a large newspaper empire, including *The Times*, the *Daily Mail*, and the *Daily Mirror*. He exercised a strong influence over British war policy in the First World War.

Lord Beaverbrook
1879–1964

1 The late Lord Northcliffe would not print anything in criticism of himself. He would always print the words of praise. Even from the publicity point of view, he was wrong.
letter, December 1952

Lord Northcliffe
1865–1922

2 When I want a peerage, I shall buy it like an honest man.
Tom Driberg *Swaff* (1974)

A. J. P. Taylor
1906–90

3 He aspired to power instead of influence, and as a result forfeited both.
English History 1914–45 (1965)

Rudolf Nureyev 1939–93

Russian-born ballet dancer and choreographer. He defected to the West in 1961, joining the Royal Ballet in London, where he began his noted partnership with **Margot Fonteyn**.

Frederick Ashton
1904–88

1 [I felt] like a ringmaster, wondering if this beautiful animal would perform his tricks or whether I would be mauled in the process.
John Percival *Nureyev: Aspects of the Dancer* (1975)

George Balanchine
1904–83

2 A one-man show. I, me, a beautiful man, alone.
in July 1968

Mikhail Baryshnikov
1948–

3 He had the charisma and the simplicity of a man of the earth and the untouchable arrogance of the gods.
Diane Solway *Nureyev: His Life* (1998)

Cecil Beaton
1904–80

4 He has no pity, no concern for others. He is ruthless and says, 'If they were dead I do not mind.' I felt very much as if I had brought an animal from the woods into the room.
in 1963; Diane Solway *Nureyev: His Life* (1998)

Ian Kilminster
1945–

5 I quite admired Nureyev for getting away with it in his underpants for so long.
interview, July 2000

Rudolf Nureyev
1939–93

6 My beauty am faded.
on being rejected by a young man he had tried to pick up
Ned Sherrin in his *Anecdotage* (1993)

Jacqueline Kennedy Onassis
1929–94

7 He's dancing against the clock. Here is a man who will dance as long as he can, to the end, to the last drop of blood.
Diane Solway *Nureyev: His Life* (1998)

Captain Lawrence Oates 1880–1912

English explorer who died on **Robert Scott**'s Antarctic expedition of 1912.

E. L. Atkinson
1882–1929
and **Apsley Cherry-Garrard**
1882–1959

1 Hereabouts died a very gallant gentleman, Captain L. E. G. Oates of the Inniskilling Dragoons. In March 1912, returning from the Pole, he walked willingly to his death in a blizzard to try and save his comrades, beset by hardships.
epitaph on cairn erected in the Antarctic, November 1912

Derek Mahon
1941–

2 'I am just going outside and may be some time.'
The others nod, pretending not to know.
At the heart of the ridiculous, the sublime.
'Antarctica' (1985)

Daniel O'Connell 1775–1847

Irish nationalist leader and social reformer; known as the Liberator. His election to Parliament in 1828 forced the British government to grant Catholic Emancipation.

Sydney Smith
1771–1845

1 The only way to deal with such a man as O'Connell is to hang him up and erect a statue to him under the gallows.
attributed

Sinéad O'Connor 1966–

Irish singer and songwriter.

Sinéad O'Connor
1966–

1 People assumed I was a lot stronger than I was because I had a big mouth and a shaved head. I acted tough to cover the vulnerability.

in November 1997

Georgia O'Keeffe 1887–1986

American painter. Her best-known paintings depict enlarged studies, particularly of flowers, and are often regarded as being sexually symbolic.

Georgia O'Keeffe
1887–1986

1 I don't very much enjoy looking at paintings in general. I know too much about them. I take them apart.

in March 1971

Bruce Oldfield 1950–

English fashion designer. In 1973 he became a freelance designer, working for the New York department store Bendel's and for **Yves St Laurent**.

Bruce Oldfield
1950–

1 I'm not interested in fashion. In fact I am bored by it. When someone says that lime green is the new black for this season you just want to tell them to get a life.

in August 2000

Andrew Loog Oldham 1944–

English pop manager. He was manager of the Rolling Stones.

Marianne Faithfull
1946–

1 I had no idea what he was talking about most of the time. He was too hip for me, he was too fast, and on top of everything else to have the Mad Hatter as your manager—it was all too much.

Faithfull (1995, with David Dalton)

Laurence Olivier 1907–89

English actor and director. He performed all the major Shakespearean roles; he was also director of the National Theatre. His films include *Rebecca*, *Henry V*, and *Hamlet*.

Glenda Jackson
1936–

1 Olivier always shows you what a marvellous actor he is by showing you how difficult it is. And I despise that.

David Nathan *Glenda Jackson* (1984)

Clive James
1939–

2 People who tell you that Olivier over-acts are telling you about themselves. He is just over-alive.

in March 1982

Charles Laughton
1899–1962

3 You've got to bring *today* into Shakespeare. That's what Olivier never does; he's the apotheosis of the nineteenth-century romantic actor.

Kenneth Tynan *Profiles* (1989)

Ralph Richardson
1902–83

4 I haven't got Laurence's splendid fury.

asked how he differed from Olivier
Kenneth Tynan *The Sound of Two Hands Clapping* (1975)

Kenneth Tynan
1927–80

5 The ability to communicate a sense of danger.

of Olivier's acting
The Sound of Two Hands Clapping (1975)

Jacqueline Kennedy Onassis 1929–94

American First Lady. She married **John F. Kennedy** in 1953. After he was assassinated she married Aristotle Onassis in 1968.

John F. Kennedy
1917–63

1 I do not think it altogether inappropriate to introduce myself to this audience. I am the man who accompanied Jacqueline Kennedy to Paris, and I have enjoyed it.

speech, Paris, June 1961

Jacqueline Kennedy Onassis
1929–94

2 The one thing I do not want to be called is First Lady. It sounds like a saddle horse.

Peter Colier and David Horowitz *The Kennedys* (1984)

*on being asked what would have happened in 1963, had **Khrushchev** and not **Kennedy** been assassinated:*

Gore Vidal
1925–

3 With history one can never be certain, but I think I can safely say that Aristotle Onassis would not have married Mrs Khrushchev.

in June 1989

Michael Ondaatje 1943–

Sri Lankan-born Canadian writer.

Michael Ondaatje
1943–

1 I think giving this computer to the last Luddite is ridiculous. It's like giving a Porsche to someone who just discovered the bicycle.

accepting a computer, in October 1988

Yoko Ono 1933–

American musician and artist, born in Japan. An established avant-garde performance artist, she married **John Lennon** in 1969 and they collaborated on various experimental recordings.

Susan Brownmiller
1935–

1 Her major conceptual piece of art, her Dance Event, her theatre happening, her technological experimentation, indeed, her life's work, was to take apart the broken pieces of John Lennon in stop-time motion and to put them back together again.

in January 1981

John Lennon
1940–80

2 It is a teacher-pupil relationship. That's what people don't understand. She's the teacher and I'm the pupil.

in September 1980

Paul McCartney
1942–

3 Maybe we should have taken to Yoko a little better. I often do feel not too clever about not talking to her, because we didn't get on too well. She was very different from anything we'd encountered.

in January 1986

John Tavener
1944–

4 It was in those very heady days of the 1960s, where she was doing Cage-like things in theatres, like shining torches into the audience's eyes, and asking people to come up on stage and jump off ladders. She told people to fly and I remember that ambulances had to be called in, because, well, people weren't flying.

Andrew Ford *Composer to Composer* (1993)

Robert Oppenheimer 1904–67

American theoretical physicist. He was director of the laboratory at Los Alamos during the development of the first atom bomb, but opposed the post-war development of the hydrogen bomb.

Robert Oppenheimer
1904–67

1 People who practice science, who try to learn, believe that knowledge is good. They have a sense of guilt when they do not try to acquire it. This keeps them busy . . . It seems hard to live any other way than thinking that it was better to know something than not to know it; and that the more you know the better, provided you know it honestly.

'Knowledge and the Structure of Culture' (1958)

Abraham Pais
1918–

2 In all my life I have never known a personality more complex than Robert Oppenheimer. Which explains, I think, why different people reacted to him in such extremely varied ways. I have known those who worshipped him and those who detested him. Having been close to him for sixteen years, I can summarize my own response to him in one word: ambivalence.
A Tale of Two Continents (1997)

Roy Orbison 1936–88

American singer and composer. After writing country music songs for other artists, he established himself as a singer with the ballad 'Only the Lonely' (1960).

Neil Young
1945–

1 His aloofness affected me profoundly . . . His music was always more important than the media. It wasn't a fashion statement. It wasn't about being in the right place at the right time making the right moves. That didn't matter to Roy.
Nick Kent *The Dark Stuff* (1994)

George Orwell 1903–50

British novelist and essayist, born in India. His work is characterized by his concern about social injustice. His most famous works are *Animal Farm* (1945) and *Nineteen Eighty-four* (1949).

Cyril Connolly
1903–74

1 He could not blow his nose without moralising on the state of the handkerchief industry.
in September 1968

Peter Hall
1930–

2 The extraordinary thing about Orwell was that he had a journalist's ability to be in the place where history was happening.
diary, March 1973

Malcolm Muggeridge
1903–90

3 Actually, as I occasionally ventured to remark to him, I think his data was derived much more from the *News of the World* and seaside picture postcards—two of his ruling passions—and even from Dickens, than from direct observation.
Miriam Gross (ed.) *The World of George Orwell* (1971)

Dennis Potter
1935–94

4 [Orwell] could recognize the putrescence seeping out of the pores of the time, and was unable to lift his nostrils clear . . . He never looked for the familiar deodorant of self-deception or sought out the sweetened balms of elegant literary evasion. He sniffed and wrote on the same quivering reflex.
in October 1968

V. S. Pritchett
1900–97

5 George Orwell was the wintry conscience of a generation which in the thirties had heard the call of the rasher assumptions of political faith. He was a kind of saint and, in that character, more likely in politics to chastise his own side than the enemy.
in 1950

John Osborne 1929–94

English dramatist. His first play, *Look Back in Anger* (1956), ushered in a new era of kitchen-sink drama.

Jill Bennett
1931–90

1 Never marry a man who hates his mother, because he'll end up hating you.
a former wife's view, in September 1982

Jeffrey Bernard
1932–97

2 It is as though God is stooping down to pick the wings off his butterflies.
of the deaths of Osborne and **Peter Cook**
in 1995

Noël Coward 1899–1973	3 We both wrote about what we saw and didn't like. Mine was a more circumscribed dislike. Everything bothers him. Dick Richards *The Wit of Noël Coward* (1968)
Jonathan Miller 1934–	4 He had to be plied with extremely expensive champagne. He became more and more like the old Edwardian father he kept attacking in Look Back in Anger. That was what he always wanted to be. His fury in the 1950s was that he wasn't a rich squire. *recording a 60th birthday TV interview, which was never used* in December 1994
John Osborne 1929–94	5 I never deliberately set out to shock, but when people don't walk out of my plays I think there is something wrong. attributed, 1975
Kenneth Tynan 1927–80	6 Mr Osborne's reservoir of bile has swelled as his audience has dwindled. in November 1973

Steve Ovett 1955–

British middle-distance runner, an Olympic gold medal winner in the 800 metres in 1980.

Steve Ovett 1955–	1 I enjoy being myself 90 per cent of the time and Steve Ovett, the runner, just 10 per cent of the time. attributed

Ovid 43 BC–AD C. 17

Roman poet. He is particularly known for his elegiac love poems (such as the *Amores* and the *Ars Amatoria*) and for the *Metamorphoses*, an epic which retells Greek and Roman myths.

John Dryden 1631–1700	1 Ovid, the soft philosopher of love. *Love Triumphant* (1694)
Johann Wolfgang von Goethe 1749–1832	2 Ovid remained classical even in exile: he looked for his suffering not in himself, but in his separation from the capital of the world. *Sayings in Prose*
William Shakespeare 1564–1616	3 Here are only numbers ratified; but, for the elegancy, facility, and golden cadence of poesy, *caret*. Ovidius Naso was the man: and why, indeed, Naso, but for smelling out the odoriferous flowers of fancy, the jerks of invention? *Love's Labour's Lost* (1595)

Robert Owen 1771–1858

Welsh-born social reformer and industrialist. He founded a model industrial community organized on principles of mutual cooperation, centred on his cotton mills at New Lanark.

Ebenezer Elliott 1781–1849	1 You came among us a rich man among the poor and did not call us a rabble. There was no sneer upon your lips, no covert scorn in your tone. in 1834
Friedrich Engels 1820–95	2 English socialism arose with Owen, a manufacturer, and proceeds therefore with great consideration towards the bourgeoisie and great injustice toward the proletariat in its methods, although it culminates in demanding the abolition of the class antagonism between bourgeoisie and proletariat. *The Condition of the Working Class in England in 1844* (1892)
Robert Owen 1771–1858	3 All the world is queer save thee and me, and even thou art a little queer. to his partner W. Allen, on severing business relations at New Lanark, 1828; attributed

Wilfred Owen 1893–1918

English poet. His experiences of fighting in the First World War inspired poems characterized by their bleak realism, indignation at the horrors of war, and pity for the victims.

Wilfred Owen
1893–1918

4 My subject is War, and the pity of War.
The Poetry is in the pity.
written 1918

on his exclusion of Owen from The Oxford Book of Modern Verse:

W. B. Yeats
1865–1939

5 I did not know I was excluding a revered sandwich-board man of the revolution . . . He is all blood, dirt and sucked sugar stick.
letter, December 1936

Niccolò Paganini 1782–1840

Italian violinist and composer. His virtuoso violin recitals, including widespread use of pizzicato and harmonics, established him as a major figure of the romantic movement.

Robert Browning
1812–89

1 From this did Paganini comb the fierce
Electric sparks, or to tenuity
Pull forth the inmost wailing of the wire—
No cat-gut could swoon out so much of soul!
Red Cotton Night-Cap Country (1873)

Lord Macaulay
1800–59

2 The newspapers say that long streamy flakes of music fall from his string, interspersed with luminous points of sound which ascend the air and appear like stars. This eloquence is quite beyond me.
letter, 1831

Camille Paglia 1947–

American cultural critic. Her controversial pro-capitalist and anti-feminist examination of art and decadence through the ages brought her to public attention.

Julie Burchill
1960–

1 The 'g' is silent—the only thing about her that is.
in January 1992

Thomas Paine 1737–1809

English political writer and radical. He called for American independence and defended the French Revolution.

John Adams
1735–1826

1 Such a mongrel between pig and puppy, begotten by a wild boar on a bitch wolf, never before in any age of the world was suffered by the poltroonery of mankind, to run through such a career of mischief.
letter, October 1805

Lord Byron
1788–1824

2 In digging up your bones, Tom Paine,
Will. Cobbett has done well:
You visit him on earth again,
He'll visit you in hell.
written 1820

G. K. Chesterton
1874–1936

3 Thomas Paine invented the name of the age of Reason; and he was one of those sincere but curiously simple men who really did think that the age of reason was beginning, at about the time when it was really ending.
William Cobbett (1925)

William Cobbett 1762–1835	4 At his expiring flambeau I lighted my taper. Audrey Williamson *Thomas Paine: His Life, Work, and Times* (1973)
Thomas Paine 1737–1809	5 My country is the world, and my religion is to do good. *The Rights of Man* pt. 2 (1792)
Thomas Paine 1737–1809	6 A share in two revolutions is living to some purpose. Eric Foner *Tom Paine and Revolutionary America* (1976)

Lord Palmerston 1784–1865

British Whig statesman. Palmerston declared the second Opium War against China in 1856, and oversaw the successful conclusion of the Crimean War in 1856 and the suppression of the Indian Mutiny in 1858.

Walter Bagehot 1826–77	1 A man of the world is not an imaginative animal, and Lord Palmerston was by incurable nature a man of the world: keenly detective in what he could realize by experience—utterly blind, dark, and impervious to what he could not so realize. *Biographical Studies* (1881)
Lord Derby 1799–1869	2 A Conservative minister working with Radical tools and keeping up a show of Liberalism in his foreign policy. in 1856
Benjamin Disraeli 1804–81	3 At the best only ginger-beer and not champagne, and now an old painted pantaloon, very deaf, very blind, and with false teeth which would fall out of his mouth when speaking if he did not hesitate and halt so in his talk. in 1855
Benjamin Disraeli 1804–81	4 Palmerston is now seventy. If he could prove evidence of his potency in his electoral address he'd sweep the country. *to the suggestion that capital could be made from one of Palmerston's affairs* attributed, probably apocryphal

Gwyneth Paltrow 1973–

American actress. Her films include *Shakespeare in Love* and *The Talented Mr Ripley*.

Ralph Lauren 1939–	1 Gwyneth is the Grace Kelly of the Nineties, so she should look like a princess, not a fashion victim. interview, May 1997

Christabel Pankhurst 1880–1958

English suffragette. With **Emmeline** and **Sylvia Pankhurst** she founded the Women's Social and Political Union, with the motto 'Votes for Women'.

Emmeline Pethwick-Lawrence 1867–1954	1 Christabel cared less for the political vote itself than for the dignity of her sex . . . Militancy to her meant the putting off of the slave spirit. *My Part in a Changing World* (1938)

Emmeline Pankhurst 1858–1928

English suffragette. With her daughters **Christabel** and **Sylvia Pankhurst** she founded the Women's Social and Political Union, and initiated the militant suffragette campaign.

David Lloyd George 1863–1945	2 What an extraordinary mixture of idealism and lunacy. Hasn't she the sense to see that the very worst method of campaigning for the franchise is to try and intimidate or blackmail a man into giving her what he would gladly give her otherwise. Richard Lloyd *Lloyd George* (1960)
Emmeline Pankhurst 1858–1928	3 I am what you call a hooligan! speech, 1909

Sylvia Pankhurst 1882–1960

English suffragette. With her mother and sister she founded the Women's Social and Political Union, with the motto 'Votes for Women'.

Ann Widdecombe
1947–

4 Just remember that all the Pankhursts were Tories.
on the proposal to erect a statue of Sylvia Pankhurst in Trafalgar Square in August 1999

Charlie Parker 1920–55

American saxophonist. From 1944 he played with Thelonious Monk and **Dizzy Gillespie**, and became one of the key figures of the bebop movement.

Philip Larkin
1922–85

1 Parker was a modern jazz player just as Picasso was a modern player and Pound a modern poet. I hadn't realized that jazz had gone from Lascaux to Jackson Pollock in fifty years.
Required Writing (1983)

Dorothy Parker 1893–1967

American humorist, literary critic, and writer. She was a leading member of the Algonquin Round Table in the 1920s, and particularly noted for her satirical wit.

George S. Kaufman
1889–1961

2 Everything I've ever said will be credited to Dorothy Parker.
attributed

Dorothy Parker
1893–1967

3 Four be the things I'd been better without:
Love, curiosity, freckles, and doubt.
'Inventory' (1937)

Dorothy Parker
1893–1967

4 Excuse my dust.
suggested epitaph for herself (1925)

S. J. Perelman
1904–79

5 Thirty-nine years old and a very toothsome dish, she immediately made every other woman in the assemblage feel dowdy, and for a moment the sound of their teeth gnashing drowned out the buzz of chitchat.
The Last Laugh (1982)

Alexander Woollcott
1887–1943

6 She is so odd a blend of Little Nell and Lady Macbeth. It is not so much the familiar phenomenon of a hand of steel in a velvet glove as a lacy sleeve with a bottle of vitriol concealed in its folds.
While Rome Burns (1934)

Charles Stewart Parnell 1846–91

Irish nationalist leader and supporter of Home Rule. He was driven from public life in 1890 after the exposure of his adultery with Katherine O'Shea.

Michael Davitt
1846–1905

1 An Englishman of the strongest type moulded for an Irish purpose.
The Fall of Feudalism in Ireland (1906)

W. E. Gladstone
1809–98

2 A marvellous man, a terrible fall.
in December 1895

Timothy Michael Healy
1855–1931

3 REDMOND: Gladstone is now master of the Party!
HEALY: Who is to be mistress of the Party?
when the Irish Parliamentary Party split over Parnell's involvement in the O'Shea divorce in December 1890

Cecil Rhodes
1853–1902

4 That man suspected his own shadow. He was unhappy and saw little good in the world, but I do think he meant well by Ireland.
J. G. McDonald *Rhodes: A Life* (1927)

W. B. Yeats
1865–1939

5 For Parnell was a proud man,
No prouder trod the ground.
'Come Gather Round Me, Parnellites' (1937)

Hubert Parry 1848–1918

English composer. Noted for his choral music, Parry's best-known work is his setting of **William Blake**'s poem 'Jerusalem', which has acquired the status of a national song.

Frederick Delius
1862–1934

1 It is a good thing Parry died when he did; otherwise he might have set the whole Bible to music.
Peter Warlock *Frederick Delius* (1923

Edward Elgar
1857–1934

2 I cannot stand Parry's orchestra: it's dead and never more than an *organ part arranged.*
letter, March 1898

George Patton 1885–1945

American general. An enthusiastic proponent of tank warfare, after the Sicilian campaign he led the US 3rd Army across France and Germany in 1944–5.

Field Marshal Earl Alexander
1891–1969

1 Patton should have lived during the Napoleonic wars—he would have made a splendid Marshal under Napoleon.
Memoirs (1962)

George Patton
1885–1945

2 War will be won by Blood and Guts alone.
Patton was called 'Old Blood and Guts' by his men
comment, 1940

Wolfgang Pauli 1900–58

Austrian-born American physicist. He made a major contribution to quantum theory with his exclusion principle, and postulated the existence of the neutrino.

Anonymous

1 He was known as the conscience of twentieth-century physics.
Abraham Pais *A Tale of Two Continents* (1997)

Wolfgang Pauli
1900–58

2 I think we will get along well, because you think slowly, just as I do.
Abraham Pais *A Tale of Two Continents* (1997)

Wolfgang Pauli
1900–58

3 When I was young, I thought that physics was easy and relations with women difficult. Now it is just the other way around.
Abraham Pais *A Tale of Two Continents* (1997)

Victor Weisskopf
1908–

4 It was absolutely marvellous working for Pauli. You could ask him anything. There was no worry that he would think a particular question was stupid, since he thought *all* questions were stupid.
in *American Journal of Physics* 1977

Linus Pauling 1901–94

American chemist. He is renowned for his study of molecular structure and chemical bonding. After the war he was involved with attempts to ban nuclear weapons.

Linus Pauling
1901–94

1 I was happy to receive the Nobel Prize for Chemistry, but I had just been having a good time carrying out studies in the field of chemistry and trying to make discoveries. The Nobel Peace Prize is the one I value more because it means there is a feeling that I have been doing my duty to my fellow human beings.
to reporters, October 1963

Luciano Pavarotti 1935–

Italian operatic tenor. He made his debut as Rodolfo in Puccini's *La Bohème* in 1961 and has since gained international acclaim and popularity for his bel canto singing.

Peter Ustinov
1921–

1 Pavarotti is not vain, but conscious of being unique.
in September 1993

Anna Pavlova 1881–1931

Russian dancer. Her highly acclaimed solo dance *The Dying Swan* was created for her by Michel Fokine in 1905.

George Balanchine
1904–83

1 She had bad taste and chose dreadful music. She liked Hungarian composers and dainty, tippety-tip dances.
Cecil Beaton's diary, September 1965

Cecil Beaton
1904–80

2 For me, Pavlova was the epitome of all that was rare and mysterious. From the moment that evening when she appeared on the stage, with her big beak of a nose, the V-shaped smile, and the long spears of blue painted eyes which gave her the head of a peacock, she was to me the personification of magic.
diary, July 1960

Jeremy Paxman 1950–

British journalist and broadcaster, noted for his confrontational interviewing style.

Henry Kissinger
1923–

1 I wonder what you do when you do a hostile interview?
in July 1999

Jeremy Paxman
1950–

2 I was wisely seen as unsuitable.
admitting he was once rejected by the Diplomatic Corps
in May 1999

Thomas Love Peacock 1785–1866

English novelist and poet. He is chiefly remembered for his prose satires, including *Nightmare Abbey* and *Crotchet Castle*, lampooning the romantic poets.

Percy Bysshe Shelley
1792–1822

1   His fine wit
Makes such a wound, the knife is lost in it.
'Letter to Maria Gisborne' (1820)

Gore Vidal
1925–

2 Every quarter century, like clockwork, there is a Peacock revival. The great tail feathers unfurl in all their Pavonian splendor, and like-minded folk delight in the display; and that's the end of that for the next twenty-five years.
Pink Triangle and Yellow Star (1982)

Peter Pears 1910–86

English operatic tenor. In his lifelong partnership with **Benjamin Britten** he performed the title roles in all Britten's operas and with Britten co-founded the Aldeburgh Festival.

Benjamin Britten
1913–78

1 I'm wiser about Peter than he is about himself. If it hadn't been for me, he'd never have been a singer, and although *he* might have been happier, lots of other people wouldn't have been.
in January 1953

Noël Coward
1899–1973

2 The one who looks as if his legs don't belong to him.
Humphrey Carpenter *Benjamin Britten* (1992)

Hans Keller
1919–85

3 For once, a singer who isn't a poor substitute for an instrumentalist!
in May 1951

Lester B. Pearson 1897–1972

Canadian diplomat and Liberal statesman, Prime Minister 1963–8.

Lester B. Pearson
1897–1972

1 To deserve success is more important than to achieve it.
Pearson's formula for life; John Robinson Beal *The Pearson Phenomenon* (1964)

Robert Peel 1788–1850

British Conservative statesman. As Home Secretary he established the Metropolitan Police. His repeal of the Corn Laws in 1846 split the Conservatives and forced his resignation.

Elizabeth Barrett Browning
1806–61

1 Did he ever see a truth before it was forced on him by circumstances rather than reasonings? Never, perhaps. It is however a noble enough commendation that he did not sacrifice the good of his country (when once seen clearly) even to the preservation of his personal consistency, and for this thing, if not for another, we should all bless his memory.

letter, August 1850

John Philpot Curran
1750–1817

2 Like the silver plate on a coffin.

describing Peel's smile
attributed

Benjamin Disraeli
1804–81

3 The right hon. Gentleman caught the Whigs bathing, and walked away with their clothes.

on Peel's abandoning protection in favour of free trade, traditionally the policy of the Whig Opposition
speech, February 1845

Benjamin Disraeli
1804–81

4 He traces the steam-engine always back to the tea-kettle.

speech, April 1845

W. E. Gladstone
1809–98

5 Peel died at peace with all mankind; even with Disraeli. The last thing he did was to cheer Disraeli. It was not a very loud cheer, but it *was* a cheer; it was distinct. I sat next to him.

H. M. and M. Swartz (eds) *Disraeli's Reminiscences* (1975)

Duke of Wellington
1769–1852

6 I have no small talk and Peel has no manners.

G. W. E. Russell *Collections and Recollections* (1898)

Pelé 1940–

Brazilian footballer. Regarded as one of the greatest footballers of all time, he appeared 111 times for Brazil and is credited with over 1,200 goals in first-class soccer.

Pelé
1940–

1 No individual can win a game by himself. Pelé is a famous name, but Pelé made his goals because another player passed to him at the proper time. And Brazil won games because Pelé didn't try to make the goals by himself, but passed to others when required so that the goal could be scored.

My Life and the Beautiful Game (1977)

Roger Penrose 1931–

British mathematician and theoretical physicist.

Roger Penrose
1931–

1 You want to tell somebody, but you can't tell most people. It's like being a very avant-garde artist.

on mathematical discovery
in November 1996

Samuel Pepys 1633–1703

English diarist and naval administrator. He is particularly remembered for his *Diary* (1660–9), which describes events such as the Great Plague and the Fire of London.

Samuel Taylor Coleridge
1772–1834

1 Pepys's only ground of morality was Prudence—a shrewd Understanding in the service of Self-love,—his conscience.

annotation to Pepys' *Memoirs*

Harold Nicolson
1886–1968

2 To be a good diarist one must have a little snouty, sneaky mind.

diary, November 1947

Samuel Pepys
1633–1703

3 Music and women I cannot but give way to, whatever my business is.

diary, March 1666

Robert Louis Stevenson 1850–94
4 He was a man known to his contemporaries in a halo of almost historical pomp, and to his remote descendants with an indecent familiarity, like a tap-room companion.
Familiar Studies of Men and Books (1882)

Eva Perón 1919–52

Argentinian politician. A former actress, after her marriage to Juan Perón, President 1946–55, she became a de facto Minister; her social reforms earned her great popularity with the poor.

Anonymous
1 I will return. And I will be millions.
inscription on the tomb of Eva Perón, Buenos Aires

Madonna 1958–
2 Many people see Eva Perón as either a saint or the incarnation of Satan. That means I can definitely identify with her.
on playing the starring role in the film Evita
in February 1996

Tim Rice 1944–
3 Don't cry for me Argentina.
title of song from the musical *Evita* (1976)

Peter the Great 1672–1725

Tsar of Russia from 1782. He modernized his armed forces and expanded his territory in the Baltic. His extensive administrative reforms were instrumental in transforming Russia into a significant power.

John Evelyn 1620–1706
1 I went to Deptford to view how miserably the tsar of Muscovy had left my house after 3 months making it his court, having gotten Sir Christopher Wren his Majesty's Surveyor and Mr London his Gardener to go down and make an estimate of the repairs, for which they allowed 150 pounds.
diary, June 1698

Petrarch 1304–74

Italian poet. His reputation is chiefly based on the *Canzoniere* (c. 1351–3), a sonnet sequence in praise of a woman he calls Laura.

Lord Byron 1788–1824
1 Think you, if Laura had been Petrarch's wife,
He would have written sonnets all his life?
Don Juan (1819–24)

Prince Philip 1921–

Husband of **Elizabeth II**. On the eve of his marriage he was created Duke of Edinburgh. He served in the Royal Navy until Elizabeth's accession in 1952.

Elizabeth II 1926–
1 I think everybody really will concede that on this, of all days, I should begin my speech with the words 'My husband and I'.
speech on her 25th wedding anniversary, November 1972

Prince Philip, Duke of Edinburgh 1921–
2 I include 'pidgin-English' in this even though I am referred to in that splendid language as 'Fella belong Mrs Queen'.
speech to the English-Speaking Union, October 1958

Jean Rook 1931–91
3 A snappish OAP with a temper like an arthritic corgi.
in June 1986

Sarah, Duchess of York 1959–
4 To walk five paces behind his far more important wife—that's so difficult for this poor man.
in April 2000

Edith Piaf 1915–63

French singer. She became known as a cabaret and music-hall singer in the late 1930s. Her songs included 'La Vie en rose' and 'Je ne regrette rien'.

Edith Piaf
1915–63

1 You can't expect too much of it, it's seen a lot of service. But I'm still a bargain.
comment on her body, c.1959

Pablo Picasso 1881–1973

Spanish painter, sculptor, and graphic artist. His prolific inventiveness and technical versatility made him the dominant figure in avant-garde art in the first half of the 20th century.

Guillaume Apollinaire
1880–1918

1 A man like Picasso studies an object as a surgeon dissects a corpse.
Les Peintres cubistes (1913)

Winston Churchill
1874–1965

2 Alfred, if you met Picasso coming down the street, would you join with me in kicking his something something something?
to Alfred Munnings, who responded 'Yes, sir, I would'
quoted by Alfred Munnings, April 1949

Salvador Dali
1904–89

3 Picasso is Spanish, I am too. Picasso is a genius. I am too. Picasso will be seventy-two and I about forty-eight. Picasso is known in every country of the world; so am I. Picasso is a Communist; I am not.
lecture, October 1951

David Hockney
1937–

4 No theoretician, no writer on art, however interesting he or she might be, could be as interesting as Picasso. A good writer on art may give you an insight to Picasso, but, after all, Picasso was there first.
Wendy O. Brown (ed.) Hockney on Photography (1988)

Pablo Picasso
1881–1973

5 When I was the age of these children I could draw like Raphael: it took me many years to learn how to draw like these children.
to Herbert Read, when visiting an exhibition of childen's drawings
quoted by Read, October 1956

Norbert Wiener
1894–1964

6 A painter like Picasso, who runs through many periods and phases, ends up by saying all those things which are on the tips of the tongues of the age to say, and finally sterilises the originality of his contemporaries and juniors.
The Human Use of Human Beings (1950)

Mary Pickford 1893–1979

Canadian-born American actress. She was a star of silent films usually playing the innocent young heroine. She also co-founded United Artists (1919).

Alistair Cooke
1908–

1 She was the girl every young man wanted to have—as his sister.
attributed

Cecil B. de Mille
1881–1959

2 There is another word for being a good trouper, a word that show business would think too grand to use. That word is dedication. And that word, I think, is Mary Pickford's secret, as it is the secret of anyone who succeeds at anything.
Mary Pickford Sunshine and Shadow (1955)

Mary Pickford
1893–1979

3 I left the screen because I didn't want what happened to Chaplin to happen to me . . . The little girl made me. I wasn't waiting for the little girl to kill me.
David Thomson A Biographical Dictionary of Film (1980)

Edith Sitwell
1887–1964

4 A confectioner's goddess of vanilla-flavoured ice-cream.
Taken Care Of (1965)

Lester Piggott 1935–

English jockey. He was champion jockey nine times between 1960 and 1971 and again in 1981 and 1982; he won the Derby a record nine times.

Hugh McIlvanney
1933–

1 A volcano trapped in an iceberg.
   in June 1985

Harold Pinter 1930–

English dramatist, actor, and director. His plays are associated with the Theatre of the Absurd and are typically marked by a sense of brooding menace.

on being telephoned by the Evening News *to ask if he had any comment to offer on the occasion of Harold Pinter's fiftieth birthday:*

Alan Bennett
1934–

1 I don't; it's only later I realize I could have suggested two minutes' silence.
   diary, October 1980

Simon Gray
1936–

2 Like Dickens, he can make one laugh in panic.
   Mel Gussow Conversations with Pinter *(1994)*

Peter Hall
1930–

3 Harold has actually rung me up to say, 'I have a re-write. Page 37. Cut the pause'.
   in September 2000

Harold Pinter
1930–

4 Oh, this dread word Pinteresque. It makes people reach for their guns. Or behave as if they were going to church. But when the audience is actually there, I am always gratified when I hear laughter. There is a great deal of humour in my plays.
   in July 1995

William Pitt 1708–78

British statesman; known as Pitt the Elder. He brought the Seven Years War to an end in 1763 and also masterminded the conquest of French possessions overseas, particularly in Canada and India.

Horace Walpole
1717–97

1 I write . . . to congratulate you on the lustre you have thrown on this country. Sir, do not take this for flattery: there is nothing in your power to give that I would accept; nay, there is nothing I could envy, but what I believe you would scarce offer me—your glory.
   of the 'year of victories', 1759
   letter, October 1759

Robert Walpole
1676–1745

2 We must muzzle this terrible young cornet of horse.
   of Pitt, who had held a cornetcy before his election to Parliament
   in c.1736

William Pitt 1759–1806

British statesman; known as Pitt the Younger. The youngest-ever Prime Minister, he introduced financial reforms to reduce the national debt.

Edmund Burke
1729–97

3 Not merely a chip of the old 'block', but the old block itself.
   on the younger Pitt's maiden speech
   in February 1781

Caroline Fox
d. 1774

4 That little boy will be a thorn in Charles's side as long as he lives.
   *on the young William Pitt as a rival to her son **Charles James Fox***
   attributed

Georgiana, Duchess of Devonshire
1757–1806

5 His eloquence was so great he could explain even every disaster into almost the contrary. His choice of words was perfect, his voice beautiful, and his way of putting aside the question when he chose, and fascinating the minds of men, extraordinary.
   letter, January 1806

Max Planck 1858–1947

German theoretical physicist who founded quantum theory, announcing the radiation law named after him in 1900.

Albert Einstein
1879–1955

1 How different, and how much better it would be for mankind if there were more like him . . . It seems that fine characters in every age and continent must remain apart from the world, unable to influence events.

letter, November 1947

Sylvia Plath 1932–63

American poet, wife of **Ted Hughes**. Her life was marked by periods of severe depression. In 1963 she committed suicide.

Seamus Heaney
1939–

1 Her last poems . . . present themselves with all the pounce and irrefutability of a tiger lashing its tail.

The Government of the Tongue (1988)

Frieda Hughes

2 My mother was not a martyr, she was a troubled, brilliant woman who would have been aghast to discover the memory of her life was as nothing compared with the memory of her death.

in September 2000

Ted Hughes
1930–98

3 Ten years after your death
I meet on a page of your journal, as never before,
The shock of your joy.

'Visit' (1998)

Philip Larkin
1922–85

4 I see her as a kind of Hammer Films poet.

letter, November 1981

Sylvia Plath
1932–63

5 We will publish a bookshelf of books between us before we perish! And a batch of brilliant healthy children!

diary, 1957

Anne Sexton
1928–74

6 Often, very often, Sylvia and I would talk at length about our first suicides, at length, in detail, in depth . . . Suicide is, after all, the opposite of the poem.

A Self-Portrait in Letters (1978)

Plato c.429–c.347 BC

Greek philosopher. A disciple of **Socrates** and the teacher of **Aristotle**, he founded the Academy in Athens.

Aristotle
384–322 BC

1 Plato is dear to me, but dearer still is truth.

attributed

Iris Murdoch
1919–99

2 Who could fathom Plato's mind? Unless one is a genius philosophy is a mug's game.

The Philosopher's Pupil (1983)

Seneca
c.4 BC–AD 65

3 Philosophy did not find Plato already a nobleman. It made him one.

Epistulae ad Lucilium

**Alfred North
Whitehead**
1861–1947

4 The safest general characterization of the European philosophical tradition is that it consists of a series of footnotes to Plato.

Process and Reality (1929)

Gary Player 1936–

South African golfer. He has won numerous championships including the British Open (1959; 1968; 1974), the Masters (1961; 1974; 1978), and the PGA (1962; 1972).

Alistair Cooke
1908–

1 In a game which more and more is engulfed by publicity, advertising, and lavish stakes, he is a gent.

in June 1965

Roy Plomley 1914–85

British writer and broadcaster. He devised and presented the radio programme *Desert Island Discs* (1941–).

Alec Guinness
1914–2000

1 When the late Roy Plomley swooped down on me with all those screeching seagulls . . . He made me feel like discarded offal thrown over the stern of a ship.
diary, February 1996

Plutarch AD c.46–c.120

Greek biographer and philosopher. He is chiefly known for *Parallel Lives*, a collection of biographies of prominent Greeks and Romans.

Ralph Waldo Emerson
1803–82

1 We need books of this tart cathartic virtue, more than books of political science or of private economy.
on Plutarch's Lives
Essays (1841)

Edgar Allan Poe 1809–49

American short-story writer, poet, and critic. His fiction and poetry are Gothic in style and characterized by their exploration of the macabre and the grotesque.

W. H. Auden
1907–73

1 Poor Poe! At first so forgotten that his grave went without a tombstone twenty-six years . . . today in danger of becoming the life study of a few professors.
introduction to *Edgar Allan Poe* (1950)

D. H. Lawrence
1885–1930

2 He was an adventurer into the vaults and cellars and horrible underground passages of the human soul. He sounded the horror and the warning of his own doom.
Studies in Classic American Literature (1924)

James Russell Lowell
1819–91

3 There comes Poe with his raven like Barnaby Rudge,
Three-fifths of him genius, and two-fifths sheer fudge.
'A Fable for Critics' (1848)

James Thurber
1894–1961

4 Poe . . . was perhaps the first great nonstop literary drinker of the American nineteenth century. He made the indulgences of Coleridge and De Quincey seem like a bit of mischief in the kitchen with the cooking sherry.
Alarms and Diversions (1957)

William Carlos Williams
1883–1963

5 Poe gives the sense for the first time in America, that literature is serious, not a matter of courtesy but of truth.
'In the American Grain' (1925)

Jackson Pollock 1912–56

American painter. He was a leading figure in the abstract expressionist movement.

Jackson Pollock
1912–56

1 There was a reviewer a while back who wrote that my pictures didn't have any beginning or any end. He didn't mean it as a compliment, but it was. It was a fine compliment.
Francis V. O'Connor *Jackson Pollock* (1967)

Alexander Pope 1688–1744

English poet. A major figure of the Augustan age, he is famous for his caustic wit and metrical skill, in particular his use of the heroic couplet.

W. H. Auden
1907–73

1 As I get older, and the times get gloomier and more difficult, it is to poets like Horace and Pope that I find myself more and more turning for the kind of refreshment I require.
in February 1969

Lord Byron
1788–1824

2 Those miserable mountebanks of the day, the poets, disgrace themselves and deny God, in running down Pope, the most *faultless* of poets, and almost of men.
letter, November 1820

John Carey
1934–

3 To escape from the grotesque tragedy which was his body, Pope perfected a series of immaculate masks and voices.
in 1985

Samuel Johnson
1709–84

4 He hardly drank tea without a stratagem.
Lives of the English Poets (1779–81)

Alexander Pope
1688–1744

5 Yes, I am proud; I must be proud to see
Men not afraid of God, afraid of me.
Imitations of Horace Epilogue to the Satires (1738)

Lytton Strachey
1880–1932

6 His verses resembled nothing so much as a spoonful of boiling oil ladled out by a fiendish monkey at an upstairs window upon such of the passers-by as the wretch had a grudge against.
in November 1909

Jonathan Swift
1667–1745

7 In Pope, I cannot read a line,
But with a sigh, I wish it mine;

When he can in one couplet fix
More sense than I can do in six:
It gives me such a jealous fit,
I cry, pox take him, and his wit.
'Verses on the Death of Dr Swift' (1731)

Ferdinand Porsche 1875–1952

Austrian car designer. In 1934 he designed the Volkswagen ('people's car'), while his name has since become famous for the high-performance sports and racing cars produced by his company.

Ernst Heinkel
1888–1958

1 He is a very amiable man but let me give you this advice. You must shut him up in a cage with seven locks and let him design his engine inside it. Let him hand you the blueprints through the bars. But for heaven's sake don't ever let him see the drawing or the engine again. Otherwise he'll ruin you.
He 1000 (1956)

Cole Porter 1892–1964

American songwriter. He made his name with a series of Broadway musicals, and also wrote songs for films.

Larry Adler
1914–

1 The Adlai Stevenson of songwriters . . . He was an aristocrat in everything he did and everything he wrote. Everything had class.
George Eells *The Life that Late He Led* (1967)

Thea Porter 1927–2000

British fashion designer, who introduced ethnic clothing in the 1960s.

Anna Harvey

2 An exotic, Bohemian creature who I always thought looked rather like a nut—a very sweet nut.
in July 2000

Marylou Luther

3 The mother of the rich hippy look. She was the first to make the rich look hip.
in July 2000

Thea Porter
1927–2000

4 What I hate is clothes that look new.
interview, 1968

Michael Portillo 1953–

British Conservative politician. A prominent right-winger, his parliamentary career was cut short when he lost his seat in the 1997 election, but he returned in a by-election.

Michael Heseltine
1933–

1 It's only when Michael Portillo comes back in the House of Commons that William [Hague] will have to watch his back.

in June 1999

Michael Portillo
1953–

2 I have that normal male thing of valuing myself according to the job I do. When I can't tell someone in one word what I am, then something is missing. I don't represent anything any more.

in June 1999

Beatrix Potter 1866–1943

English writer for children. She is known for her series of animal stories, illustrated with her own delicate watercolours.

Beatrix Potter
1866–1943

1 I am a believer in 'Breed'. I am descended from generations of Lancashire yeomen and weavers; obstinate, hard-headed, *matter-of-fact* folk.

Glen Cavaliero (ed.) *Beatrix Potter's Journal* (1986)

Ezra Pound 1885–1972

American poet and critic, resident in Europe 1908–45. He was charged with treason following his pro-Fascist radio broadcasts from Italy.

T. S. Eliot
1888–1965

1 I have never known a man, of any nationality, to live so long out of his native country without seeming to settle anywhere else.

Walter Sutton (ed.) *Ezra Pound: A Collection of Critical Essays* (1963)

Ernest Hemingway
1899–1961

2 Ezra was right half the time, and when he was wrong, he was so wrong you were never in any doubt about it.

in November 1936

Wyndham Lewis
1882–1957

3 He behaved like Baden-Powell getting everyone under canvas.

on Pound's marshalling poets under the banner of 'Imagisme' c.1912
Malcolm Bradbury and James McFarlane (eds.) *Modernism* (1991)

Ezra Pound
1885–1972

4 Somebody said that I am the last American living the tragedy of Europe.

George Plimpton (ed.) *Writers at Work* (2nd series, 1963)

Gertrude Stein
1874–1946

5 A village explainer, excellent if you were a village, but if you were not, not.

Janet Hobhouse *Everyone who was Anybody* (1975)

Nicolas Poussin 1594–1665

French painter. He is regarded as the chief representative of French classicism and a master of the grand manner.

Johann Wolfgang von Goethe
1749–1832

1 Poussin is captivating at first glance, and has an effect on us much like that of the vastness of the sea, when we have not seen it for a long time. However, one becomes tired of it in a few days and views it with indifference.

Philipp Hackert—Nachträge über Landschaftmalerei (c.1770)

Nicolas Poussin
1594–1665

2 My nature constrains me to seek and to love well-ordered things, and to flee confusion, which is as much my antithesis and enemy as light is to dark.

letter, 1642

Enoch Powell 1912–98

British Conservative and Ulster Unionist politician, noted for his condemnation of multiracial immigration into Britain and his opposition to British entry into the Common Market.

Iain Macleod 1 Poor Enoch, driven mad by the remorselessness of his own logic.
1913–70   attributed

Enoch Powell 2 Judas was paid! I am sacrificing my whole political life.
1912–98   *response to a heckler's call of 'Judas', having advised Conservatives to vote Labour at the coming general election*
            speech, February 1974

Enoch Powell 3 ANNE BROWN: How would you like to be remembered?
1912–98   ENOCH POWELL: I should like to have been killed in the war.
            radio interview, April 1986

Terry Pratchett 1948–

English science fiction writer, creator of the highly successful Discworld fantasy novels.

Terry Pratchett 1 I'm up to my neck in the real world, every day. Just you try doing your
1948–   VAT return with a head full of goblins.
            in February 2000

John Prescott 1938–

British Labour politician. Rising through the trade union movement, he became Deputy Prime Minister to **Tony Blair** in 1997.

William Hague 1 People work hard and save hard to own a car. They do not want to be
1961–   told that they cannot drive it by a Deputy Prime Minister whose idea of
            a park and ride scheme is to park one Jaguar and drive away in another.
            speech, November 1999

John Prescott 2 I am pretty middle class.
1938–   comment, April 1996

John Prescott 3 People like me were branded, pigeon-holed, a ceiling put on our
1938–   ambitions.
            on failing his 11-plus
            speech, June 1996

Elvis Presley 1935–77

American rock-and-roll and pop singer. He was the dominant personality of early rock and roll, known particularly for the vigour and frank sexuality of his performances.

James Brown 1 He was a country boy. But the way they had him livin', they never
1928–   turned off the air conditionin'. You get sick from that.
            Gerri Hirshey *Nowhere to Run: the Story of Soul Music* (1985)

Nicolas Cage 2 He was the hot rebel in the fifties, an icon, and he was King Lear and
1964–   the buffoon by the end. I felt his career was the ultimate myth.
            Douglas Thompson *Uncaged: the Biography of Nicolas Cage* (1997)

Bob Dylan 3 When I first heard Elvis's voice I just knew that I wasn't going to work
1941–   for anybody and nobody was gonna be my boss. Hearing him for the
            first time was like busting out of jail.
            in August 1987

Thom Gunn 4 Distorting hackneyed words in hackneyed songs
1929–   He turns revolt into a style, prolongs
            The impulse to a habit of the time.
            'Elvis Presley' (1957)

John Lennon 5 Nothing really affected me until Elvis.
1940–80   Hunter Davies *The Beatles* (1968)

Roy Orbison
1936–88

6 And he was this . . . this punk kid, a real weird-looking dude. Just a real raw cat, singing like a bird. I can't over-emphasize how shocking he looked and seemed to me that night.
Nick Kent *The Dark Stuff* (1994)

Robbie Williams
1974–

7 I pray to Elvis every day before I go on stage. The prayer starts with, 'Elvis, grant me serenity.'
in July 2000

Natalie Wood
1938–81

8 He felt he had been given this gift, this talent, by God. He didn't take it for granted. He thought it was something that he had to protect. He had to be nice to people. Otherwise, God would take it all back.
Peter Guralnick *Last Train to Memphis* (1994)

J. B. Priestley 1894–1984

English novelist, dramatist, and critic.

J. B. Priestley
1894–1984

1 I never read the life of any important person without discovering that he knew more and could do more than I could ever hope to know or to do in half a dozen lifetimes.
Apes and Angels (1928)

on being awarded the Order of Merit in 1977:

J. B. Priestley
1894–1984

2 I've only two things to say about it. First I deserve it. Second, they've been too long about giving me it. There'll be another vacancy very soon.
radio interview, October 1977

Joseph Priestley 1733–1804

English scientist and theologian. Priestley's most significant discovery was of 'dephlogisticated air' (oxygen).

Thomas Jefferson
1743–1826

3 Yours is one of the few lives precious to mankind.
Jacob Bronowski *The Ascent of Man* (1973)

The Artist Formerly Known as Prince 1958–

American rock, pop, and funk singer, songwriter, and musician. In 1993 he announced that he was no longer to be known as Prince, but rather by an unpronounceable symbol.

Madonna
1958–

1 He's very private, you know, and very shy. He's great when you get to know him. Charming and funny in his own way. More than anything, he really comes alive when he is working.
Mick St Michael *Madonna in Her Own Words* (1990)

The Artist Formerly Known as Prince
1958–

2 Money has some value but it's not the most valuable thing. The most valuable thing is knowledge of the truth and love—and if you have that, then give it away . . . I didn't change my name to The Artist but to an unpronounceable symbol. Because that's the spirit of the truth.
in October 1999

Matthew Prior 1664–1721

English poet. A diplomat, he is now best-known for his light verse.

Matthew Prior
1664–1721

1 Nobles and heralds, by your leave,
Here lies what once was Matthew Prior,
The son of Adam and of Eve,
Can Stuart or Nassau go higher?
'Epitaph' (1702)

Marcel Proust 1871–1922

French novelist, essayist, and critic. He devoted much of his life to writing his novel *À la recherche du temps perdu* (published in seven sections between 1913 and 1927).

Noël Coward
1899–1973

1 [Proust] is an exquisite writer but for pomposity and intricacy of style he makes Henry James and Osbert Sitwell look like Berta Ruck.
   diary, July 1950

Ezra Pound
1885–1972

2 The little lickspittle wasn't satirizing, he really thought his pimps, buggers and opulent idiots were important, instead of the last mould on the dying cheese.
   letter, November 1933

Françoise Sagan
1935–

3 After Proust, there are certain things that simply cannot be done again. He marks off for you the boundaries of your talent.
   Malcolm Cowley (ed.) *Writers at Work* (1958) 1st series

Yves Saint Laurent
1936–

4 Creating is a harrowing business. I work in a state of anguish all year. I shut myself up, don't go out. It's a hard life, which is why I understand Proust so well; I have such an admiration for what he has written about the agony of creation.
   Nicholas Coleridge *The Fashion Conspiracy* (1988)

Edith Wharton
1862–1937

5 His greatness lay in his art, his incredible littleness in the quality of his social admirations.
   A Backward Glance (1934)

Virginia Woolf
1882–1941

6 The thing about Proust is his combination of the utmost sensibility with the utmost tenacity. He searches out these butterfly shades to the last grain. He is as tough as catgut and as evanescent as a butterfly's bloom.
   diary, April 1925

Giacomo Puccini 1858–1924

Italian composer. Puccini's sense of the dramatic, gift for melody, and skilful use of the orchestra have contributed to his enduring popularity.

Thomas Alva Edison
1847–1931

1 Men die and governments change, but the songs of *La Bohème* will live for ever.
   in 1920

Giacomo Puccini
1858–1924

2 Almighty God touched me with his little finger and said: 'Write for the theatre—mind, only for the theatre.'
   letter, 1920

Augustus Pugin 1812–52

English architect, theorist, and designer. He believed that the Gothic style was the only proper architectural style because of its origins in medieval Christian society.

Kenneth Clark
1903–83

1 Pugin is the Janus of the Gothic Revival; his buildings look back to the picturesque past, his writings look forward to the ethical future.
   The Gothic Revival (1928)

Augustus Pugin
1812–52

2 I have passed my life in thinking of fine things, studying fine things, designing fine things and realizing very poor ones.
   Some remarks on the articles which have recently appeared in The Rambler (1850)

Joseph Pulitzer 1847–1911

Hungarian-born American newspaper proprietor and editor. A pioneer of campaigning popular journalism, he owned a number of newspapers.

William Randolph Hearst
1863–1951

1 He used to be a socialist when he was poor but now that he has acquired wealth he is just like the rest of the capitalists.
   W. A. Swanberg *Pulitzer* (1967)

Henry Purcell 1659–95

English composer. Organist for Westminster Abbey, he composed choral odes and songs for royal occasions, and the first English opera *Dido and Aeneas*.

John Dryden
1631–1700

1 Mr Purcell; in whose person we have at length found an Englishman equal with the best abroad.
Amphitryon (1690)

Alexander Pushkin 1799–1837

Russian poet, novelist, and dramatist. His revolutionary beliefs and atheistic writings led to his dismissal from the civil service. He was fatally wounded in a duel with his wife's admirer.

Fedor Dostoevsky
1821–81

1 A pair of boots is in every sense better than Pushkin, because . . . Pushkin is mere luxury and nonsense.
in *Epokha* 1864

Pu Yi 1906–67

Chinese emperor. He was the last emperor of China 1908–12, and Japanese puppet emperor of Manchuria 1934–45.

Pu Yi
1906–67

1 For the past 40 years I had never folded my own quilt, made my own bed, or poured out my own washing. I had never even washed my own feet or tied my shoes.
From Emperor to Citizen (1964)

Dan Quayle 1947–

American Republican politician. As vice-president to **George Bush**, his tendency to gaffes provoked much criticism.

*responding to Dan Quayle's claim to have 'as much experience in the Congress as **Jack Kennedy** had when he sought the presidency':*

Lloyd Bentsen
1921–

1 Senator, I served with Jack Kennedy. I knew Jack Kennedy. Jack Kennedy was a friend of mine. Senator, you're no Jack Kennedy.
in the vice-presidential debate, October 1988

a choice of explanations for Dan Quayle's success at various critical points in his career:

Joe Queenan

2 His family knew people/calls were made/luck would have it.
Imperial Caddy (1992)

Sergei Rachmaninov 1873–1943

Russian composer and pianist, resident in the US from 1917. Part of the Russian romantic tradition, he is primarily known for his compositions for piano.

Aaron Copland
1900–90

1 The prospect of having to sit through one of his extended symphonies or piano concertos tends, quite frankly, to depress me. All those notes, think I, and to what end?
Alan Kendall *The Tender Tyrant: Nadia Boulanger* (1976)

Sergei Rachmaninov 1873–1943	2 I feel like a ghost wandering in a world grown alien. I cannot cast out the old way of writing, and I cannot acquire the new. David Ewen *American Composers* (1982)
Igor Stravinsky 1882–1971	3 Rachmaninov was the only pianist I have ever seen who did not grimace. That is a good deal. Robert Craft *Converations with Stravinsky* (1958)

Jean Racine 1639–99

French dramatist, the principal tragedian of the French classical period.

Victor Hugo 1802–85	1 To my mind, the style of Racine has aged much more than the style of Corneille. Corneille is wrinkled, Racine has withered . . . Corneille has aged like an old man, Racine like an old woman. *Tas de pierres* (1942)
Marie de Sévigné 1626–96	2 Racine will go out of style like coffee. attributed

Walter Raleigh c.1552–1618

English explorer, courtier, and writer. He organized several voyages of exploration and colonization to the Americas, and introduced potato and tobacco plants to England. He was executed by **James I**.

Elizabeth I 1533–1603	1 RALEIGH: Fain would I climb, yet fear I to fall. ELIZABETH: If thy heart fails thee, climb not at all. lines written on a window-pane; Thomas Fuller *Worthies of England*
Prince Henry 1594–1612	2 Who but my father would keep such a bird in a cage? comment, 1611
Thomas Hobbes 1588–1679	3 I have heard my grandmother say that when she was young, they were wont to talk of this rebus, viz. The enemy to the stomach, and the word of disgrace Is the name of the gentleman with the bold face. *Raw + lye = Rawlye* John Aubrey *Brief Lives*

Marie Rambert 1888–1982

British ballet dancer, teacher, and director, born in Poland. She was founder of the Ballet Rambert in 1935.

Agnes de Mille 1908–	1 Margot Asquith used to steal her remarks all the time. Julie Kavanagh *Secret Muses* (1996)
Ninette de Valois 1898–2001	2 A marvellously intelligent woman but a born amateur because she couldn't dance herself. Julie Kavanagh *Secret Muses* (1996)
Roy Strong 1935–	3 Marie Rambert was always a side-shoot, always not quite controllable, a little wayward. diary, August 1982

Raphael 1483–1520

Italian painter and architect. Regarded as one of the greatest artists of the Renaissance, he is particularly noted for his madonnas.

Charles Baudelaire 1821–67	1 Raphael, for all his purity, is but an earthly spirit ceaselessly investigating the solid. in 1846
Salvador Dali 1904–89	2 During the Renaissance, when they wished to imitate Immortal Greece, they produced Raphael. *Dali by Dali* (1970)

Michelangelo
1475–1564

3 Raphael had good reason to be envious, since what he knew of art he learnt from me.

letter, 1542

Grigori Rasputin 1871–1916

Russian monk. His reputation for debauchery combined with his great influence over the tsarina discredited the imperial family; he was assassinated by a group loyal to the tsar.

Tsarina Alexandra
1872–1918

1 To follow our Friend's councils, lovy—I assure is right—He prays *so* hard day and night for you, only one must listen trust and ask advice—not think He does not know. God opens everything to Him . . . He will be less mistaken in people than we are—experience in life blessed by God.

letter to Tsar Nicholas II, December 1916

Terence Rattigan 1911–77

English dramatist. His plays include *The Winslow Boy* (1946) and *The Browning Version* (1948).

Noël Coward
1899–1973

1 There are only two great playwrights in Britain today, Terence Rattigan and myself.

attributed, 1964

Kenneth Tynan
1927–80

2 Mr Rattigan is the Formosa of the contemporary theatre, occupied by the old guard, but geographically inclined towards the progressives.

in 1955

Maurice Ravel 1875–1937

French composer. Noted for their colourful orchestration, his works have a distinctive tone and make use of unresolved dissonances.

Pierre Boulez
1925–

1 I prefer the early Ravel. I like people who are not trying to catch the spirit of the time, but who create the spirit of the time.

Andrew Ford *Composer to Composer* (1993)

Maurice Ravel
1875–1937

2 I make logarithms—it is for you to understand them.

Joseph Machlis *Introduction to Contemporary Music* (1963)

Erik Satie
1866–1925

3 Ravel refuses the Legion of Honour, but all his music accepts it.

Jean Cocteau *Le Discours d'Oxford* (1956)

Igor Stravinsky
1882–1971

4 The most perfect of Swiss clockmakers.

Roger Nichols *Ravel* (1977)

Man Ray 1890–1976

American photographer, painter, and film-maker. He was a leading figure in the New York and European Dada movements.

Man Ray
1890–1976

1 In whatever forms my work is finally presented . . . it is designed to amuse, bewilder, annoy or to inspire reflections, but never to arouse admiration through any technical excellence usually sought for in works of art. The streets are full of admirable craftsmen, but so few practical dreamers.

Cecil Beaton *The Magic Image* (1975)

Nancy Reagan 1923–

American First Lady. As wife of **Ronald Reagan** she was thought to have considerable influence over her husband.

Barbara Ehrenreich
1941–

1 *My Turn* is the distilled bathwater of Mrs Reagan's life. It is for the most part sweetish, with a tart edge of rebuke, but disappointingly free of dirt or particulate matter of any kind.

The Worst Years of our Lives (1991)

Nancy Reagan
1923–

2 If the President has a bully pulpit, then the First Lady has a white glove pulpit . . . more refined, restricted, ceremonial, but it's a pulpit all the same.
in March 1988; see **Roosevelt** 13

Ronald Reagan 1911–

American Republican statesman, President 1981–9. A Hollywood actor before entering politics, his presidency saw the launch of the Strategic Defense Initiative.

Alistair Cooke
1908–

3 He looks rather like a peregrinating secretary of a large union whose blue shirt and dapper suit have spent many a day squashed in the hold of a jet plane.
'Reagan: The Common Man Writ Large' (1967)

Gerald Ford
1909–

4 Ronald Reagan doesn't dye his hair, he's just prematurely orange.
attributed

Garrison Keillor
1942–

5 Ronald Reagan, the President who never told bad news to the American people.
We Are Still Married (1989)

Peggy Noonan
1950–

6 The battle for the mind of Ronald Reagan was like the trench warfare of World War I. Never have so many fought so hard for such barren terrain.
What I Saw at the Revolution (1990)

Ronald Reagan
1911–

7 I now begin the journey that will lead me into the sunset of my life.
statement to the American people revealing that he had Alzheimer's disease, 1994

Patricia Schroeder
1940–

8 Ronald Reagan . . . is attempting a great breakthrough in political technology—he has been perfecting the Teflon-coated Presidency. He sees to it that nothing sticks to him.
speech, August 1983

Gore Vidal
1925–

9 A triumph of the embalmer's art.
in April 1981

Jack Warner
1892–1978

10 No, *no. Jimmy Stewart* for governor—Reagan for his best friend.
on hearing that Reagan was seeking nomination as Governor of California
in 1966

Otis Redding 1941–67

American soul singer. 'Dock of the Bay', released after Redding's death in an air crash, became a number-one US hit in 1968.

Otis Redding
1941–67

1 I am not a blues singer or an R and B singer. I'm a soul singer. We go into the studio without anything prepared, just record what comes out. That's soul—the way you feel.
Gerri Hirshey Nowhere to Run: the Story of Soul Music (1985)

Robert Redford 1936–

American film actor and director. He made his name playing opposite Paul Newman in Butch Cassidy and the Sundance Kid and The Sting.

Robert Redford
1936–

1 If you were me for a month, you might change it to two weeks.
of his fame
attributed

Steven Redgrave 1962–

British oarsman. In 2000 he won his fifth gold medal in successive Olympic games.

Steven Redgrave
1962–

1 If anyone ever sees me going anywhere near a boat again they have permission to shoot me.
in 1996

Lou Reed 1943–

American rock singer and songwriter, a member of The Velvet Underground with a subsequent solo career.

John Cale
1942–

1 There was a commitment there. That was the powerful advantage that all of Lou's lyrics had. All Bob Dylan was singing was questions—How many miles? and all that. I didn't want to hear any more questions.
Clinton Heylin *From the Velvets to the Voidoids* (1993)

Vic Reeves 1959–

British comedian, usually appearing with Bob Mortimer.

Vic Reeves
1959–

1 People treat me like a cartoon, as if I only exist on screen.
in March 2000

Lord Reith 1889–1971

Scottish administrator and politician, first director general of the BBC. He championed the moral and intellectual role of broadcasting in the community.

Winston Churchill
1874–1965

1 That Wuthering Height.
attributed

Peter Hall
1930–

2 A record of egomania and paranoia. He hated everybody.
of Lord Reith's diaries
diary, September 1975

Osbert Sitwell
1892–1969

3 An overbearing Scottish giant of high principles and an obstinate nature.
Rat Week (1986)

Rembrandt 1606–69

Dutch painter. He used chiaroscuro to give his subjects a more spiritual and introspective quality. He is especially identified with the series of more than sixty self-portraits painted from 1629 to 1669.

Charles Baudelaire
1821–67

1 That scoundrel Rembrandt is a sturdy idealist who makes us dream and guess at what lies beyond.
in 1846

Lord Byron
1788–1824

2 There Rembrandt made his darkness equal light.
Don Juan (1819–24)

Rolf Harris
1930–

3 Only because Rembrandt didn't have his own TV show.
explaining why he was named the world's most famous artist by 38% of people in a survey in October 1997

Vincent Van Gogh
1853–90

4 What only Rembrandt has among the painters, that tenderness in the gaze . . . that heartbroken tenderness, that glimpse of a superhuman infinite that there seems so natural.
letter, 1888

Ruth Rendell 1930–

English writer of detective fiction and thrillers. She is noted for her psychological crime novels.

Ruth Rendell
1930–

1 I need people's good opinion. This is something in myself I dislike because I even need the good opinion of people who I don't admire. I am afraid of them. I am afraid of what they will say to me. I am afraid of their tongues and their indifference.
Anthony Clare *In the Psychiatrist's Chair II* (1995)

Jean Renoir 1894–1979

French film director, son of **Auguste Renoir**. His fame is based chiefly on films he made in France in the 1930s.

Jean Renoir
1894–1979

1 I would rather sell peanuts in Mexico than make films at Fox.
letter, 1941

Auguste Renoir 1841–1919

French painter. An early Impressionist, he developed a style characterized by light, fresh colours and indistinct, subtle outlines. In his later work he concentrated on the human, especially female, form.

Édouard Manet
1832–83

2 Ah, the unfortunate man! What he does is fearful. He will never make anything of it.
Wilhelm Uhde *The Impressionists* (1937)

Auguste Renoir
1841–1919

3 It's with my brush that I make love.
often quoted as 'I paint with my prick'
A. André *Renoir* (1919)

Auguste Renoir
1841–1919

4 I have spent my life amusing myself putting colours on canvas.
Herbert Read *The Meaning of Art* (3rd ed., 1951)

Joshua Reynolds 1723–92

English painter. The first president of the Royal Academy, he sought to raise portraiture to the status of historical painting by adapting poses and settings from classical statues and Renaissance paintings.

William Blake
1757–1827

1 Such artists as Reynolds are at all times hired by the Satans for the depression of Art—a pretence of Art, to destroy Art.
Annotations to Sir Joshua Reynolds' Discourses (c.1808)

Edward Burne-Jones
1833–98

2 Reynolds is all right. He's got no ideas, but he can paint.
Mary Jago *Burne-Jones Talking* (1982)

Thomas Gainsborough
1727–88

3 Damn him, how various he is!
Ellis Waterhouse *Painting in Britain, 1530–1790* (1962)

Oliver Goldsmith
1728–74

4 His pencil was striking, resistless and grand,
His manners were gentle, complying and bland;
Still born to improve us in every part,
His pencil our faces, his manners our heart.
Retaliation (1774)

Oliver Goldsmith
1728–74

5 When they talked of their Raphaels, Correggios, and stuff,
He shifted his trumpet, and only took snuff.
Retaliation (1774)

William Hazlitt
1778–1830

6 He became rich by the accumulation of borrowed wealth, and his genius was the offspring of taste. He combined and applied the materials of others to his own purposes, with admirable success; he was an industrious compiler, or a skilful translator, not an original inventor in art.
in October 1814

Horace Walpole
1717–97

7 All his own geese are swans, as the swans of others are geese.
letter, December 1786

Cecil Rhodes 1853–1902

British-born South African statesman. He expanded British territory in southern Africa.

Cecil Rhodes
1853–1902

1 So little done, so much to do.
said on the day of his death

Olive Schreiner
1855–1920

2 Too big to get through the gates of hell.
Elizabeth Longford *Jameson's Raid* (1960)

Mark Twain
1835–1910

3 I admire him, I frankly confess it; and when his time comes I shall buy a piece of the rope for a keepsake.
Following the Equator (1897)

Zandra Rhodes 1940–

English fashion designer, noted for her exotic and floating designs.

Hebe Dorsey
1925–87

4 That startlingly self-made creation who goes around looking like a real-life Andy Warhol portrait.
Nicholas Coleridge *The Fashion Conspiracy* (1988)

Jean Rhys *c.*1890–1979

British novelist and short-story writer, born in Dominica.

Jean Rhys
c.1890–1979

1 A doormat in a world of boots.
describing herself in December 1990

Richard I 1157–99

King from 1189. He led the Third Crusade, defeating Saladin, but failing to capture Jerusalem. Returning home, he was held hostage by the Holy Roman emperor until being ransomed.

Philip II
1165–1223

1 Look to yourself; the devil is loose.
message sent to **King John** on Richard's release, February 1194

Saladin
1137–93

2 I have long since been aware that your king is a man of the greatest honour and bravery, but he is imprudent . . . and shows too great recklessness of his own life . . . I would rather have abundance of wealth, with wisdom and moderation, than display immoderate valour and rashness.
remark, September 1192

Richard III 1452–85

King from 1483. He became king after his nephew Edward V was declared illegitimate and subsequently disappeared. Many historians argue that the picture of Richard as a hunchbacked cut-throat usurper was Tudor propaganda.

Anonymous

3 King Richard late mercifully reigning upon us was through great treason . . . piteously slain and murdered to the great heaviness of this city.
in August 1485; *The York House Book*

Thomas Langton
c.1440–1501

4 He contents the people where he goes best that ever did Prince, for many a poor man that hath suffered wrong many days has been relieved and helped by him . . . God hath sent him to us for the weal of us all.
in 1484

Thomas More
1478–1535

5 Richard, the third son, of whom we now entreat, was in wit and courage equal with either of them, in body and prowess far under them both: little of stature, ill-featured of limbs, crook-backed . . . He was malicious, wrathful, envious, and from afore his birth, ever froward.
'History of Richard III'

William Shakespeare
1564–1616

6 Teeth hadst thou in thy head when thou wast born
To signify thou cam'st to bite the world.
Henry VI, Part 3

Horace Walpole
1717–97

7 The truth I take to have been this. Richard, who was slender and not tall, had one shoulder a little higher than the other: a defect, by the magnifying glasses of party, by distance of time, and by the amplification of tradition, easily swelled to shocking deformity.

Historic Doubts on the Life and Reign of King Richard III (1768)

Cliff Richard 1940–

British pop singer. With his group the Drifters (later called the Shadows), he recorded such songs as 'Living Doll'. Since the 1970s he has combined a successful solo pop career with evangelism.

John Lennon
1940–80

8 We've always hated him. He was everything we hated in pop. But when we met him we didn't mind him at all. He was very nice. Now when people ask us if he's a bit soft we say no. We still hate his records but he's really very nice.

Michael Braun *Love Me Do: the Beatles' Progress* (1964)

Cliff Richard
1940–

9 I feel I've been really radical. I didn't go breaking up furniture; I didn't spit at my public. I didn't rave around the place like a lunatic 12-year-old. Now that gets up the noses of people who think they are radical.

in December 1999

Keith Richards 1943–

English rock musician and songwriter. He formed the Rolling Stones c.1962 with singer and co-songwriter **Mick Jagger**.

Elton John
1947–

1 He's like a monkey with arthritis.

in October 1997

Alexis Korner
1928–84

2 We lovingly named Keith Mr Unhealth. He always looked like the unhealthiest cat in the group. But we knew he was the strongest physically.

Stanley Booth *Keith: Till I Roll Over Dead* (1994)

Keith Richards
1943–

3 Sure thing, man. I used to be a laboratory myself once.

on being asked to autograph a fan's school chemistry book
in August 1994

Bill Wyman
1936–

4 Keith represents an image of what the public thinks the Stones are like. Gypsy, pirate, drinking, smoking, finally heavy drug taking, swearing. People see Keith and they see the Stones.

Mick St Michael *Keith Richards in His Own Words* (1994)

Viv Richards 1952–

West Indian cricketer. He captained the West Indian team from 1985 until 1991, and scored over 6,000 runs during his test career.

Dickie Bird
1933–

5 Master, oh master, if that had hit me, that would have been the end of Dickie. Poor Dickie.

Viv Richards *Sir Vivian* (2000, with Bob Harris)

Hugh McIlvanney
1933–

6 Just watching him walk slowly to the wicket can be more of a thrill than seeing other famous sportsmen at the height of their performances.

in 1985

Viv Richards
1952–

7 I do not walk the middle ground. I am either with you or against you. I go for it or I don't. That is how I played my cricket and that is how I live my life.

Sir Vivian (2000, with Bob Harris)

Ralph Richardson 1902–83

English actor. He played many Shakespearean roles as well as leading parts in modern plays and films.

James Agate
1877–1947

1 The truth is that Nature, which has showered upon this actor the kindly gifts of the comedian, has unkindly refused him any tragic facilities whatsoever. His voice has not a tragic note in its whole gamut, all the accents being those of sweetest reasonableness.
in 1938

Montgomery Clift
1920–66

2 Can't that man make any mistakes?
after the thirtieth take of a joint scene
in 1948

John Gielgud
1904–2000

3 He had always wanted to be a matinee idol, and felt inadequate because he couldn't be.
Kenneth Tynan *Show People* (1980)

Peter Hall
1930–

4 The fright I have when I see great acting is akin to the fear one has of madness. It's the person being possessed, becoming something else. Ralph could switch into that, and his truth could make other actors seem artificial—he was a great, great actor.
John Miller *Ralph Richardson* (1995)

J. B. Priestley
1894–1984

5 He doesn't surrender to roles, completely identify with them; he gives them life by bringing them into himself, adding Richardsonism to them.
in 1975

Kenneth Tynan
1927–80

6 Where Olivier would pounce on a line and rip its heart out, Richardson skips and lilts and bounces it along, shaving off pathos in great flakes.
A View of the English Stage 1944–1963 (1975)

Samuel Richardson 1689–1761

English novelist. His first novel *Pamela*, entirely in the form of letters and journals, popularized the epistolary novel.

Denis Diderot
1713–84

7 Oh Richardson! thou singular genius.
Isaac D'Israeli *Curiosities of Literature* (1849 ed.)

Samuel Johnson
1709–84

8 Why, Sir, if you were to read Richardson for the story, your impatience would be so much fretted that you would hang yourself.
comment, April 1772

Samuel Richardson
1689–1761

9 I often compare myself to a poor old woman, who, having no bellows, lays herself down on her heart, and with her mouth endeavours to blow up into a faint blaze a little handful of sticks, half green, half dry, in order to warm a mess of pottage, that, after all her pains, hardly keeps life and soul together.
letter, spring 1751

Horace Walpole
1717–97

10 The works of Richardson . . . are pictures of high life as conceived by a bookseller, and romances as they would be spiritualized by a Methodist preacher.
letter, December 1764

Duc de Richelieu 1585–1642

French cardinal and statesman. As chief minister of Louis XIII (1624–42) he dominated French government.

Pierre Corneille
1606–84

1 He has done me too much good to speak evil of him, he has done me too much evil to speak well of him.
on the death of Richelieu, in 1642

Cardinal de Retz
1613–79

2 Cardinal Richelieu, who was a very great man, but who had to a supreme degree the weakness of never disregarding the little things.
Mémoires (1715)

Mordecai Richler 1931–

Canadian writer. Much of his work reflects his Jewish upbringing in Montreal.

Louis Dudek
1918–

1 If you want to read Richler in the original, read Saul Bellow.
John Metcalf (ed.) *The Bumper Book* (1986)

Diana Rigg 1938–

British actress. In a varied stage and television career she is best remembered as Emma Peel in *The Avengers*.

Diana Rigg
1938–

1 I'm deeply honoured, but a bit confused. I was only ever a B-cup.
on being voted the sexiest television star 'of all time' by Americans
in May 1999

Robert Runcie
1921–2000

2 Being hugged by Diana Rigg is worth three sessions of chemotherapy.
after his appearance on Loose Ends *with Diana Rigg*
in April 2000

John Simon
1925–

3 Diana Rigg is built like a brick mausoleum with insufficient flying buttresses.
review of *Abelard and Heloise* in 1970

Arthur Rimbaud 1854–91

French poet. Known for poems such as 'Le Bateau ivre', and for his stormy relationship with **Paul Verlaine**, he stopped writing at about the age of 20.

Paul Claudel
1868–1955

1 Arthur Rimbaud was a primitive mystic, a lost spring which gushes from a saturated soil.
Accompagnements

Paul Verlaine
1844–96

2 Mortal, angel AND demon, in other words Rimbaud.
Dédicaces (1894)

Robert I 1274–1329

King of Scotland from 1306, known as Robert the Bruce. He defeated Edward II at Bannockburn, re-establishing Scotland as a separate kingdom.

Robert Burns
1759–96

1 Scots, wha hae wi' Wallace bled,
Scots, wham Bruce has aften led,
Welcome to your gory bed,—
Or to victorie.
'Robert Bruce's March to Bannockburn' (1799)

Michael Forsyth
1954–

2 The cult of the defeated Wallace eclipses the successes of the crowned Bruce.
on the popularity of the film Braveheart
in April 1996

Paul Robeson 1898–1976

American singer and actor. His singing of 'Ol' Man River' in the musical *Showboat* established his international reputation. His black activism and Communist sympathies led to ostracism in the 1950s.

Kenneth Tynan
1927–80

1 That mighty moral instrument, the voice of Paul Robeson, has been issuing gloriously from the radio, and I am knee-deep in its black, glutinous residue.
letter, January 1946

Alexander Woollcott
1887–1943

2 Paul Robeson strikes me as having been made out of the original stuff of the world. In this sense he is coeval with Adam and the redwood trees of California. He is a fresh act, a fresh gesture, a fresh effort of creation.
Marie Seton *Paul Robeson* (1958)

Maximilien Robespierre 1758–94

French revolutionary. As leader of the radical Jacobins he backed the execution of **Louis XVI** and initiated the Terror, but the following year he fell from favour and was guillotined.

Charles Baudelaire
1821–67

1 Robespierre, in his style of burning ice, boils and freezes like an abstraction.
Les Paradis artificiels (1860)

Thomas Carlyle
1795–1881

2 The seagreen Incorruptible.
History of the French Revolution (1837)

Heinrich Heine
1797–1856

3 Maximilien Robespierre was nothing but the hand of Jean Jacques Rousseau, the bloody hand that drew from the womb of time the body whose soul Rousseau had created.
Zur Geschichte der Religion und Philosophie in Deutschland (1834)

Victor Hugo
1802–85

4 The proofreader of the Revolution is Robespierre. He checked everything, he corrected everything.
Quatrevingt-Treize (1873)

Maximilien Robespierre
1758–94

5 I am no courtesan, nor moderator, nor Tribune, nor defender of the people: I am myself the people.
speech, April 1792

Mary Robinson 1944–

Irish Labour stateswoman, President 1990–97. She became Ireland's first woman President, noted for her platform of religious toleration and her liberal attitude.

Mary Maher

1 The proud jubilance of women voters at having a splendid candidate to vote for who also happened, icing-on-a-cake fashion, to be a woman. That was one in the eye for the ah-ya-boy-ya crowd, all right. But what's truly significant is that she got the men's vote.
in November 1990

Albert Reynolds
1933–

2 You don't argue with 92 per cent.
Olivia O'Leary and Helen Burke *Mary Robinson* (1998)

Mary Robinson
1944–

3 May it be a presidency where I the President can sing to you, citizens of Ireland, the joyous refrain of the 14th century Irish poet as recalled by W. B. Yeats: 'I am of Ireland . . . come dance with me in Ireland.'
inaugural speech as President, 1990

Sugar Ray Robinson 1920–89

American boxer. He was world welterweight champion and seven times middleweight champion.

Muhammad Ali
1942–

4 You can tell Sonny I'm here with Sugar Ray. Liston is flat-footed but me and Sugar Ray are two pretty dancers.
in 1964

Jesse Jackson
1941–

5 Sugar Ray Robinson was an original art form.
funeral tribute, 1989

when asked by the coroner if he had intended to 'get Doyle in trouble':

Sugar Ray Robinson
1920–89

6 Mister, it's my *business* to get him in trouble.
following the death of Jimmy Doyle from his injuries after fighting Robinson, June 1947
Sugar Ray (1970, with Dave Anderson)

Richard Rodgers 1902–79

American composer. He worked with librettist Lorenz Hart before collaborating with Oscar Hammerstein II on a succession of popular musicals, including *Oklahoma!* and *The Sound of Music*.

Stephen Sondheim
1930–

1 His work tended to make people think of him as an unsophisticated, platitudinous hick, whereas he was a highly intelligent, strongly principled, very firm-minded, and philosophic man. Which is just what his work seemed not to be.
Tony Palmer *All You Need Is Love* (1976)

Auguste Rodin 1840–1917

French sculptor. He was chiefly concerned with the human form, and notable works include *The Thinker* and *The Kiss*.

Isadora Duncan
1878–1927

1 I remember thinking that beneath his hands the marble seemed to flow like molten lead.
My Life (1927)

Gwen John
1876–1939

2 Everyone I have ever known before you has wanted to change me . . . But you have said that you do not want me to be different than I am.
letter; Ruth Butler *Rodin: The Shape of Genius* (1993)

Rainer Maria Rilke
1875–1926

3 No longer the forced or unwilling animal. Like man, she is awake and filled with longing, it is as though the two made common cause to find their souls.
of Rodin's sculpting of women
Rodin and Other Prose Pieces (1986, tr. G. Craig Houston)

Auguste Rodin
1840–1917

4 I owe everything to women; they move ahead as great masterpieces.
Ruth Butler *Rodin: The Shape of Genius* (1993)

George Bernard Shaw
1856–1950

5 He is perfectly simple and quite devilishly skilful at his work—not the smallest whiff of professionalism about him—cares about nothing but getting the thing accurate and making it live.
letter, April 1906

Arthur Symons
1865–1945

6 The principle of Rodin's work is sex, sex which is so conscious of itself that it finds a desperate energy to attain the impossible.
in 1900

Ginger Rogers 1911–95

American actress and dancer. She is known for her dancing partnership with **Fred Astaire**.

Alistair Cooke
1908–

1 The first time a pretty girl calls you 'sir' is of course a catastrophe. When I met Ginger Rogers, she called me 'Sir'. I've never thought much of her as an actress since.
in 1952

Irene Dunne
1898–1990

2 We always figured that Ginger gave Fred sex appeal.
Bob Thomas *Astaire* (1985)

Erwin Rommel 1891–1944

German Field Marshal; known as the Desert Fox. As commander of the Afrika Korps he succeeded in capturing Tobruk, but was defeated by **Montgomery** at El Alamein.

Winston Churchill
1874–1965

1 We have a very daring and skilful opponent against us, and, may I say across the havoc of war, a great general.
speech, 1942

Eleanor Roosevelt 1884–1962

American humanitarian and diplomat, niece of **Theodore Roosevelt** and wife of **Franklin D. Roosevelt**. She was involved in a wide range of liberal causes, including civil and women's rights.

Henry Kissinger
1923–

1 A symbol of compassion in a world of increasing righteousness.
Joseph P. Lash *Eleanor: The Years Alone* (1973)

Franklin D. Roosevelt
1882–1945

2 Eleanor has time for everybody's troubles but her own.
Alistair Cooke *Memories of the Great and the Good* (1999)

Adlai Stevenson
1900–65

3 She would rather light a candle than curse the darkness, and her glow has warmed the world.
in November 1962

Franklin D. Roosevelt 1882–1945

American Democratic statesman, President 1933–45. His New Deal of 1933 helped to lift the US out of the Great Depression, and he played an important part in Allied policy during the Second World War.

Winston Churchill
1874–1965

4 He was the greatest American friend that Britain ever found, and the foremost champion of freedom and justice who has ever stretched strong hands across the oceans to rescue Europe and Asia from tyranny and destruction.
speech, April 1948

Albert Einstein
1879–1955

5 I'm so sorry that Roosevelt is president—otherwise I would visit him more often.
attributed; in *Jewish Quarterly* Winter 1967–8

Oliver Wendell Holmes Jr.
1841–1935

6 A second-class intellect. But a first-class temperament!
in March 1933

Carl Gustav Jung
1875–1961

7 Make no mistake, he is a force—a man of superior but impenetrable mind, but perfectly ruthless, a highly versatile mind which you cannot foresee.
in 1936

Alice Roosevelt Longworth
1884–1980

8 Two-thirds mush and one-third Eleanor.
George Wolfskill and J. A. Hudson *All But the People: Franklin D. Roosevelt and his Critics, 1933–39* (1969)

Theodore Roosevelt 1858–1919

American Republican statesman, President 1901–9; known as Teddy Roosevelt. He was noted for his antitrust laws and successfully engineered the American bid to build the Panama Canal.

Mark Hanna
1837–1904

9 Now look, that damned cowboy is President of the United States.
in September 1901

H. L. Mencken
1880–1956

10 A charlatan of the very highest skill.
Prejudices, Second Series (1920)

John Morley
1838–1923

11 The two outstanding natural phenomena of America are Niagara Falls and Theodore Roosevelt
Mark Sullivan *Our Times* (1927)

Theodore Roosevelt
1858–1919

12 I am as strong as a bull moose and you can use me to the limit.
letter, June 1900

Theodore Roosevelt
1858–1919

13 I have got such a bully pulpit!
in February 1909

Diana Ross 1944–

American pop and soul singer. Originally the lead singer of the Supremes, she went on to become a successful solo artist.

Berry Gordy
1929–

1 Long before she was a star, there was a drive in her that could not be denied. Nor could her appeal. I soon realized her name needed more sparkle. 'Diane' seemed a little passive for what I saw in her. *Diana*. That was a star's name.

To be Loved: the Music, the Magic, the Memories of Motown (1994)

Christina Rossetti 1830–94

English poet. She wrote much religious poetry (reflecting her High Anglican faith), love poetry, and children's verse.

William Holman Hunt
1827–1910

1 Miss Christina was exactly the pure and docile-hearted damsel that her brother portrayed God's Virgin pre-elect to be.

Pre-Raphaelitism and the Pre-Raphaelite Brotherhood (1905)

Christina Rossetti
1830–94

2 I wrote such melancholy things when I was young that I am obliged to be unusually cheerful and robust in my old age.

Jan Marsh *Christina Rossetti* (1994)

Frances Rossetti
1800–86

3 My wish was that my husband should be distinguished for intellect, and my children too. I have had my wish,—and I now wish that there were a little less intellect in the family so as to allow for a little more common sense.

a mother's view

William Rossetti (ed.) *Dante Gabriel Rossetti: His Family Letters with a Memoir* (1895)

Dante Gabriel Rossetti 1828–82

English painter and poet. A founder member of the Pre-Raphaelite brotherhood, he is best known for his idealized images of women.

Ford Madox Ford
1873–1939

4 I should say that Rossetti was a man without any principles at all, who earnestly desired to find some means of salvation along the lines of least resistance.

Ancient Lights and Certain New Reflections (1911)

Leigh Hunt
1784–1859

5 If you paint as well as you write you may be a rich man, or at all events, if you do not wish to be rich, may get leisure enough to cultivate your writing. But I need hardly tell you that poetry, even the best . . . is not a thing for a man to live upon while he is in the flesh, however immortal it may render him in spirit.

letter to Rossetti, March 1848

George MacBeth
1932–92

6 Rossetti, dear Rossetti,
I love your work,
but you were really
a bit of a jerk.

'Pictures from an Exhibition'

John Ruskin
1819–1900

7 A great Italian lost in the inferno of London.

Alicia Craig Faxon *Dante Gabriel Rossetti* (1989)

**James McNeill
Whistler**
1834–1903

8 Rossetti is not a painter, Rossetti is a ladies' maid!

Robert Emmons *The Life and Opinions of Walter Richard Sickert* (1941)

Johnny Rotten 1957–

British rock singer. A member of the punk band The Sex Pistols, he reverted to his own name John Lydon after leaving the group.

Johnny Rotten
1957–

1 Don't touch me, I'm special.

Bob Geldof *Is That It?* (1986)

Jean-Jacques Rousseau 1712–78

French philosopher and writer, born in Switzerland. From 1750 he came to fame with works highly critical of the existing social order, notably *Émile* and *The Social Contract*.

Isaiah Berlin
1909–97

1 Rousseau was the first militant lowbrow.
in November 1952

Edmund Burke
1729–97

2 The bear loves, licks, and forms her young; but bears are not philosophers.
on Rousseau's sending his children to a hospital for foundlings
Letter to a Member of the National Assembly 1797

Lord Byron
1788–1824

3   Wild Rousseau
The apostle of affliction, he who threw
Enchantment over passion, and from woe
Wrung overwhelming eloquence.
Don Juan (1819–24)

Samuel Johnson
1709–84

4 Rousseau, sir, is a very bad man. I would sooner sign a sentence for his transportation than that of any felon who has gone from the Old Bailey these many years. Yes, I would like to have him work in the plantations.
James Boswell *Life of Johnson* (1791)

Jean-Jacques Rousseau
1712–78

5 I am commencing an undertaking, hitherto without precedent, and which will never find an imitator. I desire to set before my fellows the likeness of a man in all the truth of nature, and that man myself.
   Myself alone! I know the feeling of my heart, and I know men. I am not made like any of those I have seen; I venture to believe that I am not made like any of those in existence.
Confessions (1782)

J. K. Rowling 1965–

English novelist. Her hugely successful Harry Potter stories were originally published for children, but have proved popular with adults as well.

J. K. Rowling
1965–

1 I have yet to meet a single child who has told me that they want to be a Satanist or are interested in the occult because of the book.
in 2000

Joanna Trollope
1943–

2 I'd loathe a mega career or fortune because the problems they bring are as great as the freedoms. J. K. Rowling suffers a kind of professional rape, poor girl. But when success comes later in life, you've spent so many years being ordinary that you continue.
interview, September 2000

Peter Paul Rubens 1577–1640

Flemish painter. The foremost exponent of northern Baroque, he is best known for his portraits and mythological paintings featuring voluptuous female nudes.

William Blake
1757–1827

1 All Rubens's pictures are painted by journeymen and so far from being all of a piece, are the most wretched bungles . . . His shadows are of a filthy brown somewhat of the colour of excrement.
Annotations to Sir Joshua Reynolds' Discourses (1808)

Lord Byron
1788–1824

2 I never was so disgusted in my life as with Rubens and his eternal wives and infernal glare of colours.
letter, April 1817

Peter Paul Rubens
1577–1640

3 My endowments are such that my courage has always been equal to any enterprise, however vast in size or diversified in subject.
letter, 1621

Robert Runcie 1921–2000

English Protestant clergyman. He was Archbishop of Canterbury in a period marked by controversy over issues such as homosexuality and the ordination of women.

Frank Field 1 The archbishop is usually to be found nailing his colours to the fence.
1942–   attributed in *Crockfords 1987/88* (1987)

Robert Runcie 2 I have done my best to die before this book is published. It now seems
1921–2000   possible that I may not succeed.
   letter to Humphrey Carpenter, July 1996, in H. Carpenter *Robert Runcie* (1996)

Terry Waite 3 His faith was tinged with diffidence and, in a very Anglican way, forged
1939–   by doubt.
   in July 2000

Damon Runyon 1884–1946

American author and journalist. His short stories about New York's underworld characters are written in a highly individual style with much use of colourful slang.

Damon Runyon 1 You can keep the things of bronze and stone, and give me one man to
1884–1946   remember me just once a year.
   note to his friends shortly before he died; Ed Weiner *The Damon Runyon Story* (1948)

Salman Rushdie 1947–

Indian-born British novelist. His *The Satanic Verses* was regarded by Muslims as blasphemous, and Ayatollah Khomeini issued a fatwa condemning Rushdie to death.

P. D. James 1 I wonder whether Salman Rushdie would have written The Satanic
1920–   Verses if he had been born as handsome as Imran Khan.
   attributed, 1994

Salman Rushdie 2 The most important part of the title is the comma. Because it seems to
1947–   me that I am that comma.
   of his book East, West
   in August 1994

John Ruskin 1819–1900

English art and social critic. He was a champion of **Turner** and the Pre-Raphaelites. His *Fors Clavigera* was an attempt to spread his notions of social justice, coupled with aesthetic improvement.

Henry James 1 He has been scared back by the grim face of reality into the world of
1843–1916   unreason and illusion, and . . . he wanders there without a compass and
   a guide—or any light save the fitful flashes of his beautiful genius.
   letter, March 1869

Henry James 2 He is a chartered libertine—he has possessed himself by prescription of
1843–1916   the function of a general scold.
   in December 1878

Osbert Lancaster 3 Mr. Ruskin, whose distinction it was to express in prose of
1908–80   incomparable grandeur thought of an unparalleled confusion.
   Pillar to Post (1938)

John Ruskin 4 I am, and my father was before me, a violent Tory of the old school;
1819–1900   Walter Scott's school, that is to say, and Homer's.
   Praeterita (1885)

Tom Stoppard 5 I doubt that art needed Ruskin any more than a moving train needs one
1937–   of its passengers to shove it.
   in June 1977

J. M. W. Turner 6 He *sees* more in my pictures than I ever painted!
1775–1851   Mary Lloyd *Sunny Memories* (1879)

Bertrand Russell 1872–1970

British philosopher, mathematician, and social reformer. His work on mathematical logic had great influence on both symbolic logic and set theory. A noted pacifist, he also campaigned for women's suffrage.

Albert Einstein
1879–1955

1 Great spirits have always encountered violent opposition from mediocre minds. The mediocre mind is incapable of understanding the man who refuses to bow blindly to conventional prejudices and chooses instead to express his opinions courageously and honestly.
in March 1940

A. E. Housman
1859–1936

2 If I were the Prince of Peace, I would choose a less provocative Ambassador.
Alan Wood *Bertrand Russell: the Passionate Sceptic* (1957)

D. H. Lawrence
1885–1930

3 He is, vitally, emotionally, much too inexperienced in personal contact and conflict, for a man of his age and calibre. It isn't that life has been too much for him, but too little.
letter, 1915

Ottoline Morrell
1873–1938

4 The beauty of his mind, the pure fire of his soul began to affect and attract me, and magnetize me with an attraction almost physical, carrying me up into ecstasies such as Donne expresses; his unattractive body seemed to disappear, while our souls were united in a single flame.
Robert Gathorne-Hardy (ed.) *Ottoline at Garsington* (1974)

George Orwell
1903–50

5 So long as he and a few others like him are alive and out of jail, we know that the world is still sane in parts . . . He has an essentially *decent* intellect, a kind of intellectual chivalry which is far rarer than mere cleverness.
Collected Essays, Journalism and Letters (1968)

Anthony Quinton
1925–

6 He served as a listening-post for his age in which a vast range of movements of thought were perceptively picked up, helpfully simplified, and then sent forth to the world in a lucid and readily digestible form.
in *Dictionary of National Biography*

Bertrand Russell
1872–1970

7 Abstract work, if one wishes to do it well, must be allowed to destroy one's humanity; one raises a monument which is at the same time a tomb, in which, voluntarily, one slowly inters oneself.
letter, May 1902

Bertrand Russell
1872–1970

8 I was told that the Chinese said they would bury me by the Western Lake and build a shrine to my memory. I have some slight regret that this did not happen as I might have become a god, which would have been very *chic* for an atheist.
Autobiography (1968)

Dora Russell
1894–1986

9 To me he was exactly like the mad hatter.
in July 1985

Lytton Strachey
1880–1932

10 He belonged to the dangerous class of great gnomes.
Louis T. Stanley *Public Masks and Private Faces* (1986)

Lord John Russell 1792–1878

British Whig statesman, Prime Minister 1846–52 and 1865–6. He was responsible for introducing the Reform Bill of 1832 into Parliament.

Sydney Smith
1771–1845

11 Lord John . . . would perform the operation for the stone—build St Peter's or assume—(with or without ten minutes notice) the command of the Channel Fleet; and no one would discover by his manner that the patient had died, the church tumbled down, and the Channel Fleet been knocked to atoms.
Letters to Archdeacon Singleton (1837–40) vol. 2

Ken Russell 1927–

English film director. Characterized by extravagant and extreme imagery, his films have often attracted controversy for their depiction of sex and violence.

Glenda Jackson 12 He's got all those warts and bumps, but I like him as a person and as a
1936–   director he's like all really good directors—he leaves you alone. Bad
             directors tell you what they want; good directors always wait to be
             surprised.
             David Nathan *Glenda Jackson* (1984)

Babe Ruth 1895–1948

American baseball player. He played for the Boston Red Sox and the New York Yankees, setting a record of 714 home runs which remained unbroken until 1974.

Paul Gallico 1 God dressed in a camel's hair polo coat and flat camel's hair cap, God
1897–1976   with a flat nose and little piggy eyes, a big grin, and a fat black cigar
              sticking out of the side of it.
              in *American Dictionary of National Biography*

George Bernard Shaw 2 Who is this 'Babe' Ruth? And what does she do?
1856–1950   attributed

Ernest Rutherford 1871–1937

New Zealand physicist. He is regarded as the founder of nuclear physics, establishing the nature of alpha and beta particles, and the structure of the atom.

Edward Bullard 1 Rutherford was a disaster. He started the 'something for nothing'
1907–80   tradition . . . the notion that research can always be done on the cheap
              . . . The war taught us differently. If you want quick and effective results
              you must put the money in.
              P. Grosvenor and J. McMillan *The British Genius* (1973)

James Jeans 2 Rutherford was ever the happy warrior—happy in his work, happy in
1877–1946   its outcome, and happy in its human contacts.
              Obituary Notices of Fellows of the Royal Society (1938)

Stephen Leacock 3 When Rutherford was done with the atom all the solidity was pretty
1869–1944   well knocked out of it.
              The Boy I Left Behind Me (1947)

Ernest Rutherford 4 We haven't got the money, so we've got to think!
1871–1937   in *Bulletin of the Institute of Physics* (1962)

Ernest Rutherford 5 That shirt's too tight round the neck. Every day I grow in girth. *And* in
1871–1937   mentality.
              overheard in a tailor's in Cambridge
              C. P. Snow *Variety of Men* (1967)

C. P. Snow 6 His estimate of his own powers was realistic, but if it erred at all, it did
1905–80   not err on the modest side. 'There is no room for this particle in the
              atom as designed by *me*,' I once heard him assure a large audience.
              Variety of Men (1967)

Meg Ryan 1961–

American actress, particularly noted for her romantic roles. She has appeared in films such as *When Harry Met Sally . . .* and *Sleepless in Seattle*.

Meg Ryan 1 Through it all, I have remained consistently and nauseatingly adorable.
1961–   In fact, I have been known to cause diabetes.
             in 1999

Sue Ryder 1923–2000

English philanthropist. She co-founded an organization to care for former inmates of concentration camps, which expanded to provide homes for the mentally and physically disabled.

Richard D. North 1 Behind the piety, the seriousness, the awesome dedication, there was something a bit like flirtatiousness, and an occasional sign that she knew how essentially comic absolutely everything is. She was in that sense much more ordinary than Cheshire, which is a funny thing to say about a woman who would probably make a good candidate for canonization.
in November 2000

Sue Ryder 2 I believe that to be with people who are suffering, whoever they are,
1923–2000 makes one humble. They may be lepers or children in the last stages of tuberculosis, or starving. No matter what they look like, they have something about them which is very beautiful and gentle. It's a sort of radiance, an image of God.
interview, December 1992

S

Charles Saatchi 1943–

British advertising executive, born in Iraq. He is a noted patron of modern art.

Charles Saatchi 1 There's nothing complicated about me. There are no hidden depths. As
1943– Frank Stella said about minimalism, what you see is what you see.
in October 1999

Vita Sackville-West 1892–1962

English novelist and poet, wife of **Harold Nicolson**. She is also known for the garden which she created at Sissinghurst in Kent and for her friendship with **Virginia Woolf**.

on Vita Sackville-West's appearance in a tableau vivant:

Margot Asquith 1 Dear old Vita, all aqua, no vita, was as heavy as frost.
1864–1945 Philip Ziegler *Diana Cooper* (1981)

Clive Bell 2 Dear old, obtuse, aristocratic, passionate, grenadier-like Vita.
1881–1964 in 1924

Harold Nicolson 3 She is a dark river moving deeply in shadows. She really does not care
1886–1968 for the domestic affections. She would wish life to be conducted on a series of *grandes passions*. Or she thinks she would.
diary, December 1933

Nigel Nicolson 4 What you admire most in a person is sympathy for other people.
1917– *a son's view*
James Lees-Milne *Fourteen Friends* (1996)

Vita Sackville-West 5 I am reduced to a thing that wants Virginia.
1892–1962 letter to *Virginia Woolf*, January 1926

Stephen Spender 6 Working always in her garden, caring for her friends, her flowers and
1909–95 her poetry, modest and never interesting herself in literary disputes, her friendship had the freedom of silence and watchfulness about it.
World Within World (1951)

Yves Saint Laurent 1936–

French couturier. He opened his own fashion house in 1962, later launching Rive Gauche boutiques to sell ready-to-wear garments and expanding the business to include perfumes.

Hebe Dorsey   **1** Saint Laurent spoke a universal language, but he is a very fragile
1925–87   human being. But still, a season without Saint Laurent is like a season without God.
Nicholas Coleridge *The Fashion Conspiracy* (1988)

Yves Saint Laurent   **2** Creating is a harrowing business. I work in a state of anguish all year. I
1936–   shut myself up, don't go out. It's a hard life, which is why I understand Proust so well; I have such an admiration for what he has written about the agony of creation.
Nicholas Coleridge *The Fashion Conspiracy* (1988)

Camille Saint-Saëns 1835–1921

French composer, pianist, and organist.

Maurice Ravel   **1** I am told that Saint-Saëns has informed a delighted public that since
1875–1937   the war began he has composed music for the stage, melodies, an elegy, and a piece for the trombone. If he'd been making shell-cases instead it might have been all the better for music.
letter, October 1916

Andrei Sakharov 1921–89

Russian nuclear physicist and civil rights campaigner. Having helped to develop the Soviet hydrogen bomb, he campaigned against nuclear proliferation and was sentenced to internal exile.

Nikita Khrushchev   **1** He was obviously guided by moral and humanistic considerations. I
1894–1971   knew him and was profoundly impressed by him . . . However, he went too far in thinking that he had the right to decide whether the bomb he had developed could ever be used in the future.
Khrushchev Remembers: the Last Testament (1974)

Lord Salisbury 1830–1903

British Conservative statesman, Prime Minister 1885–6, 1886–92, and 1895–1902. He supported the policies which resulted in the Second Boer War.

Otto von Bismarck   **1** A lath of wood painted to look like iron.
1815–98   attributed, but vigorously denied by Sidney Whitman in *Personal Reminiscences of Prince Bismarck* (1902)

Benjamin Disraeli   **2** He is a great master of gibes and flouts and jeers.
1804–81   speech, August 1874

Lord Salisbury   **3** The agonies of a man who has to finish a difficult negotiation, and at
1830–1903   the same time to entertain four royalties at a country house can be better imagined than described.
letter, June 1878

Lord Salisbury   **4** I rank myself no higher in the scheme of things than a policeman—
1830–1903   whose utility would disappear if there were no criminals.
comparing his role within his party with that of **Gladstone**
Lady Gwendolen Cecil *Biographical Studies . . . of Robert, Third Marquess of Salisbury* (1962)

Alex Salmond 1954–

Scottish Nationalist politician.

David Steel   **1** Mr Salmond is looking increasingly like a maiden in distress waiting to
1938–   be rescued by James Bond. I do not think it is going to happen.
in April 1999

Pete Sampras 1971–

American tennis player. He was the youngest man ever to win the US Open, and won his seventh Wimbledon title in 2000.

Justin Gimelstob 1 When he came out of his mother's womb, God spent a little extra time on his right shoulder, just kind of touched it. So that helps.
in July 2000

George Sand 1804–76

French novelist. Her earlier novels portray women's struggles against conventional morals; she later wrote a number of pastoral novels.

Charlotte Brontë 1 Now I can understand admiration of George Sand—for though I never
1816–55 saw any of her works which I admired throughout . . . yet she has a grasp of mind which, if I cannot fully comprehend, I can very deeply respect; she is sagacious and profound; Miss Austen is only shrewd and observant.
letter, January 1848

Elizabeth Barrett 2 Thou large-brained woman and large-hearted man.
Browning *'To George Sand—A Desire' (1844)*
1806–61

Henry James 3 The time was when Madame Sand's novels were translated as fast as
1843–1916 they appeared, and circulated, half surreptitiously, as works delightful and intoxicating, but scandalous, dangerous, and seditious. To read George Sand in America was to be a socialist, a transcendentalist and an abolitionist.
in July 1868

John Ruskin 4 George Sand is often immoral; but she is always beautiful.
1819–1900 *'The Two Servants' (1881)*

Sappho early 7th century BC

Greek lyric poet who lived on Lesbos. The centre of a circle of women on her native island of Lesbos, she mainly wrote love poems in her local dialect.

Lord Byron 1 Dark Sappho! could not verse immortal save
1788–1824 That breast imbued with such immortal fire?
Could she not live who life eternal gave?
Childe Harold's Pilgrimage (1812–18)

John Singer Sargent 1856–1925

American painter. He is best known for his portraiture in a style noted for its bold brushwork. In the First World War he worked as an official war artist.

Anonymous 1 It's taking your face in your hands.
on the dangers of sitting for one's portrait to John Singer Sargent
W. Graham Robertson *Time Was (1931)*

John Singer Sargent 2 Every time I paint a portrait I lose a friend.
1856–1925 *attributed*

James McNeill 3 A sepulchre of dullness and propriety.
Whistler Richard Ormond *John Singer Sargent (1970)*
1834–1903

Malcolm Sargent 1895–1967

English conductor and composer. In 1921 he made an acclaimed debut conducting his own *Impressions of a Windy Day*. He was responsible for the BBC Promenade Concerts from 1948.

Thomas Beecham 4 I didn't know he'd been knighted. I knew he'd been doctored.
1879–1961 *on Malcolm Sargent's knighthood; attributed*

Malcolm Sargent 1895–1967	5 I spend up to six hours a day waving my arms about and if everyone else did the same they would stay much healthier. Leslie Ayre *The Wit of Music* (1966)

Jean-Paul Sartre 1905–80

French philosopher, novelist, dramatist, and critic. A leading existentialist, he dealt in his work with the nature of human life and the structures of consciousness.

Simone de Beauvoir 1908–86	1 My heart's just a mush this evening. I'm consumed by passion for you and it couldn't be more painful. This has been brewing all day and it came down on me like a tornado in the streets of Douarnenez, where I broke into sobs. letter, September 1939
Charles de Gaulle 1890–1970	2 One does not put Voltaire in the Bastille. *when asked to arrest Sartre, in the 1960s* in *Encounter* June 1975

Siegfried Sassoon 1886–1967

English poet and novelist. He is known for his starkly realistic poems written while serving in the First World War.

Siegfried Sassoon 1886–1967	1 A booby-trapped idealist. on himself; *Siegfried's Journey* (1945)
Virginia Woolf 1882–1941	2 It is realism of the right, of the poetic kind. reviewing Sassoon's war poems, in May 1917

Erik Satie 1866–1925

French composer. He formed an irreverent avant-garde artistic set associated with Les Six, Dadaism, and surrealism.

John Cage 1912–92	1 Between Satie and Beethoven there is a great break, and it's the break from a music that involves going somewhere and a music which is not going anywhere. Music which is content to stay where it is. Andrew Ford *Composer to Composer* (1993)
Jean Cocteau 1889–1963	2 Satie gave comic titles to his music in order to protect his works from persons obsessed with the sublime. Rollo Myers *Modern French Music* (1971)
Erik Satie 1866–1925	3 An artist must organize his life. Here is the exact timetable of my daily activities. Get up: 7.18 am; be inspired: 10.23 to 11.47 am. I take lunch at 12.11 pm and leave the table at 12.14 pm. *Memoirs of an Amnesiac* (1914)

Gerald Scarfe 1936–

English caricaturist.

Gerald Scarfe 1936–	1 I find a particular delight in taking the caricature as far as I can. It satisfies me to stretch the human frame about and recreate it and yet keep a likeness. *Scarfe by Scarfe* (1986)

Domenico Scarlatti 1685–1757

Italian composer. He was a prolific composer of keyboard music, and his work made an important contribution to the development of the sonata form.

Basil Bunting 1900–85	1 It is time to consider how Domenico Scarlatti condensed so much music into so few bars with never a crabbed turn or congested cadence, never a boast or a see-here. *Briggflatts* (1966)

Claudia Schiffer 1970–

German fashion model.

Karl Lagerfeld
1939–

1 Claudia would have made a wonderful Hollywood silent star.
in June 2000

Claudia Schiffer
1970–

2 I once ate a whole bar of chocolate.
in June 2000

Friedrich von Schiller 1759–1805

German dramatist, poet, historian, and critic. Initially influenced by the *Sturm und Drang* movement, he was later an important figure of the Enlightenment.

Ludwig Boltzmann
1844–1906

1 Without Schiller, there might have been a man with my nose and beard, but it would not have been me.
Populare Schriften (1905)

Arnold Schoenberg 1874–1951

Austrian-born American composer and music theorist. His major contribution to modernism was the development of atonality and serialism.

John Cage
1912–92

1 Schoenberg would say, for instance, 'Bach did such-and-such, Beethoven did such-and-such, Brahms did such-and-such, and *Schoenberg* did such-and-such,' referring to himself in the third person. So that he didn't think of himself as changing the past, but rather as one who continued the past.
Andrew Ford *Composer to Composer* (1993)

Aaron Copland
1900–90

2 Emotionally Schoenberg was still a part of the nineteenth century.
Robert Jacobson *Reverberations* (1975)

Arnold Schoenberg
1874–1951

3 I am delighted to add another unplayable work to the repertoire. I want the Concerto to be difficult and I want the little finger to become longer. I can wait.
of his Violin Concerto
Joseph Machlis *Introduction to Contemporary Music* (1963)

Richard Strauss
1864–1949

4 Only a psychiatrist can help poor Schoenberg now . . . He would do better to shovel snow instead of scribbling on music paper.
letter, 1913

Igor Stravinsky
1882–1971

5 What I never liked about Schoenberg's music was that it wasn't modern.
Andrew Ford *Composer to Composer* (1993)

Arthur Schopenhauer 1788–1860

German philosopher. According to his philosophy, the will is identified with ultimate reality and happiness is only achieved by abnegating the will.

Guy de Maupassant
1850–93

1 The greatest devastator of dreams who ever walked the earth.
'Aupres d'un mort'

Erwin Schrödinger 1887–1961

Austrian theoretical physicist. He founded the study of wave mechanics. After fleeing Nazi oppression in Europe, his general works influenced scientists of many different disciplines.

Max Born
1882–1970

1 His private life seemed strange to bourgeois people like ourselves. But all this does not matter. He was a most lovable person, independent, amusing, temperamental, kind and generous, and he had a most perfect and efficient brain.
My Life, Recollections of a Nobel Laureate (1978)

Paul Dirac
1902–84

2 Schrödinger and I both had a very strong appreciation of mathematical beauty, and this dominated all our work. It was a sort of act of faith with us that any equations which describe the fundamental laws of Nature must have great mathematical beauty in them.

in 1977

Albert Einstein
1879–1955

3 This correspondence gives me great joy, because you are my closest brother and your brain runs so similarly to mine.

letter to Schrödinger, April 1946

Erwin Schrödinger
1887–1961

4 If I am to have an interest in a question, others must also have one. My word is seldom the first, but often the second, and may be inspired by a desire to contradict or to correct, but the consequent extension may turn out to be more important than the correction, which served only as a connection.

Les Prix Nobel en 1933 (1935)

Erwin Schrödinger
1887–1961

5 I have no higher aim than to work out the *beauty* of science. I put beauty before science. *Nitimur in vetitum* [we strive for that which is forbidden]. We are always longing for our neighbour's housewife and for the perfection we are least likely to achieve.

letter, August 1944; quoting *Ovid*

James D. Watson
1928–

6 From the moment I read Schrödinger's *What is Life?* I became polarized towards finding out the secret of the gene.

lecture, October 1984

Franz Schubert 1797–1828

Austrian composer. His music is associated with the romantic movement for its lyricism and emotional intensity, but belongs in formal terms to the classical age.

Laurie Lee
1914–97

1 A rare genius whose innocent yearning for affection was expressed in music as pure as spring water.

Valerie Grove *Laurie Lee: The Well-loved Stranger* (1999)

Charles Schulz 1922–2000

American cartoonist. He is remembered as the creator of the 'Peanuts' comic strip.

Charles Schulz
1922–2000

1 I don't think I'm a true artist. I would love to be Andrew Wyeth or Picasso. But I can draw pretty well and I can write pretty well, and I think I'm doing the best with whatever abilities I have been given. And what more can one ask?

attributed

Michael Schumacher 1969–

German motor-racing driver.

Damon Hill
1960–

1 What you've got to remember about Michael is that under that cold professional Germanic exterior beats a heart of stone.

in May 2000

Michael Schumacher
1969–

2 The only thing that surprised me is that people suddenly see me as a human, which I thought I was before.

having burst into tears after winning the Italian Grand Prix
in September 2000

Clara Schumann 1819–96

German pianist and composer, wife of **Robert Schumann**.

Frédéric Chopin
1810–49

1 The only woman in Germany who can play my music.

Arthur Hedley *Chopin* (1947)

Robert Schumann 1810–56

German composer. He was a leading romantic composer, particularly noted for his songs and piano music. He drew much of his inspiration from literature.

Clara Schumann
1819–96

2 You require but a simple 'Yes'? Such a small word—but such an important one. But should not a heart so full of unutterable love as mine utter this little word with all its might? I do so and my innermost soul whispers always to you.
letter, August 1837

Robert Schumann
1810–56

3 I should not like to be understood by everybody.
Christopher Headington *The Bodley Head History of Western Music* (1974)

Arnold Schwarzenegger 1947–

American actor, noted for his physical prowess and star of action films such as *The Terminator.*

Clive James
1939–

1 He looks like a brown condom stuffed with walnuts.
attributed

Arnold Schwarzenegger 1947–

2 Sure I get treated like a male Raquel Welch. I love it.
in May 1977

Arnold Schwarzenegger 1947–

3 No one has ever been able to define me. So don't even try. People try to work me out, but I can't even work myself out. I'm full of complexities and always a surprise to myself. So you won't work me out but you can listen to me.
in December 1999

H. Norman Schwarzkopf III 1934–

American general, overall commander of coalition forces in the Gulf War.

H. Norman Schwarzkopf III 1934–

1 I don't consider myself dovish and I certainly don't consider myself hawkish. Maybe I would describe myself as owlish—that is, wise enough to understand that you want to do everything possible to avoid war.
in January 1991

Albert Schweitzer 1875–1965

German theologian, musician, and medical missionary, born in Alsace. In 1913 he qualified as a doctor and went as a missionary to Gabon, where he established a hospital.

Albert Einstein
1879–1955

1 He is the only Westerner who has had a moral effect on this generation comparable to Gandhi's. As in the case of Gandhi, the extent of this effect is overwhelmingly due to the example he gave by his own life's work.
Jamie Sayen *Einstein in America* (1985)

Paul Scofield 1922–

British actor.

Glenda Jackson
1936–

1 To me he's the ideal of what acting should be about, a total absence of an intrusive self.
David Nathan *Glenda Jackson* (1984)

Peter Scott 1909–89

English naturalist and artist, son of Sir **Robert Scott**. In 1946 he founded the Wildfowl Trust at Slimbridge in Gloucestershire.

David Bellamy
1933–

1 SMALL BOY: Is he your father?
BELLAMY: No, but he's the father of conservation.
Elspeth Huxley *Peter Scott* (1993)

John Hackett
1910–97

2 There was much of the poet in him, in the true sense of the Greek origins of the word, a doer, a creator, a maker.
Elspeth Huxley *Peter Scott* (1993)

Robert Falcon Scott
1868–1912

3 Make the boy interested in natural history if you can; it is better than games.
last letter to his wife, March 1912

Robert Falcon Scott 1868–1912

English explorer and naval officer, father of Sir **Peter Scott**. In 1910–12 Scott and four companions reached the South Pole, to discover that **Roald Amundsen** had beaten them. They died on the return journey.

Apsley Cherry-Garrard
1882–1959

4 For a joint scientific and geographical piece of organization, give me Scott.
F. A. Worsley *Shackleton's Boat Journey* (1999); see **Shackleton** 1

Robert Falcon Scott
1868–1912

5 We took risks, we knew we took them; things have come out against us, and therefore we have no cause for complaint.
'The Last Message', 1912

Sir Walter Scott 1771–1832

Scottish novelist and poet. He established the form of the historical novel in Britain, and collected and imitated old Borders tales and ballads.

Jane Austen
1775–1817

6 Walter Scott has no business to write novels, especially good ones—It is not fair.—He has fame and profit enough as a poet, and should not be taking the bread out of other people's mouths.—I do not like him, and do not mean to like *Waverley* if I can help it—but fear I must.
letter, September 1814

Lord Byron
1788–1824

7 Scott is the only very successful genius that could be cited as being as generally beloved as a man as he is admired as an author.
Lady Blessington *Conversations with Lord Byron* (1834)

Thomas Carlyle
1795–1881

8 It can be said of him, when he departed, he took a man's life along with him.
Critical and Miscellaneous Essays (1838)

William Hazlitt
1778–1830

9 His works (taken together) are almost like a new edition of human nature. This is indeed to be an author!
The Spirit of the Age (1825)

Hugh MacDiarmid
1892–1978

10 The great source of the paralysing ideology of defeatism in Scotland, the spread of which is responsible at once for the acceptance of the Union and the low standard of nineteenth-century Scots literature.
on Scott's Waverley Novels
Lucky Poet (1943)

Aleksandr Scriabin 1872–1915

Russian composer and pianist. Much of his later music reflects his interest in mysticism and theosophy.

Henry Miller
1891–1980

1 Scriabin's music sounds like I think—sometimes. Has that faroff cosmic itch. Divinely fouled up. All fire and air . . . It was like a bath of ice; cocaine and rainbows.
Nexus (1945)

Peter Sellers 1925–80

English comic actor. He made his name in *The Goon Show*, a radio series of the 1950s, but is best known for his film roles as the French detective Inspector Clouseau.

Peter Sellers 1 I can't walk on the set looking like myself.
1925–80
refusing to be interviewed by Michael Parkinson
Michael Parkinson *Sporting Profiles* (1995)

Peter Sellers 2 [I was] just a vase of flowers, and Milligan arranged me.
1925–80
Norma Farnes (ed.) *The Goons: The Story* (1997)

Billy Wilder 3 What do you mean, heart attack? You've got to have a heart before you
1906–
can have an attack.
remark, 1964

David Selznick 1902–65

American film producer. He produced such films as *King Kong* and *Anna Karenina* before establishing his own company in 1936 and producing *Gone with the Wind* and other films.

Gregory Peck 1 Selznick believed in treating his actors like little tin gods, but he was a
1916–
little hard on directors.
Donald Spoto *Notorious* (1997)

Ayrton Senna 1960–94

Brazilian motor-racing driver. He won the Formula One world championship three times. He died from injuries sustained in a crash during the Italian Grand Prix in 1994.

Damon Hill 1 People talk about Ayrton destroying his teammates psychologically, but
1960–
what's he going to do, hit me with a Vulcan Mind-grip?
in 1994

Alain Prost 2 I am not prepared to fight against people who are not afraid to die.
1955–
in October 1990

Ernest Shackleton 1874–1922

British explorer. Shackleton set out in an open boat on an 800 mile voyage to get help for his crew, trapped by ice in the Antarctic.

Apsley Cherry- 1 For a joint scientific and geographical piece of organization, give me
Garrard
Scott; for a Winter Journey, Wilson; for a dash to the pole and nothing
1882–1959
else, Amundsen: and if I am in the devil of a hole and want to get out of
it, give me Shackleton every time.
F. A. Worsley *Shackleton's Boat Journey* (1999); see **Scott** 4

William Shakespeare 1564–1616

English dramatist. Although his plays, written mostly in blank verse, were widely performed in his lifetime, many were not printed until the *First Folio* of 1623. His influence has been immense.

Matthew Arnold 1 Others abide our question. Thou art free.
1822–88
We ask and ask: Thou smilest and art still,
Out-topping knowledge.
'Shakespeare' (1849)

John Aubrey 2 He was a handsome, well-shaped man: very good company, and of a
1626–97
very ready and pleasant smooth wit.
Brief Lives

Jane Austen 3 Shakespeare one gets acquainted with without knowing how. It is part
1775–1817
of an Englishman's constitution. His thoughts and beauties are so
spread abroad that one touches them everywhere, one is intimate with
him by instinct.
Mansfield Park (1814)

Walter Bagehot
1826–77

4 To a great experience one thing is essential, an experiencing nature.
Estimates of some Englishmen and Scotchmen (1858)

Samuel Taylor Coleridge
1772–1834

5 Our *myriad-minded* Shakespeare.
Biographia Literaria (1817)

Samuel Taylor Coleridge
1772–1834

6 Shakespeare . . . is of no age—nor of any religion, or party or profession. The body and substance of his works came out of the unfathomable depths of his own oceanic mind.
Table Talk (1835)

John Dryden
1631–1700

7 He was naturally learn'd; he needed not the spectacles of books to read Nature: he looked inwards, and found her there . . . He is many times flat, insipid; his comic wit degenerating into clenches, his serious swelling into bombast. But he is always great.
An Essay of Dramatic Poesy (1668)

John Dryden
1631–1700

8 [Shakespeare] is the very Janus of poets; he wears almost everywhere two faces; and you have scarce begun to admire the one, ere you despise the other.
Essay on the Dramatic Poetry of the Last Age (1672)

Richard Eyre
1943–

9 There is a sense in which every writer in English owes a debt to Shakespeare. He is our theatrical DNA.
in November 2000

Gustave Flaubert
1821–80

10 He was not a man, he was a continent; he contained whole crowds of great men, entire landscapes.
letter, September 1852

George III
1738–1820

11 Was there ever such stuff as great part of Shakespeare? Only one must not say so! But what think you?—what?—Is there not sad stuff? what?—what?
to Fanny Burney, in her diary December 1785

Robert Greene
c. 1560–92

12 For there is an upstart crow, beautified with our feathers, that with his tiger's heart wrapped in a player's hide, supposes he is as well able to bumbast out a blank verse as the best of you; and being an absolute *Johannes fac totum*, is in his own conceit the only Shake-scene in a country.
Groatsworth of Wit Bought with a Million of Repentance (1592)

John Heming
1556–1630
and **Henry Condell**
d. 1627

13 Who, as he was a happy imitator of Nature, was a most gentle expresser of it. His mind and hand went together: And what he thought, he uttered with that easiness, that we have scarce received from him a blot.
First Folio Shakespeare (1623) preface

Samuel Johnson
1709–84

14 A quibble is to Shakespeare, what luminous vapours are to the traveller; he follows it at all adventures, it is sure to lead him out of his way and sure to engulf him in the mire.
Plays of William Shakespeare . . . (1765) preface

Ben Jonson
c. 1573–1637

15 Thou hadst small Latin, and less Greek.
'To the Memory of . . . Shakespeare' (1623)

Ben Jonson
c. 1573–1637

16 He was not of an age, but for all time!
'To the Memory of . . . Shakespeare' (1623)

Ben Jonson
c. 1573–1637

17 Sweet Swan of Avon!
'To the Memory of . . . Shakespeare' (1623)

D. H. Lawrence
1885–1930

18 When I read Shakespeare I am struck with wonder
That such trivial people should muse and thunder
In such lovely language.
'When I Read Shakespeare' (1929)

Vivien Leigh 19 Shaw is like a train. One just speaks the words and sits in one's place.
1913–67 But Shakespeare is like bathing in the sea—one swims where one
wants.
in letter from Harold Nicolson to Vita Sackville-West, February 1956

Gustav Mahler 20 Shakespeare is the positive, the productive; Ibsen merely analysis,
1860–1911 negation, barrenness.
letter, June 1904

John Milton 21 What needs my Shakespeare for his honoured bones,
1608–74 The labour of an age in pilèd stones.
'On Shakespeare' (1632)

Laurence Olivier 22 Shakespeare—the nearest thing in incarnation to the eye of God.
1907–89 in *Kenneth Harris Talking To* (1971)

Harold Pinter 23 I suppose Shakespeare's dominated my life the way he's dominated
1930– many people's lives. We don't recover from Shakespeare.
Mel Gussow *Conversations with Pinter* (1994)

Alexander Pope 24 Shakespeare (whom you and ev'ry play-house bill
1688–1744 Style the divine, the matchless, what you will)
For gain, not glory, winged his roving flight,
And grew immortal in his own despite.
Imitations of Horace (1737)

Sir Walter Scott 25 The blockheads talk of my being like Shakespeare—not fit to tie his
1771–1832 brogues.
diary, December 1826

William Shakespeare 26 Good friend, for Jesu's sake forbear
1564–1616 To dig the dust enclosed here.
Blest be the man that spares these stones,
And curst be he that moves my bones.
inscription on his grave, Stratford-upon-Avon, probably composed by himself

George Bernard Shaw 27 With the single exception of Homer, there is no eminent writer, not
1856–1950 even Sir Walter Scott, whom I can despise so entirely as I despise
Shakespeare when I measure my mind against his.
in September 1896

Horace Walpole 28 One of the greatest geniuses that ever existed, Shakespeare,
1717–97 undoubtedly wanted taste.
letter, August 1764

Mae West 29 Let Shakespeare do it his way, I'll do it mine. We'll see who comes out
1892–1980 better.
G. Eells and S. Musgrove *Mae West* (1989)

Lewis Wolpert 30 If Watson and Crick had not discovered the nature of DNA, one can be
1929– virtually certain that other scientists would eventually have determined
it. With art—whether painting, music or literature—it is quite
different. If Shakespeare had not written *Hamlet*, no other playwright
would have done so.
The Unnatural Nature of Science (1993)

Bill Shankly 1913–81

Scottish footballer and manager. He had great success in Britain and Europe as manager of
Liverpool.

Hugh McIlvanney 1 With his drill-sergeant's hairstyle, his boxer's stance and his staccato,
1933– hard-man's delivery he did not fit everybody's idea of a romantic. But
that's what he was, an out-and-out, 22-carat example of the species.
in October 1981

Bill Shankly 2 Me havin' no education, I had to use my brains.
1913–81 Hugh McIlvanney *McIlvanney on Football* (1994)

George Bernard Shaw 1856–1950

Irish dramatist and writer. His best-known plays combine comedy with intellectual debate, and he wrote lengthy prefaces expanding his ideas. A socialist, he became an active member of the Fabian Society.

James Agate
1877–1947

1 Shaw's plays are the price we pay for Shaw's prefaces.
diary, March 1933

Max Beerbohm
1872–1956

2 Shaw's judgements were often scatterbrained, but at least he had brains to scatter.
in 1954; S. N. Behrman *Conversations with Max* (1960)

Mrs Patrick Campbell
1865–1940

3 If you give him meat no woman in London will be safe.
of Shaw's vegetarianism
Frank Harris *Contemporary Portraits* (1919)

G. K. Chesterton
1874–1936

4 Mr Shaw is (I suspect) the only man on earth who has never written any poetry.
Orthodoxy (1908)

Winston Churchill
1874–1965

5 He was one of my earliest antipathies . . . I possess a lively image of this bright, nimble, fierce and comprehending being, Jack Frost dancing bespangled in the sunshine. He is at once an acquisitive Capitalist and a sincere Communist. He makes his characters talk blithely about killing men for the sake of an idea; but would take great trouble not to hurt a fly.
Great Contemporaries (1937)

Edward Elgar
1857–1934

6 Bernard Shaw is hopelessly wrong, as all these fellows are, on fundamental things:—amongst others they punch Xtianity and try to make it fit their civilization instead of making their civilization fit it. He is an amusing liar, but not much more.
letter, July 1904

Harold Laski
1893–1950

7 Shaw, with incredibly brilliant insolence, began to prove that Foreign Secretaries are by definition cynical and corrupt. Poor Austin, of course, tried to riposte; but he was like an elephant trying to catch an exceedingly agile wasp.
of an encounter between Shaw and Austen Chamberlain
letter, July 1926

Vivien Leigh
1913–67

8 Shaw is like a train. One just speaks the words and sits in one's place. But Shakespeare is like bathing in the sea—one swims where one wants.
letter from Harold Nicolson to Vita Sackville-West, February 1956

Lenin
1870–1924

9 A good man fallen among Fabians.
Arthur Ransome *Six Weeks in Russia in 1919* (1919)

Harold Nicolson
1886–1968

10 I do not think that Shaw will be a great literary figure in 2000 AD. He is an amazingly brilliant contemporary; but not in the Hardy class.
diary, December 1950

George Orwell
1903–50

11 The basis of all Bernard Shaw's attacks on Shakespeare is really the charge—quite true, of course—that Shakespeare wasn't an enlightened member of the Fabian Society.
Collected Essays, Journalism and Letters (1968)

John Osborne
1929–94

12 Shaw is the most fraudulent, inept writer of Victorian melodramas ever to gull a timid critic or fool a dull public. He writes like a Pakistani who had learned English when he was twelve years old in order to become a chartered accountant.
in June 1977

Bertrand Russell
1872–1970

13 Although like many witty men he considered wit an adequate substitute for wisdom, he could defend any idea, however silly, so cleverly as to make those who did not accept it look like fools.
Alistair Cooke *Memories of the Great and the Good* (1999)

George Bernard Shaw
1856–1950

14 The trouble, Mr Goldwyn, is that you are only interested in art and I am only interested in money.

telegraphed version of the outcome of a conversation between Shaw and **Sam Goldwyn**
Alva Johnson *The Great Goldwyn* (1937)

an unknown woman wrote to Shaw suggesting that as he had the greatest brain in the world, and she the most beautiful body, they ought to produce the most perfect child:

George Bernard Shaw
1856–1950

15 What if the child inherits my body and your brains?

Hesketh Pearson *Bernard Shaw* (1942)

A. J. P. Taylor
1906–90

16 The magic of Shaw's words may still bewitch posterity . . . but it will find that he has nothing to say.

in July 1956

Kenneth Tynan
1927–80

17 As a demolition expert he has no rivals, and we are being grossly irrelevant if we ask a demolition expert, when his work is done: 'But what have you created?' . . . Shaw's genius was for intellectual slum-clearance, not for town planning.

in July 1956

Rebecca West
1892–1983

18 Charlotte married Shaw on the understanding that the marriage was never consummated, and I am sure he always observed this condition. He was a eunuch perpetually inflamed by flirtation.

letter, February 1955

Oscar Wilde
1854–1900

19 Shaw has not an enemy in the world; and none of his friends like him.

letter from Shaw to Archibald Henderson, February 1911

W. B. Yeats
1865–1939

20 Presently I had a nightmare that I was haunted by a sewing-machine that clicked and shone, but the incredible thing was that the machine smiled, smiled perpetually. Yet I delighted in Shaw, the formidable man. He could hit my enemies, and the enemies of those I loved, as I could never hit.

Autobiographies (1926)

Mary Wollstonecraft Shelley 1797–1851

English writer, daughter of William Godwin and **Mary Wollstonecraft**. She eloped with and later married **Percy Bysshe Shelley**. She wrote the Gothic novel *Frankenstein*.

Lord Byron
1788–1824

1 Mrs Shelley is very clever, indeed it would be difficult for her not to be so; the daughter of Mary Wollstonecraft and Godwin, and the wife of Shelley, could be no common person.

Lady Blessington *Conversations with Lord Byron* (1834)

William Godwin
1756–1836

2 I am anxious that she should be brought up like a philosopher, even like a cynic. It will add greatly to the strength and worth of her character.

letter, June 1812

Percy Bysshe Shelley 1792–1822

English poet. He was a leading figure of the romantic movement with radical political views. Notable works include *Adonais*, an elegy on the death of **Keats**.

Matthew Arnold
1822–88

3 In poetry, no less than in life, he is 'a beautiful and ineffectual angel, beating in the void his luminous wings in vain'.

Essays in Criticism Second Series (1888)

Robert Browning
1812–89

4 Sun-treader, life and light be thine for ever!

Pauline (1833)

Lord Byron
1788–1824

5 Shelley is truth itself—and honour itself—notwithstanding his out-of-the-way notions about religion.

letter, June 1821

William Hazlitt
1778–1830

6 The author of the *Prometheus Unbound* has a fire in his eye, a fever in his blood, a maggot in his brain, a hectic flutter in his speech, which mark out the philosophic fanatic.
Table Talk (1821–2)

James John Hornby
1826–1909

7 I wish Shelley had been at Harrow.
view of a headmaster of Eton
Henry S. Salt *Percy Bysshe Shelley* (1896)

George Bernard Shaw
1856–1950

8 I made my then famous declaration (among 100 people) 'I am a Socialist, an Atheist and a Vegetarian' (ergo, a true Shelleyan), whereupon two ladies who had been palpitating with enthusiasm for Shelley under the impression that he was a devout Anglican, resigned on the spot.
letter, March 1908

Percy Bysshe Shelley
1792–1822

9 Less oft is peace in Shelley's mind,
Than calm in waters, seen.
'To Jane: The Recollection' (written 1822)

Richard Brinsley Sheridan 1757–1816

Irish dramatist and Whig politician. His plays are comedies of manners; they include *The Rivals* and *The School for Scandal*. In 1780 he entered Parliament, becoming a celebrated orator.

Lord Byron
1788–1824

1 Without means, without connection, without character . . . he beat them all, in all he ever attempted.
letter, June 1818

Edward Gibbon
1737–94

2 A good actor. I saw him this morning; he is perfectly well.
Sheridan had collapsed into the arms of **Burke***, after a speech lasting 11 days*
in June 1788

Horace Walpole
1717–97

3 How should such a fellow as Sheridan, who has no diamonds to bestow, fascinate all the world?—yet witchcraft, no doubt there has been, for when did simple eloquence ever convince a majority?
letter, February 1787

William Tecumseh Sherman 1820–91

American general. On a march through Georgia in the American Civil War, he crushed Confederate forces and broke civilian morale by his policy of deliberate destruction.

Ulysses S. Grant
1822–85

1 You have accomplished the most gigantic undertaking given to any general in this war, and with a skill and ability that will be acknowledged in history as unsurpassed if not unequalled.
letter written after the capture of Altanta, 1864

William Tecumsah Sherman
1820–91

2 [Grant] stood by me when I was crazy, and I stood by him when he was drunk; and now we stand by each other always.
of his relationship with his fellow Union commander
in 1864; Geoffrey C. Ward *The Civil War* (1991)

Clare Short 1946–

British Labour politician, noted for her outspokenness. She campaigned against Page Three.

Clare Short
1946–

1 I'm going to try to be good but I can't help it. I have to be me.
on being made Secretary of State for international development, in May 1997

Dmitri Shostakovich 1906–75

Russian composer. He developed a highly personal style and, although he experimented with atonality and twelve-note techniques, his music always returned to a basic tonality.

Yehudi Menuhin
1916–99

1 To anyone who knew his music, a first encounter with Dmitri Shostakovich could not fail to be startling: in contrast to the elemental force, bombast, grandeur of his works, he was a *chetif* figure, the perennial student, unassertive and shy, who looked as though all the music could be wrung out of him in a couple of song cycles.
Unfinished Journey (1976)

Elizabeth Siddall 1829–62

English painter, wife of **Dante Gabriel Rossetti** and model for many of his paintings.

John Ruskin
1819–1900

1 [She had] more the look of a Florentine fifteenth-century lady than anything I ever saw out of a fresco.
Oswald Doughty *A Victorian Romantic: Dante Gabriel Rossetti* (1960)

Sarah Siddons 1755–1831

English actress, sister of **John Kemble**. She was an acclaimed tragic actress, noted particularly for her role as Lady Macbeth.

Fanny Burney
1752–1840

1 I expected her to have been all that is interesting; the delicacy and sweetness with which she seizes every opportunity to strike and to captivate upon the stage had persuaded me that her mind was formed with that peculiar susceptibility, which, in different modes, must give equal powers to attract and to delight, in common life. But I was very much mistaken.
diary, August 1787

William Hazlitt
1778–1830

2 She is out of the pale of all theories and annihilates all rules. Wherever she sits there is grace and grandeur, there is tragedy personified. Her seat is the undivided throne of the Tragic Muse.
Table Talk (1821–2)

Richard Brinsley Sheridan
1751–1816

3 To her! To that magnificent and appalling creature! I should as soon have thought of making love to the Archbishop of Canterbury!
responding to Samuel Rogers's suggestion that **Sheridan** *might 'make open love' to Mrs Siddons*
Henry Colborn (ed.) *Sheridaniana* (1826)

Philip Sidney 1554–86

English poet, courtier, and soldier. Generally considered to represent the apotheosis of the Elizabethan courtier, he was a leading poet and patron of **Edmund Spenser**.

Robert Browning
1812–89

1 Sidney's self, the starry paladin.
Sordello (1840)

Richard Carew
1555–1620

2 Will you have all in all for prose and verse? Take the miracle of our age, Sir Philip Sidney.
William Camden *Remains concerning Britain* (1614)

Edward Dyer
d. 1607

3 Silence augmenteth grief, writing increaseth rage,
Staled are my thoughts, which loved and lost, the wonder of our age.
'Elegy on the Death of Sir Philip Sidney' (1593)

Fulke Greville
1554–1628

4 Servant to Queen Elizabeth
Councillor to King James and
Friend to Sir Philip Sidney.
his epitaph

Paul Simon 1942–

American singer and songwriter. He achieved fame with Art Garfunkel. The duo split up in 1970 and Simon went on to pursue a successful solo career.

Art Garfunkel
1941–

1 Paul is like John Lennon. They're feisty. There's a rebellious attitude. You know, that's very acceptable. It's standard rebellious attitude stuff.
Stacey Luftig (ed.) *The Paul Simon Companion* (1997)

Wallis Simpson see **Duchess of Windsor**

Frank Sinatra 1915–98

American singer and actor. He became a star in the 1940s with a large teenage following; his many hits include 'Night and Day' and 'My Way'.

Tony Bennett
1926–

1 We all fell in love, fell out of love, and fell in love again to the sound of his voice.
at Sinatra's funeral, May 1998

Humphrey Bogart
1899–1957

2 Sinatra's idea of Paradise is a place where there are plenty of women and no newspapermen. He doesn't know it, but he'd be better off if it were the other way round.
John Shepherd *Tin Pan Alley* (1982)

Bing Crosby
1903–77

3 The voice of a lifetime. Unfortunately it's my lifetime.
attributed

Ava Gardner
1922–90

4 I always knew Frank would end up in bed with a little boy.
on her former husband's marriage to **Mia Farrow**
Kitty Kelley *His Way* (1986)

Frank Sinatra
1915–98

5 If I drank as much and had as many women as I have said I have, I would be in a jar in the Massachusettes Institute of Technology.
in June 1986

Frank Sinatra
1915–98

6 You only live once, and the way I live, once is enough.
attributed

Sitting Bull (Tatanka Iyotake) c. 1831–90

Sioux chief. From about 1867, Sitting Bull led the Sioux in the fight to retain their lands; this resulted in the massacre of **General Custer** and his men at Little Bighorn.

Sitting Bull
c. 1831–90

1 What law have I broken? Is it wrong for me to love my own? Is it wicked for me because my skin is red? Because I am Sioux; because I was born where my fathers lived; because I would die for my people and my country?
to Major Brotherton, recorded July 1881

Edith Sitwell 1887–1964

English poet and critic. Her early verse was light-hearted and experimental. In 1923 she attracted attention with *Façade*, a group of poems recited to music by William Walton.

Elizabeth Bowen
1899–1973

1 A high altar on the move.
V. Glendinning *Edith Sitwell* (1981)

Noël Coward
1899–1973

2 Edith Sitwell, in that great Risorgimento cape of hers, looks as though she were covering a teapot or a telephone.
William Marchant *The Pleasure of his Company* (1975)

Noël Coward
1899–1973

3 Two wise acres and a cow.
of Edith, Osbert, and Sacheverell Sitwell
John Pearson *Façades* (1978)

Alec Guinness
1914–2000

4 Some of her clothes looked as if dragged from a dressing-up hamper—a facade and a charade. I miss her kindness and Plantagenet condescension.
diary, January 1995

Edith Sitwell
1887–1964

5 When I am told by the left-wing boys that I can't write poetry because I have no proletarian experiences, I often wonder how many of them, at the age of 17, have been sent to pawn false teeth—parental false teeth!
letter, August 1945

Edith Sitwell
1887–1964

6 I have often wished I had time to cultivate modesty . . . But I am too busy thinking about myself.
in April 1950

Virginia Woolf
1882–1941

7 Edith Sitwell came to tea: transparent like some white bone one picks up on a moor, with sea water stones on her long frail hands which slide into yours much narrower than one expects like a folded fan.
diary, March 1927

Bedřich Smetana 1824–84

Czech composer. Regarded as the founder of Czech music, he was dedicated to the cause of Czech nationalism.

Leoš Janáček
1854–1928

1 My memories of Bedřich Smetana are like a picture of how children imagine God: in the clouds.
Dalibor (1909)

Bedřich Smetana
1824–84

2 By the grace of God and with his help I shall one day be a Liszt in technique and a Mozart in composition.
diary, 1845

Delia Smith

English cookery writer and broadcaster. She is noted for her clarity and straightforward approach.

Egon Ronay

1 Her cooking is the missionary position of cooking. That is how everybody starts.
in November 1998

Delia Smith

2 I am not some prim Brownie pack leader—in fact, I am a bit of a bitch.
interview, September 2000

Anthony Worrall Thompson

3 I called her the Volvo of cooks because she is the safest chef on TV.
in 2000

F. E. Smith 1872–1930

British Conservative politician and lawyer, first Earl of Birkenhead. He was noted as an orator and wit.

Margot Asquith
1864–1945

4 Lord Birkenhead is very clever but sometimes his brains go to his head.
attributed

speaking against the Welsh Disestablishment Bill, Smith had called it 'a Bill which has shocked the conscience of every Christian community in Europe':

G. K. Chesterton
1874–1936

5 Talk about the pews and steeples
And the Cash that goes therewith!
But the souls of Christian peoples . . .
Chuck it, Smith!
'Antichrist' (1915)

Winston Churchill
1874–1965

6 F. E. had a complete armoury. The bludgeon for the platform, the rapier for a personal dispute, the entangling net and the unexpected trident for the Courts of Law and a jug of clear spring water for an anxious perplexed conclave.
Great Contemporaries (1937)

F. E. Smith
1872–1930

7 JUDGE: You are extremely offensive, young man.
SMITH: As a matter of fact, we both are, and the only difference between us is that I am trying to be, and you can't help it.
2nd Earl of Birkenhead *Earl of Birkenhead* (1933)

Zadie Smith 1975–

British writer. Her first novel *White Teeth* (2000) was highly acclaimed.

Julian Barnes
1946–

8 [*White Teeth*] gave me a burn of envy as a fiction writer.
in December 2000

Zadie Smith
1975–

9 I am all about vengeance. I have stalked boys. I have smashed their mirrors, ripped up their clothes and thrown their stereos down corridors.
in June 2000

C. P. Snow 1905–80

English novelist and scientist. His lecture *Two Cultures* discussed the division between science and the humanities.

Francis King
1923–

1 A man who so much resembled a Baked Alaska—sweet, warm and gungy on the outside, hard and cold within.
Yesterday Came Suddenly (1993)

F. R. Leavis
1895–1978

2 He doesn't know what he means, and doesn't know he doesn't know.
Two Cultures? The Significance of C. P. Snow (1963)

George Walden
1939–

3 I translated his ingratiating remarks with the same distaste I felt for his physiognomy: a great blotched moon emanating warm rays of self-regard.
Lucky George: Memoirs of an Anti-Politician (1999)

Gary Sobers 1936–

West Indian cricketer. During his test career he scored more than 8,000 runs and took 235 wickets, and he was the first batsman in first-class cricket to hit all six balls of an over for six.

C. L. R. James
1901–89

1 All geniuses are merely people who carry to an extreme definitive the characteristics of the unit of civilization to which they belong and the special act or function which they express or practise. Therefore to misunderstand Sobers is to misunderstand the West Indies.
'Garfield Sobers' (1969)

Socrates 469–399 BC

Ancient Athenian philosopher. His careful questioning was designed to reveal truth and expose error. He was sentenced to death for introducing strange gods and corrupting the young.

Max Beerbohm
1872–1956

1 The Socratic manner is not a game at which two can play.
Zuleika Dobson (1911)

Erasmus
c. 1469–1536

2 A heathen wrote to a heathen, yet it has justice, sanctity, truth. I can hardly refrain from saying, 'Saint Socrates, pray for me!'
attributed

Lord Macaulay
1800–59

3 I do not wonder that they poisoned him, a pest of a fellow—his delight in humbling everybody else, his mock humility, his quaker-like patience, more provoking than any insolence, would have driven me mad.
Arthur Bryant *Macaulay* (1932)

Montaigne
1533–92

4 I can easily imagine Socrates in the place of Alexander; Alexander in that of Socrates, I cannot.
Essais (1580)

Friedrich Nietzsche
1844–1900

5 Socrates—a mocking and amorous demon. The rat-catcher of Athens.
The Gay Science (1882)

Plato
429–347 BC

6 This was the end, Echekrates, of our friend; a man of whom we may say that of all whom we met at that time he was the wisest and justest and best.
Phaedo

Socrates
469–399 BC

7 I know nothing except the fact of my ignorance.
Diogenes Laertius *Lives of the Philosophers*

Alexander Solzhenitsyn 1918–

Russian novelist. He spent eight years in a labour camp for criticizing **Stalin** and began writing on his release. His books were banned in the Soviet Union, and he was exiled in 1974.

Anna Akhmatova
1889–1966

1 A bearer of light!
on meeting Solzhenitsyn, summer 1962

Yehudi Menuhin
1916–99

2 Here if anywhere outside *Parsifal* was a *heilge Tor*, a Prince Myshkin, a 'blessed fool' . . . One might not always agree with his tactics, but it is precisely because he is not a tactician that he is important in a world of degrees and accommodation. He is more than a writer. He is a cleansing personality, a prophet with a mission to his own country and to us all.
Unfinished Journey (1996)

Mary Somerville 1780–1872

Scottish mathematician and astronomer. Her account of Laplace's *Méchanique Céleste* was published in 1831. She supported women's education, and Somerville College at Oxford was named after her.

Maria Edgeworth
1767–1849

1 Mrs Somerville is the lady who, Laplace says, is the only woman who understands his works. She draws beautifully, and while her head is among the stars her feet are firm upon the earth.
letter, 1822

Mary Somerville
1780–1872

2 I was annoyed that my turn for reading was so much disapproved of, and thought it unjust that women should have been given a desire for knowledge if it were wrong to acquire it.
Martha Somerville (ed.) *Personal Recollections from Early Life to Old Age of Mary Somerville* (1873)

Stephen Sondheim 1930–

American composer and lyricist. He became famous with his lyrics for **Leonard Bernstein**'s *West Side Story* (1957). He has since written a number of musicals.

Stephen Sondheim
1930–

1 I don't understand what the 'cynical' label means. I aim for sentiment not sentimentality.
interview, December 2000

Sophocles c. 496–406 BC

Greek dramatist. His seven surviving plays are notable for their complexity of plot and depth of characterization.

Aristophanes
c.450–c.385 BC

1 But he was contented there, is contented here.
'there' = on earth and 'here' = in Hades
The Frogs (405 BC)

Matthew Arnold
1822–88

2 Who saw life steadily, and saw it whole:
The mellow glory of the Attic stage;
Singer of sweet Colonus, and its child.
'To a Friend' (1849)

Robert Southey 1774–1843

English poet. Associated with the Lake Poets, he is best known for his shorter poems, such as the 'Battle of Blenheim'.

Lord Byron
1788–1824

1 He had written much blank verse, and blanker prose,
And more of both than anybody knows.
The Vision of Judgement (1822)

Lord Byron
1788–1824

2 He is a person of very *epic* appearance—and has a fine head as far as the outside goes—and wants nothing but taste to make the inside equally attractive.
letter, September 1813

Thomas Carlyle
1795–1881

3 I likened him to one of those huge sandstone grinding cylinders which I had seen at Manchester. For many years these stones grind so . . . till at last . . . a grinding-stone no longer, but a cartload of quiet sand.
Reminiscences (1881)

Herbert Spencer 1820–1903

English philosopher and sociologist. He sought to apply the theory of natural selection to human societies, developing social Darwinism.

Charles Darwin
1809–82

1 The expression often used by Mr Herbert Spencer of the Survival of the Fittest is more accurate [than 'Struggle for Existence'], and is sometimes equally convenient.
On the Origin of Species (1869 ed.)

T. H. Huxley
1825–95

2 Oh! you know, Spencer's idea of a tragedy is a deduction killed by a fact.
Herbert Spencer *An Autobiography* (1904)

Stanley Spencer 1891–1959

English painter. He is best known for his religious and visionary works in the modern setting of his native village of Cookham in Berkshire.

Wyndham Lewis
1882–1957

3 Angels in jumpers.
describing the figures in Stanley Spencer's paintings
attributed

Stanley Spencer
1891–1959

4 Painting is saying 'Ta' to God.
letter from his daughter Shirin, 1988

Stephen Spender 1909–95

English poet and critic. In his critical work he defended the importance of political subject matter in literature.

*the young Spender had told **Eliot** of his wish to become a poet:*

T. S. Eliot
1888–1965

1 I can understand your wanting to write poems, but I don't quite know what you mean by 'being a poet' . . .
Stephen Spender *World within World* (1951)

Harry Pollitt
1890–1960

2 Go to Spain and get killed. The movement needs a Byron.
on being asked by Stephen Spender in the 1930s how best a poet could serve the Communist cause
Frank Johnson *Out of Order* (1982); attributed, perhaps apocryphal

Evelyn Waugh
1903–66

3 To see him fumbling with our rich and delicate language is to experience all the horror of seeing a Sèvres vase in the hands of a chimpanzee.
in May 1951

Edmund Spenser c. 1552–99

English poet. He is best known for his allegorical romance the *Faerie Queene*, celebrating Queen **Elizabeth I** and written in the Spenserian stanza.

William Cecil
1520–98

1 What! all this for a song?

*to Queen **Elizabeth I**, on being ordered to make a gratuity of £100 to Spenser in return for some poems*
Thomas Birch 'The Life of Mr Edmund Spenser' (1751)

John Dryden
1631–1700

2 Spenser more than once insinuates, that the soul of Chaucer was transfused into his body; and that he was begotten by him two hundred years after his decease.
Fables Ancient and Modern (1700)

Walter Savage Landor
1775–1864

3 Thee gentle Spenser fondly led;
But me he mostly sent to bed.
'To Wordsworth: Those Who Have Laid the Harp Aside' (1846)

Philip Larkin
1922–85

4 First I thought Troilus and Criseyde was the most *boring* poem in English. Then I thought Beowulf was. Then I thought Paradise Lost was. Now I *know* The Faerie Queene is the *dullest thing out. Blast* it.
written in pencil in St John's College library copy of *The Faerie Queene*, c.1941

Andrew Motion
1952–

5 I used to think he was the bee's knees, but now I find it's like getting lost in a greenhouse, with leaves brushing all over you.
interview, October 1999

W. B. Yeats
1865–1939

6 When Spenser wrote of Ireland he wrote as an official, and out of the thoughts and emotions that had been organized by the state. He was the first of many Englishmen to see nothing but what he was desired to see.
'Edmund Spenser' (1902)

Steven Spielberg 1947–

American film director and producer. His science-fiction and adventure films such as *ET* and *Jurassic Park* broke box office records, while *Schindler's List* won seven Oscars.

Peter Benchley
1940–

1 He has no knowledge of reality but the movies. He is B-movie literate. When he must make decisions about the small ways people behave, he reaches for the movie clichés of the forties and fifties.
in July 1974

Richard Dreyfuss
1947–

2 He's a big kid who at twelve years old decided to make movies, and he's still twelve years old—he's focused every one of of his powers and capabilities on making movies and blocked everything else in the world out of his personality.
John Baxter *Steven Spielberg* (1996)

Thomas Keneally
1935–

3 That's why you, Spielberg, are such a success—because in popular culture you're able to reduce everything to a fundamental one-line piece of mythology.
in November 1985

David Puttnam
1941–

4 Steven is an expert in micro-management. He needs to know what's going on at every moment on every project in which he's involved.
John Baxter *Steven Spielberg* (1996)

Steven Spielberg
1947–

5 I have more of a bubble-gum outlook on life than I think Welles did when he made *Citizen Kane*.
John Baxter *Steven Spielberg* (1996)

Baruch Spinoza 1632–77

Dutch philosopher, of Portuguese-Jewish descent. Expelled from the Amsterdam synagogue in 1656 for his unorthodoxy, Spinoza espoused a pantheistic system.

Albert Einstein
1879–1955

1 Spinoza is one of the most profound and pure people that our Jewish race has produced.
    letter, 1946

Novalis
1772–1801

2 A God-intoxicated man.
    attributed

Dusty Springfield 1939–99

English pop singer. She had several major hits in the 1960s, and in the 1990s her career was renewed with several collaborations with the Pet Shop Boys.

George Melly
1926–

1 Dusty went show biz all right but in an older tradition. Tantrums, breakdowns, the lot. She was the Judy Garland of the 'in' set.
    Revolt into Style (1970)

Bruce Springsteen 1949–

American rock singer, songwriter, and guitarist, noted for his songs about working-class life in the US.

Peter Gabriel
1950–

1 I think he's one of the very few mainstream artists that combines great melodies, I mean great feel, playing, lyrics and performance. There's very few people that can do all of those things.
    Mick St Michael *Peter Gabriel in His Own Words* (1994)

Joseph Stalin 1879–1953

Soviet statesman. Millions died in his enforced collectivization of agriculture and large-scale purges of the intelligentsia. After the war he maintained a firm grip on neighbouring Communist states.

Svetlana Alliluyeva
1925–

1 He is gone, but his shadow still stands over all of us. It still dictates to us and we, very often, obey.
    a daughter's view
    Twenty Letters to a Friend (1967)

Clement Attlee
1883–1967

2 He was clearly a pretty ruthless tyrant, but a man you could do business with because he said yes and no and didn't have to refer back. He was obviously the man who could make decisions, and he was obviously going to be difficult.
    Francis Williams *A Prime Minister Remembers* (1961)

Winston Churchill
1874–1965

3 A hard-boiled egg of a man . . . At once a callous, a crafty and an ill-formed man.
    Piers Brendon *Winston Churchill* (1984)

John Maynard Keynes
1883–1946

4 My picture of that interview is of a man struggling with a gramophone. The reproduction is excellent, the record is word-perfect. And there is poor Wells feeling that he has his one chance to coax the needle off the record and hear it—vain hope—speak in human tones.
    of Stalin being interviewed by **H. G. Wells**
    Stalin-Wells Talk (1934)

Nikita Khrushchev
1894–1971

5 Everyone can err, but Stalin considered that he never erred, that he was always right. He never acknowledged to anyone that he made any mistake, large or small, despite the fact that he made not a few mistakes in the matter of theory and in his practical activity.
    speech, February 1956

Nikita Khrushchev
1894–1971

6 Like Peter the Great, Stalin fought barbarism with barbarism, but he was a great man.
Khrushchev Remembers (1971)

Osip Mandelstam
1891–1938

7 Each thick finger, a fattened worm, gesticulates,
And his words strike you like they were many-pound weights.
His full cockroach moustache hints a laughter benigning,
And the shafts of his boots: always spotlessly shining.
'We exist in a country grown unreal and strange'

Jawaharlal Nehru
1889–1964

8 That great lover of peace, a man of giant stature who moulded, as few other men have done, the destinies of his age.
speech, March 1953

George Orwell
1903–50

9 This disgusting murderer is temporarily on our side.
in July 1941

George Bernard Shaw
1856–1950

10 Stalin listens attentively and seriously to Wells, taking in his pleadings exactly, and always hitting the nail precisely on the head in his reply.
of **H. G. Wells** interviewing Stalin
Stalin-Wells Talk (1934)

Leon Trotsky
1879–1940

11 It was the supreme expression of the mediocrity of the apparatus that Stalin himself rose to his position.
My Life (1930)

Leon Trotsky
1879–1940

12 The vengeance of history is more terrible than the vengeance of the most powerful General Secretary.
Stalin (1946)

Harry S. Truman
1884–1972

13 I like old Joe Stalin. He's a good fellow but he's a prisoner of the Politburo. He would make certain agreements but they won't let him keep them.
in June 1948

Lady Hester Stanhope 1776–1839

English traveller. Granted a pension on the death of her uncle, **Pitt the Younger**, she settled in a ruined convent in the Lebanon Mountains in 1814 and participated in Middle Eastern politics for several years.

Hester Stanhope
1776–1839

1 Principle? What is principle to *me*? I am a Pitt.
attributed

Henry Morton Stanley 1841–1904

Welsh explorer. As a newspaper correspondent he was sent in 1869 to central Africa to find David Livingstone.

Richard Burton
1821–90

1 He is to me, and always will be, the Prince of African travellers.
in February 1890

Henry Morton Stanley
1841–1904

2 I am partial to adventures, but I never attempt the impossible.
in April 1890

Ringo Starr 1940–

English rock and pop drummer, a member of the Beatles. After the band's split (1970) he pursued a solo career and narrated the *Thomas the Tank Engine* stories for television.

Paul McCartney
1942–

1 Ringo was a star in his own right in Liverpool before we even met . . . He would have surfaced with or without the Beatles.
in September 1980

David Steel 1938–

Scottish politician. He led the Liberal Party into an alliance and subsequent merger with the Social Democratic Party.

Michael Foot
1913–

1 He's passed from rising hope to elder statesman without any intervening period whatsoever.
speech, March 1979

Richard Steele 1672–1729

Irish essayist and dramatist. He founded and wrote for the periodicals *The Tatler* and *The Spectator*, the latter in collaboration with **Joseph Addison**.

Lord Macaulay
1800–59

1 A rake among scholars, and a scholar among rakes.
Essays Contributed to the Edinburgh Review (1850)

Alexander Pope
1688–1744

2 I am recreating my mind with the brisk sallies and quick turns of wit, which Mr Steele in his liveliest and freest humours darts about him.
letter, August 1713

Gertrude Stein 1874–1946

American writer. Stein developed an esoteric stream-of-consciousness style. Her home in Paris became a focus for the avant-garde during the 1920s and 1930s.

Clifton Fadiman
1904–

1 The mama of dada.
Party of One (1955)

Ernest Hemingway
1899–1961

2 Gertrude Stein and me are just like brothers.
John Malcolm Brinnin *The Third Rose* (1960)

Wyndham Lewis
1882–1957

3 Gertrude Stein's prose-song is a cold, black suet-pudding . . . Cut it at any point, it is the same thing . . . all fat, without nerve.
Time and Western Man (1927)

Anita Loos
1893–1981

4 A monumental, sexless Buddha.
G. Carey *Anita Loos* (1988)

Gertrude Stein
1874–1946

5 The Jews have produced only three originative geniuses: Christ, Spinoza, and myself.
J. Mellow *Charmed Circle: Gertrude Stein and Company* (1974)

Gloria Steinem 1934–

American journalist. A leading figure in the women's movement, in 1972 she founded *Ms Magazine*.

Camille Paglia
1947–

1 Gloria Steinem's marriage is proof of the emotional desperation of aging feminists who for over 30 years worshipped the steely career woman and trashed stay-at-home moms.
on Gloria Steinem's marriage at the age of 66
in September 2000

Stendhal 1783–1842

French novelist. His best-known novels are notable for their psychological realism and political analysis.

André Gide
1869–1951

1 The great secret of Stendhal, his great shrewdness, consisted in writing at once . . . thought charged with emotion.
diary, September 1937

Friedrich Nietzsche
1844–1900

2 Stendhal had perhaps the most penetrating eyes and ears of any Frenchman of this century. Is it perhaps because he had too much of the German and the Englishman in his nature for the Parisians to be able to endure him?
The Gay Science (1882)

Wallace Stevens 1879–1955

American poet. He wrote poetry privately and mostly in isolation from the literary community, developing an original and colourful style.

Marianne Moore
1887–1972

1 Wallace Stevens was really very much annoyed at being catalogued, categorized, and compelled to be scientific about what he was doing—to give satisfaction, to answer the teachers. He wouldn't do that. He was independent.

Charles Tomlinson (ed.) *Marianne Moore, A Collection of Critical Essays* (1969)

Edmund Wilson
1895–1972

2 His gift for combining words is baffling and fantastic but sure: even when you do not know what he is saying, you know that he is saying it well.

'Wallace Stevens and e. e. cummimgs' (1962)

Adlai Stevenson 1900–65

American Democratic politician. An eloquent wit and orator, he stood unsuccessfully for the presidency in 1952 and 1956.

Beatrice Eden
d. 1957

1 Mr Stevenson is just like Anthony Eden. Both are excellent Number Two men.

Fleur Cowles *She Made Friends and Kept Them* (1996)

Lyndon Baines Johnson
1908–73

2 He believed in us, perhaps more than we deserved. And so we came to believe in ourselves, more than we had.

H. J. Muller *Adlai Stevenson: A Study in Values* (1967)

Adlai Stevenson
1900–65

3 If I had any epitaph that I would rather have more than another, it would be to say that I had disturbed the sleep of my generation.

Jack W. Germand and Jules Witcover *Wake Us When It's Over* (1985)

Robert Louis Stevenson 1850–94

Scottish novelist, poet, and travel writer. He suffered from a chronic bronchial condition and spent much of his life abroad. He made his name with the adventure story *Treasure Island*.

John Carey
1934–

4 He worked at his style like a diamond-cutter, and responded to sensations with the delicacy of a poetical geiger counter.

in May 1993

G. K. Chesterton
1874–1936

5 Stevenson seemed to pick the right word up on the point of his pen, like a man playing spillikins.

The Victorian Age in Literature (1912)

Edward Elgar
1857–1934

6 What little reading I have been able to do during the last week has been in these gorgeous gold and red,—no, no, gules and or,—volumes. I feel younger also and heartened up; the man is so healthily good to one's soul and body.

letter, December 1906

W. E. Henley
1849–1903

7 A deal of Ariel, just a streak of Puck,
Much Antony, of Hamlet most of all,
And something of the Shorter-Catechist.

'In Hospital' (1888)

Robert Louis Stevenson
1850–94

8 I am an Epick writer with a k to it, but without the necessary genius.

letter, December 1892

Oscar Wilde
1854–1900

9 I see that romantic surroundings are the worst surroundings possible for a romantic writer. In Gower Street Stevenson could have written a new *Trois Mousquetaires*. In Samoa he wrote letters to *The Times* about Germans.

letter, April 1897

Jackie Stewart 1939–

Scottish motor-racing driver. He was three times world champion (1969; 1971; 1973).

Stirling Moss
1929–

1 Jackie was the first of the modern-style drivers, a man who drove fast enough to win, but at the slowest possible speed.
Bruce Jones *The Ultimate Encyclopedia of Formula One* (1999)

Jackie Stewart
1939–

2 By race time I should have no emotions inside me at all—no excitement or fear or nervousness, not even an awareness of the fatigue that's been brought on by pacing myself. I'm absolutely cold, ice-cold, totally within my shell.
'Faster' (1992, with Peter Manso)

Jackie Stewart
1939–

3 As I grew older and achieved success in competition clay pigeon shooting and later in motor racing, I glossed over it and compensated for my inabilities in a variety of ways. But it was a very thin, clear varnish in my own mind.
of his dyslexia
foreword to Philomena Ott *How to Detect and Manage Dyslexia* (1997)

Leopold Stokowski 1882–1977

British-born American conductor, of Polish descent. He is best known for arranging and conducting the music for **Walt Disney**'s film *Fantasia*.

Arthur Bliss
1891–1975

1 I also went . . . to see and hear Stokowski. I use the word 'see', for to watch was to add to the drama of the concert. The whole evening was like a great theatrical production.
As I Remember (1970)

Leopold Stokowski
1882–1977

2 Some people tell me that they *saw* me conduct somewhere. Apparently they listen with their eyes rather than their ears.
Robert Jacobson *Reverberations* (1975)

Sharon Stone 1958–

American actress. She starred in the films *Total Recall* and *Basic Instinct*.

Sharon Stone
1958–

1 I'm of peasant stock. I put my head down and work. Push. Push. Push. Push. There's nothing delicate or dainty about it.
in March 1996

Marie Stopes 1880–1958

Scottish birth-control campaigner. Her book *Married Love* (1918) was a frank treatment of sexuality within marriage.

Anonymous

1 Jeannie Jeannie, full of hopes
Read a book by Marie Stopes
But to judge from her condition
She must have read the wrong edition.
1920s skipping rhyme

Christina Hardyment

2 Stopes is Cinderella's fairy godmother, egging Western girlhood on to trust themselves to the rapturous embrace of their Prince Charmings.
Alistair Horne (ed.) *Telling Lives* (2000)

Naomi Mitchison
1897–1999

3 A light in great darkness to many of us, though a light shining through a lantern which was possibly not in the best taste.
on Married Love
Ruth Hall *Marie Stopes* (1978)

Muriel Spark
1918–

4 I used to think it a pity that her mother rather than she had not thought of birth control.
Curriculum Vitae (1992)

Marie Stopes
1880–1958

5 I will be canonised in 200 years' time.

comment written in the margin of a Catholic Truth Society pamphlet; Ruth Hall *Marie Stopes* (1978)

Tom Stoppard 1937–

British dramatist, born in Czechoslovakia. His best-known plays are comedies, often dealing with metaphysical and ethical questions.

Clive James
1939–

1 A dream interviewee, talking in eerily quotable sentences whose English has the faintly extraterritorial perfection of a Conrad or a Nabokov.

Kenneth Tynan *Show People* (1980)

Derek Marlowe
1938–

2 His public self is Charles Dodgson—he loves dons, philosophers, theorists of all kinds, and he's fascinated by the language they use. But his private self is Lewis Carroll—reclusive, intimidated by women, unnerved by emotion.

in December 1977

Harriet Beecher Stowe 1811–96

American novelist. Her novel *Uncle Tom's Cabin* (1852) strengthened the contemporary abolitionist cause with its descriptions of the sufferings caused by slavery.

Sinclair Lewis
1885–1951

1 Harriet Beecher Stowe, whose *Uncle Tom's Cabin* was the first evidence to America that no hurricane can be so disastrous to a country as a ruthlessly humanitarian woman.

introduction to Paxton Hibben *Henry Ward Beecher: an American Portrait* (1927)

Abraham Lincoln
1809–65

2 So you're the little woman who wrote the book that made this great war!

Carl Sandburg *Abraham Lincoln: The War Years* (1936)

Lytton Strachey 1880–1932

English biographer. A prominent member of the Bloomsbury Group, his *Eminent Victorians* (1918) attacked the literary Establishment through its satirical biographies.

Robert Blake
1916–

1 He was, for all his brilliance, glitter, irony and wit, an unsound biographer: he was concerned with effect rather than truth.

'The Art of Biography' (1988)

T. E. Lawrence
1888–1935

2 My memory of his books tangles with itself with my memory of Henry Lamb's marvellous portrait of an outraged wet mackerel of a man, dropped like an old cloak into a basket chair.

letter, October 1927

Ottoline Morrell
1873–1938

3 At night Lytton would become gay and we would laugh and giggle and be foolish; sometimes he would put on a pair of my smart high-heeled shoes, which made him look like an Aubrey Beardsley drawing, very wicked.

Robert Gathorne-Hardy (ed.) *Ottoline* (1963)

Edith Sitwell
1887–1964

4 He seemed to have been cut out of very thin cardboard.

Taken Care Of (1965)

Antonio Stradivari c. 1644–1737

Italian violin-maker. About 650 of his celebrated violins, violas, and violoncellos are still in existence.

Yehudi Menuhin
1916–99

1 Having lived to biblical age, siring numerous children and numerous intruments, for fifty-seven years in the same house like a sun so confident of its position it does not feel impelled to move, he made brilliant, burnished sound that conveys, for me at any rate, moral notions of loftiness.

Unfinished Journey (1976)

Thomas Wentworth, Earl of Strafford 1593–1641

English statesman. Following his failure to suppress rebellion in Scotland in 1640, he was impeached and executed.

Charles I
1600–49

1 I cannot satisfy myself in honour or conscience without assuring you now, in the midst of your troubles, that, upon the word of a king, you shall not suffer in life, honour, or fortune.
letter, April 1641

Earl of Strafford
1593–1641

2 Pity me, for never came any man to so lost a business.
letter, 1640

Johann Strauss 1825–99

Austrian composer, son of Johann Strauss the Elder. He became known as 'the waltz king', composing many famous waltzes, such as *The Blue Danube*.

Arturo Toscanini
1867–1957

1 For Strauss, the composer, I take my hat off; for Strauss the man I put it on again.
George R. Marek *Toscanini* (1975)

Richard Strauss 1864–1949

German composer. He is often regarded as the last of the 19th-century romantic composers.

George V
1865–1936

2 His Majesty does not know what the Band has just played, but it is *never* to be played again.
message sent after the Grenadier Guards had played an arrangement of Strauss' Elektra
Osbert Sitwell *Left Hand, Right Hand* (1945)

Gustav Mahler
1860–1911

3 A Vulcan lives and labours under a heap of slag, a subterranean fire—not merely a firework! It is exactly the same with Strauss's whole personality. That is why it is so difficult in his case to sift the chaff from the grain.
letter, January 1907

Pyotr Ilich Tchaikovsky
1840–93

4 Such an astounding lack of talent was never before united to such pretentiousness.
letter, 1888

Igor Stravinsky 1882–1971

Russian-born composer, resident in the US from 1939. His ballets *The Firebird* and *The Rite of Spring* both shocked audiences with their irregular rhythms and frequent dissonances.

Russell Hoban
1925–

1 Stravinsky looks like a man who was potty-trained too early and that music proves it as far as I'm concerned.
Turtle Diary (1975)

Vaslav Nijinsky
1890–1950

2 Stravinsky is a good composer, but he does not know about life. His compositions have no purpose.
Colin Wilson *Brandy of the Damned* (1964)

Sergei Prokofiev
1891–1953

3 Bach on the wrong notes.
on Stravinsky's music
V. Seroff *Sergei Prokofiev* (1968)

Meryl Streep 1949–

American actress. She won Oscars for her parts in *Kramer vs Kramer* (1980) and *Sophie's Choice* (1982).

Meryl Streep
1949–

1 Thank God I am an actress, because otherwise I would have placed all of that energy on one after another of you and made you insane.
to her children, in November 2000

Janet Street-Porter 1946–

English broadcaster. She was the BBC's first commissioning editor for youth programmes.

Kelvin Mackenzie
1946–

1 She couldn't edit a bus ticket.

on Janet Street-Porter's appointment as editor of the Independent on Sunday
in July 1999

Barbra Streisand 1942–

American singer, actress, and film director. She won an Oscar for her performance in *Funny Girl*. She later played the lead in *A Star is Born*.

Whitney Balliett
1926–

1 What she does so ingeniously is *Streisand* each song . . . She smoothes the melodic hills, raises the valleys, equalises the emotions, and encases the lyrics in a kind of silken sheen.

attributed

Walter Matthau
1920–2000

2 I'd like to work with her again in something appropriate. Perhaps Macbeth.

after starring opposite Streisand in Hello, Dolly!
Anne Edwards *Streisand: It Only Happens Once* (1996)

Barbra Streisand
1942–

3 I never wanted to be Vivien Leigh. I desperately wanted to be Scarlett O'Hara.

Anne Edwards *Streisand: It Only Happens Once* (1996)

Johan August Strindberg 1849–1912

Swedish dramatist and novelist. His satire *The Red Room* (1879) is regarded as Sweden's first modern novel. His later plays are typically tense, psychic dramas.

Sean O'Casey
1880–1964

1 Ibsen can sit serenely in his Doll's House, while Strindberg is battling with his heaven and his hell.

letter, August 1927

Eugene O'Neill
1888–1953

2 Strindberg was the precursor of all modernity in our present theatre . . . the most modern of moderns.

in 1924

Charles Edward Stuart 1720–88

Pretender to the British throne; known as the Young Pretender or Bonnie Prince Charlie. He led the Jacobite uprising of 1745–6 and was defeated at the Battle of Culloden.

Robert Burns
1759–96

1 An' Charlie he's my darling
My darling, my darling,
Charlie he's my darling—
The young Chevalier!

'Charlie he's my Darling' (1796)

Lord Elcho
1721–87

2 There you go for a damned cowardly Italian!

as Charles Edward Stuart withdrew from the field at Culloden, April 1746

Michael Forsyth
1954–

3 If Prince Charles Edward Stuart had won at Culloden 250 years ago this month there would have been precious few songs about him. We might not have gone so far as to put the Butcher Cumberland on shortbread tins, but Bonnie Prince Charlie, in the Scottish psyche, would have been irredeemably diminished by success.

in April 1996

Lady Carolina Nairne
1766–1845

4 Better lo'ed ye canna be,
Will ye no come back again?

'Will Ye No Come Back Again?'

Charles Edward Stuart
1720–88

5 I may be overcome by my enemies, but I will not dishonour myself; if I die, it shall be with my sword in my hand, fighting for the liberty of those who fight against me.

letter, 1745

Arthur Sullivan 1842–1900

English composer. His fame rests on the fourteen light operas which he wrote in collaboration with the librettist **W. S. Gilbert**.

W. S. Gilbert
1836–1911

1 You are an adept in your profession and I am an adept in mine. If we meet, it must be as master and master—not as master and servant.
  letter, March 1889

George Bernard Shaw
1856–1950

2 They trained him to make Europe yawn; and he took advantage of their teaching to make London and New York laugh and whistle.
  in September 1890

Graham Sutherland 1903–80

English painter. His portrait of **Winston Churchill** was considered unflattering and was destroyed by Churchill's family.

Winston Churchill
1874–1965

1 These modern chaps! . . . They like to make a fool of you. I *hate* this thing! And I wouldn't be surprised if no one got the opportunity of looking at it after my day.
  Cecil Beaton's diary, 1955

Joan Sutherland 1926–

Australian operatic soprano, noted for her dramatic coloratura roles.

Joan Sutherland
1926–

2 If I weren't reasonably placid, I don't think I could cope with this sort of life. To be a diva, you've got to be absolutely like a horse.
  Winthrop Sargeant *Divas: Impressions of Six Opera Superstars* (1959)

Gloria Swanson 1899–1983

American actress. She was a major star of silent films such as *Sadie Thompson* (1928), but is now chiefly known for her performance as the fading movie star in *Sunset Boulevard* (1950).

Cecil B. de Mille
1881–1959

1 Nothing was spared to bring out all the glamour that was Gloria. But I did not star her . . . The public, not I, made Gloria Swanson a star.
  The Autobiography of Cecil B. de Mille (1960)

Elinor Glyn
1864–1943

2 Your proportions are Egyptian; anyone can see that when you turn your head. *You have lived there in another time.*
  Swanson on Swanson (1980)

Gloria Swanson
1899–1983

3 I have decided that when I am a star, I will be every inch and every moment a star.
  Annette Tapert *The Power of Glamour* (1999)

Gloria Swanson
1899–1983

4 When I die, my epitaph should read: *She Paid the Bills*. That's the story of my private life.
  in July 1950

Jonathan Swift 1667–1745

Irish satirist, poet, and Anglican cleric. He is best known for *Gulliver's Travels*, a satire on human society in the form of a fantastic tale of travels in imaginary lands.

Samuel Taylor Coleridge
1772–1834

1 Swift was *anima Rabelaisii habitans in sicco*—the soul of Rabelais dwelling in a dry place.
  Table Talk (1835)

John Dryden
1631–1700

2 Cousin Swift, you will never be a poet.
  Samuel Johnson *Lives of the English Poets* (1779–81)

Samuel Johnson
1709–84

3 He washed himself with oriental scrupulosity.
  Lives of the English Poets (1779–81)

Harold Laski
1893–1950

4 To read Swift is like being locked up on a desert island with Napoleon in the capacity of secretary. There is no prospect of relief.
   letter, January 1919

Lady Mary Wortley Montagu
1689–1762

5 His character seems to me a parallel with that of Caligula, and had he had the same power, would have made the same use of it.
   letter, June 1754

George Orwell
1903–50

6 He is a Tory anarchist, despising authority while disbelieving in liberty, and preserving the aristocratic outlook while seeing clearly that the existing aristocracy is degenerate and contemptible.
   'Politics vs Literature' (1946)

Jonathan Swift
1667–1745

7 Yet malice never was his aim;
   He lashed the vice, but spared the name;
   No individual could resent,
   Where thousands equally were meant.
   'Verses on the Death of Dr Swift' (1731)

Jonathan Swift
1667–1745

8 Where fierce indignation can no longer tear his heart.
   epitaph for himself; S. Leslie *The Skull of Swift* (1928)

W. B. Yeats
1865–1939

9 Swift has sailed into his rest;
   Savage indignation there
   Cannot lacerate his breast.
   Imitate him if you dare,
   World-besotted traveller; he
   Served human liberty.
   'Swift's Epitaph' (1933)

T

Charles-Maurice de Talleyrand 1754–1838

French statesman. Involved in the coup that brought **Napoleon** to power, he was also involved in the recall of Louis XVIII, the overthrow of Charles X, and the accession of Louis Philippe.

François-René Chateaubriand
1768–1848

1 Silently there enters Vice leaning on the arm of Crime: M. de Talleyrand supported by M. Fouché.
   Mémoires d'outre tombe (1849–50)

Louis Philippe
1773–1850

2 Died, has he? Now I wonder what he meant by that?
   attributed, perhaps apocryphal

Prince Metternich
1773–1859

3 Such men as M. de Talleyrand are like sharp-edged instruments with which it is dangerous to play, but for great evils drastic remedies are necessary and whoever has to treat them should not be afraid to use the instrument that cuts the best.
   in September 1808

Napoleon I
1769–1821

4 A pile of shit in a silk stocking.
   attributed

William IV
1765–1837

5 There are few individuals whose career appears to His Majesty to have been more disreputable and although the king does not question his talents, especially for intrigue, he does not consider the selection of a man of his character . . . to be either creditable to himself or complimentary to His Majesty.
   on the appointment of Talleyrand as ambassador
   letter, September 1830

Thomas Tallis c. 1505–85

English composer. Organist of the Chapel Royal jointly with William Byrd, he served under **Henry VIII**, Edward VI, **Mary I**, and **Elizabeth I**.

Anonymous

1 As he did live, so also did he die,
In mild and quiet sort,
(O! happy man).
epitaph, St Alphege, Greenwich

William Byrd
1543–1623

2 Tallis is dead and Music dies.
'Ye Sacred Muses'

John Tavener 1944–

English composer. His music is primarily religious and has been influenced by his conversion to the Russian Orthodox Church.

John Tavener
1944–

1 I would know if I'd produced a work that was truly sacred if you could dig up a 6th century man and he could listen to it and understand it. Whereas if you dug him up and had him listen to most of the music written in the last 300 years, he would make nothing of it at all.
Andrew Ford *Composer to Composer* (1993)

Elizabeth Taylor 1932–

American actress, born in England. Notable films include *Cleopatra* and *Who's Afraid of Virginia Woolf?* She has been married eight times, including twice to the actor **Richard Burton**.

Mike Nichols
1931–

1 Elizabeth is a wonderful movie actress: she has a deal with the film lab—she gets better in the bath overnight.
in June 1994

Camille Paglia
1947–

2 Elizabeth Taylor is a pre-feminist woman. This is the source of her continuing greatness and relevance. She wields the sexual power that feminism cannot explain and has tried to destroy. Through stars like Taylor, we sense the world-disordering impact of legendary women like Delilah, Salome, and Helen of Troy.
in March 1992

Elizabeth Taylor
1932–

3 When people say: she's got everything. I've only one answer: I haven't had tomorrow.
Elizabeth Taylor (1965)

Elizabeth Taylor
1932–

4 MICHAEL WILDING: We have already been instructed to refer to her at all times as Dame.
ELIZABETH TAYLOR: If I'm not being referred to as That Broad.
responding to her son, after being made a Dame of the British Empire
in May 2000

Emlyn Williams
1905–87

5 He's miscast and she's Miss Taylor.
on the Burton-Taylor Private Lives *in 1964*
James Harding *Emlyn Williams* (1987)

Pyotr Ilich Tchaikovsky 1840–93

Russian composer. Notable works include the ballets *Swan Lake* and *The Nutcracker*, the First Piano Concerto, the overture *1812*, and his sixth symphony, the 'Pathétique'.

Pierre Boulez
1925–

1 I am not a fascist. I hate Tchaikovsky and I will not conduct him. But if the audience wants him, it can have him.
Joan Peyser *Boulez* (1976)

Sergei Diaghilev
1872–1929

2 Tchaikovsky thought of committing suicide for fear of being discovered as a homosexual, but today, if you are a composer and *not* homosexual, you might as well put a bullet through your head.
Vernon Duke *Listen Here!* (1963)

Norman Tebbit 1931–

British Conservative politician. He is noted for his blunt style.

Michael Foot
1913–

1 It is not necessary that every time he rises he should give his famous imitation of a semi-house-trained polecat.
speech, March 1978

Austin Mitchell
1934–

2 He has a nasty instinct for the exposed groin, and always puts his knee in just to stir things up.
in February 1989

Pierre Teilhard de Chardin 1881–1955

French Jesuit philosopher and palaeontologist. His views on evolution, blending science and Christianity, were declared unorthodox by the Roman Catholic Church.

Peter Medawar
1915–87

1 If it were an innocent, passive gullibility it would be excusable; but all too clearly, alas, it is an active willingness to be deceived.
review of Teilhard de Chardin *The Phenomenon of Man* (1961)

Pius XII
1876–1958

2 One Galileo in two thousand years is enough.
on being asked to proscribe the works of Teilhard de Chardin
attributed; Stafford Beer *Platform for Change* (1975)

Alfred, Lord Tennyson 1809–92

English poet. His reputation was established by *In Memoriam* (1850). Other notable works include 'The Charge of the Light Brigade' and *Idylls of the King*.

Edward Bulwer-Lytton
1803–73

1 Out-babying Wordsworth and out-glittering Keats.
The New Timon (1846)

G. K. Chesterton
1874–1936

2 He could not think up to the height of his own towering style.
The Victorian Age in Literature (1912)

Edward Fitzgerald
1809–83

3 Tennyson is emerged half-cured, or half-destroyed, from a water establishment; he's gone to a new doctor who gives him iron pills; and altogether this really great man thinks more about his bowels and nerves than about the Laureate's wreath he was born to inherit.
in 1848

Lady Gregory
1852–1932

4 Tennyson had the British Empire for God, and Queen Victoria for Virgin Mary.
W. B. Yeats' diary, March 1909

Henry James
1843–1916

5 Whenever I feel disposed to reflect that Tennyson is not personally Tennysonian, I summon up the image of Browning, and this has the effect of making me check my complaints.
letter, November 1878

George Meredith
1828–1909

6 The great length of his mild fluency: the yards of linen-drapery for the delight of women.
Frank Harris *My Life and Loves* (1922–7)

George Bernard Shaw
1856–1950

7 Brahms is just like Tennyson, an extraordinary musician, with the brains of a third rate village policeman.
letter, April 1893

Mother Teresa 1910–97

Roman Catholic nun and missionary; born of Albanian parentage. In 1928 she went to India, and devoted herself to work among the poor and the dying in Calcutta.

Malcolm Muggeridge
1903–90

1 Something beautiful for God.
title of biography (1971), quoting Mother Teresa's own words

Mother Teresa
1910–97

2 We ourselves feel that what we are doing is just a drop in the ocean. But if that drop was not in the ocean, I think the ocean would be less because of that missing drop. I do not agree with the big way of doing things.
A Gift for God (1975)

Mother Teresa
1910–97

3 By blood and origin I am Albanian. My citizenship is Indian. I am a Catholic nun. As to my calling, I belong to the whole world. As to my heart, I belong entirely to the heart of Jesus.
attributed

Ellen Terry 1847–1928

English actress. She played in many of **Henry Irving**'s Shakespearean productions and **George Bernard Shaw** created a number of roles for her.

James Agate
1877–1947

1 That voice which was like the heart of a red rose.
Ego (1935)

*on the suggestion that Ellen Terry had rejected a play by **James** 'because she did not think the part suited her':*

Henry James
1843–1916

2 Think? Think? How should the poor, toothless, chattering hag THINK?
Edmund Gosse letter April 1920

George Bernard Shaw
1856–1950

3 She was an extremely beautiful girl and as innocent as a rose. When Watts kissed her, she took for granted she was going to have a baby.
Stephen Winston *Days with Bernard Shaw* (1949)

William Makepeace Thackeray 1811–63

British novelist. He established his reputation with *Vanity Fair*, a satire of the upper middle class of early 19th-century society.

Walter Bagehot
1826–77

1 Thackeray is like the edited and illustrated edition of a great dinner.
in August 1862

Charlotte Brontë
1816–55

2 They say he is like Fielding; they talk of his wit, humour, comic powers. He resembles Fielding as an eagle does a vulture: Fielding could stoop on carrion, but Thackeray never does.
Jane Eyre (2nd ed., 1848) preface

John Ruskin
1819–1900

3 Thackeray settled like a meat-fly on whatever one had got for dinner, and made one sick of it.
Fors Clavigera (1871–84)

Harriet Thackeray
1840–75

4 Papa, why do you not write books like Nicholas Nickleby?
Anne Thackeray Ritchie *Records of Tennyson, Ruskin, and Robert and Elizabeth Browning* (1892)

William Makepeace Thackeray
1811–63

5 Mind, no biography!
injunction to his daughters; John Sutherland *Is Heathcliff a Murderer?* (1996)

Margaret Thatcher 1925–

British Conservative stateswoman, Prime Minister 1979–90. The first woman Prime Minister, she became known for her determination and her emphasis on individual responsibility and enterprise.

Anonymous

1 The iron lady.
name given to Thatcher by the Soviet defence ministry newspaper Red Star, *which accused her of trying to revive the cold war*
in January 1976

Tony Benn
1925–

2 The Prime Ministers who are remembered are those who think and teach, and not many do. Mrs Thatcher . . . influenced the thinking of a generation.
interview, 1996

of Margaret Thatcher as Prime Minister:

John Biffen   **3** She was a tigress surrounded by hamsters.
1930–
     in December 1990

James Callaghan   **4** The further you got from Britain, the more admired you found she was.
1912–
     in December 1990

Barbara Castle   **5** She is so clearly the best man among them.
1910–
     diary, February 1975

Jacques Chirac   **6** I am not prepared to accept the economics of a housewife.
1932–
     in 1987

Julian Critchley   **7** She cannot see an institution without hitting it with her handbag.
1930–2000
     in June 1982

Geri Halliwell   **8** We Spice girls are true Thatcherites. Thatcher was the first Spice Girl,
1972–
   the pioneer of our ideology—Girl Power.
     in December 1996

Denis Healey   **9** And who is the Mephistopheles behind this shabby Faust [the Foreign
1917–
   Secretary, Geoffrey Howe]? . . . To quote her own backbenchers, the
   Great She-elephant, She-Who-Must-Be-Obeyed, the Catherine the Great
   of Finchley, the Prime Minister herself.
     speech, February 1984

Denis Healey   **10** While the rest of Europe is marching to confront the new challenges,
1917–
   the Prime Minister is shuffling along in the gutter in the opposite
   direction, like an old bag lady, muttering imprecations at anyone who
   catches her eye.
     speech, February 1990

Edna Healey   **11** She has no hinterland; in particular she has no sense of history.
1918–
     Denis Healey *The Time of My Life* (1989)

Edward Heath   **12** Rejoice, rejoice, rejoice.
1916–
     telephone call to his office on hearing of Margaret Thatcher's fall from power in 1990;
     attributed

Geoffrey Howe   **13** It is rather like sending your opening batsmen to the crease only for
1926–
   them to find the moment that the first balls are bowled that their bats
   have been broken before the game by the team captain.
     on the difficulties caused him as Foreign Secretary by Margaret Thatcher's anti-European views
     resignation speech as Deputy Prime Minister, November 1990

Roy Jenkins   **14** A First Minister whose self-righteous stubbornness has not been
1920–
   equalled, save briefly by Neville Chamberlain, since Lord North.
     in March 1990

Neil Kinnock   **15** If Margaret Thatcher wins on Thursday, I warn you not to be ordinary, I
1942–
   warn you not to be young, I warn you not to fall ill, and I warn you not
   to grow old.
     on the prospect of a Conservative re-election
     speech, June 1983

David Lean   **16** She is all woman, all woman, all woman!
1908–91
     Alec Guinness *A Positively Final Appearance* (1999)

Ken Livingstone   **17** I've met serial killers and professional assassins and nobody scared me
1945–
   as much as Mrs T.
     in January 2000

François Mitterrand   **18** She has the eyes of Caligula, but the mouth of Marilyn Monroe.
1916–96
     in November 1990

of Lady Thatcher in the House of Lords:

Matthew Parris   **19** A big cat detained briefly in a poodle parlour, sharpening her claws on
1949–
   the velvet.
     Look Behind You! (1993)

Margaret Thatcher 20 To those waiting with bated breath for that favourite media
1925–   catchphrase, the U-turn, I have only this to say. 'You turn if you want;
the lady's not for turning.'
speech, October 1980

Margaret Thatcher 21 We have become a grandmother.
1925–   in March 1989

Margaret Thatcher 22 I am extraordinarily patient, provided I get my own way in the end.
1925–   in April 1989

Peter Ustinov 23 The difference between Maggie Thatcher and Joan of Arc is that
1921–   Thatcher only hears her own voice.
Quotable Ustinov (1995)

Themistocles c.528–462 BC

Athenian statesman. He helped build up the Athenian fleet, and defeated the Persian fleet at Salamis in 480.

Ralph Richardson 1 An interesting old bird. A kind of Winston Churchill of his time.
1902–83   in 1969

Dylan Thomas 1914–53

Welsh poet. In 1953 he narrated on radio *Under Milk Wood*, a portrait of a small Welsh town, interspersing poetic alliterative prose with songs and ballads.

Kingsley Amis 1 The only honest way of doing it is to attack it . . . *Someone* ought to give
1922–95   Dylan a bouquet of old bogwort before long.
on a planned review of Dylan Thomas's prose pieces for the Spectator
letter, 1955

Elizabeth Bishop 2 Thomas's poetry is so narrow—just a straight conduit between birth
1911–79   and death, I suppose—with not much space for living along the way.
letter, November 1953

Christopher 3 He seemed to be right in the midst of his life—not on one side looking
Isherwood   at it—and he grappled with it as though it were a policeman.
1904–86   diary, December 1953

Louis MacNeice 4   Young and gay
1907–63   A bulbous Taliessin, a spruce and small
Bow-tied Silenus roistering his way
Through lands of fruit and fable, well aware
That even Dionysius has his day.
Autumn Sequel (1954)

Theodore Roethke 5 He was one of the great ones, there can be no doubt of that. And he
1908–63   drank his own blood, ate of his own marrow, to get at some of that
material.
E. W. Tedlock (ed.) *Dylan Thomas: The Legend and the Poet* (1960)

Edith Sitwell 6 Alas, that he who caught and sang the sun in flight, yet was the sun's
1887–1964   brother, and never grieved it on its way, should have left us with no
goodbye, good night.
in February 1954

A. J. P. Taylor 7 He was a detestable man. Men pressed money on him, and women
1906–90   their bodies. Dylan took both with equal contempt. His great pleasure
was to humiliate people.
A Personal History (1983)

Caitlin Thomas
1913–94

8 His passion for lies was congenital: more a practice in invention than a lie. He would tell quite unnecessary ones, which did not in any way improve his situation: such as, when he had been to one cinema, saying it was another, and making up the film that was on: and the obvious ones, that only his mother pretended not to see through, like being carted off the bus into his home, and saying he had been having coffee, in a cafe, with a friend.
Leftover Life to Kill (1957)

Dylan Thomas
1914–53

9 Poetry is not the most important thing in life . . . I'd much rather lie in a hot bath reading Agatha Christie and sucking sweets.
Joan Wyndham's diary, July 1943

Dylan Thomas
1914–53

10 I am in the path of Blake, but so far behind him that only the wings of his heels are in sight.
undated letter, probably September 1933

Evelyn Waugh
1903–66

11 He's exactly what I would have been if I had not been a Catholic.
Noel Annan *Our Age* (1990)

Daley Thompson 1958–

English athlete, winner of a number of decathlon titles that included gold medals in the Olympic Games of 1980 and 1984.

Michael Parkinson
1935–

1 He is so fit he hums with energy. When he enters a room it crackles.
in March 1993

Roy Thomson 1894–1976

Canadian-born British newspaper proprietor and media entrepreneur. He settled in Edinburgh in 1952, buying the *Scotsman*, and later the *Sunday Times* and *The Times*.

Roy Thomson
1894–1976

1 If I have any advice to pass on, as a successful man, it is this: if one wants to be successful, one must think; one must think until it hurts.
After I Was Sixty: A Chapter of Autobiography (1975)

Henry David Thoreau 1817–62

American essayist and poet. He is best known for his book *Walden*, an account of a two-year experiment in self-sufficiency.

Ralph Waldo Emerson
1803–82

1 He was bred to no profession; he never married; he lived alone; he never went to church; he never voted; he refused to pay a tax to the state; he ate no flesh, he drank no wine, he never knew the use of tobacco; and, though a naturalist, he used neither trap nor gun.
Lectures and Biographical Sketches (1884)

Henry James
1843–1916

2 He was worse than provincial—he was parochial.
Hawthorne (1879)

Henry David Thoreau
1817–62

3 I wanted to live deep and suck out all the marrow of life . . . to drive life into a corner, and reduce it to its lowest terms, and, if it proved to be mean, why then to get the whole and genuine meanness of it, and publish its meanness to the world; or if it were sublime, to know it by experience.
Walden (1854)

Sybil Thorndike 1882–1976

English actress. Noted for her Shakespearean roles, she played the title part in the first London production of **George Bernard Shaw**'s *St Joan*.

Ralph Richardson
1902–83

1 Although Sybil's well-known warmth of heart is true indeed, she has a stiletto—a stiletto for fools, whom she does not suffer gladly. But she keeps it carefully concealed, as stilettos should always be.
Elizabeth Sprigge *Sybil Thorndike Casson* (1971)

James Thurber 1894–1961

American humorist and cartoonist. His collections of essays, stories, and sketches include *My World—And Welcome to It*, which contains the story 'The Secret Life of Walter Mitty'.

Larry Adler
1914–

1 Freud discovered the Id, and Thurber named it Walter Mitty.
  in October 1975

James Thurber
1894–1961

2 With sixty staring me in the face, I have developed inflammation of the sentence structure and a definite hardening of the paragraphs.
  in June 1955

Tipu Sultan c.1750–99

Sultan of Mysore. Defeated by the British in 1792, he ceded half his kingdom.

Tipu Sultan
c.1750–99

1 In this world I would rather live two days like a tiger, than two hundred years like a sheep.
  Alexander Beatson *A View of the Origin and Conduct of the War with Tippoo Sultan* (1800)

Titian c.1488–1576

Italian painter. He experimented with vivid colours and often broke conventions of composition. He painted many sensual mythological works.

John Ruskin
1819–1900

1 Nobody cares much at heart about Titian; only there is a strange undercurrent of everlasting murmur about his name, which means the deep consent of all great men that he is greater than they.
  The Two Paths (1859)

J. R. R. Tolkien 1892–1973

British novelist and literary scholar. He is famous for the fantasy adventures *The Hobbit* and *The Lord of the Rings*, set in Middle Earth.

C. S. Lewis
1898–1963

1 No one ever influenced Tolkien—you might as well try to influence a bandersnatch.
  letter, May 1959

Terry Pratchett
1948–

2 Most modern fantasy just rearranges the furniture in Tolkien's attic.
  Stan Nicholls (ed.) *Wordsmiths of Wonder* (1993)

Leo Tolstoy 1828–1910

Russian writer. He is best known for the novels *War and Peace*, an epic tale of the Napoleonic invasion, and *Anna Karenina*.

Mel Brooks
1926–

1 I decided that Tolstoy was the most gifted writer who ever lived. It's like he stuck a pen in his heart and it didn't even go through his mind on its way to the page.
  Kenneth Tynan *Show People* (1980)

Anton Chekhov
1860–1904

2 Logic and a sense of justice tell me that there is more love in electricity and steam than there is in chastity and abstention from eating meat.
  on Tolstoy as celibate and vegetarian
  Donald Rayfield *Anton Chekhov* (1997)

Albert Einstein
1879–1955

3 He remains in many ways the foremost prophet of our time . . . There is no one today with Tolstoy's deep insight and moral force.
  interview, August 1934

Maxim Gorky
1868–1936

4 With God he maintains very suspicious relations. They are like two bears in one den.
  Conor Cruise O'Brien *The Great Melody* (1993)

Maxim Gorky
1868–1936

5 I know as well as others that no man is more worthy than he of the name of genius; more complicated, contradictory, and great in everything—yes, yes, in everything. Great—in some curious sense, wide, indefinable by words—there is something in him which made me desire to cry aloud to everyone: 'Look what a wonderful man is living on earth.'

Reminiscences of Tolstoy (1934)

T. E. Lawrence
1888–1935

6 It is hopeless to grapple with Tolstoy. The man is like yesterday's east wind, which brought tears when you faced it and numbed you meanwhile.

letter, February 1924

Gustav Mahler
1860–1911

7 Tolstoy's *Confessions*; terrifyingly sad and savagely flagellant; a fallacy in his very way of putting the question and in consequence a withering blight on all human achievement whether of the heart or the head.

letter, June 1904

Sonya Tolstoy
1844–1919

8 His biographers will tell how he helped the porter by drawing his own water, but no one will know that he never once thought to give his wife a moment's rest, or his sick child a drink of water. In 32 years he never once sat for five minutes by his sick child's bedside.

on her husband
William Shirer *Love and Hatred: The Stormy Marriage Of Leo and Sonya Tolstoy* (1994)

E. M. de Vogüé
1848–1910

9 A queer combination of the brain of an English chemist with the soul of an Indian Buddhist.

The Russian Novel (1886)

Wolfe Tone 1763–98

Irish nationalist. In 1791 he helped found the Society of United Irishmen. Captured by the British during the Irish insurrection in 1798, he committed suicide.

Wolfe Tone
1763–98

1 I find, then, I am but a bad anatomist.

cutting his throat in prison, he severed his windpipe instead of his jugular, and lingered for several days
Oliver Knox *Rebels and Informers* (1998)

Arturo Toscanini 1867–1957

Italian conductor. He was musical director at La Scala in Milan before becoming a conductor at the Metropolitan Opera, New York.

Yehudi Menuhin
1916–99

1 He offered me a morsel of wisdom for use off the platform: whenever he felt miserable, he said, he thought of the thousands of people worse off than he and immediately cheered up. It was only later that it struck me his moral position wasn't exactly watertight, but no charge of smugness could be maintained against someone so unafflicted with self-analysis.

Unfinished Journey (1976)

Arturo Toscanini
1867–1957

2 I smoked my first cigarette and kissed my first woman on the same day. I have never had time for tobacco since.

in June 1946

Henri de Toulouse-Lautrec 1864–1901

French painter and lithographer. His reputation is based on his colour lithographs from the 1890s, depicting actors, music-hall singers, prostitutes, and waitresses in Montmartre.

Jules Renard
1864–1910

1 A tiny blacksmith with a pince-nez . . . He often refers to short men as if to say 'I'm not as short as all that!'

diary, November 1894

Henri de Toulouse-Lautrec
1864–1901

2 I will always be a thoroughbred hitched up to a rubbish cart.

of his physical appearance
Thadée Natanson *Un Certain Henri de Toulouse-Lautrec* (1951)

Pete Townshend 1945–

British rock musician and songwriter, a member of The Who.

Angela Carter
1940–92

1 When Pete Townshend of The Who first put on his jacket carved out of the Union Jack, he turned our national symbol into an abstraction far more effectively than did Jasper Johns when he copied the Old Glory out in paint and hung it on his wall.
in 1967

Keith Richards
1943–

2 I think Pete's mistake is to consider himself an artist . . . It's neither here nor there. I don't think you want to call yourself an artist. In show business you are an *ar-tiste*. He left the 'e' off the end.
Mick St Michael *Keith Richards in His Own Words* (1994)

Pete Townshend
1945–

3 I got into music because my nose was so big I couldn't get any girls.
in September 1986

Spencer Tracy 1900–67

American actor, particularly known for his screen partnership with **Katharine Hepburn**.

Humphrey Bogart
1899–1957

1 Spencer does it, that's all. Feels it. Says it. Talks. Listens. He means what he says when he says it, and if you think that's easy, try it.
Peter Hall's diary, April 1972

Clark Gable
1901–60

2 The guy's good and there's nobody in this business who can touch him, so you're a fool to try. And don't fall for that humble stuff either; the bastard knows it!
Larry Swindell *Spencer Tracy* (1969)

Katharine Hepburn
1909–

3 For him, life was difficult, it was acting that was easy.
interview, July 1994

Joseph L. Mankiewicz
1909–

4 KATHARINE HEPBURN: Mr Tracy, I think you're a little short for me.
MANKIEWICZ: Don't worry. He'll cut you down to size.
in 1941

W. Somerset Maugham
1874–1965

watching Tracy on the set of Dr Jekyll and Mr Hyde *(1941):*
5 Which is he playing now?
attributed

John Travolta 1954–

American actor. His 1970s successes include *Saturday Night Fever* and *Grease*, and his career was renewed by Quentin Tarantino's film *Pulp Fiction* (1994).

Pauline Kael
1919–

1 He isn't just a good actor, he's a generous-hearted actor.
in December 1977

Emma Thompson
1959–

2 Put this man in one of your movies, he needs a good movie.
to Quentin Tarantino in 1992

Lily Tomlin
1939–

3 John has a dichotomy—masculinity, femininity, refinement, crudity. You see him, you fall in love with him a little bit.
Wensley Clarkson *John Travolta: Back in Character* (1996)

John Travolta
1954–

4 It's like Quentin Tarantino gave people permission to like me again.
Wensley Clarkson *John Travolta: Back in Character* (1996)

Lee Trevino 1939–

American golfer; known as Supermex. In 1971 he became the first man to win all three Open championships (Canadian, US, and British) in the same year.

Lee Trevino
1939–

1 Yesterday, I was a poor Mexican. From now on I'm going to be a rich Spaniard.
after winning the US Open in 1968

David Trimble 1944–

Northern Irish politician, leader of the Ulster Unionists. His support was crucial to the Good Friday agreement and its subsequent implementation.

Gerry Adams
1948–

1 Well done, David.

on hearing that the Ulster Unionist Council had given its support to the Northern Ireland peace agreement

at the Sinn Féin annual conference, April 1998

Ian Paisley
1926–

2 David Trimble is drawing a line in the sand, but he's prepared to remove the line and jump over it.

in November 1999

Anthony Trollope 1815–82

English novelist. He is best-known for the six 'Barsetshire' novels and for the six political 'Palliser' novels.

Max Beerbohm
1872–1956

1 The whole of Barsetshire . . . seems to be mapped out in dear old Trollope's countenance.

*on **Julia Margaret Cameron**'s photograph of Trollope*

letter, October 1954

Henry James
1843–1916

2 Amid a little knot of Parliamentary swells conversed chiefly with Anthony Trollope—'all gobble and glare', as he was described by someone who heard him make a speech.

letter, February 1877

Henry James
1843–1916

3 His first, his inestimable merit was a complete appreciation of the usual.

Partial Portraits (1888)

James Russell Lowell
1819–91

4 A big, red-faced, rather underbred Englishman of the bald with spectacles type. A good roaring positive fellow who deafened me (sitting on his right) till I thought of Dante's Cerberus.

H. S. Scudder *James Russell Lowell* (1901)

V. S. Pritchett
1900–97

5 With all his mastery, Trollope is interested only in what people are like, not in what they are for.

attributed

Rose Trollope
1820–1917

6 He never leaves off . . . and he always has two packages of manuscript in his desk, besides the one he's working on, and the one that's being published.

on her husband

Julian Hawthorne *Shapes that Pass: Memories of Old Days* (1928)

Leon Trotsky 1879–1940

Russian revolutionary. He helped to organize the October Revolution with **Lenin**, but was expelled from the party by **Stalin** in 1927 and exiled in 1929.

Winston Churchill
1874–1965

1 He sits disconsolate—a skin of malice stranded for a time on the shores of the Black Sea and now washed up in the Gulf of Mexico. He possessed in his nature all the qualities requisite for the art of civic destruction—the organising command of a Carnot, the cold detached intelligence of a Machiavelli, the mob oratory of a Cleon, the ferocity of a Jack the Ripper, the toughness of Titus Oates.

Great Contemporaries (1937)

A. J. P. Taylor
1906–90

2 The glories of his revolutionary triumph pale before the nobility of his later defeats.

From the Boer War to the Cold War (1995)

Pierre Trudeau 1919–2000

Canadian Liberal statesman, Prime Minister of Canada 1968–79 and 1980–4. Noted for his commitment to federalism, Trudeau held a provincial referendum in Quebec in 1980, which rejected independence.

Irving Layton
1912–

1 In Pierre Elliott Trudeau, Canada has at last produced a political leader worthy of assassination.
The Whole Bloody Bird (1969)

John Lennon
1940–80

2 If all politicians were like Mr. Trudeau, there would be world peace. You people in Canada don't realize how lucky you are to have a man like Mr. Trudeau.
in December 1969

Marshall McLuhan
1911–80

3 You are immeasurably the greatest Prime Minister Canada has ever had, the first who has ever been equipped with an awareness of contemporary culture.
letter, September 1971

George Radwanski

4 As a Liberal insider once put it: 'Somebody is going to say some day, "Will the real Mr. Trudeau please stand up," and about fifty-eight people will rise.'
Trudeau (1978)

Val Sears

5 Pierre Trudeau was, for many of us, the Canadian we would like to be—a bilingual, intellectual, clever, handsome fellow and a devil with women. A Canadian who never before existed except in the eye of God.
in April 1988

Pierre Elliott Trudeau
1919–2000

6 For my part . . . I am a realist but, somehow, optimism always keeps breaking out.
in May 1982

Fred Trueman 1931–

English cricketer. A fast bowler for Yorkshire and England, he became the first bowler to take 300 test wickets.

John Arlott
1914–91

1 Fred Trueman the mature fast bowler was a sharply pointed and astutely directed weapon; Fred Trueman the man has often been tactless, haphazard, crude, a creature of impulse.
Fred: Portrait of a Fast Bowler (1983)

Michael Parkinson
1935–

2 Fred was the archetypal Yorkie: dark, glowering, resentful of authority, suspicious of the rest of the world.
in January 1995

Fred Trueman
1931–

3 I have never believed in making life easier for batsmen.
Freddie Trueman's Book of Cricket (1964)

Fred Trueman
1931–

4 Fred, t'definitive volume on t'best fast bowler that ever drew breath.
suggested title for his biography; often quoted as 't'finest bloody fast bowler . . . '
Michael Parkinson *Sporting Profiles* (1995)

Bob Willis
1949–

5 When Fred reached his 307 wickets he said afterwards that anyone who passed him would be very tired. Well, you can tell him I'm not.
in 1984

Harry S. Truman 1884–1972

American Democratic statesman, President 1945–53. He authorized the use of the atom bomb, introduced the Marshall Plan, and involved the US in the Korean War.

H. L. Mencken
1880–1956

1 If there had been any formidable body of cannibals in the country he would have promised to provide them with free missionaries fattened at the taxpayer's expense.
of Truman's success in the 1948 presidential campaign, November 1948

*of his accession to the Presidency on the death of **Franklin Roosevelt**:*

Harry S. Truman
1884–1972

2 When they told me yesterday what had happened, I felt like the moon, the stars and all the planets had fallen on me.

in April 1945

Harry S. Truman
1884–1972

3 The buck stops here.

unattributed motto on Truman's desk as President

Harry S. Truman
1884–1972

4 I never give them [the public] hell. I just tell the truth, and they think it is hell.

in April 1956

J. M. W. Turner 1775–1851

English painter. He made his name with landscapes and stormy seascapes, becoming increasingly concerned with depicting the power of light by the use of primary colours.

John Constable
1776–1837

1 He seems to paint with tinted steam, so evanescent, and so airy. The public think he is laughing at them, and so they laugh at him in return.

letter, May 1836

William Hazlitt
1778–1830

2 All is without form and void. Someone said of his landscapes that they were *pictures of nothing and very like*.

Jack Lindsay *Turner: the Man and his Art* (1985)

John Ruskin
1819–1900

3 Turner is an exception to all rules, and can be judged by no standard of art. In a wildly magnificent enthusiasm, he rushes through the aethereal dominions of the world of his own mind—a place inhabited by the *spirits of things*.

Herbert Read *The Meaning of Art* (3rd ed., 1951)

asked by a biographer of Turner to list his major characteristics:

John Ruskin
1819–1900

4 Uprightness, generosity, tenderness of heart (extreme), obstinacy (extreme), irritability, infidelity.

Herbert Read *The Meaning of Art* (3rd ed., 1951)

Sir Walter Scott
1771–1832

5 Turner's palm is as itchy as his fingers are ingenious.

letter, April 1823

Ted Turner 1938–

American businessman. His media empire includes the 24-hour news station CNN.

Ted Turner
1938–

6 Life is like a B-movie: you don't want to leave in the middle of it but you don't want to see it again.

in 1990

Mark Twain 1835–1910

American novelist and humorist, pseudonym of Samuel Langhorne Clemens. His novels about Tom Sawyer and Huckleberry Finn give a vivid evocation of Mississippi frontier life.

Louisa May Alcott
1832–88

1 If Mr Clemens cannot think of something better to tell our pure-minded lads and lasses, he had best stop writing for them.

On Adventures of Huckleberry Finn (1885)

William Faulkner
1897–1962

2 A hack writer who would not have been considered fourth rate in Europe, who tricked out a few of the old proven 'sure fire' literary skeletons with sufficient local colour to intrigue the superficial and the lazy.

in March 1922

Ernest Hemingway
1899–1961

3 All modern American literature comes from one book by Mark Twain called *Huckleberry Finn*.

Green Hills of Africa (1935)

William Dean Howells
1837–1920

4 Sole, incomparable, the Lincoln of our literature.

My Mark Twain (1910)

H. L. Mencken 5 The true father of our national literature, the first genuinely American
1880–1956 artist of the blood royal.
in February 1913

George Bernard Shaw 6 Mark Twain and I are in very much the same position. We have to put
1856–1950 things in such a way as to make people, who would otherwise hang us,
believe that we are joking.
attributed

Mark Twain 7 I am different from Washington. I have a higher and grander stand of
1835–1910 principle. Washington could not lie. I *can* lie but I won't.
in December 1871

Kenneth Tynan 1927–80

English theatre critic. He was influential in the shift of taste towards 'kitchen sink drama'
and attacked censorship.

Simon Callow 1 He never quite loses his posture of amused admiration, presenting
1949– himself as a dandy delicately negotiating the rim of a volcano; but his
seriousness is none the less real for lacking any moral dimension.
Kenneth Tynan *Profiles* (1989)

Gordon Craig 2 You have the right face for a critic. You have the look of a blooming
1872–1966 martyr.
in July 1956

Tom Stoppard 3 His paragraphs—paragraphs were the units of his prose, not
1937– sentences—were written to outlast the witness.
in 1980

Kenneth Tynan 4 Probably best summed up as a student of craftsmanship, with a special
1927–80 passion for imaginative craftsmen who put their skills to the service of
human ideas.
Tynan Right and Left (1967)

Mike Tyson 1966–

American boxer. He became undisputed world heavyweight champion in 1987. He was
imprisoned in 1992 for rape; after his release he reclaimed the WBC and WBA titles.

*intervening at a New York party, seeing Tyson forcing himself on **Naomi Campbell**:*

A. J. Ayer 1 TYSON: Do you know who the f—I am? I'm the heavyweight champion
1910–89 of the world.
AYER: And I am the former Wykeham Professor of Logic. We are both
pre-eminent in our field. I suggest we talk about this like rational
men.
Ben Rogers *A. J. Ayer: a Life* (1999)

Billy Connolly 2 People get angry at Mike Tyson for saying he's going to rip his
1942– opponent's heart out. What do they think warriors do at night—read
Tennyson?
in December 2000

Lennox Lewis 3 I'm not frightened of his punches, but he's a danger in the ring. He
1965– panics and has to bring in caveman tactics to try to win.
interview, July 2000

Mike Tyson 4 I never cared about the public. I enjoy doing what I do—I enjoy hurting
1966– people. That's what I like to do. I'm in the hurt business.
in June 2000

Galina Ulanova 1910–98

Russian ballet dancer. She gave notable interpretations of *Swan Lake* and *Giselle*, and also danced the leading roles, composed especially for her, in all three of Prokofiev's ballets.

Martha Graham
1893–1991

1 She's self-destructive, and that's how she achieves—what is the word?—*illumination.*

in August 1963

Valentino 1933–

Italian fashion designer.

Nicholas Coleridge
1957–

1 Alone among the Italian designers, I felt that Valentino was a spiritual American . . . Some of the colours of his couture—the rich reds and blues—have a high Renaissance hue to them, but they are also the colours of Disneyland.

The Fashion Conspiracy (1988)

Oscar de la Renta
1932–

2 Of all the designers I know, Valentino enjoys his success the most. He adores what his wealth has given him, and knows how to live with it.

Nicholas Coleridge *The Fashion Conspiracy* (1988)

Rudolph Valentino 1895–1926

Italian-born American actor. He played the romantic hero in silent films such as *The Sheikh* and *Blood and Sand*.

Bette Davis
1908–89

3 Valentino had silently acted out the fantasies of women all over the world. Valentino and his world were a dream. A whole generation of females wanted to ride off to a sandy paradise with him. At thirteen I had been such a female.

The Lonely Life (1962)

Mae West
1892–1980

4 Valentino had great star quality. When he died, thousands of women wept at his funeral. That's star quality.

Charlotte Chandler *The Ultimate Seduction* (1984)

John Vanbrugh 1664–1726

English architect and dramatist. His comedies include *The Relapse* and *The Provok'd Wife*; among his architectural works are Castle Howard and Blenheim Palace.

Abel Evans
1679–1737

1 Under this stone, Reader, survey
Dead Sir John Vanbrugh's house of clay.
Lie heavy on him, Earth! for he
Laid many heavy loads on thee!

'Epitaph on Sir John Vanbrugh, Architect of Blenheim Palace'

Edwin Lutyens
1869–1944

2 Vanbrugh used his weighty materials as a pigment, and the sky as his canvas, with a brush too wide to allow any niceties of detail. Surely Mammon was his Zeus.

Christopher Hussey *Life of Sir Edwin Lutyens* (1950)

Voltaire 1694–1778	3 Sir John was a man of pleasure, and likewise a poet, and an architect. The general opinion is, that he is as sprightly in his writings as he is heavy in his buildings. *Lettres Philosophiques* (1733)

Vincent Van Gogh 1853–90

Dutch painter. Best-known for his post-Impressionist work, he suffered from severe depression and eventually committed suicide.

Jeanne Calment 1875–1997	1 Ugly as sin, bad tempered, a grumbler and smelling of alcohol. remembering Van Gogh at the age of 120, February 1995
E. M. Forster 1879–1970	2 Here are pictures of potatoes, and of miners who have eaten potatoes until their faces are tuberous and dented and their skins grimed and unpeeled. They are hopeless and humble, so he loves them. *Two Cheers for Democracy* (1951)
Paul Gauguin 1848–1903	3 But I owe something to Vincent, and that is, in the consciousness of having been useful to him, the confirmation of my own original ideas about painting. And also, at difficult moments, the remembrance that one finds others unhappier than oneself. *Intimate Journals* (1923)
Paul Klee 1879–1940	4 Here is a brain consumed by the fire of a star. It frees itself in its work just before the catastrophe. Deepest tragedy takes place here, real tragedy, natural tragedy, exemplary tragedy. diary, March 1908
Peter Medawar 1915–87	5 If a scientist were to cut his ear off, no one would take it as evidence of a heightened sensibility. 'J. B. S.' (1968)
Vincent Van Gogh 1853–90	6 The more I am spent, ill, the cracked pot, by so much more am I the artist—the creative artist. Mark Roskill (ed.) *The Letters of Vincent Van Gogh* (1963)

Ralph Vaughan Williams 1872–1958

English composer. His strongly melodic music frequently reflects his interest in Tudor composers and English folk songs, which he collected and arranged.

Aaron Copland 1900–90	1 His is the music of a gentleman-farmer, noble in inspiration, but dull. in 1931

Giuseppe Verdi 1813–1901

Italian composer. His many operas are notable for strong characterization, original orchestration, and memorable tunes.

Georges Bizet 1838–75	1 Verdi . . . has wonderful bursts of passion. His passion is brutal, it is true, but that is better than having no passion at all. His music exasperates sometimes, but it never bores. letter, 1859
Giacomo Puccini 1858–1924	2 With him the purest and most luminous glory of Italy was extinguished. Peter Southwell-Sander *Puccini* (1996)

Paul Verlaine 1844–96

French symbolist poet. He served a prison sentence for wounding his lover, the poet **Arthur Rimbaud**, during a quarrel.

Dorothy Parker 1893–1967	1 And I'll stay off Verlaine too; he was always chasing Rimbauds. 'The Little Hours' (1939)

Donatella Versace 1955–

Italian fashion designer. The sister of **Gianni Versace**, she is now Creative Director of the Gianni Versace Group.

Donatella Versace
1955–

1 Look at me, I never dress down. I always have to be glamorous, even when I'm alone—especially when I'm alone.
  in July 2000

Gianni Versace 1946–97

Italian fashion designer. He was shot dead outside his home in Miami.

Gianni Versace
1946–97

2 You dress elegant and sophisticated women, I dress sluts.
  attributed by Giorgio Armani, 2000

Gianni Versace
1946–97

3 I like to dress egos. If you haven't got an ego today, you can forget it.
  attributed

Vespasian AD 9–79

Roman emperor. He was acclaimed emperor by the legions in Egypt. His reign saw the restoration of financial and military order and the initiation of a public building programme.

Vespasian
AD 9–79

1 An emperor ought to die standing.
  last words; Suetonius *Lives of the Caesars*

Queen Victoria 1819–1901

Queen from 1837 and empress of India from 1876. She took an active interest in the policies of her ministers, but largely retired from public life after **Prince Albert**'s death in 1861.

Arthur James Balfour
1848–1930

1 'I will have no melancholy in this house' is her formula—and not a bad one either in moments of anxiety.
  letter, December 1899

Thomas Carlyle
1795–1881

2 Poor little Queen! She is at an age when a girl can hardly be trusted to choose a bonnet for herself, yet a task is laid on her from which an archangel might shrink.
  on Queen Victoria's coronation, June 1838

Benjamin Disraeli
1804–81

3 No it is better not. She would only ask me to take a message to Albert.
  on his death-bed, declining a proposed visit from Queen Victoria
  Robert Blake *Disraeli* (1966)

to the Archbishop of Canterbury after the service of celebration at St Paul's for Queen Victoria's Diamond Jubilee in 1897:

Edward VII
1841–1910

4 I have no objection whatsoever to the notion of the Eternal Father, but every objection to the concept of an eternal mother.
  attributed, perhaps apocryphal

on being asked if Queen Victoria would be happy in heaven:

Edward VII
1841–1910

5 She will have to walk behind the angels—and she won't like that.
  attributed, perhaps apocryphal

George V
1865–1936

6 Today 23 years ago dear Grandmama died. I wonder what she would have thought of a Labour government.
  diary, January 1924

Henry James
1843–1916

7 She's more of a man than I expected.
  after reading Queen Victoria's letters
  E. M. Forster's diary, 1908

Rudyard Kipling
1865–1936

8 'Ave you 'eard o' the Widow at Windsor
  With a hairy gold crown on 'er 'ead?
  She 'as ships on the foam—she 'as millions at 'ome,
  An' she pays us poor beggars in red.
  'The Widow at Windsor' (1892)

Florence Nightingale
1820–1910

9 She always reminds me of the woman in the Greek chorus with her hands clasped above her head, wailing out her inexpressible despair.

*on Queen Victoria's reaction to the death of **Prince Albert***
Tyler Whittle *Victoria and Albert at Home* (1980)

Alfred, Lord Tennyson
1809–92

10 Her court was pure; her life serene;
God gave her peace; her land reposed;
A thousand claims to reverence closed
In her as Mother, Wife and Queen.

'To the Queen' (1851)

Queen Victoria
1819–1901

11 I will be good.

on being shown a chart of the line of succession
in March 1830

Queen Victoria
1819–1901

12 We are not amused.

attributed; January 1900

H. G. Wells
1866–1946

13 Queen Victoria was like a great paper-weight that for half a century sat upon men's minds, and when she was removed their ideas began to blow about all over the place haphazardly.

N. I. and J. MacKenzie *The Time Traveller* (1973)

Wilhelm II
1859–1941

14 To think that George and Nicky should have played me false! If my grandmother had been alive she would never have allowed it!

of his cousins the King of England and Tsar of Russia
remark, August 1914

Gore Vidal 1925–

American novelist, dramatist, and essayist. His essays form a satirical commentary on American political and cultural life.

Elaine Dundy
1947–

1 Just the sight of Gore had the effect of instantly cleansing my palate— like some tart lemon sorbet.

Gore Vidal *Palimpsest* (1995)

Victoria Glendinning
1937–

2 He is the most Swiftian writer we have in his savage pessimism about the human condition, his unresolved paradoxes, his hatred of hypocrisy, corruption and the kind of patriotism which means nothing more than 'persuading a man to kill a man he doesn't know'.

in February 1999

Christopher Isherwood
1904–86

3 VIDAL: I am American literature.
ISHERWOOD: I feared as much.

Fred Kaplan *Gore Vidal* (1999)

Gore Vidal
1925–

4 QUESTION: What do you think the words 'Gore Vidal' mean to most people? Especially those who haven't read your books?
VIDAL: For those who haven't read the books, I am best known for my hair preparations.

interview, November 2000

Virgil 70–19 BC

Roman poet. He wrote three major works: the *Eclogues*, the *Georgics*, and the *Aeneid*, which quickly established themselves as classics of Latin poetry.

Dante Alighieri
1265–1321

1 Thou art my master and my author. Thou art he from whom alone I took the style whose beauty has brought me honour.

Divina Commedia

Gustave Flaubert
1821–80

2 Unless one is a moron, one always dies unsure of one's own value and that of one's works. Virgil himself, as he lay dying, wanted the Aeneid burned.

letter, September 1852

Horace
65–8 BC

3 Half my own soul.

Odes

Propertius
*c.*50–after 16 BC

4 Make way, you Roman writers, make way, Greeks! Something greater than the Iliad is born.
of Virgil's Aeneid
Elegies

Alfred, Lord Tennyson
1809–92

5 I salute thee, Mantovano,
I that loved thee since my day began,
Wielder of the stateliest measure
ever moulded by the lips of man.
'To Virgil' (1882)

Voltaire 1694–1778

French writer, dramatist, and poet. A leading figure of the Enlightenment, he frequently came into conflict with the Establishment as a result of his radical views and satirical writings.

Denis Diderot
1713–84

1 This man is no more than second in all genres.
letter

Mme Du Deffand
1697–1780

2 Do you know, Monsieur . . . why I consider you a great philospher? It is because you have become rich. All those who say that one can be happy and free in poverty are liars, madmen, and fools.
letter to Voltaire

Frederick the Great
1712–86

3 Be the king of philosophers, while other princes are only the kings of men. I thank heaven every day that you exist.
letter, 1737

Victor Hugo
1802–85

4 Jesus wept; Voltaire smiled. Of that divine tear and of that human smile the sweetness of present civilisation is composed. (*Hearty applause.*)
oration, May 1878

Wolfgang Amadeus Mozart
1756–91

5 I have a piece of news for you which you may have heard already, namely that that godless arch-rascal, Voltaire, has died like a dog, like a beast.
letter, July 1778

Charles-Maurice de Talleyrand
1754–1838

6 There is someone who has more intelligence than Voltaire, it is everyone.
in July 1821

William Wordsworth
1770–1850

7 This dull product of a scoffer's pen.
of Voltaire's Candide
The Excursion (1814)

W

Richard Wagner 1813–83

German composer. He developed an operatic genre, notably in his *Ring* cycle, synthesizing music, drama, Germanic legend, and spectacle. He was strongly associated with German nationalism.

Charles Baudelaire
1821–67

1 I love Wagner; but the music I prefer is that of a cat hung up by its tail outside a window, and trying to stick to the panes of glass with its claws.
attributed

Thomas Beecham
1879–1961

2 Wagner was the most selfish man who ever lived. Everything he wrote was too long.
Robert Boothby *My Yesterday, Your Tomorrow* (1962)

Claude Debussy
1862–1918

3 Wagner: a beautiful sunset which one mistook for a dawn.
Monsieur Croche, antidilettante

Ludwig II
1845–86

4 I can only adore you . . . An earthly being cannot requite a divine spirit.
letter to Wagner; attributed

Friedrich Nietzsche
1844–1900

5 Is Wagner a human being at all? Is he not rather a disease? He contaminates everything he touches—he has made music sick . . . Wagner's art is diseased.
Der Fall Wagner (1888)

Bill Nye
1850–96

6 I have been told that Wagner's music is better than it sounds.
Mark Twain *Autobiography* (1924)

Gioacchino Rossini
1792–1868

7 Wagner has lovely moments but awful quarters of an hour.
to Emile Naumann, April 1867

Derek Walcott 1930–

West Indian poet and dramatist, who won the Nobel Prize for Literature in 1992.

Derek Walcott
1930–

1 I come from a backward place: your duty is supplied by life around you. One guy plants bananas; another plants cocoa; I'm a writer, I plant lines. There's the same clarity of occupation, and the sense of devotion.
in July 1997

Murray Walker

British television commentator, specializing in motor-racing.

Clive James
1939–

1 'I am going mad with excitement!' he told us—a necessary piece of information, because even in moments of tranquillity he sounds like a man whose trousers are on fire.
in June 1981

Alfred Russel Wallace 1823–1913

English naturalist and a founder of zoogeography. He independently formulated a theory of the origin of species that was very similar to that of **Charles Darwin**.

Charles Darwin
1809–82

1 I never saw a more striking coincidence; if Wallace had my MS. sketch written out in 1842, he could not have made a better short abstract!
note made on receiving Wallace's paper on the origin of species, June 1858

William Wallace c.1270–1305

Scottish national hero. He defeated the English army at Stirling in 1297 but after Edward I's second invasion he was captured and executed.

Robert Burns
1759–96

2 The story of Wallace poured a Scottish prejudice in my veins which will boil along there till the flood-gates of life shut in eternal rest.
letter, August 1787

Michael Forsyth
1954–

3 Wallace was a heroic failure; Bruce was a spectacular success. A loser and a winner: it is Wallace who is in fashion today. That must tell us something about the contemporary Scots ethos.
on the popularity of the film Braveheart
in April 1996

Horace Walpole 1717–97

English writer and Whig politician. He wrote *The Castle of Otranto*, one of the first Gothic novels. He also converted his home, near London, into a Gothic castle.

Fanny Burney
1752–1840

1 He was a witty, sarcastic, ingenious, deeply-thinking, highly-cultivated, quaint, though evermore gallant and romantic, though very mundane, old bachelor of other days.
Memoirs of Dr Burney (1832)

Lord Macaulay
1800–59

2 The conformation of his mind was such that whatever was little seemed to him great, and whatever was great seemed to him little.
Essays Contributed to the Edinburgh Review (1843)

Virginia Woolf
1882–1941

3 He was mischievous and obscene; he gibbered and mocked and pelted the holy shrines with nutshells. And yet with what a grace he did it— with what ease and brilliancy and wit! . . . He is the best company in the world—the most amusing, the most intriguing—the strangest mixture of ape and Cupid that ever was.
The Death of the Moth (1942)

Robert Walpole 1676–1745

British Whig statesman. Walpole is generally regarded as the first British Prime Minister in the modern sense. His period of office was marked by considerable peace and prosperity.

Lord Chesterfield
1694–1773

4 He had more of the Mazarin than of the Richelieu—He would do mean things for profit, and never thought of doing great ones for glory.
Characters of Eminent Personages of His Own Time (1777)

Robert Peel
1788–1850

5 So far as the great majority of his audience was concerned, he had blocks to cut, and he chose a fitter instrument than a razor to cut them with.
in 1833

Robert Walpole
1676–1745

6 You can read. It is a great happiness. I totally neglected it while I was in business, which has been the whole of my life, and to such a degree that I cannot now read a page—a warning to all Ministers.
to Lord Holland, after his retirement
Edmund Fitzmaurice *Life of Shelburne* (1875)

Andy Warhol c. 1928–87

American painter, graphic artist, and film-maker. A major exponent of pop art, he was noted for the standardized, consciously banal nature of his work. He coined the phrase 'famous for fifteen minutes'.

Bianca Jagger
1955–

1 I mistook his silences for intelligence.
in December 1989

Gore Vidal
1925–

2 A genius with the IQ of a moron.
in June 1989

Andy Warhol
c. 1928–87

3 If you want to know all about Andy Warhol, just look at the surface: of my paintings and films and me, and there I am. There's nothing behind it.
in March 1967

Andy Warhol
c. 1928–87

4 Whatever I do and do machine-like, is because it is what I want to do. I think it would be terrific if everybody was alike.
attributed, February 1987

Edmund White
1940–

5 The man whose heart is as warm as a hanky soaked in ethyl chloride.
States of Desire: Travels in Gay America (1980)

Tom Wolfe
1931–

6 He was the person who created Attitude . . . and that attitude was 'It's so awful, it's wonderful. It's tacky, lets wallow in it.'
in April 1987

Booker T. Washington 1856–1915

American educationist. Washington established the Tuskegee Institute in Alabama. His support for segregation and his emphasis on black people's vocational skills attracted criticism from other black leaders.

Andrew Carnegie
1835–1919

1 Booker Washington is the combined Moses and Joshua of his people. Not only has he led them to the promised land, but still lives to teach them by example and precept how properly to enjoy it.
E. L. Thornborough (ed.) *Booker T. Washington* (1969)

Theodore Roosevelt
1858–1919

2 As nearly as any man I have ever met, Booker T. Washington lived up to Micah's verse, 'What more doth the Lord require of thee than to do justice, and love mercy and walk humbly with thy God.'
Anson Phelps Stokes *A Brief Biography of Booker Washington* (1936)

George Washington 1732–99

American general and statesman, President 1789–97. He helped win the War of Independence by keeping his army together through the winter at Valley Forge and winning a decisive battle at Yorktown.

Lord Byron
1788–1824

3 The Cincinnatus of the West.
'Ode to Napoleon Bonaparte' (1814)

Benjamin Franklin
1706–90

4 George Washington, Commander of the American Armies, who, like Joshua of old, commanded the sun and the moon to stand still, and they obeyed him.
toast given at a dinner at Versailles, when the British minister had proposed a toast to **George III**, *likening him to the sun, and the French minister had likened* **Louis XVI** *to the moon*
attributed

Thomas Jefferson
1743–1826

5 His mind was great and powerful, without being of the very first order; his penetration strong, though not so acute as that of a Newton, Bacon, or Locke; and as far as he saw, no judgement was ever sounder. It was slow in operation, being little aided by invention or imagination, but sure in conclusion.
letter, January 1814

Henry Lee
1756–1818

6 A citizen, first in war, first in peace, and first in the hearts of his countrymen.
Funeral Oration on the death of General Washington (1800)

Abraham Lincoln
1809–65

7 To add brightness to the sun or glory to the name of Washington is alike impossible. Let none attempt it. In solemn awe pronounce the name, and in its naked deathless splendour leave it shining on.
speech, February 1842

Thomas Paine
1737–1809

8 As to you, sir, treacherous to private friendship (for so you have been to me, and that in the day of danger) and a hypocrite in public life, the world will be puzzled to decide whether you are an apostate or an imposter, whether you have abandoned good principles or whether you ever had any.
letter to Washington, July 1796

George Washington
1732–99

9 I can't tell a lie, Pa; you know I can't tell a lie. I did cut it with my hatchet.
M. L. Weems *Life of George Washington* (10th ed., 1810)

Muddy Waters 1915–83

American blues singer and guitarist. Waters impressed new rhythm-and-blues bands such as the Rolling Stones, who took their name from his 1950 song.

Muddy Waters
1915–83

1 All my life I was having trouble with women . . . Then, after I quit having trouble with them, I could feel in my heart that somebody would always have trouble with them, so I kept writing those blues.
Tony Palmer *All You Need is Love* (1976)

Roger Waters 1944–

English pop singer, a member of Pink Floyd.

Charles Shaar Murray

2 Had he been blessed with a rudimentary sense of humour and rather more verbal fluency than he actually possesses, Pink Floyd's former leader Roger Waters might well be pop's Martin Amis. Waters is consumed with disgust and world-weariness; his species is clearly a great disappointment to him.
in August 1992

James Dewey Watson 1928–

American biologist. Together with **Francis Crick** he proposed a model for the structure of the DNA molecule. He subsequently concentrated his efforts on cancer research.

Peter Medawar
1915–87

1 During the 1950s, the first great age of molecular biology, the English Schools of Oxford and particularly of Cambridge produced more than a score of graduates of quite outstanding ability—much more brilliant, inventive, articulate and dialectically skilful than most young scientists; right up in the Watson class. But Watson had one towering advantage over all of them: in addition to being extremely clever he had something important to be clever *about*.
review of Watson's *The Double Helix* in March 1968

Max Perutz
1914–

2 They say that all he did in Cambridge was play tennis and chase girls. But there was a serious point to that . . . He never made the mistake of confusing hard work with hard thinking; he always refused to substitute the one for the other. Of course he had time for tennis and girls.
in November 1978

James Watt 1736–1819

Scottish engineer. Among his many innovations he greatly improved the efficiency of the Newcomen steam engine.

Henry Brougham
1778–1868

1 He devoured every kind of learning. Not content with chemistry and natural philosophy, he studied anatomy, and was one day found carrying home for dissection the head of a child that had died of some hidden disorder.
Lives of Men of Letters and Science . . . in the time of George III (1845–6)

William Wordsworth
1770–1850

2 I look upon him, considering both the magnitude and the universality of his genius, as perhaps the most extraordinary man that this country ever produced.
letter, 1841

Jean Antoine Watteau 1684–1721

French painter. The light-hearted imagery of his painting contrasted with the serious religious and classical subject matter approved by the Royal Academy.

Voltaire
1694–1778

1 Watteau was quite successful with the little figures that he drew and grouped well; but he never did anything great; he was incapable of it.
Le Temple du goût (1731)

Charlie Watts 1941–

British rock musician, a member of The Rolling Stones.

Keith Richards
1943–

1 He's got a wicked jab and an uppercut and left hook. I would never want to get in front of him. He only throws 'em once every ten years, but when he does I wouldn't want to be in the way.
Stanley Booth *Keith: Till I Roll Over Dead* (1994)

Evelyn Waugh 1903–66

English novelist. His early novels were social satires. His work was profoundly influenced by his conversion to Roman Catholicism in 1930.

Harold Acton
1904–94

1 He had the sharp eye of a Hogarth alternating with that of the Ancient Mariner.
Adam (1966)

Cecil Beaton
1904–80

2 He was very conscious of what a gentleman should or should not do: no gentleman looks out of a window, no gentleman wears a brown suit. In fact, Evelyn's abiding complex and the source of much of his misery was that he was not a six-foot tall, extremely handsome and rich duke.
diary, 1949

Graham Greene
1904–91

3 There was always in Evelyn a conflict between the satirist and the romantic.
Ways of Escape (1980)

Malcolm Muggeridge
1903–90

4 Despite all Waugh's efforts to appear to be an irascible, deaf old curmudgeon, a sort of inner saintliness kept breaking through.
Miriam Gross *The World of George Orwell* (1971)

Evelyn Waugh
1903–66

5 You have no idea how much nastier I would be if I was not a Catholic. Without supernatural aid I would hardly be a human being.
Noel Annan *Our Age* (1990)

John Wayne 1907–79

American actor. Associated with the film director **John Ford** from 1930, Wayne became a Hollywood star with *Stagecoach* and appeared in many classic westerns.

John Wayne
1907–79

1 You can make me the best man in the world, or the worst, but never make me cheap.
to a director; attributed

Beatrice Webb 1858–1943

English socialist, economist, and historian. She was a prominent member of the Fabian Society and helped to establish the London School of Economics.

Hesketh Pearson
1887–1964

1 Cold, commanding, too often right to be pleasant.
Bernard Shaw: A Biography (1975)

Bertrand Russell
1872–1970

2 I knew Sidney [Webb] before his marriage. But he was then much less than half of what the two of them afterwards became. Their collaboration was quite dove-tailed. I used to think, though this was perhaps an undue simplification, that she had the ideas and he did the work.
Autobiography (1967)

Daniel Webster 1782–1852

American politician, a noted lawyer and orator.

Thomas Carlyle
1795–1881

1 A terrible, beetle-browed, mastiff-mouthed, yellow-skinned, broad-bottomed, grim-taciturn individual; with a pair of dull-cruel-looking black eyes, and as much Parliamentary intellect and silent-rage in him . . . as I have ever seen in any man.
letter, June 1824

Ralph Waldo Emerson
1803–82

2 Like the word *love* in the mouth of a courtesan.
of 'liberty' in the mouth of Webster
in 1851

Sydney Smith
1771–1845

3 Daniel Webster struck me much like a steam-engine in trousers.
Lady Holland *Memoir* (1855)

Daniel Webster
1782–1852

4 There is always room at the top.
on being advised against joining the overcrowded legal profession
attributed

John Webster c.1580–c.1625

English dramatist. His revenge tragedies were not popular in his own day, but were revived in the 19th century.

Rupert Brooke
1887–1915

5 A play of Webster's is full of the feverish and ghastly turmoil of a nest of maggots.
John Webster and the Elizabethan Drama (1916)

T. S. Eliot
1888–1965

6 Webster was much possessed by death
And saw the skull beneath the skin.
'Whispers of Immortality' (1919)

Chaim Weizmann 1874–1952

Russian-born Israeli statesman. He played an important role in persuading the US government to recognize the new state of Israel (1948) and became its first President.

Albert Einstein
1879–1955

1 The chosen one of the chosen people.
letter to Weizmann, October 1923

Raquel Welch 1940–

American actress, best remembered for her role in *One Million Years B.C.*

Raquel Welch
1940–

1 Being a sex symbol is rather like being a convict.
in February 1979

Terry Wogan
1938–

2 A smile like a razor blade, and a personality to match.
Is It Me? (2000)

Orson Welles 1915–85

American film director and actor. His realistic radio dramatization of *The War of the Worlds* caused a sensation in 1938. Notable films include *Citizen Kane* and *The Third Man*.

Jean Cocteau
1889–1963

1 An active loafer, a wise madman, a solitude surrounded by humanity.
Kenneth Tynan *Tynan Right and Left* (1967)

David Thomson
1941–

2 It is the greatest career in film, the most tragic and the one with most warnings for the rest of us.
A Biographical Dictionary of Film (1994)

Kenneth Tynan
1927–80

3 [Orson Welles] has a voice of bottled thunder, so deeply encasked that one thinks of those liquor advertisements which boast that not a drop is sold till it's seven years old.
review of *Moby Dick*, 1955

Peter Ustinov
1921–

4 He vacillated between the quick reactions of a journalist and the more contemplative approach of a thinker, but above all he was a creator.
Quotable Ustinov (1995)

Orson Welles
1915–85

5 Ladies and gentlemen, I will tell you the highlights of my life. I am a director of plays. I am a producer of plays. I am an actor on the legitimate stage. I am a writer of motion pictures. I am a motion picture actor. I write, direct, and act on the radio. I am a magician. I also paint and sketch, and I am a book-publisher. I am a violinist, and a pianist. Isn't it strange that there are so many of me—and so few of you?
introducing himself to a small audience
Kenneth Tynan *Persona Grata* (1953)

Orson Welles
1915–85

6 The biggest electric train set any boy ever had!
of the RKO studios
Peter Noble *The Fabulous Orson Welles* (1956)

Duke of Wellington 1769–1852

British soldier and Tory statesman, known as the Iron Duke. He commande the British forces in the Peninsular War and in 1815 defeated **Napoleon** at the Battle of Waterloo.

Lord Byron 1788–1824	1 Proud Wellington, with eagle beak so curled, That nose, the hook where he suspends the world! 'The Age of Bronze' (1823)
Lord Byron 1788–1824	2 Called 'Saviour of the Nations'—not yet saved, And 'Europe's Liberator'—still enslaved. *Don Juan* (1819–24)
Winston Churchill 1874–1965	3 Wellington was always at his coolest in the hottest of moments. *A History of the English Speaking Peoples* vol. 3 (1957)
Victor Hugo 1802–85	4 Waterloo is a battle of the first rank, won by a captain of the second. *Les Misérables* (1862)
Sir Walter Scott 1771–1832	5 In fact my trust is and has long been in that one man who possesses in a higher degree the gift of common sense than in anyone I have heard or read of. letter, February 1829
Alfred, Lord Tennyson 1809–92	6 The last great Englishman is low. 'Ode on the Death of the Duke of Wellington' (1852)

H. G. Wells 1866–1946

English novelist. He wrote some of the earliest science-fiction novels, such as *The War of the Worlds*, which combined political satire with warnings about the powers of science.

Brian Aldiss 1925–	1 He's the Shakespeare of science fiction. TV interview, August 1996
Henry James 1843–1916	2 Whatever Wells writes is not only alive, but kicking. G. K. Chesterton *Autobiography* (1936)
John Maynard Keynes 1883–1946	3 My picture of that interview is of a man struggling with a gramophone. The reproduction is excellent, the record is word-perfect. And there is poor Wells feeling that he has his one chance to coax the needle off the record and hear it—vain hope—speak in human tones. *of Wells interviewing* **Stalin** *Stalin-Wells Talk* (1934)
Lenin 1870–1924	4 What a little bourgeois! What a philistine! after a 'barney' with Wells in the Kremlin; Michael Foot *The History of Mr Wells* (1995)
André Maurois 1885–1967	5 Wells, in part of Europe and in the United States, will for some years have wielded an intellectual dominion comparable to that won and held by Voltaire in the eighteenth century. *Poets and Prophets* (1936)
George Orwell 1903–50	6 Here was this wonderful man who could tell you about the inhabitants of the planets and the bottom of the sea, and who *knew* that the future was not going to be what respectable people imagined. *of discovering Wells in the 1900s* in August 1941
George Orwell 1903–50	7 The minds of all of us, and therefore the physical world, would be perceptibly different if Wells had never existed. *Collected Essays, Journalism and Letters* (1968)
George Bernard Shaw 1856–1950	8 Wells does not listen to Stalin: he only waits with suffering patience to begin again when Stalin stops. He has not come to be instructed by Stalin, but to instruct him. *of Wells interviewing* **Stalin** *Stalin-Wells Talk* (1934)

Evelyn Waugh
1903–66

9 What a waste of this magical vehicle to take it prying into the future, as had the hero of the book! The future, dreariest of prospects! Were I in the saddle I should set the engine slow astern.

of Wells' Time Machine
A Little Learning (1964)

H. G. Wells
1866–1946

10 God damn you all: I told you so.

suggestion for his own epitaph, 1939; Ernest Barker *Age and Youth* (1953)

Rebecca West
1892–1983

11 He is the old maid among novelists; even the sex obsession that lay clotted on *Ann Veronica* and *The New Machiavelli* like cold white sauce was old maid's mania.

in September 1912

Rebecca West
1892–1983

12 Dear H. G., he was a devil, he ruined my life, he starved me, he was an inexhaustible source of love and friendship to me for thirty-four years, we should never have met, I was the one person he cared to see in the end, I feel desolate because he has gone.

letter, August 1946

John Wesley 1703–91

English preacher and co-founder of Methodism. Wesley was a committed Christian evangelist who won many working-class converts, often through open-air preaching.

Joseph Butler
1692–1752

1 Sir, the pretending to extraordinary revelations and gifts of the Holy Ghost is a horrid thing—a very horrid thing.

to John Wesley, August 1739

Samuel Johnson
1709–84

2 John Wesley's conversation is good, but he is never at leisure. He is always obliged to go at a certain hour. This is very disagreeable to a man who loves to fold his legs and have out his talk, as I do.

comment, March 1778

John Wesley
1703–91

3 I look upon all the world as my parish.

diary, June 1739

Mae West 1892–1980

American actress and dramatist. She made her name on Broadway in her own comedies, memorable for their spirited approach to sexual matters, before embarking on her successful Hollywood career in the 1930s.

Mae West
1892–1980

1 I've been in *Who's Who*, and I know what's what, but it'll be the first time I ever made the dictionary.

on having an inflatable life jacket named after her
letter to the RAF, early 1940s

Mae West
1892–1980

2 I'm the girl who lost her reputation and never missed it.

P. F. Boller and R. L. Davis *Hollywood Anecdotes* (1988)

Rebecca West 1892–1983

Irish-born British writer and feminist. From 1911 she wrote journalistic articles in support of women's suffrage. She reported on the Nuremberg trials.

Stevie Smith
1902–71

3 I would not call Miss West a feminist because this suggests—and is meant to—an aggrieved and strident person. I would say she is on the side of women.

in the 1950s

Anthony West
1914–87

4 She regarded me as a piece of fiction—like one of her novels—that she could edit and improve.

a son's view; June 1984

Rebecca West
1892–1983

5 I myself have never been able to find out precisely what feminism is: I only know that people call me a feminist whenever I express sentiments that differentiate me from a doormat or a prostitute.

in November 1913

Vivienne Westwood 1941–

English fashion designer. Initially a designer of punk clothing, she has since moved into more mainstream international fashion.

Vivienne Westwood
1941–

1 Life is an adventure, so I make clothes to have adventures in.
in 1981

Vivienne Westwood
1941–

2 I've never been happier than when I'm parodying the English.
in 1987

Edith Wharton 1862–1937

American novelist and short-story writer, resident in France from 1907. Her novels, many of them set in New York high society, are concerned with the conflict between social and individual fulfilment.

F. Scott Fitzgerald
1896–1940

1 Mrs Wharton, do you know what's the matter with you? You don't know anything about life.
Grace Kellogg *The Two Lives of Edith Wharton* (1965)

Henry James
1843–1916

2 Your only drawback is not having the homeliness and the inevitability and the happy limitation and the affluent poverty of a country of your own.
letter, 1912

James McNeill Whistler 1834–1903

American painter and etcher. Whistler mainly painted in one or two colours and sought to achieve harmony of colour and tone.

Edgar Degas
1834–1917

1 Whistler, if you were not a genius you would be the most ridiculous man in Paris.
George Moore *Vale* (1914)

Dante Gabriel Rossetti
1828–82

2 There's a combative artist named Whistler
Who is, like his own hog-hairs, a bristler:
A tube of white lead
And a punch on the head
Offer varied attractions to Whistler.
attributed

John Ruskin
1819–1900

3 I have seen, and heard, much of Cockney impudence before now; but never expected to hear a coxcomb ask two hundred guineas for flinging a pot of paint in the public's face.
on Whistler's Nocturne in Black and Gold
Fors Clavigera (1871–84)

James McNeill Whistler
1834–1903

4 QUESTION: For two days' labour, you ask two hundred guineas?
WHISTLER: No, I ask it for the knowledge of a lifetime.
in his case against **Ruskin**; D. C. Seitz *Whistler Stories* (1913)

Oscar Wilde
1854–1900

5 A miniature Mephistopheles, mocking the majority.
in February 1885

Gilbert White 1720–93

English clergyman and naturalist. He wrote many letters to friends on aspects of natural history in his native village of Selborne, Hampshire.

John Constable
1776–1837

1 The mind and feeling which produced *Selborne* is such a one as I have always envied. The single page alone of the life of Mr White leaves a more lasting impression on my mind than that of Charles V or any other renowned hero.
diary, April 1821

William Whitelaw 1918–99

British Conservative politician. Noted for his loyalty, he was Deputy Prime Minister to **Margaret Thatcher**.

Lord Carrington
1919–

1 He had a very loud voice and while most of his widely publicized indiscretions were intended, a number were due to his mistaken belief that he was whispering.
in October 1999

Nigel Lawson
1932–

2 [A politician] should appear stupider than he is (or be cleverer than he appears). The obvious example of this is Willie Whitelaw.
The View from No. 11 (1993)

Margaret Thatcher
1925–

3 Every Prime Minister needs a Willie.
in August 1991

Walt Whitman 1819–92

American poet. In 1855 he published the free verse collection *Leaves of Grass*. The collection celebrates democracy, sexuality, the self, and the American spirit.

Allen Ginsberg
1926–97

1 Ah, dear father, graybeard, lonely old courage-teacher, what America
did you have when Charon quit poling his ferry and you got out on a
smoking bank and stood watching the boat
disappear on the black waters of Lethe?
'A Supermarket in California' (1956)

D. H. Lawrence
1885–1930

2 This awful Whitman. This post-mortem poet. This poet with the private soul leaking out of him all the time. All his privacy leaking out in a sort of dribble, oozing into the universe.
Studies in Classic American Literature (1924)

David Lodge
1935–

3 Walt Whitman who laid end to end words never seen in each other's company before outside of a dictionary.
Changing Places (1975)

Amy Lowell
1874–1925

4 Whitman was like a prophet straying in a fog and shouting half-truths with a voice of great trumpets. He was seeking something, but he never knew quite what, and he never found it.
'Walt Whitman and the New Poetry' (1926–7)

Ann Widdecombe 1947–

British Conservative politician. Her strongly conservative policies as Shadow Home Secretary have made her very popular within the Conservative Party.

Anthony Clare
1942–

1 'Overweight', 'dumpy', 'spinster', 'ugly', are words she has chosen for self-description. She goes further and articulates a formidable onslaught on our current preoccupation with physical perfection and makes an impressive argument on behalf of all the people in our society who are physically disabled, who are physically disfigured.
In the Psychiatrist's Chair III (1998)

Alec Guinness
1914–2000

2 It looks like bare-knuckle fisticuffs . . . in the Westminster gym: Widdecombe v. Howard. On our right, God's Girl Widdecombe socking it to the Evasive Basher, also on our extreme right.
A Positively Final Appearance (1999)

William Hague
1961–

3 If we could get the common sense revolution to stand up and walk around it would look like Ann Widdecombe.
in March 2000

Ann Widdecombe
1947–

4 I would rather be round and jolly than thin and cross.
in June 1998

Ann Widdecombe
1947–

5 I think you have to be very careful when you say, 'God is on my side.' I much prefer to say, 'I am on God's side'.
Anthony Clare *In the Psychiatrist's Chair III* (1998)

William Wilberforce 1759–1833

English politician and social reformer. He was a prominent campaigner for the abolition of the slave trade.

James Boswell
1740–95

1 I saw what seemed a mere shrimp mount upon the table; but, as I listened, he grew, and grew, until the shrimp became a whale.
   letter, March 1784

William Wilberforce
1759–1833

2 They charge me with fanaticism. If to be feelingly alive to the sufferings of my fellow-creatures is to be a fanatic, I am one of the most incurable fanatics ever permitted to be at large.
   in June 1816

Oscar Wilde 1854–1900

Anglo-Irish dramatist, novelist, poet, and wit. He was imprisoned (1895–7) for homosexual offences and died in exile.

W. H. Auden
1907–73

1 From the beginning Wilde performed his life and continued to do so even after fate had taken the plot out of his hands.
   in March 1963

Max Beerbohm
1872–1956

2 An Assyrian wax statue, effeminate, but with the vitality of twenty men.
   Cecil Beaton's diary, September 1953

John Betjeman
1906–84

3 He sipped at a weak hock and seltzer
   As he gazed at the London skies
   Through the Nottingham lace of the curtains
   Or was it his bees-winged eyes?
   'The Arrest of Oscar Wilde at the Cadogan Hotel' (1937)

Ambrose Bierce
1842–c.1914

4 That sovereign of insufferables.
   in *Wasp*, San Francisco, 1882

G. K. Chesterton
1874–1936

5 Like a many-coloured humming-top, he was at once a bewilderment and a balance. He was so fond of being many-sided that among his sides he even admitted the right side. He loved so much to multiply his souls that he had among them one soul at least that was saved.
   in October 1909

Noël Coward
1899–1973

6 *De Profundis* is one long wail of self-pity. It is extraordinary indeed that such a posing, artificial old queen should have written one of the greatest comedies in the English language. In my opinion it was the only thing of the least *importance* that he did write.
   diary, July 1962

Stephen Fry
1957–

7 It's due to Oscar Wilde that today we can celebrate a society that generally appreciates diversity.
   in December 1998

Rudyard Kipling
1865–1936

8 No, I've never cared for his work. Too scented.
   Harry Ricketts *The Unforgiving Minute* (1999)

Ada Leverson
1865–1936

9 He seemed at ease and to have the look of the last gentleman in Europe.
   Letters to the Sphinx (1930)

Dorothy Parker
1893–1967

10 If, with the literate, I am
   Impelled to try an epigram,
   I never seek to take the credit;
   We all assume that Oscar said it.
   'A Pig's-Eye View of Literature' (1937)

Marquess of Queensberry
1844–1900

11 To Oscar Wilde posing as a somdomite.
   misspelt message written on his card and left at the Albemarle Club, leading Wilde to sue for libel
   in February 1895

James McNeill
Whistler
1834–1903

12 What has Oscar in common with Art? except that he dines at our tables and picks from our platter the plums for the puddings he peddles in the provinces.
in November 1886

James McNeill
Whistler
1834–1903

13 OSCAR WILDE: How I wish I had said that.
WHISTLER: You will, Oscar, you will.
R. Ellman *Oscar Wilde* (1987)

Oscar Wilde
1854–1900

14 Do you want to know the great drama of my life? It's that I have put my genius into my life; all I've put into my works is my talent.
André Gide *Oscar Wilde* (1910)

Oscar Wilde
1854–1900

15 And alien tears will fill for him
Pity's long-broken urn,
For his mourners will be outcast men,
And outcasts always mourn.
inscribed on Wilde's tomb in Père Lachaise cemetery
The Ballad of Reading Gaol (1898)

Billy Wilder 1906–

Austrian-born American film director and screenwriter. His films include *Double Indemnity*, *Sunset Boulevard*, and *Some Like It Hot*.

William Holden
1918–81

1 Billy Wilder has a mind full of razor blades.
Cameron Crowe *Conversations with Wilder* (1999)

Billy Wilder
1906–

2 I don't do cinema. I make movies.
Cameron Crowe *Conversations with Wilder* (1999)

Billy Wilder
1906–

3 I'm very uncomfortable living in any world where the Pope is twenty-five years younger than I am.
in July 1993

William I c.1027–87

King from 1066. He invaded England and defeated **Harold II** at the Battle of Hastings. He introduced Norman institutions and customs and instigated the Domesday Book.

Thomas Paine
1737–1809

1 A French bastard landing with an armed banditti and establishing himself King of England against the consent of the natives is, in plain terms, a very paltry rascally original.
Common Sense (1776)

William III 1650–1702

Stadtholder of the Netherlands from 1672 and King of England from 1689; known as William of Orange. In 1688 he deposed **James II** at the invitation of disaffected politicians and was crowned along with his wife **Mary II**.

Winston Churchill
1874–1965

2 He would break a political opponent without pity, but he was never needlessly cruel, and was glad to treat foes no longer dangerous with contempt or indifference. He wasted no time on minor revenges.
Winston Churchill *Marlborough* vol. 4 (1938)

Peter the Great
1672–1725

3 It is your military genius that has inspired my sword, and the noble emulation of your exploits has aroused in my heart the first thoughts I ever had of enlarging my Empire.
remark, September 1697

Horace Walpole
1717–97

4 He aimed not at the crown of England for ambition, but to employ its forces and wealth against Louis XIV for the common cause of the liberties of Europe.
letter, c.1792

William III
1650–1702

5 'Do you not see your country is lost?' asked the Duke of Buckingham. 'There is one way never to see it lost' replied William, 'and that is to die in the last ditch.'

Bishop Gilbert Burnet *History of My Own Time* (1838 ed.)

Prince William 1982–

Elder son of **Charles, Prince of Wales** and **Diana, Princess of Wales**.

Deborah Orr
1962–

6 One day we'll be your subjects, but the price you pay is that you're forever our object.

in June 2000

Tennessee Williams 1911–83

American dramatist. His works include *The Glass Menagerie* and *A Streetcar Named Desire*.

Kenneth Tynan
1927–80

1 Shave the beard off any of the self-portraits Gauguin painted in Tahiti, soften the features a little, and you have a sleepy outcast face that might well be Tennessee's.

in February 1956

Gore Vidal
1925–

2 Tennessee is the sort of writer who does not develop; he simply continues.

in February 1976

Harold Wilson 1916–95

British Labour statesman, Prime Minister 1964–70 and 1974–6. His administrations were pragmatic in outlook rather than rigidly socialist. In both terms of office he faced severe economic problems.

on seeing Wilson, who had resigned as Prime Minister in March, looking 'absolutely shrunk':

Tony Benn
1925–

1 Office is something that builds up a man only if he is somebody in his own right.

diary, April 1976

Tony Benn
1925–

2 For Harold Wilson the greatest term of abuse he could use was to say 'that's a theological argument' as if theology was self-evidently nonsensical.

Anthony Clare *In the Psychiatrist's Chair III* (1998)

Ivor Bulmer-Thomas
1905–93

3 If he ever went to school without any boots it was because he was too big for them.

Wilson had claimed that more than half the children with whom he went to school had been unable to afford boots or shoes (and had therefore worn clogs)
speech, October 1949

Alec Douglas-Home, Lord Home
1903–95

4 As far as the fourteenth earl is concerned, I suppose Mr Wilson, when you come to think of it, is the fourteenth Mr Wilson.

*replying to Wilson's remark (on **Home**'s becoming leader of the Conservative party) that 'the whole [democratic] process has ground to a halt with a fourteenth Earl'*
in October 1963

Roy Jenkins
1920–

5 He had a very good statistical mind . . . He could always remember who lost three by-elections running in what year . . . and liked that sort of gossip. And we also had an interest in railway timetables and railway stations.

Peter Hennessy *The Prime Ministers* (2000)

John Junor
1919–97

6 Such a graceful exit. And then he had to go and do this on the doorstep.

on Wilson's 'Lavender List' (the honours list he drew up on resigning the British premiership in 1976)
in January 1990

Harold Wilson 1916–95	7 If I had the choice between smoked salmon and tinned salmon, I'd have it tinned. With vinegar. in November 1962
Harold Wilson 1916–95	8 I'm not an intriguer . . . I only counter-intrigue against those who intrigue against me. Peter Hennessy *The Prime Ministers* (2000)

Richard Wilson 1936–

Scottish actor, best known for his role as Victor Meldrew in the television series *One Foot in the Grave*.

Richard Wilson 1936–	9 I am a socialist and even now I'm a rich, fat bastard who can afford the odd bottle of champagne, I believe in doing what I can for my fellow man. in February 1996

Woodrow Wilson 1856–1924

American Democratic statesman, President 1913–21. He took America into First World War in 1917 and played a leading role in the peace negotiations and the formation of the League of Nations.

Georges Clemenceau 1841–1929	10 What do you expect when I'm between two men of whom one [Lloyd George] thinks he is Napoleon and the other [Woodrow Wilson] thinks he is Jesus Christ? on being asked why he always gave in to **Lloyd George** at the Paris Peace Conference, 1918 letter from Harold Nicolson to his wife, May 1919
Georges Clemenceau 1841–1929	11 God Almighty was satisfied with Ten Commandments. Mr Wilson requires Fourteen Points. during the Peace Conference negotiations in 1919
John Maynard Keynes 1883–1946	12 Like Odysseus, the President looked wiser when he was seated. *The Economic Consequences of the Peace* (1919)

Barbara Windsor 1937–

English actress. She took part in many *Carry On* films, and later appeared on television in *EastEnders*.

Barbara Windsor 1937–	1 They say an actor is only as good as his parts. Well, my parts have done me pretty well, darling. in February 1999

Duchess of Windsor (Wallis Simpson) 1896–1986

American wife of Edward, Duke of Windsor (**Edward VIII**). Her relationship with the king caused a scandal in view of her impending second divorce and forced the king's abdication.

Anonymous	2 King's Moll Reno'd in Wolsey's home town. US newspaper headline on the divorce proceedings of Wallis Simpson in Ipswich, 1936
Anonymous	3 Hark the herald angels sing Mrs Simpson's pinched our king. contemporary children's rhyme
Cecil Beaton 1904–80	4 To hear her speak was enough. Her voice was raucous and appalling. I thought her awful, common, vulgar, strident, a second-rate American with no charm. in the early 1930s; Hugo Vickers *Cecil Beaton* (1993)
Rebecca West 1892–1983	5 She is a Mrs Simpson—about 34—very smart but very common and trivial. She was a quite low-class American who married a bad lot who deserted her in Shanghai, where she picked up a living anyhow until she married a business man called Ernest Simpson. letter, *c*.1933–4

Robert Winston 1940–

British obstetrician and gynaecologist, pioneer of infertility treatment.

Robert Winston
1940–

1 It's politically very incorrect to suggest that you manipulate or that you are authoritarian, but actually doctors do manipulate patients, and I think I do too. If I'm really honest I'm sure I do.
Anthony Clare *In the Psychiatrist's Chair II* (1995)

Jeanette Winterson 1959–

English novelist and critic. She won the Whitbread Prize with her first novel *Oranges Are Not the Only Fruit*.

Jeanette Winterson
1959–

on being asked to name the best living author writing in English:
1 No one working in the English language now comes close to my exuberance, my passion, my fidelity to words.
in March 1994

Ludwig Wittgenstein 1889–1951

British philosopher, born in Austria. His major works examine language and its relationship to the world.

Bertrand Russell
1872–1970

1 My German engineer, I think is a fool. He thinks nothing empirical is Knowable—I asked him to admit that there was not a rhinoceros in the room, but he wouldn't.
letter, November 1911

Bertrand Russell
1872–1970

2 I like Wittgenstein more and more. He has the pure intellectual passion in the highest degree . . . He says every morning he begins his work with hope, and every evening he ends in despair—he has just the sort of rage when he can't understand things that I have.
letter, March 1912

Karl Wallinger
1957–

3 Recently I've been getting into Wittgenstein. At first I was annoyed that he existed because he obfuscates the clarity of Bertrand Russell's arguments.
interview, August 2000

Ludwig Wittgenstein
1889–1951

4 Tell them I've had a wonderful life.
last words; Ray Monk *Ludwig Wittgenstein* (1990)

P. G. Wodehouse 1881–1975

English writer. His best-known works are humorous stories of the upper-class world of Bertie Wooster and his valet Jeeves, the first of which appeared in 1917.

Alistair Cooke
1908–

1 He is a giant Pickwick, an aging Micawber who had everything delightful turn up at once.
'Wodehouse at Eighty' (1961)

Sean O'Casey
1880–1964

2 English literature's performing flea.
P. G. Wodehouse *Performing Flea* (1953)

George Orwell
1903–50

3 It is nonsense to talk of 'Fascist tendencies' in his books. There are no post-1918 tendencies at all.
'In Defence of P. G. Wodehouse' (1945)

P. G. Wodehouse
1881–1975

4 You know, I've always been a recluse. I've never seen any sort of life—*I got it all from the newspapers!*
Alistair Cooke 'Wodehouse at Eighty' (1961)

James Wolfe 1727–59

British general. He commanded the attack on Quebec in 1759 and was fatally wounded while leading his troops to victory on the Plains of Abraham.

George II
1683–1760

1 Mad, is he? Then I hope he will *bite* some of my other generals.
replying to the Duke of Newcastle, who had complained that General Wolfe was a madman
Henry Beckles Willson *Life and Letters of James Wolfe* (1909)

James Wolfe
1727–59

2 The General . . . repeated nearly the whole of Gray's Elegy . . . adding, as he concluded, that he would prefer being the author of that poem to the glory of beating the French to-morrow.
J. Playfair *Biographical Account of J. Robinson*

Tom Wolfe 1931–

American writer. Having been a news reporter, he examined contemporary American culture in *The Electric Kool-Aid Acid Test* (1968) and the novel *The Bonfire of the Vanities* (1988).

Edward Abbey
1927–89

3 A pretentious fad-chaser . . . the pom-pom girl of American letters.
attributed

Mary Wollstonecraft 1759–97

English writer and feminist, of Irish descent; mother of **Mary Shelley**. Her best-known work is *A Vindication of the Rights of Woman*.

Robert Southey
1774–1843

1 She has made me in love with a cold climate, and frost and snow, with a northern moonlight.
on Mary Wollstonecraft's letters from Sweden and Norway
letter, April 1797

Horace Walpole
1717–97

2 That hyena in petticoats, Mrs Wollstonecraft.
letter, January 1795

Garnet Wolseley 1833–1913

British soldier. The leader of several successful military expeditions, contemporaries regarded him as the ideal of the modern professional soldier.

Anonymous

1 All Sir Garnet.
late 19th century term meaning highly satisfactory

Benjamin Disraeli
1804–81

2 He is one of those men who not only succeed but succeed quickly. Nothing can give you an idea of the jealousy, the hatred and all uncharitableness of the Horse Guards against our only soldier.
letter, 1879

W. S. Gilbert
1836–1911

3 I am the very model of a modern Major-General.
the original Major-General was made up to resemble Wolseley
The Pirates of Penzance (1879)

Garnet Wolseley
1833–1913

4 I hope I may never return home a defeated man: I would sooner leave my old bones here than go home to be jeered at.
letter, 1882

Cardinal Thomas Wolsey c. 1475–1530

English prelate and statesman. Wolsey dominated foreign and domestic policy, but failed to secure the papal dispensation necessary for **Henry VIII**'s divorce. He died on his way to trial.

Anonymous

1 Begot by butchers, but by bishops bred,
How high his Honour holds his haughty head.
traditional rhyme

Thomas Wolsey
c. 1475–1530

2 Had I but served God as diligently as I have served the King, he would not have given me over in my grey hairs.
George Cavendish *Negotiations of Thomas Wolsey* (1641)

Tiger Woods 1975–

American golfer. In 1997 he became the youngest winner of the US Masters.

Jack Nicklaus
1940–

1 It was a privilege and a pleasure just to watch Tiger Woods. He is playing a game with which I am not familiar.
  in August 2000

Tiger Woods
1975–

2 Growing up, I came up with this name: I'm a Cablinasian.
  explaining his rejection of 'African-American' as the term to describe his Caucasian, Afro-American, Native American, Thai, and Chinese ancestry
  interview, April 1997

Virginia Woolf 1882–1941

English novelist, essayist, and critic. A member of the Bloomsbury Group, her novels were characterized by their stream-of-consciousness technique and poetic impressionism.

Dirk Bogarde
1921–

1 Used to see her marching about the water-meadows quite often. Hair wispy and caught into a loose sort of knot, a big stick or sometimes a brightly coloured umbrella furled . . . She sometimes wore a big floppy straw hat and we all thought she was a witch.
  childhood memories
  letter, May 1968

Germaine Greer
1939–

2 Dr Leavis believed he could identify a woman writer by her style, even though necessarily all that she wrote must have been a parody of some man's superior achievement. After all, there was not much wrong with Virginia Woolf except that she was a woman.
  The Female Eunuch (1970)

Harold Laski
1893–1950

3 It was like watching someone organize her own immortality. Every phrase and gesture was studied. Now and again, when she said something a little out of the ordinary, she wrote it down herself in a notebook.
  letter, November 1930

Vita Sackville-West
1892–1962

4 Virginia has killed herself . . . I simply can't take it in. That lovely mind, that lovely spirit.
  letter, March 1941

Edith Sitwell
1887–1964

5 I enjoyed talking to her, but thought *nothing* of her writing. I considered her 'a beautiful little knitter'.
  letter, July 1955

Rebecca West
1892–1983

6 I could not have admired Virginia Woolf more as a writer and I was very fond of Clive Bell. But I cannot say I found the company of this group very entertaining . . . I may be prejudiced on this matter by the fact that any demented lady, even if a genius, is a difficult neighbour in the country.
  letter, April 1980

Virginia Woolf
1882–1941

7 As an experience, madness is terrific . . . and in its lava I still find most of the things I write about.
  letter, June 1930

William Wordsworth 1770–1850

English poet. Much of his work was inspired by the Lake District. His *Lyrical Ballads*, which was composed with **Coleridge**, was a landmark in romanticism. He was appointed Poet Laureate in 1843.

Matthew Arnold
1822–88

1 He spoke, and loosed our heart in tears.
  He laid us as we lay at birth
  On the cool flowery lap of earth.
  'Memorial Verses, April 1850' (1852)

Matthew Arnold
1822–88

2 His expression may often be called bald ... but it is bald as the bare mountain tops are bald, with a baldness full of grandeur.

Essays in Criticism Second Series (1888)

Robert Browning
1812–89

3 Just for a handful of silver he left us,
Just for a riband to stick in his coat ...

of Wordsworth's implied abandonment of radical principles by his acceptance of the Laureateship
'The Lost Leader' (1845)

Samuel Butler
1835–1902

4 How thankful we ought to be that Wordsworth was only a poet and not a musician. Fancy a symphony by Wordsworth! Fancy having to sit it out! And fancy what it would have been if he had written fugues!

Notebooks (1912)

Lord Byron
1788–1824

5 We learn from Horace, Homer sometimes sleeps;
We feel without him: Wordsworth sometimes wakes.

Don Juan (1819–24)

Lord Byron
1788–1824

6 Who, both by precept and example, shows
That prose is verse, and verse is merely prose,
Convincing all by demonstration plain,
Poetic souls delight in prose insane.

English Bards and Scotch Reviewers (1809)

Lord Byron
1788–1824

7 Wordsworth—stupendous genius! damned fool! These poets run about their ponds though they cannot fish.

Henry Crabb Robinson's diary, December 1816

Thomas Carlyle
1795–1881

8 He was ... a man of an immense head and great jaws like a crocodile's, cast in a mould designed for prodigious work.

in conversation, c.1849

Ralph Waldo Emerson
1803–82

9 To judge from a single conversation, he made the impression of a narrow and very English mind; of one who paid for his rare elevation by general tameness and conformity. Off his own beat, his opinions were of no value.

English Traits (1856)

William Hazlitt
1778–1830

10 Mr Wordsworth's genius is a pure emanation of the Spirit of the Age. Had he lived in any other period of the world, he would never have been heard of.

The Spirit of the Age (1825)

John Keats
1795–1821

11 For the sake of a few fine imaginative or domestic passages, are we to be bullied into a certain philosophy engendered in the whims of an egotist?

on the overbearing influence of Wordsworth upon his contemporaries
letter, February 1818

Philip Larkin
1922–85

12 Wordsworth was nearly the price of me once. I was driving down the M1 on a Saturday morning: they had this poetry slot on the radio ... and someone suddenly started reading the Immortality ode, and I couldn't see for tears. And when you're driving down the middle lane at seventy miles an hour ...

Required Writing (1983)

Ezra Pound
1885–1972

13 Mr Wordsworth, a stupid man, with a decided gift for portraying nature in vignettes, never yet ruined anyone's morals, unless, perhaps, he has driven some susceptible persons to crime in a very fury of boredom.

in September 1913

Sir Walter Scott
1771–1832

14 Wordsworth in particular is such a character as only exists in romance—virtuous, simple, and unaffectedly restricting every want and wish to the bounds of a very narrow income in order to enjoy the literary and poetical leisure which his happiness consists in.

letter, April 1806

Percy Bysshe Shelley
1792–1822

15 In honoured poverty thy voice did weave
   Songs consecrate to truth and liberty,—
   Deserting these, thou leavest me to grieve,
   Thus having been, that thou shouldst cease to be.
   'To Wordsworth' (1816)

J. K. Stephen
1859–92

16 Two voices are there: one is of the deep;
   It learns the storm-cloud's thunderous melody . . .
   And one is of an old half-witted sheep . . .
   And, Wordsworth, both are thine.
   'A Sonnet' (1891)

Oscar Wilde
1854–1900

17 Wordsworth went to the lakes, but he was never a lake poet. He found
   in stones the sermons he had already hidden there.
   Intentions (1891)

Mary Wordsworth
1782–1859

18 It is not in my power to tell thee how I have been affected by this
   dearest of all letters—it was so unexpected—so new a thing to see the
   breathing of thy inmost heart upon paper.
   letter, August 1810

Christopher Wren 1632–1723

English architect. Following the Fire of London (1666) Wren was responsible for the design
of the new St Paul's Cathedral and many of the city's churches.

Anonymous

1 *Si monumentum requiris, circumspice.*
  If you seek a monument, gaze around.
  inscription in St Paul's Cathedral, attributed to Wren's son

Edmund Clerihew Bentley
1875–1956

2 Sir Christopher Wren
  Said, 'I am going to dine with some men.
  If anybody calls
  Say I am designing St Paul's.'
  'Sir Christopher Wren' (1905)

John Evelyn
1620–1706

3 That miracle of a youth, Mr Christopher Wren.
  diary, July 1654

Robert Hooke
1635–1703

4 There scarce ever met in one man, in so great a perfection, such a
  mechanical hand, and so philosophical a mind.
  Micrographia (1665)

Frank Lloyd Wright 1867–1959

American architect. He advocated an 'organic' architecture, characterized by a close
relationship between building, landscape, and the materials used.

Alistair Cooke
1908–

1 He lay stretched out on a sofa, his fine hands folded on his lap, a shawl
  precisely draped around his shoulders. He looked like Merlin posing as
  Whistler's Mother.
  Memories of the Great and the Good (1999)

Frank Lloyd Wright
1867–1959

2 Early in life I had to choose between honest arrogance and hypocritical
  humility. I chose honest arrogance and have seen no occasion to
  change.
  Herbert Jacobs *Frank Lloyd Wright* (1965)

John Wyclif 1330–84

English religious reformer. He instituted the first English translation of the complete Bible.

John Foxe
1516–87

1 What Heraclitus would not laugh, or what Democritus would not
  weep? For though they digged up his body, burned his bones and
  drowned his ashes, yet the word of God and truth of his doctrine, with
  the fruit and success thereof, they could not burn.
  Actes and Monuments ['Foxe's Book of Martyrs']

Y

W. B. Yeats 1865–1939

Irish poet and dramatist. He was prominent in Ireland's theatrical, cultural, and literary revival. His early poetry was influenced by the Pre-Raphaelites; his later style is sparser and more lyrical.

W. H. Auden
1907–73

1 You were silly like us; your gift survived it all:
The parish of rich women, physical decay,
Yourself. Mad Ireland hurt you into poetry.
'In Memory of W. B. Yeats' (1940)

W. H. Auden
1907–73

2 Earth, receive an honoured guest:
William Yeats is laid to rest.
Let the Irish vessel lie
Emptied of its poetry.
'In Memory of W. B. Yeats' (1940)

G. K. Chesterton
1874–1936

3 Against this drab background of dreary modern materialism, Willie Yeats was calmly walking about as the Man Who Knew the Fairies.
Autobiography (1936)

Lord Alfred Douglas
1870–1945

4 Your omission of my work from the absurdly-named Oxford Book of Modern Verse is exactly typical of the attitude of the minor to the major poet. For example Thomas Moore, the Yeats of the 19th century, would undoubtedly have excluded Keats and Shelley from any anthology he had compiled.
telegram to Yeats, 1936

Oliver St John Gogarty
1878–1957

5 Yeats is becoming so aristocratic, he's evicting imaginary tenants.
Ulick O'Connor *Oliver St John Gogarty* (1964)

Maud Gonne
1867–1953

6 Poets should never marry. The world should thank me for not marrying you.
Nancy Cardozo *Maud Gonne* (1978)

Frank O'Connor
1903–66

7 Yeats was one of the most devious men I have ever known, and I deliberately mocked at his deviousness as he mocked at my simple-mindedness, probably with equal justification.
My Father's Son (1968)

Virginia Woolf
1882–1941

8 Wherever one cut him, with a little question, he poured, spurted fountains of ideas.
diary, November 1930

Boris Yeltsin 1931–

Russian statesman. As President of the Russian Federation 1991–2000 he faced opposition to his reforms and in 1993 survived an attempted coup.

Richard Milhous Nixon
1913–94

1 Gorbachev is Wall Street and Yeltsin is Main Street; Gorbachev is Georgetown drawing rooms and Yeltsin is Newark factory gate.
in April 1991

Sarah, Duchess of York 1959–

Former wife of Prince Andrew, Duke of York. The marriage attracted intense press publicity, and the couple were divorced in 1996.

Lord Charteris
1913–

1 The Duchess of York is a vulgarian. She is vulgar, vulgar, vulgar, and that is that.
in January 1995

Sarah, Duchess of York
1959–

2 I'm doing pretty well considering. In the past, when anyone left the Royal family they had you beheaded.

in July 2000

Brigham Young 1801–77

American Mormon leader. He succeeded Joseph Smith as the leader of the Mormons in 1844, and established their headquarters at Salt Lake City, Utah.

Ralph Waldo Emerson
1803–82

1 He is clearly a sufficient ruler, and perhaps civilizer of his kingdom of blockheads *ad interim*.

letter, June 1871

Artemus Ward
1834–67

2 He is dreadfully married. He's the most married man I ever saw in my life.

Artemus Ward's Lecture (1869)

Neil Young 1945–

Canadian guitarist, singer, and songwriter, noted for his wide range of styles.

Neil Young
1945–

3 Our parents were into Frank Sinatra and Rosemary Clooney and Perry Como—now I'm Perry Como.

in November 1990

Z

Frank Zappa 1940–93

American rock singer, musician, and songwriter. In 1965 he formed the Mothers of Invention, who combined psychedelic rock with elements of jazz and satire.

Lou Reed
1944–

1 I enjoyed those shows I did at the Rainbow . . . I kept thinking, Frank Zappa fell 17 feet down into that [orchestra] pit. I hate Frank Zappa, and it made me feel so happy to think about that.

in 1975

Moon Unit Zappa

2 When he died, we got to put him into the coffin. Normally, someone else gets to do that, but we put him in ourselves. We treated it like he was going on tour, and put in his espresso machine and some cayenne pepper and various other things that he would need.

a daughter's view; interview, August 2000

Emil Zatopek 1922–2000

Czech long-distance runner. In the 1952 Olympic Games he won gold medals in the 5,000 metres, 10,000 metres, and marathon.

Roger Bannister
1929–

1 Zatopek isn't human in his achievement. While he goes for a 20 mile run on his only free day, we lie here panting and moaning that the gods are unkind to us.

attributed

Zinédine Zidane 1972–

French footballer. He has played for Bordeaux, Juventus, and France, and was European Footballer of the Year in 1998 and 2000.

Zinédine Zidane
1972–

1 Everything I know about football, I learned on the street.

attributed

Author Index

Abbey, Edward 1927–89
American writer

pom-pom girl of American letters — WOLFE 3

Abse, Dannie 1923–
Welsh-born doctor and poet

in all his shining — ARCHIMEDES 1

Abzug, Bella 1920–98
American politician

Ford as his revenge — FORD 1
very serious woman — ABZUG 1

Acheson, Dean 1893–1971
American statesman

works by Mr Zane Grey — EISENHOWER 1

Acton, Harold 1904–94
English writer

sharp eye of a Hogarth — WAUGH 1

Acuff, Roy 1903–92
American singer and songwriter

sing like a bird — LANG 1

Adams, Abigail 1744–1818
American wife of John Adams

generous to the ladies — ADAMS 5

Adams, Gerry 1948–
Northern Irish politician

art of the *impossible* — ADAMS 3
Well done, David — TRIMBLE 1

Adams, John 1735–1826
American statesman

bid me burn your letters — ADAMS 1
explained ourselves — JEFFERSON 1
mongrel between pig and puppy — PAINE 1

Adams, Mrs Henry 1843–85

chaws more than he bites — JAMES 5

Adams, Victoria 1974–
English pop singer

have our wedding in a post box — BECKHAM 1

Addison, Joseph 1672–1719
English poet, dramatist, and essayist

Christian can die — ADDISON 2
Spectator of mankind — ADDISON 1

Adler, Larry 1914–
American-born mouth organist

aristocrat in everything he did — PORTER 1
Freud discovered the Id — THURBER 1

Agate, James 1877–1947
British drama critic and novelist

doesn't waste energy pretending to act — BOGART 1
like the heart of a red rose — TERRY 1
plays are the price we pay — SHAW 1
sheep painted by Raphael — LANGTRY 1
voice has not a tragic note — RICHARDSON 1
world at her feet — CAMPBELL 2

Akhmatova, Anna 1889–1966
Russian poet

bearer of light — SOLZHENITSYN 1
Fate did not leave anything out — AKHMATOVA 1

Alain 1868–1951
French philosopher

mistake is of higher quality — DESCARTES 1

Albert, Prince 1819–61
Consort of Queen Victoria

add his humble mite — ALBERT 2
not the master in the house — ALBERT 1
packed at the bottom of a trunk — EDWARD 1

Alcott, Louisa May 1832–88
American novelist

our pure-minded lads and lasses — TWAIN 1
take Fate by the throat — ALCOTT 1

Alcuin c.735–804
English scholar and theologian

so good and wise a ruler

CHARLEMAGNE 1

Aldiss, Brian 1925–
English science fiction writer

Shakespeare of science fiction

WELLS 1

Alexander, Field Marshal Earl
1891–1969
British Field Marshal

splendid Marshal under Napoleon

PATTON 1

Alexander, Tsar I 1777–1825
Tsar from 1801

curse of all the human race

NAPOLEON 1

Alexander the Great 356–323 BC
King of Macedon from 336 BC

If I were not Alexander

DIOGENES 1

not yet become lords of one

ALEXANDER 1

Alexandra, Tsarina 1872–1918

be Peter the Great

NICHOLAS 1

follow our Friend's councils

RASPUTIN 1

Ali, Muhammad 1942–
American boxer

Float like a butterfly

ALI 2

forget where October-November went

LISTON 1

gorilla in Manila

FRAZIER 2

He was the greatest

LOUIS 4

I'm the greatest

ALI 1

shook my relations in Africa

COOPER 5

should donate his face

FRAZIER 1

two pretty dancers

ROBINSON 4

Allen, Fred 1894–1956
American humorist

carries his money low

BENNY 1

Allen, Woody 1935–
American film director, writer, and actor

don't have a bad relationship

ALLEN 2

My one regret in life

ALLEN 1

other side of the comic prism

GRAHAM 1

wish it could go on forever

BROOKS 1

woman's man, a coward's coward

HOPE 1

Alliluyeva, Svetlana 1925–
daughter of Joseph Stalin

his shadow still stands

STALIN 1

Allison, Malcolm

kind of Rolls Royce Communist

CLOUGH 1

Alvarez, Luis Walter 1911–88
American physicist

no democracy in physics

FERMI 1

Amery, Leo 1873–1955
British Conservative politician

line of least resistance

ASQUITH 1

Amies, Hardy 1909–
English couturier

holds herself very well

ELIZABETH 9

Amis, Kingsley 1922–95
English novelist and poet

America, entertainment

ARMSTRONG 1

bouquet of old bogwort

THOMAS 1

common sense with wings

CLARKE 1

Dizzy is the world, art

GILLESPIE 1

gulp the stuff down

DICKENS 1

HATES the thigns I HATE

LARKIN 1

old idiot and very bad artist

GILL 1

One of the great denouncers

LAWRENCE 1

technologized the fairy-tale

FLEMING 2

works too hard and it shows

AMIS 5

Amis, Martin 1949–
English novelist

president of his own fan club	CONNORS 1
she moves like a puck	GRAF 1
stint of mental arithmetic	ASIMOV 1
stroke the squat black book	AMIS 1

Angelou, Maya 1928–
American writer

dared to love	ANGELOU 1

Annan, Noel 1916–
English historian and writer

used like an oyster-knife	LEAVIS 1

Anne, Princess Royal 1950–
British princess

cuddled by a complete stranger	ANNE 10
expect me to neigh	ANNE 9

Anonymous

All Sir Garnet	WOLSELEY 1
between me and my Calvin's	KLEIN 1
by bishops bred	WOLSEY 1
Can't act. Slightly bald	ASTAIRE 1
conscience of 20th-century physics	PAULI 1
could kiss her shadow	NIGHTINGALE 1
decent, honourable man	MAJOR 1
doubly pretty on the outside	BUSSELL 1
Egghead weds hourglass	MILLER 1
Egghead weds hourglass	MONROE 1
Ep's statues are junk	EPSTEIN 3
even become a Branch Manager	ELIOT 12
father of modern chemistry	BOYLE 2
first gentleman in Europe	GEORGE 10
flat, dishwatery utterances	LINCOLN 1
friend of the Sitwells	BEATON 1
go away and sin no more	CAROLINE 2
greatest discovery was Faraday	FARADAY 1
Hey, hey, LBJ	JOHNSON 4
His soul is marching on	BROWN 7
how very different	BERNHARDT 1
If I were to be reincarnated	BEATTY 1
If you seek a monument	WREN 1
I like Ike	EISENHOWER 2
In mild and quiet sort	TALLIS 1
introduced by a four-digit number	CLARKE 2
iron lady	THATCHER 1
ivory tower an uninhabitable slum	MILLER 2
I will be millions	PERÓN 1
Judas the Second	CECIL 1
King's Moll Reno'd	WINDSOR 2
little pink, quivering Ted	HEATH 1
make the world seem safer	MOSES 1
most superior person	CURZON 1
Mrs Simpson's pinched our king	WINDSOR 3
must have read the wrong edition	STOPES 1
nearest thing to death in life	KILMUIR 1
no careful father	EPSTEIN 2
none like unto Moses	MAIMONIDES 1
Nor can anyone understand Ein	EINSTEIN 1
paid to see Dr Grace bat	GRACE 1
persuaded to leave Moses	DE MILLE 1
piteously slain and murdered	RICHARD 3
Prudence is the other woman	BROWN 2
rare Ben Jonson	JONSON 1

Anonymous continued

Seven wealthy towns contend	HOMER 1
she saves her body for Gene Kelly	KELLY 1
Sir H. Davy's greatest discovery	DAVY 1
social skills of a whelk	BROWN 3
such soft toads	NELSON 1
Sun himself cannot forget	DRAKE 1
talked shop like a tenth muse	GLADSTONE 1
this day our daily Bradman	BRADMAN 1
Timothy has passed	LEARY 1
was alive and is dead	FREDERICK 1
weaned on a pickle	COOLIDGE 1
whole army division	NEUMANN 1
Winston is back	CHURCHILL 7
wolf that never sleeps	BADEN-POWELL 1
would wish otherwise	EDWARD 2
Would you buy a used car	NIXON 1
wrote a note for the milkman	CASTLE 1
your face in your hands	SARGENT 1

Anthony, Susan B. 1820–1906
American social reformer

prayed with his heels	DOUGLASS 1

Apollinaire, Guillaume 1880–1918
French poet

intent on the energetic	DUCHAMP 1
surgeon dissects a corpse	PICASSO 1

Arbus, Diane 1923–71
American photographer

nobody would see	ARBUS 1

Arbuthnot, John 1667–1735
Scottish physician and pamphleteer

welcome to a weary traveller	ANNE 1

Archer, Jeffrey 1940–
British Conservative politician and writer

Archangel Gabriel had stood	LIVINGSTONE 1
had a remarkable life with me	ARCHER 7

Archer, Mary 1944–
British scientist

I am cross with Jeffrey	ARCHER 2
talent for inaccurate précis	ARCHER 1

Arendt, Hannah 1906–75
American political philosopher

banality of evil	EICHMANN 1
heart's invisible furies	AUDEN 1
One only in company	ARENDT 1

Aristophanes c.450–c.385 BC
Athenian comic dramatist

contented there	SOPHOCLES 1

Aristotle 384–322 BC
Greek philosopher

dearer still is truth	PLATO 1

Arlott, John 1914–91
British writer and broadcaster

astutely directed weapon	TRUEMAN 1
memories of that timeless grace	COMPTON 1
sympathy with the bowled ball	HOBBS 1

Armstrong, Neil 1930–
American astronaut

stretched science and navigation	LINDBERGH 1

Arnold, Matthew 1822–88
English poet and essayist

apostle of the Philistines	MACAULAY 1
beautiful and ineffectual angel	SHELLEY 3
carrying coals to Newcastle	CARLYLE 1
glory of the Attic stage	SOPHOCLES 2
in St Theresa's little finger	KNOX 1
loosed our heart in tears	WORDSWORTH 1

	often be called bald	WORDSWORTH 2
	Out-topping knowledge	SHAKESPEARE 1
	pageant of his bleeding heart	BYRON 1
	Passion, vehemence, grief	BRONT&ED. 9
Arnold, Thomas 1795–1842 English historian and educator	my desire to reform them	ARNOLD 6
Ashe, Arthur 1943–93 American tennis player	closest athletic facility got blood all over you	ASHE 1 MCENROE 1
Ashton, Frederick 1904–88 British ballet dancer, choreographer, and director	intellectual strip teaser mauled in the process succeeding Queen Elizabeth	DUNCAN 1 NUREYEV 1 DE VALOIS 1
Asimov, Isaac 1920–92 Russian-born American writer and scientist	head face down on a keyboard	ASIMOV 2
Asquith, Herbert Henry 1852–1928 British Liberal statesman	sandhills of the Baldwin Cabinet Unknown Prime Minister	CHURCHILL 8 BONAR LAW 1
Asquith, Margot 1864–1945 British political hostess	all aqua, no vita brains go to his head great poster He can't see a belt only interested in buttons t is silent, as in *Harlow*	SACKVILLE-WEST 1 SMITH 4 KITCHENER 1 LLOYD GEORGE 1 GEORGE 16 HARLOW 1
Astor, Nancy 1879–1964 American-born British Conservative politician	kind of woman I would run from	ASTOR 1
Atkinson, E. L. 1882–1929 and **Cherry-Garrard, Apsley** 1882–1959 British polar explorers	walked willingly to his death	OATES 1
Attlee, Clement 1883–1967 British Labour statesman	he ended PM CH and OM I had a very good dog man who could make decisions monologue is not a decision most radical man I've known voice we heard	ATTLEE 1 BEVIN 1 STALIN 2 CHURCHILL 10 MACMILLAN 1 CHURCHILL 9
Atwood, Margaret 1939– Canadian novelist	going against the grain Jeremy Bentham of the Booker	CHARLES 14 ATWOOD 1
Aubrey, John 1626–97 English antiquary and biographer	certainly the greatest mechanic charitable to ingenious men extraordinary timorousness harmonical and ingenious king called him *the bear* *lady of* Christ's College pleasant smooth wit should be well cultivated that he was crack-brained	HOOKE 1 BOYLE 3 HOBBES 1 MILTON 1 HOBBES 2 MILTON 2 SHAKESPEARE 2 DESCARTES 2 HARVEY 1
Auden, W. H. 1907–73 English poet	apple falling towards England Children swarmed to him could not shock her more fulfil The Immanent Will his drill sergeants kind of refreshment I require	NEWTON 1 LEAR 1 AUSTEN 1 HARDY 4 KIPLING 1 POPE 1

Auden, W. H. continued

Let the Irish vessel lie	YEATS 2
Mad Ireland hurt you	YEATS 1
master of the middle style	DRYDEN 1
never wrong, the Old Masters	BRUEGEL 1
performed his life	WILDE 1
poets like Horace and Pope	HORACE 1
relation to the English language	BRITTEN 1
saved one Jew from Auschwitz	AUDEN 3
sensibility of a male adolescent	HOUSMAN 1
wedding-cake left out	AUDEN 2
When fawned on by Flush	BROWNING 5
whole climate of opinion	FREUD 2
without a tombstone	POE 1

Augustine, St of Hippo AD 354–430
Early Christian theologian

continency—but not yet	AUGUSTINE 1

Aung San Suu Kyi 1945–
Burmese political leader

do not find my work a burden	AUNG SAN 2
happy Prime Minister	BALFOUR 1
I am not a martyr	AUNG SAN 1

Austen, Jane 1775–1817
English novelist

because she *is* a woman	CAROLINE 3
dwell on guilt and misery	AUSTEN 2
intimate with him by instinct	SHAKESPEARE 3
little bit of ivory	AUSTEN 3
no business to write novels	SCOTT 6
said in his vindication	HENRY 6

Awdry, Revd W. 1911–97
English writer of children's books

He helped people see God	AWDRY 1

Ayer, A. J. 1910–89
English philosopher

I am the former Wykeham Professor of Logic	TYSON 1
mess of my personal life	AYER 1

Bacall, Lauren 1924–
American actress

life shows in your face	BACALL 1
so completely his own man	BOGART 2

Bacon, Francis 1561–1626
English lawyer, courtier, philosopher, and
essayist

all knowledge to be my province	BACON 1
fly with waxen wings	ESSEX 1
I do not look *about* me	BACON 2
stop them from getting worse	CECIL 2
thoughts, and secret observations	HENRY 5
write what men do	MACHIAVELLI 1

Bacon, Francis 1909–92
Irish painter

Who can I tear to pieces	BACON 9
without moving an eyelash	FREUD 1

Baden-Powell, Robert 1857–1941
English soldier

secret of my getting on	BADEN-POWELL 2

Bader, Douglas 1910–82
British airman

want to leave warmth behind	BADER 1

Baez, Joan 1941–
American singer and songwriter

eyes on Bob even when he is hiding	DYLAN 1
learning how to listen	BAEZ 1

Bagehot, Walter 1826–77
English economist and essayist

consecrated obstruction	GEORGE 3
edition of a great dinner	THACKERAY 1
experiencing nature	SHAKESPEARE 4
one of the smallest people	ANNE 2
serious and solemn thing	ARNOLD 7
soul of a martyr	GLADSTONE 2

| | special correspondent for posterity | DICKENS 2 |
| | utterly blind, dark, and impervious | PALMERSTON 1 |

Bailey, David 1938–
English photographer

Amusing little seams — BAILEY 1

Baker, Ginger 1939–
British rock musician

Cream was *my* band — CLAPTON 1

Bakunin, Michael 1814–76
Russian revolutionary and anarchist

world will perish — BEETHOVEN 1

Balanchine, George 1904–83
Russian-born American ballet dancer and
choreographer

dainty, tippety-tip dances — PAVLOVA 1
I, me, a beautiful man, alone — NUREYEV 2
little bit in everybody's dancing — ASTAIRE 2

Baldwin, James 1924–87
American novelist and essayist

allows them their self-respect — KING 3

Baldwin, Stanley 1867–1947
British Conservative statesman

manufacturing the plausible — LLOYD GEORGE 2
no spiritual conflict — EDWARD 6

Balfour, Arthur James 1848–1930
British Conservative statesman

no melancholy in this house — VICTORIA 1
young man of promises — CHURCHILL 11

Ball, Zoë 1970–
British entertainer

I get paid to be a fool — BALL 1

Ballesteros, Severiano 1957–
Spanish golfer

as bingo, bango, bongo — BALLESTEROS 1

Balliett, Whitney 1926–
American writer

Streisand each song — STREISAND 1

Balzac, Honoré de 1799–1850
French novelist

If I'm not a genius — BALZAC 1
not deep, but very wide — BALZAC 2

Bangs, Lester 1948–82
American critic

how far he can spread one note — MORRISON 5

Bankhead, Tallulah 1903–68
American actress

pure as the driven slush — BANKHEAD 1
Shakespeare and the Bible — BANKHEAD 2
thick as a London fog — GARBO 1

Banks, Tony 1943–
British Labour politician

elected a foetus — HAGUE 1

Banks-Smith, Nancy

up pops a python — ARCHER 3

Bannister, Roger 1929–
British runner and neurologist

glimpse of the greatest freedom — BANNISTER 1
run on his only free day — ZATOPEK 1

Barber, Lynn 1944–
British journalist

concocted the externals of a life — HOPKINS 1
heart the size of a pea — HELLER 1
improper and enormous madam — BURCHILL 1
She stands too close — MOWLAM 1
trying to pass for a grown-up — CLARK 1

Barber, Samuel 1910–81
American composer

circumference of silence — BARBER 1

Barbirolli, John 1899–1970
English conductor

excess when you are young — DU PRÉ 1
like a dancing dervish — BEECHAM 1

Bardot, Brigitte 1934–
French actress

cat transformed into a woman — BARDOT 1
I gave my beauty and my youth — BARDOT 2

Baring, Evelyn 1841–1917
British diplomat and administrator

consults the Prophet Isaiah · GORDON 1

Baring, Maurice 1874–1945
English man of letters

genius does what it must · MOZART 1
took herself as much for granted · BERNHARDT 2

Barnes, Julian 1946–
English novelist

gave me a burn of envy · SMITH 8

Barr, Roseanne 1953–
American comedian

about thirty-five pages · ARNOLD 5

Barrie, J. M. 1860–1937
Scottish writer and dramatist

can't abide children · BARRIE 1
follow him in her nightie · MARY 5
something hitherto hidden · HARDY 5

Barrymore, John 1882–1942
American actor

can do with no effort · COOPER 2
sit out front and watch me · BARRYMORE 1

Barth, Karl 1886–1968
Swiss Protestant theologian

angels play only Bach · MOZART 2

Barthes, Roland 1915–80
French writer and critic

knowledge reduced to a formula · EINSTEIN 2

Bartlett, Vernon 1894–1983
British journalist and writer

destined to rule the world · HITLER 1

Bartók, Béla 1881–1945
Hungarian composer

after the composer was dead · MENUHIN 1

Baryshnikov, Mikhail 1948–
American ballet dancer

arrogance of the gods · NUREYEV 3

Baudelaire, Charles 1821–67
French poet and critic

but an earthly spirit · RAPHAEL 1
cat hung up by its tail · WAGNER 1
Cervantes-turned-Voltairean · GOYA 2
curious mixture of scepticism · DELACROIX 2
haunted by bad angels · DELACROIX 1
nightmare full of unknown things · GOYA 1
no longer merely a passion · DELACROIX 3
special satanic grace · BRUEGEL 2
sturdy idealist · REMBRANDT 1
style of burning ice · ROBESPIERRE 1

Baxter, Beverley 1891–1964
British journalist and Conservative
politician

finally married the Mayor · BEAVERBROOK 1

Bayley, John 1925–
English academic

dark escort of Alzheimer's · MURDOCH 1

Beaton, Cecil 1904–80
English photographer

all that was rare and mysterious · PAVLOVA 2
artist of the secret, prying lens · CARTIER-BRESSON 1
beautiful and ugly · JAGGER 1
bite an apple every day · HEPBURN 3
come so readily under her spell · ELIZABETH 22
his bulging fishy eyes · COCTEAU 1
If they were dead I do not mind · NUREYEV 4
lazy and hated any power · ASHTON 1
Life is a delightful wonderland · HOCKNEY 1
like a toddler on the sands · BETJEMAN 1
made out of pink marzipan · DIOR 1

Malice in Wonderland	BEATON 2
new type of beauty	HEPBURN 1
once the very spirit of youth	COWARD 1
second-rate American with no charm	WINDSOR 4
She was a female Brummell	CHANEL 1
six-foot tall, extremely handsome	WAUGH 2
son of an ordinary Spanish boatman	BALENCIAGA 1
so well-read and generally intelligent	KORDA 1
ugly little frog	FONTEYN 1
Very *grand seigneur*	DIAGHILEV 1
wild untamed quality of genius	GARBO 2
wisdom of the world in her eyes	BLIXEN 1

Beaverbrook, Lord 1879–1964
Canadian-born British newspaper
proprietor and Conservative politician

care which way he travelled	LLOYD GEORGE 3
chorus of a third-rate revue	BALDWIN 1
cock won't fight	EDWARD 7
Mr Baldwin denouncing sanctions	BALDWIN 2
not print criticism	NORTHCLIFFE 1
sit on the wharf	CURZON 2
sudden journey to heaven	CURZON 3
suicide 25 years after	HAIG 1
you're a hard man	BENNETT 4

Beckett, Margaret 1943–
British Labour politician

Being effective	BECKETT 1

Beckett, Samuel 1906–89
Irish dramatist, novelist, and poet

her savage loving	BECKETT 3
not about something	JOYCE 1
stain upon the silence	BECKETT 2

Bee, Barnard Elliott 1823–61
American Confederate general

standing like a stone wall	JACKSON 10

Beecham, Thomas 1879–1961
English conductor

better than any damned foreigner	BEECHAM 2
If I were a dictator	MOZART 3
knew he'd been doctored	SARGENT 4
most selfish man	WAGNER 2
Mr Gladstone of music	BEETHOVEN 2
musical Malcolm Sargent	KARAJAN 1
Protestant counterpoint	BACH 1
reeking of Horlicks	BOULT 1
Towers of St Pancras Station	ELGAR 1

Beeching, H. C. 1859–1919
English clergyman

don't know isn't knowledge	JOWETT 1

Beerbohm, Max 1872–1956
English critic, essayist, and caricaturist

Assyrian wax statue	WILDE 2
game at which two can play	SOCRATES 1
had brains to scatter	SHAW 2
instinctive erudition	BEARDSLEY 1
lived in the limelight	CHURCHILL 12
old gentleman with iron-grey whiskers	BYRON 2
played it in tights	CAROLINE 4
swear-word in a rustic slum	MASEFIELD 1
whole of Barsetshire	TROLLOPE 1
wonderful all-round man	MORRIS 4

Beethoven, Ludwig van 1770–1827
German composer

immortal god of harmony	BACH 2
kneel before his tomb	HANDEL 1
ordinary human being after all	NAPOLEON 2
seize Fate by the throat	BEETHOVEN 3

Behan, Brendan 1923–64
Irish dramatist

bloody postman   BEHAN 1

Bell, Clive 1881–1964
English art critic

passionate, grenadier-like   SACKVILLE-WEST 2

Bell, Joseph 1837–1911
Scottish physician

cataract of drivel   DOYLE 1

Bell, Martin 1938–
British journalist and Independent
politician

force was with us   GUINNESS 1
white suit and the green socks   BELL 1

Bellamy, David 1933–
English botanist

father of conservation   SCOTT 1

Bellany, John 1942–
Scottish painter

let you tug the hem of his garment   MACDIARMID 1

Belloc, Hilaire 1870–1953
British poet, essayist, historian, novelist,
and Liberal politician

Gentlemen, I am a Catholic   BELLOC 2
His sins were scarlet   BELLOC 1
Remote and ineffectual Don   CHESTERTON 1

Bellow, Saul 1915–
American novelist

splash your files in the paper   BELLOW 1

Benchley, Peter 1940–
American writer

He is B-movie literate   SPIELBERG 1

Benchley, Robert 1889–1945
American humorist

no talent for writing   BENCHLEY 1

Benét, Stephen Vincent 1898–1943
American poet and novelist

all lost, wild America   BOONE 1
picklocks of biographers   LEE 5
tough as a hickory rail   LINCOLN 2

Benét, William Rose 1886–1950
American poet

treefull of angels   BLAKE 1

Benn, Tony 1925–
British Labour politician

believed that you ought to discuss   CALLAGHAN 1
great man, sitting on the floor   GANDHI 2
Not a reluctant peer   BENN 1
rescued a child from drowning   BENN 2
something that builds up a man   WILSON 1
that's a theological argument   WILSON 2
those who think and teach   THATCHER 2
to the left of new Labour   HEATH 2
wrong to blame Marx   MARX 6

Bennett, Alan 1934–
English actor and dramatist

habit of being 60   LARKIN 2
Leave us our villains   HAIG 2
life of self-indulgence   COOK 3
too timid to seem nasty   BENNETT 2
two minutes' silence   PINTER 1
unremitting humanity   DICKENS 3
Winsome, lose some   BENNETT 1

Bennett, Arnold 1867–1931
English novelist

detected only once   LLOYD GEORGE 4

Bennett, Jill 1931–90
English actress

man who hates his mother   OSBORNE 1

Bennett, Tony 1926–
American singer

all fell in love   SINATRA 1

Benny, Jack 1894–1974
American comedian and actor

I'm thinking it over — BENNY 2

Benson, E. F. 1867–1940
English novelist

purpose at white heat — GLADSTONE 3

Bentley, Edmund Clerihew
1875–1956
English writer

Abominated gravy — DAVY 2
ball got lost in his beard — GRACE 2
he is no longer alive — CLIVE 1
Ought never to have occurred — GEORGE 4
Overcame his natural *bonhomie* — MILL 1
Say I am designing St Paul's — WREN 2

Bentley, Nicolas 1907–78

about whom all is forgotten — CAMPBELL-BANNERMAN 1

Bentsen, Lloyd 1921–
American Democratic politician

you're no Jack Kennedy — QUAYLE 1

Berg, Alban 1885–1935
Austrian composer

feel I am like Beethoven — BERG 1

Berger, John 1926–
British writer and art critic

colours together like cymbals — MATISSE 1

Bergman, Ingmar 1918–
Swedish film director

images of life and death — BERGMAN 1

Bergman, Ingrid 1915–82
Swedish actress

I am a migratory bird — BERGMAN 2
rather proud of my wrinkles — BERGMAN 3

Berlin, Isaiah 1909–97
British philosopher

first militant lowbrow — ROUSSEAU 1

Berlioz, Hector 1803–69
French composer

deeply interesting romance — BERLIOZ 1
Mendelssohn is his prophet — MENDELSSOHN 1

Bernadotte, Jean Baptiste
1763–1844
French soldier, king of Sweden

not been conquered by men — NAPOLEON 3

Bernard, Jeffrey 1932–97
English journalist

as though God is stooping down — OSBORNE 2
wings off his butterflies — COOK 4
wrong bar or bed — BERNARD 1

Bernard, St of Clairvaux
1090–1153
French theologgian and abbot

From the Devil he came — HENRY 1

Berners, Lord 1883–1950
English composer, artist, and writer

backing into the limelight — LAWRENCE 14

Berra, Yogi 1925–
American baseball player

if it's good for baseball — MONROE 2
rooming with Phil Rizzuto — DIMAGGIO 1

Best, George 1946–
Northern Irish footballer

accused of being arrogant — GASCOIGNE 1
all have a go at him — BECKHAM 2
women, fast cars and booze — BEST 1

Betjeman, John 1906–84
English poet

his bees-winged eyes — WILDE 3
Spirits of well-shot woodcock — GEORGE 17
warm New England breast — LONGFELLOW 1

Bevan, Aneurin 1897–1960
British Labour politician

desiccated calculating machine	GAITSKELL 1
flamboyant labels on empty luggage	MACMILLAN 2
gives himself so generously	CHURCHILL 15
paying a visit to Woolworth's	CHAMBERLAIN 1
petrified adolescence	CHURCHILL 14
still fighting Blenheim	CHURCHILL 13
thirty pieces of silver	BEVAN 1

Bevin, Ernest 1881–1951
British Labour politician and trade unionist

Not while I'm alive	BEVAN 2

Bible, The 1611

bright Occidental Star	ELIZABETH 1

Bidot, Marcel
French cyclist

knew how to lift his backside	MERCKX 1

Bierce, Ambrose 1842–c.1914
American writer

sovereign of insufferables	WILDE 4

Biffen, John 1930–
British Conservative politician

tigress surrounded by hamsters	THATCHER 3

Billington, Rachel 1942–
British writer

character out of Bosch	MURDOCH 2

Bird, Dickie 1933–
English cricket umpire

flow past me like a ghost	HOLDING 1
have been the end of Dickie	RICHARDS 5
one of nature's witterers	BIRD 1

Birtwistle, Harrison 1934–
English composer and clarinettist

Composing's not voluntary	BIRTWISTLE 1

Bishop, Elizabeth 1911–79
American poet

can practically sit on it	MOORE 6
everything a poet should have been	KEATS 1
not much space for living	THOMAS 2

Bismarck, Otto von 1815–98
German statesman

honest broker	BISMARCK 1
lath of wood painted	SALISBURY 1
old Jew! That is the man	DISRAELI 1

Bizet, Georges 1838–75
French composer

bursts of marvellous passion	VERDI 1

Black, Cilla 1943–
British entertainer

he's not my type, chuck	GALLAGHER 1

Black, Conrad 1944–
Canadian-born businessman

king of all larrikins	KEATING 1

Blackwell, Elizabeth 1821–1910
Anglo-American physician

sad wearing away of the heart	BLACKWELL 1

Blair, Tony 1953–
British Labour statesman

critical question of judgement	HAGUE 2
People's Princess	DIANA 1
relations with the Monarch	BLAIR 1
What you do is more important	BIRTWISTLE 2

Blake, Robert 1916–

concerned with effect	STRACHEY 1

Blake, William 1757–1827
English poet

beneath my notice	BLAKE 3
gives too much of Caesar	DANTE 1
hired by the Satans	REYNOLDS 1
not drawing, but *inspiration*	CONSTABLE 1
see a round disc of fire	BLAKE 2

| | shadows are of a filthy brown | RUBENS 1 |
| | wrote in fetters | MILTON 3 |

Blakemore, Colin 1944–
British physiologist

to make a small contribution — BLAKEMORE 1

Blanchflower, Danny 1926–93
Northern Irish footballer

bad players who are a luxury — HODDLE 1
He had ice in his veins — BEST 2
usually knew how he would beat you — MATTHEWS 1

Bliss, Arthur 1891–1975
English composer

like a great theatrical production — STOKOWSKI 1

Bloy, Léon 1846–1917
French writer

no more than second-best — NAPOLEON 4

Blunden, Edmund 1896–1974
English poet

body and his bat were as truly one — HUTTON 1
feeling nervous and shy — BLUNDEN 1

Blunkett, David 1947–
British Labour politician

failed football coach — HODDLE 2

Boccaccio 1313–75
Italian writer, poet, and humanist

Mortal sight was often puzzled — GIOTTO 1

Bogarde, Dirk 1921–
British actor and writer

thought she was a witch — WOOLF 1
with tears in her eyes — MACDONALD 1

Bogart, Humphrey 1899–1957
American actor

He means what he says — TRACY 1
PLEASE FENCE ME IN — BACALL 2
plenty of women and no newspapermen — SINATRA 2
with only a sweatshirt — BRANDO 1

Boleyn, Anne 1507–36
wife of Henry VIII

withdraw your princely favour — BOLEYN 1

Bolger, Ray 1904–87
American actor

never saw a rainbow — GARLAND 1

Boltzmann, Ludwig 1844–1906
Austrian physicist

man with my nose and beard — SCHILLER 1

Bonar Law, Andrew 1858–1923
Canadian-born British Conservative
statesman, Prime Minister 1922–3

all great men are frauds — BONAR LAW 2

Bonham Carter, Helena 1966–
British actress

kept his shoes on too — ALLEN 3

Bonham-Carter, Violet 1887–1969
English Liberal politician

carried the world on his shoulders — KENNEDY 3

Bono 1960–
Irish rock star

really awful haircut — BONO 1

Boothby, Robert 1900–86
British Conservative politician

thought of as 'cards' — BEECHAM 3

Boothroyd, Betty 1929–
British Labour politician

like miners' coal dust — BOOTHROYD 1

Border, Allan 1955–
Australian cricketer

Quiet, but ruthless — BORG 1

Borges, Jorge Luis 1899–1986
Argentinian writer

live my life looking forward — BORGES 1

Borges, Leonor Acevedo 1876–1975 · waste your time with Anglo-Saxon · BORGES 2

Borgia, Cesare 1476–1507 · Caesar or nothing · BORGIA 1
Italian statesman

Born, Max 1882–1970 · most lovable person · SCHRÖDINGER 1
German theoretical physicist · theoretical physics is actual · BORN 1

Borrow, George 1803–81 · most singular genius · FIELDING 1
English writer

Boswell, James 1740–95 · glad to collect the gold dust · JOHNSON 8
Scottish lawyer and biographer · infidel wasps or venomous insects · GIBBON 1
· plain sensible man · COOK 1
· poisons our literary club · GIBBON 2
· until the shrimp became a whale · WILBERFORCE 1

Botham, Ian 1955– · out of their way to knock down · BOTHAM 1
English cricketer

Bottomley, Horatio 1860–1933 · No, reaping · BOTTOMLEY 2
British newspaper proprietor and financier · University of Life · BOTTOMLEY 1

Boulding, Kenneth 1910– · hits a very large nail · MCLUHAN 1
American academic

Boulez, Pierre 1925– · create the spirit of the time · RAVEL 1
French conductor and composer · if the audience wants him · TCHAIKOVSKY 1
· refreshing but not very bright · CAGE 1

Bourke-White, Margaret 1906–71 · attracts me like a closed door · BOURKE-WHITE 1
American photojournalist

Bowen, Elizabeth 1899–1973 · high altar on the move · SITWELL 1
Anglo-Irish novelist · stupid person's idea · HUXLEY 1

Bowie, David 1947– · fought like a *madman* · BOLAN 1
English rock musician · play my part right the way · BOWIE 1

Bowra, Maurice 1898–1971 · more dined against than dining · BOWRA 1
English scholar and literary critic · talked much but published little · BERLIN 5

Boycott, Geoffrey 1940– · means avoiding the truth · BOYCOTT 1
English cricketer

Boy George 1961– · still an A1 freak · BOY GEORGE 1
English pop singer and songwriter · trapped in a woman's body · MADONNA 1

Boyle, Jimmy 1944– · look on me as an animal · BOYLE 1
Scottish murderer

Braddock, James 1905–74 · electric bulb in your face · LOUIS 5
American boxer

Brando, Marlon 1924– · way of making a living · BRANDO 2
American actor

Braun, Wernher von 1912–77 · I could have found out · BRAUN 1
German-born American rocket engineer

Brearley, Mike 1942– · greatest match-winner · BOTHAM 2
English cricketer

Brenan, Gerald 1894–1987 · non-stop talker · MILLER 4
British travel writer and novelist · tears I shed for her · CARRINGTON 1

Brennan, Diarmuid · couldn't be much of a secret agent · BETJEMAN 2

Bridges, Robert 1844–1930
English poet

Pure Shakespeare   MASEFIELD 2

Briers, Richard 1934–
British actor

No horses or fast cars   BRIERS 1

Britten, Benjamin 1913–78
English composer, pianist, and conductor

wiser about Peter than he is   PEARS 1
words are not my medium   BRITTEN 2

Bronowski, Jacob 1908–74
Polish-born British scientist, writer, and
broadcaster

ask immensely simple questions   EINSTEIN 3
guardian of integrity   MORE 2
personal, Socratic gift   BORN 2

Brontë, Charlotte 1816–55
English novelist

all buried here   BRONTË 3
animated, and unaffected   GASKELL 1
as an eagle does a vulture   THACKERAY 2
her nature stood alone   BRONTË 10
more *real* than *true*   AUSTEN 4
she is sagacious and profound   SAND 1
stoop on carrion   FIELDING 2

Brontë, Patrick 1777–1861
Anglo-Irish clergyman

much better than likely   BRONTË 4

Brook, Peter 1925–
English theatre director

like an aircraft circling   GIELGUD 1

Brooke, Rupert 1887–1915
English poet

nest of maggots   WEBSTER 5

Brooks, Gwendolyn 1917–
American poet

He opened us   MALCOLM 1

Brooks, Louise 1906–85
American actress

distant view of harmless shadows   FIELDS 1

Brooks, Mel 1926–
American film actor and director

loudest noise to the most people   BROOKS 2
stuck a pen in his heart   TOLSTOY 1

Brophy, Brigid 1929–95
English writer

delightful department of gardening   COLETTE 1

Brougham, Henry 1778–1868
Scottish lawyer and politician

devoured every kind of learning   WATT 1
never lived in a garret   BYRON 3

Brown, Christy 1932–81
Irish writer

prisoner in a cell   BROWN 1

Brown, Craig 1957–

slogging through the praise   AMIS 2

Brown, Gordon 1951–
Scottish Labour politician

my mentor and my tormentor   CASTLE 2
now just the fireside rug   HESELTINE 1

Brown, James 1928–
American soul singer and songwriter

turned off the air conditionin'   PRESLEY 1

Brown, John Mason 1900–69

barged down the Nile   BANKHEAD 3

Brown, Tina 1953–
English writer and editor

air of witty indiscretion   CROSSMAN 1

Browning, Elizabeth Barrett
1806–61
English poet

admirable *poetical writer*	ARNOLD 1
Ariel of poets	HERRICK 1
forced on him by circumstances	PEEL 1
heart within blood-tinctured	BROWNING 6
large-brained woman	SAND 2
slipped down over the wall	BROWNING 1

Browning, Robert 1812–89
English poet

God and Robert Browning knew	BROWNING 7
handful of silver	WORDSWORTH 3
inmost wailing of the wire	PAGANINI 1
loved well because he hated	DANTE 2
she was the poet	BROWNING 2
Spitting from lips once sanctified	FITZGERALD 1
starry paladin	SIDNEY 1
Sun-treader	SHELLEY 4

Brownmiller, Susan 1935–
American writer

broken pieces of John Lennon	ONO 1

Bruce, Lenny 1925–66
American comedian

what is, not what should be	BRUCE 1

Brummell, Beau 1778–1840
English dandy

Who's your fat friend	GEORGE 11

Brunel, Isambard Kingdom
1806–59
English engineer

ambition is rather extensive	BRUNEL 1

Bruno, Frank 1961–
English boxer

man with the golden fist	BRUNO 1

Bryson, Bill 1951–
American travel writer

some really extreme danger	BRYSON 1

Buchanan, Pat 1938–
American Republican politician

skeleton in their closet	CLINTON 1

Buchman, Frank 1878–1961
American evangelist

anti-Christ of Communism	HITLER 2

Buckle, Richard 1916–
British dance critic

fear of offending orange	FONTEYN 2

Bull, Deborah 1963–
English ballet dancer

Salieri not a Mozart	BULL 1

Bullard, Edward 1907–80
English geophysicist

'something for nothing' tradition	RUTHERFORD 1

Bullock, Alan 1914–
British historian

exercised a greater influence	FREUD 3

Bulmer-Thomas, Ivor 1905–93
British Conservative politician

to school without any boots	WILSON 3

Bulwer-Lytton, Edward 1803–73
British novelist and politician

Out-babying Wordsworth	TENNYSON 1
Rupert of Debate	DERBY 1
Theseus of legislative reform	BENTHAM 1

Bunting, Basil 1900–85
English poet

so much music into so few bars	SCARLATTI 1

urchill, Julie 1960–	cry quite easily—psychopaths do	BURCHILL 2
nglish journalist and writer	*Divorced Lesbian Sluts*	ALCOTT 2
	'g' is silent	PAGLIA 1
	man's woman	MONROE 3
	perfect Disneyland childhood	JACKSON 7
	secular saint	DIANA 2
urgess, Anthony 1917–93	as much to do with visceral problems	BEETHOVEN 4
nglish novelist and critic	ideal reader of my novels	BURGESS 1
	in an insurrection of slaves	BEHN 1
	not an army of unalterable law	ELIOT 13
urke, Edmund 1729–97	bears are not philosophers	ROUSSEAU 2
sh-born Whig politician and man of	chip of the old 'block'	PITT 3
tters	ten thousand swords	MARIE-ANTOINETTE 1
urne-Jones, Edward 1833–98	beautiful romantic dream	BURNE-JONES 1
nglish painter and designer	got no ideas	REYNOLDS 2
	looks like such despair	BEARDSLEY 2
urnet, Gilbert 1643–1715	comfortable shroud to die in	CHARLES 7
cottish prelate		
urney, Fanny 1752–1840	all that is interesting	SIDDONS 1
nglish novelist and diarist	condemns whatever he disapproves	JOHNSON 9
	fallen from the moon	BANKS 1
	first lady's comet	HERSCHEL 1
	King has not a happier subject	HERSCHEL 4
	witty, sarcastic, ingenious	WALPOLE 1
urns, George 1896–1996	standing ovation for dinner	JOLSON 1
merican comedian		
urns, Robert 1759–96	Charlie he's my darling	STUART 1
cottish poet	I rhyme for fun	BURNS 2
	Poetic Genius of my Country	BURNS 1
	Scottish prejudice in my veins	WALLACE 2
	Welcome to your gory bed	ROBERT 1
urroughs, William S. 1914–97	true folk hero	NIXON 2
merican novelist		
urton, Richard 1821–90	Prince of African travellers	STANLEY 1
nglish explorer and translator	translated a doubtful book	BURTON 1
urton, Richard 1925–84	vicious about me	BURTON 5
Velsh actor		
usby, Matt 1909–94	give the ball to George	BEST 3
ritish football manager		
ush, Barbara 1925–	name things after you	BUSH 2
merican First Lady	old, white-headed and large	BUSH 1
ush, George 1924–	boring kind of guy	BUSH 4
merican Republican statesman	Oh, the vision thing	BUSH 3
ush, George W. 1946–	do not reinvent myself	BUSH 9
merican Republican statesman		
ush, Laura 1946–	running for president	BUSH 10
merican First Lady		
utler, Joseph 1692–1752	pretending to extraordinary revelations	WESLEY 1
nglish bishop and theologian		

Butler, Josephine 1828–1906
British social reformer

able to *tell* her so much more · · · · · · · · · ANDERSON

Butler, R. A. 1902–82
British Conservative politician

be a butcher and know the joints · · · · · · BUTLER
best Prime Minister we have · · · · · · · · · EDEN
biting people in the pants · · · · · · · · · · ATTLEE
fascinated by Parliament · · · · · · · · ELIZABETH 1
greatest adventurer · · · · · · · · · · CHURCHILL 1
greatest parliamentary orator · · · · · · · · BEVAN
half mad baronet · · · · · · · · · · · · · · · EDEN
seemed to know all the numbers · · · · · · MACLEOD

Butler, Samuel 1835–1902
English novelist

symphony by Wordsworth · · · · · · · WORDSWORTH
two people miserable · · · · · · · · · · · CARLYLE

Byatt, A. S. 1936–
English novelist

male turkeycocking · · · · · · · · · · · · · · AMIS

Byrd, William 1543–1623
English composer

Tallis is dead and Music dies · · · · · · · · · TALLIS

Byrom, John 1692–1763
English poet

Tweedledum and Tweedledee · · · · · · · · HANDEL

Byron, Lord 1788–1824
English poet

apostle of affliction · · · · · · · · · · · · ROUSSEAU
arbiter of others' fate · · · · · · · · · · · NAPOLEON
as generally beloved as a man · · · · · · · · SCOTT
Cincinnatus of the West · · · · · · · · WASHINGTON
compound of inspired clay · · · · · · · · · BURNS
could be no common person · · · · · · · · SHELLEY
cut his throat at last · · · · · · · · · CASTLEREAGH
darkness equal light · · · · · · · · · · REMBRANDT
eagle beak so curled · · · · · · · · · · WELLINGTON
Europe's Liberator · · · · · · · · · · · WELLINGTON
explain his explanation · · · · · · · · · COLERIDGE
found myself famous · · · · · · · · · · · · BYRON
glory and the nothing · · · · · · · · MARLBOROUGH
great, though uncouth · · · · · · · · · · · HOGG
had been Petrarch's wife · · · · · · · · · PETRARCH
he beat them all · · · · · · · · · · · · · SHERIDAN
He'll visit you in hell · · · · · · · · · · · · PAINE
He moved some hundred miles off · · · · · · BOONE
infernal glare of colours · · · · · · · · · · RUBENS
intellectual eunuch · · · · · · · · · · CASTLEREAGH
Jeanie Deans-looking body · · · · · · · · EDGEWORTH
life eternal gave · · · · · · · · · · · · · SAPPHO
lull the babe at nurse · · · · · · · · · · COLERIDGE
mental masturbation · · · · · · · · · · · · KEATS
most *faultless* of poets · · · · · · · · · · · POPE
no matter what he said · · · · · · · · · · BERKELEY
out-of-the-way notions · · · · · · · · · · SHELLEY
prince of poets · · · · · · · · · · · · · · MILTON
rottenness of eighty years · · · · · · · · · GEORGE
Sapping a solemn creed · · · · · · · · · · GIBBON
She thinks like a man · · · · · · · · · DE STA&ED.L
smiled Spain's chivalry away · · · · · · CERVANTES
snuffed out by an article · · · · · · · · · · KEATS
still was born a wit · · · · · · · · · · · · CANNING
stupendous genius! damned fool · · · · WORDSWORTH
unwilling to do any thing · · · · · · · · · · HUNT

	verse is merely prose	WORDSWORTH 6
	very *epic* appearance	SOUTHEY 2
	Wordsworth sometimes wakes	WORDSWORTH 5
	worth all your laurels	BYRON 4
	written much blank verse	SOUTHEY 1

Caesar, Julius 100–44 BC
Roman general and statesman

first in a village · CAESAR 1

Cage, John 1912–92
American composer, pianist, and writer

expert in the unknown	BOULEZ 1
music which is not going anywhere	SATIE 1
not even a burglar alarm	CAGE 2
one who continued the past	SCHOENBERG 1

Cage, Nicolas 1964–
American actor

| constantly sculpting | LYNCH 1 |
| King Lear and the buffoon | PRESLEY 2 |

Caine, Michael 1933–
English film actor

attaining the impossible dream	HUSTON 1
eel-and-pie yob	CAINE 2
My career must be slipping	CAINE 1

Cale, John 1942–
Welsh pop singer

always at an incredible level	MCGUINN 1
hear any more questions	REED 1
spoilt, clean-scrubbed schoolboy	MORRISON 1

Callaghan, James 1912–
British Labour statesman

friendliness but not friendship	ELIZABETH 11
further you got from Britain	THATCHER 4
When I am shaving in the morning	CALLAGHAN 2

Callas, Maria 1923–77
American-born operatic soprano

First I lost weight · CALLAS 1

Callow, Simon 1949–
English actor, director, and writer

| dandy delicately negotiating | TYNAN 1 |
| spirit of absolution | GISH 1 |

Calment, Jeanne 1875–1997
French centenarian

Ugly as sin · VAN GOGH 1

Cameron, Julia Margaret 1815–79
English photographer

| embodiment of a prayer | CARLYLE 3 |
| longed to arrest all beauty | CAMERON 1 |

Campbell, Alastair 1957–
British journalist

supposed to like Tory MPs · CLARK 2

Campbell, Mrs Patrick 1865–1940
English actress

Gods have whispered to	BARRIE 2
London wants flappers	CAMPBELL 3
no woman will be safe	SHAW 3
sew rings on the new curtains	GISH 2
skating on thin ice	BANKHEAD 4

Campbell, Naomi 1970–
British fashion model

make my boyfriends famous · CAMPBELL 1

Campbell, Roy 1901–57
South African poet

most violent action · AUDEN 4

Campbell, Thomas 1777–1844
Scottish poet

| once shot a bookseller | NAPOLEON 6 |
| What millions died | CAESAR 2 |

Camus, Albert 1913–60
French novelist, dramatist, and essayist

| elemental force in motion | HITLER 3 |
| I owe to football | CAMUS 1 |

Cantona, Eric 1966–
French footballer

strength to say yes · CANTONA 1

Cantor, Eddie 1892–1964
American comedian

sent a thrill up your spine · JOLSON 2

Capote, Truman 1924–84
American writer and novelist

discern Beaton's influence BEATON 3

Capra, Frank 1897–1991
Italian-born American film director

Ford is the Compleat Director FORD 8
never look phoney himself COOPER 3

Cardin, Pierre 1922–
French couturier

would never try to impress CARDIN 1

Cardus, Neville 1889–1975
English critic and writer

brilliance safe and sure BRADMAN 2
Falstaff, Puck, Malvolio BEECHAM 4
worse than breaking stones BACH 3

Carew, Richard 1555–1620
English poet

miracle of our age SIDNEY 2

Carew, Thomas c.1595–1640
English poet and courtier

universal monarchy of wit DONNE 1

Carey, George 1935–
English Anglican churchman

management bishop CAREY 1

Carey, John 1934–
British literary scholar

alchemist's laboratory GRAVES 1
body like a slag heap CHESTERTON 2
kind of human cactus HOUSMAN 2
mind didn't infect CARLYLE 4
perpetual adolescent FLAUBERT 1
poetical geiger counter STEVENSON 4
sanest person in Europe CHEKHOV 1
Scrooge seem frolicsome LARKIN 3
series of immaculate masks POPE 3
standby was Worry ELIOT 14
stay on a brain health-farm DAWKINS 1
tour operator's nightmare LAWRENCE 2

Carlyle, Jane Welsh 1801–66
Wife of Thomas Carlyle

awful and dreary blank BYRON 6
natural unassuming woman GASKELL 2
not at all the sort CARLYLE 5

Carlyle, Thomas 1795–1881
Scottish historian and political philosopher

calico millennium COBDEN 1
cartload of quiet sand SOUTHEY 3
choose a bonnet for herself VICTORIA 2
dull-cruel-looking black eyes WEBSTER 1
fat ill-shapen shoulders COLERIDGE 3
his unity with himself EMERSON 1
How great a possibility COLERIDGE 4
hungering after sweets KEATS 4
infinitely better educated BURNS 4
jaws like a crocodile's WORDSWORTH 8
largest soul in all England JOHNSON 10
live under Niagara MACAULAY 2
make his whole life a heroic poem MILTON 5
one of the solidest of men KNOX 2
pattern John Bull of his century COBBETT 1
phantasm of a man GLADSTONE 4
put in the *panels* ELIOT 1
seagreen Incorruptible ROBESPIERRE 2
secure the main chance BECKET 1
superlative Hebrew conjuror DISRAELI 2

	too fond of demonstrating everything	MILL 2
	took a man's life along	SCOTT 8
Carnegie, Andrew 1835–1919	combined Moses and Joshua	WASHINGTON 1
Scottish-born American industrialist	get to be a man and kill a king	CARNEGIE 1
Caroline of Ansbach 1683–1737	firstborn is the greatest ass	FREDERICK 2
Wife of George II		
Caroline of Brunswick 1768–1821	not at all as handsome	GEORGE 12
Wife of George IV		
Carrey, Jim 1962–	Picasso school of acting	CAGE 4
Canadian actor		
Carrington, Dora 1893–1932	hope I shall die at forty	CARRINGTON 2
English painter		
Carrington, Lord 1919–	belief that he was whispering	WHITELAW 1
British Conservative politician		
Carswell, Catherine 1879–1946	bread and wine of music	BACH 4
Scottish novelist and critic	brings me into the Pleiades	MOZART 4
	full violence of living	BURNS 5
	morose as any open clematis flower	LAWRENCE 3
Carswell, Stanley 1926–	so randy . . . and so literate	BOSWELL 1
Scottish comic actor		
Carter, Angela 1940–92	carved out of the Union Jack	TOWNSHEND 1
English novelist		
Cartier-Bresson, Henri 1908–	photographing rocks	ADAMS 2
French photographer and film director		
Cartland, Barbara 1901–	pink on the walls	CARTLAND 1
English writer		
Casals, Pablo 1876–1973	she moves *with* the music	DU PRÉ 2
Spanish cellist		
Cassatt, Mary 1844–1926	*Pour moi* it is so and so	CÉZANNE 1
American painter		
Castle, Barbara 1910–	best man among them	THATCHER 5
British Labour politician	fight for what I believe in	CASTLE 3
Castro, Fidel 1927–	intelligent bandit	KENNEDY 4
Cuban statesman	Sermon on the Mount	MARX 7
Catherine the Great 1729–96	certainly canonise Montesquieu	MONTESQUIEU 1
Empress of Russia from 1762	I shall be an autocrat	CATHERINE 1
Catullus c.84–c.54 BC	of advocates the best	CICERO 1
Roman poet		
Caulfield, Mr Justice 1914–	Has she fragrance	ARCHER 8
British judge		
Cavendish, Margaret c.1624–74	my own poor brain did make	CAVENDISH 1
English woman of letters		
Caxton, William c.1421–91	father and first founder	CHAUCER 1
first English printer		
Cecil, William 1520–98	all this for a song	SPENSER 1
English statesman	her singular kindness	ELIZABETH 2
	Seek not to be Essex	CECIL 3

Celan, Paul 1920–70
Romanian-born German poet

There's nothing in the world — CELAN 1

Cézanne, Paul 1839–1906
French painter

can't attain the intensity — CÉZANNE 2
Monet is only an eye — MONET 1

Chagall, Marc 1887–1985
Russian-born French painter and graphic
artist

married to colour — CHAGALL 1

Chandler, Raymond 1888–1959
American writer of detective fiction

If my books had been any worse — CHANDLER 1
too clean to be a genius — CHANDLER 2
too sober to be a champ — HEMINGWAY 1
tough without a gun — BOGART 3

Chandrasekhar, Subrahmanyan
1910–95
Indian-born American astronomer

I have always been alone — CHANDRASEKHAR 1

Chanel, Coco 1883–1971
French couturière

I chose the dresses — CHANEL 2
man who doesn't know women — DIOR 2

Channon, Henry ('Chips') 1897–1958
American-born British Conservative
politician and diarist

looking like the Jungfrau — MARY 1
slinking out of a bank — HUXLEY 2

Chaplin, Charlie 1889–1977
English film actor and director

I remain one thing — CHAPLIN 1

Chapman, George c.1559–1634
English scholar, poet, and dramatist

only learned architect — JONES 4

Charles I 1600–49
King from 1625

martyr of the people — CHARLES 1
not suffer in life, honour — STRAFFORD 1

Charles II 1630–85
King from 1660

kill me to make James king — JAMES 3
Let not poor Nelly starve — GWYN 1
my actions are my ministers' — CHARLES 8

Charles V 1500–58
Holy Roman Emperor from 1519

counter to all Christianity — LUTHER 1
lost such a worthy councillor — MORE 3

Charles, Prince of Wales 1948–
Heir apparent to the British throne

majesty of the language — CRANMER 1
Queen Victoria in her old age — MOUNTBATTEN 1

Charles, Ray 1930–
American pianist and singer

my one and only sister — FRANKLIN 1
My people made me what I am — CHARLES 16

Charlotte, Princess 1796–1817
Daughter of George IV

become as bad as she was — CAROLINE 5

Charlton, Bobby 1935–
English footballer

give me a life sentence — CHARLTON 1

Charteris, Lord 1913–
the Queen's former private secretary

bit of an ostrich — ELIZABETH 23
Duchess of York is a vulgarian — YORK 1

Chateaubriand, François-René
1768–1848
French writer and diplomat

Vice leaning on the arm — TALLEYRAND 1

Chaucer, Geoffrey c.1343–1400
English poet

grete poete of Ytaille — DANTE 3

Chekhov, Anton 1860–1904
Russian dramatist and short-story writer

literature is my mistress — CHEKHOV 2
more love in electricity and steam — TOLSTOY 2

Cher 1946–
American pop singer and actress

counterfeit $20 bill

CHER 1

Cherry-Garrard, Apsley 1882–1959
British polar explorer

For a dash to the pole

AMUNDSEN 1

in the devil of a hole

SHACKLETON 1

scientific and geographical

SCOTT 4

Cherwell, Lord 1886–1957
German-born British physicist

improprieties of Clodius

CHERWELL 1

Chesterfield, Lord 1694–1773
English writer and politician

do mean things for profit

WALPOLE 4

Chesterton, G. K. 1874–1936
English essayist, novelist, and poet

abysses may exist

BRONT&ED. 5

Chuck it, Smith

SMITH 5

daintily dressed Walt Whitman

MEREDITH 1

English poet but a French soldier

BELLOC 3

far more gloomy character

HUXLEY 3

Man Who Knew the Fairies

YEATS 3

multiply his souls

WILDE 5

never have bullied a pupil

COBBETT 2

never written any poetry

SHAW 4

number of jolly good ideas

CHESTERTON 3

own towering style

TENNYSON 2

pick the right word

STEVENSON 5

sincere but curiously simple

PAINE 3

sort of village atheist

HARDY 6

Chetwode, Lord 1869–1950

Call me 'Field Marshal'

BETJEMAN 3

Chevalier, Maurice 1888–1972
French singer and actor

Considering the alternative

CHEVALIER 1

that nightingale talent

MACDONALD 2

Chirac, Jacques 1932–
French statesman

economics of a housewife

THATCHER 6

Chisholm, Melanie 1974–
English pop singer

would like to like reading

CHISHOLM 1

Chopin, Frédéric 1810–49
Polish-born French composer

money means nothing to me

CHOPIN 1

only woman who can play my music

SCHUMANN 1

rouged, on stilts, and blowing

LISZT 1

Chrétien, Jean 1934–
Canadian Liberal statesman

acting as a head waiter

MULRONEY 1

Christie, Agatha 1890–1976
English writer of detective fiction

perfect sausage machine

CHRISTIE 1

Churchill, Jennie 1854–1921
American-born society hostess

most beautiful woman in the room

CHURCHILL 1

no real purpose in life

CHURCHILL 17

Churchill, Lord Randolph 1849–94
British Conservative politician

forest laments

GLADSTONE 5

old man in a hurry

GLADSTONE 6

those damned dots

CHURCHILL 2

Churchill, Winston 1874–1965
British Conservative statesman

always at his coolest

WELLINGTON 3

Bessie, you're ugly

BRADDOCK 1

Churchill, Winston continued

bloodthirsty guttersnipe	HITLER 4
bludgeon for the platform	SMITH 6
boneless wonder	MACDONALD 8
called upon to give the roar	CHURCHILL 20
candle in that great turnip	BALDWIN 3
coincidence of his facts	CROSSMAN 2
Cross of Lorraine	DE GAULLE 2
disappointing when you meet	BERLIN 1
female llama surprised	DE GAULLE 1
fierce and comprehending being	SHAW 5
foremost champion of freedom	ROOSEVELT 4
good and immoral	ASQUITH 2
good deal to be modest about	ATTLEE 3
Happy Warrior of Squandermania	LLOYD GEORGE 5
hard-boiled egg of a man	STALIN 3
I am a glow-worm	CHURCHILL 21
ingenuity to re-rat	CHURCHILL 18
in victory unbearable	MONTGOMERY 1
Italy's pinchbeck Caesar	MUSSOLINI 2
kicking his something something	PICASSO 2
like a plague bacillus	LENIN 1
lose the war in an afternoon	JELLICOE 1
maggot in the Nazi apple	HESS 1
modern conception of a robot	MOLOTOV 1
morning had been golden	CURZON 4
nothing but abject surrender	CHAMBERLAIN 2
opportunity of looking at it	SUTHERLAND 1
poison in your coffee	ASTOR 2
poison in your coffee	CHURCHILL 19
posing as a fakir	GANDHI 3
powerful graceful cat	BALFOUR 3
read Homer for fun	GLADSTONE 7
shaped by this one man	LLOYD GEORGE 6
sheep in sheep's clothing	ATTLEE 4
skin of malice	TROTSKY 1
sunk in a bigger ship	MOUNTBATTEN 2
That Wuthering Height	REITH 1
very daring and skilful opponent	ROMMEL 1
very like England	ANNE 3
wasted no time on minor revenges	WILLIAM 2
whipped jackal is frisking	MUSSOLINI 1
wicked and moral	BALFOUR 2
Wonderful on paper	BERLIN 6

Cicero 106–43 BC
Roman orator and statesman

born when I was consul	CICERO 2
decorated, and got rid of	AUGUSTUS 1
living in Plato's Republic	CATO 1

Clairmont, Claire 1798–1879
lover of Byron

wild originality	BYRON 7

Clapton, Eric 1945–
English guitarist, singer, and
composer

everything he did was correct	HENDRIX 1
one man and his guitar versus the world	CLAPTON 2

Clare, Anthony 1942–
British psychiatrist

'Overweight', 'dumpy', 'spinster'	WIDDECOMBE 1

Clarendon, Earl of 1609–74
English statesman and historian

brave bad man	CROMWELL 1
head to contrive	HAMPDEN 2
immoderate lover of the Scottish	CHARLES 2
threw away the scabbard	HAMPDEN 1
was not confident enough	CHARLES 3

Clark, Alan 1928–99
British Conservative politician

dignity and competence	MOWLAM 2
eyelashes as thick as caterpillars	CARTLAND 2
If you have bright plumage	CLARK 3

Clark, Joe 1939–
Canadian statesman

his life was Canada	DIEFENBAKER 1

Clark, Kenneth 1903–83
English art historian

Janus of the Gothic Revival	PUGIN 1
most relentlessly curious man	LEONARDO 1
pale and withdrawn, dissolves	BOTTICELLI 1

Clarke, Arthur C. 1917–
English science fiction writer

never stopped growing	CLARKE 3
our first engineering saint	FULLER 1

Clary, Julian 1959–
British entertainer

mess around with women	CLARY 1

Claudel, Paul 1868–1955
French poet and dramatist

primitive mystic, a lost spring	RIMBAUD 1

Clay, Henry 1777–1852
American politician

easily swayed by the basest men	JACKSON 1

Cleaver, Eldridge 1935–98
American political activist

Black history began	MALCOLM 2

Clemenceau, Georges 1841–1929
French statesman

I have no political system	CLEMENCEAU 1
satisfied with Ten Commandments	WILSON 11
thinks he is Jesus Christ	WILSON 10
thinks he is Napoleon	LLOYD GEORGE 7

Clift, Montgomery 1920–66
American actor

Can't that man make any mistakes	RICHARDSON 2

Clinton, Bill 1946–
American Democratic statesman

career as a golf instructor	BLAIR 2
comeback kid	CLINTON 3
full of the broken promises	MILOSEVIC 1
I didn't inhale	CLINTON 2
Presidents have feelings	CLINTON 11

Clinton, Hillary Rodham 1947–
American lawyer

hard dog to keep	CLINTON 5
standing by my man	CLINTON 4
stayed home and baked cookies	CLINTON 12

Clive, Lord 1725–74
British general

astonished at my own moderation	CLIVE 2
reserved for some end	CLIVE 3

Clough, Arthur Hugh 1819–61
English poet

led us all out into the desert	EMERSON 2
quite capable of talking	GASKELL 3

Clough, Brian 1935–
English football player and manager

my dear Mam's mangle	CLOUGH 2
stings like one too	BROOKING 1

Clunes, Martin 1962–
English actor

led as wild a life	CLUNES 1

Cobbett, William 1762–1835
English political reformer and radical
journalist

At his expiring flambeau	PAINE 4
leave his country as good	COBBETT 3

Cocteau, Jean 1889–1963
French dramatist and film director

active loafer, a wise madman	WELLES 1
gave comic titles to his music	SATIE 2
madman who thought he was	HUGO 1
noble, acute, and deadly	MODIGLIANI 1

Coe, Sebastian 1956–
British athlete and politician

athletics has always been about	COE 1

Coetzee, J. M. 1940–
South African novelist

sex as demonic as Sade	AUSTEN 5

Coghill, Nevill 1899–1980
British literary scholar

clearly no laughing matter	JONSON 2

Cohen, Leonard 1934–
Canadian singer and writer

Beethoven of pop music	MITCHELL 1
blaze in a very bright light	JOPLIN 1
sheer perfection of his style	CHARLES 17
soaked to the skin	COHEN 2
voice can make *me* cry	COHEN 1

Coleman, Michael and **Burke, Brian**

matchstalk cats and dogs	LOWRY 1

Coleridge, Nicholas 1957–
British journalist

colours of Disneyland	VALENTINO 1

Coleridge, Samuel Taylor
1772–1834
English poet, critic, and philosopher

breezy day in May	FIELDING 3
catches fire by its own motion	DRYDEN 2
dared not hope to live	HAZLITT 1
flashes of lightning	KEAN 1
Found death in life	COLERIDGE 5
his own oceanic mind	SHAKESPEARE 6
iron pokers into true-love knots	DONNE 2
my gentle-hearted Charles	LAMB 1
myriad-minded Shakespeare	SHAKESPEARE 5
only ground of morality	PEPYS 1
soul of Rabelais	SWIFT 1
to make one Milton	NEWTON 2

Collins, Joan 1933–
British actress

What I need is a wife	COLLINS 1

Collins, Michael 1890–1922
Irish revolutionary

always drawing lines and circles	DE VALERA 1

Collins, William 1721–59
English poet

almost lost in Art	JONSON 3

Colman, George , the Younger
1762–1836
English dramatist

hewed passages through the Alps	JOHNSON 11
moved to flute and hautboys	GIBBON 4

Colum, Mary 1880?–1957
Irish writer

like an extinct volcano	MARKIEVICZ 1

Comfort, Nicholas

brain might blow up	COMFORT 1

Compton-Burnett, Ivy 1884–1969
English novelist

like to give him a push	JAMES 6
not much to say	COMPTON-BURNETT 1

Congreve, William 1670–1729
English dramatist

avoid coveting my neighbour's wife	CONGREVE 1

Conlon, Gerry 1954–
Irish member of the Guildford Four

like a runaway train	CONLON 1

Connally, Ray

to finish being invented | BEATTY 2

Connery, Sean 1930–
Scottish actor

Almost Buddha-like | GORBACHEV 1
old man with a good face | CONNERY 2
one is not Bond | CONNERY 1

Connolly, Billy 1942–
Scottish comedian

falling down a flight of stairs | CARNEGIE 2
warriors do at night | TYSON 2

Connolly, Cyril 1903–74
English writer

appeared honourably ineligible | HOME 1
could not blow his nose | ORWELL 1
have always disliked myself | CONNOLLY 1
ravishing verbal woodcuts | LEE 1
twist the milksop's arm | HEMINGWAY 2

Connor, William Neil 1909–67
British journalist

piece of calculating candy-floss | LIBERACE 1

Connors, Jimmy 1952–
American tennis player

if you're going to be a louse | CONNORS 2
Nobody reminds me of me | CONNORS 3

Conrad, Joseph 1857–1924
Polish-born English novelist

cased in British tar | CONRAD 1
deep gloom or in violent sunshine | JAMES 7
grimacing, haunted creature | DOSTOEVSKY 1

Constable, John 1776–1837
English painter

calm sunshine of the heart | CLAUDE 1
deadly slime of his touch | BYRON 8
more lasting impression | WHITE 1
paint with tinted steam | TURNER 1
water escaping from mill-dams | CONSTABLE 2

Cook, Margaret

card with a robin on it | COOK 6

Cook, Peter 1937–95
English satirist and actor

passing the time enjoyably | COOK 5
selfish, vain, greedy | MOORE 2

Cooke, Alistair 1908–
American journalist and broadcaster

as much golf as possible | EISENHOWER 3
candid, decent Everyman underneath | CAGNEY 1
colourful human adjunct | FROST 4
giant Pickwick, an aging Micawber | WODEHOUSE 1
girl every young man wanted | PICKFORD 1
he is a gent | PLAYER 1
his marvellous low-key cunning | BURTON 6
like a peregrinating secretary | REAGAN 3
matinee idol toughened | COOPER 4
Merlin posing as Whistler's Mother | WRIGHT 1
not always 'The Golden Bear' | NICKLAUS 1
only in permanent soft-focus | DIETRICH 1
playing a sour piano | MORTON 1
Popeye in the flesh | CHICHESTER 1
reveals the Garbo's face | GARBO 3
she called me 'Sir' | ROGERS 1

Coolidge, Calvin 1872–1933
American Republican statesman

minding my own business | COOLIDGE 2

Coon, Caroline 1945–
British artist

mutant alien from another planet | BOWIE 2

Cooper, Henry 1934–
English boxer

Louisville Lip | ALI 3

Copland, Aaron 1900–90
American composer

All those notes, think I	RACHMANINOV 1
music of a gentleman-farmer	VAUGHAN WILLIAMS 1
still a part of the nineteenth century	SCHOENBERG 2

Coppola, Francis Ford 1939–
American film director, writer, and producer

genius, but no talent	COPPOLA 1
this strange, moody Titan	BRANDO 3
water's the same shape	COPPOLA 2

Copps, Sheila
Canadian politician

company boy from a company town	MULRONEY 2

Corneille, Pierre 1606–84
French dramatist

has done me too much good	RICHELIEU 1

Cornford, Frances 1886–1960
English poet

young Apollo, golden-haired	BROOKE 1

Correggio c.1489–1534
Italian painter

I, too, am a painter	CORREGGIO 1

Courbet, Gustave 1819–77
French painter

without having lied	COURBET 1

Coward, Noël 1899–1973
English dramatist, actor, and composer

apocryphal jokes I never made	COWARD 2
Be one quarter as good	DIETRICH 2
covering a teapot	SITWELL 2
Everything bothers him	OSBORNE 3
extinguished like a candle-snuffer	CHARLES 15
finest light-comedy actor	HARRISON 3
hated people more easily	MAUGHAM 1
legs don't belong to him	PEARS 2
mad rocking-horse	MACDONALD 3
May I call you 338	LAWRENCE 15
next war will be photographed	BEATON 4
one long wail of self-pity	WILDE 6
only two great playwrights	RATTIGAN 1
part well above his capabilities	EDEN 3
pomposity and intricacy	PROUST 1
Two wise acres	SITWELL 3
un-nailed from the cross	EVANS 2

Cowper, William 1731–1800
English poet

reader of the works of God	NEWTON 3
thresh his old jacket	JOHNSON 12

Coxhead, Elizabeth 1909–

image of Irish womanhood	MARKIEVICZ 2

Craig, Gordon 1872–1966
English actor and theatre director

look of a blooming martyr	TYNAN 2

Cranborne, Lord 1946–
British Conservative peer

miserable limpet	MAJOR 2

Crane, Hart 1899–1932
American poet

Being, of all, least sought for	DICKINSON 1

Cranmer, Thomas 1489–1556
Anglican prelate and martyr

hand that wrote it	CRANMER 2

Crawford, Christina 1939–

consummate match for my mother	DAVIS 1
flowers and plants were plastic	CRAWFORD 1

Crawford, Joan 1908–77
American actress

Wally Beery's grandmother	CRAWFORD 2

Crazy Horse c.1842–1877
Oglala Sioux leader

They say we massacred him	CUSTER 1

Crick, Francis 1916–
English biophysicist

only five fingers   CRICK 1

Cripps, Stafford 1889–1952
British politician

power of the spirit   GANDHI 4
treat Jesus better   CHURCHILL 22

Critchley, Julian 1930–2000
British Conservative politician and
journalist

could not see a parapet   HESELTINE 2
hitting it with her handbag   THATCHER 7

Cromwell, Oliver 1599–1658
English soldier and statesman

Cruel necessity   CHARLES 4
warts and all   CROMWELL 2

Crosby, Bing 1903–77
American singer and film actor

He was an average guy   CROSBY 1
voice of a lifetime   SINATRA 3

Crosby, David 1941–
American rock singer

as modest as Mussolini   MITCHELL 2

Cross, J. W. 1840–1924

took possession of her   ELIOT 2

Crossman, Richard 1907–74
British Labour politician

While there is death   GAITSKELL 2

Cukor, George 1899–1983
American film director

mind is wonderfully unclouded   MONROE 4
no flesh-and-blood lover ever saw   CRAWFORD 3
soft about her toughness   HARLOW 2
what a master storyteller   DE MILLE 2

cummings, e. e. 1894–1962
American poet

more than we notice you notice   AYER 2

Cunninghame Graham, R. B.
1852–1936
Scottish writer, traveller, and politician

beautiful set of false teeth   CAMPBELL-BANNERMAN 2

Curie, Marie 1867–1934
Polish-born French physicist

interested in things   CURIE 1
leaned on the sweet serenity   CURIE 6

Curie, Pierre 1859–1906
French physicist

derive more good than bad   NOBEL 1

Curio

Every woman's man   CAESAR 3

Curran, John Philpot 1750–1817
Irish judge

silver plate on a coffin   PEEL 2

Currie, Edwina 1946–
British Conservative politician

apart from abolish cellulite   HURLEY 1

Curtis, Tony 1925–
American actor

It's like kissing Hitler   MONROE 5

Curzon, Lord 1859–1925
British Conservative politician

utmost insignificance   BALDWIN 4

Dali, Salvador 1904–89
Spanish painter

dispossessed the Jewish people   FREUD 4
imitate Immortal Greece   RAPHAEL 2
Picasso is a genius   PICASSO 3
Picasso is Spanish, I am too   DALI 2
sacks of reinforced concrete   LE CORBUSIER 1
wanted to be a cook   DALI 1

Dalton, Hugh 1887–1962
British Labour politician

Dante Alighieri 1265–1321
Italian poet

Danton, Georges Jacques 1759–94
French revolutionary

Darlington, W. A. 1890–1979

Darwin, Charles 1809–82
English natural historian

Darwin, Francis 1848–1925
English botanist

David, Elizabeth 1913–92
British cookery writer

Davies, Hunter 1936–
British journalist and writer

Davies, Marion 1897–1961
American actress

Davies, Robertson 1913–95
Canadian novelist

Davis, Bette 1908–89
American actress

Davis, Colin 1927–
English conductor

Davis, Miles 1926–91
American jazz trumpeter

Davis, Sammy Jnr. 1925–90
American entertainer

Davis, Steve 1957–
English snooker player

Davitt, Michael 1846–1905
Irish nationalist

Davy, Humphrey 1778–1829
English chemist

Dawson of Penn, Lord 1864–1945
Physician to King George V

Day, Robin 1923–2000
British journalist and broadcaster

little mouse shall lead them	ATTLEE 5
loyal to his own career	CROSSMAN 3
Homer, the sovereign poet	HOMER 2
master of those who know	ARISTOTLE 1
my master and my author	VIRGIL 1
now Giotto has the palm	GIOTTO 2
show my head to the people	DANTON 1
like a demented typewriter	BRIERS 2
better short abstract	WALLACE 1
damnable heresies	HUXLEY 7
interesting lecture on silence	BABBAGE 1
made to bear directly	DARWIN 1
mind seemed a very narrow one	CARLYLE 6
parts of my brain now atrophied	DARWIN 2
Survival of the Fittest	SPENCER 1
take only a single volume	MILTON 6
tried to bribe him with sixpence	DARWIN 3
voice of authority	BEETON 1
One of nature's Boy Scouts	LINEKER 1
take a trip to Russia	MAYER 1
bellyaching about something	AMIS 3
bend the bow of Ulysses	FRYE 1
excellent life of somebody else	DAVIES 2
he was lazy, self-indulgent	FLYNN 1
Playing our parts	DAVIS 2
silently acted out the fantasies	VALENTINO 3
last scene of Siegfried	DAVIS 6
vision of the Garden of Eden	MOZART 5
doesn't need any horns	HOLIDAY 1
average Negro could never *hope*	DAVIS 10
colored, one-eyed Jew	DAVIS 9
don't come with instructions	HIGGINS 1
Englishman of the strongest type	PARNELL 1
never could learn to swim	DALTON 1
moving peacefully towards	GEORGE 18
always an institution	DAY 2

Dayan, Moshe 1915–81
Israeli statesman and general

most exciting and dramatic	DAYAN 1

de Beauvoir, Simone 1908–86
French novelist and feminist

consumed by passion for you	SARTRE 1
kind of emptiness	GARBO 4
nothing can be read	BARDOT 3

de Bernières, Louis 1954–
British novelist and short-story writer

transformed into archangel	DE BERNIÈRES 1

Debray, Régis 1940–
French Marxist theorist

observed all the things	BALZAC 3

Debussy, Claude 1862–1918
French composer and critic

colour of my soul is iron-grey	DEBUSSY 1
creates the illusion of music	BERLIOZ 2
mistook for a dawn	WAGNER 3
pink sweet stuffed with snow	GRIEG 1

Defoe, Daniel 1660–1731
English novelist and journalist

long, lascivious reign	CHARLES 9

Degas, Edgar 1834–1917
French painter and sculptor

can draw so well	CASSATT 1
most ridiculous man in Paris	WHISTLER 1
talent at twenty-five	DEGAS 1

de Gaulle, Charles 1890–1970
French soldier and statesman

Jeanne d'Arc and Bonaparte	DE GAULLE 4
taken up the broken blade	DE GAULLE 3
Voltaire in the Bastille	SARTRE 2

Delacroix, Eugène 1798–1863
French painter

truest artist I have ever met	CHOPIN 2
What beauty	MICHELANGELO 1

de la Renta, Oscar 1932–
American fashion designer

enjoys his success the most	VALENTINO 2

Delius, Frederick 1862–1934
English composer

seen the best of the earth	DELIUS 1
set the whole Bible to music	PARRY 1

de Mille, Agnes 1908–
American dancer and choreographer

mid-air like jugglers' balls	DE MILLE 3
used to steal her remarks	RAMBERT 1

de Mille, Cecil B. 1881–1959
American film producer and director

bring out all the glamour	SWANSON 1
high C for fifty-five seconds	MACDONALD 4
how to photograph thought	GRIFFITH 1
That word is dedication	PICKFORD 2

Dempsey, Jack 1895–1983
American boxer

Tall men come down to my height	DEMPSEY 1

Dench, Judi 1934–
British actress

get a little bit of him	DENCH 1

Deneuve, Catherine 1943–
French actress

life is not about men	DENEUVE 1

de Pisan, Christine c.1364–c.1430
Italian writer

Nurtured on iron	JOAN 1

De Quincey, Thomas 1785–1859
English essayist and critic

ever condescended to cut it	LOCKE 1

Derby, Lord 1799–1869
British Conservative statesman

keeping up a show of Liberalism	PALMERSTON 2

de Valera, Eamon 1882–1975
American-born Irish statesman

misunderstood Madame	MARKIEVICZ 3
only to examine my own heart	DE VALERA 2

de Valois, Ninette 1898–2001
Irish choreographer, ballet dancer, and
teacher

Dreadful name — BULL 2
she couldn't dance herself — RAMBERT 2

Devonshire, Georgiana, Duchess of 1757–1806

eloquence was so great — PITT 5
like a brilliant player of billiards — FOX 1

Diaghilev, Sergei 1872–1929
Russian ballet impresario

composer and *not* homosexual — TCHAIKOVSKY 2
Half tart, half royal family — DE VALOIS 2

Diana, Princess of Wales 1961–97

queen in people's hearts — DIANA 3

Dickinson, Emily 1830–86
American poet

They shut me up in prose — DICKINSON 2

Diderot, Denis 1713–84
French philosopher and man of letters

charms of Cleopatra — CATHERINE 2
second in all genres — VOLTAIRE 1
thou singular genius — RICHARDSON 7

Didion, Joan 1934–
American writer

brilliantly, surpassingly antisocial — HUGHES 1

Diefenbaker, John G. 1895–1979
Canadian statesman

there's snow on the roof — DIEFENBAKER 2

Dietrich, Marlene 1901–92
German-born American actress and singer

all real men are gentle — HEMINGWAY 3
my legs are my fortune — DIETRICH 3

Diogenes c.400–c.325 BC
Greek philosopher

stand out of my sun — DIOGENES 2

Dirac, Paul 1902–84
British theoretical physicist

great mathematical beauty — SCHRÖDINGER 2

Disney, Walt 1901–66
American animator and film producer

invention of a mouse — DISNEY 1

Disraeli, Benjamin 1804–81
British Tory statesman and novelist

caught the Whigs bathing — PEEL 3
great master of gibes — SALISBURY 2
If Gladstone fell — GLADSTONE 10
inebriated with the exuberance — GLADSTONE 9
noble Lord is the Prince Rupert — DERBY 2
only ginger-beer and not champagne — PALMERSTON 3
prove evidence of his potency — PALMERSTON 4
rushed into the debate — GLADSTONE 8
take a message to Albert — VICTORIA 3
to the top of the greasy pole — DISRAELI 3
traces the steam-engine — PEEL 4
uncharitableness of the Horse Guards — WOLSELEY 2
We authors, Ma'am — DISRAELI 4

Disraeli, Mary Anne d. 1872

see Dizzy in his bath — DISRAELI 5

Dobson, Frank 1940–
British Labour politician

ego has landed — LIVINGSTONE 2
I am unspun — DOBSON 1

Docherty, Tommy 1928–
Scottish football player and manager

forty-eight hours at Old Trafford — KISSINGER 1
King Herod was to babysitting — HILL 1

Dodd, Ken 1931–
British comedian

play the old Glasgow Empire — FREUD 5

Donne, John 1572–1631
English poet and divine

Anne Donne, Un-done — DONNE 3
worth an history — HILLIARD 1

Donovan 1946–
British pop singer and songwriter

certainly had a wicked tongue — LENNON 1

Dorsey, Hebe 1925–87
American fashion journalist

like a season without God — SAINT LAURENT 1
real-life Andy Warhol portrait — RHODES 4

Dostoevsky, Anna 1846–1918

incapable of love — DOSTOEVSKY 2

Dostoevsky, Fedor 1821–81
Russian novelist

pair of boots is better — PUSHKIN 1

Douglas, James, Earl of Morton
c.1516–81
Scottish courtier

neither feared nor flattered — KNOX 3

Douglas, Lord Alfred 1870–1945
English poet

minor to the major poet — YEATS 4

Douglass, Frederick c.1818–95
American former slave and civil rights
campaigner

national temple of cruelty and blood — BROWN 8
slave was made a man — DOUGLASS 2

Dowd, Maureen 1952–
American journalist

queen of surfaces — DIANA 4

Drayton, Michael 1563–1631
English poet

drunk deep of the Pierian spring — JONSON 4
Such a King Harry — HENRY 3
that fine madness — MARLOWE 1

Dreyfuss, Richard 1947–
American actor

he's still twelve years old — SPIELBERG 2

Dryden, John 1631–1700
English poet, critic, and dramatist

equal with the best abroad — PURCELL 1
fountain of good sense — CHAUCER 3
great, ere fortune made him so — CROMWELL 3
here is God's plenty — CHAUCER 2
invades authors like a monarch — JONSON 5
soft philosopher of love — OVID 1
soul of Chaucer was transfused — SPENSER 2
spectacles of books — SHAKESPEARE 7
very Janus of poets — SHAKESPEARE 8
will never be a poet — SWIFT 2

Du Deffand, Mme 1697–1780
French literary hostess

because you have become rich — VOLTAIRE 2

Dudek, Louis 1918–
Canadian poet

read Richler in the original — RICHLER 1
seem to have any questions — FRYE 2

Duncan, Isadora 1878–1927
American dancer and teacher

marble seemed to flow — RODIN 1
only dance masters I could have — DUNCAN 2

Dundy, Elaine 1947–

tart lemon sorbet — VIDAL 1

Dunne, Dominick 1925–
American journalist and writer

got inside the establishment — CAPOTE 1

Dunne, Irene 1898–1990
American actress and singer

gave Fred sex appeal — ROGERS 2

du Pré, Jacqueline 1945–87
English cellist

everything to be played his way — CASALS 1
never bothered me what happened — DU PRÉ 3

Duras, Marguerite 1914–
French writer

so beautiful as this ugly woman — CALLAS 2

Dürer, Albrecht 1471–1528
German engraver and painter

not in the manner of the classics	DÜRER 1
still the best in painting	BELLINI 1

Durrell, Gerald 1925–95
English zoologist and writer

write for money	DURRELL 2

Durrell, Lawrence 1912–90
English novelist and writer

fresh, crisp lettuce	DURRELL 1

Dvořá, Antonín 1841–1904
Czech composer

Mozart is sunshine	MOZART 6

Dyer, Edward d. 1607
English poet

wonder of our age	SIDNEY 3

Dylan, Bob 1941–
American singer and songwriter

as much from Cézanne	CÉZANNE 3
like busting out of jail	PRESLEY 3
washed-up has-been	DYLAN 2

Dyson, Esther 1951–
American businesswoman

think of who I am	DYSON 1

Dyson, Freeman 1923–
British-born American physicist

sort of *Bhagavad-Gita* ideal	FEYNMAN 1

Eddy, Nelson 1901–67
American singer and actor

cutting into frozen custard	MACDONALD 5

Eden, Beatrice d. 1957
First wife of Anthony Eden

excellent Number Two men	EDEN 4
just like Anthony Eden	STEVENSON 1

Edgeworth, Maria 1767–1849
English-born Irish novelist

while her head is among the stars	SOMERVILLE 1

Edison, Thomas Alva 1847–1931
American inventor

natural businessman	FORD 6
songs will live for ever	PUCCINI 1

Edmonds, Frances
English writer

without being actually comatose	GOWER 1

Edmonds, John 1944–
British trade unionist

failed diploma in ballooning	BRANSON 1

Edward III 1312–77
King of England from 1327

win his spurs	BLACK PRINCE 1

Edward VII 1841–1910
King from 1901

concept of an eternal mother	VICTORIA 4
walk behind the angels	VICTORIA 5

Edward VIII 1894–1972
King, 1936; afterwards Duke of Windsor

disapproved of Soviet Russia	GEORGE 19
Ice in the place of blood	MARY 3
invincible virtue	MARY 2
one matchless blessing	GEORGE 25
support of the woman I love	EDWARD 8

Ehrenreich, Barbara 1941–
American sociologist and writer

bedevilled by bladder problems	BUSH 5
distilled bathwater	REAGAN 1

Einhard c.770–840
Frankish chronicler

lofty stature	CHARLEMAGNE 2

Einstein, Albert 1879–1955
German-born theoretical physicist

as cold as a herring	CURIE 2
between politics and equations	EINSTEIN 6
bursting with envy	HITLER 5
choose to be a plumber	EINSTEIN 5
chosen one	WEIZMANN 1
comparable to Gandhi	SCHWEITZER 1

condescending attitude	GOETHE 1
deep insight and moral force	TOLSTOY 3
deplorable philosophe	MACH 1
did not acknowledge the work	GALILEO 1
do things in his spirit	GANDHI 5
experimenter, the theorist	NEWTON 4
fame has not corrupted	CURIE 4
father of modern physics	GALILEO 2
France will say that I am a German	EINSTEIN 4
Full of goodness and obstinacy	CURIE 3
I don't believe a word of it	HEISENBERG 1
joy by his mere presence	BOHR 1
knows what she is doing	NOETHER 1
living work of art	LORENTZ 1
loved mysterious Nature	FARADAY 2
most profound and pure people	SPINOZA 1
no illusions lulled him	FREUD 6
one who perpetually gropes	BOHR 2
opposition from mediocre minds	RUSSELL 1
remain apart from the world	PLANCK 1
stand up openly	KEPLER 1
with the moneybags of Carnegie	CARNEGIE 3
would visit him more often	ROOSEVELT 5
you are my closest brother	SCHRÖDINGER 3

Eisenhower, Dwight D. 1890–1969
American general and Republican
statesman

into the very heart of man	BOHR 3
just as little inside	MONTGOMERY 2

Eisenstaedt, Alfred 1898–1995
German-born American photographer

brain is 30 years old	EISENSTAEDT 1
click with people	EISENSTAEDT 2

Elcho, Lord 1721–87

damned cowardly Italian	STUART 2

Elgar, Edward 1857–1934
English composer

decent hearing of my work	ELGAR 2
giant, lofty and unapproachable	BRAHMS 1
heals and pacifies all men	BACH 5
make it fit their civilization	SHAW 6
organ part arranged	PARRY 2
so healthily good to one's soul	STEVENSON 6
sounds one is permitted to weave	ELGAR 3

El Greco 1541–1614
Cretan-born Spanish painter

not know how to paint	MICHELANGELO 2

Eliot, George 1819–80
English novelist

long sad years of youth	ELIOT 3

Eliot, T. S. 1888–1965
Anglo-American poet, critic, and dramatist

Crawling up like a louse	BECKET 2
genius for what precisely	LEWIS 5
If and Perhaps and But	ELIOT 15
live so long out of his native country	POUND 1
mean by 'being a poet'	SPENDER 1
model for all poets	DANTE 4
much possessed by death	WEBSTER 6
no idea could violate it	JAMES 8
rhythmical grumbling	ELIOT 16
unclouded by current opinions	BLAKE 4

Elizabeth, Queen, the Queen Mother 1900–
Queen Consort of George VI

extraordinary calmness and serenity   ELIZABETH 13
first the girls got the giggles   ELIOT 17

Elizabeth I 1533–1603
Queen from 1558

daughter of debate   MARY 6
faithful to the state   CECIL 4
glory of my crown   ELIZABETH 5
God may pardon you   ESSEX 2
heart and stomach of a king   ELIZABETH 4
If thy heart fails thee   RALEIGH 1
not for your bad legs   CECIL 5
turned out in my petticoat   ELIZABETH 3

Elizabeth II 1926–
Queen from 1952

devoted to your service   ELIZABETH 12
My husband and I   PHILIP 1

Elliott, Ebenezer 1781–1849
English poet

rich man among the poor   OWEN 1

Elton, Ben 1959–
British writer and performer

bottom of a stand-up comedian   ELTON 1

Emerson, Ralph Waldo 1803–82
American philosopher and poet

bred to no profession   THOREAU 1
documents in the history of freedom   BURNS 6
kingdom of blockheads   YOUNG 1
love in the mouth of a courtesan   WEBSTER 2
narrow and very English mind   WORDSWORTH 9
sulphuric acid in his tea   ADAMS 8
tart cathartic virtue   PLUTARCH 1
That new saint   BROWN 9

Emin, Tracey 1963–
English artist

on every bloody A-list   EMIN 1

Empson, William 1906–84
English poet and literary critic

experience of propaganda   MILTON 7

Engels, Friedrich 1820–95
German socialist

English socialism arose with Owen   OWEN 2

Enright, D. J. 1920–
British writer

unetiolated visionary   KAFKA 1

Epstein, Brian 1934–67
English manager of the Beatles

He wants to know   HARRISON 1

Epstein, Jacob 1880–1959
British sculptor

leave art to us   EPSTEIN 4
stick to murder   KHRUSHCHEV 1

Erasmus c.1469–1536
Dutch Christian humanist

already something of royalty   HENRY 7
man of all hours   MORE 4
Saint Socrates, pray for me   SOCRATES 2
sense of the ridiculous   MORE 5

Ernst, Max 1891–1976
German artist

Looking   ERNST 1

Evangelista, Linda 1965–
Canadian supermodel

don't get out of bed   EVANGELISTA 1

Evans, Abel 1679–1737
English poet and divine

Laid many heavy loads   VANBRUGH 1

Evelyn, John 1620–1706
English diarist

laughing and jolly   MARY 12
miracle of a youth   WREN 3
tsar of Muscovy had left my house   PETER 1

Evert, Chris 1954–
American tennis player

I'm a control freak — EVERT 1
work three times as hard — KING 1

Ewart, Gavin 1916–95
British poet

he thinks he's Yeats — HEANEY 1
now Betjemanless — BETJEMAN 4

Eyre, Richard 1943–
English theatre director

He is our theatrical DNA — SHAKESPEARE 9

Fadiman, Clifton 1904–
American critic

mama of dada — STEIN 1
our greatest literary sadist — FAULKNER 1

Fairbairn, Nicholas 1933–95
Scottish Conservative politician

He is vin ordinaire — MAJOR 3

Fairbanks, Douglas Jr 1909–
American actor

rather vault over the desk — FAIRBANKS 1

Faithfull, Marianne 1946–
English singer

always took place in the extreme — JONES 1
at least one other meaning — DYLAN 3
Mad Hatter as your manager — OLDHAM 1
well-known pneumatic personality — JAGGER 2

Faldo, Nick 1957–
English golfer

being 'Mechanical Man' — FALDO 1

Faraday, Michael 1791–1867
English physicist and chemist

remain plain Michael Faraday — FARADAY 3

Farrow, Mia 1945–
American actress

big career, a big man — FARROW 1
his conscience on his sleeve — ALLEN 5
wanted to get cotton sheets — ALLEN 4

Faulkner, William 1897–1962
American novelist

fourth rate in Europe — TWAIN 2
made the books and he died — FAULKNER 2
What do you do — GABLE 1

Fauré, Gabriel 1845–1924
French composer and organist

been reserved all my life — FAURÉ 1

Fayed, Mohamed Al 1933–
Egyptian businessman

we were building the pyramids — FAYED 1

Fellini, Federico 1920–93
Italian film director

fairy godmother who had just come — BERGMAN 4

Ferry, Bryan 1945–
English pop singer and songwriter

getting the best out of himself — BOWIE 3

Feynman, Richard 1918–88
American theoretical physicis

What I cannot create — FEYNMAN 2

Field, Frank 1942–
British Labour politician

give the public a rest — BLAIR 3
nailing his colours to the fence — RUNCIE 1

Fields, W. C. 1880–1946
American humorist

best ballet dancer that ever lived — CHAPLIN 2
living in Philadelphia — FIELDS 2

Fingleton, Jack 1908–81
Australian cricketer

poem of athletic grace — LARWOOD 1

Firmont, L'Abbé Edgeworth de
1745–1807
Irish-born confessor to Louis XVI

Son of Saint Louis — LOUIS 3

Fischer, Bobby 1943–
American chess player

watch my opponent's egos crumble — FISCHER 1

Fisher, Lord 1841–1920
British admiral

always did the right thing — EDWARD 3

Fitzgerald, Edward 1809–83
English scholar and poet

more about his bowels and nerves — TENNYSON 3
no more Aurora Leighs — BROWNING 3

Fitzgerald, F. Scott 1896–1940
American novelist

don't know anything about life — WHARTON 1
only whistling or humming — KEATS 5
some sort of epic grandeur — FITZGERALD 2
stick hardened in the fire — HEMINGWAY 4

Fitzgerald, Penelope 1916–2000
English novelist and biographer

back-of-the-envelopes writer — FITZGERALD 6

Fitzgerald, Zelda 1900–47
Wife of F. Scott Fitzgerald

bullfighting, bullslinging — HEMINGWAY 5
I was made for you — FITZGERALD 3

Flaubert, Gustave 1821–80
French novelist

he was a continent — SHAKESPEARE 10
I doubt everything — FLAUBERT 2
if he had known how to write — BALZAC 4
wanted the Aeneid burned — VIRGIL 2

Florey, Howard 1898–1968
Australian pathologist

If you do the experiment — FLOREY 1

Flynn, Errol 1909–59
Australian-born American actor

reconciling my gross habits — FLYNN 2

Fonda, Jane 1937–
American actress

trying to shoot at American planes — FONDA 1

Fonteyn, Margot 1919–91
English ballet dancer

explained it when I danced it — FONTEYN 3
sauntering through the park — ASTAIRE 3

Foot, Michael 1913–
British Labour politician

adventurer pure and simple — DISRAELI 6
fascination of a public execution — BEVIN 2
most passionate nuclear disarmer — GORBACHEV 2
passed from rising hope — STEEL 1
perspiration of firm confidence — MACLEOD 2
semi-house-trained polecat — TEBBIT 1

Foote, Samuel 1720–77
English actor and dramatist

revenge against vanity — GARRICK 1

Ford, Ford Madox 1873–1939
English novelist

finding the *mot juste* — CONRAD 2
lines of least resistance — ROSSETTI 4

Ford, Gerald 1909–
American Republican statesman

not a Lincoln — FORD 2
prematurely orange — REAGAN 4

Ford, Harrison 1942–
American actor

waiting on six million people — FORD 5
You can type this shit — LUCAS 1

Ford, John 1895–1973
American film director

director of Westerns — FORD 9
half pagan, half puritan — HEPBURN 4

Foreman, George 1948–
American boxer

I can spell it. M-o-n-e-y — FOREMAN 1

Forster, E. M. 1879–1970
English novelist

cover the universe with mud	JOYCE 2
gave pleasure a bad name	CONNOLLY 2
guts to betray my country	FORSTER 1
most sublime noise	BEETHOVEN 5
never learnt it	COLERIDGE 6
pictures of potatoes	VAN GOGH 2
secret casket of his genius	CONRAD 3

Forsyth, Frederick 1938–
English novelist

heard Kennedy was dead	KENNEDY 5
keep a measly affair secret	COOK 7

Forsyth, Michael 1954–
Scottish Conservative politician

diminished by success	STUART 3
successes of the crowned Bruce	ROBERT 2
Wallace was a heroic failure	WALLACE 3

Fox, Caroline d. 1774
wife of Henry Fox, Lord Holland

thorn in Charles's side	PITT 4

Fox, Charles James 1749–1806
British Whig statesman

most unmanageable colleague	BURKE 1

Fox, George 1624–91
English founder of the Society of Friends

hadst thou been faithful	CROMWELL 4

Foxe, John 1516–87
English religious writer

drowned his ashes	WYCLIF 1

Francis, Clare 1946–
English yachtswoman and writer

love conversation and people	LEE 2

Franklin, Benjamin 1706–90
American politician, inventor, and scientist

sun and the moon to stand still	WASHINGTON 4

Franklin, Rev. C. L.

still a gospel singer	FRANKLIN 2

Franz Josef 1830–1916
Emperor of Austria

Nothing has been spared me	FRANZ 1

Frederick the Great 1712–86
King of Prussia from 1740

Be the king of philosophers	VOLTAIRE 3
say what they please	FREDERICK 3

Freud, Sigmund 1856–1939
Austrian psychiatrist

nothing but a conquistador	FREUD 7

Frost, Carina 1952–

thinks he's God Almighty	FROST 1

Frost, David 1939–
English broadcaster and writer

potentially lethal consequences	FROST 2

Fry, Roger 1866–1934
English art critic

Fra Angelico of Satanism	BEARDSLEY 3
persuades me to be a Christian	BACH 6

Fry, Stephen 1957–
English comedian, actor, and writer

generally appreciates diversity	WILDE 7
not megalomaniacally insane	MAXWELL 2
Pink Champagne Socialist	FRY 2
sort of public kitten	FRY 3

Frye, Northrop 1912–91
Canadian literary critic

message to the modern world	FRYE 3
Read Blake or go to hell	BLAKE 5

Fulford, Robert 1932–
Canadian commentator

talking to Citizen Black	BLACK 1
tart, aphoristic, defiant	ATWOOD 2

Fuller, R. Buckminster 1895–1983
American designer and architect

world's most successful failure	FULLER 2

Fuller, Roy 1912–91
English poet and novelist

lot of them were small — HERRICK 2

Fuseli, Henry 1741–1825
Swiss-born British painter and art critic

makes me call for my greatcoat — CONSTABLE 3

Gable, Clark 1901–60
American actor

big beautiful close-up — MACDONALD 6

don't fall for that humble stuff — TRACY 2

Gabriel, Peter 1950–
English rock singer

combines great melodies — SPRINGSTEEN 1

Gainsborough, Thomas 1727–88
English painter

everybody's faces but their own — GARRICK 2

how various he is — REYNOLDS 3

sick of portraits — GAINSBOROUGH 1

Gaitskell, Hugh 1906–63
British Labour politician

fight and fight and fight again — GAITSKELL 3

Galbraith, J. K. 1908–
American economist

do not feel quite well — MARX 8

still possible to drop his name — DAVIES 3

Galileo Galilei 1564–1642
Italian astronomer and physicist

if there were many like you — KEPLER 2

now shrivelled up for me — GALILEO 3

Gallagher, Noel 1967–
English pop singer

Has God played Knebworth — GALLAGHER 4

If I wasn't related to Liam — GALLAGHER 2

We are lads — GALLAGHER 3

Gallagher, Thomas

roots that started it all — GALLAGHER 5

Gallico, Paul 1897–1976
American writer

God with a flat nose — RUTH 1

Galsworthy, John 1867–1933
English novelist

strange bird — LAWRENCE 4

Gandhi, Indira 1917–84
Indian stateswoman

Every drop of my blood — GANDHI 1

Gandhi, Mahatma 1869–1948
Indian statesman

first article of my faith — GANDHI 6

Garbo, Greta 1905–90
Swedish film actress

I am a misfit in life — GARBO 6

I had made enough faces — GARBO 7

I want to be alone — GARBO 5

Garcia, Jerry 1942–95
American rock singer and guitarist

going up, it's like a skyrocket — JOPLIN 2

Gardner, Ava 1922–90
American actress

in bed with a little boy — SINATRA 4

Garfield, James Abram 1831–81
American Republican statesman

can no more be guarded against — GARFIELD 1

Garfunkel, Art 1941–
American singer

standard rebellious attitude — SIMON 1

Garland, Judy 1922–69
American singer and actress

why am I so lonely — GARLAND 2

Garrick, David 1717–79
English actor-manager

correct the heart — HOGARTH 1

talked like poor Poll — GOLDSMITH 1

Gaskell, Elizabeth 1810–65
English novelist

said to be frightfully shy   BRONTË 6
sense of a great shock and grief   LINCOLN 3
shut my eyes to the awkward blot   ELIOT 4

Gauguin, Paul 1848–1903
French painter

heart which beats   DEGAS 2
others unhappier than oneself   VAN GOGH 3
What does it matter   GAUGUIN 1

Gautier, Emile

bohemian sculptor or a nihilist   CURIE 7

Gay, John 1685–1732
English poet and dramatist

Life is a jest   GAY 1

Gellhorn, Martha 1908–98
American journalist

tourist of wars   GELLHORN 1

Gemmill, Archie 1947–
Scottish footballer

never feel too sure of himself   CLOUGH 3

Genghis Khan 1162–1227
founder of the Mongol empire

conquering one's enemies   GENGHIS 1

Gentileschi, Artemisia 1593–1652/3
Italian painter

woman makes one doubtful   GENTILESCHI 1

George I 1660–1727
King from 1714

hate all Boets and Bainters   GEORGE 1

George II 1683–1760
King from 1727

bite some of my other generals   WOLFE 1

George III 1738–1820
King from 1760

as contemptible as he is odious   FOX 2
glory in the name of Briton   GEORGE 6
Was there ever such stuff   SHAKESPEARE 11

George IV 1762–1830
King from 1820

get me a glass of brandy   CAROLINE 6
will throw you all overboard   CANNING 2

George V 1865–1936
King from 1910

all the brains I've met   GEORGE 22
come between Bertie and the throne   GEORGE 26
damned if I'm an alien   GEORGE 20
dear Grandmama died   VICTORIA 6
dignity of the office   MACDONALD 9
frightened of me   GEORGE 21
more guts than the rest of them   GEORGE 27
never to be played again   STRAUSS 2
ruin himself in twelve months   EDWARD 9
think of all I owe her   MARY 4

George VI 1894–1952
King from 1936

'Clam' would be more appropriate   ATTLEE 6

Geronimo c.1829–1909
Apache leader

moved about like the wind   GERONIMO 1

Gershwin, George 1898–1937
American composer and pianist

AM OUT TO WRITE HITS   GERSHWIN 1

Gershwin, Ira 1896–1983
American songwriter

Brothers of the Great   GERSHWIN 2

Getty, John Paul 1892–1976
American industrialist

not a wealthy woman   ELIZABETH 14

Giamatti, A. Bartlett 1938–89
American baseball player

like talking to Homer   BERRA 1

Gibbon, Edward 1737–94
English historian

admire his eloquence — BURKE 2
adorned by the female graces — ADDISON 3
captain of the Hampshire grenadiers — GIBBON 6
he is perfectly well — SHERIDAN 2
idle and unprofitable — GIBBON 5
I must love the dog — FOX 3

Gide, André 1869–1951
French novelist and critic

Hugo—alas — HUGO 2
thought charged with emotion — STENDHAL 1

Gielgud, John 1904–2000
English actor and director

badger's way of sniffing out — EVANS 3
if I really looked like that — HOCKNEY 2
intense, egocentric boy — BRANDO 4
married some terrible film star — BURTON 7
performance was pure revenge — EVANS 4
speaks five languages — BERGMAN 5
wanted to be a matinee idol — RICHARDSON 3
want to play the big parts — GUINNESS 2

Gilbert, W. S. 1836–1911
English dramatist

Baytch is by way of decomposing — BACH 7
it must be as master and master — SULLIVAN 1
model of a modern Major-General — WOLSELEY 3

Gillespie, Dizzy 1917–93
American jazz trumpet player

If it hadn't been for him — ARMSTRONG 2

Gimelstob, Justin
American tennis player

God spent a little extra time — SAMPRAS 1

Ginsberg, Allen 1926–97
American poet and novelist

lonely old courage-teacher — WHITMAN 1
maybe just poet — GINSBERG 1
sold out to God — DYLAN 4

Giovanni, Nikki 1943–
American poet

death is a slave's freedom — KING 4

Gish, Lillian 1896–1993
American actress

influence the whole world — GRIFFITH 2
long, dark Swedish winters — GARBO 8
usually ends — GISH 3

Gladstone, Catherine 1812–1900

if you weren't such a great man — GLADSTONE 11

Gladstone, W. E. 1809–98
British Liberal statesman

died at peace with all mankind — PEEL 5
man who is *never beaten* — DISRAELI 7
morals or principles — CHURCHILL 3
terrible fall — PARNELL 2
There never was a Churchill — MARLBOROUGH 2

Glendinning, Victoria 1937–
English biographer and novelist

most Swiftian writer we have — VIDAL 2

Glennie, Evelyn 1965–
Scottish percussion player

loneliest period for a musician — GLENNIE 1

Gloucester, William Henry, Duke of 1743–1805

Always scribble, scribble — GIBBON 7

Glyn, Elinor 1864–1943
British novelist

Your proportions are Egyptian — SWANSON 2

Godwin, William 1756–1836
English philosopher and novelist

philosopher, even like a cynic — SHELLEY 2

Goebbels, Joseph 1897–1945
German Nazi leader

born popular leader — HITLER 6
Jewish intellectual infection — HINDEMITH 1

Goethe, Johann Wolfgang von
1749–1832
German poet, novelist, and dramatist

captivating at first glance	POUSSIN 1
classical even in exile	OVID 2
great only as a poet	BYRON 10
harmony were conversing	BACH 8
I do not know myself	GOETHE 2
look for what she does	KAUFMAN 1
political tittle-tattle	BYRON 9
utterly untamed personality	BEETHOVEN 6

Gogarty, Oliver St John 1878–1957
Irish writer and surgeon

Beauty's Bolshevik	JOHN 3
evicting imaginary tenants	YEATS 5
rose to bring about Eutopia	DE VALERA 3

Golden, Harry

what I call brotherhood	MONROE 6

Goldsmith, Oliver 1728–74
Anglo-Irish writer, poet, and dramatist

born to improve us in every part	REYNOLDS 4
only took snuff	REYNOLDS 5
On the stage he was natural	GARRICK 4
Our Garrick's a salad	GARRICK 3
Too nice for a statesman	BURKE 3
when his pistol misses fire	JOHNSON 13

Goldwater, Barry 1909–98
American Republican politician

dime store New Dealer	EISENHOWER 4
lied to his own men	NIXON 3

Goldwyn, Sam 1882–1974
American film producer

he can't take less	CHAPLIN 3
wasted my time with *that* one	DAVIS 3

Gonne, Maud 1867–1953
Irish nationalist and actress

I was the Father sowing	GONNE 1
Poets should never marry	YEATS 6

Gooch, Daniel 1816–89
English engineer

originality of thought	BRUNEL 2

Gorbachev, Mikhail Sergeevich
1931–
Soviet statesman

without the presence of this Pope	JOHN PAUL 1

Gordy, Berry 1929–
American record producer

her name needed more sparkle	ROSS 1

Gorky, Maxim 1868–1936
Russian writer and revolutionary

two bears in one den	TOLSTOY 4
what a wonderful man	TOLSTOY 5

Gorman, Teresa 1931–
British Conservative politician

high-kick her out of the House	BOOTHROYD 2

Gould, Stephen Jay 1941–
American palaeontologist

because he is persecuted	GALILEO 4
largely displacement activity	DARWIN 4
see connections among things	GOULD 1

Gower, David 1957–
English cricketer

enigma to puzzle the sphinx	BOYCOTT 2
For fun, style and excellence	GOWER 2

Goya 1746–1828
Spanish painter

Velasquez and Rembrandt	GOYA 3

Grade, Lew 1906–98
British television producer and executive

All my shows are great	GRADE 1

Grade, Michael 1943–
British film and television executive

played with his Meccano set	BIRT 1

Graham, Billy 1918–
American evangelical preacher

more about the life of Christ	DE MILLE 4

Graham, Martha 1893–1991
American dancer, teacher, and choreographer

achieves—*illumination*　　　　ULANOVA 1

Grainger, Percy 1882–1961
Australian-born American composer and pianist

happy to have with us today　　　ELLINGTON 1
kill him and get the song　　　　GRAINGER 2
think of turnips if you like　　　GRAINGER 1

Grant, Cary 1904–86
British-born American actor

She made it look so easy　　　　KELLY 5

Grant, Ulysses S. 1822–85
American Unionist general and statesman

backbone of an angle-worm　　　GARFIELD 2
He was a gallant soldier　　　　JACKSON 11
unsurpassed if not unequalled　　SHERMAN 1
verb is anything that signifies　　GRANT 2

Graves, Robert 1895–1985
English poet

bum person　　　　　　　　　LAWRENCE 5
made so many mysteries　　　LAWRENCE 16
no known cure　　　　　　　　AMIS 4
shrinking, womanish poet　　　KEATS 6

Gray, Patrick, Lord d. 1612

dead woman bites not　　　　　MARY 7

Gray, Simon 1936–
English dramatist

make one laugh in panic　　　PINTER 2

Gray, Thomas 1716–71
English poet

blasted with excess of light　　MILTON 8
blind to all his faults　　　　DRYDEN 3
She-wolf of France　　　　ISABELLA 1
Too poor for a bribe　　　　GRAY 1

Greaves, Jimmy 1940–
English footballer

best known Briton of the 20th century　CHARLTON 2
hammer in his left boot　　　HURST 1
I am an alcoholic　　　　　GREAVES 1

Greene, Graham 1904–91
English novelist

corrupt and phosphorescent prettiness　DAVIS 4
her haggard equine renunciations　GARBO 9
human Mickey Mouse　　　ASTAIRE 4
satirist and the romantic　　WAUGH 3
to be a *creative artist*　　HARDY 1
toted a breast like a man totes a gun　HARLOW 3

Greene, Robert c.1560–92
English poet and dramatist

only Shake-scene　　　SHAKESPEARE 12

Greer, Germaine 1939–
Australian feminist

did not know how to keep him　HENDRIX 2
except that she was a woman　WOOLF 2
haven't lost my sense of humour　GREER 2
Just William of the side　GASCOIGNE 2
lipstick must rot the brain　MOORE 9
mother who was motherly　GREER 1

Gregory, Dick 1932–
American comedian and civil rights activist

walked like a king　　　MALCOLM 3

Gregory, Lady 1852–1932
Irish dramatist

British Empire for God　　TENNYSON 4

Greville, Fulke 1554–1628
English poet, writer, and politician

Friend to Sir Philip Sidney　　SIDNEY 4

Grey, Lady Jane 1537–54
queen of England 9–19 June 1553

so gentle a schoolmaster　　GREY 1

Grieg, Edvard 1843–1907
Norwegian composer, conductor, and
violinist

fresh healthy outlook on Art GRAINGER 3
music has a taste of codfish GRIEG 2

Griffith, D. W. 1875–1948
American film director

belongs with the slapstick cops FAIRBANKS 2
has the most brain GISH 4

Grigg, John 1924–
British writer and journalist

better rating in British mythology LLOYD GEORGE 8
priggish schoolgirl ELIZABETH 15

Grigson, Geoffrey 1905–85
British poet and critic

more natural or else more abstract MOORE 3

Gromyko, Andrei 1909–89
Soviet statesman

he's got iron teeth GORBACHEV 3

Guedalla, Philip 1889–1944
British historian and biographer

milk of human kindness BARRIE 3
simple dynastic arrangement JAMES 9

Guinness, Alec 1914–2000
English actor

all those screeching seagulls PLOMLEY 1
bloody awful, banal lines LUCAS 2
brings Yorkshire and Camden Town BENNETT 3
from his head to his crotch JOYCE 3
God's Girl Widdecombe WIDDECOMBE 2
his work still shines out GILL 2
If you get in that car DEAN 1
Plantagenet condescension SITWELL 4
silver trumpet muffled GIELGUD 2
small-part actor who's been lucky GUINNESS 3
vain actor playing to the gallery MONTGOMERY 3

Gunn, Thom 1929–
English poet

turns revolt into a style PRESLEY 4

Guthrie, James 1859–1930
Scottish painter

ought to be an artist MACKINTOSH 1

Guthrie, Woody 1912–67
American folk singer and writer

been in the red all my life GUTHRIE 2
Left wing, chicken wing GUTHRIE 1
won't make it with his writing DYLAN 5

Gwyn, Nell 1650–87
English actress and courtesan

Protestant whore GWYN 2

Hackett, John 1910–97
British general

much of the poet in him SCOTT 2

Hackman, Gene 1931–
American actor

keep myself as common HACKMAN 1

Hague, William 1961–
British Conservative politician

common sense revolution WIDDECOMBE 3
If Roland Rat were appointed MANDELSON 1
park one Jaguar PRESCOTT 1
probity and integrity ARCHER 4
run as his 'night mayor' LIVINGSTONE 3

Haig, Earl 1861–1928
British Field Marshal

like the feather pillow DERBY 3

Haldane, J. B. S. 1892–1964
Scottish mathematical biologist

NHS is quite like heaven HALDANE 1

Hall, Jerry 1956–
American model

whore in the bedroom   HALL 1

Hall, Peter 1930–
English theatre and film director

always likes his own work   MILLER 7
appearance sometimes hawk-like   BECKETT 4
completely inhabited   BARKER 1
Cut the pause   PINTER 3
egomania and paranoia   REITH 2
like a precise headmaster   BRITTEN 3
make other actors seem artificial   RICHARDSON 4
quicksilver in his wit   GIELGUD 3
theatrical whore   BRECHT 1
where history was happening   ORWELL 2
wished to avoid life   IRVING 1

Halliwell, Geri 1972–
English pop singer

first Spice Girl   THATCHER 8
not going to be Meryl Streep   HALLIWELL 1

Hamilton, Neil 1949–
British Conservative politician

poor Martin doesn't have a clue   BELL 2

Hamilton, Nigel 1944–
British biographer

toyed with men's lives   MOUNTBATTEN 3

Hammerstein, Oscar II 1895–1960
American songwriter

Irving just loves hits   BERLIN 2
so in love with the world   GERSHWIN 3

Hand, Learned 1872–1961
American judge

prefer a self-made name   GOLDWYN 1

Hanna, Mark 1837–1904
American politician and businessman

that damned cowboy is President   ROOSEVELT 9

Hardie, Keir 1856–1915
Scottish Labour politician

called upon to pay the bill   EDWARD 10
memories of boyhood are gloomy   HARDIE 1

Harding, D. W. 1906–
British psychologist and critic

Regulated hatred   AUSTEN 6

Hardy, G. H. 1877–1947
English mathematician

fifth best pure mathematician   HARDY 2
when Aeschylus is forgotten   ARCHIMEDES 2
whole class above every batsman   BRADMAN 3

Hardy, Thomas 1840–1928
English novelist and poet

no more novel-writing   HARDY 7

Hardyment, Christina
British writer

egging Western girlhood on   STOPES 2
Greer is a Snow Queen   GREER 3

Hargrave, John 1894–82
British artist and writer

primitive fraternity gang spirit   BADEN-POWELL 3

Harman, Mr Justice 1930–
British judge

operetta called *La Gazza Ladra*   GASCOIGNE 3

Harold II c.1019–66
King of England, 1066

seven feet of English ground   HARALD 1

Harris, Rolf 1930–
Australian entertainer and artist

didn't have his own TV show   REMBRANDT 3

Hart, Lorenz 1895–1943
American songwriter

taps all the other chaps to death   ASTAIRE 5

Harvey, Anna

Hastings, Max 1945–
British journalist and broadcaster

Hastings, Warren 1732–1818
British colonial administrator

Hatton, Christopher 1540–91
English statesman

Havel, Václav 1936–
Czech dramatist and statesman

Hawthorne, Nathaniel 1804–64
American novelist

Haydn, Franz Joseph 1732–1809
Austrian composer

Hazlitt, William 1778–1830
English essayist

looked rather like a nut	PORTER 2
passion for 'tidiness'	MONTGOMERY 4
saved her venom to create	BURKE 4
fish for men's souls	ELIZABETH 6
special time caught me up	HAVEL 1
as English as a beefsteak	JOHNSON 14
greatest composer I know	MOZART 7
understands my language	HAYDN 1
annihilates all rules	SIDDONS 2
by darkening knowledge	BROWNE 1
downright blows of matter	HOBBES 3
hand would have burnt yours	BURNS 7
icicle upon the bust of tragedy	KEMBLE 1
infinite variety of talent	KEAN 2
kind of fourth estate	COBBETT 4
landscapes want gusto	CLAUDE 2
mind which keeps open house	COLERIDGE 8
new edition of human nature	SCOTT 9
not an original inventor in art	REYNOLDS 6
philosophic fanatic	SHELLEY 6
pictures of nothing and very like	TURNER 2
pith is in the postscript	LAMB 2
power, passion, self-will	DANTE 5
sitting for her picture	GAINSBOROUGH 2
Spirit of the Age	WORDSWORTH 10
surveyor, not the builder	BACON 3
talked on for ever	COLERIDGE 7
thirst after unrighteousness	MARLOWE 2
This is true eloquence	BURKE 5
tricks of a political rope-dancer	CANNING 3

Headlam, Cuthbert Morley
1876–1964
British Conservative politician

Healey, Denis 1917–
British Labour politician

Healey, Edna 1918–
British writer

Healy, Timothy Michael 1855–1931
Irish nationalist politician

Heaney, Seamus 1939–
Irish poet

be the bride at a wedding	CHURCHILL 23
bores people too quickly	MACMILLAN 3
corpse at the funeral	CHURCHILL 4
Great She-elephant	THATCHER 9
savaged by a dead sheep	HOWE 1
shuffling along in the gutter	THATCHER 10
She has no hinterland	THATCHER 11
mistress of the Party	PARNELL 3
cross between Oscar Wilde	MARLOWE 3
healthy Anglican life	HERBERT 1
My passport's green	HEANEY 2
OED in carpet slippers	AUDEN 5
stained cape of his heart	GOYA 4
tiger lashing its tail	PLATH 1

Hearst, William Randolph
1863–1951
American newspaper publisher

I'll furnish the war   HEARST 1
used to be a socialist   PULITZER 1

Heath, Edward 1916–
British Conservative statesman

Music means everything   HEATH 3
Popular, effective   BLAIR 4
Rejoice, rejoice   THATCHER 12

Hebblethwaite, Margaret 1951–
British writer and theologian

foot in the Monty Python series   JOHN PAUL 2

Hecht, Ben 1894–1964
American screenwriter

wonderful panic   GOLDWYN 2

Hedren, Tippi 1935–
American actress

looking like Cary Grant   HITCHCOCK 1

Heine, Heinrich 1797–1856
German poet

hand of Jean Jacques Rousseau   ROBESPIERRE 3
lark as great as an eagle   BERLIOZ 3

Heinkel, Ernst 1888–1958
German aeronautical engineer

cage with seven locks   PORSCHE 1

Heisenberg, Werner 1901–76
German mathematical physicist and
philosopher

Primarily a philosopher   BOHR 4

Heller, Joseph 1923–99
American novelist

as good as *Catch-22*   HELLER 2
Comedy doesn't make me laugh HELLER 3
If Nixon was second-rate   NIXON 4
Kissinger brought peace   KISSINGER 2

Hellman, Lillian 1905–84
American dramatist

cut my conscience to fit   HELLMAN 1

Héloise c. 1098–1164
French nun

thing I least valued   ABELARD 1

Heming, John 1556–1630
and **Condell, Henry** d. 1627

scarce received a blot   SHAKESPEARE 13

Hemingway, Ernest 1899–1961
American novelist

All modern American literature   TWAIN 3
best that ever came into the ring DIETRICH 4
come from big words   FAULKNER 3
If he wags that silly finger COWARD 3
in any ring with Mr Tolstoy   HEMINGWAY 6
just like brothers   STEIN 2
most beautiful fighting machine   LOUIS 6
right half the time   POUND 2
seen a nastier-looking man   LEWIS 6
took LITERATURE so solemnly   FITZGERALD 4

Hendrix, Jimi 1942–70
American rock musician

Maybe to Venus or somewhere   HENDRIX 4
play the guitar with your teeth   HENDRIX 3

Henley, W. E. 1849–1903
English poet and dramatist

something of the Shorter-Catechist   STEVENSON 7

Hennessy, Peter 1947–
English historian and writer

very last of the steam locomotives   HOME 2

Henri IV 1553–1610
King of France from 1589

wisest fool in Christendom   JAMES 1

Henry, Joseph 1797–1878
American physicist

overflowings of a mind so rich   BABBAGE 2

Henry, Prince 1594–1612
Son of James I

keep such a bird in a cage
RALEIGH 2

Henry II 1133–89
King of England from 1154

this turbulent priest
BECKET 3

Henry VIII 1491–1547
King of England from 1509

Flanders mare
ANNE 8

sow by the right ear
CRANMER 3

Hepburn, Audrey 1929–93
British actress

sank into my two left feet
ASTAIRE 6

Hepburn, Katharine 1909–
American actress

acting that was easy
TRACY 3

Funny as a baby's open grave
HUSTON 2

His yes meant yes
BOGART 4

lived my life as a man
HEPBURN 5

Hepworth, Barbara 1903–75
English sculptor

left hand is my thinking hand
HEPWORTH 1

Herschel, Caroline 1750–1848
German-born astronomer

own myself to be vain
HERSCHEL 2

Herschel, John 1792–1871
English astronomer and physicist

Light was my first love
HERSCHEL 3

Hervey, Lord 1696–1743
English politician and writer

to carry candles
HERVEY 1

Herzog, Chaim 1918–97
Irish-born Israeli statesman and writer

routine, discipline, training
DAYAN 2

Heseltine, Michael 1933–
British Conservative politician

have to watch his back
PORTILLO 1

king of the gutter of politics
KINNOCK 1

Hewson, John 1946–
Australian Liberal politician

call Paul Keating
KEATING 2

Heywood, Thomas c.1574–1641
English dramatist

Seven cities warred for Homer
HOMER 3

Hill, Christopher 1912–
British historian

founded the British Empire
CROMWELL 5

wanted the millennium
BUNYAN 1

Hill, Damon 1960–
English motor-racing driver

cold professional Germanic
SCHUMACHER 1

hit me with a Vulcan Mind-grip
SENNA 1

Hilliard, Nicholas 1547–1619
English painter

most excellent painter
HOLBEIN 1

Hindemith, Paul 1895–1963
German composer

feel like a cornerstone
HINDEMITH 2

Hindenburg, Paul von 1847–1934
German Field Marshal and statesman

make him a postmaster
HITLER 7

Hirst, Damien 1965–
English artist

imagination and a chainsaw
HIRST 1

Hislop, Ian 1960–
English satirical journalist

bogus category in between
ARCHER 5

Hitchcock, Alfred 1899–1980
British-born film director

guts of a bank robber
MACLAINE 1

If I made Cinderella
HITCHCOCK 2

Hitler, Adolf 1889–1945
German dictator

assurance of a sleepwalker
HITLER 8

Hoban, Russell 1925–
American novelist

potty-trained too early
STRAVINSKY 1

Hobbes, Thomas 1588–1679
English philosopher

enemy to the stomach — RALEIGH 3
kept himself wholly to geometry — DESCARTES 3
see his own doctrine established — HARVEY 2

Hobbs, Jack 1882–1963
English cricketer

greatest run-getting machine — BRADMAN 4

Hobsbawm, Eric 1917–
British historian

most overrated US president — KENNEDY 6
This great romantic — CHURCHILL 24

Hockney, David 1937–
British artist

finish up painting blue stripes — NEWMAN 1
I've got Bradford — HOCKNEY 3
Picasso was there first — PICASSO 4

Hodges, Roy

if she'd gone into crime — JACKSON 2

Hodgkin, Dorothy 1910–94
British chemist

I think with my hands — HODGKIN 1

Hogarth, William 1697–1764
English painter and engraver

never deviated into grace — DÜRER 2

Hoggart, Simon 1946–
British journalist

skulk in broad daylight — MANDELSON 2

Holden, William 1918–81
American actor

mind full of razor blades — WILDER 1

Holiday, Billie 1915–59
American singer

always making a comeback — HOLIDAY 2
no sugar cane for miles — HOLIDAY 3

Holland, Lord 1705–74
English Whig politician

obliged to go to bed — FOX 4

Holliday, Judy 1922–65
American actress

She sings so delicious — FERRIER 1

Holloway, David 1924–

wild life of Balmoral — HUGHES 2

Holmes, Oliver Wendell Jr.
1841–1935
American lawyer

first-class temperament — ROOSEVELT 6

Home, Alec Douglas-Home, Lord
1903–95
British Conservative statesman

fourteenth Mr Wilson — WILSON 4
have to have a box of matches — HOME 3

Hooke, Robert 1635–1703
English scientist

such a mechanical hand — WREN 4

Hopcraft, Arthur 1932–
British journalist

opposite of glamorous — MATTHEWS 2

Hope, Anthony 1863–1933
English novelist

His foe was folly — GILBERT 1

Hope, Bob 1903–
American comedian

Astaire starts counting his money — KELLY 2
I'm still here — HOPE 2
in a little Cellophane bag — CROSBY 2
millionaire has just as good a chance — KENNEDY 7

Hopkins, Gerard Manley 1844–89
English poet and priest

fancy and aesthetic tastes — HOPKINS 2
most masculine of our poets — DRYDEN 4
time's eunuch — HOPKINS 3

Hopkins, Hoppy
American screenwriter

iron butterfly — MACDONALD 7

Hopper, Hedda 1885–1966
American actress and columnist

no one ever filled his shoes   GRIFFITH 3

Horace 65–8 BC
Roman poet

even excellent Homer nods   HOMER 4
Half my own soul   VIRGIL 3
hold my head so high   HORACE 2

Horder, Lord 1871–1955
British physician

reason why I have found nothing   MACDONALD 10

Hornby, James John 1826–1909
English headmaster

wish Shelley had been at Harrow   SHELLEY 7

Housman, A. E. 1859–1936
English poet

justify God's ways to man   MILTON 9
less provocative Ambassador   RUSSELL 2
photograph is not quite true   HOUSMAN 4
razor ceases to act   HOUSMAN 5
Wordsworth drunk and Porson sober   HOUSMAN 3

Howe, Geoffrey 1926–
British Conservative politician

bats have been broken   THATCHER 13

Howells, William Dean 1837–1920
American novelist and critic

Lincoln of our literature   TWAIN 4

Howerd, Frankie 1922–92
British comedian

Such cruel glasses   DAY 3

Hoy, Claire
Canadian journalist

layer of more plastic   MULRONEY 3

Hoyle, Fred 1915–
English astrophysicist

outrageous young fellow   HOYLE 1

Hughes, Frieda

memory of her death   PLATH 2

Hughes, Howard Jr. 1905–76
American industrialist, aviator and film
producer

look like a taxi-cab   GABLE 2

Hughes, Ted 1930–98
English poet

shock of your joy   PLATH 3
utility son-in-law   HUGHES 3

Hughes, William Morris 1862–1952
Australian statesman

from here to Broken Hill   HITLER 9
lead a flock of homing pigeons   MENZIES 1

Hugo, Victor 1802–85
French poet, novelist, and dramatist

aged like an old man   CORNEILLE 1
captain of the second   WELLINGTON 4
captured the rays of the sun   CAMERON 2
French soul is stronger   JOAN 2
Molière speaks to society   MOLIÈRE 1
nothing but the fact   MACHIAVELLI 2
proofreader of the Revolution   ROBESPIERRE 4
Racine has withered   RACINE 1
Voltaire smiled   VOLTAIRE 4

Hume, Basil 1923–99
English cardinal

could have been me   HUME 1

Hume, David 1711–76
Scottish philosopher, economist, and
historian

all because I am a Scotsman   HUME 2

Humphries, Barry 1934–
Australian entertainer and writer

reinvent ourselves   ARCHER 6

Humphrys, John 1943–
British broadcaster

perfect face for radio	HUMPHRYS 1
questions politicians wanted asked	DAY 4

Hunt, Leigh 1784–1859
English poet and essayist

great piece of placid marble	COLERIDGE 9
laughing queen that caught	CLEOPATRA 1
paint as well as you write	ROSSETTI 5
This Adonis in loveliness	GEORGE 13

Hunt, William Holman 1827–1910
English painter

pure and docile-hearted damsel	ROSSETTI 1

Hurd, Douglas 1930–
British Conservative politician

been a don or a schoolmaster	HEATH 4

Hurley, Elizabeth 1965–
British actress and model

as fat as Marilyn Monroe	MONROE 7
my north, my south	GRANT 1
She is a very pretty girl	KOURNIKOVA 1

Hussey, Christopher 1899–1970
British architectural historian

artist in horticulture	JEKYLL 1

Huston, John 1906–87
American-born film director

become king of Scotland	CONNERY 3
break out and eat everybody	DAVIS 5

Hutton, Len 1916–90
English cricketer

as easy as drinking tea	GOWER 3
debonair way he played	COMPTON 2

Huxley, Aldous 1894–1963
English novelist

choose to be Faraday	FARADAY 4
compelled to write about him	LAWRENCE 6

Huxley, T. H. 1825–95
English biologist

deduction killed by a fact	SPENCER 2
nothing but his shirt	GLADSTONE 12
one wild whirl to me	HUXLEY 8
suppose his audience knows	FARADAY 5
too much of a sceptic	HUXLEY 9

Ice-T 1958–
American rap musician

talks good for a black guy	ICE-T 1

Ingrams, Richard 1937–
English satirical journalist

bug-eyed serial killer	INGRAMS 2
publish and be sued	INGRAMS 1

Ingres, Jean 1780–1867
French painter

wolf into the sheepfold	DELACROIX 4

Irving, Henry 1838–1905
English actor-manager

most resounding note	MARLOWE 4

Irving, John 1942–
American novelist

novelist with a scientific background	FREUD 8

Isherwood, Christopher 1904–86
English novelist

butterfly attention wandered	GARBO 10
he grappled with it	THOMAS 3
I am a camera	ISHERWOOD 1
I feared as much	VIDAL 3
sucks at the dry teats of books	HUXLEY 4

Ives, Burl 1909–95
American singer and actor

so small and delicate	GUTHRIE 3

Ivins, Molly 1944–
and **Dubose, Lou**
American journalists

trouble with 'the vision thing'	BUSH 11

Jackson, Glenda 1936–
English actress and politician

absence of an intrusive self — SCOFIELD 1
he leaves you alone — RUSSELL 12
Oh my God, I must have died — JACKSON 3
one of Blair's babes — JACKSON 4
showing you how difficult it is — OLIVIER 1

Jackson, Jesse 1941–
American Democratic politician and
clergyman

original art form — ROBINSON 5

Jackson, Michael 1958–
American pop singer

my greatest teacher — BROWN 5
only had to get married — JOHN 7

Jackson, Thomas 1824–63
American Confederate general

I would follow blindfold — LEE 6

Jacob, Max 1876–1944
French poet

as fragile as glass — MODIGLIANI 2

Jagger, Bianca 1955–
Nicaraguan-born wife of Mick Jagger

mistook his silences — WARHOL 1

Jagger, Mick 1943–
English rock musician

must have been very lonely — MCCARTNEY 1
that essential dumbness — MADONNA 2

Jakobovits, Lord 1921–
British rabbi

Hitler's principal allies — HITLER 10

James, Clive 1939–
Australian critic and writer

adrenalin instead of blood — HIGGINS 2
care much about Britain — LARKIN 4
complete Krakatoa number — MCENROE 2
condom stuffed with walnuts — SCHWARZENEGGER 1
eerily quotable sentences — STOPPARD 1
fed with warm peppermint creams — LIBERACE 2
good after-sales service — BORG 2
Goth swaggering around Rome — MURDOCH 6
He is just over-alive — OLIVIER 2
man whose trousers are on fire — WALKER 1
midget is good at being short — MONROE 8
smoother than a pint of Guinness — HEANEY 3
verb chasing its own tail — BUSH 6
way it goes boink-boink — MUGGERIDGE 1

James, C. L. R. 1901–89
Trinidad-born writer

carry to an extreme — SOBERS 1

James, Henry 1843–1916
American novelist

all gobble and glare — TROLLOPE 2
appreciation of the usual — TROLLOPE 3
as handsome as his photographs — ARNOLD 2
chartered libertine — RUSKIN 2
chattering hag THINK — TERRY 2
country of your own — WHARTON 2
greatest of superficial novelists — DICKENS 4
great gossip — BROWNING 8
grim face of reality — RUSKIN 1
image of Browning — TENNYSON 5
loved to be popular — JAMES 10
magnificently ugly — ELIOT 5
more of a man than I expected — VICTORIA 7
not only alive, but kicking — WELLS 2
Of course, of course — BROOKE 2
original or a copy — MORRIS 1

James, Henry continued

scandalous, dangerous, and seditious	SAND 3
spiteful fairy is vulgarity	MILLAIS 1
terrible fault for an archfiend	IRVING 2
very genial, comfortable being	HUXLEY 10
wondrous museum	BURNE-JONES 2
worse than provincial	THOREAU 2
wounded by a pin-prick	FLAUBERT 3

James, P. D. 1920–
English writer

as handsome as Imran Khan	RUSHDIE 1
interest in death	JAMES 17

James, William 1842–1910
American philosopher

known the limits of his genius	EMERSON 3

James I 1566–1625
King of Scotland from 1567 and of
England from 1603

like the peace of God	DONNE 4
no other prison than this library	JAMES 2

James V 1512–42
King of Scotland from 1513

It came with a lass	MARY 8

Janáček, Leoš 1854–1928
Czech composer

how children imagine God	SMETANA 1

Jarrell, Randall 1914–65
American poet

never steps twice into the same	AUDEN 6

Jay, Douglas 1907–96
British Labour politician

never used one syllable	ATTLEE 7

Jeans, James 1877–1946
English physicist and astronomer

ever the happy warrior	RUTHERFORD 2
saw too deeply into things	MAXWELL 1

Jefferson, Thomas 1743–1826
American Democratic Republican
statesman

few lives precious to mankind	PRIESTLEY 3
no judgement was ever sounder	WASHINGTON 5
no one could replace him	FRANKLIN 4
This is all the ill	ADAMS 6

Jekyll, Gertrude 1843–1932
English garden designer

more or less a gardener	JEKYLL 2

Jenkins, Roy 1920–
British politician

bravest of all categories	GAITSKELL 4
indifferent to the waves	HEATH 5
self-righteous stubbornness	THATCHER 14
so little intelligence	CALLAGHAN 3
very good statistical mind	WILSON 5

John, Augustus 1878–1961
Welsh painter

If it's beauty, it's love	JOHN 4
In case it is one of mine	JOHN 5
remembered only as the brother	JOHN 10

John, Barry 1945–
Welsh rugby union player

pulled off the streets of Belfast	BEST 4

John, Elton 1947–
English pop singer and songwriter

amount of energy he radiated	BOLAN 2
extremely funky pub pianist	JOHN 8
it's like a child to me	JOHN 9
kinda got a non-voice	COHEN 3
monkey with arthritis	RICHARDS 1

John, Elton 1947–
and **Taupin, Bernie** 1950–

candle in the wind	DIANA 6
candle in the wind	MONROE 9
Goodbye England's rose	DIANA 5

John, Gwen 1876–1939
Welsh painter

do not want me to be different — RODIN 2

John, Pope XXIII 1881–1963
Pope from 1958

Anybody can be pope — JOHN 2

Johnson, Amy 1903–41
English aviator

spirit found outlet in the air — JOHNSON 1

Johnson, Earvin 1959–
American basketball player

Magic is who I am — JOHNSON 2

Johnson, Lyndon Baines 1908–73
American Democratic statesman

can't fart and chew gum	FORD 3
enviably attractive nephew	KENNEDY 9
football without a helmet	FORD 4
free man, an American	JOHNSON 5
He believed in us	STEVENSON 2
holds out an olive branch	KHRUSHCHEV 2
never said a word of importance	KENNEDY 8
outside pissing in	HOOVER 1

Johnson, Samuel 1709–84
English poet, critic, and lexicographer

any suspicion of her powers	BURNEY 1
attain an English style	ADDISON 4
black dog	JOHNSON 15
clipped hedge	CORNEILLE 2
Colossus from a rock	MILTON 11
desired to know nothing	GEORGE 2
dull in a new way	GRAY 2
eclipsed the gaiety of nations	GARRICK 5
father of English criticism	DRYDEN 5
finest gentleman I have ever seen	GEORGE 7
frame of adamant	CHARLES 12
I refute it *thus*	BERKELEY 2
limb lopped off	BOSWELL 2
morals of a whore	CHESTERFIELD 2
never at leisure	WESLEY 2
oriental scrupulosity	SWIFT 3
pen in his hand	GOLDSMITH 3
Poet, Naturalist, and Historian	GOLDSMITH 2
quibble is to Shakespeare	SHAKESPEARE 14
read Richardson for the story	RICHARDSON 8
ruled by the tongue of Fox	FOX 5
sentence for his transportation	ROUSSEAU 4
surly republican	MILTON 10
tea without a stratagem	POPE 4
wit among Lords	CHESTERFIELD 1
with Burke under a shed	BURKE 6

Jolson, Al 1886–1950
American singer

ain't heard nuttin' yet — JOLSON 3

Jones, Grace 1952–
Jamaican-born rock star

once I get my oysters — JONES 3

Jones, Tom 1940–
Welsh pop singer

counted how many knickers	JONES 7
He says he's not a singer	DYLAN 6

Jones, Vinnie 1965–
Welsh footballer

harder growing in concrete	JONES 10
so many games and never be booked	LINEKER 2

Jonson, Ben c.1573–1637
English dramatist and poet

Dominus do-all	JONES 5
He was not of an age	SHAKESPEARE 16
lest he should make an end	BACON 4
Marlowe's mighty line	MARLOWE 5
not keeping of accent	DONNE 5
only faithful watchman for the realm	CECIL 6
small Latin, and less Greek	SHAKESPEARE 15
Sweet Swan of Avon	SHAKESPEARE 17
Who never kept his word	DUDLEY 1

Joplin, Janis 1943–70
American singer

Fourteen heart attacks	EISENHOWER 5
made love to 25,000 people	JOPLIN 3

Jopling, Michael 1930–
British Conservative politician

had to buy all his furniture	HESELTINE 3

Joseph II 1741–90
Holy Roman Emperor

much too many notes	MOZART 8

Josephine 1763–1814
Empress of France

feared to be importunate	NAPOLEON 7

Joyce, James 1882–1941
Irish novelist

hand that wrote *Ulysses*	JOYCE 4
neat generalizations about life	BALZAC 5
slick as a Frenchman	CHAUCER 4
undercurrents of gurgle	JOYCE 6

Jung, Carl Gustav 1875–1961
Swiss psychologist

discoverer of the Unconscious	BOSCH 1
superior but impenetrable mind	ROOSEVELT 7

Junor, John 1919–97
British journalist

do this on the doorstep	WILSON 6

Juvenal AD c.60–c.130
Roman satirist

practising speech-making	HANNIBAL 1

Kael, Pauline 1919–
American film critic

generous-hearted actor	TRAVOLTA 1

Kammerer, Frau

would have made a good Hausfrau	KRUPSKAYA 1

Kaufman, George S. 1889–1961
American dramatist

Everything I've ever said	PARKER 2

Kazan, Elia 1909–
Turkish-born American film director

crawled over broken glass	LEIGH 1
guy with that much pain in him	DEAN 2
hell of a lot of turmoil	BRANDO 5

Keane, Fergal 1961–
Irish journalist

skeletons are calcium deficient	GORE 1

Keating, Paul 1944–
Australian Labor statesman

gets the mail through	KEATING 3
shiver looking for a spine	HEWSON 1

Keats, John 1795–1821
English poet

content with half knowledge	COLERIDGE 10
describes what he sees	BYRON 11
full of mean and thrify maxims	FRANKLIN 5
how very sad thy fate	CHATTERTON 1
made myself remembered	KEATS 8
Mister John Keats five feet high	KEATS 7
name was writ in water	KEATS 9
paint in his gauntlets	DÜRER 3
whims of an egotist	WORDSWORTH 11

Keble, John 1792–1866
English clergyman

found in my parish	KEBLE 1

Keegan, Kevin 1951–
English footballer and manager

improve on perfection — BECKHAM 3

Keeler, Christine 1942–
English model and showgirl

lady with the moustache — LEWINSKY 1

Keillor, Garrison 1942–
American humorous writer and
broadcaster

never told bad news — REAGAN 5

Keller, Hans 1919–85
Austrian-born British musicologist

isn't a poor substitute — PEARS 3

Keller, Helen 1880–1968
American writer and social reformer

wonderful cool something — KELLER 1

Kelly, Gene 1912–96
American dancer and choreographer

I'm the Marlon Brando — KELLY 3

Kelly, Grace 1928–82
American film actress

epitome of Ewardian elegance — BEATON 5

Keneally, Thomas 1935–
Australian novelist

one-line piece of mythology — SPIELBERG 3

Kennedy, Charles 1959–
British Liberal Democrat politician

you call me love — BOOTHROYD 3

Kennedy, John F. 1917–63
American Democratic statesman

between Nixon and the White House — NIXON 5
man who accompanied Jacqueline — ONASSIS 1
They sank my boat — KENNEDY 10
when Thomas Jefferson ate alone — JEFFERSON 2

Kennedy, Joseph P. 1888–1969
American financier and diplomat

sell Jack like soapflakes — KENNEDY 11

Kennedy, Nigel 1956–
British violinist

never portrayed anger — MENUHIN 2
violin is going to be there — KENNEDY 16

Kennedy, Rose 1890–1995
wife of Joseph Kennedy

might as well be president first — KENNEDY 2
mother of a great son — KENNEDY 20
Now Teddy must run — KENNEDY 1

Kenny, Mary

social illiterate, a political simpleton — FISCHER 2

Kern, Jerome 1885–1945
American composer

good Jewish music — KERN 1
no place in American music — BERLIN 3

Keynes, John Maynard 1883–1946
English economist

coax the needle off the record — WELLS 3
elusive colt — FORSTER 2
given facts of the outside world — ASQUITH 3
knew more about economics — KEYNES 1
last of the magicians — NEWTON 5
man struggling with a gramophone — STALIN 4
this goat-footed bard — LLOYD GEORGE 9
what Pericles felt of Athens — CLEMENCEAU 2
wiser when he was seated — WILSON 12

Khrushchev, Nikita 1894–1971
Soviet statesman

considered that he never erred — STALIN 5
fought barbarism with barbarism — STALIN 6
he went too far in thinking — SAKHAROV 1
I was a clerk in an office — KHRUSHCHEV 3

Kierkegaard, Sören 1813–55
Danish philosopher

I am in love with Mozart — MOZART 9

Kilminster, Ian 1945–
English pop singer

can't believe Alice Cooper plays golf	COOPER 1
getting away with it in his underpants	NUREYEV 5
He was the perfect gentleman	HENDRIX 5
your lawn would die	KILMINSTER 1

King, Billie Jean 1943–
American tennis player

ask me to stop playing	KING 2

King, Coretta Scott 1927–
American civil rights activist

champion of justice	ALI 4

King, Don 1931–
American boxing promoter

want to take us to the bank	KING 5

King, Francis 1923–
British writer

resembled a Baked Alaska	SNOW 1

King, Martin Luther 1929–68
American civil rights leader

be the white man's brother	KING 6
I've seen the promised land	KING 7

Kingsmill, Hugh 1889–1949
English man of letters

still alive at twenty-two	HOUSMAN 6

Kinnock, Neil 1942–
British Labour politician

first Kinnock in a thousand generations	KINNOCK 2
looking up at me from the sewer	HESELTINE 4
reserved for dead people	KINNOCK 3
warn you not to be ordinary	THATCHER 15
young, bald Leader	HAGUE 3

Kipling, Rudyard 1865–1936
English writer and poet

'eard o' the Widow at Windsor	VICTORIA 8
My Daemon was with me	KIPLING 2
prerogative of the harlot	BEAVERBROOK 2
smote 'is bloomin' lyre	HOMER 5
taught me to loathe Horace	HORACE 3
tinker out of Bedford	BUNYAN 2
Too scented	WILDE 8

Kirstein, Lincoln 1907–96
American dance impresario

Montgomery and Mrs Bowdler	DE VALOIS 3

Kissinger, Henry 1923–
American politician

do a hostile interview	PAXMAN 1
my first mistake	KISSINGER 3
symbol of compassion	ROOSEVELT 1
whole room might tilt	DE GAULLE 5

Kitchener, Lord 1850–1916
British soldier and statesman

commander so sincerely lamented	GORDON 2
don't mind your being killed	EDWARD 11

Klee, Paul 1879–1940
Swiss painter

Colour has taken hold	KLEE 1
Deepest tragedy takes place	VAN GOGH 4

Klein, Marci

dad's name all over his underwear	KLEIN 2

Knowles, Mary 1733–1807
English Quaker

tears out the heart	JOHNSON 16

Knox, John c.1505–72
Scottish Protestant reformer

Greater abomination	MARY 9

Kodály, Zoltán 1882–1967
Hungarian composer

regeneration from the people	BARTÓK 1

Kollwitz, Käthe 1867–1945
German sculptor and graphic artist

always worked with my blood	KOLLWITZ 1

Korchnoi, Viktor 1931–
Russian chess player

state against the individual	KARPOV 1

Korner, Alexis 1928–84
French-born jazz and blues musician

named Keith Mr Unhealth — RICHARDS 2

Kournikova, Anna 1981–
Russian tennis player

all blondes are stupid — KOURNIKOVA 2
She's sooo ugly — HURLEY 2

Krebs, Hans 1900–81
German-born British biochemist

chance of hitting the right one — KREBS 1

Kubrick, Stanley 1928–99
American film director

not an anecdotable character — CLARKE 4

Kundera, Milan 1929–
Czech novelist

Heartlessness masked — DICKENS 5

Labouchere, Henry 1831–1912
British politician

card up his sleeve — GLADSTONE 13

la Fontaine, Jean de 1621–95
French poet

made a god among the pagans — DESCARTES 4

Lagerfeld, Karl 1939–
German fashion designer

Chanel never liked knees — CHANEL 3
not take ourselves too seriously — LAGERFELD 1
wonderful Hollywood silent star — SCHIFFER 1

Lagrange, Joseph Louis 1736–1813
Italian-born French mathematician

Only a moment to cut off — LAVOISIER 1

Lahr, John 1941–
American critic

made such a spectacular entrance — NEESON 1

Laing, R. D. 1927–89
Scottish psychiatrist

descended to the 'Underworld' — FREUD 9

Lamartine, Alphonse de 1790–1869
French statesman and writer

possessed so much soul — BALZAC 6

Lamb, Charles 1775–1834
English writer

Archangel a little damaged — COLERIDGE 12
Cultivate simplicity — COLERIDGE 11
more to do than feel — LAMB 3
Not a fatter fish than he — GEORGE 14
Other pictures we look at — HOGARTH 2
propagated like trees — BROWNE 2
thrice noble, chaste, and virtuous — CAVENDISH 2

Lamb, Lady Caroline 1785–1828
wife of Lord Melbourne

dangerous to know — BYRON 12

Lampell, Millard 1919–97
American songwriter

lonesome train — LINCOLN 4

Lancaster, Osbert 1908–80
English writer and cartoonist

ruthless as any American — DIAGHILEV 2
unparalleled confusion — RUSKIN 3

Landor, Walter Savage 1775–1864
English poet

mostly sent to bed — SPENSER 3

lang, k. d. 1962–
Canadian singer

idea of torch *and* twang — LANG 2

Langevin, Paul 1872–1946
French physicist

habit of believing nothing — CURIE 8
pope of physics — EINSTEIN 7

Langton, Thomas c. 1440–1501
Bishop of St David's

God hath sent him to us — RICHARD 4

Larkin, Philip 1922–85
English poet

addiction to things Latin-American	GILLESPIE 2
Beatles could not get down	LENNON 2
Beatles could not get down	MCCARTNEY 2
dullest thing out	SPENSER 4
from Lascaux to Jackson Pollock	PARKER 1
gigantic indestructible crystal	BRADMAN 5
Hammer Films poet	PLATH 4
Happiness writes white	LARKIN 6
incompetent blaster	BEIDERBECKE 1
make art out of art instead	AUDEN 7
making great jazz with a Genius	ARMSTRONG 3
nearly the price of me once	WORDSWORTH 12
poet of unhappiness	HOUSMAN 7
present from Easter Island	HUGHES 4
survivor from the passenger list	HOPKINS 4
way to start a punch-up	BETJEMAN 5
what daffodils were	LARKIN 5

Larwood, Harold 1904–95
English cricketer

wouldn't burst a paper bag	BOTHAM 3

Laski, Harold 1893–1950
British Labour politician and academic

desert island with Napoleon	SWIFT 4
exceedingly agile wasp	SHAW 7
how high above all others	HOBBES 4
monkey looking for fleas	CHURCHILL 25
organize her own immortality	WOOLF 3
scandal is the second breath	ASQUITH 6

Laud, William 1573–1645
English prelate

mild and gracious prince	CHARLES 5

Lauda, Niki 1949–
Austrian motor-racing driver

rat was always my role model	LAUDA 1

Laughton, Charles 1899–1962
British-born American actor

nineteenth-century romantic actor	OLIVIER 3

Lauren, Ralph 1939–
American fashion designer

Grace Kelly of the Nineties	PALTROW 1
My life helps me with my job	LAUREN 1

Laver, Rod 1938–
Australian tennis player

more unpopular every time	CONNORS 4

Law, Denis 1940–
Scottish footballer

like looking at a stranger	LAW 1

Lawrence, D. H. 1885–1930
English novelist and poet

Bright Phoebus smote him	BROOKE 3
cheap Byron of his day	MASEFIELD 3
commonplace genius	HARDY 8
horrible underground passages	POE 2
How much nicer, finer, bigger	LOWELL 1
journalistic dirty-mindedness	JOYCE 5
much too inexperienced	RUSSELL 3
one of the greatest pioneers	FRANKLIN 6
people whom I dislike	DE QUINCEY 1
pig in clover	BENNETT 5
private soul leaking out	WHITMAN 2
such trivial people	SHAKESPEARE 18
uncanny magic of sea-creatures	MELVILLE 1
when I feel spiteful	LAWRENCE 7
Writers among the Ruins	CONRAD 4

Lawrence, Frieda 1879–1956
Wife of D. H. Lawrence

loved me absolutely · LAWRENCE 8

Lawrence, Ruth 1971–
English mathematician

not like passing an O-level · LAWRENCE 13

Lawrence, T. E. 1888–1935
English soldier and writer

like yesterday's east wind · TOLSTOY 6
outraged wet mackerel · STRACHEY 2
rolled thunderstorms in teacups · FORSTER 3
very mean fellow · KIPLING 3

Lawson, Nigel 1932–
British Conservative politician

cleverer than he appears · WHITELAW 2

Layton, Irving 1912–
Canadian poet

worthy of assassination · TRUDEAU 1

Leacock, Stephen 1869–1944
Canadian humorist

done with the atom · RUTHERFORD 3

Lean, David 1908–91
English film director

all woman, all woman · THATCHER 16

Lear, Edward 1812–88
English artist and writer

pleasant to know Mr Lear · LEAR 2

Leary, Timothy 1920–96
American psychologist

only painter of LSD · DALI 3

Leavis, F. R. 1895–1978
English literary critic

doesn't know · SNOW 2
I'd have been Cromwell · LEAVIS 2
Public School accent · BROOKE 4
Self-contempt, well-grounded · ELIOT 18

Le Carré, John 1931–
English novelist

to propose the character · GUINNESS 4

Le Corbusier 1887–1965
French architect

to make the family sacred · LE CORBUSIER 2

Lee, Henry 1756–1818
American soldier and politician

first in the hearts · WASHINGTON 6

Lee, Laurie 1914–97
English writer

always carries on with the job · ELIZABETH 16
hoarder of myths · FRINK 1
music as pure as spring water · SCHUBERT 1
person of concealment · LEE 3
Possessed of an archaic beauty · FRINK 2
spiky selfish personality · LEIGH 2
still mewling and puking · HUGHES 5

Lee, Robert E. 1807–70
American Confederate general

I have lost my *right* arm · JACKSON 12
trading on the blood of my men · LEE 7

Lee-Potter, Lynda
British journalist

slightly effeminate Geordie trucker · MOWLAM 3

Lees-Milne, James 1908–97
British writer

white face of a grey mare · KEPPEL 1

Lehmann, Lotte 1888–1976
German-born American soprano

long hands like tigers' claws · KLEMPERER 1

Lehmann, Rosamond 1901–90
English novelist

dangerous person for women · LEE 4
gets off with women · FLEMING 3

Lehrer, Tom 1928–
American humorist

already been dead for a year — MOZART 10
That's not my department — BRAUN 2

Leigh, Vivien 1913–67
English actress

like bathing in the sea — SHAKESPEARE 19
Shaw is like a train — SHAW 8

Lenin 1870–1924
Russian revolutionary

fallen among Fabians — SHAW 9
What a little bourgeois — WELLS 4

Lennon, John 1940–80
English pop singer and songwriter

always been a freak — LENNON 3
don't realize how lucky you are — TRUDEAU 2
everything we hated in pop — RICHARD 8
George, the invisible man — HARRISON 2
Nothing really affected me — PRESLEY 5
teacher-pupil relationship — ONO 2

Lennon, Sean Taro Ono 1975–

most important thing — LENNON 4

Leno, Jay 1950–
American comedian and writer

computer in every classroom — CLINTON 6

Leonard, Sugar Ray 1956–
American boxer

endowed with God-given talents — LEONARD 1

Leonardo da Vinci 1452–1519
Italian painter, scientist, and engineer

learning how to die — LEONARD 2

Le Saux, Graeme 1968–
English football player

described as 'cerebral' — LE SAUX 1

Lester, Dick 1932–
American film director

thin skin surrealism — MILLIGAN 1

Levant, Oscar 1906–72
American pianist

accompaniment to his conducting — BERNSTEIN 1
fall in love with yourself again — GERSHWIN 4

Leverson, Ada 1865–1936
English novelist

last gentleman in Europe — WILDE 9

Levin, Bernard 1928–
British journalist

enthusiasm of a Boy Scout — BENN 3
fox at large — MACMILLAN 4
remembered to turn the gas off — GETTY 1
Whom the mad would destroy — MAO 1
who talks more rapidly — BERLIN 7

Lewinsky, Monica 1973–
American political trainee

become an accidental celebrity — LEWINSKY 2

Lewis, Carl 1961–
American athlete

have to be like King Kong — LEWIS 1

Lewis, C. S. 1898–1963
English literary scholar

influence a bandersnatch — TOLKIEN 1
intensely loved and hated — KIPLING 4
rodent and a firefly — AYER 3

Lewis, Lennox 1965–
English boxer

bring in caveman tactics — TYSON 3
call myself a mother's boy — LEWIS 4

Lewis, Sinclair 1885–1951
American novelist

ruthlessly humanitarian woman — STOWE 1

Lewis, Wyndham 1882–1957
English novelist, painter, and critic

Angels in jumpers — SPENCER 3
behaved like Baden-Powell — POUND 3
cold, black suet-pudding — STEIN 3
Rogue Elephant, a Cannibal Shark — LEWIS 7

Liberace 1919–87
American showman

cry all the way to the bank
LIBERACE 3

Lichtenstein, Roy 1923–97
American painter and sculptor

programmed or impersonal
LICHTENSTEIN 1

Liddell, Eric 1902–45
Scottish athlete and missionary

with God's help, I run faster
LIDDELL 1

Lincoln, Abraham 1809–65
American Republican statesman

can't spare this man
GRANT 3

events have controlled me
LINCOLN 5

little woman who wrote
STOWE 2

naked deathless splendour
WASHINGTON 7

Lindbergh, Anne Morrow 1906–
American writer

his terrific drive
LINDBERGH 2

Lindbergh, Charles 1902–74
American aviator

Science, freedom, beauty
LINDBERGH 3

Lindsay, Vachel 1879–1931
American poet

Booth died blind
BOOTH 1

prairie-lawyer, master of us
LINCOLN 6

Lippmann, Walter 1889–1974
American journalist

genius for inactivity
COOLIDGE 3

Liston, Sonny 1932–70
American boxer

refused to accept defeat
MARCIANO 1

Liszt, Franz 1811–86
Hungarian composer and pianist

do not let them intimidate you
GRIEG 3

pillars of smoke and fire
BEETHOVEN 7

Livingstone, Ken 1945–
British Labour politician

become a socialist terror
BENN 4

nobody scared me as much
THATCHER 17

vampire in charge of a blood bank
MANDELSON 3

Lloyd, Marie 1870–1922
English music-hall entertainer

by command of the British Public
LLOYD 1

Lloyd George, David 1863–1945
British Liberal statesman

adequate Lord Mayor of Birmingham
CHAMBERLAIN 4

drum out of the skin of his mother
CHURCHILL 27

greatest living orators
CLEMENCEAU 3

intimidate or blackmail a man
PANKHURST 2

keep him straight
MACDONALD 11

like to call on the Holy Ghost
CHURCHILL 26

never make up his mind
BONAR LAW 3

no room for the cat
ASQUITH 4

One of those revolving lighthouses
KITCHENER 2

on the water, I presume
BEAVERBROOK 3

pick up mercury
DE VALERA 4

retail mind
CHAMBERLAIN 3

scent on a pocket handkerchief
BALFOUR 4

to the top of his boots
HAIG 3

wrong end of a drainpipe
CHAMBERLAIN 5

Lockhart, John Gibson 1794–1854
Scottish writer and critic

starved apothecary
KEATS 10

Lodge, David 1935–
English novelist

laid end to end words
WHITMAN 3

whaling a universal metaphor
MELVILLE 2

Logue, Christopher 1926–
English poet

breaks your little toe
ALI 5

Come to the edge
APOLLINAIRE 1

Longfellow, Henry Wadsworth
1807–82
American poet

Dead he is not, but departed — DÜRER 4
Lady with a Lamp — NIGHTINGALE 2

Longworth, Alice Roosevelt
1884–1980
American daughter of Theodore Roosevelt

been a revolutionary priest — KENNEDY 18
may call me Alice — MCCARTHY 1
one-third Eleanor — ROOSEVELT 8

Loos, Anita 1893–1981
American writer

monumental, sexless Buddha — STEIN 4
once in a while isn't very smart — HUXLEY 5
So bloated with conceit — COWARD 4
without calculation — CRAWFORD 4

Louis, Joe 1914–81
American boxer

insulted if you missed him — MARCIANO 2

Louis Philippe 1773–1850
King of France 1830–48

what he meant by that — TALLEYRAND 2

Louis XIV 1638–1715
King of France from 1643

I am the State — LOUIS 1
ladies declare war on me — ANNE 4

Lovelace, Ada 1815–52
English mathematician

influence of *ambition* — LOVELACE 1

Lovelock, James 1919–
English scientist

merge with the chemistry — LOVELOCK 1

Lowell, Amy 1874–1925
American poet

prophet straying in a fog — WHITMAN 4
would set doors ajar — DICKINSON 3

Lowell, James Russell 1819–91
American poet

good roaring positive fellow — TROLLOPE 4
two-fifths sheer fudge — POE 3

Lowry, L. S. 1887–1976
English painter

use simple materials — LOWRY 2

Lucas, E. V. 1868–1938
English journalist, essayist, and critic

God will know the truth — CHESTERTON 4

Lucas, George 1944–
American film director, producer, and screenwriter

biggest insecurities — COPPOLA 3

Luce, Clare Booth 1903–87
American diplomat, politician, and writer

deer in the body of a woman — GARBO 11

Ludwig II 1845–86
King of Bavaria

cannot requite a divine spirit — WAGNER 4
have my hair curled every day — LUDWIG 1

Lumley, Joanna 1946–
British actress

painted smile is always genuine — LUMLEY 1

Luther, Martin 1483–1546
German Protestant theologian

I can do no other — LUTHER 2
turn astronomy inside out — COPERNICUS 1

Luther, Marylou
American fashion journalist

mother of the rich hippy look — PORTER 3

Lutyens, Edwin 1869–1944
English architect

best friend a man could ever — JEKYLL 3
weighty materials as a pigment — VANBRUGH 2

Lycett Green, Candida 1942–

always having lunch — BETJEMAN 6

Lydgate, John c.1370–c.1451
English poet

he was the lodesterre — CHAUCER 5

Lynch, David 1946–
American film director

grabs onto it like crazy — CAGE 5

Lynton, Mrs Lynn 1822–98
English writer

so purely artificial — ELIOT 6

Lyttelton, George 1883–1962
British writer

crackling with intelligence — MURDOCH 3

Lytton, Lady 1874–1971

see all his faults — CHURCHILL 28

MacArthur, Douglas 1880–1964
American general

best clerk who ever served — EISENHOWER 6
old soldiers never die — MACARTHUR 1

Macaulay, Lord 1800–59
English politician and historian

agony is abated — MACAULAY 3
epithet for a knave — MACHIAVELLI 3
essence of war is violence — HAMPDEN 3
expression of fondness — BYRON 13
first of biographers — BOSWELL 3
huge massy face — JOHNSON 17
last Englishmen who sold justice — BACON 5
long streamy flakes of music — PAGANINI 2
love your neighbour's wife — BYRON 14
not wonder that they poisoned him — SOCRATES 3
patriarchs seemed children — BURNEY 2
rake among scholars — STEELE 1
rich, quiet, and infamous — HASTINGS 1
rob a neighbour — FREDERICK 4
seemed to him little — WALPOLE 2
sluttish magnificence — DRYDEN 6

MacBeth, George 1932–92
Scottish poet and novelist

really a bit of a jerk — ROSSETTI 6

MacCaig, Norman 1910–96
Scottish poet

torchlight procession of one — MACDIARMID 2

McCarthy, Joseph 1908–57
American politician

Americanism with its sleeves rolled — MCCARTHY 2

McCarthy, Mary 1912–89
American novelist

'and' and 'the' — HELLMAN 2
horror of Gandhi's murder — GANDHI 7
modern American woman — FLAUBERT 4

McCartney, Paul 1942–
English pop singer and songwriter

Ballads and babies — MCCARTNEY 3
manoeuvring swine — LENNON 5
never get totally involved — JAGGER 3
She was very different — ONO 3
star in his own right — STARR 1

McColgan, Liz 1964–
Scottish athlete

proved I wanted it more — MCCOLGAN 1

MacColl, Ewan 1915–89
Scottish singer and writer

He is against everything — DYLAN 7

McCullin, Don 1935–
British photojournalist

try to be is human — MCCULLIN 1

MacDiarmid, Hugh 1892–1978
Scottish poet and nationalist

campaign is a personal issue — HOME 4
Mair nonsense has been uttered — BURNS 8
paralysing ideology of defeatism — SCOTT 10
problems o' the Scottish soul — LAUDER 1
vitalises the other torpid denizens — MACDIARMID 3

MacDonald, Jeannette 1903–65
American actress and singer

fastest derrière-pincher — CHEVALIER 2

McDonald, Trevor 1939–
West Indian-born broadcaster

bottle it and sell it — MCDONALD 1

McEnroe, John 1959–
American tennis player

if they want to boo me — MCENROE 4
worth forty thousand of you — MCENROE 3

Macfarlane, Gwyn 1907–87

creates a gold mine — FLOREY 2
stumbles on a nugget of gold — FLEMING 1

McGinley, Phyllis 1905–78
American poet

best in your bulging versery — NASH 1

McGough, Roger 1937–
English poet

on the outside of things — MCGOUGH 1

McGuinness, Tom 1941–
British rock musician

it was him against the world — CLAPTON 3

McIlvanney, Hugh 1933–
Scottish journalist

ability to treat you as an equal — BUSBY 1
fit everybody's idea of a romantic — SHANKLY 1
sensitive as a pick-pocket's hands — BEST 5
volcano trapped in an iceberg — PIGGOTT 1
walk slowly to the wicket — RICHARDS 6

McInerney, Jay 1955–
American writer

remember which dance — FITZGERALD 5

Mackenzie, Kelvin 1946–
British journalist and media executive

couldn't edit a bus ticket — STREET 1

MacLaine, Shirley 1934–
American actress

half-Canadian—the top half — BEATTY 3
push a peanut all the way — MACLAINE 2

McLaren, Malcolm 1946–
English manager and pop singer

everything This society hates — MCLAREN 1

McLean, Don 1945–
American songwriter

day the music died — HOLLY 1

Macleod, Iain 1913–70
British Conservative politician

part of First Gravedigger — BEVAN 4
remorselessness of his own logic — POWELL 1

McLuhan, Marshall 1911–80
Canadian communications scholar

awareness of contemporary culture — TRUDEAU 3
detractors work night and day — MCLUHAN 3
formula for the electronic age — NIGHTINGALE 3
his place in the sun — FRYE 4
I am an intellectual thug — MCLUHAN 2

McMenemy, Lawrie
British football manager

even the blind men were calling — KEEGAN 1

Macmillan, Harold 1894–1986
British Conservative statesman

could have a translation — KHRUSHCHEV 4
creeping about the Vatican — BUTLER 2
Duke of Wellington of America — KENNEDY 12
gardener in his Sunday clothes — MOLOTOV 2
iron painted to look like wood — HOME 5
I was always a shit — MACMILLAN 5
might as well have a film star — ELIZABETH 17
prophesying the imminent fall — BEVAN 5
they don't like clever people — DISRAELI 8

McNamara, Robert 1916–
American Democratic politician

McNamara's War — MCNAMARA 1
We were terribly wrong — MCNAMARA 2

MacNeice, Louis 1907–63
British poet, born in Belfast

Bow-tied Silenus roistering his way — THOMAS 4

Madonna 1958–
American pop singer and actress

alive when he is working — PRINCE 1
do everything he can do — JACKSON 8
saint or the incarnation of Satan — MADONNA 3
— PERÓN 2

Maher, Mary

splendid candidate to vote for — ROBINSON 1

Mahler, Gustav 1860–1911
Austrian composer

analysis, negation, barrenness — IBSEN 1
breath from the lungs of Wagner — BRAHMS 2
greater than inarticulate nature — BEETHOVEN 8
My life has all been paper — MAHLER 2
not merely a firework — STRAUSS 3
only the discarded husk — MAHLER 1
positive, the productive — SHAKESPEARE 20
withering blight on all — TOLSTOY 7

Mahon, Derek 1941–
Northern Irish poet

At the heart of the ridiculous — OATES 2

Mailer, Norman 1923–
American novelist and essayist

anybody that pompous — DAVIES 4
every man's love affair with America — MONROE 10
fat off a taxicab driver's neck — ABZUG 2
intellectual throwing a good punch — ALI 6

Maintenon, Francoise de
1635–1719
French queen

Behold the fine appointment — LOUIS 2

Mallory, George Leigh 1886–1924
British mountaineer

Because it's there — MALLORY 1

Mandela, Nelson 1918–
South African statesman

dedicated my life — MANDELA 1
until I changed myself — MANDELA 2

Mandelson, Peter 1953–
British Labour politician

charismatic human being — CLINTON 7
taking the high ground — BLAIR 5

Mandelstam, Nadezhda 1899–1980
Russian wife of Osip Mandelstam

as helpless as everybody else — EHRENBURG 1
stern and overbearing abbess — AKHMATOVA 2

Mandelstam, Osip 1891–1938
Russian poet

full cockroach moustache — STALIN 7
Upon you is the mark of God — AKHMATOVA 3

Manet, Édouard 1832–83
French painter

each marrying an academician — MORISOT 1
impressions of a moment — MANET 1
never make anything of it — RENOIR 2

Mankiewicz, Joseph L. 1909–
American screenwriter and director

cut you down to size — TRACY 4

Mann, Thomas 1875–1955
German novelist

inaugurated the twentieth century — CONRAD 5

Manning, Cardinal 1808–92
English cardinal

He was a great hater — NEWMAN 2

Mansfield, Katherine 1888–1923
New Zealand-born short-story writer

warming the teapot — FORSTER 4

Manzarek, Ray 1935–
American rock musician

enjoying every intoxicated moment — MORRISON 2
that soul, that torment — MORRISON 6

Map, Walter c.1140–c.1209
Welsh author

fear of becoming too fat — HENRY 2

Maradona, Diego 1960–
Argentine football player

head of Maradona

MARADONA 1

Marceau, Marcel 1923–
French mime artist

express the tragic moment

MARCEAU 1

Marciano, Rocky 1923–69
American boxer

they call him cheap

MARCIANO 3

Margach, James d. 1979
British journalist

authoritarian and intolerant

HEATH 6

little indiarubber man

ATTLEE 8

Margaret, Princess 1930–
British princess

have the Queen as their aunt

MARGARET 1

Marlborough, John, Duke of
1650–1722
British general

That was once a man

MARLBOROUGH 3

Marlborough, Sarah, Duchess of
1660–1744

flames of extravagant passion

ANNE 5

never share the heart and hand

MARLBOROUGH 5

pleasure me in his top-boots

MARLBOROUGH 4

Marlowe, Derek 1938–
British writer

his private self is Lewis Carroll

STOPPARD 2

Martin, Pete 1901–
American journalist

wrap up 115 pounds of smoke

KELLY 6

Martineau, Harriet 1802–76
English writer

If you put the question in wrong

BABBAGE 3

Marvell, Andrew 1621–78
English poet

nothing common did or mean

CHARLES 6

such a vast expense of mind

MILTON 12

Marx, Chico 1891–1961
American film comedian

whispering in her mouth

MARX 1

Marx, Groucho 1895–1977
American film comedian

ACCEPT ME AS A MEMBER

MARX 4

before she was a virgin

DAY 1

guy I knew in Pittsburgh

GARBO 12

never kissed an ugly girl

MARX 3

phone, a horse or a broad

MARX 2

Marx, Karl 1818–83
German political philosopher

I am not a Marxist

MARX 9

leather-tongued oracle

BENTHAM 2

Mary, Queen 1867–1953
Queen Consort of George V

refused a lesser sacrifice

EDWARD 12

Mary I 1516–58
Queen of England

'Calais' lying in my heart

MARY 10

Masefield, John 1878–1967
English poet

Shone, with a Hope

CHURCHILL 29

Masters, Brian 1939–
British writer

tendency to forgive other people

LONGFORD 1

Matthau, Walter 1920–2000
American actor

something appropriate. Perhaps Macbeth

STREISAND 2

Matthews, Stanley 1915–2000
English footballer

Danny projected his mind

BLANCHFLOWER 1

Maugham, W. Somerset 1874–1965
English novelist

fence is just too high	JAMES 11
kettle to a dog's tail	DOSTOEVSKY 3
knew to be bogus	LAWRENCE 17
meanness and frippery	DOSTOEVSKY 4
nostalgia of the slums	CHAPLIN 4
observed life from a window	JAMES 12
Which is he playing now	TRACY 5

Maupassant, Guy de 1850–93
French novelist and short-story writer

greatest devastator of dreams	SCHOPENHAUER 1

Maurois, André 1885–1967
French writer

wielded an intellectual dominion	WELLS 5

Mawdsley, James
British civil rights activist

Not just a treasure to Burma	AUNG SAN 3

Maxton, James 1885–1946
Scottish Labour politician

You're a bloody tragedy	MACDONALD 12

Maxwell, James Clerk 1831–79
Scottish physicist

his crude ideas as well	FARADAY 6

Maxwell, Robert 1923–91
Czech-born British publisher

Left wing, as you would expect	MAXWELL 3

Mayall, John 1933–
British rock musician

always a chameleon thing	CLAPTON 4

Maynard Smith, John 1920–
English biologist

on our side against the creationists	GOULD 2

Medawar, Peter 1915–87
English immunologist and author

born anew every morning	MEDAWAR 1
cut his ear off	VAN GOGH 5
demanded danger money	HALDANE 3
important to be clever *about*	WATSON 1
in some ways the cleverest	HALDANE 2
willingness to be deceived	TEILHARD DE CHARDIN 1

Mehta, Zubin 1936–
Indian-born American conductor

This girl plays like five men	DU PRÉ 4

Meitner, Lise 1878–1968
Austrian-born Swedish physicist

lack of personal relationships	EINSTEIN 8

Melbourne, Lord 1779–1848
British Whig statesman

as cocksure of anything	MACAULAY 4

Melly, George 1926–
British jazz singer

Judy Garland of the 'in' set	SPRINGFIELD 1
nothing could be that funny	JAGGER 5
pop's Byronic hero, its Rimbaud	JAGGER 4
so desperate, so sincere, so drunk	BURDON 1
vulgar caricature of a show-biz success	JONES 8

Melville, Herman 1819–91
American novelist and short-story writer

he is no common humbug	EMERSON 4
meteor of the war	BROWN 10

Mencken, H. L. 1880–1956
American journalist and literary critic

charlatan of the very highest skill	ROOSEVELT 10
Coolidge only snored	COOLIDGE 4
first genuinely American artist	TWAIN 5
formidable body of cannibals	TRUMAN 1
lands in the Thirteenth	CHESTERTON 5

Mendeleev, Dmitri 1834–1907
Russian chemist

double number of Newtons	NEWTON 6

Menuhin, Diana | Y sat on Cloud Nine | MENUHIN 3

Menuhin, Yehudi 1916–99 | civilized and respectful | MOZART 11
American-born British violinist | creating Utopias | MENUHIN 4
| If wind and water could write music | BRITTEN 4
| most fulfilled and relaxed | HEATH 7
| passion and directness | DU PRÉ 5
| people worse off than he | TOSCANINI 1
| primeval strength of its origins | BARTÓK 2
| Prince Myshkin, a 'blessed fool' | SOLZHENITSYN 2
| product of the misty landscapes | BRAHMS 3
| spontaneous expressiveness | KENNEDY 17
| sun so confident of its position | STRADIVARI 1
| totally uncompromising power | BEETHOVEN 9
| unassertive and shy | SHOSTAKOVICH 1

Merckx, Madame Eddy | vaccinated with a bicycle spoke | MERCKX 2

Meredith, George 1828–1909 | dandy Isaiah | ARNOLD 3
English novelist and poet | teeth of the Apocalyptic horse | ELIOT 7
| yards of linen-drapery | TENNYSON 6

Metternich, Prince 1773–1859 | instrument that cuts the best | TALLEYRAND 3
Austrian statesman

Michelangelo 1475–1564 | good reason to be envious | RAPHAEL 3
Italian sculptor, painter, and architect | greatest goldsmith | CELLINI 1
| my children shall be the works | MICHELANGELO 3

Middleton, Thomas c.1580–1627 | visible eclipse of playing | BURBAGE 1
English dramatist

Mies van der Rohe, Ludwig | don't want to be interesting | MIES VAN DER ROHE 1
1886–1969
German-born architect and designer

Mill, John Stuart 1806–73 | proved that it *may* be true | DARWIN 5
English philosopher and economist

Millais, John Everett 1829–96 | never seen or heard of Rossetti | MILLAIS 2
English painter

Millay, Edna St Vincent 1892–1950 | looked on Beauty bare | EUCLID 1
American poet | so pure, so relentless | BACH 9

Miller, Arthur 1915– | help her solve her problems | MONROE 11
American dramatist

Miller, Henry 1891–1980 | eye of Paris | BRASSAÏ 1
American novelist | Has that faroff cosmic itch | SCRIABIN 1
| master of the nightmare | DISNEY 2
| perpetual sea of sex | MILLER 5

Miller, Jonathan 1934– | as Alice in Wonderland | MILLIGAN 2
English writer and director | jack of all trades | MILLER 8
| wasn't a rich squire | OSBORNE 4
| what Freud did for sex | MCLUHAN 4

Milligan, Spike 1918– | smartest thing I've heard him say | EVANS 1
Irish comedian

Milne, A. A. 1882–1956 | had more publicity than he wants | MILNE 2
English writer for children | King John was not a good man | JOHN 1

Milne, Christopher 1920–96
English bookseller

escape from being fifty   MILNE 1

Milton, John 1608–74
English poet

consider how my light is spent   MILTON 13
labour of an age   SHAKESPEARE 21
our chief of men   CROMWELL 6
prisoner to the Inquisition   GALILEO 5

Minnelli, Vincente 1910–84
American film director

would always belong to the people   GARLAND 3

Minsky, Marvin 1927–
American computer scientist

least stuck person   FEYNMAN 3

Mirabeau, Comte de 1749–91
French revolutionary

altars to this mighty genius   FRANKLIN 7

Mitchell, Austin 1934–
British Labour politician

instinct for the exposed groin   TEBBIT 2

Mitchell, Warren 1926–
English actor

Hancock hated the world   HANCOCK 1

Mitchison, Naomi 1897–1999
Scottish writer and feminist

light in great darkness to many   STOPES 3

Mitford, Mary Russell 1787–1855
English novelist and dramatist

poker or a fire-screen   AUSTEN 7

Mitford, Nancy 1904–73
English writer

washes it down with Deuteronomy   MONTGOMERY 5

Mitterrand, François 1916–96
French socialist statesman

mouth of Marilyn Monroe   THATCHER 18

Modigliani, Amedeo 1884–1920
Italian painter and sculptor

use of spoiling canvas   MODIGLIANI 3

Monet, Claude 1840–1926
French painter

paint as a bird sings   MONET 2

Monkhouse, Bob
British comedian

petty-minded game show host   BARRYMORE 2

Monroe, Marilyn 1926–62
American actress

work for those people who work hard   MONROE 12

Montagu, Elizabeth 1720–1800
English writer

she is a great Prince   CATHERINE 3

Montagu, Lady Mary Wortley
1689–1762
English writer

lobster to attendant shrimp   CAROLINE 1
parallel with that of Caligula   SWIFT 5

Montaigne 1533–92
French moralist and essayist

can easily imagine Socrates   ALEXANDER 2
in the place of Alexander   SOCRATES 4

Montesquieu 1689–1755
French political philosopher

learned men who are clean   LEIBNIZ 1

Montgomery, Lord 1887–1976
British field marshal

explain all those men I killed   MONTGOMERY 6
man I'd go in the jungle with   MAO 2

Montgomery, Robert 1807–55
English clergyman and poet

monk who shook the world   LUTHER 3

Moore, George 1852–1933
Anglo-Irish novelist

began by imitating Manet	MONET 3
hiatus in the history of art	MORISOT 2
On every page James is a prude	JAMES 13
sort of literary Cinderella	BRONTË 1
wreck of Stevenson	CONRAD 6

Moore, Henry 1898–1986
English sculptor and draughtsman

first hole made through	MOORE 4

Moore, Marianne 1887–1972
American poet

being catalogued, categorized	STEVENS 1
very difficult to write	MOORE 7

Moore, Roger 1928–
English actor

Left eyebrow raised	MOORE 8

Moorehead, Alan 1910–83

orchestra without a conductor	BURTON 2

Moran, Margaret 1955–
British Labour politician

I am a Blair Witch	MORAN 1

More, Kenneth 1914–82
English actor

If I was in a tight corner	BADER 2

More, Thomas 1478–1535
English scholar and statesman

Devil should have right	MORE 6
ill-featured of limbs, crook-backed	RICHARD 5
wish him a castle in France	HENRY 8

Morecambe, Eric 1926–84
English comedian

get it wrong as well	MORECAMBE 1

Morgan, Piers 1965–
British newspaper editor

most reviled man	LE SAUX 2

Morisot, Berthe 1841–95
French painter

record something fleeting	MORISOT 3

Morley, John 1838–1923
British politician and writer

outstanding natural phenomena	ROOSEVELT 11

Morley, Sheridan 1941–

wrote from the gut	BERLIN 4

Morrell, Ottoline 1873–1938
English society hostess

always a spectator in life	ASQUITH 5
like an Aubrey Beardsley drawing	STRACHEY 3
lost in the world outside	NIJINSKY 1
pure fire of his soul	RUSSELL 4
same intense poignancy	CHAPLIN 5
searching and speculating	KEYNES 2

Morris, Desmond 1928–
English anthropologist

manners of the dominant male	MAXWELL 4

Morris, William 1834–96
English writer, artist, and designer

I cannot paint you	MORRIS 2
ministering to the swinish luxury	MORRIS 5

Morrison, Jim 1943–71
American rock singer and songwriter

revolt, disorder, chaos	MORRISON 3

Morrison, Van 1945–
Irish singer, songwriter, and musician

nothing to do with rock	MORRISON 7

Morshead, Owen 1893–1977
English librarian

trample on their young	GEORGE 23

Mortimer, John 1923–
English novelist, barrister, and dramatist

descendent of the Roundheads	BENN 5

Moses, Grandma 1860–1961
American painter

best out of what life offered · MOSES 2

Mosley, Diana 1910–
English wife of Oswald Mosley

incredibly frank, and wonderful · HITLER 11

Mosley, Leonard 1913–

charm, charm, charm · MOUNTBATTEN 4

Moss, Stirling 1929–
English motor-racing driver

drove fast enough to win · STEWART 1

Motion, Andrew 1952–
English poet

hunted by your own quick hounds · DIANA 7
like getting lost in a greenhouse · SPENSER 5

Mountbatten, Lord 1900–79
British sailor, soldier, and statesman

be jolly at my funeral · MOUNTBATTEN 5

Mowlam, Mo 1949–
British Labour politician

put up with 'the sinner' · MOWLAM 4

Mozart, Wolfgang Amadeus
1756–91
Austrian composer

audience who understand nothing · MOZART 12
Keep your eyes on him · BEETHOVEN 10
makes them *Mozartish* · MOZART 13
that godless arch-rascal · VOLTAIRE 5

Muggeridge, Kitty 1903–94

risen without trace · FROST 3

Muggeridge, Malcolm 1903–90
British journalist

bored for England · EDEN 5
much more from the *News of the World* · ORWELL 3
parody of a Conservative politician · MACMILLAN 6
playing a piano in a brothel · MUGGERIDGE 2
preoccupation with physical appetite · MAUGHAM 2
saintliness kept breaking through · WAUGH 4
Something beautiful for God · TERESA 1
taking the floor in a night-club · BEAVERBROOK 4

Muir, Frank 1920–98
English writer and broadcaster

thinking man's crumpet · BAKEWELL 1

Murdoch, Iris 1919–99
English novelist

fathom Plato's mind · PLATO 2
I'm just wandering · MURDOCH 5
in the second league · MURDOCH 4

Murdoch, Rupert 1931–
Australian-born American publisher and
media entrepeneur

shuffling around in Gucci shoes · DALAI 1

Murray, Charles Shaar
British journalist

might well be pop's Martin Amis · WATERS 2
preaches safe sex and hard work · MADONNA 4

Murray, James 1837–1915
Scottish lexicographer

through an untrodden forest · MURRAY 1

Murrow, Ed 1908–65
American broadcaster and journalist

mobilized the English language · CHURCHILL 30
terrorize a whole nation · MCCARTHY 3

Mussolini, Benito 1883–1945
Italian Fascist dictator

more intelligent than Hitler · MUSSOLINI 3

Muste, A. J. 1885–1967
American pacifist

If I can't love Hitler · HITLER 12

Nabokov, Vladimir 1899–1977
Russian novelist

fundamentally medieval world · FREUD 10
think like a genius · NABOKOV 1

Nader, Ralph 1934–
American lawyer and reformer

Only Al Gore can beat Al Gore · GORE 2

Naidu, Sarojini 1879–1949
Indian politician

setting him up in poverty   GANDHI 8

Nairne, Lady Carolina 1766–1845
Scottish songwriter

Will ye no come back again   STUART 4

Nansen, Fridtjof 1861–1930
Norwegian Arctic explorer

where he wanted to 'remain'   NANSEN 1

Napoleon I 1769–1821
Emperor of France

France has more need of me   NAPOLEON 9
no heart, only head   JOSEPHINE 1
shit in a silk stocking   TALLEYRAND 4
successor of Charlemagne   NAPOLEON 8

Nastase, Ilie 1946–
Romanian tennis player

plays something else   BORG 3

Nathan, George Jean 1882–1958

triumph of sugar   BARRIE 4

Navratilova, Martina 1956–
Czech-born American tennis player

I don't like labels   NAVRATILOVA 1

Neame, Ronald 1911–
British film director and producer

He was like a chameleon   GUINNESS 5

Nehru, Jawaharlal 1889–1964
Indian statesman

great lover of peace   STALIN 8
last Englishman to rule   NEHRU 1
light has gone out   GANDHI 9
restored all that was beautiful   CURZON 5

Neill, A. S. 1883–1973
Scottish teacher and educationist

lost my fear of my pupils   NEILL 1

Nelson, Horatio, Lord 1758–1805
British admiral

legacy to my king and country   HAMILTON 1
Nelson touch   NELSON 3
right to be blind sometimes   NELSON 2

Newbolt, Henry 1862–1938
English lawyer and poet

he's in his hammock   DRAKE 2

Newman, John Henry 1801–90
English prelate and theologian

any other sort of religion   NEWMAN 3

Newton, Isaac 1642–1727
English mathematician and physicist

elasticity of his fingers   HANDEL 3
on the shoulders of giants   NEWTON 7
playing on the sea-shore   NEWTON 8

Nichols, Mike 1931–
American director

gets better in the bath   TAYLOR 1

Nicklaus, Jack 1940–
American golfer

I am not familiar   WOODS 1

Nico 1938–1988
German singer and actress

wanted visions for his poetry   MORRISON 4

Nicolson, Harold 1886–1968
English diplomat, politician, and writer

brilliant contemporary   SHAW 10
dark river moving deeply   SACKVILLE-WEST 3
dimming of the lights   MACDONALD 13
excuse for thinking hard   ELIOT 19
kill animals and stick in stamps   GEORGE 24
little snouty, sneaky mind   PEPYS 2
manner of a clothes-brush   CHAMBERLAIN 6
moustache of a Neapolitan tenor   KIPLING 5
spinnaker of 'Yes Ma'am'   ELIZABETH 24
village fiddler after Paganini   ATTLEE 9

Nicolson, Nigel 1917–
British Conservative politician and writer

sympathy for other people — SACKVILLE-WEST 4

Nietzsche, Friedrich 1844–1900
German philosopher and writer

arrogant old muddle-head and grumbler — CARLYLE 7
contaminates everything he touches — WAGNER 5
feeds on pure ambrosia — EMERSON 5
limits that morality sets — HAYDN 2
most penetrating eyes and ears — STENDHAL 2
music about music — BEETHOVEN 11
rat-catcher of Athens — SOCRATES 5
synthesis of monster and the Superman — NAPOLEON 10

Nightingale, Florence 1820–1910
English nurse

procession of one — MACAULAY 5
woman in the Greek chorus — VICTORIA 9

Nijinsky, Vaslav 1890–1950
Russian ballet dancer

compositions have no purpose — STRAVINSKY 2

Nilsen, Dennis 1945–
British mass-murderer

reducing them to objects — NILSEN 1

Nin, Anaïs 1903–77
French-born American writer

very touch of the letter — MILLER 6

Niven, David 1910–83
English actor

he *always* let you down — FLYNN 3

Nixon, Richard Milhous 1913–94
American Republican statesman

even go to the bathroom — CASTRO 1
Georgetown drawing rooms — GORBACHEV 4
he'll no longer matter — BUSH 7
I gave them a sword — NIXON 7
I'm not a crook — NIXON 6
Newark factory gate — YELTSIN 1

Nolan, Sidney 1917–93
Australian painter

nature of the 'otherness' — NOLAN 1

Noonan, Peggy 1950–
American writer

battle for the mind — REAGAN 6

Norman, Barry 1933–
British film critic and writer

totally memorable — KELLY 7

Norman, Greg 1955–
Australian golfer

Nick played great — FALDO 2

North, Richard D.

good candidate for canonization — RYDER 1

Northcliffe, Lord 1865–1922
British newspaper proprietor

buy it like an honest man — NORTHCLIFFE 2

Novalis 1772–1801
German poet and novelist

God-intoxicated man — SPINOZA 2

Nunn, Trevor 1940–
English theatre director

attack, thrust, determination — JACKSON 5

Nureyev, Rudolf 1939–93
Russian-born ballet dancer

beauty am faded — NUREYEV 6

Nye, Bill 1850–96
American humorist

better than it sounds — WAGNER 6

Oates, Captain Lawrence
1880–1912
English polar explorer

head screwed on right — AMUNDSEN 2

O'Brien, Conor Cruise 1917–
Irish politician, writer, and journalist

wear a clove of garlic .... HAUGHEY 1

O'Brien, Edna 1932–
Irish novelist and short-story writer

wished he was an intellectual .... HUSTON 3

O'Brien, Flann 1911–66
Irish novelist and journalist

Book of Kells .... FORD 7

O'Casey, Sean 1880–1964
Irish dramatist

battling with his heaven .... STRINDBERG 1
literature's performing flea .... WODEHOUSE 2
physical courage .... MARKIEVICZ 4
sit serenely in his Doll's House .... IBSEN 2
two gay guardian angels .... JOYCE 7

O'Connor, Frank 1903–66
Irish man of letters

one of the most devious men .... YEATS 7

O'Connor, Sinéad 1966–
Irish singer and songwriter

big mouth and a shaved head .... O'CONNOR 1
turn him into a peach .... CLINTON 8

O'Keeffe, Georgia 1887–1986
American painter

I take them apart .... O'KEEFFE 1

Oldfield, Bruce 1950–
English fashion designer

lime green is the new black .... OLDFIELD 1

Oldham, Andrew Loog 1944–
English pop manager

had a vision for the Beatles .... EPSTEIN 1
next adventure, a true star .... FAITHFULL 1

Oliphant, Mrs Margaret 1828–97
Scottish novelist and critic

in a mental greenhouse .... ELIOT 8

Olivier, Laurence 1907–89
English actor and director

could be played as a bore .... GUINNESS 6
nearest thing to the eye of God .... SHAKESPEARE 22

Onassis, Jacqueline Kennedy
1929–94
Wife of John Fitzgerald Kennedy

dancing against the clock .... NUREYEV 7
never be another Camelot .... KENNEDY 13
sounds like a saddle horse .... ONASSIS 2

Ondaatje, Michael 1943–
Sri Lankan-born Canadian writer

computer to the last Luddite .... ONDAATJE 1

O'Neill, Eugene 1888–1953
American dramatist

most modern of moderns .... STRINDBERG 2

Ono, Yoko 1933–
Japanese poet and songwriter

very honest about everything .... LENNON 6

Oppenheimer, Robert 1904–67
American theoretical physicist

more you know the better .... OPPENHEIMER 1
wholly without worldliness .... EINSTEIN 9

Orbison, Roy 1936–88
American singer and songwriter

real raw cat, singing like a bird .... PRESLEY 6

Orderic Vitalis 1075–c.1142
Anglo-Norman monk and chronicler

remarkable for his physical strength .... HAROLD 1

Orleans, Duchess of 1652–1722

most incompetent man .... JAMES 4

O'Rourke, P. J. 1947–
American humorous writer

because they were pretty .... KENNEDY 14

Orr, Deborah 1962–
British journalist

you're forever our object — WILLIAM 6

Orwell, George 1903–50
English novelist

according to his very dim lights — CHAMBERLAIN 7
always fighting against something — DICKENS 6
antisocial as a flea — DALI 4
dash of Theocritus — HOUSMAN 8
elephantine pedant — JOYCE 8
gutless Kipling — AUDEN 8
how clean a smell — GANDHI 10
if Wells had never existed — WELLS 7
kind of intellectual chivalry — RUSSELL 5
looking only on the black side — MUGGERIDGE 3
member of the Fabian Society — SHAW 11
physical stink off its pages — DALI 5
recently dead fish — ATTLEE 10
simply a hole in the air — BALDWIN 5
something deeply appealing — HITLER 13
talk of 'Fascist tendencies' — WODEHOUSE 3
temporarily on our side — STALIN 9
Tory anarchist, despising authority — SWIFT 6
what respectable people imagined — WELLS 6
worshipped Kipling at thirteen — KIPLING 6
would probably choose Fascism — ELIOT 20

Osborne, John 1929–94
English dramatist

looking forward to the past — SHAW 12
set out to shock — OSBORNE 5

Ouida 1839–1908
English novelist

like the Three Mousquetaires — BURTON 3

Ovett, Steve 1955–
British runner

Seb was never the saint — COE 2
Steve Ovett, the runner — OVETT 1

Owen, Robert 1771–1858
Welsh-born social reformer

All the world is queer save thee — OWEN 3

Owen, Wilfred 1893–1918
English poet

Poetry is in the pity — OWEN 4

Pacheco, Ferdi

cash register for a brain — LEONARD 2

Page, Russell 1906–85
British garden designer

two pairs of spectacles — JEKYLL 4

Paget, Reginald 1908–90
British Labour politician

original banana man — EDEN 6

Paglia, Camille 1947–
American author and critic

as asexual as an adenoid — FIENNES 1
future of feminism — MADONNA 5
no female Mozart — MOZART 14
proof of emotional desperation — STEINEM 1
raisin-eyed, carrot-nosed — CLINTON 13
sense the world-disordering impact — TAYLOR 2

Paine, Thomas 1737–1809
English political theorist

apostate or an imposter — WASHINGTON 8
fell like the stick — BURKE 7
forgets the dying bird — BURKE 8
My country is the world — PAINE 5
share in two revolutions — PAINE 6
to begin with hypocrisy — ADAMS 7
very paltry rascally original — WILLIAM 1

Pais, Abraham 1918–
American physicist

in one word: ambivalence — OPPENHEIMER 2
prepared for a surprise — BOHR 5

Paisley, Ian 1926–
Northern Irish politician

drawing a line in the sand — TRIMBLE 2
International Socialist Playgirl — MCALISKEY 1
She has become a parrot — ELIZABETH 18

Palden Gyatso
Tibetan monk

written all over my suffering — MAO 3

Pankhurst, Emmeline 1858–1928
English suffragette

what you call a hooligan — PANKHURST 3

Pankhurst, Sylvia 1882–1960
English suffragette

finest fighting platform speaker — BRADDOCK 2

Parker, Dorothy 1893–1967
American critic and humorist

always chasing Rimbauds — VERLAINE 1
assume that Oscar said it — WILDE 10
call him spurious and shoddy — DICKENS 7
capacity for enjoyment — HEMINGWAY 7
emotions from A to B — HEPBURN 6
Excuse my dust — PARKER 4
How do they know — COOLIDGE 5
looking for the right word — FLAUBERT 5
Love, curiosity, freckles — PARKER 3
one of the prettiest love stories — ASQUITH 7
see John Knox in Paradise — KNOX 4

Parkinson, Michael 1935–
British journalist and broadcaster

both Isaiah and Irving Berlin — COOKE 1
council estate in Sheffield — ELIZABETH 19
dark, glowering, resentful — TRUEMAN 2
light meter, low cloud — BIRD 2
like a king among commoners — MOORE 1
littered with gibbering wrecks — GOWER 4
performing a one-man show — COMPTON 3
so fit he hums with energy — THOMPSON 1

Parr, Samuel 1747–1825
English educator

old lion is dead — JOHNSON 18

Parris, Matthew 1949–
British journalist and former Conservative
politician

big cat detained briefly — THATCHER 19
Bring on the fruitcakes — CLARK 4
comes straight from Tony — MANDELSON 4

Parry, Hubert 1848–1918
English composer

one composer at a time — ELGAR 4

Parsons, Tony 1953–
English critic and writer

half a pint of semi-skimmed milk — MINOGUE 1

Pascal, Blaise 1623–62
French mathematician, physicist, and
moralist

Had Cleopatra's nose been shorter — CLEOPATRA 2
to be able to do without God — DESCARTES 5

Patil, Sadashiv Kanoji
Indian politician

like the great banyan tree — NEHRU 2

Patten, Chris 1944–
British Conservative politician

As tough as old boots — MAJOR 4

Patton, George 1885–1945
American general

Blood and Guts — PATTON 2

Pauli, Wolfgang 1900–58
Austrian-born American physicist

relations with women difficult — PAULI 3
think slowly — PAULI 2

Pauling, Linus 1901–94
American chemist

duty to my fellow human beings — PAULING 1

Paxman, Jeremy 1950–
British journalist and broadcaster

wisely seen as unsuitable — PAXMAN 2

Payn, Graham

danced a boring Charleston — EDWARD 13

Pearson, Hesketh 1887–1964
English actor and biographer

Cold, commanding, too often right — WEBB 1

Pearson, Lester B. 1897–1972
Canadian Liberal statesman

To deserve success is more important — PEARSON 1

Peck, Gregory 1916–
American actor

actors like little tin gods — SELZNICK 1

Peel, John 1939–
English disc jockey

him reinventing himself — BOWIE 4

Peel, Robert 1788–1850
British Conservative statesman

fitter instrument than a razor — WALPOLE 5

Pelé 1940–
Brazilian footballer

another player passed to him — PELÉ 1
how football should be played — MATTHEWS 3

Pembroke, Lord 1734–94

his bow-wow way — JOHNSON 19

Penrose, Roger 1931–
British mathematician

very avant-garde artist — PENROSE 1

Pepys, Samuel 1633–1703
English diarist

all she doth is romantic — CAVENDISH 3
crown he got to himself — CROMWELL 7
is the most, and promises the least — HOOKE 2
Music and women — PEPYS 3
Pretty witty Nell — GWYN 3
understand but little — BOYLE 4

Perelman, S. J. 1904–79
American humorist

every other woman feel dowdy — PARKER 5

Perutz, Max 1914–
Austrian-born British biochemist

play tennis and chase girls — WATSON 2

Peter the Great 1672–1725
tsar of Russia

inspired my sword — WILLIAM 3

Pethwick-Lawrence, Emmeline
1867–1954
English suffragette

putting off of the slave spirit — PANKHURST 1

Petronius d. AD 65
Roman satirist

careful felicity — HORACE 4

Pevsner, Nikolaus 1902–
German-born architectural historian

greatest folly builder — LUTYENS 1

Peyton, Lord 1919–
British Conservative politician

spelling the word 'image' — HOME 6

Philip, Prince , Duke of Edinburgh 1921–
husband of Elizabeth II

Fella belong Mrs Queen — PHILIP 2
given him the hell of a time — ANNE 11
tolerance in abundance — ELIZABETH 20

Philip II 1165–1223
King of France

devil is loose — RICHARD 1

Piaf, Edith 1915–63
French singer

seen a lot of service — PIAF 1

Picasso, Pablo 1881–1973
Spanish painter

could draw like Raphael — PICASSO 5
leads to Hiroshima — EINSTEIN 10

Pickford, Mary 1893–1979
Canadian-born American actress

little girl made me — PICKFORD 3
running away from it — FAIRBANKS 3

Pilic, Nikki
Yugoslav-born German tennis player

He is *all* contradiction — BECKER 1

Pilley, W. Charles

festering putrid heaps — LAWRENCE 9

Pinter, Harold 1930–
English dramatist

don't recover from Shakespeare — SHAKESPEARE 23
dread word Pinteresque — PINTER 4
part of his nervous system — HUTTON 2
ruthless and savage — CLINTON 9
undoubtedly ruthless — MILOSEVIC 2

Pius XII 1876–1958
Italian cleric; Pope from 1939

One Galileo in two thousand years — TEILHARD DE CHARDIN 2

Plath, Sylvia 1932–63
American poet

between us before we perish — PLATH 5
publish a bookshelf of books — HUGHES 6

Plato 429–347 BC
Greek philosopher

wisest and justest and best — SOCRATES 6

Plomer, William 1903–73
British poet

nothing scandalous or equivocal — COOK 2

Plutarch AD c.46–c.120
Greek philosopher and biographer

cylinder containing a sphere — ARCHIMEDES 3
fear the smiling surface — CICERO 3

Pollitt, Harry 1890–1960
British Communist politician

Go to Spain and get killed — SPENDER 2

Pollock, Jackson 1912–56
American painter

any beginning or any end — POLLOCK 1

Pope, Alexander 1688–1744
English poet

brisk sallies and quick turns — STEELE 2
damned to everlasting fame — CROMWELL 8
For gain, not glory — SHAKESPEARE 24
Formed to delight — GAY 2
last and greatest art — DRYDEN 7
Let Newton be — NEWTON 9
make up a common account — NEWTON 10
Men not afraid of God — POPE 5
no imagination, but as much wit — DONNE 6
reptile all the rest — HERVEY 2
Statesman, yet friend to Truth — ADDISON 5
whom three realms obey — ANNE 6
wisest, brightest, meanest — BACON 6

Porter, Thea 1927–2000
British fashion designer

hate is clothes that look new — PORTER 4

Portillo, Michael 1953–
British Conservative politician

believes in everything — BLAIR 6
in one word what I am — PORTILLO 2

Potter, Beatrix 1866–1943
English writer for children

hard-headed, *matter-of-fact* — POTTER 1
seven years at his picture — HUNT 4

Potter, Dennis 1935–94
English television dramatist

familiar deodorant of self-deception — ORWELL 4

Pound, Ezra 1885–1972
American poet

act as if we were dead already — HOUSMAN 9
anything but AVARICE — BENNETT 6
but the one 'Sordello' — BROWNING 9
He was a martyr — HITLER 14
in a very fury of boredom — WORDSWORTH 13
last American — POUND 4
last mould on the dying cheese — PROUST 2
Rudyard the dud yard — KIPLING 7
think she was born in free verse — LOWELL 2
vile scum on a pond — CHESTERTON 6
wish he would wash — EPSTEIN 5

Poussin, Nicolas 1594–1665
French painter

love well-ordered things — POUSSIN 2

Powell, Anthony 1905–2000
English novelist

Greek tragedy — COMPTON-BURNETT 2
Muggeridgian Trinity — MUGGERIDGE 4

Powell, Enoch 1912–98
British Conservative politician

have been killed in the war — POWELL 3
Judas was paid — POWELL 2
sufficiently outrageous — BYRON 15

Pratchett, Terry 1948–
English science fiction writer

furniture in Tolkien's attic — TOLKIEN 2
head full of goblins — PRATCHETT 1

Prescott, John 1938–
British Labour politician

branded, pigeon-holed — PRESCOTT 3
He didn't like heads — MOORE 5
pretty middle class — PRESCOTT 2

Priestley, J. B. 1894–1984
English novelist, dramatist, and critic

another vacancy very soon — PRIESTLEY 2
black-shirted bullfrog — MUSSOLINI 4
bringing them into himself — RICHARDSON 5
God can stand being told — AYER 4
happiest writer I have ever met — CLARKE 5
knew more and could do more — PRIESTLEY 1

Prince, The Artist Formerly Known as 1958–
American rock singer and musician

spirit of the truth — PRINCE 2

Prior, Matthew 1664–1721
English poet

Stuart or Nassau go higher — PRIOR 1

Pritchett, V. S. 1900–97
English writer and critic

art as inverted poetry — CHEKHOV 3
grown by making judgements — ELIOT 9
what people are like — TROLLOPE 5
wintry conscience of a generation — ORWELL 5

Prokofiev, Sergei 1891–1953
Russian composer

Bach on the wrong notes — STRAVINSKY 3

Propertius c.50–after 16 BC
Roman poet

greater than the Iliad — VIRGIL 4

Prost, Alain 1955–
French motor-racing driver

not afraid to die — SENNA 2

Proust, Marcel 1871–1922
French novelist, essayist, and critic

admire, adore and venerate — FAURÉ 2

Puccini, Giacomo 1858–1924
Italian composer

luminous glory of Italy — VERDI 2
Write for the theatre — PUCCINI 2

Pugin, Augustus 1812–52
English architect and designer

thinking of fine things   PUGIN 2

Puttnam, David 1941–
English film producer

know what's going on   SPIELBERG 4

Pu Yi 1906–67
Chinese emperor

never even washed my own feet   PU YI 1

Queenan, Joe

His family knew people   QUAYLE 2

Queensberry, Marquess of 1844–
1900

posing as a somdomite   WILDE 11

Quinton, Anthony 1925–
British philosopher

listening-post for his age   RUSSELL 6

Rachmaninov, Sergei 1873–1943
Russian composer and pianist

wandering in a world grown alien   RACHMANINOV 2

Radwanski, George
Canadian journalist and policy consultant

real Mr. Trudeau please stand up   TRUDEAU 4

Raine, Craig 1944–
English poet

greatest pyrotechnician   AMIS 7
Pioneer of the bizarre   JONSON 6

Rainier, Prince 1923–
Prince of Monaco

Pay your parking tickets   COULTHARD 1

Raleigh, Walter c.1552–1618
English explorer and courtier

lady whom Time had surprised   ELIZABETH 7
patterns of a merciless prince   HENRY 9

Rambert, Marie 1888–1982
British ballet dancer and director

he made them into gods   DIAGHILEV 3
I know it was near the stars   NIJINSKY 2

Ramsey, Alf 1920–
English footballer and manager

bends the rules to suit himself   MARADONA 2
silly grin to make your mark   GASCOIGNE 4

Ransome, Arthur 1884–1967
English writer

quite without personal ambition   LENIN 2

Rattle, Simon 1955–
English conductor

conducted a Beethoven performance   BEETHOVEN 12

Ravel, Maurice 1875–1937
French composer

I make logarithms   RAVEL 2
making shell-cases instead   SAINT-SAËNS 1

Ray, Man 1890–1976
American photographer, painter, and film-maker

to amuse, bewilder, annoy   RAY 1

Reagan, Nancy 1923–
American actress

white glove pulpit   REAGAN 2

Reagan, Ronald 1911–
American Republican statesman

into the sunset of my life   REAGAN 7
opponent's youth and inexperience   MONDALE 1

Redding, Otis 1941–67
American soul singer

just record what comes out   REDDING 1

Redford, Robert 1936–
American film actor and director

If you were me for a month   REDFORD 1

Redgrave, Steven 1962–
British oarsman

anywhere near a boat again   REDGRAVE 1

Redwood, John 1951–
British Conservative politician

all the really dirty plates   BROWN 4

Reed, Lou 1944– American rock singer and songwriter	all-knowing, suffering fish eyes	JONES 2
	fell 17 feet down into that pit	ZAPPA 1
Rees-Mogg, William 1928– British journalist	butterfly on a wheel	JAGGER 6
Reeves, Vic 1959– British comedian	only exist on screen	REEVES 1
Reid, Alastair 1926– Scottish writer	able to afford a cat	GRAVES 2
Reid, Jimmy Scottish trade unionist	Syrian long distance lorry driver	BENN 6
Reith, Lord 1889–1971 British administrator and politician	sacrificed to his megalomania	CHURCHILL 31
Renan, Ernest 1823–92 French historian and philosopher	ordinary schoolchild now knows	ARCHIMEDES 4
Renard, Jules 1864–1910 French novelist	not as short as all that	TOULOUSE-LAUTREC 1
Rendell, Ruth 1930– English writer	need people's good opinion	RENDELL 1
Renoir, Auguste 1841–1919 French painter	elegant and 'feminine' artist	MORISOT 4
	putting colours on canvas	RENOIR 4
	stuck to his flying machines	LEONARDO 3
	with my brush I make love	RENOIR 3
Renoir, Jean 1894–1979 French film director	rather sell peanuts in Mexico	RENOIR 1
Retz, Cardinal de 1613–79 French churchman and politician	disregarding the little things	RICHELIEU 2
	with good intentions	MAZARIN 1
Reynolds, Albert 1933– Irish statesman	don't argue with 92 per cent	ROBINSON 2
Reynolds, Joshua 1723–92 English painter	last words which I should pronounce	MICHELANGELO 4
Rhodes, Cecil 1853–1902 South African statesman	So little done, so much to do	RHODES 1
	suspected his own shadow	PARNELL 4
Rhys, Jean c.1890–1979 British novelist and short-story writer	doormat in a world of boots	RHYS 1
Rice, Tim 1944– English songwriter	Don't cry for me Argentina	PERÓN 3
Rich, Adrienne 1923– American poet and critic	silence for entertainment	DICKINSON 4
Richard, Cliff 1940– British pop singer	I've been really radical	RICHARD 9
Richards, Ann 1933– . American Democratic politician	silver foot in his mouth	BUSH 8
Richards, Keith 1943– English rock musician	almost like a national monument	FRANKLIN 3
	felt I owed him so much	BERRY 1
	I used to be a laboratory	RICHARDS 3
	wicked jab and an uppercut	WATTS 1
	you are an *ar-tiste*	TOWNSHEND 2

Richards, Viv 1952–
West Indian cricketer

do not walk the middle ground	RICHARDS 7
say he was my white brother	BOTHAM 4

Richardson, Ralph 1902–83
English actor

do things against their will	KORDA 2
kind of brilliant butterfly	GIELGUD 4
Laurence's splendid fury	OLIVIER 4
stiletto for fools	THORNDIKE 1
Winston Churchill of his time	THEMISTOCLES 1

Richardson, Samuel 1689–1761
English novelist

blow up into a faint blaze	RICHARDSON 9
spurious brat	FIELDING 4

Rigg, Diana 1938–
British actress

only ever a B-cup	RIGG 1

Rilke, Rainer Maria 1875–1926
German poet

awake and filled with longing	RODIN 3

Rimbaud, Arthur 1854–91
French poet

first seer, king of poets	BAUDELAIRE 1

Rimsky-Korsakov, Nikolai
1844–1908
Russian composer

Better not listen to it	DEBUSSY 2

Robertson-Glasgow, R. C. 1901–65

slice the bowling to ribbons	BRADMAN 6

Robespierre, Maximilien 1758–94
French revolutionary

I am myself the people	ROBESPIERRE 5

Robinson, Edward G. 1893–1972
Romanian-born American actor

Whatever John Ford wants	FORD 10

Robinson, John 1919–83
English theologian; Bishop of Woolwich

flesh was sacramental	LAWRENCE 10

Robinson, Mary 1944–
Irish stateswoman

come dance with me in Ireland	ROBINSON 3

Robinson, Sugar Ray 1920–89
American boxer

get him in trouble	ROBINSON 6

Robson, Bobby 1933–
English football player and manager

win a game on his own	MARADONA 3

Rochester, Lord 1647–80
English poet

lies a great and mighty king	CHARLES 11
merry monarch	CHARLES 10

Rodin, Auguste 1840–1917
French sculptor

antique frescoes and sculpture	NIJINSKY 3
life in all its tumultuousness	BALZAC 7
owe everything to women	RODIN 4
so constrained by agony	MICHELANGELO 5

Roeg, Nicolas 1928–
British film director

he was so hard to reach	BOWIE 5

Roethke, Theodore 1908–63
American poet

drank his own blood	THOMAS 5

Rogers, Ginger 1911–95
American actress and dancer

She is snippy	HEPBURN 7

Rogers, Samuel 1763–1855
English poet

with his *one* hand	NELSON 4

Rogers, Will 1879–1935
American actor and humorist

Zulus know Chaplin better	CHAPLIN 6

Ronay, Egon British publisher and journalist	missionary position	SMITH 1
Rook, Jean 1931–91 English journalist	temper like an arthritic corgi	PHILIP 3
Roosevelt, Eleanor 1884–1962 American humanitarian and diplomat	trick at the last minute	NIXON 8
Roosevelt, Franklin D. 1882–1945 American Democratic statesman	fun to be in the same decade time for everybody's troubles	CHURCHILL 32 ROOSEVELT 2
Roosevelt, Theodore 1858–1919 American Republican statesman	as strong as a bull moose chocolate éclair lived up to Micah's verse such a bully pulpit	ROOSEVELT 12 MCKINLEY 1 WASHINGTON 2 ROOSEVELT 13
Rosebery, Lord 1847–1929 British Liberal statesman	died by inches in public	CHURCHILL 5
Ross, Diana 1944– American pop and soul singer	kind of idolized me	JACKSON 9
Rossellini, Isabella 1952– Italian actress	just got off the Greyhound bus	LYNCH 2
Rossetti, Christina 1830–94 English poet	unusually cheerful and robust	ROSSETTI 2
Rossetti, Dante Gabriel 1828–82 English painter and poet	combative artist named Whistler young fellows in Dreamland	WHISTLER 2 BURNE-JONES 3
Rossetti, Frances 1800–86	little more common sense	ROSSETTI 3
Rossini, Gioacchino 1792–1868 Italian composer	awful quarters of an hour	WAGNER 7
Rostand, Maurice French poet	outshines the burning brands	CURIE 5
Rosten, Leo 1908–97 American writer and social scientist	hates dogs and babies	FIELDS 3
Roth, Philip 1933– American novelist	This isn't Deep Throat	LEWINSKY 3
Rotten, Johnny 1957– British rock singer	Don't touch me, I'm special	ROTTEN 1
Rousseau, Jean-Jacques 1712–78 French philosopher and novelist	I am not made like any	ROUSSEAU 5
Rowland, Tiny 1917–98 British businessman	hero from zero	FAYED 2
Rowling, J. K. 1965– English novelist	want to be a Satanist	ROWLING 1
Royko, Mike 1932– American journalist	No self-respecting fish	MURDOCH 7
Rubens, Peter Paul 1577–1640 Flemish painter	equal to any enterprise	RUBENS 3

Runcie, Robert 1921–2000
English Protestant clergyman

done my best to die   RUNCIE 2
worth three sessions of chemotherapy   RIGG 2

Runyon, Damon 1884–1946
American writer

one man to remember me   RUNYON 1

Rushdie, Salman 1947–
Indian-born British novelist

I am that comma   RUSHDIE 2

Ruskin, John 1819–1900
English art and social critic

enjoys dinner—and breakfast   MORRIS 6
exception to all rules   TURNER 3
flinging a pot of paint   WHISTLER 3
Florentine fifteenth-century lady   SIDDALL 1
George Sand is often immoral   SAND 4
Italian lost in the inferno   ROSSETTI 7
murmur about his name   TITIAN 1
no more sense in it   MACAULAY 6
settled like a meat-fly   THACKERAY 3
tenderness of heart (extreme)   TURNER 4
Tory of the old school   RUSKIN 4
want of veneration   CONSTABLE 4
yet been done in figure-painting   MILLAIS 3

Russell, Bertrand 1872–1970
British philosopher and mathematician

adequate substitute for wisdom   SHAW 13
Alps, Andes and Apennines   HUXLEY 6
examining his wives' mouths   ARISTOTLE 2
Her talk was marvellous   MANSFIELD 1
I might have become a god   RUSSELL 8
indulge in eloquent soliloquy   LAWRENCE 11
intellect was the sharpest   KEYNES 3
most fortunate of all philosophers   LOCKE 2
mystery from gravitatio   EINSTEIN 11
not a rhinoceros in the room   WITTGENSTEIN 1
one slowly inters oneself   RUSSELL 7
pure intellectual passion   WITTGENSTEIN 2
she had the ideas   WEBB 2
thin crust of barely cooled lava   CONRAD 7
What Galileo and Newton were   DARWIN 6

Russell, Dora 1894–1986
Wife of Bertrand Russell

exactly like the mad hatter   RUSSELL 9

Russell, Ken 1927–
English film director

had that touch of vulgarity   DUNCAN 3

Russell, Lord John 1792–1878
British Whig statesman

ought to have a vote   ANDERSON 2

Rutherford, Ernest 1871–1937
New Zealand physicist

Every day I grow in girth   RUTHERFORD 5
We haven't got the money   RUTHERFORD 4

Ryan, Meg 1961–
American actress

known to cause diabetes   RYAN 1

Ryder, Sue 1923–2000
English philanthropist

to be with people who are suffering   RYDER 2

Ryle, Gilbert 1900–76
English philosopher

Ghost in the Machine   DESCARTES 6

Saatchi, Charles 1943–
British advertising executive

no hidden depths	SAATCHI 1

Sackville-West, Vita 1892–1962
English writer and gardener

imaginative jester of genius	LUTYENS 2
self-conscious fribble	BEERBOHM 1
That lovely mind	WOOLF 4
thing that wants Virginia	SACKVILLE-WEST 5

Sagan, Françoise 1935–
French novelist

boundaries of your talent	PROUST 3

Saint Laurent, Yves 1936–
French couturier

work in a state of anguish	SAINT LAURENT 2
written about the agony of creation	PROUST 4

Saladin 1137–93
Sultan of Egypt and Syria

too great recklessness	RICHARD 2

Salisbury, Lord 1830–1903
British Conservative statesman

entertain four royalties	SALISBURY 3
imagines a perpetual conspiracy	DISRAELI 10
than a policeman	SALISBURY 4
Too clever by half	DISRAELI 9

Salisbury, Lord 1893–1972
British Conservative politician

Too clever by half	MACLEOD 3

Sandburg, Carl 1878–1967
American poet

copperheads and the assassin	LINCOLN 7

Sargent, John Singer 1856–1925
American painter

I lose a friend	SARGENT 2

Sargent, Malcolm 1895–1967
English conductor and composer

six hours a day waving my arms about	SARGENT 5

Sassoon, Siegfried 1886–1967
English poet

booby-trapped idealist	SASSOON 1
with rechristened eyes	DE LA MARE 1

Satie, Erik 1866–1925
French composer

be inspired: 10.23 to 11.47 am	SATIE 3
refuses the Legion of Honour	RAVEL 3

Sayers, Dorothy L. 1893–1957
English writer

very great comic writer	DANTE 6

Sayle, Alexei 1952–
British comedian and writer

fat, wear silly trousers	MUSSOLINI 5

Scarfe, Gerald 1936–
English caricaturist

stretch the human frame	SCARFE 1

Scargill, Arthur 1938–
British trade union leader

running for mayor of Toytown	LIVINGSTONE 4

Schiffer, Claudia 1970–
German fashion model

whole bar of chocolate	SCHIFFER 2

Schlesinger, Arthur M. Jr. 1917–
American historian

died of typhus in Siberia	LENIN 3

Schnabel, Artur 1882–1951
Austrian-born pianist

quality of the notes	MOZART 15
Too easy for children	MOZART 16

Schoenberg, Arnold 1874–1951
Austrian-born American composer

it is his native language	GERSHWIN 5
little finger to become longer	SCHOENBERG 3
not a composer, but an inventor	CAGE 3
preserve one's self and to learn	IVES 1

Schreiner, Olive 1855–1920
South African novelist and feminist

Too big to get through   RHODES 2

Schrödinger, Erwin 1887–1961
Austrian theoretical physicist

deep truth in a bad joke   EDDINGTON 1
hod-carriers have something to do   EINSTEIN 12
often the second   SCHRÖDINGER 4
our neighbour's housewife   SCHRÖDINGER 5

Schroeder, Patricia 1940–
American Democratic politician

Teflon-coated Presidency   REAGAN 8

Schubert, Franz 1797–1828
Austrian composer

inspiring suggestions   MOZART 17

Schulz, Charles 1922–2000
American cartoonist

don't think I'm a true artist   SCHULZ 1

Schumacher, Michael 1969–
German motor-racing driver

suddenly see me as a human   SCHUMACHER 2

Schumann, Clara 1819–96
German pianist and composer

require but a simple 'Yes'   SCHUMANN 2
unsympathetic and querulous   BERLIOZ 4

Schumann, Robert 1810–56
German composer

Hats off, gentlemen   CHOPIN 3
Johannes to be the true Apostle   BRAHMS 4
Nature would burst   BEETHOVEN 13
should not like to be understood   SCHUMANN 3

Schumpeter, J. A. 1883–1950
American economist

cold metal of economic theory   MARX 10

Schwarzenegger, Arnold 1947–
American actor

can't even work myself out   SCHWARZENEGGER 3
like a male Raquel Welch   SCHWARZENEGGER 2

Schwarzkopf, H. Norman III 1934–
American general

consider myself hawkish   SCHWARZKOPF 1

Schweitzer, Albert 1875–1965
German theologian and medical
missionary

have the same given name   EINSTEIN 13

Scott, Robert Falcon 1868–1912
English polar explorer

interested in natural history   SCOTT 3
we knew we took them   SCOTT 5

Scott, Sir Walter 1771–1832
Scottish novelist and poet

almost the Voltaire of Germany   GOETHE 3
Big Bow-Wow strain   AUSTEN 8
gift of common sense   WELLINGTON 5
honest grunter   HOGG 3
might have been a great man   NAPOLEON 11
no remains of personal beauty   BURNEY 3
not fit to tie his brogues   SHAKESPEARE 25
only exists in romance   WORDSWORTH 14
palm is as itchy   TURNER 5
so shone with reflected light   BOSWELL 4
spoil him for his own trade   HOGG 2
Too many flowers   HEMANS 1
very sagacious country farmer   BURNS 9
well-bred and accomplished gentleman   GEORGE 15
writes all the while she laughs   EDGEWORTH 2

Scribner, Charles 1921–95
American publisher

most fussy of authors   LINDBERGH 4

Sears, Val
Canadian journalist

Canadian we would like to be TRUDEAU 5

Secombe, Harry 1921–
Welsh singer and entertainer

refused to shake hands GRADE 2

Seikaly, Rony
American basketball player

unprotected sex JOHNSON 3

Self, Will 1961–
British writer

éminence cerise ELIZABETH 25

Sellar, W. C. 1898–1951
and **Yeatman, R. J.** 1898–1968
British writers

secretly changed the Question GLADSTONE 14
word 'CALLOUS' engraved MARY 11

Sellers, Peter 1925–80
English comic actor

just a vase of flowers SELLERS 2
looking like myself SELLERS 1
Milligan arranged me MILLIGAN 3

Selznick, David O. 1902–65
American film producer

they all like him GABLE 3

Seneca c.4 BC–AD 65
Roman philosopher and poet

already a nobleman PLATO 3

Sévigné, Marie de 1626–96
French letter-writer

out of style like coffee RACINE 2

Sewell, Brian
British art historian and critic

I don't know what art is EMIN 2

Sexton, Anne 1928–74
American poet

talk about our first suicides PLATH 6

Shakespeare, William 1564–1616
English dramatist

Age cannot wither her CLEOPATRA 3
flowers of fancy OVID 3
for Jesu's sake forbear SHAKESPEARE 26
Harry! England and Saint George HENRY 4
Teeth hadst thou in thy head RICHARD 6
This royal infant ELIZABETH 8

Shankly, Bill 1913–81
Scottish footballer and manager

Me havin' no education SHANKLY 2

Shaw, George Bernard 1856–1950
Irish dramatist

always hitting the nail precisely STALIN 10
And what does she do RUTH 2
Atheist and a Vegetarian SHELLEY 8
auto da fé of teetotallers CHESTERTON 8
Brahms is just like Tennyson BRAHMS 5
Class War Correspondent MARX 11
Einstein has made a universe EINSTEIN 14
freak of French nature CHESTERTON 7
her acting was worse CAMPBELL 4
I despise Shakespeare SHAKESPEARE 27
incomparable Max BEERBOHM 2
innocent as a rose TERRY 3
London and New York laugh and whistle SULLIVAN 2
man without originality CAESAR 4
most silent woman MORRIS 3
my body and your brains SHAW 15
my prudish hands would refuse JOYCE 9
not come to be instructed WELLS 8

Shaw, George Bernard continued

only interested in art	GOLDWYN 3
only interested in money	SHAW 14
plenty of orchestral sugar	GRIEG 4
quite devilishly skilful	RODIN 5
Seven Humbugs of Christendom	ELGAR 5
someone had licked it	DUNCAN 4
third rate village policeman	TENNYSON 7
trifling with literary fools	JOHNSON 20
un-English individual	BELLOC 4
would otherwise hang us	TWAIN 6
would turn in his coffin	IRVING 3
wretched half-achievement	MARLOWE 6

Shaw-Lefevre, Charles , Lord Eversley 1794–1888

in such a passion about	FOX 6

Shelley, Mary 1797–1851
English novelist

gloomy and yet more gay	BYRON 16

Shelley, Percy Bysshe 1792–1822
English poet

cloud-encircled meteor	COLERIDGE 13
delusions of Christianity	BYRON 17
In honoured poverty	WORDSWORTH 15
knife is lost in it	PEACOCK 1
met Murder on the way	CASTLEREAGH 3
old, mad, blind, despised	GEORGE 8
one of those happy souls	HUNT 2
peace in Shelley's mind	SHELLEY 9
weep for Adonais	KEATS 11
words are instinct with spirit	DANTE 7

Shephard, Gillian 1940–
British Conservative politician

throw down his pencil	MAJOR 5

Sheridan, Richard Brinsley 1751–1816
Anglo-Irish dramatist

I meant—voluminous	GIBBON 8
making love to the Archbishop	SIDDONS 3
not even as a second-rate one	BURKE 9

Sherman, William Tecumsah 1820–91
American Union general

stood by me when	GRANT 4
when I was crazy	SHERMAN 2

Sherrin, Ned 1931–
British writer and broadcaster

celebrating the Englishness	DAVIES 1

Short, Clare 1946–
British Labour politician

I have to be me	SHORT 1

Sickert, Walter 1860–1942
British painter

he meant British Art	MILLAIS 4

Simon, John 1873–1954
British Conservative politician

If Joan of Arc had been born	HITLER 15

Simon, John 1925–

built like a brick mausoleum	RIGG 3

Simon, Paul 1942–
American singer and songwriter

generally a well-intentioned guy	LENNON 7

Sinatra, Frank 1915–98
American singer and actor

above all, a gentle soul	LENNON 8
I would be in a jar	SINATRA 5
way I live, once is enough	SINATRA 6

Sitting Bull c. 1831–90
Hunkpapa Sioux leader

Because I am Sioux	SITTING 1
stood like a sheaf of corn	CUSTER 2

Sitwell, Edith 1887–1964
English poet and critic

beautiful little knitter	WOOLF 5
chilblained, mittened musings	ARNOLD 4
innocent fertility-daemon	MONROE 13
like a short express train	BOWRA 2
mailed fist in a cotton glove	LEWIS 8
primeval grandeur of countenance	ELIOT 10
sandy desert of Dr Leavis's mind	LEAVIS 3
sang the sun in flight	THOMAS 6
sent to pawn false teeth	SITWELL 5
time to cultivate modesty	SITWELL 6
vanilla-flavoured ice-cream	PICKFORD 4
very thin cardboard	STRACHEY 4

Sitwell, Osbert 1892–1969
English man of letters

overbearing Scottish giant — REITH 3

Skidelsky, Robert 1939–
British economist

so much practical good — KEYNES 4

Slim, Viscount 1891–1970
British field marshal

irresistible frankness and charm — MOUNTBATTEN 6

Smetana, Bedřich 1824–84
Czech composer

be a Liszt in technique — SMETANA 2

Smith, Adam 1723–90
Scottish philosopher and economist

perfectly wise and virtuous man — HUME 3

Smith, Arthur and **England, Chris**

Queen Mother of football — LINEKER 3

Smith, Delia
English cookery expert

not some prim Brownie pack leader — SMITH 2

Smith, F. E. 1872–1930
British Conservative politician and lawyer

extremely offensive, young man	SMITH 7
takes one jump in the dark	BALDWIN 6

Smith, John Maynard 1920–
English biologist

like sitting on a landmine — HALDANE 4

Smith, Logan Pearsall 1865–1946
American-born man of letters

ready as ever for a scrap — JEKYLL 5

Smith, Patti 1946–
American poet and pop singer

what planet did he come from — HENDRIX 6

Smith, Stevie 1902–71
English poet and novelist

Colours of hell	EL GRECO 1
not like being a woman	DE BEAUVOIR 1
on the side of women	WEST 3

Smith, Sydney 1771–1845
English clergyman and essayist

consent to speak as inarticulately	MALTHUS 1
divided mankind into two parts	ARNOLD 8
flashes of silence	MACAULAY 7
soul of Hogarth has migrated	DICKENS 8
statue to him under the gallows	O'CONNELL 1
steam-engine in trousers	WEBSTER 3
with or without ten minutes notice	RUSSELL 11

Smith, Zadie 1975–
British writer

all about vengeance — SMITH 9

Smollett, Tobias 1721–71
Scottish novelist

great Cham of literature — JOHNSON 21

Snow, C. P. 1905–80
English novelist and scientist

brilliant and concentrated	HARDY 3
He was a cheat	GRACE 3
not err on the modest side	RUTHERFORD 6
of the industrial revolution	IBSEN 3

Socrates 469–399 BC
Greek philosopher

I know nothing	SOCRATES 7

Somerville, Mary 1780–1872
Scottish mathematician and astronomer

reading was so much disapproved of	SOMERVILLE 2

Sondheim, Stephen 1930–
American songwriter

sentiment not sentimentality	SONDHEIM 1
unsophisticated, platitudinous hick	RODGERS 1

Sorley, Charles Hamilton
1895–1915
English poet

dying on active service	BROOKE 5
wanted was more warmth	GOETHE 4

South, Robert 1634–1716
English court preacher

rubbish of an Adam	ARISTOTLE 3

Southey, Robert 1774–1843
English poet and writer

in love with a cold climate	WOLLSTONECRAFT 1
loss of a dear friend	NELSON 5
'twas a famous victory	MARLBOROUGH 6
Without being intentionally obscene	HERRICK 3

Spark, Muriel 1918–
British novelist

He's a Pole first	JOHN PAUL 3
not thought of birth control	STOPES 4
take the edge off cold charity	GREENE 1

Sparrow, John 1906–92
English academic

Hell would not be Hell	BOWRA 3

Spencer, Herbert 1820–1903
English philosopher

taking two irons out of the fire	HUXLEY 11

Spencer, Lord 1964–
English peer

most hunted person	DIANA 9
needed no royal title	DIANA 8

Spencer, Stanley 1891–1959
English painter

saying 'Ta' to God	SPENCER 4

Spender, Stephen 1909–95
English poet

always the same baby elephant	BERLIN 8
laugh-at-with	AUDEN 9
silence and watchfulness	SACKVILLE-WEST 6

Spenser, Edmund c.1552–99
English poet

well of English undefiled	CHAUCER 6

Spielberg, Steven 1947–
American film director and producer

bubble-gum outlook on life	SPIELBERG 5
he's an original	CONNERY 4

Springsteen, Bruce 1949–
American rock singer and songwriter

Bob freed your mind	DYLAN 8

Squire, J. C. 1884–1958
English man of letters

Devil howling 'Ho!'	EINSTEIN 15

Stalin, Joseph 1879–1953
Soviet dictator

use the same lavatory as Lenin	KRUPSKAYA 2

Stanhope, Hester 1776–1839
English traveller

What is principle to *me*	STANHOPE 1

Stanley, Henry Morton 1841–1904
Welsh explorer

If he were not so wicked	BURTON 4
never attempt the impossible	STANLEY 2

Stanton, Edwin Mcmasters
1814–69
American lawyer

belongs to the ages
LINCOLN 8

Starr, Ringo 1940–
English rock and pop drummer

especially his poems
BEETHOVEN 14

he goes on and on
MCCARTNEY 4

Steel, David 1938–
British Liberal politician

to be rescued by James Bond
SALMOND 1

Stein, Gertrude 1874–1946
American writer

Christ, Spinoza, and myself
STEIN 5

marries three girls from St Louis
HEMINGWAY 8

village explainer
POUND 5

Steinbeck, John 1902–68
American novelist

nothing sweet about the songs
GUTHRIE 4

Steinem, Gloria 1934–
American journalist

huge as a colossus doll
MONROE 14

Steiner, George 1926–
American French-born critic and writer

genius and happiness united
MENUHIN 5

Stephen, J. K. 1859–92
English journalist and poet

Two voices are there
WORDSWORTH 16

Stevens, Jocelyn 1932–
British businessman

bird in a gilded cage
MARGARET 2

Stevenson, Adlai 1900–65
American Democratic politician

cornerstone of a public building
EISENHOWER 8

cut down a redwood tree
NIXON 10

heart-beat from the Presidency
NIXON 9

Let us march
KENNEDY 15

rather light a candle
ROOSEVELT 3

sleep of my generation
STEVENSON 3

talk under their feet
EISENHOWER 7

Stevenson, Robert Louis 1850–94
Scottish novelist

cannot write like Hazlitt
HAZLITT 2

Epick writer with a k
STEVENSON 8

grim reliance in himself
KNOX 5

like a tap-room companion
PEPYS 4

making so much of Natural Selection
DARWIN 7

Prudence is a wooden Juggernaut
FRANKLIN 8

Stewart, Jackie 1939–
Scottish motor-racing driver

absolutely cold, ice-cold
STEWART 2

clear varnish in my own mind
STEWART 3

Stewart, James 1908–97
American actor

played a love scene with her
KELLY 8

Stokowski, Leopold 1882–1977
British-born American conductor

listen with their eyes
STOKOWSKI 2

Stone, Sharon 1958–
American actress

Push. Push. Push
STONE 1

Stopes, Marie 1880–1958
Scottish birth-control campaigner

canonised in 200 years' time
STOPES 5

Stoppard, Tom 1937–
British dramatist

Life's a curse
HOUSMAN 10

moving train needs passengers
RUSKIN 5

written to outlast the witness
TYNAN 3

Strachey, Lytton 1880–1932
English biographer

believe the Arabian Nights	NEWMAN 4
class of great gnomes	RUSSELL 10
Deity and the Drains	NIGHTINGALE 4
meaninglessness of fate	BROOKE 6
mystery of Botticelli	MALLORY 2
no striped frieze	BACON 7
seductive genius	BEERBOHM 3
spoonful of boiling oil	POPE 6

Strafford, Earl of 1593–1641
English statesman

so lost a business	STRAFFORD 2

Strasberg, Lee 1901–82
American actor, director, and drama teacher

hear Shakespeare thinking	GIELGUD 5

Strauss, Richard 1864–1949
German composer

do better to shovel snow	SCHOENBERG 4

Stravinsky, Igor 1882–1971
Russian composer

did not grimace	RACHMANINOV 3
dirtiest man	AUDEN 10
heyday of Strauss and Debussy	IVES 2
it wasn't modern	SCHOENBERG 5
perfect of Swiss clockmakers	RAVEL 4

Streep, Meryl 1949–
American actress

placed all of that energy	STREEP 1
potential to be America's Chekhov	ALLEN 6

Streisand, Barbra 1942–
American singer and actress

President, not a Pope	CLINTON 10
wanted to be Scarlett O'Hara	STREISAND 3

Strindberg, August 1849–1912
Swedish dramatist and novelist

Swedenborg's visions	MUNCH 1

Stringfellow, Peter
British nightclub owner

Not a good combination	BEST 6

Strong, Roy 1935–
English art historian

always a side-shoot	RAMBERT 3
any glimmer of repentance	BLUNT 1
he thrives on adulation	ASHTON 2

Stross, Randall E.

practical intellectual	GATES 1

Stuart, Charles Edward 1720–88
pretender to the British throne

with my sword in my hand	STUART 5

Sullivan, Arthur 1842–1900
English composer

more or less sacrifice yourself	GILBERT 2

Sutherland, Graham 1903–80
English painter

very special sense of luxury	BACON 10

Sutherland, Joan 1926–
Australian operatic soprano

be absolutely like a horse	SUTHERLAND 2

Suzman, Janet 1939–
South African actress

draws the role towards her	JACKSON 6

Swanson, Gloria 1899–1983
American actress

every inch and every moment	SWANSON 3
like playing house	DE MILLE 5
She Paid the Bills	SWANSON 4

Swift, Jonathan 1667–1745
Anglo-Irish poet and satirist

can in one couplet fix	POPE 7
Lives in a state of war	HOBBES 5
malice never was his aim	SWIFT 7
no longer tear his heart	SWIFT 8

Swinburne, Algernon Charles
1837–1909
English poet

wrinkled and toothless baboon

EMERSON 6

Symons, Arthur 1865–1945
Welsh critic and poet

sex which is so conscious

RODIN 6

Symons, Julian 1912–94
English crime writer

shows us the ace of spades

CHRISTIE 2

Talleyrand, Charles-Maurice de
1754–1838
French statesman

It is not an event

NAPOLEON 12

who has more intelligence

VOLTAIRE 6

Tavener, John 1944–
English composer

dig up a 6th century man

TAVENER 1

his is a neurotic joy

MAHLER 3

most extraordinary human cry

BEETHOVEN 15

people weren't flying

ONO 4

Taylor, A. J. P. 1906–90
British historian

bewitch posterity

SHAW 16

every feeling except trust

LLOYD GEORGE 10

great showman whose technique

MUSSOLINI 6

Hitler's level of accuracy

HITLER 16

nobility of his later defeats

TROTSKY 2

no faith in the future

BISMARCK 2

pleasure was to humiliate

THOMAS 7

power instead of influence

NORTHCLIFFE 3

Taylor, Elizabeth 1932–
American actress

haven't had tomorrow

TAYLOR 3

referred to as That Broad

TAYLOR 4

Taylor, Roger
British tennis coach

never beaten until the last gasp

CONNORS 5

Tchaikovsky, Pyotr Ilich 1840–93
Russian composer

astounding lack of talent

STRAUSS 4

childhood toward the God Jehovah

BEETHOVEN 16

giftless bastard

BRAHMS 6

Tebbit, Norman 1931–
British Conservative politician

called him a one-ball juggler

HESELTINE 5

he's got an unusual voice

HAGUE 4

Tenniel, John 1820–1914
English draughtsman

Dropping the pilot

BISMARCK 3

Tennyson, Alfred, Lord 1809–92
English poet

denied the faculty of verse

CARLYLE 8

God-gifted organ-voice of England

MILTON 14

In her as Mother, Wife and Queen

VICTORIA 10

last great Englishman

WELLINGTON 6

plenty of music in him

BROWNING 10

white flower of a blameless life

ALBERT 3

wide sea of glue

JONSON 7

Wielder of the stateliest measure

VIRGIL 5

Tennyson, Emily 1813–96
wife of Alfred, Lord Tennyson

endless Madonnas

CAMERON 3

Teresa, Mother 1910–97
Roman Catholic nun and missionary

By blood and origin

TERESA 3

just a drop in the ocean

TERESA 2

Terry, Ellen 1847–1928
English actress

anyone over the age of ten

CARROLL 1

what the shell is to a lobster

IRVING 4

when there's a fog

BURNE-JONES 4

Thackeray, Harriet 1840–75

write books like Nicholas Nickleby

THACKERAY 4

Thackeray, William Makepeace
1811–63
English novelist

Mind, no biography	THACKERAY 5
some Tomkins to love her	BRONTË 7

Thatcher, Margaret 1925–
British Conservative stateswoman

do business together	GORBACHEV 5
get my own way in the end	THATCHER 22
getting awfully bossy	BLAIR 7
lady's not for turning	THATCHER 20
makes me feel positively 'wet'	BLACK 2
no sympathy in politics	HEATH 8
Prime Minister needs a Willie	WHITELAW 3
socialist—a crypto-Communist	KINNOCK 4
very good back-seat driver	MAJOR 6
We have become a grandmother	THATCHER 21

Thayer, William Roscoe 1859–1923
American biographer and historian

From log-cabin to White House	GARFIELD 3

Thomas, Caitlin 1913–94
wife of Dylan Thomas

passion for lies	THOMAS 8

Thomas, Dylan 1914–53
Welsh poet

deprecate the boy bushranger	AUDEN 11
everything in this cankered world	KIPLING 8
in the path of Blake	THOMAS 10
rather lie in a hot bath	THOMAS 9

Thomas, R. S. 1913–2000
Welsh poet and clergyman

thin, cerebral laughter	DONNE 7

Thompson, Anthony Worrall
British chef

Volvo of cooks	SMITH 3

Thompson, Emma 1959–
British actress

big she is in Uruguay	AUSTEN 9
he needs a good movie	TRAVOLTA 2

Thomson, David 1941–
British film critic

ghost of Rockefeller	BENNY 3
huge man trying to inspire order	CLEESE 1
leer face-lifted into a smile	CHEVALIER 3
most warnings for the rest of us	WELLES 2
rat in the skirting boards	GREENAWAY 1
wind tunnel at dawn	GERE 1

Thomson, James 1700–48
Scottish poet

Untwisted all the shining robe	NEWTON 11

Thomson, J. J. 1856–1940
English atomic physicist

no doubt be found interesting	DALTON 2
start off on a new tack	KELVIN 1

Thomson, Roy 1894–1976
Canadian-born British newspaper
proprietor

he's six months older	GETTY 2
think until it hurts	THOMSON 1

Thoreau, Henry David 1817–62
American writer

suck out all the marrow	THOREAU 3

Thorpe, Jeremy 1929–
British Liberal politician

lay down his friends	MACMILLAN 7

Thurber, James 1894–1961
American humorist

definite hardening of the paragraphs	THURBER 2
nonstop literary drinker	POE 4

Tickell, Thomas 1686–1740
English poet

taught us how to die	ADDISON 6

Tinling, Ted
American fashion designer

Sugar Plum Fairy of the lot	EVERT 2

Tipu Sultan c.1750–99 | two days like a tiger | TIPU 1

Tolkien, J. R. R. 1892–1973
British philologist and writer | *Ulsterior motive* | LEWIS 2

Tolstoy, Leo 1828–1910
Russian novelist | can't stand Shakespeare's plays | CHEKHOV 4

Tolstoy, Sonya 1844–1919 | never once sat for five minutes | TOLSTOY 8

Tomlin, Lily 1939–
American actress | masculinity, femininity | TRAVOLTA 3

Tone, Wolfe 1763–98
Irish nationalist | bad anatomist | TONE 1

Torke, Michael 1961–
American composer | waste money on psychotherapy | BACH 10

Tortelier, Paul 1914–90
French cellist | she was a Wagner heroine | DU PRÉ 6

Toscanini, Arturo 1867–1957
Italian conductor | I take my hat off | STRAUSS 1
kissed my first woman | TOSCANINI 2
With one more drop of blood | BEETHOVEN 17

Toulouse-Lautrec, Henri de
1864–1901
French painter and lithographer | hitched up to a rubbish cart | TOULOUSE-LAUTREC 2

Townshend, Pete 1945–
British rock musician and songwriter | most psychedelic experience | HENDRIX 7
my nose was so big | TOWNSHEND 3

Tracy, Spencer 1900–67
American actor | impression with what he *did* | GABLE 4

Travolta, John 1954–
American actor | permission to like me | TRAVOLTA 4

Trefusis, Violet 1894–1972 | might have been posted in Kensington | NICHOLAS 2
she was 'cosy' | COLETTE 2

Trevelyan, G. M. 1876–1962
English historian | plotted to make men like | ANNE 7
BALDWIN 7

Trevino, Lee 1939–
American golfer | I was a poor Mexican | TREVINO 1

Trimble, David 1944–
Northern Irish politician | like Hitler in a synagogue | ADAMS 4

Trollope, Anthony 1815–82
English novelist | left in privacy | ELIOT 11

Trollope, Joanna 1943–
British writer | kind of professional rape | ROWLING 2
sex appeal of old socks | LENNON 9

Trollope, Rose 1820–1917 | never leaves off | TROLLOPE 6

Trotsky, Leon 1879–1940
Russian revolutionary | mediocrity of the apparatus | STALIN 11
revolver in his trouser pocket | HITLER 17
something of the flunkey | MACDONALD 14
there was no turning back | LENIN 4
vengeance of history | STALIN 12

Trudeau, Pierre Elliott 1919–2000
Canadian Liberal statesman | I am a realist but | TRUDEAU 6

Trueman, Fred 1931–
English cricketer

best fast bowler	TRUEMAN 4
couldn't bowl a hoop downhill	BOTHAM 5
making life easier for batsmen	TRUEMAN 3
real tiger who hates bowlers	BOYCOTT 3

Truffaut, François 1932–84
French film director

as if they were love scenes	HITCHCOCK 3

Truman, Harry S. 1884–1972
American Democratic statesman

against the law for generals	MACARTHUR 2
all the planets had fallen on me	TRUMAN 2
buck stops here	TRUMAN 3
I never give them hell	TRUMAN 4
prisoner of the Politburo	STALIN 13

Turgot, A. R. J. 1727–81
French economist and statesman

snatched the lightning shaft	FRANKLIN 9

Turner, J. M. W. 1775–1851
English landscape painter

sees more in my pictures	RUSKIN 6

Turner, Ted 1938–
American businessman

idea of a better world	MURDOCH 8
Life is like a B-movie	TURNER 6

Twain, Mark 1835–1910
American writer

all that can be known	KIPLING 9
barkeeper entering heaven	AUSTEN 10
buy a piece of the rope	RHODES 3
Creator made Italy from designs	MICHELANGELO 6
I *can* lie but I won't	TWAIN 7
probably fond of them	CARLYLE 9

Tynan, Kenneth 1927–80
English theatre critic

as neurotic as a chipmunk	BROOK 1
bleak, illuminating footnotes	DAVIS 8
built-in shit detector	BOGART 5
communicate a sense of danger	OLIVIER 5
corpses piling at his ankles	CAGNEY 2
doughnut pickled in vinegar	FIELDS 4
Formosa of the contemporary theatre	RATTIGAN 2
from the neck up	GIELGUD 6
gnome expelled from Eden	MUGGERIDGE 5
heart of an unfrocked evangelist	BRUCE 2
Helpmann is dancing incarnate	HELPMANN 1
Huckleberry Finn complex	HEPBURN 8
ice-berg characters	GUINNESS 7
intellectual slum-clearance	SHAW 17
Lincoln in horn-rims	MILLER 3
manner of Friar Tuck	LEWIS 3
mighty moral instrument	ROBESON 1
only sophisticated playwright	CONGREVE 2
passion for high living	CONNOLLY 3
pith as well as the husk	COOKE 2
reservoir of bile has swelled	OSBORNE 6
salmon standing on its tail	LAUGHTON 1
scholar at a jam session	GREENE 2
sees in Garbo sober	GARBO 13
sex, but no particular gender	DIETRICH 5
silk, satin and even bombazine	EVANS 5
skips and lilts and bounces it	RICHARDSON 6
sleepy outcast face	WILLIAMS 1
Slightly in *Peter Pan*	COWARD 6
straight man *who is funny*	MORECAMBE 2

student of craftsmanship		TYNAN 4
tart, vocally, as a hollowed lemon		COWARD 5
voice of bottled thunder		WELLES 3
Was it unadventurous		ASTAIRE 7
we forbid her to develop		GARLAND 4
would have preferred Dunlopillo		LEIGH 3

Tyrrell, Robert Yelverton
1844–1914

elucidating Browning's translation — BROWNING 11

Tyson, Mike 1966–
American boxer

Anyone who can fly — JORDAN 1
chopped off one of my arms — BRUNO 2
I enjoy hurting people — TYSON 4

Updike, John 1932–
American novelist and short-story writer

tap-dancing up a storm — KELLY 4

Ustinov, Peter 1921–
Russian-born actor, director, and writer

above all he was a creator — WELLES 4
cathedral in your mouth — MACMILLAN 8
cigarette in the background — BOGART 6
conscious of being unique — PAVAROTTI 1
died young at any age — HEPBURN 2
face was frozen with terror — MACMILLAN 9
only hears her own voice — THATCHER 23
reverse of an iceberg — LAUGHTON 2
wears his belt like a crown — JOHNSON 6
working for *Vogue* — BOTTICELLI 2

Vadim, Roger 1927–2000
French film director

sacrificed her body to the god — BARDOT 4

Van Dyck, Anthony 1599–1641
Flemish painter

sweetness, and sureness of touch — JONES 6

Van Gogh, Vincent 1853–90
Dutch painter

glimpse of a superhuman infinite — REMBRANDT 4
spent, ill, the cracked pot — VAN GOGH 6

Vasari, Giorgio 1511–74
Italian painter, architect, and biographer

might have been a scientist — LEONARDO 4

Venables, Terry 1943–
English football player and manager

boy's a very sensitive boy — GASCOIGNE 5

Venturi, Robert 1925–
American architect

Less is a bore — MIES VAN DER ROHE 2

Verlaine, Paul 1844–96
French poet

angel AND demon — RIMBAUD 2

Versace, Donatella 1955–
Italian fashion designer

always have to be glamorous — VERSACE 1

Versace, Gianni 1946–97
Italian fashion designer

elegant and sophisticated women — ARMANI 1
I dress sluts — VERSACE 2
I like to dress egos — VERSACE 3

Vespasian AD 9–79
Roman emperor from AD 69

ought to die standing — VESPASIAN 1

Victoria, Queen 1819–1901
Queen of the United Kingdom from 1837

Albert—who is beautiful	ALBERT 4
as if I was a public meeting	GLADSTONE 16
had her at the War Office	NIGHTINGALE 5
I will be good	VICTORIA 11
large loving mind	DICKENS 9
not a nature made to bear sorrow	EDWARD 4
old, wild, and incomprehensible man	GLADSTONE 15
We are not amused	VICTORIA 12

Vidal, Gore 1925–
American novelist and critic

all their Pavonian splendor	PEACOCK 2
always in court	FORSTER 5
been at home in New York	BENTHAM 3
best known for my hair preparations	VIDAL 4
bigger and more original	NIXON 11
Good career move	CAPOTE 2
Gore is thicker than Nader	GORE 3
IQ of a moron	WARHOL 2
not have married Mrs Khrushchev	ONASSIS 3
not seen the joke	HEMINGWAY 9
triumph of the embalmer's art	REAGAN 9
world is black or white	KENNEDY 19
writer who does not develop	WILLIAMS 2

Vidor, King 1895–1982
American film director

wanted to quit the business	DE MILLE 6

Virgil 70–19 BC
Roman poet

understand the causes	LUCRETIUS 1

Vogüé, E. M. de 1848–1910

brain of an English chemist	TOLSTOY 9

Voltaire 1694–1778
French writer and philosopher

art of pleasing	CHESTERFIELD 3
as sprightly in his writings	VANBRUGH 3
found in ten centuries	NEWTON 12
free from all human weakness	CHARLES 13
never did anything great	WATTEAU 1
well acquainted with human nature	CONGREVE 3

von Sternberg, Josef 1894–1969
Austrian-born American film director

until the alchemy was complete	DIETRICH 6

Vreeland, Diana 1903–89

just like a Shetland pony	BAILEY 2

Wagner, Richard 1813–83
German composer

Jew may be highly talented	MENDELSSOHN 2

Waite, Terry 1939–
British religious adviser

forged by doubt	RUNCIE 3

Walcott, Derek 1930–
West Indian poet and dramatist

I plant lines	WALCOTT 1

Waldegrave, William 1946–
British Conservative politician

not very frightened of him	MAJOR 7

Walden, George 1939–
British Conservative politician

books, trees and women	MITTERRAND 1
great blotched moon	SNOW 3
such a dated decor	MACMILLAN 10

Walker, Scott 1944–
American singer

want to jump out of a window	JONES 9

Waller, William 1598–1668
English general

cautious of his own words	CROMWELL 9

Wallinger, Karl 1957–
British musician

annoyed that he existed   WITTGENSTEIN 3
hang him upside down from a tree   LENNON 10

Walpole, Horace 1717–97
English writer and connoisseur

All his own geese are swans   REYNOLDS 7
at the head of school   ALEXANDER 3
complete genius and a complete rogue   CHATTERTON 2
do not take this for flattery   PITT 1
fascinate all the world   SHERIDAN 3
fear of being splashed   GAINSBOROUGH 3
forces and wealth against Louis XIV   WILLIAM 4
gingerbread, filigraine   ADAM 1
going to draw naked savages   BANKS 2
high life as conceived by a bookseller   RICHARDSON 10
hyena in petticoats   WOLLSTONECRAFT 2
I believe you would go to heaven   MORE 1
laboured as his extempore sayings   CHESTERFIELD 4
mortifications and humiliations   GEORGE 9
mountebank and his zany   BOSWELL 5
mountebank and his zany   JOHNSON 22
still admiring pismire Herschel   HERSCHEL 5
swelled to shocking deformity   RICHARD 7
undoubtedly wanted taste   SHAKESPEARE 28

Walpole, Hugh 1884–1941
New Zealand-born British novelist

only real person here to him   KIPLING 10

Walpole, Robert 1676–1745
English Whig statesman

I cannot now read a page   WALPOLE 6
terrible young cornet of horse   PITT 2

Walsh, Raoul 1887–1980
American film director

you can kill off Bogart   BOGART 7

Walton, Izaak 1593–1683
English writer

great Secretary of Nature   BACON 8
marked him for his own   DONNE 8
unspotted of the world   HERBERT 2

Ward, Artemus 1834–67
American humorist

most married man   YOUNG 2

Ward, Mrs Humphrey 1851–1920
English writer and anyi-suffrage
campaigner

like them, but not with them   BRONTË 2

Warhol, Andy c. 1928–87
American artist

just look at the surface   WARHOL 3
terrific if everybody was alike   WARHOL 4

Warner, Jack 1892–1978
Canadian-born American film producer

all the Walter Mittys of the world   FLYNN 4
Reagan for his best friend   REAGAN 10

Warner, Sylvia Townsend
1893–1978
English writer

bolt him in pellets   HERRICK 4
charged straight through him   CONSTABLE 5
embattled codfish   DE GAULLE 6

Washington, Booker T. 1856–1915
American educationist

saw it all, lived it all   DOUGLASS 3

Washington, George 1732–99
American general and statesman

I can't tell a lie   WASHINGTON 9

Waterhouse, Keith 1929–
English novelist, dramatist, and
screenwriter

Jeffery Bernard is unwell   BERNARD 2

Waters, Muddy 1915–83
American blues singer and guitarist

He took my music — JAGGER 7
kept writing those blues — WATERS 1

Waters, Roger 1944–
English pop singer

key that unlocked the door — BARRETT 1

Watson, James D. 1928–
American biologist

in a modest mood — CRICK 2
polarized towards finding out — SCHRÖDINGER 6

Waugh, Auberon 1939–2001
English journalist and novelist

greatest improvement in English life — DAVID 1

Waugh, Evelyn 1903–66
English novelist

delicious little old dandy — BEERBOHM 4
exactly what I would have been — THOMAS 11
give up writing about God — GREENE 3
I believe in the Devil — BEAVERBROOK 5
know Mr Auden to appreciate him — AUDEN 12
part that was not malignant — CHURCHILL 6
Sèvres vase in the hands — SPENDER 3
waste of this magical vehicle — WELLS 9
Without supernatural aid — WAUGH 5

Wayne, John 1907–79
American actor

never make me cheap — WAYNE 1

Webb, Beatrice 1858–1943
English socialist

limited-minded German bourgeois — EDWARD 5
organization 'agin the government' — HARDIE 2
Restless, almost intolerably so — CHURCHILL 33

Webster, Daniel 1782–1852
American politician

always room at the top — WEBSTER 4

Weisskopf, Victor 1908–
American physicist

thought *all* questions were stupid — PAULI 4

Welch, Raquel 1940–
American actress

rather like being a convict — WELCH 1

Welles, Orson 1915–85
American actor and film director

biggest electric train set — WELLES 6
if you don't understand grammar — ANTONIONI 1
I like the old masters — FORD 11
there are so many of me — WELLES 5

Wellington, Duke of 1769–1852
British general and statesman

Peel has no manners — PEEL 6

Wellington, Duke of 1769–1852
British soldier and statesman

forty thousand men — NAPOLEON 13
may all your wives be like her — CAROLINE 7

Wells, H. G. 1866–1946
English novelist

gentle bright kitten — EINSTEIN 16
I told you so — WELLS 10
leviathan retrieving pebbles — JAMES 14
like a great paper-weight — VICTORIA 13
merger between Heaven and Hell — BEAVERBROOK 6
unaccountably unpuncturable — HALDANE 5

Welsh, Irvine 1957–
Scottish novelist

all that's perfectly hideous — MACDIARMID 4

Wesley, John 1703–91
English preacher

all the world as my parish — WESLEY 3

West, Anthony 1914–87

could edit and improve — WEST 4

West, Mae 1892–1980
American film actress

created his own character	CHAPLIN 7
created their own characters	MARX 5
I've been in *Who's Who*	WEST 1
Let Shakespeare do it his way	SHAKESPEARE 29
never missed it	WEST 2
she was her own person	GARBO 14
thousands of women wept	VALENTINO 4

West, Rebecca 1892–1983
English novelist and journalist

demented lady, even if a genius	WOOLF 6
doormat or a prostitute	WEST 5
eunuch perpetually inflamed	SHAW 18
hardly a brain in his head	FORSTER 6
married a bad lot	WINDSOR 5
old maid among novelists	WELLS 11
ruined my life	WELLS 12

Westwood, Vivienne 1941–
English fashion designer

clothes to have adventures in	WESTWOOD 1
parodying the English	WESTWOOD 2
showed me the other side	MCLAREN 2

Wharton, Edith 1862–1937
American novelist

dance I had always dreamed of	DUNCAN 5
his incredible littleness	PROUST 5
how great he would have been	JAMES 15

Whinney, Robert
Captain in the British Navy

one glorious defeat	MOUNTBATTEN 7

Whistler, James McNeill 1834–1903
American-born painter

knowledge of a lifetime	WHISTLER 4
ladies' maid	ROSSETTI 8
puddings he peddles in the provinces	WILDE 12
sepulchre of dullness	SARGENT 3
You will, Oscar, you will	WILDE 13

White, Edmund 1940–
American writer and critic

all of his characters into geniuses	BALZAC 8
hanky soaked in ethyl chloride	WARHOL 5

White, Patrick 1912–90
Australian novelist

desperate semi-coded messages	NOLAN 2
Little-Thing-in-Blue	ELIZABETH 21

White, Theodore H. 1915–86
American writer and journalist

primordial as a salmon	JOHNSON 7

Whitehead, Alfred North
1861–1947
English philosopher and mathematician

series of footnotes to Plato	PLATO 4

Whitehorn, Katharine 1928–
English journalist

knocked off his horse by God	MUGGERIDGE 6

Whitington, R. S. 1912–
Australian cricketer

oyster would have envied	BRADMAN 7

Whitman, Walt 1819–92
American poet

He *built* poems	LOWELL 3
himself more a French revolution	CARLYLE 10
This dust was once the man	LINCOLN 9

Whittington, Robert
English grammarian

man for all seasons	MORE 7

Widdecombe, Ann 1947–
British Conservative politician

circumference to rival the Equator	DOBSON 2
I am on God's side	WIDDECOMBE 5
Pankhursts were Tories	PANKHURST 4
rather be round and jolly	WIDDECOMBE 4
something of the night	HOWARD 1

Wiener, Norbert 1894–1964
American mathematician

tips of the tongues of the age   PICASSO 6

Wilberforce, Samuel 1805–73
English prelate

descent from a monkey   HUXLEY 12

Wilberforce, William 1759–1833
English politician and social reformer

one of the most incurable fanatics   WILBERFORCE 2

Wilde, Oscar 1854–1900
Anglo-Irish dramatist and poet

chaos illuminated by flashes   MEREDITH 2
died at the age of a flower   BEARDSLEY 4
genius who drops his aspirates   KIPLING 11
knew nothing of Plato and Darwin   MILL 3
miniature Mephistopheles   WHISTLER 5
my genius into my life   WILDE 14
never a lake poet   WORDSWORTH 17
not an enemy in the world   SHAW 19
outcasts always mourn   WILDE 15
painful duty   JAMES 16
prose Browning   BROWNING 12
sins that I had never committed   CHOPIN 4
take off his face   BEERBOHM 5
three-headed Cerberus of Civilization   LOWELL 4
worst surroundings possible   STEVENSON 9

Wilder, Billy 1906–
American screenwriter and director

got to have a heart   SELLERS 3
Hollywood's Joan of Arc   MONROE 15
I don't do cinema   WILDER 2
twenty-five years younger   WILDER 3

Wilder, Gene 1933–
American actor

lighting ten thousand matches   ALLEN 7

Wilhelm II 1859–1941
German emperor

If my grandmother had been alive   VICTORIA 14
running away with *him*   HITLER 18
Tsar is not treacherous   NICHOLAS 3

William III 1650–1702
King from 1689

die in the last ditch   WILLIAM 5

William IV 1765–1837
King from 1830

does not question his talents   TALLEYRAND 5

Williams, Bernard 1929–
English philosopher

preferred having Jesuits   AYER 5

Williams, Emlyn 1905–87
Welsh dramatist and actor

He's miscast   BURTON 8
she's Miss Taylor   TAYLOR 5
Tomb of the Well-Known Soldier   EISENHOWER 9
unbridled oboe of a voice   GIELGUD 7

Williams, Robbie 1974–
British rock singer

Elvis, grant me serenity   PRESLEY 7

Williams, Tennessee 1911–83
American dramatist

about that heavenly voice   FERRIER 2
someday arrive at the gloomy Dane   BRANDO 6

Williams, William Carlos 1883–1963
American poet

grim humour   BRUEGEL 3
literature is serious   POE 5

Williamson, Malcolm 1931–
Australian composer

but then so is Aids   LLOYD WEBBER 1

Willis, Bob 1949–
English cricketer

would be very tired   TRUEMAN 5

Wilson, A. N. 1950–
British writer

unfashionable race   HEANEY 4

Wilson, Colin 1931–
English novelist and writer

apples of decadence   DELIUS 2
certain arrested development   BRITTEN 5
deposited it in bank vault   BARTÓK 3
strong smell of burning rubber   BEETHOVEN 18

Wilson, Edmund 1895–1972
American critic and writer

do not know what he is saying   STEVENS 2
fictional character   ELIOT 21

Wilson, Harold 1916–95
British Labour statesman

immatures with age   BENN 7
inordinately weak   CALLAGHAN 4
I only counter-intrigue   WILSON 8
kick Ted in the groin   HEATH 9
symbol of everything that is best   BUSBY 2
tinned. With vinegar   WILSON 7

Wilson, Richard 1936–
Scottish actor

rich, fat bastard who can afford   WILSON 9

Wilson, Woodrow 1856–1924
American Democratic statesman

writing history with lightning   GRIFFITH 4

Winchilsea, Anne Finch, Lady
1661–1720
English poet

little too loosely she writ   BEHN 2

Windsor, Barbara 1937–
English actress

only as good as his parts   WINDSOR 1

Windsor, Duchess of 1896–1986
wife of the former Edward VIII

born to be a salesman   EDWARD 14
gave up so much for me   EDWARD 15

Winston, Robert 1940–
British gynaecologist

doctors do manipulate patients   WINSTON 1

Winterson, Jeanette 1959–
English novelist and critic

comes close to my exuberance   WINTERSON 1
entirely fenced in with posts   FRY 1
Salieri of letters   CONRAD 8

Wittgenstein, Ludwig 1889–1951
Austrian-born philosopher

I've had a wonderful life   WITTGENSTEIN 4

Wodehouse, P. G. 1881–1975
English writer; an American citizen from
1955

do seem to loathe the poor blighter   KIPLING 12
got it all from the newspapers   WODEHOUSE 4
still think it swell   DOYLE 2

Wogan, Terry 1938–
Irish broadcaster

anything else that ends in -ic   BROOKS 3
smile like a razor blade   WELCH 2

Wolf, Hugo 1860–1903
Austrian composer

One single cymbal clash   BRUCKNER 1

Wolfe, Humbert 1886–1940
British poet

place was run by Jews   CHESTERTON 9

Wolfe, James 1727–59
British general

prefer being the author   GRAY 3
                                                      WOLFE 2

Wolfe, Tom 1931–
American writer

created Attitude   WARHOL 6

Wolpert, Lewis 1929–
English biologist

had not written *Hamlet*   SHAKESPEARE 30

Wolseley, Garnet 1833–1913
British soldier

born at Blenheim	MARLBOROUGH 7
God must be very angry	GLADSTONE 17
sooner leave my old bones here	WOLSELEY 4

Wolsey, Thomas c.1475–1530
English prelate and statesman

served God as diligently	WOLSEY 2
want part of his appetite	HENRY 10

Wood, Natalie 1938–81
American actress

had to be nice to people	PRESLEY 8

Woods, Tiger 1975–
American golfer

I'm a Cablinasian	WOODS 2

Woolf, Virginia 1882–1941
English novelist

absorbing morality at every pore	CHAUCER 7
Apes are preferable	CONNOLLY 4
as tough as catgut	PROUST 6
first of the masculinists	MILTON 15
I love, I hate, I suffer	BRONTË 8
light man, I daresay	HUNT 3
madness is terrific	WOOLF 7
mind is a very thin soil	MANSFIELD 2
Nobody reads her	BROWNING 4
one shriek, sparks, smoke	LAWRENCE 12
prose is now prosaic	ADDISON 7
realism of the right kind	SASSOON 2
scratching of pimples	JOYCE 10
spurted fountains of ideas	YEATS 8
strangest mixture of ape and Cupid	WALPOLE 3
transparent like some white bone	SITWELL 7
turned from the contacts of man	BROWNE 3

Woollcott, Alexander 1887–1943
American writer

firing on the rescuers	CAMPBELL 5
Little Nell and Lady Macbeth	PARKER 6
original stuff of the world	ROBESON 2

Wordsworth, Dorothy 1771–1855
English writer

courage to address himself	DE QUINCEY 2

Wordsworth, Mary 1782–1859
English wife of William Wordsworth

breathing of thy inmost heart	WORDSWORTH 18

Wordsworth, William 1770–1850
English poet

admitted into respectable society	HAZLITT 3
England hath need of thee	MILTON 16
marble index of a mind	NEWTON 13
marvellous boy	CHATTERTON 3
product of a scoffer's pen	VOLTAIRE 7
this poor man was mad	BLAKE 6
universality of his genius	WATT 2

Wright, Frank Lloyd 1867–1959
American architect

chose honest arrogance	WRIGHT 2

Wyman, Bill 1936–
British rock musician

does the most incredible dancing	BROWN 6
public thinks the Stones are like	RICHARDS 4

Yancey, William 1814–63
American Confederate politician

man and the hour	DAVIS 7

Yeats, W. B. 1865–1939
Irish poet

antithesis of daily life	MORRIS 7
definition of mysticism	BUNYAN 3
dirt and sucked sugar stick	OWEN 5
great soft tiger cat	JOYCE 11
half-awakened Adam Can disturb	MICHELANGELO 7
haunted by a sewing-machine	SHAW 20

	I see a schoolboy	KEATS 12
	loved the pilgrim soul in you	GONNE 2
	most innocent, wicked man	JOHN 6
	No prouder trod the ground	PARNELL 5
	sailed into his rest	SWIFT 9
	Who beat upon the wall	BLAKE 7
	wrote as an official	SPENSER 6

Yevtushenko, Yevgeny 1933–
Russian poet

whites with black souls   KING 8

York, Sarah, Duchess of 1959–

they had you beheaded   YORK 2
walk five paces behind   PHILIP 4

Young, Neil 1945–
Canadian singer and songwriter

music was always more important   ORBISON 1
now I'm Perry Como   YOUNG 3

Young, Terence 1915–94
Film director

hasn't changed Sean one iota   CONNERY 5

Zappa, Moon Unit

treated it like he was going on tour   ZAPPA 2

Zhdanov, Andrei 1896–1948
Soviet Politburo official

Half nun, half harlot   AKHMATOVA 4

Zhvanetsky, Mikhail 1934–
Russian writer

walking backward into the future   GORBACHEV 6

Zidane, Zinédine 1972–
French footballer

learned on the street   ZIDANE 1

Ziegler, Philip 1929–
British historian

In Spite of Everything   MOUNTBATTEN 8

Zola, Émile 1840–1902
French novelist

crushes the entire century   BALZAC 9
towers of Notre Dame to dance   CÉZANNE 4